# Understanding Homeland Security

*Understanding Homeland Security* is a unique textbook on homeland security that blends the latest research from the areas of immigration policy, counterterrorism research, and border security with practical insight from homeland security experts and leaders such as former Secretaries of the Department of Homeland Security Tom Ridge and Janet Napolitano.

The textbook also includes:

- A historical overview of the origins of the homeland security enterprise as well as its post-9/11 transformation and burgeoning maturity as a profession
- In-depth descriptions of the state, local, and federal government entities, such as the U.S. Department of Homeland Security, that enforce and carry out the nation's homeland security laws and policies
- Detailed discussion of relevant, contemporary topics such as asylum and refugee affairs, cybersecurity and hacking, border security, transportation and aviation security, and emergency management policy
- A chapter on homeland security privacy and civil liberties issues
- Unique current affairs analysis of controversial topics such as the National Security Agency's warrantless wiretapping program, Edward Snowden, the 2016 U.S. presidential election, Russian cyberhacking efforts, and Black Lives Matter
- Advice, guidance, and insight for students through interviews with homeland security leaders as well as terrorism experts such as Bruce Hoffmann and biowarfare specialists such as Dr. Rebecca Katz

The target audience for this text is advanced undergraduate or entry-level graduate students in criminology, intelligence analysis, public policy, public affairs, international affairs, or law programs. This textbook meets requirements for entry-level introductory courses in homeland security.

**Ehsan Zaffar** is a civil rights lawyer, educator, and homeland security policymaker. He primarily studies the impact of homeland security law and policy on civil rights, human rights, and civil liberties and has taught courses on these issues at George Mason University and George Washington University.

# Understanding Homeland Security

## Foundations of Security Policy

*Ehsan Zaffar*

Routledge
Taylor & Francis Group

NEW YORK AND LONDON

First published 2020
by Routledge
52 Vanderbilt Avenue, New York, NY 10017

and by Routledge
2 Park Square, Milton Park, Abingdon, Oxon, OX14 4RN

*Routledge is an imprint of the Taylor & Francis Group, an informa business*

© 2020 Taylor & Francis

*Library of Congress Cataloging-in-Publication Data*
Names: Zaffar, Ehsan, author.
Title: Understanding homeland security : foundations of security policy / Ehsan Zaffar.
Description: Abingdon, Oxon ; New York. NY : Routledge, 2019. |
Identifiers: LCCN 2019015184 | ISBN 9780323296458 (hardback) |
    ISBN 9780367259044 (paperback) | ISBN 9780323296243 (ebook)
Subjects: LCSH: National security—United States. | Civil defense—United States. | Security sector—United States.
Classification: LCC UA23 .Z33 2019 | DDC 363.340973—dc23
LC record available at https://lccn.loc.gov/2019015184

ISBN: 978-0-323-29645-8 (hbk)
ISBN: 978-0-367-25904-4 (pbk)
ISBN: 978-0-323-29624-3 (ebk)

Typeset in Stone Serif
by Apex CoVantage, LLC

Visit the eResources: www.routledge.com/978036725904

*The subtlest change in New York is something people don't speak much about but that is in everyone's mind. The city, for the first time in its long history, is destructible. A single flight of planes no bigger than a wedge of geese can quickly end this island fantasy, burn the towers, crumble the bridges, turn the underground passages into lethal chambers, cremate the millions. The intimation of mortality is part of New York now: in the sounds of jets overhead, in the black headlines of the latest edition.*

— E. B. White, 1949

This book is dedicated to the memory of all those lost in the events of September 11, 2001, and those who continue to suffer from the aftermath of that event and the collective American reaction to it.

# Contents

# *Figures*

# *Acknowledgments*

I would like to thank those friends, family, and professionals who have helped in the arduous endeavor of crafting this textbook, including Professor Maryam Jamshidi for her insight, knowledge, and unwavering belief in me. I'd also like to thank my acquisitions editor, Dr. Pamela Chester, for her bottomless patience and kindness. I'm also grateful to Secretary Napolitano, Governor Tom Ridge, Dr. Kevin Fandl, and Dr. Erroll Southers as well as all of the other professionals who contributed interviews for this textbook. This textbook would not have been possible without research, citation, and drafting assistance from Meri Nagapetyan, Justin Hienz, and Caroline Marshall.

Finally, this book is dedicated to my students who honor me with the opportunity to teach them . . . oh and to everyone with a red line under their name in Microsoft Word, don't change your name, live the dream.

# *Introduction*

It has been 18 years since the attacks of September 11, 2001. Those attacks changed the fabric of the U.S. government, the American people's conception of their place in the world, and their knowledge of the wider world. The 9/11 attacks brought about the greatest reorganization of the U.S. federal government since World War II. In the process, this reorganization also dramatically changed the way state, local, and tribal governments functioned. Huge sums of taxpayer money were poured into national security efforts and the entirely new professional field of "homeland security" was created. By some estimates, almost 20% of all federal spending in the Washington, D.C., area today is for homeland security purposes, and a burgeoning crop of upper middle-class professionals rely on homeland security jobs to earn a living.

After 9/11, vast legacy government agencies such as the Immigration and Naturalization Service were broken apart and reconstituted under the newly created Department of Homeland Security. Entire missions of other government agencies were changed to focus only on homeland security issues. Buildings were purchased throughout Washington, D.C., to house the growing homeland security enterprise. Academic programs, such as the one this book is likely being used for, were created by schools nationwide to train students about homeland security issues. The various agencies that handle homeland security continue to come to terms with their vast and growing responsibility, which covers everything from terrorism, to immigration enforcement, investigating counterfeiting and human trafficking crimes, to responding to natural disasters.

Over the past 18 years, a growing regulatory framework has focused on securing public and private facilities against acts of terror. Private owners and operators of critical infrastructure such as power plants, dams, and highways have partnered with the federal government to protect these critical facilities. The general public has had to come to terms with dealing with government presence in everyday life, whether that's undergoing screening at the airport by the Transportation Security Administration, seeing actors play homeland security agents on TV, or hearing about how to handle suspicious packages on their local commuter train. Homeland security has become an everyday part of our lives.

These intrusive activities to secure the country have resulted in pushback from advocacy and civil liberties groups. Individuals like Edward Snowden have leaked classified information in an attempt to expose government practices they deem questionable. Important questions continue to be asked about how far governments at all levels can go and what the "balance" is between rights and security.

In this book we explore homeland security as a concept and as a practical reality. We begin our journey before 9/11 and discuss the idea of homeland security in its previous iterations. We consider why the U.S. created the various homeland security bodies in response to 9/11 and what the structure of these agencies tells us about how they ought to work. We then delve into the substantive areas that form the homeland security enterprise, from immigration issues to border enforcement and cybersecurity. Near the end of the text we explore the impact homeland security policies have had on broader governance and ask important questions about the impact of security policy on civil rights and civil liberties in the U.S.

Homeland security as a field and enterprise is just beginning and will change dramatically over the next few decades. In fact, it is likely that large portions of this book will be out of date within the next half-decade of its release. This makes it a tumultuous but exciting time to be a student learning about homeland security as well as someone starting a career in the homeland security field.

Thank you for allowing me to be a part of this journey with you.

C H A P T E R   1

# *Homeland Security Before 9/11*

---

**IN THIS CHAPTER YOU WILL LEARN ABOUT**

The origins emergency management as a precursor to homeland security policy and practice.

The federal government's response to the rising threat of terrorism prior to 9/11.

The differences between the related concepts of national security, homeland security, and homeland defense.

---

## INTRODUCTION

One of the most significant events of the 21st century occurred on September 11, 2001 when a group of individuals flew two planes into the World Trade Center Towers in Manhattan, New York (the "9/11" attacks). These attacks, perpetrated by a group commonly known as al-Qa'ida, were the first perpetrated on U.S. soil since the Japanese bombing of Pearl Harbor in 1941. Similar to the attack on Pearl Harbor, the 9/11 attacks prompted an enormous and concerted government response. After 9/11, the United States went to war in Iraq and Afghanistan, and launched counterterrorism and intelligence initiatives around the globe. State and federal government bodies passed legislation and crafted policies designed to protect the nation against all hazards, from terrorism to natural disasters.

The 9/11 attacks had a particularly dramatic impact on the U.S. security apparatus. In direct response to 9/11, the White House announced the creation of the Office of Homeland Security, which later became the Department of Homeland Security. When the Department of Homeland Security was stood up in November 2002, it constituted the largest government reorganization since the Department of Defense was created in 1947. While this reorganization created entirely new agencies, practice areas, and mission sets, it was also the culmination of decades of legislation and debate over the federal government's role in responding to large-scale disasters. What is today referred to as "homeland security" is a relatively new phenomenon, and its origins rest primarily not in counterterrorism but, instead, in emergency management.

In this chapter we will explore the origins of homeland security as both a concept and a modern policy practice. Later chapters of this text will delve deeper into the more practical aspects of homeland security, such as transportation security and border security. The last few chapters will highlight the impact homeland security policy has had in other related policy areas such as civil rights and civil liberties and privacy policy.

## THE ORIGINS OF FEDERAL EMERGENCY MANAGEMENT

The United States government has always held some responsibility for responding to security threats, as well as manmade disasters and natural disasters. Today, this broad, crosscutting responsibility is generally called "homeland security," but that term is a recent addition to the security and emergency response lexicon. To understand the emergence of homeland security after the September 11, 2001, terrorist attacks, it is important to review the long arc of U.S. emergency management that preceded these attacks.

As a formal responsibility of federal government, emergency management began with efforts to address threats from fire and disease in 19th-century towns and cities.[1] For the most part, an American living in the mid- to early 1800s perceived the federal government as a remote and far-removed organization that did not intrude on daily affairs. Instead, Americans engaged on a regular basis with their state and local governments.

With the Industrial Revolution, Americans increasingly moved to cities. As time passed, fewer people worked on rural farmlands and increasing numbers worked instead in urban factories. As people overflowed the capacity of cities to handle them, manmade disasters like city fires, structural building collapse, and riots became more common. Municipal governments were unable to cope with the sudden rise in population and public facilities to accommodate basic needs remained inadequate throughout the late 19th and early 20th century. The lack of clean drinking water as well as unmanaged sewage made disease commonplace and hard to control in growing cities like New York. Buildings went up quickly to house factories and laborers, but they were often built poorly and were susceptible to fire (Figure 1.1).

While facing rising threats to health and safety, towns relied on minimal tax income and a few scattered social service organizations, such as churches and non-governmental organizations for support. Eventually, the challenges of a growing population became so large that local governments across the country looked to the federal government for help. The first instance of the federal government stepping in to assist a state or local government with

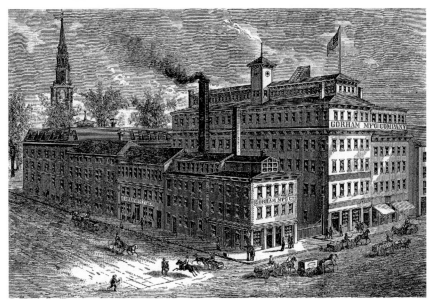

**FIG. 1.1**
Increased urbanization and poor safety policies contributed to an increase in manmade and natural disasters that only organizations as large as governments could respond to.

*Source*: Welcome Arnold Greene, The Providence Plantations for 250 Years 274 (1886), https://upload.wikimedia.org/wikipedia/commons/8/8b/Gorham_Manufacturing_Company_1886.jpg.

an emergency was in 1803. On December 26, 1802, a fire started at the New Hampshire Bank building in Portsmouth, New Hampshire (Figure 1.2). The blaze spread quickly, destroying 200 buildings with an estimated $200,000 in damages.[2] The disaster was so significant that the local Portsmouth community was unable to cope using its limited local government resources. A local newspaper later described the heroic efforts of local residents fighting the fire:

> The women of Portsmouth did not flee in the face of the 1802 fire, but pitched in and worked on the bucket brigades until they dropped from sheer exhaustion. Volunteers from nearby towns were instrumental in spelling the spent firefighters and in guarding valuables from the dozens of reported looters who many believed were themselves the incendiaries arsonists.[3]

**FIG. 1.2**
The New Hampshire Bank Building Fire in Portsmouth, New Hampshire, was one of the first man-made disasters that taxed the response capabilities of local officials to such an extent that they sought federal assistance.

*Source*: Wikimedia, https://upload.wikimedia.org/wikipedia/commons/thumb/2/2e/Portsmouth,_NH_-_oldest_bank(s).JPG/1024px-Portsmouth,_NH_-_oldest_bank(s).JPG (last visited Dec. 12, 2018).

Facing insurmountable costs, New Hampshire's U.S. congressmen appealed to the federal government for assistance. The result was the Congressional Fire Disaster Relief Act, the first piece of national disaster legislation and the first time federal resources were made available to help a local government with a local emergency.[4] This legislation was the first of several congressional actions to respond to growing natural and manmade hazards across the country. Congress increasingly became involved in responding to state and local requests for disaster assistance. Throughout the late 1800s and early 1900s city buildings kept growing larger and taller, housing more people, making it easier for fires to spread and burn down entire towns full of tightly packed and poorly constructed housing. Large fires killed hundreds in major cities like New York, Chicago, and San Francisco throughout the early 20th century.

During this time, the federal government functioned as a small, loosely knit organization (unlike the strong, centralized federal government we see today). As such, instead of passing comprehensive legislation that created a department or agency to handle disasters, the federal government responded by passing legislation to deal with specific events.[5] For instance, between 1803 and 1950, the Congress addressed more than 100 disasters of various types using one-off decrees to provide federal resources to address local crises. For example, Congress chartered the American Red Cross to assist victims of disasters that occurred in 1905; sent soldiers to maintain order after the 1906 San Francisco earthquake and ensuing fire; and granted the Army Corps of Engineers authority over flood control in the Mississippi Valley in 1927.

### Federal Emergency Response Function Grows During Wartime

Thus, in the United States, the development of emergency management (and later, of homeland security) has been and continues to be event-driven. As such, alongside responding to natural and manmade disasters, U.S. participation in the two World Wars of the 20th century also precipitated a change in how the federal government managed disasters. To manage these wars and provide for the general defense of the country, states yielded increasing power to the federal government. After these wars were over, the federal government often failed to relinquish its wartime powers. For instance, during wartime the federal government provided financial assistance to the states. In return, the federal government sought cooperation from the states on a variety of measures designed to standardize behavior, such as federal speed limits for roads and bridges in various states. As wars and conflicts throughout the 20th century ended, the federal government kept these financial quid-pro-quo relationships in place. Likewise, states continued to rely on federal aid for a variety of issues, including responding to disasters. This dependence only grew throughout the 20th and 21st centuries. Today, this "**power of the purse**" continues to be a major reason why states seek aid from the federal government even today, especially when the state's budget is unable to provide for assistance for recovery and rebuilding.

*One gov body withholding funding or putting stipulations on the use of funds to control & manipulate actions of another body*

In response to these growing urban disasters, Congress established the Council on National Defense in 1916 to coordinate "industries and resources for the national security and welfare" and to "create relations which will render possible in time of need the immediate concentration and utilization of the resources of the Nation."[6] (Notice the pairing of the terms "national security" and "welfare"; this was one of the first examples of these two concepts being joined in the federal government's ethos.) The establishment of the Council led to the creation and coordination of civil defense councils. Eventually totaling 182,000 units, these state and local civil defense councils directed "home front" activities that were important during both World War I (and later World War II), such as conserving resources, providing economic stability, and responding to threats to Americans on U.S. soil. This coordination of local councils throughout the country by the federal government to respond to emergencies (though only those driven by armed conflict or war) was decidedly different from the previous trend of congressional legislation designed to address emergencies on an ad-hoc basis. This more coordinated approach served as a precursor for the establishment of the far more complicated national security and homeland security federal agencies that arose later.

World War II also brought about increasing federal involvement in emergency management. The Reconstruction Finance Corporation and the Bureau of Public Roads (both formed during World War II) were authorized to provide financial assistance to certain public facilities and infrastructure in the wake of natural disasters.[7] During his tenure, President Franklin D. Roosevelt also established offices within the White House to manage and coordinate federal emergency support activities, specifically:

To advise and assist the President in the discharge of extraordinary responsibilities imposed upon him by any emergency arising out of war, the threat of war, imminence of war, flood, drought, or other condition threatening the public peace or safety.[8]

## LEGISLATIVE AND EXECUTIVE ACTION ON FEDERAL RESPONSE TO DISASTERS

As the Cold War blossomed in the 1950s, emergency management in the United States was staffed largely by retired military service members working part-time in poorly resourced and organizationally marginalized civil defense offices. These offices focused more on war planning than disaster preparedness, and disasters only became a priority for civil defense, as well as other public safety agencies, when an emergency occurred.[9]

### From Ad-Hoc to Organized

The advent of the nuclear age and ensuing threats from a potential nuclear war motivated the federal government to expand civil defense programs across the country. Particularly in the wake of 1962 Cuban Missile Crisis, local communities built bomb shelters in an attempt to create some infrastructure that could shield the public during a nuclear attack by a communist nation. The federal government also began creating formal emergency preparedness infrastructure. For instance, President Harry S. Truman created the Federal Civil Defense Administration (FCDA), which merged in 1958 with the Office of Civil and Defense Mobilization (OCDM)—one of the first examples of permanent federal emergency management organizations and the precursors of today's Department of Homeland Security. The goal of these government bodies was to provide technical assistance to state and local governments in the wake of a natural disaster or armed attack through the provision of resources and expertise.

Though President John F. Kennedy created an Office for Emergency Preparedness[10] inside the White House to specifically coordinate federal responses to large-scale events, the majority of congressional responses to these

**FIG. 1.3**
President John F. Kennedy decided to change the federal approach to disasters and emergency management. In 1961, he created the Office of Emergency Preparedness inside the White House to handle the growing risk of natural disasters. Civil Defense responsibilities, however, remained in the Office of Civil Defense within DOD.

*Source*: Wikimedia, https://upload.wikimedia.org/wikipedia/commons/e/ec/John_F._Kennedy_signs_bills_1961.JPG (last visited Dec. 12, 2018).

disasters continued to come in the form of ad-hoc legislation. However, a series of natural disasters throughout the 1960s led to the passage of increasingly specific legislation. In 1965, Hurricane Betsy killed 75 people and caused billions of dollars in damage in south Florida. An increasing demand for petroleum products and the resulting transportation of hazardous materials created the potential for human-caused disasters, and in 1967, a 100,000-ton oil spill of a U.S. tanker off the coast of England shocked Congress. Then, in 1969, Hurricane Camille made landfall, causing $1.5 billion in damages, destroying the world's longest bridge, and killing more than 250 people throughout the Mississippi Gulf Coast. Silverstein notes that,

At the time of Hurricane Camille, the federal government viewed its responsibility in natural disasters as limited to issuing regional alerts to populations that were in projected paths of storms and, after disaster struck, assisting in emergency recovery efforts for people exposed to health hazards and other threats to personal safety. Hurricane Camille marked the beginning of an era when the U.S. federal government recognized that its responsibility ran deeper than the traditional emergency food kitchens and temporary shelters it had previously provided.[11]

The consequences from Hurricane Camille and other disasters led to the passage of several pieces of legislation and an Executive Branch reorganization that enhanced the federal responses to natural disasters. Among these were: The Disaster Relief Act of 1969; the Flood Protection Act of 1973; the Disaster Relief Act of 1974;[12] and the 1977 National Earthquake Hazards Reduction Act (NEHRA), which created a unified federal response plan for catastrophic earthquakes. At the same time, the Executive Branch made organizational changes to better respond to natural disasters. The Federal Disaster Assistance Administration was established within the U.S. Department of Housing and Urban Development (HUD) in 1973. And the Nixon administration reorganized the Office of Civil Defense into a "dual use" agency, the Defense Civil Preparedness Agency. This reorganization was based on the premise that "a community prepared to deal with peacetime hazards is that much better prepared to cope with the effects of a nuclear attack."[13]

Reforming the Office of Civil Defense into the dual use Defense Civil Preparedness Agency was another notable recognition by the federal government that responding to both manmade and natural emergencies required similar government infrastructure and policies. This reorganization can be seen as the beginning of the notion that the functions of an emergency management agency could also be used to address national security priorities. Congress officially sanctioned "dual-use" emergency management agencies under Public Law 94–361 on July 13, 1976. Yet, despite these actions, experts in the new field of emergency management aspired to do more than just respond to disasters; they sought to prevent disasters from occurring and to mitigate the impact of those that did. Both the President and Congress increasingly understood that ad-hoc responses to disasters were ineffective long-term strategies.

## CREATION OF THE FEDERAL EMERGENCY MANAGEMENT AGENCY

Guided by this quest to proactively manage disasters, President Jimmy Carter submitted a comprehensive plan for the reorganization of all federal emergency response agencies in 1979. Reorganization Plan Number 3 consolidated all of the disparate and scattered emergency preparedness, mitigation, and response activities of the federal government into a single agency: The Federal Emergency Management Agency (FEMA).[14]

The scope of this reorganization was massive. Reorganization Plan Number 3 consolidated numerous agencies into a single organization, including: The National Fire Prevention Control Administration (from the Department of Commerce); the Federal Insurance Administration and the Federal Disaster Assistance Administration (both from HUD); the Federal Broadcast System (from the Executive Office); the Defense Civil Preparedness Agency (from DOD); and the Federal Preparedness Agency (from the General Services Administration, or GSA). Reorganization Plan Number 3 gave FEMA four primary responsibilities: 1) establish federal disaster policies; 2) mobilize federal resources for disaster response; 3) coordinate federal efforts with those of state and local governments; and 4) manage federal disaster response activities.[15]

While the concept and intention were sound, poor leadership and disorganization throughout the 1980s degraded FEMA's ability to address nationwide natural disasters. In particular, three natural disasters at the end of the decade—the Loma Prieta earthquake (Figure 1.4), Hurricane Andrew, and Hurricane Hugo—raised serious questions about FEMA's ability to effectively respond to natural disasters. When surveying the damage caused by Hurricane Hugo, South Carolina Senator Fritz Hollings expressed his frustration at the lack of FEMA's response, calling the agency "the sorriest bunch of bureaucratic jackasses I've ever known."[16]

Despite these difficulties, FEMA made inroads in developing comprehensive disaster management plans and response capabilities. For instance, FEMA pioneered the Integrated Emergency Management System (IEMS) philosophy, which sought to practically apply the "dual-use" ethos behind the agency's creation. IEMS emphasized that both attack and peacetime emergencies required similar responses. Under IEMS, the response plan for a major storm

**FIG. 1.4**
Ground view of collapsed building and burned area at Beach and Divisadero
Streets, Marina District, San Francisco, following the October 17, 1989,
Loma Prieta earthquake. At 5:04:15 p.m. (PDT), the magnitude 6.9 (moment
magnitude; surface-wave magnitude, 7.1) earthquake severely shook the San
Francisco and Monterey Bay regions. The epicenter was located at 37.04°
N. latitude, 121.88° W. longitude near Loma Prieta peak in the Santa Cruz
Mountains, approximately 14 km (9 mi.) northeast of Santa Cruz and 96 km
(60 mi.) south-southeast of San Francisco.

*Source*: C.E. Meyer, USGS, https://prd-wret.s3-us-west-2.amazonaws.com/assets/palladium/
production/s3fs-public/styles/full_width/public/thumbnails/image/LomaPrietaSFDivisidero
CollapseMeyer.jpg (last visited Dec. 12, 2018).

or an accident at a nuclear power plant would also be useful in a response to
an attack on U.S. soil by a foreign country. While no one could foresee it at
the time, this foundational concept would eventually evolve into the "all-
hazards" philosophy adopted by the Department of Homeland Security after
the 9/11 attacks.

## FEDERAL RESPONSES TO TERRORISM BEFORE 9/11

As the 1990s began, the U.S government's primary emergency management concern remained the threat posed by natural hazards such as earthquakes and hurricanes. This was the case even as large-scale terrorist attacks on U.S. soil increasingly became a concern for security experts in the government. Indeed, while 9/11 is remembered as a watershed moment in American

**FIG. 1.5**
The Oklahoma City National Memorial and Museum was dedicated on April 19, 2000, five years to the day after the bombing. "The memorial is really built to remember those who were killed and those who survived and those who were changed forever," said Executive Director Kari Watkins. Two towers on either side of a reflecting pool where the Murrah building stood show the time immediately before and after the explosion. In the museum, visitors can see a room of twisted metal and concrete fragments left untouched after the bombing, along with a variety of interactive exhibits. In the memorial area, there is a chair for each of the 168 victims. Between the memorial and museum stands the Survivor Tree, which survived the blast and subsequent fires and symbolizes the notion that good will always triumph over evil.

*Source*: FBI, The Oklahoma City Bombing 20 Years Later, https://stories.fbi.gov/oklahoma-bombing/img/OKCNM-Chairs-Evening.jpg (last visited Dec. 12, 2018).

history, there were two terrorist attacks in the decade prior to 9/11, and neither led to significant changes in how the United States investigated, interdicted, or prosecuted terrorist actors on U.S. soil.

In 1993, Ramzi Ahmed Yousef and several co-conspirators detonated a truck bomb in the parking structure beneath the North Tower of the World Trade Center in New York City. With financing from Khaled Sheikh Mohammed, who later conceived and orchestrated the 9/11 attacks, Yousef hoped the destruction of one tower would result in the collapse of the other. Six people were killed in the attack, but the bomb fortunately failed to destroy the building. This incident did little to change public discourse about the threat from international terrorism.

Then in 1995, Timothy McVeigh and Terry Nichols detonated a truck bomb in front of the federal building in Oklahoma City, killing 168 people, injuring hundreds, and causing massive damage to the building. While this attack shocked Americans, it also did not lead to a lasting shift in how Americans viewed terrorism or how governments responded to a rising terrorist threat. As such, the Oklahoma City bombings did not marshal the political will to reform how the government protected the nation against terrorist attacks on critical targets, such as government buildings. There continued to be little to no public discourse about how terrorists or other criminal threats should be monitored, assessed, and deterred.

## SIDEBAR 1.1 Oklahoma City Bombing

The Oklahoma City bombing is still the deadliest act of homegrown terrorism in U.S. history. On April 19, 1995, Timothy McVeigh parked a Ryder truck packed with 5,000 pounds of explosives in front of the Murrah federal building. In a matter of seconds, the blast from the truck destroyed most of the nine-story concrete and granite building, killing 168 people, including 19 children who were in the building's daycare center. Dozens of cars were incinerated and more than 300 nearby buildings were damaged or destroyed.[17]

Timothy McVeigh targeted the Murrah building largely because it was full of U.S. government workers. Fourteen federal agencies had offices there and 98 of the victims worked for the federal government. McVeigh was a decorated Army veteran and believed the government was attacking the personal rights and freedoms of Americans. His anger was further stoked when 76 women, men, and children died in a fire during an armed standoff with federal agents in Waco, Texas in 1993. McVeigh, like many others radicalized by this incident, came to believe that federal officers had set the fire, and he planned to "fire the first shot" in a revolutionary war against the American government.

As the FBI and FEMA responded to the attacks, evidence quickly led to McVeigh. Investigators determined the explosion was caused by a truck bomb and collected vehicle parts with telltale bomb damage. A vehicle identification number led to a Ryder rental facility in Junction City, Kansas. On April 20, the FBI released a sketch of the man who rented the truck. The owner of the Dreamland Motel in Junction City recognized him as a guest registered as Timothy McVeigh.

A search of police records showed that McVeigh was in the Noble County jail in Perry, Oklahoma. A state trooper had stopped him shortly after the bombing because his car was missing a license plate. He arrested McVeigh for carrying a concealed firearm, and McVeigh was still in custody when the FBI called.

McVeigh used a Michigan address when he checked into the Dreamland Motel. He listed the same address—which belonged to a brother of Terry Nichols—when he was arrested shortly after the bombing. Terry Nichols was one of McVeigh's Army buddies also known for his antigovernment sentiments, and the investigation showed that Nichols helped McVeigh buy and steal the material for the bomb and helped mix the ingredients. Before the bombing, McVeigh spent time in Arizona with Michael Fortier, another Army friend, where he shared his plans and described how he would place the barrels of explosives in the truck. To help finance the plot, Fortier sold guns that McVeigh and Nichols had stolen.

Investigators discovered plenty of other evidence. The clothes McVeigh was wearing when he was arrested—along with a set of earplugs in his pocket—tested positive for chemical residue used in the explosive. Jim Norman said of McVeigh's clothes: "When we sent that clothing back to the FBI Laboratory and they did a chemical analysis test, they determined that he was basically the explosive equivalent of a powdered sugar donut."

McVeigh's fingerprints were also found on a receipt at Nichols' home for 2,000 pounds of fertilizer used to make the bomb. Other evidence linked McVeigh and Nichols to each other and to different elements of the crime.[18]

In August 1995, McVeigh and Nichols were charged with the same 11 federal crimes:

- Conspiring to use a weapon of mass destruction to kill people and destroy federal property;
- Using a weapon of mass destruction that caused death and injury;
- The malicious destruction of federal property by explosives; and
- Eight counts of first-degree murder of federal law enforcement officers.

A federal jury found McVeigh guilty of all counts on June 2, 1997. He was executed on June 11, 2001. A different jury found Nichols guilty of conspiracy and eight counts of manslaughter on December 23, 1997. He was sentenced to life in prison. Fortier testified against McVeigh and was sentenced to 12 years in prison for failing to report the planned attack and for lying to the FBI.

**CRITICAL THINKING QUESTION**

The Department of Homeland Security did not exist at the time the Oklahoma City bombing took place. Nor was there a governmental effort to create an agency like DHS after the bombing took place. However, as we will see, the 9/11 attacks mobilized a significant government reorganization to address terrorist attacks similar to the one that took place in Oklahoma. What was different about 9/11? What factors associated with 9/11 or the response to it led to the creation of a government department like DHS?

1.2 Discussion: "Why Now?"

Despite these attacks on both the American people and the federal government, Congress remained unable to deal with the rising threat from terrorism on U.S. soil. One exception was the increasing use of the Joint Terrorism Task Force (JTTF), a standing multi-agency team of local and federal law enforcement capable of responding to and initiating terrorism investigations. The concept was first put into practice in 1980 as an effort between the New York City Police Department and the Federal Bureau of Investigation. The first JTTFs focused on a range of terrorist groups threatening New York. The model proved effective throughout the 1980s. The 1993 World Trade Center attack and the Oklahoma City bombing further reinforced the need for more JTTF units. By 9/11, there were 35 JTTFs around the country.[19]

Meanwhile, in the decades before 9/11 the Department of Justice and the Department of Defense vied for the lead role in responding to terrorist attacks. Ultimately, Congress passed the Defense Against Weapons of Mass Destruction Act (also known as the Nunn-Lugar-Domenici Act). This legislation was a nascent attempt at coordinating the government's response to terrorism at home. In what would seem prescient after 9/11, the Act provided funds to assist first responders dealing with a weapon of mass destruction (WMD) attack on U.S. soil.

In addition to a rise in domestic terrorist attacks, similar attacks against U.S. interests abroad also accelerated throughout the 1990s and the early 2000s. In 1998, a terrorist organization known as al-Qa'ida organized an attack on the U.S. Embassy in Dar es Salaam, Tanzania and the U.S. Embassy in Nairobi, Kenya. The attacks killed more than 200 embassy personnel, as well as dozens of citizens from both countries.[20] Even though al-Qa'ida had been known to U.S. foreign policy and national security experts for some time, for the most part, these attacks were the first time the American public heard of this organization.

*U.S. knew about al-Qa'ida prior to 9/11 & had faced attacks by them.*

## RECOMMENDATIONS FROM COUNTERTERRORISM COMMISSIONS

Responding to these domestic and international terrorist incidents, the Executive Branch and Congress united to form several commissions to determine how best to address the rising threat of terrorism. In 1999, Congress created the Advisory Panel to Assess Domestic Response Capabilities for Terrorism Involving Weapons of Mass Destruction (also called the Gilmore Commission) to assess the capabilities for responding to terrorist incidents in the United States involving WMD, as well as the federal government's capacity to support state- and local-level counterterrorism efforts.[21]

The National Commission on Terrorism (also called the Bremer Commission) recognized the growing threat international terrorism posed to the United States and advocated the use of financial and intelligence tools to disrupt terrorist plots overseas and at home. The Bremer Commission's recommendations on monitoring individuals were somewhat controversial, particularly the recommendation for "monitoring of all foreign students, using criminals and terrorists as American spies, and making wiretapping easier."[22] Despite the controversy, a number of the Commission's recommendations, specifically those relating to surveillance and disrupting terrorist finances, were eventually adopted as part of the USA PATRIOT ACT after 9/11 (see Chapter 5).

Another such body, the U.S. Commission on National Security (also called the Hart-Rudman Commission; see the Sidebar on the Hart-Rudman Commission), was tasked with:

> Analyzing the emerging international security environment; develop a US national security strategy appropriate to that environment; and assess the various security institutions for their current relevance to the effective and efficient implementation of that strategy, and recommend adjustments as necessary.[23]

*[handwritten margin note: Emphasized needs for more security prior to 9/11]*

## SIDEBAR 1.2 The Hart-Rudman Commission

The U.S. Commission on National Security/21st Century (USCNS/21), also called the Hart-Rudman Commission for its co-chairs Gary Hart and Warren Rudman, was tasked in 1998 to conduct a review of 21st-century national security priorities for the United States. The Commission's findings were conducted and released in three phases:

*Phase 1*: Analyzed the evolving international security environment and identified trends demanding national security attention over the ensuing 25 years. The Phase 1 report, "New World Coming: American Security in the 21st Century," was released on September 15, 1999.

*Phase 2*: Designed a national security strategy to meet the challenges and needs identified in Phase 1. The phase's report, "Seeking a National Strategy: A Concert for Preserving Security and Promoting Freedom," was released on April 15, 2000.

*Phase 3*: Assessed the existing national security institutions to determine their capacity to implement the Phase 2 strategy and to recommend any changes needed to do so. The final report, "Roadmap for National Security: Imperative for Change," was released on January 31, 2001.

While the Commission's findings were wide-ranging and touched on numerous priorities and topics, the growing threat from international terrorism was a recurring topic in the Commission's work. Findings in the Phase 1 report stated that "America will become increasingly vulnerable to hostile attack on our homeland, and our military superiority will not entirely protect us," as well as that U.S. intelligence would not be able to "prevent all surprises." The Commission wrote, "States, terrorists, and other disaffected groups will acquire weapons of mass destruction and mass disruption, and some will use them. Americans will likely die on American soil, possibly in large numbers."[24]

When the final report was released in 2001, the Commission concluded, in part:

> Mass-casualty terrorism directed against the U.S. homeland [is] of serious and growing concern. [The Commission] therefore proposed in Phase II a strategy that prioritizes deterring, defending against, and responding effectively to such dangers. Thus, in Phase III, it recommends a new National Homeland Security Agency to consolidate and refine the missions of the nearly two dozen disparate departments and agencies that have a role in U.S. homeland security today.[25]

The September 11 terrorist attacks occurred mere months after the Commission made this recommendation.

The Hart-Rudman Commission issued its report on January 31, 2001, recommending the creation of a new, independent "National Homeland Security Agency" with the responsibility for planning, coordinating, and integrating various government activities involved in homeland security.[26] The report proposed moving previously independent federal agencies and departments into the new National Homeland Security Agency, including the U.S. Customs Service, the U.S. Border Patrol, the U.S. Coast Guard, and FEMA. This report's proposals ended up forming the basis of the hurried legislation passed in the immediate aftermath of the 9/11 attacks, including the Homeland Security Act that created the Department of Homeland Security.

The fact that all these commissions issued recommendations designed to prevent a 9/11 scenario just a few years—and in some cases, just a few months—before the 9/11 attacks was breathtakingly prescient, revealing that while the United States had begun to correctly identify major challenges to an integrated federal response to terrorism, the effort to do so was insufficient to thwart a well-planned and well-financed effort to attack the United States. Indeed, it took the massive, culture-rending terrorist attack of 9/11 to push the government to put all of these commissions' recommendations into action.

Thus, on September 11, 2001, the country was inadequately prepared to confront a terrorist attack on U.S. soil. The United States had spent much of the preceding decades preparing for natural disasters as well as attacks by foreign powers in the form of nuclear attacks and chemical and biological warfare. While these types of threats were worthy of careful planning and preparation, the narrow focus on civil defense and emergency response, especially during the last decades of the 20th century, blinded the United States to the ever-growing threat of terrorism . . . until it was too late.

## DEFINING HOMELAND SECURITY

*\* Need to be more pro-active*

The concept of securing the country against a range of threats has long been evolving, and, as noted, the United States' internal security posture has been and largely remains *event-driven*. Looming threats can inspire fear or economic protectionism, which in turn drives law and policy that alters and/or expands the role of the U.S. government in furthering homeland security. The event-driven nature of U.S. homeland security persists, though there are numerous fruitful efforts to anticipate emerging threats and adapt the U.S. security apparatus before those threats materialize. Thus, though there is some consensus on core ideas, challenges, and mission areas involved in securing the homeland, the very definition of "homeland security" continues to evolve.

First seen in the Hart-Rudman Commission report (which issued its recommendations prior to 9/11), the term "**homeland security**" has broadly come to mean two things:

- Programs, policies, and procedures put into place to detect, disrupt, and prevent terrorist attacks on U.S. soil; or
- Mitigation of, response to, and recovery from natural hazards and other catastrophic events (such as that caused by a weapon of mass destruction or WMD).

As will be discussed in Chapter 2, the Department of Homeland Security (DHS) is ostensibly organized around these two focus areas and the actions of this federal department play a large role in how the term "homeland security" is defined. Based on the previously discussed history of emergency management and natural disaster mitigation, DHS became responsible for coordinating local, state, and federal responses to large-scale disasters, such as hurricanes and other public health emergencies. This reassignment of duties has continued to expand the concept of homeland security to include responding to, preventing, and recovering from significant disasters and other events that threaten the United States and its economy, the rule of law, and government operations.[27]

At the same time, the terrorist attacks on September 11, 2001, which were the primary catalyst for the creation of DHS, imbued DHS with its second core mission of preventing terrorist attacks on the United States. As such, even as DHS has wide-ranging responsibilities, from emergency management to immigration enforcement, all Department Components contribute to the counterterrorism mission, making terrorism prevention a principal aspect of how homeland security is defined in the federal government.

Despite these definitions employed by DHS, it is important to note that even several years after the 9/11 attacks, the U.S. government as a whole still

**FIG. 1.6**

The DHS seal is symbolic of the Department's mission—to prevent attacks and protect Americans—on the land, in the sea, and in the air. The seal was developed with input from senior DHS leadership, employees, and the U.S. Commission on Fine Arts. The Ad Council—which partners with DHS on its Ready.gov campaign—and the consulting company Landor Associates were responsible for graphic design and maintaining heraldic integrity.

*Source*: Wikimedia, https://upload.wikimedia.org/wikipedia/commons/8/8a/Seal_of_the_United_States_Department_of_Homeland_Security.svg (last visited Dec. 12, 2018).

does not have a single definition for "homeland security."[28] Even with the establishment of DHS, a Homeland Security Council at the White House, and several dozen Homeland Security Presidential Directives, the term "homeland security" remains difficult to define (see the "Federal Definitions of Homeland Security" in this chapter for more information).

## CALL-OUT BOX
## Federal Definitions of Homeland Security

2007 National Strategy for Homeland Security (White House)

*Many definitions*

> *A concerted national effort to prevent terrorist attacks within the United States, reduce America's vulnerability to terrorism, and minimize the damage and recover from attacks that do occur.*[29]

2008 U.S Department of Homeland Security Strategic Plan, Fiscal Years 2008–2013 (DHS)

> *A united national effort to prevent and deter terrorist attacks, protect and respond to hazards, and to secure the national borders.*[30]

2010 National Security Strategy (White House)

> *A seamless coordination among federal, state and local governments to prevent, protect against and respond to threats and natural disasters.*[31]

2010 Quadrennial Homeland Security Review (DHS)

> *A concerted national effort to ensure a homeland that is safe, secure and resilient against terrorism and other hazards where American interests, aspirations, and ways of life can thrive.*[32]

2010 Bottom-Up Review (DHS)

> *Preventing terrorism, responding to and recovering from natural disasters, customs enforcement and collection of customs revenue, administration of legal immigration services, safety and stewardship of the Nation's waterways and marine transportation system, as well as other legacy missions of the various components of DHS.*[33]

2011 National Strategy for Counterterrorism (White House)

> *Defensive efforts to counter terrorist threats.*[34]

2012 Strategic Plan (DHS)

> *Efforts to ensure a homeland that is safe, secure and resilient against terrorism and other hazards.*[35]

Government watchdogs have argued that multiple homeland security definitions and missions impede the development of a coherent national homeland security strategy and hamper the effectiveness of congressional oversight. Definitions and missions are part of strategy development. Policymakers develop strategy by identifying national interests, prioritizing goals to achieve those national interests, and arraying instruments of national power to achieve national interests.

Though DHS is attempting to coordinate and align its definition and missions, there remains significant confusion about DHS and larger homeland security definitions and strategies. Many argue that the result of these unclear foundational directives has become evident in the resulting organization and mission confusion of DHS. An absence of agreed-upon definitions and mission priorities can also result in Congress funding parts of the homeland security enterprise that DHS or other federal agencies do not wish to be funded. For instance, Congress may appropriate funding for counterterrorism programs, such as the State Homeland Security Grant Program, when DHS may have identified an all-hazards grant program, such as Emergency Management Performance Grant Program, as a priority.[36] Additionally, definitions that do not specifically include immigration enforcement or natural disaster response and recovery may result in homeland security stakeholders and other federal government entities not adequately resourcing and focusing on these activities.

*[handwritten margin note: Need solid definition to better appropriate funding.]*

## AN "ALL HAZARDS" APPROACH

Despite the numerous definitions of homeland security, we can rely on a series of overarching themes and concepts that can help us to reach a common understanding:

- **Coordination** The homeland security enterprise seeks to coordinate the actions of all levels of government (federal, state, local, and tribal government) and the private sector. The federal government (usually through DHS) serves as the primary coordinating body;
- **Mitigation** Absolute security or complete threat reduction is unobtainable. Homeland security activities should seek to reduce, manage, and mitigate risk, rather than eliminate it; and

- **All-hazards** Homeland security envisions preparing for and responding to all types of threats, those caused by humans (such as cybersecurity threats or terrorist acts) as well as those that occur naturally (such as hurricanes).

This "all-hazards" approach is discussed further in Chapter 7.

Even though counterterrorism is arguably perceived to be the dominant focus in homeland security activities, DHS and partner organizations are philosophically oriented around the all-hazards concept. The all-hazards approach is a natural outgrowth of an agency designed to mitigate national problems while also coordinating the security and threat response efforts of state and local law enforcement and public safety agencies. The all-hazards approach is also an outgrowth of a simple practical fact: The bureaucratic infrastructure used to respond to a hurricane, for example, is the same as that used when responding to a terrorist attack. The ways in which federal, state, and local agencies communicate and collaborate have crosscutting institutional value.

While there is common agreement that this is the appropriate organizational philosophy for government agencies involved in homeland security, a broad all-hazards definition is frustrated by the fact that there is little common agreement on definitions of the hazards themselves. For example, the federal government does not have one definition for terrorism; it has many.

*Many definitions of terrorism*

The FBI defines **terrorism** as "the unlawful use of force or violence against persons or property to intimidate or coerce a government, the civilian population, or any segment thereof, in furtherance of political or social objectives."[37] The Department of Defense defines terrorism as "the unlawful use of violence or threat of violence, often motivated by religious, political, or other ideological beliefs, to instill fear and coerce governments or societies in pursuit of goals that are usually political."[38] And the Central Intelligence Agency defines terrorism as "premeditated, politically motivated violence perpetrated against noncombatant targets by subnational groups or clandestine agents."[39]

DHS captures aspects of these definitions in its own somewhat broader definition:

> Any activity that involves an act that is dangerous to human life or potentially destructive to critical infrastructure or key resources, and is a violation of the criminal laws of the United States or of any state or other subdivision of the United States and appears to be intended to intimidate

**FIG. 1.7**
A FEMA promotional image for communities and local governments wishing to raise awareness of hurricane-related flood risk. The statement in this image can also apply to a host of other hazards, not just floods.

*Source*: Federal Emergency Management Agency, https://agents.floodsmart.gov/sites/default/files/inline-images/nobody-thinks-facebook-fb.png (last visited Dec. 12, 2018).

or coerce a civilian population to influence the policy of a government by intimidation or coercion, or to affect the conduct of a government by mass destruction, assassination, or kidnapping.[40]

The multiple definitions of terrorism and the all-hazards approach to emergency management pose a bureaucratic problem. A broad mandate paired with lack of clarity on the definition of the mission results in confusion across state and local government sectors as well as overlap of the mission set, where more than one agency or part of an agency ends up doing the same job. Though this is a problem endemic in all large bureaucracies, it is particularly troubling when considering the safety-oriented mission of many homeland security government agencies, including DHS.

## NATIONAL SECURITY AND HOMELAND DEFENSE

As with the term "homeland security," "**national security**" is also difficult to define. The National Security Act of 1947[41] simply defined "national security" as the state's efforts to protect itself. However, many government agencies define national security differently. The Department of Defense defines national security as

> a collective term encompassing both national defense and foreign relations of the United States with the purpose of gaining:
>
> 1. A military or defense advantage over any foreign nation or group of nations;
> 2. A favorable foreign relations position; or
> 3. A defense posture capable of successfully resisting hostile or destructive action from within or without, overt or covert.[42]

As concepts, homeland security and national security are intimately related, and in practice many of the organizations charged with ensuring national security (such as the Department of Defense) have important roles in the homeland security apparatus. Ultimately, however, national security focuses on policy shaping the overall territorial integrity of a country by pursuing goals externally and in relationship with the international community, whereas homeland security agencies focus on domestic policy by pursuing goals focused on internal security concerns.

Complicating definitions further is the concept of "homeland defense," which is distinct from homeland security. Whereas homeland security is the responsibility of civilian agencies at all levels, addressing law enforcement, disaster, immigration, and terrorism issues, homeland defense is the purview of the armed forces. **Homeland defense** is primarily a Department of Defense activity and is defined as "the protection of U.S. sovereignty, territory, domestic population, and critical defense infrastructure against external threats and aggression, or other threats as directed by the President."[43]

The differences between homeland security and homeland defense are not completely distinct. An international terrorist organization attack on and within the United States would result in a combined homeland security and homeland defense response, such as on 9/11 when civilian agencies were responding to the attacks while the U.S. military established a combat air patrol over New York and Washington, D.C. This distinction between homeland security and homeland defense, and the evolution of homeland security as a concept, was reflected in the strategic documents developed and issued following 9/11.

We will explore these concepts, as well as how they remain distinct but also overlap, in further chapters. We will also discuss the impact vague and ambiguous definitions have on the way the government carries out homeland security policy.

## CONCLUSION

So central has the idea of "homeland security" become to American culture that many Americans are left bewildered when confronted with the absence of this term in government policy prior to 9/11. Today, homeland security forms the basis of entire hit television shows, podcasts, and documentaries. Large academic programs (such as the one you are probably in now) are founded upon the discipline, and several hundred thousand individuals work to secure the homeland every day.

Thus, it is also surprising that despite how quickly the concept has invaded popular American culture, so little consensus exists on exactly what "homeland security" is. This is due, in part, to its roots in the slow-growing discipline of emergency management, and perhaps in its confusing co-option of this discipline into the larger homeland security enterprise. As if all this confusion wasn't enough, the discipline of homeland security continues to change with every passing year. As we will see in the remainder of this text, new terrorist threats and the rising problem of climate change are pushing the boundaries of this new discipline. It is both a scary and exciting time to be involved in the growing field of homeland security, and also a time when individuals can shape the discipline in important and meaningful ways.

## HOMELAND SECURITY VOICES: Governor Tom Ridge (Part 1)

*Thomas Ridge has held a number of public service positions throughout his career, the most relevant of these for the purposes of this text being his service as the first Secretary of Homeland Security as well as the Assistant to the President for Homeland Security to George W. Bush. Prior to his service at the Executive Branch, Tom Ridge was a member of the U.S. House of Representatives from 1983 to 1995 and 43rd Governor of Pennsylvania from 1995 to 2001.*

*Following the September 11 attacks President George W. Bush named Ridge the first Director of the newly created Office of Homeland Security. In January 2003, the Office of Homeland Security became an official Cabinet-level department—the Department of Homeland Security—and Ridge became the first Secretary of Homeland Security. He served in this role during Bush's first term as President, retiring thereafter.*

*In part 1 of this interview from 2014, Gov. Ridge discusses his efforts in standing up DHS and his views on some of the challenges facing the Department as it continues to grow.*

**FIG. 1.8**
Tom Ridge introduces President Bush just prior to the President's speech regarding the PATRIOT ACT, the war in Iraq, and the war on terror. Taken at the Union Pier in Charleston, South Carolina.

*Source*: Former DHS Secretary Tom Ridge with Former President George W. Bush, CPL Jose O. Mediavilla, USMC. Released to the public as part of the combined military service digital photographic files archive, https://nara.getarchive.net/download-image?src=https://cdn9.picryl.com/photo/2004/02/05/the-honorable-tom-ridge-secretary-of-homeland-security-introduces-george-w-ba58f1.jpg.

*What challenges did you have standing up the Department of Homeland Security?*

TR: The seminal challenge, in my mind, was convincing Congress and ultimately Americans in the 21st century, particularly after 9/11, that it was absolutely essential for the United States to build a border-centric agency that effectively monitored people and goods coming in and out of the country. The inter-connectedness and inter-dependency of the global community and the forces of globalization necessitated the creation of the Department of Homeland Security. In fact, I would have argued for its creation even before 9/11.

The second most significant challenge was creating a collective sense of mission among the disparate entities that form DHS so that every agency appreciated the necessity of newfound internal collaboration among government agencies entities that had previously existed in siloed and closed-off entities.

A third challenge was to integrate the capabilities of each component agency of DHS in a way that was both efficient in terms of the resources committed, while being effective in terms of the outcome desired. If one thinks of DHS initially as a holding company, those who were involved at the outset of DHS would remind you that underneath the holding company umbrella we had mergers, acquisitions, start-ups, and a few other things going on all under one entity called DHS. Thus, the mechanics of starting up DHS were very complicated, but the first two challenges were the most important substantively and intellectually.

*Do you believe that a government entity such as DHS was the best way to solve the lack of coordination among government agencies that existed prior to 9/11?*

TR: One of the observations I made when standing up DHS, predicated both on my experience previously as a Congressman and then as Governor of Pennsylvania and then certainly as Assistant to the President for Homeland Security, is that not too much moves in Washington, D.C., as far as integrating capabilities unless you control budgets.

DHS was a new department in name, but it was created through the assimilation of multiple agencies for whom border responsibilities were very essential. To the extent that agencies with authority over and around the border were included in a border-centric agency, DHS' initial structure was appropriately framed—the agencies and units of government that were integrated into DHS were clearly appropriate. At the outset of DHS, there were multiple human resource systems, multiple procurement systems, and different approaches toward the budget as well as the creation of different digital and cyber divisions. The organizational tasks were astounding. Had DHS been a series of merging businesses, by the time they received regulatory approval, they would have had more than a year to sort out all the issues associated with merging a large organization. Unfortunately DHS had less than 90 days to sort those same issues out with a staff of over 180,000 personnel and at the same time we had to fill vacancies and build out policies. I think that business line integration of the Department continues to this day. Given these challenges, the defensive role that DHS plays in combating terrorist threats is a vital one, despite the challenges that remain in making the Department a more complete entity.

*One of the roles of the Department was to focus on the private sector, because the private sector bears the brunt of both manmade and natural hazards. Do you think that the Department's current initiatives have been sufficient in increasing the resiliency of the private sector to all these hazards or is there more work to do? And if there is more work to be done, is there a structure that should be put in place that is different than the public/private partnerships that are currently in place?*

TR: The term "public/private partnership" is very much a refrain that political figures use on a fairly regular basis and I happen to believe that public/private partnerships, if structured around mutual goals and mutual responsibility, are far more effective than either the government or the private sector working independently. Let me give an example: We wanted to expedite throughput across the Detroit/Ontario border region and there were many complaints about infrastructure. Alfonso Martinez-Fonts, he's from the Department in charge of private sector collaboration, sat down with the private sector and facilitated a change in delivery schedules, customs and border protections in the toll booths, in order to make change work.

However, if you are trying to combat terrorism, one of your largest, most significant concerns is sharing information. Information-sharing is still a challenge, although not so much DHS' challenge because DHS is really a consumer of intelligence. DHS doesn't generate intelligence, so DHS can't be blamed for not dispersing information they don't know. DHS needs to receive information about potential attacks from other government agencies, alphabet agencies, and other resources. There are still too many occasions when federal government agencies do not share information about a potential physical attack such as the Boston Marathon attack with the private sector.

So public/private partnerships work, if they are managed effectively toward mutually beneficial outcomes and are far more effective than either organization working on its own. Ultimately, I think that DHS, and the rest of the government channeling information through DHS, still has a lot of work to do in building stronger partnerships with the private sector.

*Speaking of the Boston Marathon bombing, two criticisms have arisen in the aftermath of the bombing: First is the allegation that the federal law enforcement community, including DHS, is not doing enough to capture terrorists despite the massive resources they have at their disposal. The second criticism is that federal law enforcement agencies continue to focus too much on ideologically based violent extremism. These critics cite incidents such as the non-ideologically motivated shooting in Aurora, Colorado and the 2013 Washington Navy Yard shooting as two incidents that don't receive as much attention or resources. What are your thoughts on the validity of these criticisms?*

TR: It's extremely difficult for me to compare the Boston Marathon bombings to the shooting in Aurora, Colorado or those in the Naval Yard since I believe the latter two weren't terrorist attacks because they did not represent action taken based upon the embrace of a certain extremist ideology. Of course, the family of the deceased thought it was an act of terror clearly, but in terms of terrorism as I think of it in terms of action on the basis of flawed ideology, the shootings in Colorado and DC were not terrorism.

As to the first criticism applied to the Boston Marathon: I believe the desire to stay focused on an independent investigation and the reluctance to share relevant information with the commissioner of police or local authorities was a huge mistake. This is relevant not just to the Boston Marathon bombing but generally as well. At some point Washington, D.C., must come to trust the integrity and the ability of law enforcement at the state and local level and share law enforcement information so that it can be used in a way by local officials to further an ongoing investigation. Frankly speaking, state and local police have as many or more resources available than any of the alphabet agencies at the federal level. Federal authorities are no better than their counterparts at the local level. They might have higher training, higher salaries, or access to more information but they need to share it, and when it came to the Boston Marathon bombings, they didn't.

*What if I play devil's advocate and say, "we have Fusion Centers, see we are involving local law enforcement in the work that we do and we value their contributions to the Intelligence Community, Fusion Centers didn't exist before DHS?"*

TR: I think Fusion Centers are great, although we have too many of them. However, at the end of the day Fusion Centers are only as good as when someone in the federal government shares the information gathered at the Fusion Center. The notion of a Fusion Center rhetorically, conceptually, is a great idea—but who is hitting the send button with all that information at the federal level?

*Well, what more can be done? What would you want to see done on information-sharing?*

TR: For starters, there is a lot of information that should not be classified secret or top secret. I think government agencies often use the classification system to deny access to information to people who deserve access. In many instances the claim by government in general that "we would be compromising sources and ethics" is a cop out. There are ways around that, but until the President of the United States pulls everybody together, and maybe the Intelligence Community and all the intelligence committees in Congress say "this has got to stop," we cannot secure the country as effectively as possible from inside the Beltway.

We talk about public/private partnerships; how about a public/public partnership? In a federal system—governors, big city mayors, and chiefs of police, and state police—should have a say when it comes to information security as well. They need to be empowered with relevant information from time to time so that they can be another set of boots on the ground, eyes and ears in the community; and the federal government makes a horrible mistake not sharing some of the information it classifies with these public agencies.

*Edward Snowden's revelations about domestic surveillance have resulted in the American people losing trust with the federal government generally and specifically with the domestic programs that the U.S. government has in place to combat terrorism. From your perspective, as a former DHS Secretary and as somebody who has served in almost all the leadership roles of federal government: What role do domestic surveillance programs play in reducing terrorist threats and how best can these programs be reformed?*

TR: I'm a traditionalist. I've spent most of my life in public service and I understand the sophistication, the technology, and the potential use domestic surveillance programs may be put to in an anecdotal way to prevent a terrorist attack. However, I am not prepared to surrender what little privacy we have left in this country. I think there's a lot of young people giving up their privacy by telling everybody about themselves through social media. For instance, I don't know if people who signed up for Google know that their information is going to be used to sell them products. I respect what the NSA (National Security Agency) tried to do. I believe their actions are consistent with the law, but I'm not convinced these domestic surveillance programs are terribly effective. There is a lot of uncertainty as to the procedures they have used, but I for one think that going forward the NSA will have to make a stronger case that they should be engaged in domestic surveillance while meeting the standards set out in the Fourth Amendment.

*This interview continues at the conclusion of Chapter 2.*

## KEYWORDS

- **"power of the purse"**: The power of the purse is the ability of one government body to manipulate and control the actions of another body by withholding funding, or putting stipulations on the use of funds. The power of the purse can be used positively (e.g. awarding extra funding to programs that reach certain benchmarks) or negatively (e.g. removing funding for a department or program, effectively eliminating it).

- **homeland security**:
  - Programs, policies, and procedures put into place to detect, disrupt, and prevent terrorist attacks on U.S. soil; or
  - Mitigation of, response to, and recovery from natural hazards and other catastrophic events (such as that caused by a weapon of mass destruction or WMD).

- **terrorism**: Any activity that involves an act that is dangerous to human life or potentially destructive to critical infrastructure or key resources, and is a violation of the criminal laws of the United States or of any state or other subdivision of the United States and appears to be intended to intimidate or coerce a civilian population to influence the policy of a government by intimidation or coercion, or to affect the conduct of a government by mass destruction, assassination, or kidnapping (this is one of many definitions).

- **national security**: The creation of policies by governments to ensure the survival and safety of the state, using the state's diplomatic, economic, and military power to achieve security.

- **homeland defense**: The protection of U.S. sovereignty, territory, domestic population, and critical defense infrastructure against external threats and aggression, or other threats as directed by the President.

---

**KNOWLEDGE CHECK**

1. How did the federal government respond to emergencies in the 19th and 20th centuries?
2. What are some examples of federal government efforts to respond to emergencies prior to 9/11?
3. How are the concepts of homeland security, national security, and homeland defense different? How are they the same?
4. What is the "all-hazards" approach to emergency management?

---

## NOTES

1. B. Wayne Blanchard, "Historical Overview of U.S. Emergency Management" (lecture taught at the Emergency Management Institute), https://training.fema.gov/hiedu/docs/hazdem/session%209—historical%20overview%20of%20us%20em.doc.
2. SeacoastNH.com, www.seacoastnh.com/History/As-I-Please/The-Three-Fires-of-Christmas/ (last visited Dec. 12, 2018).
3. *Id.*
4. Drabek, Thomas, *The Evolution of Emergency Management*, in *Emergency Management: Principles and Practice for Local Government* 6 (Thomas E. Drabek & Gerard J. Hoetmer eds., 1991).
5. *Id.*
6. B. Wayne Blanchard, "Historical Overview of U.S. Emergency Management" (lecture taught at the Emergency Management Institute), https://training.fema.gov/hiedu/docs/hazdem/session%209—historical%20overview%20of%20us%20em.doc.
7. *Id.*

8. Exec. Order No. 8629, 6 Fed. Reg. 191 (January 7, 1941).

9. *Societal Factors Influencing Emergency Management Policy and Practice*, in Facing the Unexpected—Disaster Preparedness and Response in the United States 240 (Kathleen J. Tierney, Michael K. Lindell, Ronald W. Perry eds., 2001).

10. The Office for Emergency Preparedness' responsibilities were distinct from the civil defense responsibilities of the Department of Defense Office of Civil Defense.

11. B. Wayne Blanchard, "Historical Overview of U.S. Emergency Management" (lecture taught at the Emergency Management Institute), https://training.fema.gov/hiedu/docs/hazdem/session%209—historical%20overview%20of%20us%20em.doc (citing Silverstein, 1992).

12. The act was in response to damages caused by Hurricane Agnes and was a watershed moment for the provision of federal emergency aid to the states because it authorized the federal government, for the first time, to *directly* provide individual and family disaster assistance. *See* John J. Rumbarger, Prologue: Crisis in Emergency Preparedness, Part 2 (1983) (citing John J. Rumbarger, Crisis in Emergency Preparedness, Part I, "Emergency Preparedness and Industrial Mobilization," Report by the Joint Committee on Defense Production, Congress of the United States, at 169–172, *Civil Preparedness Review Part I,* 1977, and *Excerpts from the President's Message to Congress Transmitting Reorganization Plan. No. 1 of 1973,* After Disaster Strikes: Federal Programs and Organizations 111–12 (1974)).

13. DEFENSE CIVIL PREPAREDNESS AGENCY, DEPARTMENT OF DEFENSE, CIVIL PREPAREDNESS—A NEW DUAL MISSION (1972) https://training.fema.gov/hiedu/docs/dcpa%20-%201972%20-%20civil%20preparedness%20a%20new%20dual%20mission-annual%20r.pdf.

14. *See* Exec. Order No. 12127, 44 Fed. Reg. 19367 (1979); *See also* 5 U.S.C. § 903 (2018).

15. SAUNDRA K. SCHNEIDER, Flirting with Disaster—Public Management in Crisis Situations 22 (1995).

16. B. Wayne Blanchard, "Historical Overview of U.S. Emergency Management" (lecture taught at the Emergency Management Institute), https://training.fema.gov/hiedu/docs/hazdem/session%209—historical%20overview%20of%20us%20em.doc.

17. Federal Bureau of Investigation, *The Oklahoma City Bombing 20 Years Later,* https://stories.fbi.gov/oklahoma-bombing/ (last visited Dec. 12, 2018).

18. Federal Bureau of Investigation, *The Oklahoma City Bombing 20 Years Later,* https://stories.fbi.gov/oklahoma-bombing/ (last visited Dec. 12, 2018).

19. Interview with Joe Valiquette, special agent, and J. Peter Donald, public affairs specialist, Federal Bureau of Investigation (Dec. 9, 2010).

20. FEDERAL BUREAU OF INVESTIGATION, *East African Embassy Bombings*, www.fbi.gov/history/famous-cases/east-african-embassy-bombings (last visited Dec. 12, 2009).

21. Advisory Panel to Assess Domestic Response Capabilities for Terrorism Involving Weapons of Mass Destruction, Forging America's New Normalcy: Securing Our Homeland, Preserving Our Liberty (2003).

22. National Commission on Terrorism, Countering the Changing Threat of International Terrorism (2000) www.gpo.gov/fdsys/pkg/CDOC-106hdoc250/pdf/CDOC-106hdoc250.pdf.

23. United States Commission on National Security/ 21st Century, New World Coming: American Security in the 21st Century (1999).

24. United States Commission on National Security/ 21st Century, New World Coming: American Security in the 21st Century, Phase I Report 138 (1999) http://govinfo.library.unt.edu/nssg/NWR_A.pdf.

25. United States Commission on National Security/ 21st Century, Road Map for National Security: Imperative for Change, Phase III Report vi (2001) http://govinfo.library.unt.edu/nssg/PhaseIIIFR.pdf.

26. United States Commission on National Security/ 21st Century, Road Map for National Security: Imperative for Change, Phase III Report iv (2001) http://govinfo.library.unt.edu/nssg/PhaseIIIFR.pdf.

27. Nadav Morag, *Does Homeland Security Exist Outside the United States?*, 7 Homeland Security Affairs 1 (2011).

28. Shawn Reese, Cong. Research Serv., R42462, Defining Homeland Security: Analysis and Congressional Considerations (2013).

29. The Office of the President, Homeland Security Council, National Strategy for Homeland Security, at 1 (2007) www.dhs.gov/xlibrary/assets/nat_strat_homelandsecurity_2007.pdf.

30. U.S. Department of Homeland Security, One Team, One Mission, Securing the Homeland: U.S. Homeland Security Strategic Plan, Fiscal Years 2008–2013, at 3 (2008) file:///Users/carolinemarshall/Downloads/235371.pdf.

31. The White House Office of the President, National Security Strategy, at 2 (2010) file:///Users/carolinemarshall/Downloads/24251.pdf.

32. U.S. Department of Homeland Security, Quadrennial Homeland Security Review Report: A Strategic Framework for a Secure Homeland, at 13 (2010) www.dhs.gov/sites/default/files/publications/2010-qhsr-report.pdf.

33. U.S. Department of Homeland Security, Bottom-Up Review Report, at 3 (2010) www.dhs.gov/sites/default/files/publications/bur_bottom_up_review.pdf.

34. The White House Office of the President, National Strategy for Counterterrorism, at 11 (2011) https://obamawhitehouse.archives.gov/sites/default/files/counterterrorism_strategy.pdf.

35. U.S. Department of Homeland Security, Department of Homeland Security Strategic Plan: Fiscal Years 2012–2016, at 2 (2012) www.dhs.gov/sites/default/files/publications/DHS%20Strategic%20Plan.pdf. This document does not explicitly state a definition for "homeland security" but it does define DHS' "vision."

36. Shawn Reese, Cong. Research Serv., R42462, Defining Homeland Security: Analysis and Congressional Considerations, at 10 (2013).

37. 28 C.F.R. § 0.85 (2018).

38. Joint Chiefs of Staff, Counterterrorism Joint Publication 3–26 (2014) www.jcs.mil/Portals/36/Documents/Doctrine/pubs/jp3_26.pdf.

39. Central Intelligence Agency, *CIA & The War on Terrorism—Terrorism FAQs* (Apr. 19, 2013, 12:29 PM) www.cia.gov/news-information/cia-the-war-on-terrorism/terrorism-faqs.html?tab=list-3.

40. Office of Intelligence and Analysis (U/FOUO) Domestic Terrorism and Homegrown Violent Extremism Lexicon (2011) https://info.publicintelligence.net/DHS-ExtremismLexicon.pdf.

41. Implementing Recommendations of the 9/11 Commission Act of 2007, Pub. L. No. 110–53, § 101, 121 Stat. 266 (2007).

42. Department of Defense, DoD Dictionary of Military and Associated Terms, at 162 (2018) www.jcs.mil/Portals/36/Documents/Doctrine/pubs/dictionary.pdf.

43. Assistant Secretary of Defense for Homeland Defense and Global Security, *Frequently Asked Questions*, U.S. Department of Defense (last visited Dec. 13, 2018) http://policy.defense.gov/OUSDP-Offices/ASD-for-Homeland-Defense-Global-Security/Homeland-Defense-Integration-DSCA/faqs/.

# CHAPTER 2

# The Formation of the Homeland Security Enterprise After 9/11

---

**IN THIS CHAPTER YOU WILL LEARN ABOUT**

---

What the September 11, 2001 attacks revealed about the United States' readiness to resist and respond to the evolving terrorist threat.

The structure of federal agencies that secure the homeland.

The role of other federal, state, and local government agencies, as well as the private sector, in homeland security.

## INTRODUCTION

When al-Qa'ida terrorists hijacked airplanes on the morning of September 11, 2001, the U.S. public was generally aware of a growing threat from international terrorism. A 2001 Pew Research Center and Council on Foreign Relations survey conducted before 9/11 revealed that 74% of the general public viewed weapons of mass destruction (WMD) as a major threat, and 64% of the public believed international terrorism was a major threat.[1] The September 11 attacks were thus something both familiar (international terrorism) and also unwitnessed (the use of airplanes as weapons of mass destruction).

The U.S. had not experienced a foreign attack of this magnitude since Japan bombed the U.S. naval base at Pearl Harbor in 1941. There was enormous shock, sadness, and anger in the wake of the September 11 attacks. But aside from the emotional reaction, the attacks drove the largest government reorganization since the Department of Defense was created in 1947, transforming much of the federal government and dramatically altering the functions of many state, local and municipal agencies.

The attacks also prompted rapid and dramatic change in security priorities. The threat of terrorism was real, and Americans were scared and calling for the government to protect the homeland.[2] Eleven days after the attacks, Pennsylvania Governor Tom Ridge was appointed to be the first director of the Office of Homeland Security in the White House. The office oversaw and coordinated a comprehensive national strategy to safeguard the country against terrorism and respond to any future attacks.

In the months and years that followed, there was a focused and robust effort to understand how a small group of well-funded terrorists could elude the U.S. national security establishment, including intelligence organizations such as the Central Intelligence Agency (CIA). The attacks on 9/11 and resulting public anger, confusion, and fear led, in part, to the passage of the Homeland Security Act in November 2002. The Homeland Security Act created the Department of Homeland Security (DHS), a new cabinet-level agency tasked with coordinating national homeland security efforts. All or part of 22 federal entities were merged into DHS as part of a national effort to more closely integrate federal counterterrorism efforts with efforts of local governments, intelligence agencies, and foreign intelligence counterparts.

As a first step in understanding the vast complexity of the U.S. homeland security enterprise, it is important to investigate the lessons learned from the 9/11 attacks and the resulting national effort to create government bodies and relationships capable of responding to all of the human-caused and natural threats facing the U.S. in the 21st century. The concepts covered below present a lot of new information and will be covered in much greater detail in subsequent chapters.

## INVESTIGATIONS INTO FAILURES ON 9/11

Osama bin Laden (Figure 2.1), the leader of al-Qa'ida, was known to the U.S. Intelligence Community prior to the September 11 attacks. In February 1998, bin Laden issued a *fatwa* (religious edict), stating:

**FIG. 2.1**
Osama bin Laden sits with his adviser Dr. Ayman al-Zawahiri during an interview with Pakistani journalist Hamid Mir. Hamid Mir took this picture during his third and last interview with Osama bin Laden in November 2001 in Kabul. Dr. Ayman al-Zawahiri was present in this interview and acted as the translator of Osama bin Laden.

*Source*: Hamid Mir, Osama bin Laden, and Ayman al-Zawahiri in 2001 (2001) https://upload.wikimedia.org/wikipedia/commons/a/a1/Hamid_Mir_interviewing_Osama_bin_Laden_and_Ayman_al-Zawahiri_2001.jpg.

1998
Statement

Killing the Americans and their allies—civilians and military—is an individual duty for every Muslim who can carry it out in any country where it proves possible, in order to liberate Al-Aqsa Mosque and the holy sanctuary from their grip, and to the point that their armies leave all Muslim territory, defeated and unable to threaten any Muslim.[3]

Throughout the 1990s, bin Laden's threats and others from similar terrorist leaders began inspiring violent action throughout the Middle East and North Africa, highlighting al-Qa'ida's role as a growing transnational terrorist organization whose adherents operated globally.

At least some members of the U.S. Intelligence Community treated Osama bin Laden as a credible threat. The CIA created a "bin Laden station," the first time a U.S. government intelligence agency established an operational unit to address threats posed by a single individual. In August 1998, al-Qa'ida operatives drove truck bombs into the U.S. embassies in Nairobi, Kenya, and Dar es Salaam, Tanzania. In response, then-CIA Director George Tenet declared war on bin Laden. Unknown to the CIA, the terrorist plot that would occur on September 11, 2001, had already been under development for two years.[4]

*[handwritten margin note: → After '98 bombing]*

The plotting and events that led up to the 9/11 attacks are well documented elsewhere and worthy of study. For our purposes, however, there are two critical facts to note about the morning of September 11:

- Intelligence Community agencies were actively engaged in monitoring and attempting to disrupt al-Qa'ida and its affiliates. Each agency had some level of awareness about an impending plot, though none had the full picture.
- Existing aviation security protocols were followed on the morning of September 11. One of the hijackers, Mohamed Atta, even triggered the Computer Assisted Passenger Prescreening System (CAPPS), which identified air travelers for additional security measures.[5] And when the hijackers on four planes charged the cockpits and began issuing demands, those instructions were followed by airline personnel per existing hijacking policy, which mistakenly assumed any hijacker would ultimately want to land the airplane.

Thus, al-Qa'ida did not appear unexpectedly over the horizon, as Japanese aircraft had done in their sneak attack on Pearl Harbor decades earlier. Indeed, well before 9/11, the United States was aware of al-Qa'ida's intentions, its previous attacks on U.S. personnel and interests abroad, and the likelihood that they would strike again. The fact that the attacks on 9/11 occurred despite this awareness is what made them so surprising and shocking for the public and the national security community. In the aftermath of 9/11 everyone wanted to know: How did this happen? Congress and other government bodies soon convened a series of meetings, committees, and task forces to determine the answer to this question.

### Congressional Inquiries Into 9/11

The first of these congressional committees were the House Permanent Select Committee on Intelligence and the Senate Select Committee on Intelligence.

**FIG. 2.2**
Osama bin
Laden was even-
tually found
and killed in
Abbottabad,
Pakistan, on
May 2, 2011.

*Source*: Josh Pesavento, Celebrations in Times Square for the Death of Osama bin Laden
(2011) https://upload.wikimedia.org/wikipedia/commons/4/4d/Times_Square_on_the_
night_Osama_bin_Laden_killed.jpg.

On December 2002, they released the "Report of the Joint Inquiry Into the
Terrorist Attacks of September 11, 2001."[6]

One of the principal findings of the report was that the CIA, the Federal
Bureau of Investigation (FBI), and other intelligence agencies, through their
respective national security responsibilities, had each independently uncovered significant pieces in the overall picture of the growing threat posed by
al-Qa'ida prior to 9/11. However, the agencies had failed to collaborate and
share information and this failure to share information prevented the United
States from thwarting the attack on 9/11. Beyond the structural reasons discussed later in this text, a dichotomy between how international security
operations were different from domestic security operations also led to confusion within the U.S. Intelligence Community. For instance, the view prior to

9/11 was that because al-Qa'ida attacks occurred abroad and not within the United States, al-Qa'ida did not pose a direct threat to U.S. interests that warranted affirmative or offensive actions on behalf of the U.S. national security establishment.

The Joint Inquiry report contained additional recommendations, but much of it was redacted (hidden from public view), leaving many without a clear understanding of how such a devastating attack could have occurred on U.S. soil.

## The 9/11 Commission

Even as the congressional inquiry was underway, there was growing public interest in why the attacks succeeded. In response to this search for answers, President George W. Bush signed the National Commission on Terrorist Attacks Upon the United States (Public Law 107–306) in 2002. PL 107–306 created an independent, bipartisan commission charged with determining how the U.S. national security apparatus had failed to foresee and prevent the 9/11 attacks. The 9/11 Commission (as it came to be called) was also tasked with offering recommendations for how the United States could prevent similar terrorist attacks in the future (Figure 2.3).[7]

Chaired by former New Jersey Governor Thomas Kean and vice-chaired by former Congressman Lee Hamilton, the 9/11 Commission reviewed more than 2.5 million pages of documents, interviewed more than 1,200 people, held 19 days of hearings, and took public testimony from 160 witnesses. In 2004, after a thorough review of all the aforementioned data and documents, the 9/11 Commission issued its final report, noting:

> We learned about an enemy who is sophisticated, patient, disciplined, and lethal . . . we learned that the institutions charged with protecting our borders, civil aviation, and national security did not understand how grave this threat could be, and did not adjust their policies, plans and practices to deter or defeat it.[8]

As part of its mandate, the Commission developed a list of 41 recommendations for how to enhance "U.S. readiness and resilience against transnational and domestic terrorism." The U.S. national security establishment has relied

**FIG. 2.3**
The 9/11 Commission Report is the official report of the events leading up to the September 11, 2001, terrorist attacks. It was prepared by the National Commission on Terrorist Attacks Upon the United States at the request of United States President George W. Bush and Congress.

# THE
# 9/11
# COMMISSION
# REPORT

**FINAL REPORT OF THE NATIONAL COMMISSION ON TERRORIST ATTACKS UPON THE UNITED STATES**

*Source:* 9/11 Commission, www.9-11commission.gov/press/911report_cover_HIGHRES.jpg.

on these recommendations in developing homeland security policy over the last decade. More importantly, the recommendations of the 9/11 Commission have been critical in developing a strategic overarching federal homeland security mission.

Even before the 9/11 Commission completed its investigation, there was a larger revelation that the United States had not sufficiently built the analytical and strategic capacity to respond to the 21st-century terrorist threat. Indeed, while the first congressional inquiry was primarily focused on failures in the Intelligence Community, it revealed larger systemic issues that spanned the entire federal government, as well as state and local governments. The identified problems were not that those bodies charged with guarding against terrorism had failed, but that neither they, nor their established policies and procedures, were sufficient to address the rapidly evolving global threat landscape.

In short, the general understanding enshrined by bodies like the 9/11 Commission was that the U.S. was simply unprepared for the terrorist threat that arrived on September 11. Remedying this structural problem required a massive reorientation of the U.S. security and intelligence apparatus. Below we discuss the legal and policy vehicles used to make these changes and then the resulting structure of the newly formed Department of Homeland Security.

## SIDEBAR 2.1 The Death of Osama bin Laden

Osama bin Laden, a man who had vexed the U.S. homeland security establishment for more than a decade, was killed on the morning of May 2, 2011 in Pakistan. The mission's success was the end result of many years of complex, thorough, and advanced intelligence operations and analyses led by the Central Intelligence Agency (CIA) with support from partners across the Intelligence Community (IC).[9]

While bin Laden had been a key focus of the IC since the 1990s, shortly after 9/11, the CIA began collecting information on key individuals connected to or providing support to bin Laden. Reporting identified a key courier by his *kunya* (operational pseudonym). It would be years later that the *kunya* was matched to a real name. By late 2010, further intelligence linked the courier to a compound in Abbottabad, a large town in Pakistan's Cyber-Pakhtunkhwa Province, about 35 miles north of the capital Islamabad. The compound and its main residence had extensive security features unusual for the area: High walls topped with barbed wire, double entry gates, opaque windows, no apparent Internet or telephone connections, and all trash seemed to be burned rather than collected. Moreover, the two owners of the property did not appear to have jobs or an income stream that would allow them to afford such a property. This, along with other intelligence, led the IC to assess that the compound was probably being used to hide bin Laden, as well as the courier.[10]

Intense training for the raid began, including the building of an exact life-size replica of the compound with movable interior walls to prepare the assault teams for any internal layout they might encounter. The operation, authorized by President Obama on April 29, was a surgical raid by a small team of special operations forces chosen to minimize collateral damage, to pose as little risk as possible to non-combatants on the compound or to Pakistani civilians in the neighborhood, and to increase the likelihood of confirming the identity of bin Laden. The military helicopters arrived at the Abbottabad compound at 0030 Pakistan time on May 2. One crashed, but the assault continued without delay. Bin Laden was found and killed within 9 minutes. In the aftermath, bin Laden was positively identified via several independent means.[11]

The death of bin Laden marked a significant victory in the US-led campaign to disrupt, dismantle, and defeat al-Qa'ida. He was largely responsible for the organization's mystique, its ability to raise money and attract new recruits, and its focus on the United States as a target for terrorist attacks.

**CRITICAL THINKING QUESTION**

Read the Sidebar on the death of Osama bin Laden. Why do you think bin Laden was killed on site rather than arrested? In the past those who committed mass atrocities such as the Nazis in the aftermath of World War II were often charged in international or domestic courts and sentenced to prison or death. Were there good policy reasons for killing bin Laden instead of holding a trial to determine the extent of his crimes? What are the disadvantages or advantages for the U.S. when considering the summary execution of charismatic criminal leaders?

## NATIONAL HOMELAND SECURITY STRATEGY AND DHS

Many of the post-9/11 structural changes mentioned above were first expressed in the National Homeland Security Strategy of 2002. This docu-

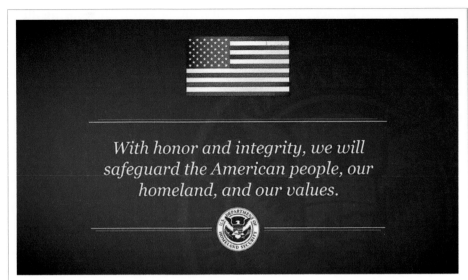

**FIG. 2.4**
The aspirational mission statement of the Department of Homeland Security.

*With honor and integrity, we will safeguard the American people, our homeland, and our values.*

*Source*: Department of Homeland Security, Department of Homeland Security Mission Statement, www.dhs.gov/sites/default/files/images/opa/16_0511_S1_mission_statement_web_03.jpg.

ment has since been continually updated. Three primary concepts constitute the foundation of the national homeland security strategy: Security, resilience, and customs & exchange. In turn, these concepts drive five broad areas of responsibility for the Department of Homeland Security (DHS):

### Prevent Terrorism

DHS was founded after 9/11 primarily to prevent future major terrorist attacks on U.S. soil. As a result, DHS works to prevent the unauthorized acquisition, importation, movement, or use of chemical, biological, radiological, and nuclear materials and capabilities within the United States. DHS also works to reduce the vulnerability of critical infrastructure and key resources, essential leadership, and major events to terrorist attacks and other hazards.

***Secure and Manage Borders*** Border security became a counterterrorism-oriented enterprise after 9/11. To that end, DHS Components, primarily Customs and Border Protection (CBP), are tasked with securing all U.S. air, land, and sea ports of entry. CBP and other Components are also responsible for safeguarding and streamlining lawful trade and travel while working to disrupt and dismantle transnational criminal and terrorist organizations.

***Enforce and Administer Immigration Laws*** DHS is responsible for enforcing U.S. immigration laws. This includes determining whether an individual may work legally in the United States under a visa, be granted permanent alien status, or be awarded citizenship through naturalization. Most of this work falls under the authority of a DHS subcomponent known as Immigration and Customs Enforcement (ICE). DHS works closely with other government agencies, including the Department of State, to investigate the background of any individuals seeking to remain in the United States. DHS also manages the deportation process for individuals found to be in the country illegally.

***Safeguard and Secure Cyberspace*** With government agencies, the private sector, and critical infrastructure all networked through the Internet, DHS faces increasing responsibility to secure civilian and government computer systems and work with industry and state, local, tribal, and territorial (SLTT) governments to secure critical infrastructure information systems. DHS also works to analyze and reduce cyber threats and vulnerabilities, distribute threat warnings to government and private groups, and coordinate the response to cyber incidents to ensure that government computers, networks, and cyber systems remain secure.

***Ensure Resilience to Disasters*** Primarily through the Federal Emergency Management Agency (FEMA) (a semi-autonomous entity within DHS and a DHS component), DHS coordinates the federal government's comprehensive response to a terrorist attack, natural disaster, or other large-scale emergency while working with federal, SLTT, and private sector partners to ensure recovery takes place after such an incident. DHS is responsible for bolstering information sharing and collaboration during and after a natural disaster or terrorist attack, providing grants, plans, and training to state and local law enforcement partners and facilitating rebuilding and recovery.

## LEGISLATION ESTABLISHING HOMELAND SECURITY MISSIONS

There are three statutes that authorize DHS to conduct its work and outline the powers and limits of DHS as it conducts its mission:

### Homeland Security Act of 2002

Passed in the immediate aftermath of the 9/11 attacks, the Homeland Security Act of 2002 (HSA) established DHS and set forth its primary mission to combat terrorist threats to the homeland. The HSA ushered in the largest reorganization of the federal government since the creation of the Department of Defense in 1947. Importantly, the HSA created many of the bodies that carry out the provisions of the related "Uniting and Strengthening America by Providing Appropriate Tools Required to Intercept and Obstruct Terrorism Act of 2001" (USA PATRIOT ACT).

### Intelligence Reform and Terrorism Prevention Act of 2004 (IRTPA)

Among other things, the Intelligence Reform and Terrorism Prevention Act of 2004 (IRTPA) addressed transportation security, border surveillance, alien detention, visa requirements, and alien smuggling. Importantly, IRTPA also established three organizations related to DHS: The Office of the Director of National Intelligence (ODNI), the National Counterterrorism Center (NCTC), and the Privacy and Civil Liberties Oversight Board. IRTPA required DHS to take over conducting pre-flight comparisons of airline passenger information *very* to that of federal government watch lists and also mandated several other *transportation focused* transportation-related security laws.

*Deals w/ anything fluid.*

**FIG. 2.5**
Former Secretary of Homeland Security Jeh C. Johnson shares a hug with TSA supervisor Carol Richel and Jefferson Parish Sheriff's Office Lieutenant Heather Sylve during a visit to Louis Armstrong New Orleans International Airport. When a deranged man attacked TSA officers and wounded Officer Richel, Lieutenant Heather Sylve took the attacker down and saved Officer Richel's life.

*Source*: Barry Bahler, DHS Secretary Jeh C. Johnson Hugs Staff, www.dhs.gov/download/15_0327_blb_0001_high.jpg.

## Implementing Recommendations of the 9/11 Commission Act of 2007 (Public Law 110–53)

PL 110–53 sought to implement a number of recommendations of the 9/11 Commission and addressed a range of the Department's missions, including cargo security, critical infrastructure protection, grant administration, intelligence and information sharing, privacy, and transportation security. In particular, PL 110–53 mandated that DHS inspect 100% of all air and sea cargo entering the United States, redistributed counterterrorism funding more appropriately, and tasked DHS with creating Fusion Centers. → *multiple agencies*

Other important laws, such as the Post-Katrina Emergency Management Reform Act of 2006 and the Immigration and Nationality Act, also provide significant enforcement authority to DHS. In addition to these laws, DHS carries out its mission through the promulgation of numerous regulatory actions, referred to collectively as "rulemaking." The DHS regulatory agenda includes regulations issued by DHS Components, including major DHS operational components, such as the U.S. Coast Guard and FEMA.

Related to rulemaking, DHS must also comply with Presidential Executive Orders in the form of Homeland Security Presidential Directives, such as Directive 7, which establishes a national policy for federal departments and agencies to identify and prioritize critical infrastructure and to protect them from terrorist attacks.

## SIDEBAR 2.2 Rulemaking

Rulemaking is the policymaking process for Executive Branch and other independent agencies of the federal government. Agencies use this process to develop and issue Rules (also referred to in this text and elsewhere as "regulations"). The process of rulemaking is governed by the Administrative Procedure Act (APA). Rulemaking can lead to a new rule, an amendment to an existing rule, or the repeal of an existing rule. Regulations usually fill gaps in the law and provide details on how the Executive agency will implement the law. For instance, the Immigration and Nationality Act (INA) legally obligates DHS to remove (deport) undocumented immigrants. In what manner or how quickly they are to be removed is not specified in the INA. These questions are answered by regulations.

To issue a regulation anbx agency or department must have the legal authority to do so. This authority is usually granted to an agency by Congress in the statute that created the agency. For instance, the Homeland Security Act (HSA) created the Department of Homeland Security and also grants DHS certain rulemaking powers. The rulemaking process is expensive and time-consuming. Before a government agency like DHS can begin the process, a preliminary assessment is made of whether the regulation is even necessary in the first place.[12]

After an agency researches the issues underlying the regulation and determines whether a regulation is necessary, it often proposes a regulation, also known as a Notice of Proposed Rulemaking. These proposals are often published online in the Federal Register so that they can be viewed by the public. Thereafter the agency will allow a certain period of time (usually a few months) to allow the public to comment on the proposed rule. Some public comments contain one-sentence or one-paragraph comments, while others contain thousands of pages of detailed analysis, with supporting documents submitted as attachments.

After the comment period closes, the agency reviews all comments and conducts a comment analysis. Then agencies decide whether to proceed with the rulemaking process or issue a new or modified proposal. In some cases, the proposal is withdrawn. If the regulation clears the public comment period it is published as a regulation. A final regulation must include response to significant, relevant issues raised in the public comments and statement providing a basis and the purposes of the regulation. The final regulation is also published in the Federal Register and made publicly available in print and online.[13]

### CRITICAL THINKING QUESTION

How is rulemaking different from the way a bill becomes a law in Congress? What protections and oversight mechanisms does it lack? Does the rulemaking process provide more or less oversight by other government agencies and the public compared to the lawmaking process in Congress? What are the implications of these differences as you think about rulemaking in the homeland security context?

## DEPARTMENT OF HOMELAND SECURITY ORGANIZATIONAL STRUCTURE

DHS is an organization in continual flux. The Department's operating structure underwent significant changes in the first several years of its existence. For instance, after Hurricane Katrina, DHS was reorganized by the Post-Katrina Emergency Management Reform Act (PKEMRA) of 2006. The Act created positions specifically tasked with helping the U.S. Gulf Coast region recover from Hurricane Katrina and, later, the Deepwater Horizon oil spill of 2010 that occurred in the same region. In 2008, Homeland Security Presidential Directive 23 issued by President George W. Bush created the National Cyber Security Center at DHS. The NCSC is responsible for coordinating cybersecurity efforts and improving situational awareness and information sharing on cybersecurity issues across the federal government.[14]

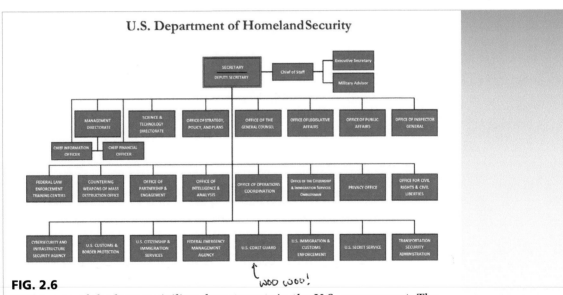

**FIG. 2.6**

DHS is one of the largest civilian departments in the U.S. government. The top two rows of this chart outline the Office of the Secretary and contain all of the policymaking offices in Washington, D.C. The bottom two rows are DHS Components, many of which are large operational units that function throughout the country.

*Source*: Department of Homeland Security, DHS Organizational Chart, www.dhs.gov/organizational-chart.

Today, DHS is organized into two main sections: The Office of the Secretary and DHS operational components. The Office of the Secretary provides the policymaking and logistical support for the Department, tying together the vast organization along similar lines of effort and priorities. DHS' operational components, such as ICE and CBP, are tasked with carrying out the Department's mandate. Staff at these operational components apprehend undocumented immigrants at the border, review applications for citizenship, and prepare intelligence products. Many of these operational components are legacy organizations that were merged when DHS was formed.

## OFFICE OF THE SECRETARY

DHS is a cabinet-level department led by the Secretary of Homeland Security. There have been several DHS Secretaries and as of this writing the Department is led by Secretary Kirstjen Nielsen. The Secretary and his or her staff are collectively referred to as the "Office of the Secretary." This office "sits" atop the DHS chain of authority and decision-making. The Office of the Secretary is responsible for coordinating the Department's functions and activities and managing its overall focus. In conjunction with guidance from the President and other government agencies, as well as all DHS Components, the Secretary also sets the direction for priorities in intelligence analysis and gathering and critical infrastructure protection.

The Office of the Secretary is divided into several sub-offices and issue-specific divisions that coordinate and oversee the components. These sub-offices include:

### The Office for Civil Rights and Civil Liberties (CRCL)

Led by the Officer for Civil Rights and Civil Liberties, CRCL supports the Department's mission to secure the nation while preserving individual liberty, fairness, and equality under the law.[15] CRCL is a congressionally mandated office that integrates civil rights and civil liberties into all of the Department's activities and works closely with Components that maintain distinct civil rights oversight offices (such as TSA). CRCL accomplishes its mission by:

- Promoting respect for civil rights and civil liberties in policy creation and implementation by advising Department leadership and personnel, as well as state and local partners.
- Communicating with individuals and communities whose civil rights and civil liberties may be affected by Department activities, informing them about policies and avenues of redress, and promoting appropriate attention within the Department to their experiences and concerns.
- Investigating and resolving civil rights and civil liberties complaints filed by the public regarding Department policies or activities, or actions taken by Department personnel.
- Leading the Department's equal employment opportunity programs and promoting workforce diversity and merit system principles.

**Privacy Office**

The DHS Privacy Office was the first statutorily mandated privacy office in any federal agency. The Privacy Office is responsible for evaluating Department programs, systems, and initiatives for potential impact on privacy and providing mitigation strategies to reduce detrimental privacy impacts.[16] Among other things, the Privacy Office:

- Evaluates Department legislative and regulatory proposals involving the collection, use, and disclosure of personally identifiable information (PII).
- Centralizes Freedom of Information Act (FOIA) and Privacy Act operations to provide policy and programmatic oversight and support implementation across the Department.
- Operates a Department-wide Privacy Incident Response Program to ensure that incidents involving PII are properly reported, investigated, and mitigated, as appropriate.
- Responds to complaints of privacy violations and provides redress, as appropriate.
- Provides training, education, and outreach to build a culture of privacy across the Department and transparency to the public.

> **DEFINITION BOX: Personally Identifiable Information (PII)**
>
> **Personally identifiable information** (PII) is any data that could potentially identify a specific individual. Information that can be used to distinguish one person from another and can be used for de-anonymizing anonymous data can be considered PII.

### Citizenship and Immigration Services Ombudsman

The Office of the Citizenship and Immigration Services Ombudsman works to improve the quality of citizenship and immigration services delivered to the public by providing individual case assistance, as well as making recommendations to improve the administration of immigration benefits.[17] Another statutory creation, the Ombudsman (an individual appointed to head this office) is meant to be an impartial and confidential resource independent of U.S. Citizenship and Immigration Services (USCIS) (a DHS component) that individuals may approach with an immigration or citizenship-related issues.

***Office of the Inspector General***   The DHS Office of the Inspector General (OIG) is the Department's "watchdog," working to internally monitor the Department for malfeasance and abuse. Established by Congress in 2002, the OIG is led by the Inspector General, who is appointed by the President and confirmed by the Senate. The OIG conducts and supervises independent audits, investigations, and inspections of DHS programs and operations and recommends ways for the Department to carry out its responsibilities in the most "effective, efficient, and economical manner possible."[18] Like Inspector General offices in other departments, the DHS OIG works to deter, identify, and address fraud, abuse, mismanagement, and waste of taxpayer funds invested at DHS.

***Office of Intergovernmental Affairs***   The Office of Intergovernmental Affairs (IGA) coordinates DHS initiatives and operations with that of state and local governments. IGA is responsible for initiating the dialogue on homeland security issues with local senior leadership (such as city mayors and state governors), along with the national associates (such as the League of Cities) that represent them.[19] IGA focuses on three major stakeholder groups: State officials, local officials, and tribes. The state, local, and tribal teams are each served by a director who is charged with overseeing outreach and engagement with other government officials on a variety of DHS-related programs and policy issues.

***Office of Legislative Affairs***   The Office of Legislative Affairs serves as the primary liaison to members of Congress and staff (Figure 2.7).[20] This

**FIG. 2.7** DHS' Office of Legislative Affairs often engages with members of Congress on Capitol Hill.

*Source*: The George F. Landegger Collection of District of Columbia Photographs in Carol M. Highsmith's America, Library of Congress, Prints and Photographs Division, www.loc.gov/rr/print/.

office also responds to inquiries from Congress and notifies the Legislative Branch about the Department's work. As of 2015, DHS reported to between 88 to 188 committees and subcommittees, a number that has continually grown since the founding of DHS.[21] This represents the largest oversight burden of any Executive Branch department.

**Office of General Counsel**   The Office of General Counsel is responsible for all of the Department's legal determinations and serves as the Department's regulatory policy officer, manages the rulemaking program, and ensures all DHS regulatory actions comply with relevant statutes and executive orders.[22] The office is led by the General Counsel with a staff of more than 1,700 attorneys.

**Office of Public Affairs**   The Office of Public Affairs represents the Department in all public matters, shares information with the public, and interfaces with the press. The Office of Public Affairs also serves as the federal government's lead public information office during a national emergency or disaster.[23] The Office of Public Affairs is further divided into the press office, incident and strategic communications, multimedia, speech writing, Web operations, and communications and internal communications.

**Office of Counternarcotics Enforcement (CNE)**   CNE is the Secretary's principal advisor on the adequacy of DHS counternarcotics resources.[24] Among other responsibilities, CNE coordinates policy and operations between DHS and other federal departments and agencies and between DHS and state and local agencies with respect to stopping narcotics smuggling into the United States.

**Executive Secretariat (ESEC)**   Also known as the Office of the Executive Secretary, the ESEC provides direct support to the DHS Secretary, Deputy Secretary, and other senior leaders in the Department. In particular, this support comes in the form of handling, routing, and compiling requests for information and drafting documents to ensure all parts of DHS with a say in the document in question receive the opportunity to comment and contribute to it.[25]

## SIDEBAR 2.3 Homeland Security at the Movies

You may remember Harrison Ford in *Air Force One*. Sorry to burst your bubble, but in reality there is no escape pod on the President's plane. A fan of Showtime's *Homeland*? Unfortunately, the central plot of the show isn't possible because the National Security Agency (NSA) and the Central Intelligence Agency (CIA) cannot legally spy on U.S. citizens like actress Claire Danes does routinely on the air. Danes' character, with all her flaws and psychological issues, is also unlikely to be able to hold down a job at the CIA or other security agencies. That's because DHS and other government employees pass rigorous background checks and the behavior portrayed by Danes and other actors on TV would likely result in termination in real life.

Hollywood's version of homeland security is glamorous, conflicted, and slick. Though the work of homeland security professionals is often more interesting, varied, and dangerous than other professions, it does not approach the neurotic and high-stakes version portrayed in the movies and on TV. Asked about the show *Homeland* one CIA analyst recently remarked:

**FIG. 2.8**
Dwayne Johnson (The Rock) shares a photo with Coast Guard recruits. Hollywood stars often portray homeland security personnel in ways that do not reflect the reality of challenging and thankless work.

*Source*: Hollywood Shares Stage with Coasties at Spike TV awards, http://coast-guard.dodlive.mil/files/2010/06/spikeawards3.jpg

Homeland takes the high-intensity, high-adrenalin moments and packages them into an hour. The real job as an analyst was maybe 15–20 per cent awe-inspiring and dramatic moments. Other times, it's about writing reports. You wouldn't want to watch an analyst at a computer writing a President's Daily Brief.[26]

Officials in these agencies also don't find themselves poring over murder-boards at their homes (information about suspects would likely be classified and viewed in secure environments), chatting loudly on phones in the office (because this information would be sensitive and classified), or violating many of the warrant-based constitutional protections afforded U.S. citizens. What these shows often do get right are the conflicts and concerns surrounding security and rights. At a time of significant debate over national security and intelligence issues in terms of public opinion, the moral quandaries of the characters in these shows often reflect the ambiguities of national security policy. Chapter 10 explores these challenging moral and ethical issues further.

## Office of Policy

The Office of Policy is composed of five subcomponent offices and HSAC and is a central resource to the Secretary and other Department leaders for strategic planning and analysis.[27] The Office of Policy Implementation and Integration (PII), the Office of Strategy, Planning, Analysis and Risk (SPAR), and the Office of International Affairs (OIA) work in different capacities across all mission areas to develop and align Department-wide strategies, policies, and activities. In addition, the Office of Policy includes the Private Sector Office and the Office for State and Local Law Enforcement, which are focused on partnerships with stakeholders in the broader homeland security enterprise.[28]

The Private Sector Office (PSO) works with businesses, conglomerates, trade associations, non-governmental organizations (NGOs), and other private sector organizations to build resilience and emergency preparedness within the business community. PSO also liaises with the private sector to coordinate and enhance methods of securing privately held buildings, venues, and critical infrastructure. To this end, the PSO made several recommendations for jurisdictions seeking to improve collaboration with their private sector counterparts:

- Prepare formalized agreements describing ways to exchange information between government agencies and the private sector about vulnerabilities and risks to private critical infrastructure;
- Use community policing initiatives, strategies, and tactics to identify suspicious activities related to terrorism;
- Establish a regional prevention information command center; and
- Coordinate the flow of information regarding infrastructure.

PSO also advises the DHS Secretary on the economic impact of policies and regulations while promoting public-private partnerships (PPPs), Department policies, and best practices that advance the homeland security mission. As a part of this, PSO provides several programs that contribute to a more resilient private sector:

- *The Loaned Executive Program* offers an opportunity for executive-level experts to volunteer to work with the Department for a limited period to collaboratively develop innovative approaches to addressing homeland security challenges.
- *The Voluntary Private Sector Preparedness Accreditation and Certification Program* establishes criteria for private sector preparedness, including disaster management, emergency management, and business continuity programs.[29]
- *The Protected Critical Infrastructure Information (PCII) Program* created by the Critical Infrastructure Information Act of 2002, advances the voluntary sharing of private sector infrastructure information with the government.[30]

In line with emergency preparedness, Ready.gov is a website presenting information and tools to advance an all-hazards approach to private sector preparedness, following program elements within National Fire Protection Association 1600, Standard on Disaster/Emergency Management and Business Continuity Programs, which is an American National Standard adopted by DHS.[31]

> **DEFINITION BOX: Public-Private Partnership**
>
> A **public-private partnership** (PPP) is a joint effort or venture between any level of government and one or more private sector organizations.

### Office of the Military Advisor

The Military Advisor and his or her staff provide counsel and support to the Secretary and DHS senior leadership in affairs relating to policy, procedures, and preparedness activities, and operations between DHS and the Defense Department.

## ADVISORY BODIES

In addition to the civil servants and political staff at the Office of the Secretary, the DHS Secretary also relies on a number of volunteer advisory and consultative bodies in their decision-making process. These advisory bodies can be made up of subject matter experts with experience in specific areas (e.g. transportation security, immigration enforcement) or can be general in nature. Many of these councils are created under the aegis of the Federal Advisory Committee Act (FACA), which was enacted in 1972 to ensure that advice by the various advisory committees formed over the years was objective and accessible to the public.

Some of these DHS committees include:

### Homeland Security Advisory Council (HSAC)

The Secretary's preeminent advisory board, HSAC is composed of notable experts from across the country. Several subcommittees arise from the HSAC and advise on further specific issues, such as cybersecurity and violent extremism. The HSAC seeks to provide advice and recommendations to the Secretary independent from DHS management and leadership. In this way, HSAC serves an important function in providing an unfiltered perspective to the Secretary (Figure 2.9).

**FIG. 2.9**
Secretary John-
son addresses
his final meet-
ing of the
Homeland
Security Advi-
sory Council
(HSAC).

*Source*: Homeland Security (@DHSgov), Twitter (Dec. 1, 2016, 12:52 PM) https://twitter.com/DHSgov/status/804427899159900160.

### Homeland Security Academic Advisory Council (HSAAC)

HSAAC provides advice and recommendations to the Secretary and senior leadership on matters related to homeland security and the academic community.[32] For example, in recent years, HSAAC has made recommendations regarding the best way to recruit students from graduate and undergraduate programs to work for the Department, encouraged the development of academic disciplines related to homeland security, and worked to increase the resilience of campuses to terrorism and natural disasters.

### National Infrastructure Advisory Council

NIAC provides advice to the DHS Secretary (as well as to leaders outside the Department, such as the President) on the security of information systems for public and private institutions that constitute the critical national infrastructure.[33] Notably, this advisory council is not appointed by the DHS Secretary but is directly appointed by the President.

### Homeland Security Science and Technology Advisory Committee (HSSTAC)

HSSTAC seeks to provide independent, consensus-based scientific and technical advice and recommendations to the Under Secretary for Science and Technology (who leads the DHS Science & Technology Directorate). In particular, the Under Secretary for Science & Technology relies on this committee to help identify new technologies in areas that strengthen homeland security.[34]

## DHS OPERATIONAL COMPONENTS

The Homeland Security Act consolidated a multitude of government agencies, departments and offices with homeland security responsibilities into a single department. Today, DHS is composed of large bodies with broad mission sets, called Components. They are treated as semi-autonomous units within the greater DHS organizational structure. (Note: Outside of DHS, Components are often referred to as government "agencies" or "bureaus," which is the accepted nomenclature for the organizational substructure of a federal department. For instance, the Federal *Bureau* of Investigation is an organizational component of the larger U.S. Department of Justice.)

Government bodies that pre-date DHS, such as the Secret Service, FEMA, and the Coast Guard, have long and storied histories and traditions. Even with the urgent homeland security need in the wake of the 9/11 attacks, time was taken in Congress to debate which parts of the federal government would be merged into one department. The FBI, for example, fought to remain as a semi-autonomous part of the Department of Justice, as did other law enforcement agencies with homeland security responsibilities, such as the Bureau of Alcohol, Tobacco, and Firearms, the CIA, and the National Park Service Police. As a result, DHS contains many (but not all) of the government entities with homeland security responsibilities.

The largest and most significant Components include:

## United States Coast Guard (USCG)

*woo woo!*

One of the five branches of the armed forces, the USCG is the only military organization within DHS. The USCG protects the maritime economy and environment and defends the nation's maritime borders (Figure 2.10). The USCG has been operating continuously since 1790, and its mission did not change when it was integrated with DHS. Though it has 11 specific statutory missions, they can be organized into three primary areas:

- *Maritime Safety*: Ensure the safety of those who work and live on the sea, often referred to as "mariners." For example, the USCG has a substantial commercial fishing vessel safety program designed to safeguard commercial fisherman, many of whom earn their living performing some of the most dangerous work in the world. The USCG also operates the International Ice Patrol to protect ships transiting the North Atlantic shipping lanes, which are often ice-covered. The USCG is the nation's lead agency for maritime search and rescue in U.S. waters (which extend up to 100 nautical miles

**FIG. 2.10**
The Coast Guard Cutter Bainbridge Island, home-ported in Sandy Hook, N.J., provides homeland security near the Statue of Liberty in the New York Harbor, U.S.

*Source*: Tom Sperduto, Coast Guard Cutter Bainbridge Island, https://upload.wikimedia.org/wikipedia/commons/1/11/US_Navy_030828-C-9409S-509_The_Coast_Guard_Cutter_Bainbridge_Island.jpg.

from the U.S. coast). In addition to its response duties, the USCG also investigates the causes of maritime emergencies and incidents, often working closely with the National Transportation Safety Board.

- *Maritime Security*: As the nation's primary maritime law enforcement service, it enforces federal laws, treaties on waters under U.S. jurisdiction, and other international maritime agreements. After 9/11, in addition to suppressing violations of drug, immigration, and fisheries laws, the USCG has also begun to secure the nation from terrorist threats that may enter the country by sea or terrorist actions that may take place at sea. The USCG role in interdicting migrants has taken on new importance in the wake of recent refugee and migration crises. Migrants and refugees often take great risks and endure significant hardships in their attempts to flee their countries and enter the United States, and the USCG's work in intercepting these entrants (most of whom are trying to enter the country unlawfully) has an important humanitarian dimension.[35] Upon interdiction, the USCG will often work with the DHS Components United States Citizenship and Immigration Services (USCIS) and Immigration and Customs Enforcement (ICE) to process, adjudicate, and, as necessary, deport individuals to their countries of origin.

- *Maritime Stewardship*: Protect the natural resources and environment of U.S. territorial waters.[36] Working with other federal agencies, the USCG also protects marine resources to preserve U.S. waters from overfishing and ensure healthy stocks of fish and other living marine resources. Throughout the 1970s and 1980s, the USCG's mission expanded to protect the marine environment at large and for the common good. As a result, the USCG today also safeguards sensitive marine habitats, mammals, and endangered species and also protects waters from the discharge of oil and hazardous substances. Practically, this means that under the National Contingency Plan, the USCG serves as the designated Federal On-Scene Coordinator for any marine environmental disaster. As such, the USCG is responsible for coordinating the response and cleanup operations of other state and federal government agencies.

### Federal Emergency Management Agency (FEMA)

FEMA is the federal government's primary disaster response and recovery organization and usually steps in when local governments are unable to meaningfully respond to a natural or terrorist disaster (and often when an official state of emergency has been declared). FEMA is led by the FEMA Administrator, who attends meetings of the President's Cabinet. Beyond responding to disasters, FEMA also provides state and local governments with expertise and advice in preparing for natural hazards and works with the private sector on programs to provide disaster insurance to those affected by floods and hurricanes. FEMA's work is organized by region, and its zones of responsibilities are divided into ten distinct national regions. This organization is discussed further in Chapter 7.

### U.S. Secret Service

One of the oldest federal law enforcement agencies in the country, the Secret Service was initially founded to prevent currency counterfeiting in 1865. Since then, the organization's mission has expanded to include the protection of the nation's leaders and U.S. critical financial infrastructure. Secret Service agents are often seen guarding national leaders, foremost among them the President. A Secret Service detail also accompanies several members of the

**FIG. 2.11** A member of the Secret Service stands guard outside the Eisenhower Executive Office Building in Washington, D.C.

*Source*: Gabriel A. Silva, Secret Service Agent Guards EEOB, https://upload.wikimedia.org/wikipedia/commons/b/b5/Secret_Service_Agent_Guards_EEOB.jpg.

President's Cabinet, including the DHS Secretary. Today, the Secret Service investigates both crimes against those it protects (such as threats to the President), as well as financial crimes, such as counterfeiting, telecommunications fraud, computer fraud, and identity theft.[37]

### Immigration and Customs Enforcement (ICE)

ICE was created in 2003 through the merger of the investigative and interior enforcement elements of the former U.S. Customs Service and the Immigration and Naturalization Service (INS). ICE is one of DHS' largest components, employing more than 20,000 individuals. ICE personnel enforce federal laws governing border control, customs, trade and immigration, and the Component's recent $6 billion budget is primarily allocated between two directorates: Enforcement and Removal Operations (ERO) and Homeland Security Investigations (HSI).

ERO enforces the nation's immigration laws. The ERO directorate is responsible for identifying and apprehending immigrants who are in the country illegally, or "undocumented immigrants," because they lack an official document (i.e. passport, visa, or residency papers) that evidences a legal status. ERO is also responsible for housing undocumented immigrants while they are being processed for removal to their home countries or for other adjudication to determine their status in the United States.[38]

HSI is one of DHS' primary law enforcement arms. HSI special agents are responsible for investigating domestic and international activities arising from the unauthorized movement of people and goods into, within, and out of the United States. For example, HSI agents routinely investigate instances of human and child trafficking, child pornography, and other similar crimes.[39]

### Customs and Border Protection (CBP)

CBP is one of the world's largest law enforcement organizations and is the largest DHS component. After integration into DHS, the customs mission shifted from merely preventing illicit goods and people from entering the country to also apprehending terrorists and preventing bad actors from using the nation's transportation network. Today, CBP regulates and facilitates international trade, collects **import duties** (taxes on goods from overseas that are sold in the United States), and enforces U.S. trade regulations. Most CBP personnel work to apprehend individuals attempting to illegally cross U.S. land and sea borders or ports of entry. While doing this work, CBP personnel also interdict narcotics, contraband, and other harmful products.

CBP is divided into three directorates: Border Patrol, the Office of Field Operations (OFO), and the Office of Air and Marine (which is an important but smaller directorate). The Border Patrol's mission focuses on preventing undocumented immigration while also preventing terrorists and weapons (including weapons of mass destruction) from entering the United States.[40] The Border Patrol uses sophisticated surveillance and law enforcement techniques to achieve its mission, preventing the entry of undocumented individuals and contraband into the country while facilitating the flow of legal immigration and trade.

OFO manages the customs operations at air, land, and sea ports of entry, as well as foreign ports of entry (known as preclearance stations). In practice, this means that CBP OFO officers question individuals when they try to enter the country and also search personal and industrial cargo and goods before they enter the country (Figure 2.12).

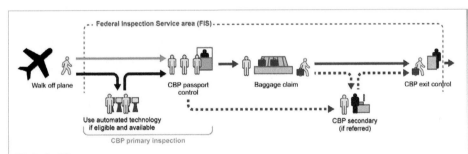

**FIG. 2.12**
This diagram shows how CBP OFO works to screen airport passengers as they enter the United States from overseas travel. (Credit: GAO analysis of CBP information.)

*Source*: U.S. Government Accountability Office, CBP Screening of International Air Travelers, www.gao.gov/assets/690/683801.pdf.

### U.S. Citizenship and Immigration Services (USCIS)

USCIS oversees lawful U.S. entry, immigration, and citizenship. USCIS staff verify an individual's eligibility to become a lawful permanent resident and also administer the process whereby someone becomes a naturalized citizen.[41] Working with the State Department, USCIS also vets individuals who request a visa to visit the United States or conduct business inside the country. Unique among DHS Components (as well as the federal government), USCIS operates almost exclusively on income obtained from those seeking its services, mostly through fees. Congress provides little to no funding to this component. This reliance on income from those who seek its services has increasingly encouraged a culture oriented towards customer service, making USCIS one of the DHS Components most frequently cited as responsive to taxpayer and citizen concerns.

### Transportation Security Administration (TSA)

Though it is most commonly association with aviation security, TSA provides security to the traveling public irrespective of the transportation mode. TSA was initially housed at the Department of Transportation and was moved to DHS in 2003 (Figure 2.13). Today, 55,000 uniformed TSA Transportation

**FIG. 2.13**
The uniforms of TSA officers still sport the seal that was used when TSA was part of the Department of Transportation.

*Source*: Department of Homeland Security, Transportation Security Officer.Uniform, www.dhs.gov/blog/2015/02/25/tsa-workers-deserve-more-iou.

Security Officers (TSOs) are present at more than 450 U.S. airports to screen passengers and baggage, as well as conduct other aviation security functions. TSA also oversees security for highways, railroads, buses, mass transit systems, pipelines, and certain ports of entry. TSA's mission puts it in constant contact with the traveling public.

## DHS SUPPORT COMPONENTS AND DIRECTORATES

Lacking the semi-autonomy of DHS Components, Directorates are often led by Under Secretaries or Assistant Secretary-level leaders and are responsible for specialized DHS operations. These are sometimes called "Support Components" because their work often supports the fieldwork of DHS Components.

### National Protection and Programs Directorate (NPPD)

NPPD carries out the department's statutory responsibility to secure the nation's physical and cyber critical infrastructure. In many cases, this means NPPD works with private owners of U.S. physical infrastructure (such as dams, schools, and power plants). NPPD personnel may work with the owners of critical infrastructure to create contingency plans for a terrorist attack or natural hazard.

NPPD also works with public and private partners to ensure the security and continuity of the nation's cyber and communications infrastructure.[42] Though NPPD has several components itself, one of the more significant components is the Federal Protective Service (FPS), a law enforcement agency within NPPD that protects and secures more than 9,000 federal buildings and other facilities, as well as those who visit and work there.[43] Occasionally, FPS also provides protection for "National Security Special Events," such as the presidential inauguration. NPPD is in the midst of being reorganized into a field component similar to USCIS and ICE.

## SIDEBAR 2.4 Reorganizing NPPD

The most recent reorganization of the department is the restructuring of the National Protection and Programs Directorate. NPPD works with interagency partners, SLTT government bodies, and critical infrastructure owners and operators to collectively maintain secure, functioning, and resilient infrastructure.[44] Created in 2007 as a headquarters directorate by combining several existing entities, NPPD's mission over the years has evolved to take on more operational responsibilities in the field, especially as terrorist threats to the homeland have evolved. For instance, malicious cyber activity has become more sophisticated, requiring an equally sophisticated and agile response.

To accomplish this vision of an agile and responsive field department, NPPD recently proposed three new priorities:

- Greater unity of effort across the NPPD organization, particularly across cyber and physical threats, vulnerabilities, consequences, and mitigation;
- Enhanced operational activity; and
- Excellence in acquisition program management and other mission support functions.

To achieve these priorities, NPPD is being reorganized into three separate but interconnected operational directorates (i.e. working "in the field" rather than from Washington, D.C.):

**Infrastructure Security Directorate**: Focuses on activities to protect critical national infrastructure from cyber and physical risks by working with private and public sector owners and operators to build the capacity to assess and manage these risks. For instance, this directorate may fulfill its own goal by having trained personnel (e.g. Protective Security Advisors) deliver training in best practices for securing a range of venues (e.g. a house of worship, nuclear power plant) against a terrorist attack.

**National Cybersecurity and Communications Integrations Directorate (NCCID)**: Focuses on cyber-specific operations and DHS' responsibility to mitigate and respond to threats to information technology and communication assets, networks, and systems. In particular, this directorate will work to secure federal government networks against cyber threats.

**Federal Protective Service Directorate**: A pre-existing component of NPPD that will continue to focus on the direct protection of physical federal facilities and those who work in and visit them through integrated law enforcement and security operations. Under this reorganization, this directorate focuses on protecting cybersecurity aspects of federal facilities in coordination with the NCCID.

### Science and Technology Directorate (S&T)

S&T is staffed by technical specialists, academics, and engineers who work to further DHS' primary mission to combat terrorism and build resilience using the latest technology and research. S&T works closely with academic "Centers of Excellence" at major U.S. universities to conduct basic and applied research, development, demonstration, testing, and evaluation activities relevant to the DHS mission.[45] For instance, S&T has worked to create 3-D printed robots that

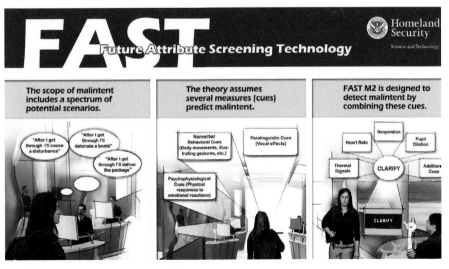

**FIG. 2.14** Artist's conception of how Future Attribute Screening Technology (F.A.S.T.) might be employed at a security checkpoint.

*Source*: Department of Homeland Security, DHS S&T Future Attribute Screening Technology, https://upload.wikimedia.org/wikipedia/commons/9/98/Dhs-fast.png.

can be assembled on site at a port of entry and provide DHS bomb squad personnel with a way to address threats without having to wait for support or backup.[46]

Within S&T is the seldom mentioned SAFETY Act Office, which administers the Support Anti-terrorism by Fostering Effective Technologies Act of 2002 (SAFETY Act).[47] Established by the Homeland Security Act, the SAFETY Act provides liability protections for providers of "Qualified Anti-Terrorism Technologies." The SAFETY Act program is designed to encourage the private sector to develop and deploy anti-terrorism products and services by creating a system of "risk management" and a system of "litigation management." Currently, if a private sector organization proactively implements security technologies into their operations and those technologies fail to guard life and property during a terrorist attack, the private organization may be legally liable. With SAFETY Act coverage, companies gain liability protection for lawsuits brought against them in the aftermath of a terrorist attack.

### Intelligence and Analysis (I&A)

I&A is an essential part of DHS' terrorism fighting mission and is a member of the larger Intelligence Community (IC). Because lack of intelligence sharing partially led to the 9/11 attacks, Congress tasked DHS with ensuring intelligence information obtained by the federal government was appropriately shared with state and local law enforcement partners. This mandate was meant to ensure that all levels of government, especially local first responders, had the information they needed to interdict and prevent an attack. DHS I&A is the directorate that today carries out this mandate. Most of I&A's information sharing occurs through the National Network of Fusion Centers.[48] I&A also created its own intelligence products, and runs the DHS' Nationwide Suspicious Activity Reporting Initiative (SARS) known for its "See Something, Say Something," campaign.

### Federal Law Enforcement Training Center (FLETC)

FLETC is a large, interagency institute that trains personnel from more than 90 federal government agencies, including officers of the Federal Protective

Service. FLETC was established to ensure the standardized minimum levels of training of law enforcement agencies protecting the homeland, and it existed before DHS was founded. Notably, FLETC does not provide training for the FBI, whose agents are trained separately at the FBI's Quantico training facility.

### Directorate for Management

DHS' Management Directorate is responsible for budget, appropriations, fund expenditures, accounting, and finance; procurement; human resources and personnel; information technology systems; facilities, property, equipment, and other material resources; and identification and tracking of performance measurements relating to DHS responsibilities.[49]

## OTHER FEDERAL AGENCIES ENGAGED IN HOMELAND SECURITY

While DHS is the central federal government agency managing the nation's homeland security efforts, there are also many other government bodies with homeland security-specific offices and mandates. In line with the broader understanding that coordination, collaboration, and information and asset sharing are essential to addressing all hazards, numerous federal departments contribute to the broader homeland security mission in ways specific to their authorities and areas of operation and expertise. These include:

### The White House

Several bodies exist within the White House that oversee specific homeland security mission areas. The National Security Council and the Homeland Security Council are tasked with advising the President on matters relating to homeland security. The Homeland Security Council was established by Presidential Directive in 2001 and was formalized and codified by Congress as part of the Homeland Security Act. Members of the Homeland Security Council include the President and Vice President, as well as the Secretaries

**FIG. 2.15**
President Barack
Obama delivers
remarks on the
FY 2016 budget
at the Depart-
ment of Home-
land Security
in Washington,
D.C., Febru-
ary 2, 2015.

*Source*: Pete Souza, President Barack Obama Discusses Homeland Security Issues
(2015) https://obamawhitehouse.archives.gov/sites/default/files/image/image_file/
p020215ps-0262.jpg.

of most government federal departments. Additional attendees often include
the President's advisors on domestic and economic policy and military
advisors.

In February 2009, Presidential Study Directive 1 merged the HSC staff with
the NSC staff, creating the National Security Staff (later renamed the National
Security Council Staff). The NSC Staff is made up of policymakers and subject
matter experts who advise the President and the HSC/NSC about pressing
homeland security matters. They also work with federal departments, such
as DHS, to coordinate interagency and federal government-wide homeland
security efforts.

### Department of Justice

The Department of Justice (DOJ) conducts investigations into acts of terrorism, and through U.S. Attorneys, prosecutes those charged with participating

in or supporting terrorism. DOJ's constituent components work similarly to the traditional state and local criminal justice system in that they activate usually (but increasingly not always) in the aftermath of an incident. Thus, the FBI may be called upon to investigate a crime, such as a terrorist attack, after it has been committed. Once a suspect is identified, arrested, and charged, the attorneys working for the U.S. Attorney's Office prosecute the suspect and the U.S. judicial system administers appropriate punishment, be it civil or criminal. Once sentenced, this individual is then housed in one of the many federal prisons run by the Bureau of Prisons (BOP). All of the aforementioned organizations from the FBI to the BOP are housed at the Department of Justice and are analogous to the DHS Components discussed earlier.

## The Department of State

The State Department coordinates activities with foreign governments and international organizations, in particular to secure and protect U.S interests and personnel abroad from harm. The State Department maintains and staffs embassies in many nations, and Foreign Service Officers monitor the social, political, and economic atmosphere in foreign countries for threats to the U.S. homeland. They also establish relevant contacts with local personnel and are focal points for gathering intelligence. Unlike other government departments, the State Department uses diplomacy and the diplomatic process, as well as dialogue and negotiation, as its primary means of interdicting terrorist threats to the homeland.

## Department of Defense

The Department of Defense (DOD) role in homeland security is referred to as "homeland defense." DOD and its armed components serve a military defense and deterrent role, preventing larger nations and nation-state actors from initiating a physical or cyberattack against the United States. In addition to its military role, DOD also supports FEMA and other federal agencies during domestic terrorist attacks or natural disasters, though it is always in an "assistance-only" role and only when the response capabilities of a state government and the rest of the federal government are overwhelmed. DOD's role in domestic affairs is limited by the *Posse Comitatus* Act, which places strict limits on when and how military personnel can be used in domestic affairs.

---

**DEFINITION BOX: *Posse Comitatus* Act**

The ***Posse Comitatus* Act** is a federal law passed in 1878 that limits the powers of the federal government in using military personnel to enforce domestic policies within the territory of the United States.

---

*1.3 Discussion:*
*"Posse Comitatus"*

**CRITICAL THINKING QUESTION**

Should a law like the *Posse Comitatus* Act exist? Why do you think this law was passed? Shouldn't the U.S. armed forces be allowed to take large-scale actions inside the U.S.? Why or why not?

## Department of Treasury

The Treasury Department works to reduce the use of the financial system for illicit activities by terrorist groups and state sponsors of terrorism, WMD proliferators, and other homeland security threats. The Treasury Department's role was enhanced after 9/11 when it initiated the Terrorist Finance Tracking Program, which monitors the flow of U.S. funds related to terrorist groups worldwide and then works to interdict and stop terrorist financing. The Office of Terrorism and Financial Intelligence (TFI) is charged with safeguarding the financial system against criminal exploitation that seeks to support terrorist organizations or activities.

## Intelligence Agencies

Intelligence agencies, such as the CIA, NSA, NCTC, and ODNI, play a critical role in ensuring that the nation's leaders have actionable information with which to make critical homeland security decisions. Their role is discussed in Chapter 5.

## The Department of Commerce

The Department of Commerce's Bureau of Industry and Security (BIS) is charged with guarding U.S. national security through: Export control in order to prevent the proliferation of WMD and the transfer of other weapons; ensuring treaty compliance, efforts to guard the economic security of the United States; and encouraging the defense industrial base, which produces technologies contributing to U.S. military superiority.[50]

## Department of Health and Human Services (HHS)

HHS is a partner to DHS Components in several areas. The Homeland Security Act transferred the responsibility for the care and placement of unaccompanied children to the Office of Refugee Resettlement (ORR) within HHS.[51] Undocumented unaccompanied children apprehended by ICE or other law enforcement are transferred to ORR custody. Additionally, HHS collaborates with the DHS Office of Health Affairs to administer the DHS BioWatch program (Figure 2.16). BioWatch is a system of aerosol sensors designed to serve as an early warning system for a biological attack. Sensors are deployed across U.S. cities and in transportation networks to detect the release of deadly pathogens, such as anthrax or smallpox.

## U.S. Department of Agriculture (USDA)

The USDA is a cabinet-level agency that oversees the production and management of the nation's food supply. The vast majority of the U.S. food and agriculture sector is privately owned. It relies on critical infrastructure to function and constitutes one-fifth of the country's economic activity.[52] Within USDA, the Office of Homeland Security and Emergency Coordination (OHSEC) leads the department's security and preparedness programs, and responds to threats and disasters that impact the food sector through training and interagency coordination.[53] OHSEC initiatives include protecting classified information within USDA, safe use of radiation sources, and homeland security planning and preparedness with regard to U.S. food and agriculture.

**FIG. 2.16** The Department of Homeland Security's BioWatch program is a system of aerosol sensors designed to serve as an early warning for a biological attack.

# BioWatch

*Office of Health Affairs*

*BioWatch's critical mission is to build the preparedness of jurisdictions in case of a biological attack and to provide early warning in case of the intentional release of select, airborne biological agents in more than 30 metropolitan areas across the United States.*

**Building Jurisdictional Preparedness**
BioWatch builds jurisdictional preparedness by leading exercises, providing training, and by offering written guidance and standardized methodologies for response.

The BioWatch community consists of hundreds of individuals representing federal, state, and local organizations nationwide, including public health officials, laboratorians, first responders, and environmental health representatives.

**Saving Lives through Early Detection**
BioWatch provides early warning through accurate detection and enables key decision-makers to initiate a coordinated response that can save lives.

Outdoor Release of Biological Agent (~100 grams with 50,000 people exposed)

| With Early Detection: **More Lives are Saved** | Without Early Detection: **More Lives are Lost** |
|---|---|
| Illness Rate with Early Detection: **45-58%** — Expected Fatalities: **8,500** | Illness Rate without Early Detection: **81%** — Expected Fatalities: **18,320** |

Data based on Sandia Report SAND2012-0125, BioWatch Technical Analysis of Biodetection Architecture Performance

**BioWatch Operations**

Routine, Daily Operations — If laboratory analysis reveals a BioWatch biological agent, then a series of response actions occur — Detection — Response Activities

Continuous air monitoring (24/7) — Filter collection — Transportation to the laboratory — Filter sample process and analysis — Data interpretation and results reporting — Laboratory director may seek consultation • The director reports a detection — Local jurisdictions activate their response plans, determine resource needs in preparation for a national conference call to assess threat level and the public health risk • Additional tests may be conducted • BioWatch stakeholders are notified and the public is informed

Homeland Security

dhs.gov

*Source*: Department of Homeland Security, DHS BioWatch Program, www.dhs.gov/sites/default/files/publications/BioWatch%20Infographic_0.pdf.

## Department of Energy (DOE)

The DOE's national security mission spans several critical areas. The DOE manages the Strategic Petroleum Reserve, contributes to physical and cyber-security assets for energy infrastructure, runs programs for worker health and safety, contributes to emergency response and preparedness, and develops methods for mitigating the impact of climate change.[54] Within the DOE is the National Nuclear Security Administration (NNSA), a semi-autonomous agency responsible for enhancing security through nuclear science. NNSA manages the U.S. nuclear weapons stockpile, helps guard against the threat from WMD, provides nuclear propulsion to the U.S. Navy, and responds to nuclear and radiological emergencies.[55]

### Environmental Protection Agency (EPA)

The EPA is responsible for preparing the water sector for acts of terrorism and is the lead agency for decontaminating areas after an attack or disaster. The EPA's Office of Homeland Security (OHS) leads the agency's planning, prevention, preparedness, and response for homeland security-related incidents. OHS advises agency leadership on national security and intelligence; is the primary liaison to the White House, DHS, the Intelligence Community, and other agencies; and coordinates with EPA programs and regions on homeland security activities.[56] The EPA's National Homeland Security Research Center (NHSRC) was created after the 9/11 attacks to research scientific matters related to homeland security.[57] NHSRC leads critical scientific research to enhance responses to disaster scenarios involving hazardous chemicals, pathogens, and radiological materials.

## STATE AND LOCAL PARTNERS

Emergencies are almost always initially dealt with at the local level, with only Major Disasters requiring a Presidential Disaster Declaration and ensuing federal management. The structure of state and local homeland security organizations and response capabilities varies by jurisdiction, but all states and many local municipal organizations have some infrastructure to prepare, prevent, respond to, and recover from natural disasters and terrorist attacks.

State governors are responsible for ensuring that their state is adequately prepared for emergencies and disasters. Governors have considerable authority to organize and oversee homeland security functions according to their state's needs and priorities. Governors make several important decisions both before, during, and after a terrorist attack or natural disaster. For instance, governors are responsible for overseeing a state-level department of homeland security and/or department of emergency management (though not every state has such a department).

Many state homeland security activities are funded by federal grants. Some of these are based on formulas, some are discretionary, and some are awarded based on factors such as population and risk, or the unique physical characteristics of each state (such as whether it borders a body of water). State governors must decide how to use federal homeland security resources and funds in the most effective way possible. Accordingly, governors spend considerable time recruiting stakeholders to work with the state to respond to disasters and attacks, often through mechanisms similar to ones employed by the federal government, such as advisory committees.

State governments devote significant resources to Fusion Centers that track and collate intelligence from different levels of government. In particular, Fusion Centers serve as an effective way for governors to obtain intelligence information from the federal government regarding an impending attack or natural disaster in their state. During a disaster or an attack, governors are given considerable authority to convene or request additional resources. They can deploy the National Guard or request expertise, equipment, and personnel from the federal government or other states. Governors also serve as the point of contact with FEMA and the federal government.

## City-Level Partners

City leaders, such as mayors or council-members, play a critical role in preventing and responding to attacks and natural disasters. Undoubtedly, the most critical responsibility of local officials is to serve as first responders in the aftermath of a terrorist attack. Relatedly, they also serve to interdict illicit activity that often leads to the larger crime of terrorism. No single local government agency possesses the authority or expertise to act alone on the many complex issues surrounding terrorism. Therefore, coordination between federal, state, and local governments is essential.

DHS fulfills part of this coordinating role by sharing information and intelligence with state and local governments through institutions like Fusion Centers. Local governments also have information-sharing bodies and mechanisms, such as the National League of Cities and the U.S. Conference of Mayors, the two umbrella organizations that help coordinate and unify local homeland security efforts.

**FIG. 2.17**
One of the first meetings of the U.S. Conference of Mayors in Boston. The photo highlights the growing diversity in the makeup of mayoralties throughout the United States. Today, mayors are an even more diverse group of public leaders.

*Conference of Mayors
September 14 - 1985.*

*Source*: City of Boston Archives, U.S. Conference of Mayors 1985, www.flickr.com/people/48039697@N05.

The U.S. Conference of Mayors is a non-partisan group of executives whose cities' populations exceed 30,000 people. Since 9/11, the Conference has focused on raising preparedness levels, including a project designed to address responses to WMD. The Conference also created a mayors' training institute to discuss preparedness issues between mayors and federal officials.[58] In January 2002, the Conference laid out a comprehensive strategy to combat terrorist threats at the local level.

The National League of Cities (NLC) is an organization representing cities, villages, and towns, serving as an advocate and resource for building stronger communities. As a part of NLC, the Public Safety and Crime Prevention Committee develops policy positions on public safety issues, many of which present a nexus to homeland security mission areas, including emergency preparedness and response and domestic terrorism.[59]

Like state governments, local governments rely on pre-existing structures, such as police and fire departments, to respond to terrorism, violent extremism, and natural disasters. To manage these additional responsibilities, cities also seek funding from the federal government and other non-governmental actors. Larger cities, like New York and Los Angeles, have dedicated departments that handle homeland security matters. They are responsible for creating an emergency response plan that can be deployed during a homeland security incident. Cities also spend time sharing specific preparedness information with their citizens, one example being the Houston Police Department's Stop/Run/Hide video, which shows what citizens can do during active shooter situations.

As first responders, municipal leaders also play a crucial role in local efforts to prevent or respond to a terrorist incident by communicating effectively with the public and other stakeholder audiences. Even when there are no current homeland security incidents occurring, local leaders are often the best source of direct information regarding threats to citizens in their cities and towns.

### State and Local Law Enforcement and Emergency Response

The first lines of defense and response in any terrorist attack or natural disaster are state and local law enforcement and emergency responders. Police officers, fire departments, medical responders, and others are the first to arrive on scene. To effectively respond to all hazards, they require the tools and information to take immediate action. Recognizing this, the 9/11 Commission recommended (and Congress created) the DHS Office for State and Local Law Enforcement (OSLLE), which is the department's primary liaison with state and local law enforcement agencies.[60] OSLLE creates event response policies for state and local law enforcement while also identifying law enforcement challenges impacting the homeland security mission and promoting DHS initiatives such as the "See Something, Say Something" campaign (Figure 2.18).

State and local law enforcement are also critical in gathering and sharing information with the wider homeland security enterprise. They are essential in passing on information in real time during an emergency, and they constitute an enormous intelligence gathering asset. Because they live and work in their communities on a daily basis, local law enforcement are able to share crucial local information and intelligence via Fusion Centers and

**FIG. 2.18**
The use of the "See Something, Say Something" slogan was licensed in 2010 by the U.S. Department of Homeland Security (DHS). To aid in spreading the campaign across the U.S, DHS collaborated with a number of organizations, professional sports teams, states, and cities and has awarded millions of dollars in federal grants to help with its message. Today, over half of all Americans are familiar with the slogan.

*Source*: Department of Homeland Security, DHS "See Something, Say Something" Promotional Poster, www.dhs.gov/if-you-see-something-say-something/if-you-see-something-say-something-officials-psa.

through other means. Therefore, through numerous partnerships with local law enforcement, DHS and other homeland security-related federal agencies are able to gather a truly comprehensive picture of the day-to-day threat environment throughout the U.S.

## ROLE OF THE PRIVATE SECTOR IN HOMELAND SECURITY

Central to homeland security are the priorities of preparedness and resilience; that is, a readiness to respond to all hazards and the capacity to rapidly restore operations after an event. The homeland security enterprise can provide the tools, advice, oversight, funding, and other functions that support preparedness and resilience, but ultimately what is required is the willing participation of non-government organizations. Recognizing this, the 9/11 Commission recommended a series of steps for enhancing private sector preparedness. In line with that recommendation, there are a series of programs run by the aforementioned DHS Private Sector Office. DHS' Science and Technology Directorate also funds the development of new counterterrorism and emergency response technologies, eventually assisting the private sector to bring these technologies to market.

While the private sector holds great responsibility in participating in the homeland security mission, businesses and other organizations also constitute a significant asset to the national effort to restore operations as quickly as possible following an attack or natural disaster. This capability is often referred to as **resilience**. After a natural disaster, such as a hurricane or earthquake, the faster businesses can reopen their doors, the faster the community can return to normal operation. When supermarkets, restaurants, gas stations, hardware stores, pharmacies, and other businesses cannot quickly restore operation, it compounds the damage and threat to the community, making a bad situation worse. Conversely, when these and other businesses rapidly restore operation, citizens in need are able to access the food and other necessities that cannot be provided in full by government organizations.

**DEFINITION BOX: Resilience**

**Resilience** The Department of Homeland Security defines resilience as the ability to withstand and recover rapidly from deliberate attacks, accidents, and natural disasters, as well as unconventional stresses, shocks, and threats to our economy and democratic system.

## SIDEBAR 2.5 A Resilient Homeland Security Workforce

The concept of resilience isn't only central to the mission of DHS as it is carried out with the general public; it is also central to the internal processes of the department as well. Most recently, DHS has sought to hire psychologists and other experts to teach a variety of courses on mindfulness and meditation to its employees to help "enhance psychological health and resilience," as well develop compassion and leadership skills.[61]

Much of the capacity that human beings have for overcoming adversity stems from connections to other people and interactions with them. Mindfulness meditation can be the first step in helping the victims of 2017's Hurricane Maria recover from long-lasting trauma and despair. Moreover, meditation can also help DHS employees, such as FEMA specialists, recover from witnessing tragedy and dealing with the emotional needs of disaster victims. Mindfulness as a resilience and coping response also helps individuals focus their attention and regulate emotion.[62]

Experts argue, however, that mindfulness training alone isn't enough for those in the homeland security professions. Often, what is required for those in stressful security and intelligence-related professions is a culture where people can feel like mistakes can be fixed, time off for the development of personal relationships and families, and the ability to exercise autonomy and professional freedom.[63] These are all difficult qualities to imbue in a government bureaucracy where orders are often followed to the letter, secrecy is essential, and national crises make long workdays the norm.

Following a disaster, a rapid restoration of business also has an important economic benefit. Often, more damaging to a community than the disaster itself are the cascading economic consequences that stem from it. Without a resilient private sector, a disaster in one city can have real impacts on another part of the country, making natural disasters and terrorist attacks inherently national events. For example, a disrupted supply chain in New York City in the aftermath of a terrorist attack slows the delivery of goods to other businesses around the country, in turn impacting their economic productivity. Restoring normal operations rapidly can limit the economic consequences of disasters. There is also a psychological aspect to resilience, particularly with regard to acts of terrorism. Terrorism is a tactic used to instill a sense of fear and shake confidence in government. Quickly returning public life to a measure of normality helps limit that fear and preserve public confidence.

The U.S. private sector is thus an essential partner in the homeland security enterprise. Partnerships with the private sector are particularly important with regard to critical infrastructure, the vast majority of which is privately owned. Private ownership means that federal, state, and local authorities can only advise on, support, and sometimes regulate the measures taken to secure critical infrastructure against all hazards; most critical infrastructure is not (and cannot be) directly secured by government bodies. That requires voluntary action on the part of the infrastructure owners.

Given this inherent challenge, there are a range of programs and groups established to enhance the security of the nation's critical infrastructure. These include:

- *The Critical Infrastructure Partnership Advisory Council* (CIPAC), a forum where public and private stakeholders can jointly engage in and coordinate activities enhancing infrastructure protection and resilience.[64]
- *The National Infrastructure Advisory Council* (NIAC), which advises the President, via the DHS Secretary, on infrastructure security and information systems.[65] The NIAC is made up of 30 members from industry, academia, and state and local governments.
- *The Regional Consortium Coordinating Council* (RC3), which provides a framework for regional groups to engage and advance resilience activities.

## CONCLUSION

More than 15 years after the 9/11 attacks, the homeland security enterprise is vast, touching every aspect of the nation's public and private sectors. As with any massive endeavor, the homeland security enterprise is far from a perfect system. While many of the 9/11 Commission's recommendations have been implemented, more work remains. For instance, the evolving threat of homegrown radicalization to violence requires DHS and other government agencies to continually reassess strategic deployment of assets and strategies.

Nonetheless, as you will learn throughout the rest of this text, the homeland security enterprise is designed such that it can grow and adapt to an ever-changing threat environment.

Understanding this broad picture of the stakeholders in the homeland security arena, we now move on to exploring the myriad roles, responsibilities, priorities, mandates, and challenges present within each homeland security mission area.

## HOMELAND SECURITY VOICES: Governor Tom Ridge (Part 2)

*Continued from Chapter 1*

**Let's talk about domestic issues. A number of unaccompanied minors have been crossing the United States' southern border over the past few years. In many cases the government is unable to care for those who do make it across and those who don't are often taken advantage of or hurt in the border crossing process. Do you think asking for additional funding from Congress is the way to diminish the number of individuals crossing the border?**

TR: The unaccompanied minor issue is another reflection of the failure of political leadership from both political parties to grasp the national implications of an immigration system that is in need of overhaul. I have enormous empathy for these minors and I have empathy for DHS, which is being blamed for by some for what happens to these minors. Its reprehensible that one political party is worried about citizenship and the other about enforcement, when our broken immigration system could be solved in a meaningful way. Nobody from Congress wants to tackle it, they would rather run for election around either doing or not doing certain things rather than to say "we solved the problem." I'm dissatisfied with both parties and particularly the failure of presidential leadership.

**What would be a potential solution to this problem?**

TR: Republicans have to accept the reality that we are not going to send 10 to 12 million undocumented immigrants back home. It's an unrealistic position. Instead, we can legitimize the presence of individuals who are here illegally and create a structure allowing them to travel back and forth across the border legally. This legitimization does not necessarily mean citizenship but rather giving individuals opportunities of employment, similar to the system in Europe.

Specifically, I think it would be smart to: Legitimize the presence of all undocumented immigrants who have not committed crimes, give them two years to register with the government. Collect their names and biometrics in a database and allow them to seek employment in the U.S. However, if they have committed a crime then send them back to their country of origin. A second part of the solution would build a framework for businesses to hire those legitimized individuals. Thirdly,

**FIG. 2.19**
Tom Ridge served as the first Secretary of Homeland Security and prior to that was the governor of Pennsylvania.

*Source*: Department of Homeland Security, Tom Ridge, Former Secretary of Homeland https://upload.wikimedia.org/wikipedia/commons/f/f3/Tom_Ridge.jpg.

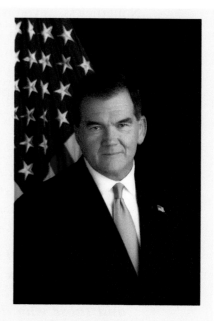

that framework must include heavy sanctions against businesses who h ire outside this permitted group of employees. For instance, after the second offense the government could even put them out of business.

When it comes to enforcement on the southern border, we have plenty of Border Patrol officers on the border, but we need to put a little bit more diplomatic pressure on our friends in Mexico. The reason people come to the United States illegally is because it is so difficult to enter lawfully. Moreover, we shouldn't believe that everybody who comes across the border necessarily wants to be an American citizen. This is a crazy mindset, which speaks to me of a certain elitism and arrogance. Instead, I believe most undocumented individuals are seeking employment and want to come to the U.S. work eight or nine months and then go back to their country of origin.

*Let's move on to a different topic: The No-Fly and Watchlist. What are your views on the efficacy of the watchlist? Is it an important tool in the fight against terrorists, especially domestic terrorists? And if it is, how could it, or should it be, modified to make it more effective?*

TR: Clearly, there are reasonable grounds for any country that may have secured information about individuals coming in and out of the United States of America, to at least allow for customs officers to question those individuals when they get to a U.S. port of entry. I do think there is a role that watchlists play both in the U.S. and globally, especially when legitimate suspicions arise from a person's connection to terrorists, their travel in connection with terrorist activity, or their involvement in fundraising or support of a terrorist or terrorist activity. In the 21st century you have to have a system of that sort.

*One of the issues that DHS has been dealing with, and that you may have dealt with in your tenure as Secretary, was congressional oversight and how oversight responsibilities of DHS are shared by more committees in Congress than any other cabinet-level department. What are your thoughts on how congressional oversight can be reformed?*

TR: The relationship that DHS has with the Hill is compounded with overlapping committee and subcommittee jurisdictional responsibilities. This is in part responsible, in my judgment, for the fact that the department itself hasn't had a chance to mature and become as effective and as efficient as it needs to be. There are too many vested interests in the department that could probably even circumnavigate the Secretary of Homeland Security. As a former member of Congress, legislative oversight is imperative, it's absolutely essential to the growth and maturity and effectiveness of DHS, but when you have the Secretary and the deputy secretaries and all the agency heads running around to over 100 congressional committees and subcommittees, reporting to Congress becomes inefficient, irresponsible, and unwarranted.

However, unmanaged oversight is a symptom of government at large. The U.S. government is organized for the mid-1950s, but a 21st-century government, given its size and complexity, requires not only looking at jurisdiction over DHS, but jurisdictional oversight over the entire Executive Branch. I'm not saying that the secretaries at DHS should be less immune from congressional oversight, but the oversight is dysfunctional.

One of the other ironies based on my experience, is that individual congresspeople will complain to one another about the outrageous number of committee and subcommittees on which they serve. Rarely do they stay in any of those hearings for over an hour or two. Rarely does a member develop any level of expertise, but you take away that committee or subcommittee assignment from them and they will go ballistic. This is where the House and Senate leadership of both parties in conjunction with the President of the United States ought to just mandate the changes and get it done. It's an agency that needs oversight, but nobody on the Hill, no small group of men and women in either body has a broader comprehensive view of the department (DHS) and the need to accelerate the integration of capabilities. All three secretaries have sought it, think-tanks have recommended it, people on the Hill want it, everybody knows, military leaders have suggested it, there's so many people who have said "Congress deal with it," and they just ignore the reality of a dysfunctional relationship with an emerging department that is critical to America's security.

*There was a recent debate in New York between General Hayden, Peter Bergen, and a few others, on "is the war on terror" a "real" war? Some experts believe that the "war on terror" is an idea that sets up a framework, that allows the government to bring disparate government agencies together. This is similar to what the "war on drugs" did for the fight against illicit drugs. In other words, it's kind of a rallying cry. Do you think the war on terror serves as this rallying cry or is it irrelevant and/or more harmful than good?*

TR: Waging war against terror or on terrorism is a misnomer. This is really a war against Islamic extremists, it's unlike anything the broader world community has ever experienced. The connected tissue that formed al-Qa'ida in 2001 has grown faster and metastasized in more areas and created even more extremist organizations than anybody imagined could happen 10 or 12 years ago. So the notion that you do call it a war against these extremists, and the notion that there are multiple ways you need to defend yourself against this enemy lends itself to the use of the word "war." This is instead a war against an extremist ideology and there are many ways we have to go about being proactive to defend ourselves and mitigate potential consequences of that war.

*Were you involved in any way in the development of the term "war on terror"?*

TR: No. The "war on terror" was a mantra established under President Bush. I don't understand the background of the term. I think now more than ever it's misplaced and it's time to redefine what we are fighting against. We are not fighting against a tactic; it is just simply a tactic used by Islamic extremists. Not Jewish extremists, not Christian extremists, not atheist extremists. It's Islamic extremists, and we just need to accept it as that and move on.

Call it a war against extremism. You cannot call it a war against *Islam*, because it's not. Frankly the terrorist community is much better organized, much better funded, has much greater reach, seems to be having greater appeal, because of a lot of factors. It's not only the United States, the broader Western community particularly because it seems to be that is primarily where the extremists are focused. I don't think China particularly is worried about Islamic extremism, Russia probably is in a province or two, but they are going to deal with it a little differently than the Western world would. It's really a war against extremists and it's gotten worse, not better.

## KEYWORDS

- **personally identifiable information** (PII): Is any data that could potentially identify a specific individual. Information that can be used to distinguish one person from another and can be used for de-anonymizing anonymous data can be considered PII.
- **public-private partnership** (PPP): A public-private partnership is a joint effort or venture between any level of government and one or more private sector organizations.
- **import duties**: Taxes on goods from overseas that are sold in the United States.
- *Posse Comitatus* Act: A federal law passed in 1878 that limits the powers of the federal government in using military personnel to enforce domestic policies within the territory of the United States.
- **resilience**: Defined as the ability to withstand and recover rapidly from deliberate attacks, accidents, or natural disasters, as well as unconventional stresses, shocks, and threats to our economy and democratic system.

### KNOWLEDGE CHECK

1. What did the 9/11 attacks reveal about the government's ability to defend itself against terrorist attacks?
2. What is the mission of the Department of Homeland Security?
3. DHS is made up of some large, semi-autonomous subcomponents. What are they?
4. What is the role of the private sector in homeland security? Why is it important?

## NOTES

1. Pew Research Center for The People & The Press, Council on Foreign Relations, The View Before 9/11: America's Place in the World, A Special Analysis on Foreign Policy Attitudes Before the Attacks (2001) www.pewresearch.org/wp-content/uploads/sites/4/legacy-pdf/20011018.pdf.

2. Raphael Perl, *The Department of Homeland Security: Background and Challenges*, in Terrorism: Reducing Vulnerabilities and Improving Responses: U.S.-Russian Workshop Proceedings 177 (2004).

3. Al-Qa'ida in its Own Words 55 (Gilles Kepel and Jean-Pierre Milelli eds., 2008).

4. Terry McDermott, Perfect Soldiers, The 9/11 Hijackers: Who They Were, Why They Did It 176–177 (2005).

5. National Commission on Terrorist Attacks Upon the United States, The 9/11 Commission Report, at 18 (2004) www.9-11commission.gov/report/911Report.pdf.

6. S. Rep. No 107–351 (2002); H.R. Rep. No. 107–792 (2002).

7. Intelligence Authorization Act for Fiscal Year 2003, Pub. L. No. 107–306 http://govinfo.library.unt.edu/911/about/107-306.title6.htm.

8. National Commission on Terrorist Attacks Upon the United States, The 9/11 Commission Report (2004) www.9-11commission.gov/report/911Report.pdf.

9. *Minutes and Years: The Bin Ladin Operation*, Central Intelligence Agency (Apr. 29, 2016, 8:40 PM). www.cia.gov/news-information/featured-story-archive/2016-featured-story-archive/minutes-and-years-the-bin-ladin-operation.html.

10. *Id.*

11. *Id.*

12. *Regulatory Process*, Regulations.gov (last visited Dec. 16, 2018) www.regulations.gov/?tab=learn.

13. *Id.*

14. U.S. Dep't of Homeland Security, Brief Documentary History of the Department of Homeland Security 2001–2008, www.historyassociates.com/wp-content/uploads/2015/09/US-Department-of-Homeland-Security-Brief-History-2001-2008.pdf.

15. *Office for Civil Rights and Civil Liberties*, U.S. Dep't of Homeland Security (May 30, 2018) www.dhs.gov/office-civil-rights-and-civil-liberties.

16. *Privacy Office*, U.S. Dep't of Homeland Security (Sept. 17, 2018) www.dhs.gov/privacy-office.

17. *CIS Ombudsman*, U.S. Dep't of Homeland Security (July 17, 2018) www.dhs.gov/topic/cis-ombudsman.

18. *Office of Inspector General*, U.S. Dep't of Homeland Security (last visited Dec. 16, 2018) www.oig.dhs.gov/index.php?option=com_content&view=article&id=94&Itemid=63.

19. *Office of Intergovernmental Affairs*, U.S. Dep't of Homeland Security (Jan. 27, 2018) www.dhs.gov/office-intergovernmental-affairs-1.

20. *Office of Legislative Affairs*, U.S. DEP'T OF HOMELAND SECURITY (Sept. 20, 2018) www.dhs.gov/about-office-legislative-affairs.

21. FEDERAL TIMES (last visited Mar. 22, 2016) www.federaltimes.com/story/government/dhs/blog/2015/02/03/congress-dhs-oversight/22801817/.

22. *Office of the General Counsel*, U.S. DEP'T OF HOMELAND SECURITY (Feb. 26, 2018) www.dhs.gov/office-general-counsel.

23. *Office of Public Affairs,* U.S. DEP'T OF HOMELAND SECURITY (Jan. 19, 2018) www.dhs.gov/office-public-affairs.

24. U.S. Dep't of Homeland Security Office of Inspector General, The Responsibilities of the Office of Counternarcotics Enforcement (2010) www.oig.dhs.gov/assets/Mgmt/OIG_10-80_Apr10.pdf.

25. *Office of the Executive Secretary,* U.S. DEP'T OF HOMELAND SECURITY (July 23, 2018) www.dhs.gov/office-executive-secretary.

26. Jon Swaine, *Homeland nothing like real intelligence work, say CIA employees*, THE TELEGRAPH (Oct. 6, 2013, 3:59 PM) www.telegraph.co.uk/news/worldnews/northamerica/usa/10357816/Homeland-nothing-like-real-intelligence-work-say-CIA-employees.html.

27. *Office of Strategy, Policy, and Plans,* U.S. DEP'T OF HOMELAND SECURITY (July 9, 2018) www.dhs.gov/office-policy.

28. Bureau of Justice Assistance, Engaging the Private Sector to Promote Homeland Security: Law Enforcement-Private Security Partnerships, at vii (2005) www.ncjrs.gov/pdffiles1/bja/210678.pdf.

29. *Voluntary Private Sector Preparedness Accreditation and Certification Program*, FEMA (July 16, 2012, 6:46 PM) www.fema.gov/news-release/2008/07/30/voluntary-private-sector-preparedness-accreditation-and-certification.

30. *Protected Critical Infrastructure Information (PCII) Program*, U.S. DEP'T OF HOMELAND SECURITY (Oct. 4, 2018) www.dhs.gov/pcii-program.

31. *Preparedness Planning for Your Business*, READY.GOV (last visited Dec. 16, 2018) www.ready.gov/business.

32. *Academic Engagement*, U.S. DEP'T OF HOMELAND SECURITY (July 30, 2018) www.dhs.gov/academic-engagement.

33. *National Infrastructure Advisory Council*, U.S. DEP'T OF HOMELAND SECURITY (Dec. 11, 2018) www.dhs.gov/national-infrastructure-advisory-council.

34. *Homeland Security Science and Technology Advisory Charter*, U.S. DEP'T OF HOMELAND SECURITY (last visited Dec. 16, 2018) www.dhs.gov/science-and-technology/homeland-security-science-and-technology-advisory-committee-charter.

35. *Maritime Security*, U.S. COAST GUARD (last visited Mar. 22, 2016) www.uscg.mil/top/missions/MaritimeSecurity.asp.

36. *Maritime Stewardship*, U.S. COAST GUARD (last visited Mar. 22, 2016) www.uscg.mil/top/missions/MaritimeStewardship.asp.

37. *Frequently Asked Questions*, SECRETSERVICE.GOV (last visited Dec. 16, 2018) www.secretservice.gov/about/faqs/.

38. *Who We Are*, U.S. Immigration and Customs Enforcement (Dec. 14, 2018) www.ice.gov/about.

39. *What We Do*, U.S. Immigration and Customs Enforcement (Dec. 4, 2018) www.ice.gov/overview.

40. *Border Patrol Overview*, U.S. Customs and Border Protection (Apr. 26, 2018) www.cbp.gov/border-security/along-us-borders/overview.

41. *About Us*, U.S. Citizenship and Immigration Services (Mar. 6, 2018) www.uscis.gov/aboutus.

42. *Cybersecurity Division*, U.S. Dep't of Homeland Security (last visited Dec. 16, 2018) www.dhs.gov/office-cybersecurity-and-communications.

43. *The Federal Protective Service*, U.S. Dep't Homeland Security (Nov. 16, 2018) www.dhs.gov/topic/federal-protective-service.

44. *Examining the Mission, Structure, and Reorganization Effort of the National Protection and Programs Directorate: Hearing Before the Comm. on Homeland Security*, 114th Cong. (2015) (written testimony of The Honorable Suzanne E. Spaulding, Dr. Ronald J. Clark, and Dr. Phyllis A. Schneck) available at http://docs.house.gov/meetings/HM/HM08/20151007/103965/HHRG-114-HM08-Wstate-SpauldingS-20151007.pdf.

45. *About S&T*, U.S. Dep't of Homeland Security (last visited Dec. 16, 2018) www.dhs.gov/science-and-technology/about-st.

46. *Our Work*, U.S. Dep't of Homeland Security (last visited Dec. 16, 2018) www.dhs.gov/science-and-technology/our-work.

47. *The Office of SAFETY Act Implementation*, U.S. Dep't of Homeland Security (last visited Dec. 18, 2018) www.dhs.gov/science-and-technology/safety-act.

48. *Office of Intelligence and Analysis Mission*, U.S. Dep't of Homeland Security (Dec. 7, 2018) www.dhs.gov/office-intelligence-and-analysis-mission.

49. *Operational and Support Components*, U.S. Dep't of Homeland Security (Nov. 20, 2018) www.dhs.gov/operational-and-support-components

50. *Mission Statement*, Bureau of Industry and Security, U.S. Dep't of Commerce (last visited Dec. 16, 2018) www.bis.doc.gov/index.php/2011-09-12-15-43-33.

51. *About*, Office of Refugee Resettlement, U.S. Dep't of Health and Human Services (Oct. 23, 2017) www.acf.hhs.gov/orr/about.

52. *Food and Agriculture Sector*, U.S. Dep't of Homeland Security (last visited Dec. 16, 2018) www.dhs.gov/food-and-agriculture-sector.

53. *Office of Homeland Security & Emergency Coordination*, U.S. Dep't of Agric. (last visited Dec. 16, 2018) www.dm.usda.gov/ohsec/.

54. *National Security and Safety*, Dep't of Energy (last visited Dec. 16, 2018) www.energy.gov/public-services/national-security-safety.

55. *About NNSA*, U.S. Dep't of Energy (last visited Dec. 18, 2018) www.energy.gov/nnsa/about-nnsa.

56. *About the Office of Homeland Security (OHS)*, U.S. Environmental Protection Agency (last visited Dec. 16, 2018) www.epa.gov/aboutepa/about-office-homeland-security-ohs.

57. *About the National Homeland Security Research Center (NHSRC)*, U.S. Environmental Protection Agency (last visited Dec. 16, 2018) www.epa.gov/aboutepa/about-national-homeland-security-research-center-nhsrc.

58. United States Conference of Mayors at 1 (last visited Mar. 22, 2016) http://usmayors.org/70thAnnualMeeting/securitysurvey_061302.pdf.

59. *Public Safety and Crime Prevention Committee*, Nat'l League of Cities (last visited Dec. 16, 2018) www.nlc.org/influence-federal-policy/policy-committees/public-safety-and-crime-prevention.

60. *The Office for State and Local Law Enforcement*, U.S. Dep't of Homeland Security (last visited Dec. 16, 2018) www.dhs.gov/office-state-and-local-law-enforcement.

61 *Mindfulness Training*, Federal Business Opportunities (Last visited Dec. 16, 2018) www.fbo.gov/index?s=opportunity&mode=form&id=a5ecab6564e1acc730da81bd2c013ad0&tab=core&_cview=1.

62. *Faculty & instructors*, U. of Minnesota (last visited Dec. 16, 2018) http://icd.umn.edu/people/.

63. *Homeland Security wants its employees to learn mindfulness, but is that the best way to build resilience?*, The Verge (Dec. 13, 2017, 1:41 PM) www.theverge.com/2017/12/13/16772178/mindfulness-resilience-stress-reduction-programs-employers.

64. *Critical Infrastructure Partnership Advisory Council*, U.S. Dep't of Homeland Security (Nov. 1, 2018) www.dhs.gov/critical-infrastructure-partnership-advisory-council.

65. *National Infrastructure Advisory Council*, U.S. Dep't of Homeland Security (Dec. 11, 2018) www.dhs.gov/national-infrastructure-advisory-council.

# CHAPTER 3

# Immigration

**IN THIS CHAPTER YOU WILL LEARN ABOUT**

The history of legal and illegal immigration to the United States.

The removal process and the federal agencies involved in removing undocumented individuals.

Policy exceptions to removal for humanitarian and refugee applicants.

## INTRODUCTION

**Immigration** is the international movement of people to a country where they are not natives or where they do not possess citizenship, in order to settle or reside in that country for a significant length of time. Immigration has been an important part of the United States' history. Aside from Native Americans, who can be considered to be indigenous to the United States, all other Americans arrived to the U.S. via immigration.

Individuals can immigrate to a country legally or illegally, i.e. in a way that violates the immigration laws of the destination country. Illegal immigration as well as immigration in general trends upward from a poorer country to a richer country. If you arrive in the United States illegally, you risk being deported (physically removed) to your home country. Most illegal immigrants in the U.S. are considered "out of status" and work in a shadow market economy to avoid being apprehended by Immigration and Customs Enforcement (ICE).

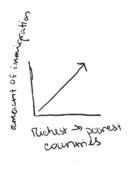

Ample economic evidence suggests that migration of peoples, whether legal or illegal, is significantly beneficial to the destination country. With few exceptions, research finds that immigration on average has positive economic effects on the native population (concomitantly migration away from a country is bad for that country's economy, referred to colloquially as "brain drain"). Nonetheless, and especially after 9/11, the United States has adopted a posture of increasingly limiting and criminalizing the immigration of undocumented persons and prioritizing the deportation of those undocumented immigrants who have committed crimes while in the United States.

In this chapter we discuss the nature of America's land and sea borders, the history of both legal and illegal immigration, how and why those who enter the U.S are removed and the government agencies involved in apprehending undocumented individuals and confiscating illegal contraband in the U.S.

## HISTORY OF IMMIGRATION AND IMMIGRATION ENFORCEMENT

Immigration has played an important role in American history, and the U.S. continues to have the most open immigration policy in the world. Before the era of rapid communications and transportation, America encouraged relatively open immigration as an incentive to settle open and empty lands in the West and Midwest. Following the Civil War, several states passed immigration laws, some of which conflicted with each other. In response, in 1875 the Supreme Court declared the regulation of the entry of individuals into and out of the country a federal responsibility.

The Immigration and Naturalization Service (INS) was established in 1891 to deal with the large increase in immigration from Ireland and Eastern Europe that occurred primarily after 1880. Indeed, from 1900 to 1920 nearly 24 million immigrants arrived to U.S. shores, referred to collectively as the "Great Wave" of immigration. World War I resulted in reduced immigration from Europe, but mass immigration resumed upon the war's end and Congress responded with a new immigration policy: The national-origins quota system passed in 1921 and revised in 1924.

*[handwritten margin note: less immigration during wars]*

Immigration under this system was limited by assigning each nationality a quota based on its representation in past U.S. census figures. Practically speaking, this meant that European, and especially Western European, immigrants had more immigration slots open to them because Americans from those backgrounds already comprised the larger portion of the U.S. population. Conversely, this severely limited immigration from countries that had no significant pre-existing representation in the U.S. such as India, China, and Egypt. Also in 1924, Congress created the U.S. Border Patrol as a semiautonomous entity within the INS. The Border Patrol was tasked with patrolling the southern border between Mexico and the U.S. to interdict undocumented crossers and contraband.

Unsurprisingly, with the advent of the quota system and the creation of the Border Patrol, all immigration flows into the U.S. practically ceased. In fact, during the Great Depression immigration flows actually went into negative territory as Americans left the country seeking better economic opportunities abroad. Though immigration picked up after World War II, it still did not approach pre-WWI levels. This was primarily because the 1920s national-origin quota system remained in place after WWII. Congress combined these older quota laws and combined all previous immigration and naturalization law into the Immigration and Nationality Act of 1952. American farmers and agriculture companies continued to import seasonal labor from Mexico, as they had during WWII, under a 1951 formal agreement between the U.S. and Mexico called the "Bracero Program."

As the American economy grew in the decades following WWII, Congress realized that attracting talent from abroad was vital to the success of the American economy. Thus, in 1965 Congress replaced the national-origin quota system with a preference system designed to unite immigrant families and attract skilled immigrants to the U.S. This change in national immigration policy led to a dramatic demographic shift in the U.S. population that we continue to see to this day. Since 1965 the majority of applicants for immigration visas now come from Asia and Latin America rather than Europe. Despite this change in immigration policy, the preference system still had an overall cap on the total number of immigration visas that could be granted in on year.

From the 1960s onwards, both the number of legal immigrants as well as the number of illegal immigrants increased—drawn by American economic

*Not a lot of immigration during Great Depression*

might and the prospect of jobs and a better life. By the early 1980s, millions of undocumented immigrants resided in the U.S. In response to the large number of undocumented immigrants, Congress passed the Immigration Reform and Control Act (IRCA) in 1986. *GOALS*

The IRCA had two major goals: Amnesty and enforcement. IRCA promised that out-of-status immigrants in the country present at the time the IRCA was passed would not be subject to deportation if they 1) had resided continually in the U.S. since January 1982 or 2) had completed 90 days of agricultural work between May 1985 and May 1986. Ninety-four percent of applicants who applied for amnesty were accepted, eventually providing almost 3 million undocumented immigrants legal status in the United States. The IRCA also contained enforcement provisions that made the hiring and harboring of undocumented immigrants a federal crime. *Overall IRCA seems positive*

The federal government's immigration-related responsibilities expanded under the IRCA. The IRCA charged the INS with enforcing sanctions against United States employers who hired undocumented aliens. Carrying out employer sanction duties involved investigating, prosecuting, and levying fines against corporate and individual employers, as well as deportation of those found to be working illegally.[1]

In 1990 Congress further reformed immigration statutes. The Immigration Act of 1990 was an amendment to the 1965 Act and increased the number of legal immigrants that could enter the US every year from 500,000 to 700,000. In addition, the 1990 Act introduced the "lottery" system that assigned visas to immigrants randomly, irrespective of their status, wealth, or country of origin. The primary reason for instituting the lottery system was to further ameliorate the effects of the national-quota system put into place in the 1920s. *Lottery system to undo 1920s National-Quota system*

The 1990 Act also increased the number of visas that could be issued to foreigners from 54,000 to 140,000 per year. Additional categories were added to the visas prioritizing those foreigners who were experts in their field, possessed extraordinary abilities, or were advanced professionals in fields prioritized by the U.S. government. The 1990 Act was one among many other trends that resulted in a sharp rise in the number of immigrants seeking legal entry into the U.S. From the early 1990s until the end of the decade, slightly more than 1.1 million migrants came to the U.S. every year on average.

*More immigrants when economy is good*

*Less imigrants when economy is bad or disaster strike*

This number of legal migrants (as well as the number of illegal immigrants) declined sharply after 2001. Both the rise of immigration in the 1990s and its subsequent decline coincides with a variety of conditions that influence immigration flows. The most notable of these is the performance of the American economy. As the economy grew in the 1990s, jobs for migrants grew plentiful and attracted both legal and illegal immigrants to the country. Secondly, the events of 9/11 played some role in declining immigration flows.

The events of September 11, 2001 injected new urgency into INS' mission and initiated another shift in United States immigration policy. The emphasis of American immigration law enforcement became border security and removing criminal aliens to protect the nation from terrorist attacks. At the same time, the INS and subsequent organizations such as USCIS had to retain their commitment to welcoming lawful immigrants and supporting their integration and participation in American civic culture.

Since 9/11 the primary emphasis of immigration legislation has been to reduce government benefits to immigrants, increase border security, and provide broader reasoning for excluding immigrants on terrorism grounds. Notable exceptions to that pattern were President Obama's executive orders on unauthorized immigration: Deferred Action for Early Childhood Arrivals (DACA) in 2012 and Deferred Action for Parents of Americans and Lawful Permanent Residents (DAPA) in 2014.

*DACA vs. DAPA*

DACA allowed young adults, ages 15 to 30 at the time of the order's passage, who had been brought to the United States illegally as children to apply for temporary relief from deportation proceedings and also apply for a temporary work permit. In 2014, President Obama eliminated the age limits for DACA eligibility. Under DAPA, some undocumented immigrants with U.S.-born children were allowed to apply for deportation relief and seek a work permit.[2] The rationale behind both executive orders was to allow those children brought to the U.S. through no fault of their own to remain in the country to which they were now accustomed. To be eligible for DACA or DAPA, recipients cannot have felonies or serious misdemeanors on their records.

*Rationale: children are not at fault, this is the country they're accustomed to.*

**CRITICAL THINKING QUESTION**

Note the word "deferred" in the DACA and DAPA executive actions discussed in this chapter. What do you think this implies? If you were a lawyer counseling someone to apply for DACA or DAPA would you also counsel them that those benefits may be revoked at a future time?

## SIDEBAR 3.1 Deferred Action for Early Childhood Arrivals

The Deferred Action for Early Childhood Arrivals program began as a congressional bill. Senator Dick Durbin, along with other members of Congress, introduced several forms of the Development, Relief and Education for Alien Minors (DREAM) Act in both the House of Representatives and the Senate. The bill was reintroduced several times since 2009, but failed to pass.

On June 15, 2012, seeing no action by Congress, President Obama announced that his administration would stop deporting undocumented immigrants who match certain criteria in the proposed DREAM Act. This policy was called the Deferred Action for Early Childhood Arrivals (DACA) program, discussed elsewhere in this chapter. Since then, hundreds of thousands of people have applied for the program and by January 2017, over 700,000 people had registered for the program.[3] Because DACA was designed in large part to address the immigration status of the same people covered by the DREAM Act, the two programs are often debated together, with some policy experts making little distinction between the DACA program and the DREAM Act. *cover same people*

To apply for DACA, eligible individuals must pay a $495 application fee, submit several forms, and produce documents showing they meet the requirements. They do not need legal representation. To be eligible, recipients must have entered the United States before their 16th birthday and prior to June 2007, be currently in school, a high school graduate, or be honorably discharged from the military, be under the age of 31 as of June 15, 2012, and not have been convicted of a felony, significant misdemeanor, or three other misdemeanors, or otherwise pose a threat to national security. The program does not currently provide permanent lawful status or a path to citizenship, nor does it provide eligibility for federal welfare or student aid.

Considerable debate about the homeland security implications of DACA have been raised. In particular, some experts questioned providing a semblance of legal status to individuals who may otherwise be dangerous or seek to harm the United States. Research has so far failed to show evidence that DACA recipients are more likely to commit crimes than U.S. citizens. This tallies with a body of research literature from the past century that shows immigrants do not commit crimes at a higher rate than nonimmigrant Americans.[4]

In fact, considerable research has shown that DACA increased the wages and labor force participation of DACA-eligible immigrants and reduced the number of unauthorized immigrant households living in poverty.[5] Additional studies have shown that DACA increased the mental health outcomes for DACA-eligible immigrants and their children.

Recently, President Donald Trump sought to eliminate DACA and encouraged Congress to find a permanent solution for those young adults brought to the U.S. illegally as children. As of this writing these presidential efforts to rescind DACA are currently subject to legal challenge.

The events of 9/11 brought about the creation of the Department of Homeland Security. DHS replaced the INS with three separate agencies: USCIS, ICE, and CBP—each with some responsibility for enforcing immigration laws.

Due, in part, to the recommendations made by the 9/11 Commission to increase data sharing between government agencies responsible for securing the homeland, DHS received considerable funding to create and manage additional databases regarding immigrants and visitors to the United States at a scale unprecedented prior to 9/11. Notable among these was the National Security Entry-Exit Registration System (NSEERS) program, which required select male non-citizens from countries with a "significant terrorist presence" to be fingerprinted and photographed. The NSEERS program was delisted in

2011, which means that the authority to engage the program remained in effect but no additional individuals were screened.

DHS also increased security screening for refugees and asylum seekers. Refugee applicants to the United States are subject to intensive biographic and security checks. Through close coordination with federal law enforcement and intelligence communities, these checks are continually reviewed and enhanced to address specific populations that may pose particular threats.[6] More about the refugee admissions process is discussed elsewhere in this chapter.

## LAWS THAT GOVERN IMMIGRATION

### Immigration and Nationality Act — *Most important body of immigration law*

As discussed previously, the Immigration and Nationality Act (INA) was created in 1952. Before the INA, a variety of statutes governed immigration law. Congress passed the INA, in part, to consolidate the nation's disparate immigration statutes in one written document. The INA remains the most important body of immigration law in the United States. The INA is divided into titles, chapters, and sections. Although it stands alone as a body of law, the INA is also contained in the United States Code (U.S.C.). The U.S.C. is a collection of all the laws of the United States. It is arranged in 50 subject titles by general alphabetical order. The INA is Title 8 of the U.S.C. and deals with "Aliens and Nationality." When browsing the INA or other statutes one may often see reference to the U.S.C. citation. For example, Section 208 of the INA deals with asylum, and is also contained in 8 U.S.C. 1158. Although it is correct to refer to a specific section by either its INA citation or U.S.C. citation, the INA citation is more commonly used.

Laws like the INA are not static. They are open to amendment by Congress. The INA and other similar laws are also interpreted by federal government agencies to account for specific "on the ground" situations faced by the agency personnel carrying out the law (such as ICE ERO officers). This agency interpretation process is done through rulemaking and policy creation (discussed in Chapter 2). Lastly, the INA is also open to judicial review by all federal courts, but also federal administrative courts.

The INA has been amended a number of times. When Congress enacts a law, it generally does not re-write the entire body of law, or even entire sections of a law, but instead adds to or changes specific words within a section. These changes are then reflected within the larger body of law. The language changing the larger body of law is generally referred to as the "amendment" or "amendatory" language.

Laws like the INA are usually broad and do not cover specific fact circumstances that ICE or USCIS personnel may have to deal with on a daily basis. Thus, the general provisions of laws enacted by Congress (such as the INA) are interpreted and implemented by regulations issued by various Executive Branch departments and agencies, such as DHS. Unlike laws, department and agency regulations are open for public comment and review. This is to provide public oversight and involvement in the regulatory process, because unlike federal legislation, the public has not elected the heads of federal departments and agencies (they are appointed by the President and serve at his or her pleasure). After the regulations are proposed, assessed by the public, discussed, and revised as necessary, they are then published in the Federal Register and also published in the Code of Federal Regulations (C.F.R.). This process of regulation creation is referred to as rulemaking (discussed in Chapter 2).

A number of government agencies are responsible for executing the nation's immigration laws and policies. Among those previously discussed are Immigration and Customs Enforcement (ICE), Customs and Border Protection (CBP), and United States Citizenship and Immigration Services (USCIS). Here we discuss the immigration enforcement related responsibilities of ICE and USCIS (CBP is discussed in Chapter 4), including describing the apprehension and deportation process in detail. Additional agencies that have ancillary functions related to immigration enforcement are also discussed.

### Administrative Decisions

In addition to rulemaking, USCIS interprets the INA and other immigration statutes through administrative decisions regarding specific immigration cases brought by individuals.

The Administrative Appeals Office (AAO) at USCIS usually issues non-precedent (a decision that does not create new law) decisions. These administrative law decisions apply existing law and policy to the facts of a given immigration case. Though a non-precedent decision is binding on the parties involved in the case, it does not create or modify agency guidance or practice. Thus, non-precedent decisions interpret statutes like the INA for the particular circumstances of one case, but that interpretation does not become policy or regulation that can be looked to later by other parties involved in immigration proceedings.

On the other hand, "precedent decisions" are AAO administrative decisions that are selected and designated by the Secretary of Homeland Security and other federal agencies to apply repeatedly as policy to other similar immigration cases that may arise. Thus, precedent decisions are binding future cases on DHS and its components such as ICE, USCIS, and CBP. But like many other policies, precedent decisions can be modified or overruled by other precedent decisions, the Attorney General, federal courts, and statutes that Congress passes. Precedent decisions are often made for cases heard at the Board of

**FIG. 3.1**
An audience member at the 2015 NAACP Convention raises a hand to ask a question about the Board of Immigration Appeals and immigration reform as President Barack Obama finishes his closing remarks.

*Source*: Lawrence Jackson, Questions About Immigration Reform, https://obamawhitehouse.archives.gov/sites/default/files/image/image_file/1lja1547.jpg.

Immigration Appeals (BIA) (discussed elsewhere in this chapter). Even though the BIA is not a federal court, the decisions administrative law judges make at the BIA are subject to judicial review by other federal courts (including the United States Supreme Court).

### *Policy Memoranda*

In addition to rulemaking and administrative law decisions, leadership from ICE, USCIS, and other federal agencies involved in immigration matters often issue policy memoranda and procedural manuals that give guidance to personnel adjudicating immigration matters, processing immigration applications or petitions for immigration benefits. Each of these policy memos are written in different formats to suit the work of a specific agency or department. Some of them are published and can be viewed by the public. For instance, USCIS issues a USCIS Policy Manual that provides comprehensive guidance on how USCIS personnel should act when confronted with specific fact circumstances. In doing so, the Policy Manual interprets the broad mandates of the INA and other similar statutes for very narrow and specific "on the ground" situations. For example, the Policy Manual recently addressed what USCIS programs should get priority if the government shuts down due to temporary budget disagreements in Congress.[7]

## SIDEBAR 3.2 Secure Communities

Secure Communities is a U.S. government program that relies on partnerships among local, state, and federal law enforcement agencies in order to advance ICE's mission to detain and remove undocumented immigrants. The story of how Secure Communities came to be is a little complicated, but worth telling in detail as it provides insight into how homeland security policy is crafted as well as the unintended consequences of these policies. In 2002 Congress passed a law requiring the FBI and the newly formed Department of Homeland Security to establish an electronic system to allow for the sharing of data across both agencies.

This was done, in part, to diminish the "silo effect" between law enforcement and intelligence agencies. The silo effect refers to a government agency's tendency to operate within its own boundaries, while remaining hesitant to share information or collaborate effectively with partner agencies to investigate and apprehend criminals and terrorists. The 9/11 Commission (discussed in Chapter 2) blamed the silo effect, in part, for the government's inability to prevent 9/11, specifically citing the inability of federal agencies to share information with each other about the 9/11 hijackers as the proximate cause of the attacks.[8]

This information sharing was codified in 8 U.S.C. § 1722: US Code—Section 1722, which requires DHS and the FBI to:

1. Create interoperable law enforcement and intelligence electronic data systems; and
2. Integrate all databases that process or contain information about aliens into the aforementioned data system.

Therefore, any information in the FBI database of national suspects or criminals is readily accessible by ICE personnel. Likewise, any information that ICE had on potential undocumented aliens is accessible by the FBI. The FBI database we are referring to here is the same one that local law enforcement officers check when booking suspects. For decades, local police officers and sheriffs have shared the fingerprints of individuals who are arrested or booked into custody with the FBI to check if they have a previous criminal record or are wanted somewhere else in the country.

Remember also that ICE's mission is to "identify, arrest and remove aliens who present a danger to national security or are a risk to public safety, as well as those who enter the United States illegally or otherwise undermine the integrity of the immigration laws and . . . border control efforts."[9] But ICE cannot remove (deport) every undocumented immigrant present in the country. ICE receives annual appropriations from Congress sufficient to remove a limited number of the more than 12 million individuals estimated to be in the U.S. who lack lawful status or are removable because of a criminal conviction.[10] Given this reality, ICE must set sensible priorities, such as removing those individuals with the most egregious criminal offenses amounting to an aggravated felony and providing discretion to others who have an extensive family history in the U.S. although they may have arrived unlawfully.

*[handwritten margin note: shared databases]*

### Process in Practice

When state and local law enforcement arrest or take someone into custody for a violation of a criminal offense, they generally fingerprint the person. After fingerprints are taken, the state and local authorities electronically submit the fingerprints to the FBI. This data is then stored in the FBI's criminal databases. After running the fingerprints against those databases, the FBI sends the state and local authorities a record of the person's criminal history.

Pursuant to 8 U.S.C. §1722, once the FBI checks the fingerprints, the FBI automatically sends them to U.S. Immigration and Customs Enforcement (ICE). Under its statutory authority, ICE then determines if that person is also subject to removal (deportation). This change, whereby the fingerprints are sent to DHS in addition to the FBI, fulfills the 2002 Congressional mandate for the FBI to share information with ICE, and is consistent with a 2008 federal law that instructs ICE to identify criminal aliens for removal. DHS refers to this process and program as "Secure Communities." It technically bestows no additional authorities upon local law enforcement and only identifies those who have their fingerprints submitted for criminal justice purposes.[11]

If the undocumented alien has been previously encountered and fingerprinted by an immigration official and there is a digitized record, then the immigration database will register a "match." ICE then reviews other databases to determine whether the person is here illegally or is otherwise removable. In cases where the person appears from these checks to be removable, ICE generally issues a detainer on the person. The detainer requests the state or local jail facility to hold the individual up to an extra 48 hours (excluding weekends) to allow for an interview of the person. Following the interview, ICE decides whether to seek the person's removal.[12]

In making these decisions, ICE considers a number of factors, including the person's criminal history, immigration history (such as whether the person was previously deported or has an outstanding removal order from an immigration judge), family ties, duration of stay in the U.S., significant medical issues, and other circumstances. In many instances involving lower-level criminals or people who are not convicts, re-entrants, or fugitives, ICE offers the person the option of voluntary return. A voluntary return allows the person to enter the U.S. lawfully in the future.

When someone is subject to immigration proceedings, the court process is independent of the state criminal justice system. As a result, undocumented immigrants can be removed before their state/local criminal case is concluded. There are a variety of reasons that the local arrest may not result in a criminal conviction. However, all of those removed are guilty of an immigration violation, and removed pursuant to the Immigration and Nationality Act.

### Expansion of Secure Communities

DHS has expanded Secure Communities from 14 jurisdictions in 2008 to more than 3,000 as of 2012, including all jurisdictions along the southwest border. DHS was on track to expand Secure Communities to all law enforcement jurisdictions nationwide during fiscal year 2013.[13]

Through August 31, 2012, more than 166,000 immigrants convicted of crimes were removed from the United States after identification through Secure Communities. Of the more than 166,000, more than 61,000 immigrants were convicted of aggravated felony (level 1) offenses, including murder, rape, and the sexual abuse of children. Some states and local jurisdictions have tried to "opt out" of Secure Communities, believing that participation was not mandatory. This belief exists, in part, because in the past DHS officials have contradicted each other about whether Secure Communities is mandatory or voluntary.

### Replacement With "Priority Enforcement Program"

Secure Communities has met with criticism and has become a point of contention with governors, mayors, and other state and local law enforcement who have refused to cooperate with the program. In some cases, state and local officials have issued executive orders or laws prohibiting local law enforcement cooperation with federal authority on immigration matters.[14] In response, DHS has recently created the Priority Enforcement Program (PEP) to replace Secure Communities. The goal of this new program is to effectively identify and remove criminals in state and local jails in a way that sustains community trust. DHS will continue to rely on biometric data (fingerprints) submitted during bookings by state and local law enforcement agencies to verify individuals who are enforcement priorities. In addition, DHS will work with the Department of Justice's Bureau of Prisons (BOP) to find and remove federal criminals serving time as soon as possible.[15]

Unlike Secure Communities, PEP only authorizes ICE to ask for a transfer of custody from state or local law enforcement rather than the continued detention of an undocumented immigrant by state or local law enforcement until ICE can obtain jurisdiction over a case. Therefore, under PEP, ICE can only seek to transfer an undocumented immigrant in the custody of state or local law enforcement when they have been *convicted* of Priority 1 and Priority 2 offenses. Priority 1 and Priority 2 offenses are those offenses involving threats to national security, border security, and public safety, misdemeanants, and new immigration violators.[16] More detail:

Priority 1 offenses:

1.  Aliens engaged in or suspected of terrorism, espionage, or who pose a danger to national security;
2.  Aliens convicted of an offense related to active gang participation;
3.  Aliens convicted of an offense classified as a felony in the convicting jurisdiction; or
4.  Aliens convicted of an aggravated felony.

Priority 2 offenses:

1.  Aliens convicted of three or more misdemeanor offenses other than minor traffic offenses or state or local offenses; or
2.  Aliens convicted of a significant misdemeanor (domestic violence, sexual abuse/exploitation, burglary, unlawful possession or use of firearm, drug distribution/trafficking, or DUI).

ICE can also request local law enforcement to transfer undocumented immigrants into ICE custody if an ICE Field Officer Director feels that an undocumented immigrant poses a danger to national security. Unless the undocumented immigrant presents a demonstrable risk to national security, under PEP, action will only be taken against those who are convicted of specific crimes.[17]

Additionally, PEP addresses the issue of detainer-based detention. Detainers were requests by ICE to local law enforcement to keep an individual temporarily in detention in order to give the immigration authorities sufficient time to assume custody. A number of federal courts held detainers to be a violation of the Fourth Amendment.[18] To rectify the issue ICE now must issue notification requests inquiring when the individual will be released instead of requesting continued detention. However, in special circumstances ICE can still request for the continued detention of an undocumented immigrant in state or local custody, but ICE must specify that the person is either 1) subject to a final order of removal or 2) have sufficient probable cause to find that person "removable." Nothing prevents ICE from seeking the transfer of an undocumented immigrant deemed a priority, and nothing can prevent a transfer if the state or locality agrees to cooperate with ICE.

To ensure that transfer requests are properly submitted, DHS created accountability and safeguard measures to address biased policing and abuse. This includes exceptions to enforcement priorities as well as personnel to protect an individual from deportation.[19] Additionally, DHS plans to also monitor activities at the state and local levels by collecting and analyzing data to better detect inappropriate use of transfer requests and biased policing. DHS also plans to establish effective remedial measures in response to any abuse found.

*[handwritten margin note: search & seizures]*

## CRITICAL THINKING QUESTION

Read the Sidebar on the Secure Communities Program. Even though state and local law enforcement have no additional authorities to remove undocumented aliens under Secure Communities, can you think of ways that this policy can influence their law enforcement duties? What incidental effects can such a policy have on those who wish to report crime or those who were witnesses to crimes?

## IMMIGRATION AND CUSTOMS ENFORCEMENT (ICE)

Prior to 9/11 immigration duties were handled by the Immigration and Naturalization Service (INS). As discussed in Chapter 2, INS was broken up after 9/11 into three separate component agencies: CBP, USCIS, and ICE—all three of which then came under the jurisdiction and authority of the Secretary of Homeland Security and his or her department. Being the largest of these agencies, ICE became the principal immigration-related investigative arm of DHS.[20]

Today ICE handles a variety of duties, all related to immigration and customs issues. ICE is divided into two components.[21] The first, Enforcement and Removal Operations (ERO), is responsible for enforcing the nation's

**FIG. 3.2** ICE keeps detailed statistics of the number of undocumented individuals apprehended and removed each year. This document displays the statistics from fiscal year 2017.

*Source*: ICE By the Numbers FY 2017, U.S. Customs and Immigration Enforcement.

immigration laws and also responsible for removing or deporting undocumented aliens back to their country of origin.[22] Uniformed Immigration Enforcement Agents (IEA) carry out the task of investigating, apprehending, and then assisting in the removal of undocumented aliens. This process is informally known as **deportation** and formally referred to as "removal."

ERO has several other component offices, such as those that provide legal or ethics advice to ERO and other offices that ensure coordination between ERO and other state, local and federal government agencies (see Figure 3.3).

Homeland Security Investigations (HSI) comprises the other primary component of ICE. In many ways HSI special agents operate similarly to FBI special agents, but with a narrower subject matter mandate. HSI agents and other associated personnel investigate issues that threaten the national security of the United States—especially those issues related to human rights violations,

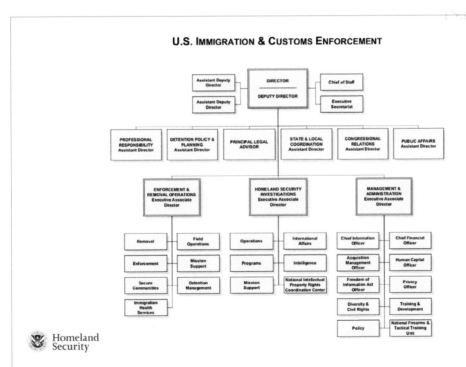

**FIG. 3.3**
An org chart that describes the priority and placement of various offices with DHS' ICE subcomponent.

*Source*: Department of Homeland Security, U.S. Immigration and Customs Enforcement Organizational Chart, www.dhs.gov/xlibrary/assets/org-chart-ice.pdf.

human trafficking and arms trafficking, the theft of precious cargo or art, drug smuggling, and cybercrimes such as the possession and dissemination of child pornography.[23] With over 6,000 special agents, HSI is the second largest law enforcement body in the United States (behind only the FBI).[24]

### ERO and the Deportation Process

*Initial Contact*    The deportation process, formally referred to as "removal proceedings," is a complicated process and begins when an undocumented immigrant comes to the notice of immigration officers, usually Border Patrol or ICE IEA's or HSI special agents.[25] Border Patrol agents usually encounter undocumented immigrants as they attempt to cross the northern land border with Canada or the southern land border with Mexico.[26] Sometimes, undocumented migrants attempt to enter the United States via a port of entry, such as an airport, usually with false or misleading identification. Other times, ICE and CBP agents receive leads or tips from citizens or as a result of ongoing investigations that inform them of the presence of an undocumented immigrant.[27] More recently, certain government initiatives, such as the Secure Communities/Priority Enforcement Program (see the Sidebar on Secure Communities elsewhere in this chapter) has allowed local law enforcement to forward

*Handwritten margin note: Initial Contact: • Becomes aware of illegal alien*

**FIG. 3.4**
A table that describes the number of apprehensions of undocumented immigrants by various DHS Components, including ICE and CBP.

| | 2006 | 2007 | 2008 | 2009 | 2010 |
|---|---|---|---|---|---|
| CBP | 1,089,136 | 876,787 | 723,840 | 556,032 | 463,382 |
| ICE/HSI | 101,854 | 53,562 | 33,573 | 21,877 | 17,836 |
| ICE/ERO | 15,467 | 30,407 | 34,155 | 35,094 | 35,774 |
| Total | 1,206,457 | 960,756 | 791,568 | 613,003 | 516,992 |

**Source: DHS**

*Source*: Apprehensions by DHS 2006–2019, www.cis.org/sites/cis.org/files/articles/2011/reasoner-removals-t1.jpg.

arrest information to ICE, which when compared to ICE databases sometimes results in a match between an arrested individual and their undocumented status.[28]

### Serving Complaint, Processing

Upon custody, the ICE or CBP officer processes the suspected undocumented individual, obtaining identifying information such as fingerprints, photo-. *undocument-* graphs, and contact information.[29] This procedure is similar to what occurs *ed person* when local police arrest a suspect. However, unlike a local arrest, ICE also *gets* checks the individual's information against numerous federal databases, *processed* including its own Automated Biometric Identification System (IDENT), as *. put in* well as the FBI's Integrated Automated Fingerprint Identification System (the *database* largest criminal database in the world).[30] The results from this database are compared to the information agents obtain during the processing of the indi-. *determin-* vidual to determine whether the arrestee has been concealing their identity *ation* while living illegally in the United States or if they previously came to the United States under false pretense.[31]

*. Decicision*

After processing and database comparisons are complete, ICE agents must make two decisions:

1. Will the individual be released or detained? And if they are to be detained, ①
   under what conditions will that detention take place?
2. What kinds of charges will be levied against the individual to be removed?[32] ②

Let's discuss the first decision ICE agents must consider, whether the individual should be detained or released. Though a number of factors must be considered in coming to this decision, the two primary criteria are whether:

1. The alien constitutes a flight risk; and/or
2. Whether the alien constitutes a public safety risk.[33]

The number of undocumented aliens entering the country far exceed ICE and CBP's ability to interdict, process, and remove them. For instance, in 2017 about 143,000 undocumented aliens were arrested in the United States and during the same time the Department of Homeland Security removed approximately 81,000.[34] Likewise, the number of spaces available to house captured undocumented aliens are much lower than the number of undocumented aliens arrested. ICE agents must also be careful when housing undocumented aliens awaiting adjudication of their status because unlike a traditional criminal population, undocumented aliens in detention often include families, women, the elderly, and the young.[35]

The first criteria, whether the alien is a flight risk, is largely irrelevant. This is primarily because the alien is present in the U.S. because of economic opportunity and fleeing back to their home country is not an appealing option. Sometimes, undocumented aliens are present in the United States because they fled violence or felt that their life was threatened in their home country. In these cases, returning to their home country is also an unlikely option. Thus, the majority of the time, ICE agents are left to consider the second criteria: Whether the undocumented alien who is in custody constitutes a public safety risk.

ICE agents have several options when considering what to do with an undocumented alien in custody:

- *Notice to Appear*: This is similar to a ticket a police officer may give you when you are caught speeding. It essentially informs the undocumented alien that they must appear before an immigration judge to contest their current, undocumented (or illegal) status in the United States. The Notice often provides a date and time for appearance before a federal immigration judge.[36]
- *Warrant of Arrest*: Sometimes issued alongside a Notice to Appear, and sometimes issued in advance of an arrest (when an ICE officer knows that an arrest is likely). This document informs the undocumented alien that they will be subject to confinement, likely in some form of detention facility (there are many different kinds throughout the United States, most of them run as private institutions).[37]

At this point, ICE agents often apply the second criteria mentioned earlier: Whether the undocumented alien in custody poses a risk to public safety. If the alien poses a safety or flight risk then they are detained in one of several detention facilities throughout the country while their case winds its way through the administrative judicial process.[38] At any given time, there is space to house approximately 30,000 detainees in facilities that are either owned by

*[Handwritten margin notes: "More undocumented aliens then places to house them" and "Flight Risk → irrelevant & unlikely"]*

the U.S. government or owned in part or in whole by various private government contractors.[39]

If the undocumented alien does not pose enough of a safety risk to be placed in detention, then a number of the following alternative actions can be taken:

- An undocumented alien may be released on their **own recognizance** (OA). This means that the ICE agent or official trusts that the undocumented alien will attend their removal hearing without requiring detention or the posting of a **bond** (a deposit of funds to ensure or guarantee that the undocumented alien will attend the hearing).[40]
- The undocumented alien can also be released, but nonetheless monitored as an alternative to detention while they await their hearing. For instance, the undocumented alien may be required to wear an electronic ankle bracelet that monitors and reports their location on a 24-hour basis. Additionally, the undocumented alien may be required to remain within a limited geographic area.[41]

### CRITICAL THINKING QUESTION

Do you think the detention and alternative detention methods outlined above are effective ways to police and remove undocumented aliens? Does your answer change when you consider the cost of detaining undocumented aliens?

### SIDEBAR 3.3 Is Illegal Immigration Actually "Illegal"?

Crossing the U.S. land, sea, or air border without proper permission (i.e. documents such as a passport, green card, visa etc.) is a crime under 8 U.S. Code Section 1325 (a) (Improper Entry by Alien). Yet unlawful presence in the U.S. isn't a crime. For instance, if an individual enters the country legally (say on a tourist visa) and then decides to remain beyond the expiration of their visa (visa overstay), they are not subject to criminal penalties. Individuals who overstay their visas are also undocumented immigrants like those who cross the border. However, visa overstays tend to be more affluent (they can afford expensive international plane tickets and have the resources to apply for and obtain a visa) than those migrants who cross the southern land border (who tend to be very poor individuals largely from Central America).

Visa overstays are more difficult to apprehend because they are not visibly present at a physical location such as the land border where easy interdiction is possible. Once legally present in the U.S. they can remain, sometimes indefinitely. Their relatively higher access to resources, generally higher education and English-language proficiency, also allows them to blend in with American society and obtain meaningful employment. For instance, in 2017, DHS reported that the number one nationality for overstays for visa overstays was Canada, followed by the UK and China—all affluent nations.[42] Overstays are also growing. As of 2007, the number of yearly overstays have exceeded border crossings. Lastly, these kinds of visa overstay violators also face milder civil (instead of criminal) penalties.

This has interesting policy implications as the bulk of apprehension resources tend to be directed towards those individuals who are visible, easily apprehended, and lack the resources to blend, i.e. those crossing the U.S. southern land border, and not towards visa overstays. Experts have cautioned that a policy that focuses apprehension resources on one specific subset of undocumented immigrants may not only be discriminatory in scope, but also present grave security risks. For instance, the 9/11 hijackers were individuals who came into the country legally on tourist visas. If visa overstays are not being tracked and apprehended, they can "fall through the cracks" like the 9/11 hijackers did. Moreover, these same experts make a legal argument that though crossing the border is an "illegal act" it is notorious (out in the open) and remediating the crime is relatively easy, i.e. you remove the individual back to their home country. On the other hand, visa overstay is an act of fraud with the intention to deceive the federal government, an arguably more serious crime than an open and notorious border crossing.

### Immigration Hearings

Undocumented aliens in detention, or those released on their own recognizance and those being monitored by electronic means—are all awaiting a hearing in front of an immigration judge. These judges, and those attorneys who represent the U.S. government against undocumented aliens, act under the Immigration and Nationality Act (INA).[43] Undocumented aliens can choose to be represented by private counsel or attorneys who work for non-governmental organizations and non-profits.[44]

The purpose of most immigration hearings is to:

1. Determine the legal status of the undocumented alien by considering whether their initial entry into the United States was legal. The hearing tries to answer the question: Does the undocumented alien have the legal right to be in the country?
2. Determine whether the undocumented alien is guilty of any additional crimes committed while in the United States. This may include adjudicating the crime that led to the arrest of the undocumented alien in the first place.[45]

During the course of the hearing the immigration judge may:

- Allow the undocumented alien to leave voluntarily (referred to as "Voluntary Departure")—again, as long as the undocumented alien is not a flight risk or threat to the safety or national security of the United States. Though the departure is "voluntary"—often the undocumented aliens given this option are nonetheless detained pending their departure. Moreover, their transportation back to their country of origin is under guard, with armed escorts of ICE or CBP agents.[46]
- Proceed with formal removal proceedings. These proceedings are similar to those in a normal court of the law. The parties, in this case the U.S. government and the undocumented alien, are both represented by legal counsel. Both parties present evidence through their counsel to the administrative law judge, who then considers and weighs the evidence in light of the undocumented alien's particular circumstances and the law—and then makes a decision regarding the undocumented alien's status in the

United States. It is important to note that throughout this process, the undocumented alien is contesting their status—in other words, they are arguing that they have the right to be in the United States legally.[47] In some cases, undocumented aliens will be given the option to stipulate (or agree) to the removal charges against him. In essence, these stipulated orders of removal act as guilty pleas. Once an undocumented alien signs the stipulation, they are held in detention until they can formally be removed—often by the same means as those undocumented aliens who opted for voluntary departure.[48]

*"plead guilty"* (handwritten annotation with arrow)

- Those undocumented aliens who are encountered at ports of entry or within a 100 miles of U.S. land borders are often subject to expedited removal proceedings. These proceedings, as their name suggests, are undertaken quickly and often at the physical location where the undocumented alien is first encountered. The undocumented alien subject to expedited removal must meet certain criteria stipulated by the Illegal Immigration Reform and Immigrant Responsibility Act (IIRIRA). The interdicting officer will often apply this criterion to the circumstances of the undocumented alien, often at the physical location where the undocumented alien was arrested, and then make a decision regarding the legal status of the undocumented alien. The officer's decision is often reviewed by a supervisory officer or sometimes a judicial officer.[49]

If an undocumented alien is removed using any of these methods, but then thereafter re-enters the country and is apprehended—then the previous order from their previous immigration hearing is reapplied, and the undocumented alien is often removed under the same previous decision.[50]

---

**CRITICAL THINKING QUESTION**

Why would the U.S. government grant voluntary departure to undocumented aliens instead of pursuing formal removal proceedings against them?

## HSI AND INVESTIGATIVE PROGRAMS

In addition to apprehending and removing undocumented aliens from the United States, ICE agents, primarily those personnel who serve as HSI agents, also source and investigate a number of federal crimes (Figure 3.5).

### Cyber Crime[51]

The **Cyber Crimes Center** (C3) at HSI combats criminal activity conducted on or facilitated by the Internet. C3 additionally supports the wider U.S. government's efforts in investigating international and domestic cross-border crime. Additionally, C3 also offers training to federal, state, local, and

**FIG. 3.5** DHS HSI personnel often work closely with local law enforcement to provide safety and security at national events. Here, HSI Gang Unit personnel work with local law enforcement to provide security at the 2017 Presidential Inauguration.

*Source*: Barry Bahler for the Department of Homeland Security, DHS Homeland Security Investigations Personnel Provide Safety at 2017 Presidential Inauguration, https://upload.wikimedia.org/wikipedia/commons/d/d7/DHS_Law_Enforcement_Personnel_Ensures_Safety_at_2017_Presidential_Inauguration_(31598659454).jpg.

international law enforcement agencies while also allowing them access to a renowned computer forensics laboratory that specializes in digital evidence recovery.[52] C3 is comprised of the Cyber Crimes Unit, the Child Exploitation Investigations Unit, and the Computer Forensics Unit.

**The Cyber Crimes Unit** manages HSI's cyber-related investigations by focusing on transnational criminal organizations (those organizations with criminal activities that cross international borders) that use cyber-capability to further their criminal enterprise. In addition to investigating national and international cyber criminals, the Cyber Crimes Unit also provides expertise in the form of training or advice to HSI agents in the following areas:

- Identity and benefit document fraud
- Money laundering
- Financial fraud (including e-payment and Internet gambling)
- Commercial fraud
- Counter-proliferation investigations
- Narcotics trafficking
- Illegal exports

**Child Exploitation Investigations Unit** targets those who violate U.S. laws forbidding child exploitation, child pornography, and child sex tourism online or via other electronic means.[53] Major initiatives of the Child Exploitation Investigations Unit include:

- Operation Predator: An international initiative to identify, investigate and arrest child predators who possess or trade children for the purposes of child pornography or sex trafficking.
- The Virtual Global Taskforce: An international alliance of law enforcement agencies and private sector partners that work together to fight online child sexual exploitation and abuse.
- The National Child Victim Identification System: A database to assist law enforcement agencies in identifying victims of child sexual exploitation.
- The Victim Identification Program: A program that focuses on identifying and rescuing children who have been depicted in child abuse material.[54]

**The Computer Forensics Unit** is staffed by HSI investigators and analysts who perform forensic examinations of seized digital storage devices, such as

**FIG. 3.6**
An ICE Cyber Crimes specialist removes a chip of a confiscated hard drive. Once the hard drive is fixed he will put it back together so they can get the evidence they need off of it.

*Source*: Josh Denmark, ICE Cyber Crimes Center at Work, www.flickr.com/photos/134940118@N08/28111717109.

computer hard drives, flash drives, and mobile phones. They use specialized techniques to overcome computer encryption and data loss in order to preserve information that may be used as evidence in later case.

### National Security

ICE is involved in almost every foreign terrorism investigation related to crime that crosses the U.S. border.[55] For instance, when terrorists from abroad move money, weapons, people, or any other contraband across U.S. borders, ICE employs a set of law enforcement tools to intercept and investigate this activity through the ICE National Security Unit (NSU).[56]

Importantly, the NSU also oversees ICE's participation on the Joint Terrorism Task Force (JTTF). As discussed in Chapter 1, the JTTF is a collection state, local, and federal law enforcement and security entities that investigates, detects, interdicts, and then prosecutes terrorists and dismantles terrorist organizations.[57] In fiscal years 2009 and 2010, ICE special agents initiated 1,133 criminal investigations related to terrorism through their participation in the JTTF.[58] During that same period, ICE agents made 534 arrests and conducted thousands of seizures of money, arms, contraband, and other assets related to illegal schemes.[59]

## UNITED STATES CITIZENSHIP & IMMIGRATION SERVICES

A component of the Department of Homeland Security, USCIS is charged with processing immigrant visa petitions, naturalization petitions, asylum applications, and refugee applications (both of these latter categories have been discussed in depth in other parts of this chapter). USCIS focuses on two points on an immigrant's journey towards civic integration into the culture

**FIG. 3.7**
Former Deputy Secretary of Homeland Security Alejandro Mayorkas delivers remarks and gives the Oath of Allegiance at a Naturalization Ceremony in Washington, D.C., October 6, 2015.

*Source*: Barry Bahler, Naturalization Ceremony.

of the United States: When they first become permanent residents (i.e. a green card holder) and when they are ready to begin the naturalization process to become a U.S. citizen. A lawful permanent resident can apply for citizenship after they have resided in the U.S. with this status for at least five years with no trips outside the United States lasting 180 days or more.


## Refugees and Asylum

Refugee status or asylum may be granted by the United States to people who have been persecuted or fear they will be persecuted on account of race, religion, nationality, and/or membership in a particular social group or political opinion.

**Refugees** are displaced persons who have been forced to cross national boundaries and who cannot return home safely. Since 1975, the United States has admitted and resettled over 3 million refugees from around the world. In 2016, the U.S. government admitted 84,995 refugees in various U.S. cities.

**Asylum seekers** are those people who flee their home country and randomly enter another country seeking asylum, or the right to international protection in the country other than their home. Individuals can seek asylum for a number of reasons, including political animus or a government policy to injure, threaten, or kill religious and ethnic minorities should they return to their home country. Since 9/11 policing the entry of foreigners, and particularly refugees, has become an important national security priority.[60]

The first refugee legislation in the United States was the Displaced Persons Act of 1948, which brought 400,000 Eastern Europeans to the United States. Other refugee-related legislation included the Refugee Relief Act of 1953 and the Fair Share Refugee Act of 1960. The United States also used the Attorney General's parole authority to bring large groups of persons into the country for humanitarian reasons, beginning in 1956 with Hungarian nationals and culminating with hundreds of thousands of Indochinese parolees in the 1970s.[61]

The 1967 United Nations Protocol relating to the Status of Refugees (which the United States ratified in 1968) prohibits any nation from returning a refugee to a country where his or her life or freedom would be threatened. Congress enacted the Refugee Act of 1980 to comply with the requirements and principles of the Protocol, which established a geographically and politically neutral refugee definition. The Refugee Act of 1980 also made a distinction between refugee and asylum status and allowed certain refugee applicants to be processed while in their countries of nationality.

Not everyone who applies for refugee status to the United States is admitted. There is a long process involving multiple U.S. government agencies to screen, vet, and then transport those refugees finally admitted into the country (Figure 3.8). This process begins with the establishment of admission ceil-

**FIG. 3.8**
Refugees seeking admission into the U.S. must undergo a long and complicated screening and vetting process, during which they may be denied status at any time.

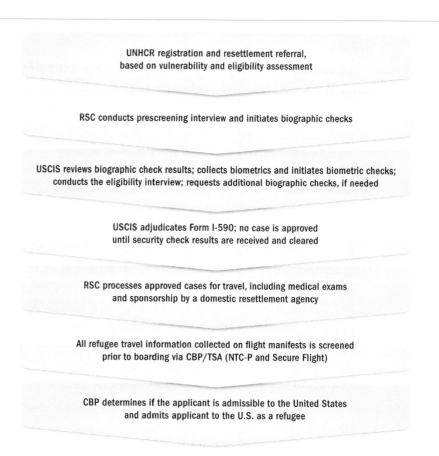

UNHCR registration and resettlement referral, based on vulnerability and eligibility assessment

RSC conducts prescreening interview and initiates biographic checks

USCIS reviews biographic check results; collects biometrics and initiates biometric checks; conducts the eligibility interview; requests additional biographic checks, if needed

USCIS adjudicates Form I-590; no case is approved until security check results are received and cleared

RSC processes approved cases for travel, including medical exams and sponsorship by a domestic resettlement agency

All refugee travel information collected on flight manifests is screened prior to boarding via CBP/TSA (NTC-P and Secure Flight)

CBP determines if the applicant is admissible to the United States and admits applicant to the U.S. as a refugee

*Source*: U.S. Citizenship and Immigration Services, General Refugee Screening & Admission Process, www.uscis.gov/sites/default/files/USCIS/Humanitarian/Refugees%20&%20Asylum/ FactSheetFlow_LtGray_En_V2.png.

ings by the President (in consultation with Congress). For instance, the total number of refugees authorized for admission in 2014 was 70,000. Forty-seven percent of this allocation was designated for those refugees from the Near East and South Asia region to account for those individuals fleeing persecution in Iraq, Bhutan, and Iran.

In order to qualify for refugee status, a principal applicant must be 1) of special humanitarian concern to the United States; 2) meet the refugee definition set forth in 101(a)(42) of the INA (explained earlier); 3) be admissible under the INA; and 4) not be firmly resettled in any foreign country. Since 9/11, security concerns have pervaded the screening process for refugees. The following explains the refugee application, screening, and admission process in detail, highlighting the steps taken to ensure the safety of the homeland while fulfilling what the government sees as a moral responsibility to resettle refugees:

1. Refugees apply for refugee status with the United Nations High Commissioner for Refugees (UNHCR). UNHCR then collects identifying documents and performs an initial assessment of the applicants. This may include collecting biodata such as place of birth, age, gender etc., Because those fleeing certain conflict zones, such as Syria, may have ties to foreign terrorist organizations, refugee applicants from these regions receive enhanced scrutiny. They may have to provide biometric information such as scans of their iris and fingerprints. UNHCR confirms the refugee's inability to return to their home country and their need to be resettled in another nation. Different nations have criteria for the kinds of refugees they will accept. The U.S. is particularly stringent and less than 1% of UNHCR applicants are considered for U.S. resettlement. UNHCR's recommendations are then passed to the U.S. Refugee Admissions Program (USRAP), which is an interagency effort involving a number of governmental and non-governmental partners both abroad and in the United States. USRAP is managed by the U.S. Department of State.

2. USRAP then begins a complicated screening process. Screening is a shared responsibility. It includes both biometric and biographic checks at multiple stages of the process, including immediately before a refugee's departure to the United States and upon his or her arrival in the United States.

The screening of refugee applicants involves numerous biographic checks that are ignited by Resettlement Support Centers (RSCs) overseas. RSCs work with the State Department to carry out administrative and processing functions, such as file preparation, data collection, and out-processing activities during the refugee admissions process. RSCs in coordination with USCIS initiate checks on the Department of State's Consular Lookout and Support System (CLASS). CLASS is owned and operated by the State Department and is a database that provides access to information critical for adjudicating immigration and refugee applications. CLASS contains records provided by numerous U.S. and other agencies and includes information on individuals who have been denied visas, immigration violations, criminal histories, and terrorism concerns, as well as intelligence information and child support enforcement data. CLASS also includes information from the: National Counterterrorism Center's (NCTC) Terrorist Screening Center, Interpol, Drug Enforcement Administration, U.S. Health and Human Services, and the FBI (extracts of the National Crime Information Center's Wanted Persons File, Immigration Violator File, Foreign Fugitive File, Violent Gang and Terrorist Organization File, and the Interstate Identification Index). Name checks are conducted using CLASS on the applicant's primary names as well as any variations used by the applicant. Responses are received before the applicant's in-person interview with a USCIS official. Possible derogatory matches are reviewed and assessed prior to the interview by USCIS in the United States. If a new name or variation is later identified at the in-person interview, USCIS may request another CLASS name check on the new name and place the case on hold until that response is received. Those selected undergo further review and questioning by U.S. officials from various government agencies such as USCIS, the NCTC, the FBI, and the U.S. Department of State. These screenings look for indicators that may show a past history of criminal activity. At this time USCIS also reviews biographic check results, conducts an eligibility interview, and collects additional biometrics.

3. Any applicant who is a member of a group or nationality that the U.S. government has designated as requiring a higher level check must also pass receive a cleared Security Advisory Opinion (SAO). The Department of State initiates SAO name checks for these refugee applicants when they are

being prescreened by an RSC. The SAO biographic check is conducted by the FBI and Intelligence Community partners. SAOs are processed, and a response must be received before finalizing the clearance decision. If there is a new name or variation of a name identified at a later in-person USCIS interview, USCIS may request another SAO for the new name and place the case on hold until that response is received.

4. Yet another step may include another check by several other U.S. government agencies. This is referred to as the Interagency Check (IAC). The IAC screens biographic data, including names, dates of birth, and other additional data of all refugee applicants within designated age ranges. This information is captured at the time the applicant is prescreened and is provided to Intelligence Community partners. This screening procedure began in 2008 and has expanded over time to include a broader range of applicants and records. These checks occur throughout the refugee screening process.

5. As the SAO, IAC, and CLASS checks continue or complete, USCIS begins preparing for the refugee interview. USCIS collects fingerprints of all applicants and begins a series of biometric checks. These checks include: An FBI fingerprint check through the Next Generation Identification (NGI) database that checks recurring biometric records pertaining to criminal history and previous immigration data; a check through the DHS Automated Biometric Identification System (IDENT/USVISIT) database, which checks the applicant's information and matches it with travel and immigration history as well as any immigration violations and law enforcement and national security concerns (enrollment in IDENT also allows U.S. Customs and Border Protection to confirm the applicant's identity at U.S. ports of entry later); and a check through the Department of Defense's Automated Biometric Identification System (ABIS), which matches applicant information against records collected in areas of conflict such as Iraq, Afghanistan, Syria, or Sudan. ABIS screening began in 2007 for Iraqi applicants and has now been expanded to all nationalities. CBP's National Targeting Center-Passenger (NTC-P) conducts biographic vetting of all ABIS biometric matches against various classified and unclassified U.S. government databases.

6. You can imagine how long this process takes, often months and sometimes more than a year. During that time refugees may pass away, opt

to remain in the country where they first sought refuge, or emigrate to another country with less stringent entrance policies. This may be especially so because they realize more screening is on the horizon in the form of the USCIS Interview. The USCIS refugee interview is an important part of the refugee screening process. Highly trained USCIS officers conduct extensive interviews with each refugee applicant to learn more about the applicant's claim for refugee status and admissibility. These officers have undergone specialized and extensive training on: Refugee law, grounds of inadmissibility, fraud detection and prevention, security protocols, interviewing techniques, credibility analysis, and country conditions research. Before deploying overseas, these officers also receive additional training on the specific population that they will be interviewing, detailed country of origin information, and updates on any fraud-related trends in immigration security issues that have been identified. As of the time of this writing, those officers conducting interviews of Syrian applicants undergo an expanded one-week training focusing on Syria-specific topics, including a classified intelligence briefing. During the interview, the officer develops lines of questioning to obtain information on whether the applicant has been involved in terrorist activity, criminal activity, or the persecution or torture of others. The officer will also conduct a credibility assessment on each applicant.

7. Either before, during, or after the USCIS Interview, if any national security concerns are raised, either based on security and background checks or personal interviews or testimony, USCIS conducts an additional review through the internal Controlled Application Review and Resolution Process (CARRP). CARRP is an internal USCIS process that a case can go through to ensure that immigration benefits or services are not granted to individuals who pose a threat to national security and/or public safety, or who seek to defraud the U.S. immigration system.

8. Those refugees fleeing the conflict in Syria receive an enhanced review. USCIS' Refugee, Asylum and International Operations Directorate along with the Fraud Detection and National Security Directorate (FDNS) work together to provide enhanced review of certain Syrian cases. This review involves FDNS providing intelligence-driven support to refugee adjudicators, including identifying threats and suggesting topics for questioning.

FDNS also monitors terrorist watch lists and disseminates intelligence information reports on any applicants who are determined to present a national security threat.

9. Finally, those applicants who pass all of these tests and are approved for resettlement in the United States receive additional vetting by Customs and Border Patrol. CBP inspects all applicants who are approved for refugee resettlement to the United States to determine their admissibility before they are physically allowed to enter the U.S. as refugees. CBP receives a manifest of all approved resettlement individuals who have been booked for travel to the United States. This manifest is received eight days before the scheduled travel. CBP then begins vetting the individuals before they arrive at a U.S. airport and then conducts an inspection and additional background checks of these individuals upon their arrival at a U.S. airport.

Prior to arrival in the United States, an approved refugee must also undergo a medical exam, a cultural orientation that familiarizes them with the United States, and obtain travel assistance or a loan for travel to the U.S. Upon arrival to the United States, admitted refugees are eligible for some government assistance from the Office of Refugee Resettlement at the U.S. Department of Health and Human Services. This housing assistance and financial aid is temporary and limited, usually carrying a refugee family through its first three months of life in the United States. Refugees admitted to the United States must apply for a green card (i.e. permanent legal status) one year after their arrival to the United States.

## Asylum Seekers

What about asylum seekers, the second category of individuals seeking entry into the United States we discussed above? The United States provides refuge to persons who have been persecuted or have a "well-founded fear of persecution" through the refugee program (discussed earlier) for those who are outside the United States, and an asylum program for those persons (and their immediate relatives) already in the U.S. (Figure 3.9). This is because individuals will often arrive legally in the U.S. through a visa program and then seek refuge because they fear returning to their home country.

**FIG. 3.9**
Since 9/11 and particularly after the election of Donald Trump, the U.S. has reduced the ability of individuals to claim asylum status at land borders. This has led to a number of protests around the country and the world.

*Source*: John Englart "Takver," Individuals Protesting U.S. Asylum Policies, https://upload. wikimedia.org/wikipedia/commons/1/10/Courage_is_Contagious,_Anonymous_-_Refugee_ Action_protest_27_July_2013_Melbourne_(9374736297).jpg.

To be eligible for **asylum status**, an applicant must meet the definition set forth in 101(a)(42) of the Immigration and Nationality Act (INA):

> a person who is unable or unwilling to return to his or her country of nationality because of persecution or a well-founded fear of persecution on account of race, religion, nationality, membership in a particular social group, or political opinion.

*To get asylum status*

This definition applies to refugees as well. Thus, an applicant meeting this definition who is outside the United States is considered to be someone seeking refugee status, while an applicant seeking asylum status is someone who does so while in the United States or at a U.S. port of entry.

Generally, any alien already present in the United States or arriving at a port of entry may seek asylum regardless of his or her immigration status (i.e. even if they are in the country without proper documentation such as a green card or visa). Asylum can be obtained in one of three ways: 1) affirmatively through a USCIS asylum officer; 2) defensively in removal proceedings before an immigration judge of the Executive Office for Immigration Review (EOIR) of the Department of Justice (this is when an undocumented immigrant in deportation proceedings can claim that returning would subject them to violence or death); or 3) an individual may derive asylum status as the spouse or child of an asylum. To obtain asylum, an alien must apply within one year from the date of last arrival or establish that an exception applies based on changed or extraordinary circumstances.

The Asylum Division within USCIS adjudicates asylum claims filed with the agency through the affirmative asylum process. During an asylum inter-

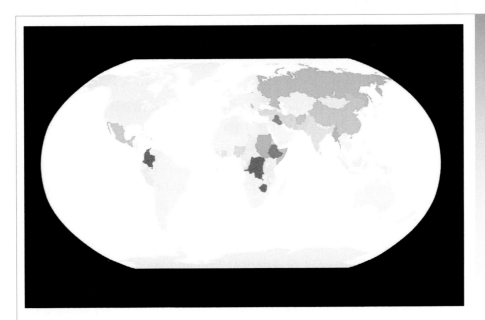

**FIG. 3.10**
Colombia is the country of origin of the greatest number of asylum seekers—43,100 to 44,200. Darker countries have the greatest number of asylum seekers. Since 2009 these numbers have changed dramatically, with Syria and Central America now producing the greatest number of asylum seekers.

*Source*: Stephen Morley, Map Showing Number of Asylum Seekers 2009, https://upload.wiki-media.org/wikipedia/commons/thumb/8/8d/Asylum-seekers-by-country-of-origin.svg/2000px-Asylum-seekers-by-country-of-origin.svg.png.

view, an asylum officer determines if the applicant meets the definition of a refugee, is credible, and is not barred from obtaining asylum. Individuals may be barred for committing certain crimes, posing a national security threat, engaging in the persecution of others, or firmly resettling in another country before coming to the United States.

An individual granted asylum is authorized to work in the United States. In addition, an asylum is eligible for certain public benefits including employment assistance, a social security card, and social services. If an applicant in a valid immigration status, such as a foreign student with a student visa, fails to establish eligibility for asylum before USCIS, the application will be denied by USCIS, and the applicant will remain in his or her valid status. On the other hand, if the applicant is not in a valid status, such as an individual who is living in the United States on an expired visa, and USCIS finds the applicant ineligible for asylum, USCIS will then place the applicant in removal proceedings before an immigration judge with EOIR, where the application will be considered anew.

Aliens who have not previously filed for asylum may be placed in removal proceedings by immigration enforcement officials because they are undocumented, are in violation of their status when apprehended, or were caught attempting entry into the United States without proper documentation. Such individuals may file for asylum directly with EOIR. During the proceedings an immigration judge may grant asylum or deny the asylum application and issue an order of removal. The applicant may appeal the denial to the Board of Immigration Appeals and seek further review by a U.S. Court of Appeals.

In 2014, the three leading countries of nationality of persons granted asylum were China (34%), Egypt (12%), and Syria (4%).[62]

---

**CRITICAL THINKING QUESTION**

Is the United States obliged to accept refugees and those seeking asylum? Legal issues and questions aside, should the United States accept those refugees? What could be the potential benefits and challenges of doing so?

### Humanitarian Functions

USCIS provides a number of humanitarian programs to assist individuals in need of shelter or aid from disasters, oppression, emergency medical issues, and other urgent circumstances. Some of these programs, such as the refugee and asylum programs and Deferred Action for Childhood Arrivals, have been discussed elsewhere in this chapter. Here, we focus on some of the smaller, yet nonetheless important remaining USCIS humanitarian policy priorities. It is important to note that the subject areas discussed below all create *exceptions* to the deportation requirement. In other words, the law generally mandates that DHS remove those individuals found to be in the country without status. However, due to certain humanitarian reasons, USCIS will delay, defer, or grant additional protections to undocumented migrants in the country if they fall under the following categories.

### Temporary Protected Status

The Secretary of Homeland Security may designate a foreign country for temporary protected status (TPS) due to conditions in the country that temporarily prevent a country's nationals from returning safely, or in certain circumstances, where the country is unable to handle the return of its nationals adequately. This grant of status most often occurs in country suffering grave natural disasters, war, or other calamity. The Secretary usually designates a country for TPS due to the following temporary conditions in the country:

- Ongoing armed conflict such as a civil war;
- An environmental disaster such as an earthquake or hurricane; or
- Other extraordinary and temporary conditions.

For instance, most recently DHS granted TPS to those in the U.S. from Syria (due to the Syrian civil war), Haiti (due to the 2010 Haiti earthquake), and Sudan (due to the Sudanese conflict of 2013).

During a designated period, individuals who are TPS beneficiaries or who are found preliminarily eligible for TPS upon initial review of their cases are eligible for the following temporary status:

- Not removable from the United States (they cannot be deported, even if they are in the country illegally);

- Can obtain employment through an official government authorization; and
- Can be granted an authorization to travel abroad and return to the United States without the possibility of adverse action due to their immigration status.

Thus, even though an individual with TPS is technically in the country illegally, because they are temporarily protected, they cannot be detained by DHS or its component agencies such as ICE, on the basis of their immigration status in the United States.

The temporary nature of TPS is important. Because TPS is a temporary benefit, it does not allow an individual to later obtain lawful permanent resident status. Because TPS is temporary the Secretary's designation is also often revoked when the war, natural disaster, or other emergency situation ends and return is possible. Thus, those migrants whose countries' TPS designations are set to expire have few options to remain in the United States, especially because they do not have the ability to apply for permanent residency in the U.S. despite their many years of continuous residence under TPS (though a TPS beneficiary can apply for a visa).

---

**CRITICAL THINKING QUESTION**

TPS beneficiaries often end up residing in the United States for many years while the conflict or disaster in their country continues. Many form families and become an important part of their communities. Removal of their TPS status forces many to return to a still-recovering country, often faced with leaving behind U.S. citizen children and other connections. Imagine yourself as a member of Congress. What legislation could you draft that would allow TPS beneficiaries to remain legally in the United States while maintaining the integrity of the nation's immigration laws discussed previously in this chapter?

---

## Victims of Human Trafficking and Other Crimes

USCIS helps protect victims of human trafficking and other crimes by providing immigration relief. **Human trafficking**, also known as trafficking in persons, is a form of modern-day slavery in which traffickers lure individuals to the United States from foreign countries with false promises of employment and a better life. Individuals and their families may also fall victim to many other types of crime in the United States. These crimes include rape, murder, manslaughter, domestic violence, sexual assault, and many others.

USCIS relief for those brought to the United States in this manner focuses on two primary types of visas: The T Nonimmigrant Status Visa and the U Nonimmigrant Status Visa. T nonimmigrant status provides immigration protection

**FIG. 3.11**
Through the Blue Campaign, DHS raises public awareness about human trafficking, leveraging formal partnerships and making awareness-raising resources available to educate the public to recognize human trafficking and report suspected instances.

*Source*: DHS Blue Campaign Public Service Advertisement, Department of Homeland Security.

*T visa*

*Victims of trafficking*

*U visa*

*Crime victims suffered substantial mental or physical abuse*

to victims of trafficking. The T visa allows victims to remain in the United States and assist law enforcement authorities in the investigation or prosecution of human trafficking cases. U nonimmigrant status provides immigration protection to crime victims who have suffered substantial mental or physical abuse as a result of the crime. The U visa allows victims to remain in the United States and assist law enforcement authorities in the investigation or prosecution of the criminal activity. Congress created the U nonimmigrant visa with the passage of the Victims of Trafficking and Violence Protection Act (including the Battered Immigrant Women's Protection Act) in October 2000. The same legislation also created the T nonimmigrant status.

## SIDEBAR 3.4 DHS Blue Campaign

The Blue Campaign (Figure 3.12) is DHS' effort to combat human trafficking. Working in collaboration with law enforcement, government, non-governmental organizations, and private groups, the Blue Campaign strives to protect the basic right to freedom and bring those who exploit human lives to justice. The Blue Campaign is primarily a public awareness program. Campaign staff offer training to local law enforcement and others to increase detection and investigation of human trafficking, and to protect victims and bring suspected traffickers to justice.

The Blue Campaign aligns with DHS' overarching responsibility for investigating human trafficking, arresting traffickers, and protecting victims. DHS also provides immigration relief to non-U.S. citizen victims of human trafficking (outlined elsewhere in this chapter). The Blue Campaign is built on a "victim-centered" approach to combating human trafficking that places equal value on identifying and stabilizing victims and on investigating and prosecuting traffickers.

Because the Blue Campaign is a DHS-wide program, it involves participation from a number of DHS Components, including ICE, USCIS, CBP, and FLETC. For instance, ICE HSI victim assistance specialists assess the needs of those victims of human trafficking that are found through investigations. They then work with local law enforcement and HSI special agents to integrate victim assistance considerations through a criminal investigation. During case investigations, victim assistance specialists assess a victim's needs and work with law enforcement agents to integrate victim assistance considerations throughout a criminal investigation. ICE HSI can also assist a victim in getting short-term immigration relief, referred to as "Continued Presence"—available only upon request by law enforcement. In the absence of other resources, DHS also has an emergency assistance fund that is available for emergency victim assistance needs.

**FIG. 3.12**
DHS describes the Blue Campaign Logo as one that "conveys unity, strength, and innovation. The logo is representative of the unprecedented collaboration among our dedicated government and non-government partners in the fight against human trafficking. The color blue is internationally symbolic of human trafficking awareness, and the Blue Campaign's name references the global anti-human trafficking symbols the Blue Heart and the Blue Blindfold, as well as the "thin blue line" of law enforcement.

*Source*: DHS Blue Campaign Logo, https://pbs.twimg.com/media/DXy_NNfW4AAdItY.jpg.

### Female Genital Mutilation or Cutting (FGM/C)

Female genital mutilation or cutting (FGM/C) refers to cutting and other procedures that injure the female genital organs for non-medical reasons (also referred to as "female circumcision" in some parts of the world). The practice has no discernible health benefit and can lead to a range of serious physical and mental health problems. DHS and the U.S. government have expressed staunch opposition to FGM/C, irrespective of the type, degree, or severity and motivation for performing the practice. In the United States, and in many other parts of the world, FGM/C is considered a human rights abuse and/or gender-based violence and punishable as a crime. Empowering or enabling FGM/C at larger scales may also be considered a national security issue. In the United States, anyone who performs FMG/C on a woman 18 years of age or older without her consent may be charged with a crime under a range of laws.

### Battered Spouse, Children, and Parents

Those spouses, children, or parents experiencing mental or physical violence at the hands of another family member or relative may be able to file an immigrant visa petition under the Immigration and Nationality Act (INA) as amended by the Violence Against Women Act (VAWA). The VAWA provisions in the INA allow certain spouses, children, and parents of U.S. citizens as well as certain spouses and children of permanent residents (i.e. those with a green card) to file a petition for themselves, without the abuser's knowledge. This allows victims to seek both safety and independence from their abuser, who is not notified about the filing. Notably, the VAWA provisions apply equally to women and men and, moreover, unlike many other immigration-related statutory provisions, are permanent laws that do not require congressional reauthorization.

### Humanitarian Parole

Individuals who are outside the United States may be able to request parole into the United States based on humanitarian or significant public health reasons. This "catch-all" entry method sits apart from the previously discussed

**FIG. 3.13**
A pie chart that represents federal government anti-human trafficking strategy based on the Federal Strategic Action Plan on Services for Victims of Human Trafficking in the United States 2013–17.

**Prevention**
Prevent human trafficking through public awareness, outreach, education, and advocacy campaigns

**Protection**
Protect and assist victims by funding nongovernmental organizations that provide victim services, such as shelter, as well as health, psychological, legal, and vocational services

3P paradigm

**Prosecution**
Investigate and prosecute human trafficking crimes and provide training and technical assistance for law enforcement officials, such as police, prosecutors, and judges

*Source*: 3P Paradigm of Combating Human Trafficking, www.flickr.com/photos/usgao/16823993999/in/photolist-qqbRop-qqz9Us-vKqu2p-rCFnh4-rV8Ke8-rV1uaS-rUD9ra-Vyqozr-VyqoxT-qcrknR-q8P6Bo-ptB4bg-Bt63pR-ErhXdo-FfBbaK-qYksvc-sdPFrU-PA4jEV-N1N9xz.

humanitarian or public health rationales that may allow other non-U.S. persons to legally enter the United States. USCIS uses its discretion to authorize parole. Parole allows an individual, who may be inadmissible or otherwise ineligible for admission into the United States, to be paroled into the United States for a temporary period. The INA allows the Secretary of Homeland Security to use their discretion to parole any foreign national applying for admission into the United States temporarily for urgent humanitarian reasons or a significant public health benefit.[63]

An individual who is paroled into the U.S. has not been formally admitted into the United States for purposes of immigration law and is considered a temporary visitor. Parole is not intended to be used solely to avoid normal visa processing procedures and timelines, to bypass inadmissibility waiver processing, or to replace established refugee processing channels. The most common form of parole that the public often hears about is when young children are brought to the United States to undergo an innovative emergency medical procedure to save their life. The duration of parole is often identified in all cases by USCIS and usually not granted for more than a year. Parole ends on the date the parole period expires or when the beneficiary departs the United States, or acquires an immigration status, whichever occurs first. In some cases, USCIS may place conditions on parole, such as reporting requirements (e.g. requiring a parolee to share their location with USCIS on a regular basis). Unlike many other forms of permanent or temporary immigration benefits, parole often requires that the parolee be sponsored by someone who can financially support the parolee if they are unable to do so themselves.

The two reasons parole is granted is because of 1) urgent humanitarian reasons or granting parole is of 2) significant public benefit. Neither of these phrases have statutory or regulatory definitions. USCIS will look at all of the circumstances, taking into account factors such as whether or not the parolee circumstances are pressing, the effect of the circumstances on the individual's well-being, and the degree of suffering that may result if parole is not authorized. Regarding the second "public benefit" category, while a parole applicant may personally benefit from the authorization of parole, the statutory standard focuses on the public benefit in extending parole. For example, a beneficiary's participation in legal proceedings may constitute a significant public benefit, because the opportunity for all relevant parties to participate in legal proceedings may be required for justice to be served. There may also be circumstances where a request is based on both urgent humanitarian reasons *and* significant public benefit reasons. For example, a person may be paroled if they have a request for medical care that involves experimental treatment or medical trials from which a larger community in the United States may benefit.[64]

# OTHER AGENCIES WITH IMMIGRATION RESPONSIBILITIES

### Department of Health and Human Services

The Department of Health and Human Services' Office of Refugee Resettlement (ORR) provides funding and overusing to state-licensed shelters throughout the United States for children referred to ORR by DHS. These include children who enter the country without their parent or legal guardian and children who, for other reasons, have been separated from their parent or legal guardian.[65]

Under the Homeland Security Act of 2002, Congress transferred the care and custody of unaccompanied minors to ORR from the former INS in order to ensure that children were not detained in the same manner as adults. In the Trafficking Victims Protection Reauthorization Act of 2008, which expanded and redefined HHS' statutory responsibilities, Congress directed that each

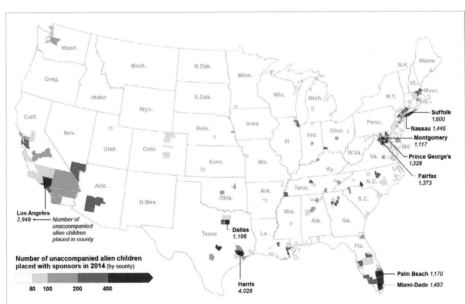

**FIG. 3.14**
A map of the counties where HHS' Office for Refugee Resettlement released unaccompanied minor children after detention.

*Source*: Counties to Which ORR Resettlement Release Unaccompanied Children, Dep't of Health and Human Services (2014) www.flickr.com/photos/usgao/25227777114/in/photolist-Bt63pR-ErhXdo-FfBbaK-Vyqozr-VyqoxT-QZRzo9-RvHSvC-PA4jEV-q82hzZ-RovbGR.

child must be "promptly placed in the least restrictive setting that is in the best interest of the child."[66]

HHS has interpreted this guidance to operate a network of state-licensed ORR-funded care providers, most of which are located close to areas where immigration officials apprehend large numbers of undocumented individuals. These care facilities must meet ORR standards and provide a continuum of care for children including foster care, group homes, shelter, staff secure, secure, and residential treatment centers. As of 2014 HHS operates a network of just over 100 shelters in 17 states that house and provide care for unaccompanied undocumented minors.[67]

## SIDEBAR 3.5 Unaccompanied Undocumented Minors

Most of this chapter refers to adult undocumented immigrants. However, how does and how should the government respond when the undocumented immigrant is a minor? Moreover, what should the response be when the child is not accompanied by a parent or guardian at the time they are apprehended by ICE or Border Patrol agents? These policy questions have become increasingly important ones as the number of apprehended unaccompanied undocumented children (UUC) have increased dramatically over the past decade, reaching a peak in 2014. Prior to 2014, UUC apprehensions were steadily increasing (Figure 3.15). For example, in 2011, the Border Patrol apprehended 16,067 unaccompanied children at the southwest U.S. land border, whereas in 2014 this number was 68,500.[68]

U.S. law defines UUCs as those children who lack lawful immigration status in the U.S. who are under the age of 18, and who are either without a parent or legal guardian in the U.S. or without a parent or legal guardian in the U.S. who is available to provide care and physical custody. Two statutes and a legal settlement directly affect U.S. policy for the treatment and administrative processing of a UUC:

- The Trafficking Victims Protection Reauthorization Act of 2008;
- The Homeland Security Act of 2002; and
- The *Flores Settlement Agreement* of 1997.

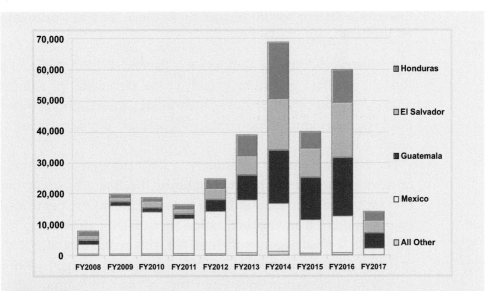

**FIG. 3.15**
Chart that shows the increase in the number of UUC apprehensions overall, as well as the countries of origin of the children being apprehended.

*Source*: UUC Apprehensions at the Southwest Border by Country of Origin 2008–2017 (Jan. 18, 2017) https://fas.org/sgp/crs/homesec/R43599.pdf.

DHS and HHS share responsibility for processing, treatment, and placement of UUC. CBP apprehends and detains unaccompanied children arrested at the border (CBP's work with UUC is discussed in greater detail in Chapter 4). ICE handles custody, transfer, and removal responsibilities, apprehends UUC in the interior of the country, and represents the government in any court proceedings for removal. HHS' ORR coordinates and implements the housing and care of UUC.

To address this crisis at its peak in 2014, the Obama Administration developed a working group to coordinate the efforts of federal agencies involved. It also opened additional shelters and holding facilities to accommodate the large number of UUC apprehended at the border. In June 2014, the Obama Administration announced plans to provide funding to the affected Central American countries for a variety of programs and security-related initiatives to mitigate the flow of UUC.

UUC continue to cross the United States' southwest land border in great numbers as of this writing.

### Executive Office for Immigration Review (at the Department of Justice)

The Executive Office for Immigration Review (EOIR), discussed elsewhere in this chapter, is a government body made up mostly of administrative law judges and lawyers that hears and decides immigration-related cases. The EOIR conducts immigration court proceedings, appellate reviews, and administrative hearings.

The EOIR was created on January 9, 1983 through an internal Department of Justice reorganization that combined the Board of Immigration Appeals (BIA) with the Immigration Judge function previously performed by the former Immigration and Naturalization Service (INS). In addition to establishing EOIR as a separate agency within DOJ, this reorganization made the Immigration Courts independent of INS, the agency charged with enforcement of federal immigration laws. The Office of the Chief Administrative Hearing Officer (OCAHO) was added in 1987. EOIR is also separate from the Office of Special Counsel for Immigration-Related Unfair Employment Practices in the DOJ Civil Rights Division and the Office of Immigration Litigation in the DOJ Civil Division. The Director of the EOIR reports directly to the Deputy Attorney General of the United States.[69]

EOIR is made up of several components that work together to adjudicate immigration law decisions, some of which are:

- *Office of the Director.* The EOIR is headed by a Director who is responsible for the supervision of the Deputy Director, the Chairman of the Board of Immigration Appeals, the Chief Immigration Judge, the Chief Administrative Hearing Officer, and all agency personnel in the execution of their duties in accordance with 8 C.F.R. 3. He or she represents the position and policies of the EOIR to the Attorney General, Members of Congress and other governmental bodies, the news media, the bar, and private groups interested in immigration matters.

- *The Board of Immigration Appeals.* The BIA is a component of the EOIR and the highest administrative body for interpreting and applying immigration laws. The BIA can include up to 21 Board Members, including the Chairman and Vice Chairman who share responsibility for BIA management. The BIA has nationwide jurisdiction to hear appeals from certain decisions rendered by immigration judges and by district directors of the Department of Homeland Security in a wide variety of proceedings in which the U.S. government is one party and the other party is an alien, citizen, undocumented immigrant, or a (usually foreign) business firm. The BIA is where immigration cases end up when they are being appealed for a rehearing. Generally the BIA does not conduct courtroom proceedings. Instead, it decides appeal cases by conducting a "paper review" of the underlying case. This means that the original parties to the case, witnesses, or evidence etc. are not reviewed again. Only the legal documents from the underlying case are considered. Sometimes, the BIA will hear oral arguments of the attorneys on both sides of the underlying case, but this is rare.[70] BIA decisions are binding on all DHS officers and officials, as well EOIR immigration judges, unless modified or overruled by the Attorney General, a federal court, or Congress. Most BIA decisions are subject to additional review (often referred to as **judicial review**) by federal courts. The majority of appeals reaching the BIA involve orders of removal and applications for relief from removal—in other words, requests by undocumented immigrants to remain inside the United States when an EOIR decision requires that they be deported. Additional BIA cases include the exclusion of aliens applying for admission to the United States, petitions to classify the status of alien relatives for the issuances of preference immigrant visas, fines imposed upon carriers for the violation of immigration laws, and motions for reopening and reconsideration of decisions previously rendered. The BIA is required to exercise its independent judgment in hearing appeals for the Attorney General.

- *Office of the Chief Immigration Judge.* The Chief Immigration Judge establishes operating policies and oversees policy implementation for the immigration courts. He or she provides overall program direction and established priorities for approximately 330 immigration judges located in 58 immigration courts throughout the U.S.
- *Office of the Chief Administrative Officer.* The Chief Administrative Hearing Officer is responsible for the general supervision and management of the judges who hear immigration cases (i.e. Administrative Law Judges or ALJs). ALJs, discussed elsewhere in this chapter, hear all immigration law cases and decide issues arising under several provisions of the Immigration and

Nationality Act (INA). For instance, an ALJ may decide issues related to the hiring, recruiting, or referring of undocumented immigrants, unfair employment practices relating to undocumented immigrants, or the presence of undocumented immigrants in the country without proper legal permission.

* *Office of General Counsel.* The Office of the General Counsel provides legal advice on a wide variety of matters involving the EOIR and its employees in the performance of their official duties. The OGC staff serves as agency counsel in federal court litigation, assists the Office of Policy in developing agency regulations, responds to all Freedom of Information Act (FOIA) and Privacy Act requests, and serves as the designated point of contact regarding Standards of Conduct and other ethics guidance for all EOIR employees.

---

**CRITICAL THINKING QUESTION**

Why is it important that EOIR, which is part of the Department of Justice, be separate and independent from ICE and USCIS?

---

## CONCLUSION

*To say the least...*

As this chapter makes clear, the United States' legal and policy apparatus for the screening, vetting, and entry of non-U.S. persons such as refugees, undocumented immigrants, documented legal permanent residents, and others is vastly complex. Not discussed here, but nonetheless an important fact for discussion and thought, is the social, economic, and political impact that immigrants, both documented and undocumented, have on the U.S. The 2016 presidential election has brought a great deal of attention to immigration issues in American society. Much of this debate focused on stereotypes of outsiders and echoed a nativist rhetoric that some believed had disappeared from public discourse.

Nonetheless, some economic concerns relating to the influx of immigrant labor and additional concerns about the security of the U.S. do persist. As you look again at the history portion of this chapter, do you see history repeating itself, albeit with some differences? Indeed, despite being one of the most welcoming countries for immigrants, American history is nonetheless rife with anti-immigrant rhetoric in the public sphere. America's immigration history is more contested, nuanced, and complicated than many Americans realize. This complexity is the reason, in part, for the similarly complicated legal and policy structures discussed in this chapter.

## HOMELAND SECURITY VOICES: Kevin Fandl, Ph.D.

*Dr. Kevin Fndl is an Assistant Professor of Legal Studies and Global Business Strategy at the Fox School of Business at Temple University. He has a decade of federal service experience, most recently as a federal attorney and Counsel to the Assistant Secretary for U.S. Immigration and Customs Enforcement (ICE). Previously, he worked as an attorney for the U.S. Trade and Development Agency and for U.S. Customs and Border Protection. He has been an adjunct law professor at the American University Washington College of Law since 2004, teaching courses on international trade and development law, intellectual property and international trade law, and advanced legal writing.*

**FIG. 3.16**

Dr. Kevin Fandl.

*Source: Dr. Kevin Fandl.*

*Dr. Fandl has written and published numerous articles on subjects such as economic development, international trade law, and the informal economy. His most recent work includes The Role of Informal Legal Institutions in Economic Development (Fordham International Law Journal). He was also awarded a Fulbright grant in 2006 to travel to Bogota, Colombia, to conduct investigation of the Colombian informal economy while teaching classes in the Master of Law program at la Universidad de los Andes. Dr. Fandl completed his Doctorate in Public Policy at George Mason University and received his Master's degree in International Relations at American University with a certificate in International Human Rights Law from Oxford University.*

***What advice would you give students who would like to work on immigration-related issues?***

KF: Study languages and take the time to understand immigration law, both statutes and case law. Immigration is shaped both by domestic policy and foreign policy. To get a complete picture of the subject, therefore, it helps to work overseas. A good place to start is internship programs overseas and study abroad programs. On the other hand, if you are interested in learning more about customs, then having a solid understanding of how trade law and the import/export process works is crucial. A law degree is useful, but not necessary—a background in economics or mathematics may be more helpful. You can gain experience in this field by working as a broker or focusing on economic policy and obtaining training on economics and trade.

***Could you discuss how you came to be affiliated with Customs and Border Protection (CBP) and your work with the organization?***

KF: In law school I applied to be a Presidential Management Fellow (PMF) because I wanted to work for the government rather than go work for a large law firm. CBP had just begun accepting PMFs and they offered me a position in their international trade office. While there, I learned the intricacies of trade issues and other subjects. I enjoyed the practical nature of my work since we worked with real trade goods, real cases etc. While at CBP I also spent some time at the Office of General Counsel's Intellectual Property Office where I handled decisions on trademark and copyright infringement cases brought by major companies. I had the opportunity to even go out to the port itself, examine the goods at the port, and watch the inspections take place.

***How did you then make your way from CBP to ICE?***

KF: I left CBP at the conclusion of my fellowship and went to work for the U.S. Trade and Development Agency (USTDA). At that time I was more focused on economic development and had begun a Ph.D. program focused on economic development issues and trade. I had a wonderful mentor at the Trade and Development Agency and that is the key to career success especially when working at a small government agency. After a period with USTDA, I was offered a Fulbright to Colombia where I taught trade law for one year. Doing so also helped me develop the Spanish-language skills, which I believe are essential in a career like mine.

My time in Colombia also exposed me to teaching and I realized that teaching was my passion. Since I didn't yet have my Ph.D. I decided I needed to keep working before I could begin teaching and applied to an attorney position at the ICE General Counsel Office. My supervisor served as an outstanding mentor who helped me expand my skills into areas not traditionally employed by attorneys, such as management and operations.

When my mentor moved into the leadership of the agency, he called upon me time and time again and placed me in a variety of positions. He gave me an appointment to run the Executive Secretariat, which was the correspondence division of the agency. While there, I often wondered if I was developing any expertise—but soon realized that I was developing a much more important skill—versatility. That is what is needed for a fruitful career in the government. You need to be flexible and adaptable. Talking to the other practitioners at the General Counsel's Office, all of them saw me as someone who moved very rapidly up into management. It wasn't based on my legal skills alone, but also on my ability to take on new tasks, new challenges, and use my legal skills to address them. To succeed in government, you have to be open to opportunities and taking the initiative. Having a mentor who believed this as well, and seeing him move his way up through the ranks using the ideas of versatility and adaptability made me believe it was the right approach.

***You've mentioned languages being important, specifically you focused on Spanish as a second language. Why do you believe it is important?***

KF: I believe language skills are crucial. I learned Spanish in college but perfected it through immersion while I was in Colombia. Spanish is particularly helpful for immigration issues because many legal and undocumented immigrants in the U.S. are Spanish speakers—but students can focus on learning other languages, including Mandarin Chinese, Arabic, Urdu etc. When you learn a language you learn another culture along with it. I think monolingual individuals tend to have a singular view of the world and, as such, have less upward mobility in a global economy.

***You've worked both at ICE and CBP, so could you explain how customs and trade are connected to immigration?***

KF: ICE focuses on people, including immigrants and people trading in goods; CBP focuses on the goods themselves. From a theoretical perspective, this distinction has less meaning—goods or people moving across the border are related. The movement of both people and goods affects the economy, and both are effectively regulated by similar laws and guidelines. Though we have two separate agencies, one focusing on people and the other on goods, it makes sense to eventually enforce the lawful movement of both goods and people under one unified government agency. ICE has been working in this direction by unifying training amongst customs and immigration officers.

**Immigration reform is an issue both political parties want to work on. What do you think Congress can do to reform our current system of immigration laws and immigration enforcement policies?**

KF: The answer to this question relates to the connection between people and goods I spoke about earlier. If labor immigrants were treated (legally) as goods, and viewed in a commercial light, then you would see a desire to integrate them into the tax and tariff system, as goods already are. In this hypothetical case, our immigration enforcement system would examine individuals in their economic context rather than their impact on American society or American culture. Much like a job applicant should be evaluated based upon their skills and their potential contributions to the workplace, an immigrant should be evaluated based upon their skills and their potential contribution to the economy.

For example, imagine that an undocumented immigrant seeks to enter the U.S. but has considerable education and specialized skills, then a system like the one I envision would make it very easy for them to enter the United States. In fact, this kind of system would likely encourage more of these folks to emigrate by providing incentives to highly skilled, high-wage workers, since they would provide an economic benefit to the U.S. Let's look at another example. Let's imagine that there are plenty of folks willing to enter the United States illegally to pick vegetables or harvest nuts. If we already have enough of these individuals in the country, then we would impose a tariff or tax to limit their supply in the country. In this way you regulate the entry of immigrants based on the free market supply and demand, rather than through artificial regulation of immigrants based on irrelevant factors, which is what we are currently doing.

Effective reform of our labor immigration policy requires us to look at the economic side of labor immigration and to regulate entry based upon the contributions the immigrants might make to our economy, their impact on the domestic job market, and of course, national security concerns. Tariffs would be set much like charges are levied for visas today. The funds generated from tariffs imposed upon immigrants wishing to come to the U.S. can then be used to offset any potential negative externalities, such as increased enrollment in schools or increased use of the public health system. More importantly, such a system should also provide these immigrants a pathway to citizenship, or at least residency while also educating the American public about the positive impact of immigrants.

All that being said, I think such a system is not likely to come to fruition in the current toxic political environment. Discrimination against immigrants is rampant, and the economic argument often gets lost among heated accusations about criminality, culture, and rhetoric. Historically, most immigration reform efforts are sidelined by laws that discriminate against certain immigrant populations. Ironically, these laws are passed in the immediate aftermath of efforts to meaningfully reform or encourage immigration. For instance, the Chinese Exclusion Act of 1882 was introduced only after pressure from states facing large immigrant populations despite a national effort to lower barriers to immigration. California politicians, and subsequently national politicians, quickly realized the political capital they could generate with discriminatory rhetoric against individuals who, after all, could not vote. The Chinese Exclusion Act prohibited all immigration of Chinese laborers into the United States and was really one of the first times discriminatory efforts in immigration were introduced. Since then the idea that people should be blocked from entering based on their national origin has been ingrained into American society. The target of that discrimination has evolved, shifting from Asian immigrants in the 19th century to Southern Europeans in the early 20th century to Latinos in the late 20th and early 21st centuries.

### *Could there be other reasons besides discrimination? What about high unemployment believed to be caused due to an influx of undocumented immigrants as a reason to limit immigration?*

KF: High unemployment is often blamed on immigrants. There is a lot of misinformation out there about the impact of immigrants on the domestic economy. Most studies, whether from conservative think-tanks such as the American Enterprise Institute or more liberal ones such as Brookings and the Center for American Progress, show that immigrants have a net positive impact on the American economy. This applies to both highly skilled and less-skilled immigrants. These immigrants enter the country as consumers, tax-payers, and contributors to so many aspects of American society. The misconception that immigrants harm the domestic economy is leading to significant discrimination and Congress is using this to justify keeping immigrants from entering the United States. But the economics are clear—immigrants are good for domestic jobs, wages, and economic growth.

*One other reason for limiting immigration, legal or illegal, could be 9/11. Thoughts?*

KF: This is the latest justification, recasting immigration into a national security issue. Immigrants are now increasingly seen as potential threats. I think that this is just another excuse for lack of Congressional action on effective immigration reform. Currently, Congress' idea of immigration reform is just a two-pronged approach: Increased border security and a pathway to legalization or amnesty of some kind for the undocumented immigrants already present in the U.S. Neither of these ideas make much sense. For instance, complete border security is not possible from a practical perspective since it would significantly slow trade and lead exporters elsewhere. And legalization, while an important aspect of reform, only addresses the immigrants already here, not those that continue to come year after year. National security is a concern that is best addressed by investigating specific threats, not by further isolating ourselves from the global economy.

## KEYWORDS

- **immigration**: Is the international movement of people to a country where they are not natives or where they do not possess citizenship, in order to settle or reside in that country for a significant length of time.

- **own recognizance** (OA): The release of a suspect in return for a promise that he or she will appear in court for all future proceedings related to the case.

- **immigration bond**: A deposit of funds to ensure or guarantee that an undocumented alien will attend their upcoming court hearing.

- **refugees**: Those displaced persons who have been forced to cross national boundaries and who cannot return home safely.

- **asylum seekers**: Those people who flee their home country and randomly enter another country seeking asylum, or the right to international protection in the country other than their home.

- **human trafficking**: Is modern-day slavery and involves the use of force, fraud, or coercion to obtain some type of labor or commercial sex act.

- **judicial review**: A process under which executive or legislative actions are subject to review by the judiciary (courts).

---

**KNOWLEDGE CHECK**

1. How did the demographic makeup of immigrants to the U.S. change over time?
2. What are the legal authorities DHS and ICE rely upon to remove undocumented individuals from the U.S.?
3. What is the difference between a refugee and an individual seeking asylum?

## NOTES

1. U.S. Citizenship and Immigration Services, Overview of INS History, at Sec. 9 (2012) www.uscis. gov/sites/default/files/USCIS/History%20and%20Genealogy/Our%20History/INS%20 History/INSHistory.pdf.
2. Mark Hugo Lopez and Jens Manuel Krugstad, *States suing Obama over immigration programs are home to 46% of those who may qualify*, Pew Research Center (Feb. 11, 2015) www.pewresearch.org/fact-tank/2015/02/11/states-suing-obama-over-immigration-programs-are-home-to-46-of-those-who-may-qualify/.
3. Editorial, *Fortunately, Trump gives young, undocumented DREAMers a reprieve—for now*, Miami Herald (Jan. 23, 2017, 9:32 PM) www.miamiherald.com/opinion/editorials/article128334459. html.
4. Robert Farley, *No Evidence Sanctuary Cities 'Breed Crime'*, FactCheck.org (Feb. 10, 2017) www. factcheck.org/2017/02/no-evidence-sanctuary-cities-breed-crime/.
5. Catalina Amuedo-Dorantes and Francisca Antman, *Can authorization reduce poverty among undocumented immigrants? Evidence from the Deferred Action for Childhood Arrivals program*, 147 Economics Letters 1–4 (2016) www.sciencedirect.com/science/article/pii/S0165176516302968 ?via%3Dihub.
6. *Refugee Processing and Security Screening*, U.S. Citizenship and Immigration Services (Aug. 31, 2018) www.uscis.gov/refugeescreening.
7. *Policy Memoranda*, U.S. Citizenship and Immigration Services www.uscis.gov/legal-resources/ policy-memoranda.
8. National Commission on Terrorist Attacks Upon the United States, The 9/11 Commission Report (2004) www.9-11commission.gov/report/911Report.pdf.
9. *ICE Air Operations*, U.S. Immigration and Customs Enforcement, (July 7, 2016) www.ice.gov/ factsheets/ice-air-operations.

10. *Secure Communities*, U.S. Immigration and Customs Enforcement (Mar. 20, 2018) www.ice.gov/secure-communities.

11. U.S. Dep't of Homeland Security (2011) www.dhs.gov/news/2011/11/29/statement-record-ice-house-judiciary-subcommittee-immigration-policy-and-enforcement; *See also Improving Security and Facilitating Commerce at America's Northern Border and Ports of Entry, Hearing before the S. Comm. on the Judiciary*, 112th Cong. (2011) (statement of John Morton, Assistant Secretary, U.S. Immigration and Customs Enforcement) *available at* www.dhs.gov/news/2011/05/16/statement-record-ice-senate-judiciary-subcommittee-immigration-refugees-and-border.

12. *Secure Communities*, U.S. Immigration and Customs Enforcement (Mar. 20, 2018) www.ice.gov/secure-communities.

13. John Morton, U.S. Immigration and Customs Enforcement www.ice.gov/doclib/news/library/speeches/120308morton.pdf.

14. Memorandum from Secretary Jeh Johnson to Acting Director Thomas S. Winkowski (Nov 20, 2014) (Secure Communities) available at www.dhs.gov/sites/default/files/publications/14_1120_memo_secure_communities.pdf.

15. *Fact Sheet: Immigration Accountability Executive Action,* The White House Office of the Press Secretary (Nov 20, 2014) available at https://obamawhitehouse.archives.gov/the-press-office/2014/11/20/fact-sheet-immigration-accountability-executive-action.

16. Memorandum from Secretary Jeh Johnson to Acting Director Thomas S. Winkowski (Nov 20, 2014) (Policies for the Apprehension Detention and Removal of Undocumented Immigrants) available at www.dhs.gov/sites/default/files/publications/14_1120_memo_prosecutorial_discretion.pdf.

17. Memorandum from Secretary Jeh Johnson to Acting Director Thomas S. Winkowski (Nov 20, 2014) (Secure Communities) available at www.dhs.gov/sites/default/files/publications/14_1120_memo_secure_communities.pdf.

18. Straub, E., Odrcic, D., & Laxton, S. *Immigration Detainers and Unlawful Detention: A Guide for Criminal Attorneys* (Jan. 1, 2011) available at www.legalactioncenter.org/sites/default/files/docs/lac/Guide-Criminal-Attys-Wisc-Straub-2011.pdf.

19. *Life After PEP-Comm*, Immigrant Legal Resource Center (Jan. 6, 2015) www.ilrc.org/files/documents/ilrcorganizersadvisory-2015-0106.pdf.

20. *Who We Are*, U.S. Immigration and Customs Enforcement, (Dec. 14, 2018) www.ice.gov/about#wcm-survey-target-id.

21. *Id.*

22. *Enforcement and Removal Operations*, U.S. Immigration and Customs Enforcement (July 31, 2018) www.ice.gov/ero.

23. *Homeland Security Investigations,* U.S. Immigration and Customs Enforcement (Sep. 21, 2018) www.ice.gov/hsi.

24. *Id.*

25. *Fiscal Year 2017 ICE Immigration Removals,* U.S. IMMIGRATION AND CUSTOMS ENFORCEMENT (Dec. 13, 2017) www.ice.gov/removal-statistics/.

26. *Border Patrol Overview,* U.S. CUSTOMS AND BORDER PROTECTION, (Apr. 26, 2018) www.cbp.gov/border-security/along-us-borders/overview.

27. *Homeland Security Investigations Tip Line: 866-DHS-2-ICE,* U.S. IMMIGRATION AND CUSTOMS ENFORCEMENT (Jan. 1, 2018) www.ice.gov/tipline/.

28. *Secure Communities,* U.S. IMMIGRATION AND CUSTOMS ENFORCEMENT (Mar. 20, 2018) www.ice.gov/secure-communities.

29. W.D. Reasoner, *Deportation Basics: How Immigration Enforcement Works (Or Doesn't) in Real Life),* CENTER FOR IMMIGRATION STUDIES, (July 18, 2011) http://cis.org/deportation-basics.

30. *DHS/NPPD/Privacy Impact Assessment,* DEP'T OF HOMELAND SECURITY (last visited April 5, 2014) www.dhs.gov/publication/dhsnppdpia-002-automated-biometric-identification-system-ident.

31. *IDENT-IAFIS,* GLOBALSECURITY.ORG (last updated July 13, 2011) www.globalsecurity.org/security/systems/ident-iafis.htm.

32 W.D. Reasoner, *Deportation Basics: How Immigration Enforcement Works (Or Doesn't) in Real Life),* CENTER FOR IMMIGRATION STUDIES, (July 18, 2011) http://cis.org/deportation-basics.

33. *Id.*

34. *FY 2017 ICE Immigration Removals,* U.S. Immigration and Customs Enforcement, www.ice.gov/removal-statistics/ (Dec 13, 2017).

35. W.D. Reasoner, *Deportation Basics: How Immigration Enforcement Works (Or Doesn't) in Real Life),* CENTER FOR IMMIGRATION STUDIES, (July 18, 2011) http://cis.org/deportation-basics.

36. Policy Memorandum, *Revised Guidance for the Referral of Cases and Issuance of Notices to Appear (NTAs) in Cases Involving Inadmissible and Removable Aliens,* U.S. IMMIGRATION AND CUSTOMS ENFORCEMENT (Nov. 7, 2011) *available at* www.uscis.gov/sites/default/files/USCIS/Laws/Memoranda/Static_Files_Memoranda/NTA%20PM%20%28Approved%20as%20final%2011-7-11%29.pdf.

37. W.D. Reasoner, *Deportation Basics: How Immigration Enforcement Works (Or Doesn't) in Real Life),* CENTER FOR IMMIGRATION STUDIES, (July 18, 2011) http://cis.org/deportation-basics.

38. 8 C.F.R. § 236.1 (2018).

39. *Detention Management,* U.S. IMMIGRATION AND CUSTOMS ENFORCEMENT, (Dec. 18, 2018) www.ice.gov/detention-management; *See also Detention Management,* U.S. IMMIGRATION AND CUSTOMS ENFORCEMENT (last visited May 4, 2012) www.ice.gov/factsheets/detention-management.

40. *The Immigration Court Practice Manual,* U.S. DEP'T OF JUSTICE EXECUTIVE OFFICE OF IMMIGRATION REVIEW, (2009) *available at* www.justice.gov/eoir/pages/attachments/2015/02/02/practice_manual_review.pdf.

41. Memorandum from Acting Director Wesley Lee to Field Office Directors (May 11, 2005) *(*Eligibility Criteria for Enrollment into the Intensive Supervision Appearance Program (ISAP) and the Electronic Monitoring Device (EMD) Program*) available at* www.ice.gov/doclib/foia/dro_policy_memos/dropolicymemoeligibilityfordroisapandemdprograms.pdf.

42. Neil G. Ruiz, Jeffrey S. Passel, and D'vera Cohn, *Higher share of students than tourists, business travelers overstayed deadlines to leave U.S. in 2016*, Pew Research, www.pewresearch.org/fact-tank/2017/06/06/higher-share-of-students-than-tourists-business-travelers-overstayed-deadlines-to-leave-u-s-in-2016/.

43. 8 U.S.C.A. § 1534 (2018).

44. *Id.*

45. *The Immigration Court Practice Manual*, U.S. Dep't of Justice Executive Office of Immigration Review, (2009*) available at* www.justice.gov/eoir/pages/attachments/2015/02/02/practice_manual_review.pdf.

46. *How to Apply For Voluntary Departure*, Executive Office of Immigration Review (last updated Oct 2011) *available at* www.justice.gov/sites/default/files/eoir/legacy/2013/01/22/Voluntary%20Departure%20-%20English%20%2813%29.pdf.

47. *The Immigration Court Practice Manual*, U.S. Dep't of Justice Executive Office of Immigration Review, (2009) *available at* www.justice.gov/eoir/pages/attachments/2015/02/02/practice_manual_review.pdf.

48. 8 U.S.C. §1229a (2018).

49. *What to do if You Are in Expedited Removal or Reinstatement of Removal*, Executive Office of Immigration Review (last updated Oct 2011) *available at* www.justice.gov/sites/default/files/eoir/legacy/2013/01/22/Expedited%20Removal%20-%20English%20%2817%29.pdf.

50. 8 U.S.C. §1326 (2018).

51. ICE inherited former USCS and FPS investigative authorities providing the legal basis for the Cyber Crimes Unit. Duties to ICE where transferred under various statutes, including 18 U.S.C. § 2516, the Authorized Interception of Wire, Oral, or Electronic Communication, and 40 U.S.C. § 1315 Offenses Committed Against Property Owned or Occupied by the Federal Government or Persons on the Property. *ICE Investigations: Mission Roles in Multi-Agency Areas of Responsibility*, U.S. Immigration and Customs Enforcement (Aug. 2007) *available at* www.fbiic.gov/public/2008/may/ice_mission_roles.pdf.

52. *Cyber Crimes Center*, U.S. Immigration and Customs Enforcement (Jun. 29, 2017) www.ice.gov/cyber-crimes/.

53. *Child Exploitation Investigations Unit*, U.S. Immigration and Customs Enforcement (April 3, 2017) www.ice.gov/predator.

54. *Cyber Crimes Center*, U.S. Immigration and Customs Enforcement (Jun. 29, 2017) www.ice.gov/cyber-crimes/. The Child Exploitative Investigations Units inherited former USCS investigative authorities when they were merged into ICE. This included U.S. federal authorities under child pornography and exploitation statutes outlined in 18 U.S.C. §§ 2251–2253. Other statutes include 18 U.S.C. § 2260. The Protect Act of 2003 enacted under 18 U.S.C. § 1466A criminalizes obscene visual representations of the sexual abuse of children.

55. *National Security Unit*, U.S. Immigration and Customs Enforcement (Jan. 3, 2018) www.ice.gov/national-security-unit/.

56. *Joint Terrorism Task Force,* U.S. Immigration and Customs Enforcement (Jan. 3, 2018) www.ice.gov/jttf/.

57. *Id.*

58. *Id.*

59. *Id.*

60. Information collated and adapted from: *Refugee Processing and Security Screening,* U.S. Immigration and Customs Enforcement (Aug. 31, 2018) www.uscis.gov/refugeescreening.

61. Nadwa Mossad, *Annual Flow Report: Refugees and Asylees: 2014,* U.S. Dep't of Homeland Security (Apr. 2016) www.dhs.gov/sites/default/files/publications/Refugees_Asylees_2014.pdf.

62. Nadwa Mossad, *Annual Flow Report: Refugees and Asylees: 2014,* U.S. Dep't of Homeland Security at 6 (Apr. 2016) www.dhs.gov/sites/default/files/publications/Refugees_Asylees_2014.pdf.

63. *Humanitarian or Significant Public Benefit Parole for Individuals Outside the United States,* U.S. Citizenship and Immigration Services (Dec. 15, 2018) www.uscis.gov/humanitarian/humanitarian-or-significant-public-benefit-parole-individuals-outside-united-states.

64. *Humanitarian or Significant Public Benefit Parole for Individuals Outside the United States,* U.S. Citizenship and Immigration Services (Dec. 15, 2018) www.uscis.gov/humanitarian/humanitarian-or-significant-public-benefit-parole-individuals-outside-united-states.

65. *Unaccompanied Alien Children Information Fact Sheets,* U.S. Dep't of Health and Human Services (Dec. 20, 2018) www.hhs.gov/programs/social-services/unaccompanied-alien-children/index.html.

66. 8 U.S.C. § 1232(b)(2) (2018).

67. *About Unaccompanied Alien Children's Services,* Office of Refugee Resettlement (June 15, 2018) www.acf.hhs.gov/orr/programs/ucs/about.

68. William A. Kandel, Cong. Research Serv., R43599, Unaccompanied Alien Children: An Overview, at 1 (2017) https://fas.org/sgp/crs/homesec/R43599.pdf.

69. *About the Office,* U.S. Dep't of Justice (Aug. 14, 2018) www.justice.gov/eoir/about-office.

70. *Board of Immigration Appeals,* U.S. Dep't of Justice (Oct. 15, 2018) www.justice.gov/eoir/board-of-immigration-appeals.

# Border Threats, Border Security, and Risk Assessment

> **IN THIS CHAPTER YOU WILL LEARN ABOUT**
>
> The history and nature of U.S. land, sea, and air borders.
>
> The growth of the federal border security apparatus.
>
> The government agencies that are responsible for securing the border today.

## INTRODUCTION

America shares 7,000 miles of land border with Canada and Mexico, as well as rivers, lakes, and coastal waters around the country. These borders are vital economic gateways that account for trillions of dollars in trade and travel each year. A number of these land and sea borders are also home to the nation's largest, most economically viable and prosperous cities and towns. Protecting borders from the illegal movement of weapons, drugs, contraband, and people, while promoting lawful entry and exit, is essential to homeland security, economic prosperity, and national sovereignty.

The inherent need to control the border stems from the international legal principle of **territorial integrity**, which prohibits states from using force or other means of pressure (such as economic pressure) to alter the territorial integrity or political independence of another state. In other words, much like human beings are entitled to control over their bodies, so too are states entitled to control the borders of their territory. Under this principle, border controls are put into place to control the movement of people, animals, and goods into as well as out of a country. Specialized government agencies are usually created to maintain the territorial integrity of a nation's air, land, sea (and, increasingly, digital) borders. In the United States, those responsibilities are shared by Customs and Border Protection and the U.S. Border Patrol, both Components of the Department of Homeland Security. CBP and BP perform various functions such as **customs**, immigration, security, quarantine, and other functions.

The degree of how aggressively a nation controls its borders depends on the country and the border concerned. For instance, in the United States the southern border with Mexico is far more regulated than the larger northern land border with Canada. Similarly, screening when entering Mexico from the United States takes a much shorter period of time, than entering the United States from Mexico. As discussed in Chapter 3, certain documents that verify a traveler's status, such as a visa, or passport, are often reviewed and verified at land, air, and sea borders by customs agencies. Some customs activities may concentrate on screening cargo and luggage, including imported goods, to ensure nothing that could present a health or agricultural risk is being imported into the U.S. After 9/11, customs activity has increasingly focused on terrorist actors or contraband entering the country.

In this chapter, we discuss the nature of the various borders, the history of how borders have been secured and managed in the United States, and the modern homeland security agencies that implement the policies to secure U.S. borders today.

## HISTORY OF THE UNITED STATES BORDER

As far back as the earliest written records, there have been political units such as city-states and empires claiming a definite territory. Unwanted intrusion into these territories was considered an act of war, and normally resulted in combat. Historically, there were also sometimes several layers of authority, with units waging war on each other while recognizing some higher authority. Ancient and medieval nobility in China and Europe would fight private wars amongst each other while still acknowledging the same king or emperor. Borders became more important after the end of World War I when the massive movement of global goods and people required clearly defined borders to mark where one country's territory ended and another's began. The League of Nations, a precursor international body to the United Nations, was intended to uphold the territorial integrity of member nations. Its successor, the United Nations, and other similar organizations serve today as ultimate arbiters on territorial integrity around the world.

### 1776–1840s: What Border?

The size and borders of the U.S. have varied greatly since its creation in 1776. New land grants from treaties like the Louisiana Purchase of 1803 often formed semi-autonomous territories that then applied for statehood. For much of its history, the United States had essentially open borders that were relatively porous and unsecured. What we today consider "illegal" migration was the norm. This was partially because of lack of manpower, partially because borders themselves were often never perfectly drawn, and partially because labor transfer on both sides of the border was economically beneficial for all North American nations, including the United States. Even today, a large number of individuals enter the United States illegally, especially from the southern border (discussed in Chapter 3). Indeed, the illegal entry of individuals is the predominant preoccupation of the United States' homeland security apparatus today.

In the colonial era, border control in North America had a largely different focus: Authorities were more worried about the cross-border movement of goods than people (Figure 4.1). Strict imperial trade laws meant that economic relations with the Colonies' southern neighbors (such as the Caribbean Islands) were to a significant extent founded on various sorts of smuggling. For instance, the rum distilleries in Colonial New England were kept in business by large-scale smuggling of molasses from the French West Indies in violation of British customs rules.

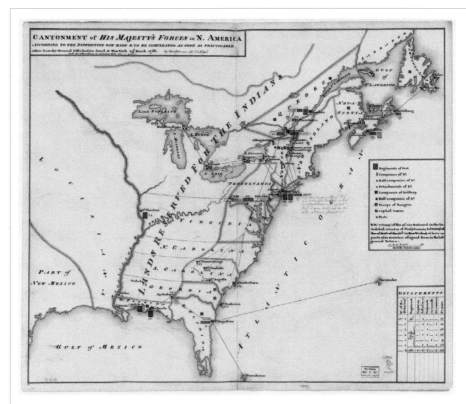

**FIG. 4.1**
A colonial era map of the U.S. Eastern Seaboard shows the relatively inaccurate conception of U.S. land and sea borders, which often hugged rivers and shorelines. In comparison, today the U.S. sea borders exist many miles offshore and are not referenced to any structural body in the water.

*Source*: Daniel Patterson, Cantonment of His Majesty's Forces in North America, Library of Congress, https://cdn.loc.gov/service/gmd/gmd3/g3301/g3301r/ar011800.jp2.

One of the first efforts to impose border controls on the flow of people was actually aimed at American colonists themselves, as they continued trying to push westward into territories not yet owned by the British Crown. The British feared loss of control over their subjects and also wished to avoid conflicts between the colonists and Native Americans. With the British Proclamation of 1763, King George III imposed a frontier line separating the Colonies from the Indian territories west of the Appalachian Mountains. The King prohibited colonists from moving across the line to settle, and deployed thousands of troops to try to enforce the law.

Colonists simply ignored the proclamation, and thousands moved into what became Kentucky and Tennessee, seeking land and a better life. To them, the frontier controls were just another attempt by the British crown to tell Americans what they could or couldn't do. Tensions between the colonists and British authorities over freedom of movement intensified all the way up to the outbreak of the Revolutionary War. After the U.S. gained its independence, that tension persisted over a different kind of unauthorized migration: Thousands of ambitious British artisans smuggled themselves out of Britain in violation of their country's strict exit controls. They were eagerly welcomed in the United States, and helped jump-start the American Industrial Revolution.

The United States' freedom from Britain opened up new opportunities for illegal westward movement. In the 1780s Congress passed laws enabling the federal government to survey and sell off territory beyond the original states in order to raise revenue, deter squatters and promote westwardly migration. Nonetheless, a flood of unlawful settlers undermined these plans. Congress increasingly began passing harsher laws and the problem grew. The Intrusion Act of 1807 criminalized illegal settlement and authorized fines and imprisonment for lawbreakers. But these measures were largely ineffective. Indeed, some of the illegal settlers were ultimately rewarded for their malfeasance . . . the territory that is now Vermont and Maine was settled primarily by illegal squatters who refused to buy land from the legally recognized owners and violently resisted government eviction efforts.

This pattern repeated itself for decades: Illegal settlement, intense and often violent resistance to federal government authority, and finally official resignation to the reality that illegal movement created communities and legitimate populations that were difficult, if not impossible, to move. This westward migration (both legal and illegal) included those European immigrants who entered the country legally through the 1800s but then settled illegally on U.S territories or Native American lands not owned by the United States (Figure 4.2). Parallels can be drawn between these legal entry/illegal stay migrants and the "visa overstays" who enter the U.S. legally but then remain after their visa has expired, discussed more fully in Chapter 3.

Faced with an inability to deter and remove illegal settlers, Congress passed preemption acts in 1830 and again in 1841. These were essentially pardons for illegal settlement, providing legitimate land deeds at discounted prices. This pattern of the law adjusting to facts on the ground has been a hallmark

**FIG. 4.2**
1886 in Loup Valley, Nebraska. A family poses with the wagon in which they live and travel daily during their pursuit of a (likely illegally obtained) homestead.

*Source:* Library of Congress, www.archives.gov/files/research/american-west/images/134.jpg.

of U.S. immigration legislation and executive action, including President Reagan's 1980s amnesty laws and President Obama's Deferred Action for Early Childhood Arrivals (discussed in Chapter 3). Not until the 1880s did the federal government begin controlling immigration in a serious and sustained way, triggered mostly by worries about rising Chinese migration to California. Until then, managing immigration had largely been left to those states bordering Mexico or Canada.

## 1850–1920: A Period of Exclusionary Border Policies

When many thousands of Chinese laborers began arriving in the mid- to late 1800s to help build massive continent-spanning railroads, they found life rough and citizenship impossible to obtain. As the railroads were completed and the demand for labor dried up, anti-Chinese backlash quickly followed. As political pressure to respond to the "yellow peril" intensified, Congress first passed the Page Act of 1875, followed by the far more sweeping Chinese Exclusion Act of 1882 (Figure 4.3), which barred the entry of Chinese laborers into the United States (mostly through seaports such as San Francisco and Los Angeles).

With the door to legal migration closed, many Chinese immigrants who had family overseas began transporting their loved ones to the United States illegally through Canada. Though Canadian officials knew full well that most of the arrivals from China were just passing through on their way to California, they turned a blind eye to their entry to North America. Eventually, vAmerican pressure on the Canadians to deny entry to Chinese prompted the people-smuggling business to shift south to Mexico and the United States' southern border. The U.S.-Mexico border already had a history for being an unpatrolled gateway for smuggling, but starting in the late 1800s and early 1900s it became a gateway for the smuggling of people as well. Foreshadowing future developments, a January 1904 editorial in the El Paso Herald Post warned, "If this Chinese immigration to Mexico continues, it will be necessary to run a barb wire fence along our side of the Rio Grande."[1]

Chinese immigrants weren't the only "undesirables" coming in through the southern border. By the last decades of the 19th century, federal law also prohibited the admission of paupers, criminals, prostitutes, "lunatics," "idiots," and contract workers. These restrictions were often used as a smokescreen to target those non-European migrants attempting to obtain entry into the United States. Those of Lebanese descent, Greeks, Italians, Slavs from the Balkans, and Jews were especially targeted by these restrictions. When turned away at official ports of entry, these individuals found illegal (and at that time unpatrolled) land crossings along the southern border to be a convenient alternative. Worries over these migrants (who at that time were not anywhere as large a number as today) became so acute that when the U.S. Border Patrol was created in 1924, its priority target for enforcement wasn't illegal immigrants of Mexican descent, but Europeans.

Nonetheless, along with European undocumented immigrants came a growing influx of Mexican and Central American workers. Prior to 1950 these immigrant workers were largely tolerated, with employers in the

**FIG. 4.3**
A lithograph produced a few years after the passage of the Chinese Exclusion Act that displays the height of anti-Chinese sentiment: It was used favorably to advertise detergent.

Southwest and throughout California informally recruiting large numbers of Mexicans to work in agriculture and other jobs Americans would not do. Formal, legal entry through ports of entry was complicated and a cumbersome process, while crossing the border to make a living was relatively simple and largely ignored. Strict controls against Central Americans crossing the border prior to the 1950s were widely perceived as neither viable nor desirable. As a substitute for European and Asian workers, Central Americans were considered an ideal labor force: Flexible, temporary, and acclimated to the American Southwest (which not too long ago was part of Mexico itself).

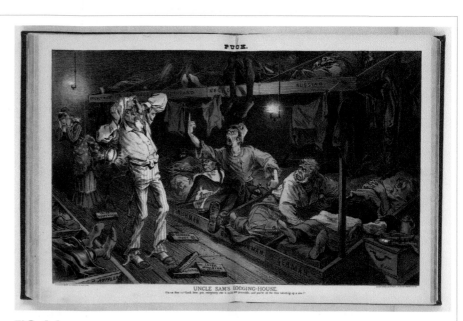

**FIG. 4.4**
A print that shows an Irishman confronting Uncle Sam (i.e. the U.S.) in a boarding house filled with laborers, immigrants from several countries who are attempting to sleep; the "Frenchman, Japanese, Negro, Russian, Italian," and "German" sleep peacefully. The "Irishman" makes trouble, throwing bricks labeled "The Chinese must go" at Uncle Sam and the figure of Lady Liberty.

*Source*: Uncle Sam's Lodging House (1882) www.loc.gov/resource/ppmsca.28483/.

## 1920–2000: Rise of Formal Border Security Policy

Thus, by 1930 nearly 1.5 million Mexican and Central American immigrants lived north of the border. As this mostly illegal immigration surged to fulfill economic demand, many in Congress began receiving pressure from local constituents living in border states to curb non-white immigration for Central Americans, in a way similar to that of Chinese Americans. This xenophobia was driven in part by a gradual but growing shift in demographics in the American Southwest. Though most Central American migrants continued to return home after seasonal work, a small number found it more profitable to settle down in California or Arizona and obtain jobs on the off season as temporary labor. As they started families and had children, leaving became harder and they began forming communities in the U.S., often reuniting with lost relatives who had remained behind when parts of the American Southwest were seized or purchased by the United States from Mexico.

In 1929, as western farmers who relied on Mexican labor clashed with border communities afraid of a "brown encroachment" into "white lands," Congress issued a compromise: Those individuals who did not cross the border through a port of entry would be said to have committed a crime and be deported back to their country of origin. Thus, those who just walked across the land border, as many did at that time, would be considered to be entering the country illegally. Government agencies such as the Border Patrol (and other ones to be created throughout the 20th century) were tasked with enforcing border security. Outlined in the Immigration Act of 1930, these policies set up the modern system of border enforcement discussed in this chapter, as well as the system of apprehending undocumented immigrants and deporting them back to their country of origin discussed in Chapter 3.

Prior to the Immigration Act, being in the U.S. without proper documents or permission was not considered a crime. Instead, those individuals in the U.S. without proper documents were not granted the benefits citizens enjoyed, such as the ability to obtain government funds or the right to vote. This was not the case after the passage of the Immigration Act of 1930. By the end of 1930, the Attorney General had prosecuted 7,001 cases of unlawful entry (up from one case the year before). By the end of the decade, U.S. Attorneys across the country had prosecuted more than 44,000 cases. These numbers were the highest per capita for some time. Indeed, with few exceptions, prosecutions for unlawful entry and re-entry across the southern land border remained low until 2005.

Conflicts between those who relied on undocumented immigrant labor and the communities in the area who feared immigrant entry continued over the first half of the 20th century. The Mexican government filed official complaints with Congress alleging that the Border Patrol was working at the behest of major growers in California and Arizona by allowing too many workers without proper documents to cross the southern border, but making exceptions to score political points. In response to this diplomatic and constituent pressure, the Immigration and Naturalization Service ("INS," which was at the time the precursor to today's CBP and ICE) initiated "Operation Wetback," in which INS claimed to have deported more than 1 million people in the summer of 1954.[2]

Soon thereafter, Congress placed a national origin quota on Mexicans entering the U.S., similar to the one placed earlier on Chinese immigrants. Congress also ended the Bracero Program, which had allowed for guest workers to enter legally and efficiently from across the border. Nonetheless, because economic demand had not diminished, long-established patterns of migrant labor continued, often illegally. Criminals on both sides of the border also found the population of illegal migrant workers vulnerable to suggestion and blackmail and the drug trade began to take advantage of a surge of unlawful border crossers by using them as drug mules. This in turn led to calls for a "War on Drugs" that President Nixon declared in 1971, giving the Border Patrol increased funding and authority to apprehend unlawful migrant crossers to search for drugs and other contraband. Due to the increasing militarization and security at the border, unlawful migrant workers increasingly saw the border crossing to be a dangerous and fraught exercise. Over time, a number decided it was less dangerous to remain on the U.S. side of the border and continue working in farms or other businesses, than to risk a daily or seasonal unlawful crossing. Thus, the number of illegal (or undocumented) immigrants in the United States continued to grow, reaching 3.6 million by 1986.[3] Though President Reagan granted amnesty to a large number of these undocumented immigrants, again the economic realities paired with a lack of

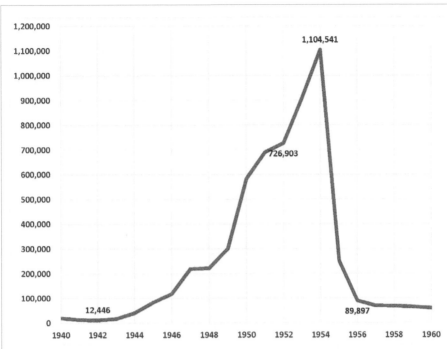

**FIG. 4.5**
The federal government became increasingly active in the interdiction, apprehension, and removal of undocumented immigrants in the immediate aftermath of World War II and coinciding with the rise of McCarthyism and the Cold War.

*Source*: U.S. Immigration Enforcement Actions 1940–1960, Dep't of Homeland Security, www.dhs.gov/immigration-statistics/yearbook/2015/table39.

reasonable guest worker programs encouraged individuals to continue crossing the border illegally and remaining inside the country without proper authorization.

In response the Border Patrol initiated Operation Hold the Line in 1993 as a show of force in cities like El Paso, San Diego, and Juarez. Operation Hold the Line concentrated agents and technology in specific urban areas to deter potential unlawful border crossers. A temporary drop in unlawful border crossings resulted in similar programs throughout the 1990s, including Operation Gatekeeper and Operation Safeguard in Arizona. In response to the perceived success of these operations, Congress continued to increase Border Patrol funding, which in the 1990s was made up of over 5,000 border agents patrolling a southern land border over 2,000 miles long.

## 2001–2016: Border Security as a National Security Issue

September 11 and the War on Terror necessitated a shift in border security strategy, transforming the Border Patrol and CBP from a customs-oriented organization to one focused on identifying and apprehending terrorists and other criminals. Then DHS Secretary Tom Ridge in speaking about the creation of DHS and ultimately Customs and Border Protection (CBP) stated

> The U.S. had no architecture for the asymmetric terrorist threat that the United States now faced; it made sense to build a border-centric agency to meet the threats of the 21st century.[4]

In 2009, United States Attorneys across the country prosecuted more than 50,000 cases of unlawful entry or re-entry.[5] By 2015, prosecutions for unlawful entry of undocumented immigrants accounted for half of all federal prosecutions across the country and the federal government spent at least $7 billion a year to apprehend and detain unlawful border crossers.

The time after 9/11 saw a shift not only in the culture and mission of border enforcement, but also in the sophistication of the technology used to deter and apprehend unlawful border crossers. Notably, CBP repurposed drones used by the Department of Defense in the "War on Terror" to identify those illegally crossing the 2,000-mile southern land border (Figure 4.6). Additional equipment to detect heat signatures and identify targets at night was also deployed by CBP. Secure fencing was installed along parts of the border throughout the 2000s and recently discussion of a border wall has brought renewed interest to securing the southern border.

The debate about how best to secure the southern border continues unabated today. For instance, border enforcement and topics like building additional secure fencing, a border wall, and hiring additional agents dominated the 2016 presidential election. Border security remains an important part of the United States' political discourse. This is due, perhaps, in part to the unique culture that surrounds the border and those who patrol it. Border law enforcement has many features that set it apart from other law enforcement organizations and cultures, namely the disproportionate focus on non-citizens, zero tolerance policies, and lower standards of probable cause (rights at the land border and ports of entry are somewhat diminished). Moreover, policing

**FIG. 4.6**
Unmanned and unarmed "Predator" drones like these have been used by CBP to monitor illegal border crossings of individuals, drugs, and other contraband across the U.S. southern land border.

*Source*: Gerald Nino, CBP Air & Marine Unmanned Aircraft System, Customs and Border Protection (2006).

along the border follows the logic of a larger system. The dramatic increase in Border Patrol agents discussed above also tracks a similar increase in prison populations across the country, as well as increasing privatization of incarceration and migrant detention more generally. Scholars have defined this trend as the "culture of control" in which increasing policies trend towards a punitive criminal justice system response.[6]

## THE SOUTHERN BORDER TODAY

The southern land border of the United States includes 23 U.S. counties and 39 Mexican municipalities. The population at the border continues to grow steadily, due not just to births, but also mass migrations and the number of employment opportunities along the border (particularly in Mexico). The economy of border communities on both sides is affected dramatically by changes in government policies surrounding immigration and border security. This is especially the case because communities on one side often encourage the formation of a community on the other side. These mutually dependent communities are referred to as "twinnings." Thus, if one of these sister communities faces an economic issue, chances are the community on the other side of the border will as well.

Today, the southern border extends 1,954 land miles from the Pacific Ocean to the Gulf of Mexico. The southern border is often an inhospitable place, characterized by deserts, rugged hills, lots of sun, and two major rivers: The Colorado and the Rio Grande. The Rio Grande marks much of the southern border as a natural boundary and its status as a border is maintained through treaties between Mexico and the United States. The southern border of the U.S. is the most frequently crossed international boundary in the world (with approximately 350 million legal crossings per year). Much of this traffic goes through 330 official ports of entry manned by border security personnel from both nations that dot the border along its almost 2,000-mile length. At these

**FIG. 4.7**
Several Border Patrol sectors of varying sizes are required to cover a land border as large as the one between the U.S. and Mexico.

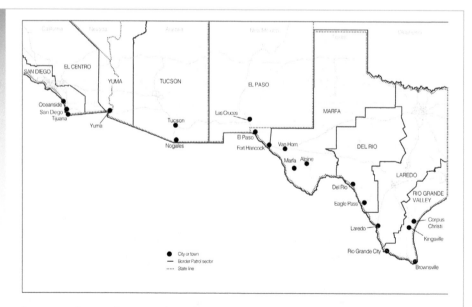

*Source*: Border Patrol Sectors Along the Southwest Border, src="https://farm6.staticflickr.com/5015/5452095492_e4a3cc7f40_o_d.jpg".

ports of entry, individuals and commercial traffic are usually inspected by CBP (on the U.S. side) and similar border agencies on the Mexican side. Border crossings can take place via automobile, pedestrian walkways, railroads, and ferries.

## SIDEBAR 4.1 The 100-Mile Border Zone

In 1953 the Department of Justice adopted regulations as a result of interpreting the Immigration and Nationality Act that changed the legal scope and definition of the "border."[7] Prior to the passage of these regulations the "border" consisted of the actual ports of entry (such as seaports and land border ports of entry) and the few hundred yards surrounding these areas. The 1953 regulations extended the border as far as 100 miles inland from all land borders, and notably these regulations have been seen to apply to airports as well. Since the United States has over 200 international airports scattered throughout the nation, the "border" thus extends through much of the United States, irrespective of whether it actually sits adjacent to a foreign country. By some estimates, two-thirds of the United States' population lives within this border zone. Indeed, some states like Delaware, Florida, and Rhode Island lie almost completely within the border as defined by the 1953 regulations.[8] Since the Border Patrol is statutorily authorized and obligated to carry out its border enforcement responsibilities, it may do so anywhere the "border" exists. Within the border CBP can, for instance, operate immigration-related checkpoints.

Furthermore, the Fourth Amendment's prohibitions against arbitrary stops and seizures by law enforcement officers have been held not to apply in or at a border. For example, at ports of entry, airports, or seaports, CBP does not need a warrant or even suspicion of wrongdoing to justify conducting what courts term a "routine search," such as searching luggage or a vehicle. Nonetheless, outside an actual port of entry, but still within the definition of the border as outlined above, there are some additional limitations placed on Border Patrol. For instance, within the extended border, Border Patrol may not pull over a driver without "reasonable suspicion." Likewise, the Border Patrol cannot search vehicles in the extended border without a warrant or "probable

*[handwritten margin note:] → inland are considered borders, gives BP authority*

cause" (a reasonable belief, that based on the circumstances observed by the Border Patrol officer, leads him or her to believe an immigration violation or crime has likely occurred).

## U.S. BORDER PATROL

The southern and northern land borders are patrolled by the United States Border Patrol. The Border Patrol is a federal law enforcement agency that is a large and semi-autonomous component of CBP (which itself is a component of DHS). With 21,000 agents, the Border Patrol is at times the largest law enforcement body in the United States.

The mission of the Border Patrol has shifted over time, from preventing the entry of contraband and illegal aliens into the United States to an emphasis in preventing the entry of terrorists and terrorist weapons (such as weapons of mass destruction) from entering the United States after 9/11. Today, the Border Patrol is responsible for physically patrolling nearly 6,000 miles of Mexican and Canadian international land borders and over 2,000 miles of coastal waters surrounding the Florida Peninsula and the island of Puerto Rico. Established in 1924, the Border Patrol has grown from a handful of mounted agents patrolling desolate areas along the U.S. borders to a large federal law enforcement force today.

The Border Patrol accomplishes its mission by leveraging technology (such as advanced surveillance tools like sensor alarms, aircraft, and drones) and also traditional training such as Native American tracking techniques (referred to as "signcutting"). Electronic sensors are placed at strategic locations along the border to detect people or vehicles entering the country unlawfully. Video monitors and night vision scopes are also used to detect unlawful border crossers. Agents patrol the border in vehicles, boats, and afoot. In some areas, the Border Patrol even employs horses, all-terrain motorcycles, bicycles, and snowmobiles. Along the coastal waterways of the United States and Puerto Rico and interior waterways common to the United States and Canada, the Border Patrol conducts border control activities from the decks of marine craft of various sizes. The Border Patrol maintains over 109 vessels, ranging from blue-water craft to inflatable hull craft, in 16 sectors, in addition to Headquarters special operations components. In addition to physically patrolling the land border, some other major Border Patrol activities include maintaining immigration checkpoints along highways leading into or out of border areas (see the Sidebar on the 100-Mile Border Zone), conducting city patrols and transportation checks, and conducting anti-smuggling investigations.

Border Patrol operations are divided into several sectors throughout the country. Each sector contains numerous stations and other offices to coordinate the work of the Border Patrol. For instance, the Detroit Sector covers 863 miles of international water boundaries (the Great Lakes) with Canada and covers over 3,802 miles of lakeshore and riverbanks. The sector encompasses the U.S. states of Michigan, Indiana, Ohio, and Illinois. The lakes and rivers that compose the international border in Michigan allow easy waterway access into the United States from Canada for nine months out of the year.

**FIG. 4.8** CBP, Border Patrol agents from the McAllen station horse patrol unit on patrol on horseback in South Texas.

*Source*: Donna Burton, U.S. Customs and Border Protection, South Texas, Border Patrol Agents, McAllen Horse Patrol Unit, https://farm6.staticflickr.com/5489/11933914763_cd46af3697_o_d.jpg.

During the rest of the year many of those waterways freeze over, impeding navigation by boat. In many places, however, "ice bridges" are created that allow for unlawful crossings by foot or snowmobile.[9]

## Patrolling the Southern vs. Northern Borders

The history of the Detroit Sector mimics that of the development of other Border Patrol sectors, and in particular highlights the changing role of the northern land border from a priority for border enforcement to an area that is often neglected when it comes to land border enforcement resources today. On May 22, 1924, presumably in anticipation of passage of the Labor Appropriations Act (which established the Border Patrol), the Commissioner General of the Immigration Service announced plans to increase the Detroit District force from 18 to 40 officers and plans to procure patrol automobiles, boats, and motorcycles to conduct enforcement operations. In his announcement he specified Detroit as the most vulnerable spot for unlawful entry into the United States by land.[10] In June 1924, Major Ruel Davenport was designated the first Chief Patrol Inspector in Detroit. He was given the task of organizing and directing a Border Patrol Sector that extended from Port Sanilac, Michigan to Port Clinton, Ohio. The Sector was divided into three subsectors with headquarters at Marine City, Detroit, and Sibley, Michigan. Shortly after creation of the sector, a second sector was created at Sault Ste. Marie, Michigan. This sector was to control the mounting volume of unlawful entries and smuggling across the St. Mary's River between Drummond Island and Whitefish Bay, and was organized under the jurisdiction of the Immigration Service's Montreal District.

During the height of Prohibition, organized crime was a growing concern, as the Mafia controlled the majority of alcohol being smuggled into the United States. As a result, liquor smuggling from Canada became a well-organized, thriving industry. The opportunity to earn substantial sums of money became a temptation for many. Lawlessness and violence became more common along the water borders of the Detroit Sector. Three Detroit Sector Patrol Inspectors were killed in the line of duty during this period, as smugglers attempting to bring contraband across the border resorted to violence to protect their cargo. As border violations continued to mount through the

1920s, the sector's manpower increased. By March 1926, there were 70 Patrol Inspectors and by July 1928, the total had reached 113 officers. This number represented nearly 15% of the Border Patrol's 850 men nationwide. Despite all efforts, Detroit continued to have the highest incidence of unlawful entry and smuggling in the country.

With the passage of the 21st Amendment ending Prohibition on December 5, 1933, border area traffic gradually declined. By that time, the sector force had reached a record strength of 141 Patrol Inspectors, which made Detroit the largest in the nation. This included the Sault Ste. Marie office, which had been added to the sector. In 1935 the Border Patrol received patrol boats to help control the traffic along the Detroit River, and the first Border

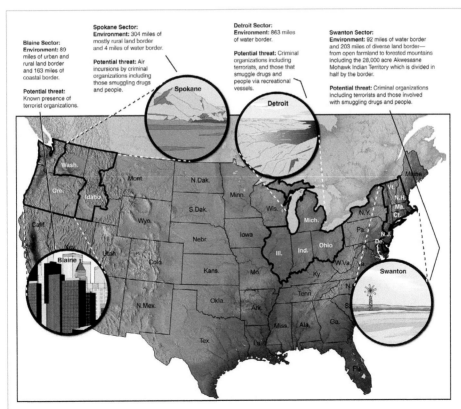

**FIG. 4.9**

There are distinct cultural and geographic differences between the southern and northern U.S. land borders.

*Source*: Description of Northern Border Patrol Sectors, https://farm6.staticflickr.com/5092/543 1047735_00371fea84_o_d.jpg.

Patrol shortwave radio was installed at Detroit in 1936. Eventually, the subsectors were dissolved and all operations were controlled from the one Sector Headquarters in Detroit. In April 1964, Detroit Sector Headquarters was moved to new quarters on the first floor of a three-story brick building located at Jefferson and Mt. Elliott in downtown Detroit. In 1996, Sector Headquarters moved to their current location at 26000 South St., Bldg 1516 on Selfridge ANGB, Mt. Clemens, Michigan. The one-story brick building is owned and maintained by the Air National Guard.

Notice how in the last 60 years, though still an important port of entry for goods and people from Canada, the Detroit Sector no longer has the largest Border Patrol presence in the nation. Border security resources have shifted dramatically from the north to the south.

---

**CRITICAL THINKING QUESTION**

The northern U.S. land border with Canada is almost three times the length of the southern border (at 5,525 miles) but receives far less Border Patrol resources. For instance, the northern border has one Border Patrol agent for every 16 miles whereas the southern border is staffed with enough Border Patrol agents to cover every 1,000 feet. If you were a smuggler, drug kingpin, or terrorist, which border would you use to conduct illicit trade or crime? If you were a policy advisor at the Border Patrol, how would you advise leadership on securing the northern border without diminishing their capacity to secure the southern border?

---

## Special Operations Group

In 2007 the Border Patrol joined two units, the Border Patrol Tactical Unit (BORTAC) and the Border Patrol Search, Trauma and Rescue Unit (BORSTAR), to form the U.S. Border Patrol's Special Operations Group (SOG), headquartered in El Paso, Texas. SOG provides DHS and the rest of CBP with specially trained and equipped teams capable of rapid response to emergent and uncommon law enforcement situations at the border that may require special tactics and techniques, search and rescue, and medical response capabilities. The SOG advances the missions of the Border Patrol by handling uncommon and dangerous situations outside the normal scope of Border Patrol agent duties (which are inherently dangerous to begin with). SOG deploys to domestic and international intelligence-driven and anti-terrorism efforts as well as to disaster and humanitarian special operations. SOG's in-house intelligence unit (SOG IU) provides vital mission-critical field intelligence to SOG assets. SOG IU conducts electronic targeting and collections and provides additional support for selected CBP missions and Border Patrol sector intelligence activities. The command staff for the Mobile Response Unit is also located at SOG. The Mobile Response Unit is a rapidly deployable Border Patrol asset capable of addressing problematic areas along U.S. borders.

**FIG. 4.10**
Officers from the San Diego Field Office Special Response Team (SRT) conduct training exercises for CBP officers attached to the San Diego Field Office Mobile Field Force.

*Source*: SRT Provides Mobile Field Force Training, https://farm2.staticflickr.com/1948/4485849 9405_54f9f45af7_o_d.jpg.

## SIDEBAR 4.2 Sanctuary Cities

You may have heard the term "Sanctuary City" on the news. The term has become politicized and come to mean either an unsafe city that allows dangerous undocumented individuals to remain in violation of federal law, or safe havens for undocumented immigrants from the unjust prosecution by federal authorities of the nation's immigration laws.

In reality neither of those two descriptions quite fit. **Sanctuary Cities** are cities and counties in the U.S. that limit their cooperation with federal immigration enforcement. Each city carries out this decision to limit its cooperation in different ways. For instance, Chicago government officials do not share individual residency status with ICE and CBP. In Washington, D.C., local police officers are forbidden from asking residents about their immigration status. Generally, these laws try to determine how a local police officer should handle the arrest of a potentially undocumented individual: Should a police officer ask the apprehended person whether they are undocumented? If they learn that they are, should they report them to ICE or other federal immigration authorities?

These decisions are complicated by the existence of interoperable and shared databases between local law enforcement, the FBI, and ICE (discussed more thoroughly in the Sidebar on Secure Communities in Chapter 3). Irrespective of the method, when ICE learns that local law enforcement is holding someone in custody, they must act to remove them from the country.

Potential cooperation between local law enforcement and immigration authorities has significant side effects. Undocumented immigrants number in the millions and are often productive members of society who report crimes, are witnesses to crimes, or are victims of crimes. When they become afraid that an interaction with local law enforcement may potentially lead to deportation, they become hesitant to engage with the police and report crimes or come forward if they are the victim of a crime. Disconnected from approaching law enforcement, undocumented individuals also become the target of unscrupulous actors who know they have nothing to fear from the police if they prey on these immigrants.

It becomes difficult for local police to do their job when they don't have community trust:

"Five hundred thousand Angelinos (people who live in Los Angeles) are undocumented immigrants. I need their cooperation. I need them to work with their local police stations. I need them to be witnesses to violent crime."—Charlie Beck, Chief LAPD.[11]

While many counties, especially those with larger undocumented populations, are choosing not to cooperate with federal immigration enforcement authorities on immigration issues, many other cities, especially those in the Midwest and South, are. This has created a patchwork of cities and counties, some of which are more cooperative with federal immigration enforcement and others that are not. It should be noted that irrespective of a city's cooperation with immigration authorities, agencies like ICE and CBP are always able to deport individuals within their respective jurisdictions.

Recently, many states and the federal government have been considering imposing monetary penalties or limiting funding to cities that choose not to cooperate with federal immigration enforcement authorities.

## Canine Program

The CBP Canine Program is headquartered in El Paso, Texas and considered to be critical to the overall DHS mission of securing the homeland. The CBP Canine Program has the responsibility of training canine instructors, canine handlers, and canines to assist Border Patrol in its mission. With more than 1,500 canine teams, the Canine Program is the largest and most diverse law enforcement canine training program in the country. The primary goal of the canine program is terrorist detection and apprehension. The working Border Patrol canine team is considered by CBP to be the best tool available to detect and apprehend persons attempting entry into the United States to organize, incite and carry out acts of terrorism within U.S. borders. The Canine Program's secondary goal is detection and seizure of controlled substances and other contraband, often used to finance terrorist and/or criminal drug trafficking organizations. In reality, the number and scope of criminal and organized crime or drug syndicate threats far exceed those from terrorist actors. Thus, the Canine Program's secondary goal of contraband detection is more frequently put into practice.[12]

Under the direction of the Office of Training and Development (OTD), the CBP Canine Program offers certified training based upon numerous federal and internationally recognized standards (Figure 4.11). The Canine Program also provides formal training for various local, state, and federal agencies. As a resource center, the Canine Program serves as liaison to the field, providing guidance for training issues, legal requirements, and certification standards. The Border Patrol maintains a breeding program to supplement the number of suitable dogs entering detection training. Working and sporting breed dogs are whelped and cared for in a variety of approved housing facilities. The puppies' final evaluation takes places between 7 and 14 months of age when they enter into one of the formal canine detection courses.

**FIG. 4.11**
A CBP agricultural canine team spots contraband food at Miami International Airport.

Source: James Tourtellotte, Customs and Border Protection, CBP Agricultural Canine, https://farm9.staticflickr.com/8080/8406682858_5c35f1d5dd_o_d.jpg.

**Air and Marine Operations**

With approximately 1,800 federal agents and mission support personnel, 240 aircraft and 300 marine vessels operating throughout the United States, Puerto Rico, and the U.S. Virgin Islands, the Air and Marine Operations (AMO) Unit of CBP conducts its mission in the air and maritime environments at and beyond the border, and within the nation's interior (Figure 4.12). AMO interdicts unlawful people and cargo approaching U.S. borders, investigates criminal networks and provides domain awareness in the air and maritime environments, and responds to contingencies and national taskings. For instance, in 2017, AMO enforcement actions resulted in the approximate seizure or disruption of 269,790 pounds of cocaine, 384,230 pounds of marijuana, 1,089 illicit weapons, 2,573 arrests for criminal violations, and 37,009 apprehensions of unlawful entrants.

AMO's missions fall into four broad categories that reflect CBP's core competencies of interdiction, investigation, domain awareness, and contingency operations/national tasking missions:

**FIG. 4.12**
CBP Office of Air and Marine helicopter patrols the air space around New York City.

*Source*: James Tourtellotte, U.S Customs and Border Protection, https://farm7.staticflickr.com/6103/6257713471_c9e2d393c3_o_d.jpg.

- **Interdiction**: Encompasses efforts to intercept, apprehend or disrupt threats in the land, sea, and air domains as they move toward or across the United States borders;
- **Investigation**: Leverages the expertise of agents in the air and marine domains to conduct investigations to defeat criminal networks;
- **Domain awareness**: Refers to the effective understanding of the environment and information associated with the various domains (air, land, and maritime) that could affect safety, security, the economy, or the environment. AMO employs advanced systems to contribute to overall domain awareness; and
- **Contingency/National Tasking**: These include disaster relief, contingency of operations, humanitarian operations, enforcement relocation, search and rescue, and national special security events.

Notably, AMO also helps to inspect and certify those pilots flying in the border areas, or in and around U.S. air borders. CBP's responsibility for smuggling interdiction has roots in the legacy U.S. Customs Service, created in 1789. Preventing air smuggling became a critical element to the U.S. Customs Service mission in the 1920s as general use aircraft began to come into use.[13] In 2003, that vital mission passed to CBP and AMO. AMO is authorized to conduct pilot certificate inspections under a variety of statutes and regulations, including:

- 14 C.F.R. § 61.3(1) Requirement for certificates, ratings, and authorizations;
- 14 C.F.R. § 91.203 Civil aircraft: Certifications required; and
- 49 U.S.C. § 44103(d) Registration of aircraft.

### International Initiatives

CBP coordinates and supports foreign initiatives, programs, and activities with external partners worldwide. CBP focuses on international cooperation and strengthening multi and bilateral relationships to achieve international agreements and joint efforts that both facilitate and secure legitimate trade and travel. CBP protects U.S. borders by implementing programs and initiatives that promote anti-terrorism, global border security, nonproliferation, export controls, immigration, and capacity building. One such program is CBP Preclearance (discussed in the Sidebar on Preclearance). CBP also promotes the expansion of the World Customs Organization Framework of Standards for supply chain security and facilitation by providing targeted countries with training and advisory support through programs such as capacity building and Export Control and Border Security.

## SIDEBAR 4.3 Preclearance

Clearance takes place every time someone travels into the United States from overseas, whether they are a U.S. citizen or a foreigner. If you have done so, you are familiar with the procedure. Immediately upon landing at a U.S. airport, you stand in line and are questioned by a CBP officer. Sometime the screening takes a longer period of time and your baggage may also be searched. This screening of foreign travelers and goods is the essential function of CBP and is what "Customs" in the title Customs and Border Protection often refers to.

Preclearance is when this same process takes place overseas on foreign soil, at foreign airports. CBP operates a number of preclearance facilities in airports on foreign soil. These facilities are staffed by CBP officers and travelers heading to the U.S. must pass through the same clearance checks they would have when landing on U.S. soil. The Preclearance process is intended to streamline border procedures, reduce congestion at U.S. airports and facilitate easier travel and business between preclearance foreign airports and U.S. airports (particularly those U.S. airports not equipped to conduct significant screening). Preclearance facilities exist at most major Canadian airports. Arrangements also exist with Bermuda, The Bahamas, Aruba, Ireland, and the United Arab Emirates. Passengers traveling from a preclearance port arrive in the U.S. as domestic travelers, though they may still be subject to inspection again at the discretion of CBP.

The Preclearance process presents a number of benefits, but also some drawbacks, some of which have drawn criticism. Preclearance is beneficial to those individual travelers who have a connecting flight to another U.S. airport (i.e. they land in Washington, D.C., and connect to a Los Angeles flight). A drawback is the delays that often occur at Preclearance facilities, primarily because these facilities are often poorly staffed or have to contend with both U.S. laws and the laws and regulations of the foreign country where the Preclearance facility is based. A major security advantage is that CBP obtains derogatory informa-

**FIG. 4.13**
U.S. Customs and Border Protection (CBP) preclearance operations at Vancouver International Airport. Here, passengers are seen arriving at the airport.

*Source*: Donna Burton, U.S. Customs and Border Protection, https://farm5.staticflickr.com/4661/26003318348_1cecbcd9a9_o_d.jpg.

tion about passengers before they arrive in the U.S. and in many cases, before they even board the plane in the foreign country. They can thereby exclude inadmissible passengers or goods from the flight before a long voyage to the U.S. commences.

Preclearance facilities exist because of the agreements that the U.S. government and CBP have made with the governments of the countries that host these facilities. Travelers who have passed through U.S. government checks at the foreign departure gate, but whose flight or boat has not departed, are still within the legal jurisdiction of the foreign nation. U.S. officials have limited permission to search and question travelers headed to the United States (as they would once the travelers arrived in the U.S.), but they do not have the power to arrest or detain travelers—even if they learn that the traveler has committed a violation of U.S. law. Local criminal and other laws apply and would have to be enforced by local officials in the host country. This means, that in most cases, travelers can choose to abandon their flight to the U.S. and leave the foreign airport, whereas in the U.S. they may have been detained or prosecuted further (some Preclearance facilities even have signs explaining these rights).

Though no foreign country has similar facilities on U.S. soil or at any U.S. port of entry, plans are in place to expand Preclearance facilities to other foreign countries over the coming years.

**CRITICAL THINKING QUESTION**

Read the Sidebar on Preclearance facilities. Why don't you think other nations have similar Preclearance facilities in the United States?

## SECURING THE BORDERS[14]

America's borders and ports are busy places, with tens of millions of cargo containers and hundreds of millions of lawful travelers entering the U.S. each year,[15] while much smaller but not insignificant amounts of unlawful cargo entries and hundreds of thousands of unauthorized migrants are seized and arrested. Many illicit goods and unlawful travelers are not interdicted by border security forces such as the Border Patrol, and enter the United States unlawfully. The breadth and variety of these interactions are reflected in DHS' broad and complicated border security mission, which tasks DHS with:

> preventing the illegal flow of people and goods across U.S. air, land and sea borders while expediting the safe flow of lawful travel and commerce; ensuring security and resilience of global movement systems; and disrupting and dismantling transnational organizations that engage in smuggling and trafficking across the border.[16]

To execute this broad mission, DHS and Congress must balance a number of competing priorities and allocate resources accordingly. For example, how should border security programs weigh the facilitation of legal trade and travel against the competing goal of preventing illegal entries? How should the allocation of border security resources be divided among programs designed to counter differing threats? Should additional personnel be added to the southern border or at the northern border? Is it more efficient to invest enforcement dollars at ports of entry or on building physical barriers and increasing surveillance between land border ports?

After 9/11 the answer to most of these questions has been "all of the above" due primarily to the immense amount of funding that has been poured into the nation's homeland security infrastructure. As time has passed and anti-terrorism

**FIG. 4.14**
This border fence line runs through Arizona and Mexico. The fence is regularly patrolled by U.S. Customs and Border Protection, U.S. Border Patrol agents on the lookout for illegal crossings, human trafficking, and drug smuggling.

*Source*: Donna Burton, U.S. Customs and Border Protection, U.S. Border Patrol Takes Watch at Arizona Border Fence Line, https://farm6.staticflickr.com/5053/5412842651_6a78a76b2 d_o_d.jpg.

budgets have shrunk (especially in the wake of the 2008 financial crisis) and terrorist tactics have shifted from using foreign actors to attack domestic targets to using domestic actors to attack domestic targets, policy leaders have found themselves reevaluating how best to fund and secure the nation's borders to prevent terrorism. Like the strategy DHS employs for dealing with transportation security issues, the department's border security strategy is also based on reducing risk rather than completely eliminating all risk. Thus, DHS and the other agencies that play a role in securing U.S. borders seek to deploy limited resources in order to diminish broad and unpredictable risk. DHS defines this mission as

> the process for identifying, analyzing and communicating risk and accepting, avoiding, transferring, or controlling it to an acceptable level considering associated costs and benefits of any actions taken.[17]

DHS' (and by extension the Border Patrol's) border security mission is multifold and includes efforts to prevent the entry of unlawful border crosses, shut down criminal networks (particularly drug cartels), and interdict potential terrorists at U.S. borders. When considering this complicated border security mission, certain trends become evident.[18] First, while migration, drugs and terrorism are DHS' highest-profile concerns at U.S. borders, border security encompasses a number of additional goals, including efforts to facilitate lawful travel and trade and to prevent the entry of persons with serious communicable diseases. Second, while DHS combats illegal migration, criminal networks, and potential terrorists at U.S. borders, its work on all three of these issues also extends beyond the border, both within the United States and through international partnerships. Third, DHS efforts at U.S. borders and its efforts to combat unauthorized migration, drugs and criminal networks, and terrorism represent a subset of the department's overall homeland security mission space (Figure 4.15).

In Figure 4.15, while the different elements of DHS' border security mission overlap, they also include distinct regions. For example, the "criminal

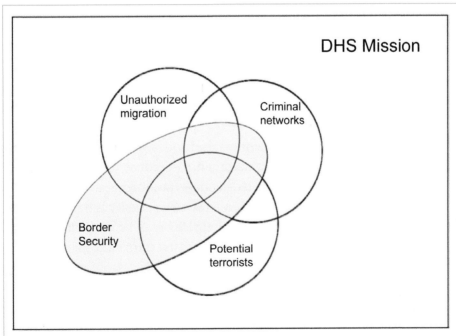

**FIG. 4.15** Diagram that shows border security overlapping responsibilities. See accompanying text in the chapter for a detailed discussion.

Source: Marc R. Rosenblum, Jerome P. Bjelopera, and Kristin M. Finklea, Cong. Research, Serv., www.hsdl.org/?view&did=731927.

networks" circle in the figure includes characteristics of this threat that are unique to it. Trafficking organizations that specialize in specific crimes fall in this region of the diagram. The circle intersects with "unauthorized migrants," describing possible ways in which these two threats relate, such as drug trafficking organizations that expand into migrant smuggling. At the core of the diagram all three circles overlap and highlight areas in which the threats converge—drug smugglers, unauthorized aliens, and terrorists may use the same smuggling routes or techniques, for example.

The peripheral areas of each circle are also important because threats encompass distinct features, and certain policy responses may be more appropriate to combat particular threats. For example, while there is some overlap among unlawful migrants, drug smugglers, and potential terrorists as threat issues, the great majority of unlawful migrants do not fall into the other categories. For instance, none of the 9/11 hijackers or known post-9/11 terrorist threats (such as Richard Reid, the "shoe bomber," or Faisal Shahzad, the "Times Square bomber") entered the United States unlawfully.

Likewise, while most unlawful migrants enter the country between ports of entry or by overstaying nonimmigrant visas, many illicit drugs are smuggled into the United States hidden within cargo containers, private vehicles, or in other non-commercial vehicles.[19] As a result, the enforcement tools targeting unlawful migration such as personnel and infrastructure between ports of entry, worksite enforcement, and visa overstay analysis . . . likely do little to reduce narcotic smuggling, and vice versa.] Another set of enforcement measures may be ideally designed to combat terrorism, and yet another to prevent other border threats, such as fraudulent goods.

Another way of thinking about border security is in terms of organizational components. In general, border threats may be divided into *actors* and *goods*. Threat actors include potential terrorists, transnational criminals, and unlawful migrants, among other types of people whose entry into the U.S. may produce harmful consequences. Threatening goods include weapons of mass destruction (WMD) and certain other weapons, illegal drugs, and other contraband, counterfeit products, and products brought into the United States illegally and/or with potentially harmful effect. While risk management methodologies may be used to analyze a wide variety of threats, we focus here on exclusively physical threats at U.S. borders, including the inflow of dangerous and/or unlawful people and goods.

## Threat Actors

Any person who intends to harm the United States, or whose presence may lead to harmful consequences, may be considered a **threat actor** and thus a potential target for border enforcement policies. At least three distinct types of threat actors may be described: Transnational terrorists, transnational criminals, and unlawful migrants (i.e. those who cross the border without proper documentation. One subset of this category, undocumented immigrants, is discussed in detail in Chapter 3). Although certain actors fall into more than one category (such as transnational criminals who migrate illegally or transnational terrorists who commit crimes), from an analytical standpoint—and for the purposes of designing countermeasures—these actors may be distinguished and categorized by their motives and their behavior.

## Transnational Terrorists

The Immigration and Nationality Act prohibits the admission of any alien who has engaged in a terrorist activity, is considered likely to engage in terrorist activity, has incited terrorist activity, or is a representative of a terrorist organization or a group that endorses or espouses terrorist activity.[20] A defining feature of terrorists, as distinct from transnational criminals, is that terrorists are motivated by particular grievances about aspects of societies that surround them, and they articulate their views "on moral grounds."[21] To help explain their grievances, terrorists adopt extremist ideologies or narratives. Based on their grievances and ideologies, terrorists generally have goals other than personal monetary gain, which may include both immediate goals that can be met without overthrowing the political system and transformational goals such as the destruction of an entire political or economic system.

The INA describes a variety of specific terrorist activities, including hijacking or sabotage of any conveyance (i.e. vehicle), the seizure or threatened violence against another individual in order to compel a third person or governmental

**FIG. 4.16**
Based on analysis by the U.S. Department of State, these nations served as "safe harbors" for transnational terrorists and terrorist organizations as of August 2010. Today's transnational threats likely come from some of the same, yet also some different nations.

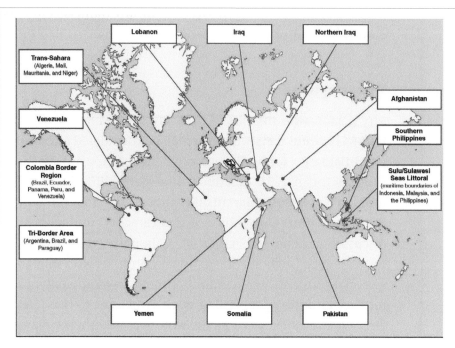

*Source:* Terrorist Safe Havens, https://farm6.staticflickr.com/5106/5808163473_d0d8237296_o_d.jpg.

organization to do or abstain from an activity, violence against an internationally protected person, assassination, and the use of a weapon of mass destruction or other dangerous device other than for personal monetary gain.[22] Terrorists often seek to instill fear among a targeted population to destroy the collective confidence individuals invest in social institutions and national leadership. Terrorists use violent tactics to direct public attention towards their grievances, gain recruits, or coerce people. Terrorists also promote their causes by fashioning propaganda.

### Transnational Criminals

The INA also prohibits the admission of certain criminals, including aliens who have committed crimes of moral turpitude, aliens with multiple serious criminal convictions, controlled substance traffickers, aliens engaged in prostitution or commercialized vice, significant traffickers in persons, and money launderers, among others.[23] In contrast with terrorists, criminals generally are non-ideological, and fundamentally motivated by the pursuit of profit. People also participate in criminal organizations for reasons that involve other sorts of personal gain. They may believe, for example, that being a gangster confers a positive social image, or they may desire the sensation of belonging to a powerful and even prestigious entity. Criminal gangs attract youth by glorifying gang life and by offering a sense of belonging, and the gang also provides membership incentives such as drugs, alcohol, and sex. Additionally, kinship, ethnic ties, or friendship can also play a role in the formation of criminal groups.

Profit incentives can often drive criminals to "provide goods and services that either illegal, regulated, or in short supply."[24] They devote resources to enhancing their market-related activities, which can involve carving out and defending turf, devising novel smuggling techniques, running and protecting supply chains, eliminating rivals, laundering money, and shielding secrets from competitors such as rival gangs and law enforcement. Thus, criminal earnings depend on defying the rule of law, but not necessarily affecting it via a government overthrow or revolution. Violence—or its threatened use—plays a key role in the efforts of organized criminals to generate profits. This violence can send a specific message to rivals or enemies, for example about control of markets and supply routes or questions of reputation and status, but it is rarely ideologically driven. In addition, criminals may secure access to illegal markets by corrupting or intimidating public officials, gaining influence over state activity, or even having states co-opt criminals themselves.[25]

Having said that, the line between "terrorists" and "criminals" remains murky. The vast majority of terrorists do not use airplanes or other weapons of mass destruction to achieve their aims. Instead, like criminals, most terrorists employ the use of small arms fire and handguns to terrorize their victims. Like criminals, terrorists are often recruited and radicalized into terrorist cells, which mimic gang groupings. Like criminals, terrorists may identify on the basis of shared culture, language, kinship, economic class, or other subcultural grouping. Often, the grievance that may drive a terrorist to commit a terrorist act is vague and hard to define, even by the terrorist themselves. In this way, many terrorists share a general incentive to commit a maladaptive act. Lastly, many terrorists are lured to terrorism (especially overseas) with offers of money, new cars, or other goods. Again, in this way terrorists, like criminals, have a financial or pecuniary incentive to commit a terrorist act.

### Unlawful Migrants

In addition to terrorists and certain criminals, the INA defines as inadmissible, among others, aliens with certain health-related concerns, aliens who raise certain foreign policy concerns, aliens considered likely to become a public charge, certain employment-based immigrants who have not received a labor certification, and aliens arriving at an illegal time or place or not in possession of a valid unexpired visa or other valid entry document.[26] Unlawful (or unauthorized) migrants, like lawful migrants, may be motivated by some combination of employment opportunities, a general desire to improve their economic circumstances, family connections, and dangerous or difficult conditions in their home countries, among other factors. Apart from immigration-related offenses such as illegal entry, or the use of fraudulent documents to obtain employment, many unauthorized aliens never commit a criminal offense, though some unauthorized migrants become involved with transnational criminals during the course of their migration or while obtaining employment. Indeed, unlawful presence in the U.S. absent additional factors is often a civil violation, not a criminal offense (see Chapter 3 for a detailed discussion).[27]

Thus, while a terrorist may be unauthorized, "regular" unauthorized aliens are distinguished from terrorists in that they are not motivated by extremist ideologies and do not engage in terrorist activities. And, unlike criminals (who may also be unauthorized), "regular" unauthorized individuals do not seek to profit by exploiting illegal markets or providing illegal services, and they do not use violence or the threat of violence to generate profits.

### DEFINITION BOX: Public Charge

**Public charge** is a term used by U.S. immigration officials to refer to a person who is considered *primarily* dependent on the government for survival and subsistence, as demonstrated by a receipt of public cash assistance for income maintenance or institutionalization for long-term care at government expense.

## Illegal Goods

Any **good** (i.e. non-person thing) that is smuggled into or out of the United States is illegal and may pose security risks. Illegal goods fall into two broad categories distinguished by their inherent illegitimacy: Certain weapons, illegal drugs, and counterfeit goods are always illegal and categorically prohibited, while other foods are generally legal, but become illegitimate because they are smuggled to avoid the enforcement of specific laws, taxes, or regulations.

## Categorically Prohibited Goods

U.S. law enforcement seeks to prevent a variety of illegal goods from entering the United States. DHS, for instance, has identified high consequence weapons of mass destruction (WMDs) as one of the primary threats to homeland security. WMDs may come in many forms, and the term often covers chemical, biological, radiological, nuclear, and explosive (referred to as CBRNE) weapons. Concerns over WMD or their component materials crossing the border into the United States generally emphasize terrorists' use of these weapons, yet some have raised concerns that criminal networks may—for the right price—attempt to smuggle WMD or related materials.[28]

In addition to the smuggling of weapons into the United States, there are also border security and national security concerns over the smuggling of weapons *out* of the United States. One such concern involved Mexican drug trafficking organizations purchasing firearms in the United States and smuggling these weapons to Mexico, where their possession by civilians is largely prohibited. Firearms smuggled from the United States into Mexico have been cited as helping in fueling the rise of drug-trafficking violence in Mexico. Illegal drugs comprise another set of illicit goods that challenge U.S. border security. The U.S., through the Controlled Substances Act (CSA, 21 U.S.C. Section 801 et. seq.), prohibits the possession, production, distribution, and trafficking of a number of drugs and substances. Nonetheless, drug demand in the United States fuels a multi-billion-dollar illicit industry, and many of the drugs consumed in the United States are produced internationally and smuggled into the country. As such, illegal drugs are among the top catego-

**FIG. 4.17**
Two U.S. Customs and Border Protection Officers inspecting the remains of a pickup truck that was found to have 5.4 pounds of heroin concealed in the transfer case. The vehicle was trying to bring the heroin in from Mexico. The vehicle was searched at the Paso Del Norte Port of Entry.

*Source*: Steven Green, U.S. Customs and Border Protection, CBP Officers Inspecting the Remains of a Smuggler's Vehicle, https://farm8.staticflickr.com/7012/6812392389_c6900f2817_o_d.jpg.

ries of seizures by border security officials. CBP seized an average of 13,717 pounds of drugs each day in 2011.[29]

The smuggling of counterfeit and pirated goods into the United States, particularly by transnational criminal organizations, has also been identified as a threat to border security. This smuggling violates intellectual property rights and "threatens America's economic vitality and national security, and the American people's health and safety."[30] In 2011, ICE and CBP had over 23,000 seizures of counterfeit goods, 25% more than the year before. The domestic value of these seizures was more than $178 million. Products originating from China, both mainland China and Hong Kong, accounted for 80% of the products seized.

## Goods Considered Illegal via Smuggling

Goods that *are not* categorically prohibited are illegal if they are smuggled into or out of the United States. These otherwise legitimate goods can pose a variety of threats when they are moved through illicit channels and means. For instance, alcohol, while generally legal and regulated in the United States and other countries, is smuggled to circumvent taxes or to evade laws prohibiting alcohol. One snapshot of alcohol-linked financial losses comes from Michigan, where illegal alcohol imports are estimated to cost the state at least $14 million per year in lost taxes, not including sales tax or business income tax.[31] Cigarettes and other tobacco products are similarly smuggled to circumvent taxes and regulations. Cigarettes, which comprise about 80% of the value of tobacco product shipments in the United States, are smuggled internationally, including to and from the United States, as well as across state lines. Proceeds from the smuggling of cigarettes have been linked to the financing of terrorist operations abroad.

Cross-border movement of money is not inherently illegal, but certain practices are. For instance, bulk cash smuggling is one of the primary means by which criminals move their illicit proceeds out of the United States. Estimates are that between $20 billion and $25 billion in bank notes may be smuggled across the southwest border into Mexico each year. In 2011, CBP seized an average of $345,687 in undeclared or illicit currency each day, over $126 million total in 2011.[32]

---

**CRITICAL THINKING QUESTION**

Are unlawful migrants or border crossers (often referred to as "undocumented aliens" or "illegal immigrants") security threats? Why or why not?

---

## CONTEMPORARY BORDER PATROL SECURITY STRATEGIES

In 2004 the U.S. Border Patrol issued its first strategy as a component of DHS. This strategy was a resource-based approach focused on what the Border Patrol termed "operational control." **Operational control** was defined as the ability to detect, respond to, and interdict border intrusions in areas deemed as high priority for threat potential or other national security objectives, through varied deployment combinations of personnel, technology, and infrastructure. This strategy was a significant step for the Border Patrol as it endeavored to correlate and quantify a metric that illustrated a level of control or security at specific points along the border. The 2004 strategy also focused on turning the Border Patrol into a centralized, command-driven agency that emphasized a flow of information from the CBP Commissioner to the Chief of the Border Patrol, and on to field commanders, while providing flexibility at the lower levels for mission execution. This provided a well-defined common operating picture in which national strategic guidance could be disseminated uniformly and national threats could be addressed strategically throughout the 20 U.S. Border Patrol Sectors. This organizational realignment helped guide the Border Patrol into a national-security posture and prepare for the significant growth necessitated by post-9/11 priorities.

From 2004 through 2010, the Border Patrol saw an unprecedented buildup of resources that increased its ability to decrease the flow of illegal activity and combat drug and aliens smuggling organizations along the border. New technology and long-range reconnaissance equipment acquired from the U.S military assisted with increased situational awareness, especially after the Border Patrol re-tooled and distributed it to sectors along the southwest border. The use of land-based radar systems became widespread and provided a greater capability in the deserts of Arizona and the boot heel region of New Mexico. Additionally, during the latter part of 2010, the U.S. Border Patrol implemented post-apprehension measures, specifically the Consequence Delivery System, which was designed to apply consequences to apprehended unlawful border crossers that were seen to reduce the likelihood that a person would attempt re-entry.

Integrated missions conducted with the Department of Defense, such as Operation Jumpstart in 2006, which marked the largest deployment of National Guard troops to a domestic border security mission in modern history, played a role in increased security along the U.S. border throughout the period after 9/11. Between 2005 and 2011, National Guard Entry Identification Teams (EITs) were deployed across the southern border, alongside Border Patrol agents, in an effort to fill capacity gaps. Concurrently, 6,000 new Border Patrol agents were trained and placed in the field. DHS also implemented the Secure Border Initiative (SBI) during this time. SBI was designed

**FIG. 4.18**
U.S. Customs and Border Protection personnel along with DOD personnel secure the San Ysidro Port of Entry near San Diego, CA.

*Source*: Mani Albrecht, U.S. Customs and Border Protection, https://farm5.staticflickr.com/4865/31114435637_eb139fa846_o_d.jpg.

to enable the Border Patrol to gain greater situational awareness along the border through an integrated technology deployment that included underground sensors, camera towers, and other detection equipment connected to a central location to facilitate a common operating picture and streamline interdiction efforts.

This program was later terminated by DHS because of cost overruns and unforeseen obstacles that simply could not deliver on the promise of increased situational awareness. Instead, DHS opted to focus on mobile solutions instead of fixed assets; many of the mobile land-based radar trucks that were a product of SBI are still used by the Border Patrol at the time of this writing. As increasing resources were deployed to the southern border, Border Patrol observed a concurrent drop in the apprehension of unlawful entrants. The increased securitization of the southern border, as a whole and by segment, resulted in several unintended consequences. While areas in which significant increases in resources were deployed saw illegal entries and apprehensions diminish, the gains were offset by increased activity within other, less-controlled areas. In some instances, there appeared to be a full displacement of trafficking organizations to other geographic areas where fewer resources were deployed (often referred to as the "balloon effect"). Still, in other areas, entrenchment became an issue. The "entrenchment problem" occurs when smuggling or other criminal organizations and their resources facilitate the rapid influx of infrastructure on the non-native (e.g. the Mexican side) of the border. Thus, after the increased deployment of law enforcement resources in urban areas such as San Diego, Nogales, and El Paso, smugglers changed tactics and moves to the sparse desert regions of Arizona to conduct operations.

## Case Study: Altar, Mexico

Consider the case of Altar, Mexico: A town 60 miles south of the Arizona/Mexico border. Altar quickly became a staging point for smugglers where as many as 60 buses arrived each day with immigrants intending to cross illegally into the U.S. Because there was no major urban area similar to Altar immediately north of the international border on the U.S. side, this organized buildup of infrastructure by smugglers in Altar was different from anything the Border Patrol had experienced in the past. Rather, the deserts of Arizona on the other side of the southern border provided little infrastructure that could be used by Border Patrol agents to maneuver and intercept smugglers once they crossed onto the U.S. side. The smugglers developed a network of "spotters" and supply routers in Mexico to facilitate their illicit trade faster than the U.S. Border Patrol could counter through the deployment of infrastructure, technology, and personnel at the time.

These results led the Border Patrol to acknowledge that no amount of resources could guarantee and immediate or sustained interdiction capability. The Border Patrol instead sought an acceptable, but measured enforcement and interdiction capability, to achieve an increased level of security sought by Congress and the public. Essentially, the 2004 strategy was designed to reduce the flow of illegal entries and maintain an acceptable level of cross-border incursions, through the deployment of interdiction resources. However, operational experience and the adaptability of smuggling organizations made clear that a continual buildup of resources along the border alone could not address root causes of cross-border illicit activity. What could an individual interdiction agency do to combat the root causes of illegal entries?

With increased resources and larger budgets came the heightened expectation of greater security and results. Historically, the Border Patrol used apprehensions of unlawful crossers as a metric for gauging success, focusing on outputs rather than outcomes. In 2011, with unprecedented agency growth, through an increase in Border Patrol agents and resources, aligned with an increase in Defense Support for Civil Authorities (DSCA) operations initiated through several joint task forces across the government, the Border Patrol saw its nationwide apprehensions reduced by 78% compared to 2000 (while narcotic and illegal drug seizures increased, due primarily to the increase of the agents post-9/11).

## Recent Changes in Strategy

The Border Patrol's 2012–2016 Strategic Plan was thus released at a time when apprehensions of unlawful crossers had been reduced to levels not seen the 1970s and while the number of 21,730 Border Patrol agents deployed along the southern border was the largest in American history. Thus, in 2012 Border Patrol and DHS leadership shifted the Border Patrol's work from generalized deterrence and apprehension to a risk-based strategy that sought to direct interdiction efforts towards those unlawful crossers who posed the greatest risk of injury, harm, or crime to the nation. The 2012 Strategic Plan outlined two high-level goals for the Border Patrol:

1. Secure the U.S. southern border through the application of "information, integration and rapid response"; and
2. Strengthen the Border Patrol through an investment in the workforce and expansion of the organization's capabilities, including its personnel.

These goals, coupled with a shift from resource-intensive deployment method to deployment of agents and resources only to those areas that posed the greatest risk, began a new strategy for Border Patrol that continues in some ways at the writing of this book.

Risk-based strategies (discussed elsewhere in this text) are plentiful in both private and public sectors, especially in cases where cost is a significant factor in whether a mission is undertaken. The National Aeronautics and Space Administration (NASA) has used a risk-based strategy for years; most notably in the case of the International Space Station. NASA demonstrated the ability to identify the highest risk areas for space debris damage on military satellites and space station facilities with a high probability.[33] In some instances, if the risk was deemed high enough, the International Space Station would be asked to shift position to mitigate the risk in what is known as a "debris-avoidance maneuver." Today it costs about $10,000 to put a pound of payload in Earth's orbit; the alternative to this risk-based approach for building the International Space Station would require equal reinforcement of all areas, regardless of debris-impact probability. This would raise the cost of many NASA projects exponentially and could make many NASA projects impractical, such as the deployment of the International Space Station.

A direct comparison shows that the process NASA uses to mitigate risks through an analysis of the probabilities and vulnerability is similar to the methodology the Border Patrol adopted after 2012 to address the greatest risks along the southern border. Arizona (where the deployment of resources and personnel tends to be the strongest) employs approximately 5,000 Border Patrol agents in Tucson and Yuma Sectors. These agents patrol 388 miles of the southern border. To reach this level of resources along the remaining 5,600 linear miles of the southern (with Mexico) and northern land borders (with Canada) would require more than 77,000 Border Patrol agents with a minimum yearly estimated budget of $12.6 billion.[34] A substantial increase considering all major offices of CBP reported 61,534 full-time employees with an enacted budget of $11.6 billion in 2012. Even with these increased numbers, detection and apprehension could not be guaranteed.

This new risk-based approach to border security was a direct result of the shifting environment in which Border Patrol agents work. Since the early 2000s, Transnational Criminal Organization (TCOs) use social networking and many forms of advanced electronic equipment to gain real-time counter-intelligence on Border Patrol operations. This facilitates a greater situational awareness within their ranks and creates an elusive network, one in which illicit operations can be halted and diverted to other areas at a moment's notice. Thus, a strategy that necessitated that Border Patrol agents lie in wait for hours for a criminal to cross the border, or saturating an area with patrols or surveillance technology, increasingly bears negligible results.

Thus, since 2012 the Border Patrol began relying heavily on technology developed initially for the military (to combat "asymmetric threats" abroad). For instance, the Border Patrol received new ISR equipment to help patrol the southern border. This included advanced thermal imaging technology used by the military for targeting individuals as well as unmanned aerial vehicles (drones) that had previously proved successful in Iraq and Afghanistan. The Border Patrol continues to use these technologies today to provide real-time tracking and monitoring of the border.

Many of these post-2012 tactics, techniques, and procedures employed by the Border Patrol mirror what the Department of Defense has done for years. For instance, the South Texas Campaign (STC), the first campaign executed against the new 2012–2016 Strategic Plan, was partly a product of lessons learned by DOD on the battlefield. While Border Patrol has coordinated investigative and interdiction efforts amongst its various components, STC made strides in accomplishing the coordinated efforts of intelligence, investigation, and interdictions through a unified command and a three-star commander who was delegated command and control over CBP components in the South Texas corridor.[35]

## Estimating the Likelihood of Border Threats

DHS defines **likelihood** as:

> the chance of something happening, whether defined, measured or estimated objectively or subjectively, or in terms of general descriptors (such as rare, unlikely, likely, almost certain), frequencies, or probabilities.[36]

In general, there are two main approaches to estimating likelihood: Based on observations of historical trends (past frequency), which may be used to calculate the probability that an event will occur, or based on analytic predictions about expected frequencies. Both approaches confront certain limits, however.

How often a particular threat event has actually occurred within a given time period can be defined as its frequency. Over the long run, the frequency with which an event occurs may be used to estimate its probability, as scientists do, for example, in describing the probability that a dangerous hurricane will occur based on previous observation. For certain types of border threats, analysts may have historical data that allow them to describe such frequencies. In the case of unauthorized migration, for example, CBP and the legacy Immigration and Naturalization Service (INS) have used apprehensions of unauthorized migrants by the Border Patrol as a proxy to estimate unlawful inflows.[37]

Yet deriving probabilities from historical observations is problematic. On a basic level, how exactly should illegal flows be counted? Historical frequencies may focus on illegal incidents—the number of unlawful crossings—or on quantities, such as the number of individual migrants, or pounds (or tons) of illegal drugs or contraband. A given threat such as drug smuggling or illegal migration does not occur with equal frequency along all parts of the border, but varies between the southern vs. northern land and coastal borders, as well as among different portions of the southern border and by mode of entry (e.g. air, land, or sea). More importantly, measures of past frequencies are only of *known* frequencies and not *actual* unlawful immigration flows into the country. For instance, while data from the National Seizure System indicate that over 1.7 million kilograms of illegal drugs were seized along the southern border in 2010, this is not indicative of the total amount of illicit drugs smuggled across the southern border and into the United States for that time period. Estimates of successful unlawful inflows, whether of unlawful individuals, drugs, or something else illegal, are just estimates.

Learning from past history is even more problematic when it comes to rare events like attempted terrorist attacks. Probability models based on historical frequencies are poorly equipped to describe one-in-a-million chances, or to distinguish between chances that are one-in-a-million versus one-in-a-billion or one-in-a-thousand. Especially when combined with the fact the stakes may be high, as in the case of terrorism, rare event probability models may not be sufficiently accurate to generate quantitative predictions about the probability of a future incident. Partly for this reason, the Intelligence Community often describes likelihood in terms of qualitative rather than quantitative ranges, i.e. using words like "remote" or "unlikely."[38] More generally, historical analysis is limited because as the famous phrase goes, "past performance is no guarantee of future results." Changes to the underlying model may invalidate long-term probabilities. Scientists use long-term frequencies to calculate the probability of severe weather, for example; but some people believe that rising temperatures and sea level may have altered climate dynamics so that probability models describing "500 year" floods and "100 year" storms may no longer be accurate. Similarly, some social scientists believe labor market and demographic changes in the United States and migration of countries of origin, along with the decades-long escalation in U.S. border security enforcement, may have fundamentally altered regional immigration dynamics.

## Likelihood as Expected Frequency

An argument can be made that historical frequency, in other words the number of terrorists that potentially traversed the U.S. southern border in 2010, fails to capture the likelihood of certain border threats. Frequency only attempts to measure events that have occurred in the past. But how can the likelihood of a dreaded event such as the smuggling of a weapon of mass destruction into the U.S. be evaluated if it has only a few precedents, or has never occurred and is unprecedented? And even where a track record exists, as with unlawful migration and illegal drugs and other contraband, what can be done to increase the accuracy of estimated probabilities?

The observation of past frequencies may be supplemented with analysis by subject field experts to make more informed predictions about the *expected* frequency of future events. With respect to the threat of terrorism, for example, federal law enforcement and intelligence analysts help estimate the likelihood of a terrorist attack. This involves many factors aside from historical frequency, such as probing and evaluating the motivations of threat actors, their organizational structures, and their capabilities, as well as estimating the impact of broad social, political, or economic forces on these actors. Intelligence analysts and others may look at similar data to estimate the future likelihood of illegal drug flows and other contraband, and social scientists may examine market and social forces to model future migration flows.

A key component in these processes is the development of indicators or milestones to warn of increased likelihood. For example, indicators may be used to evaluate whether a specific terrorist group is coming closer to realizing its plans to smuggle operatives into the United States. In such a scenario, milestones may include evidence of the group's efforts to recruit document forgers or specialists with experience smuggling people into the United States. Ideally, as indicators are met or not met, the chances of an attack are reevaluated and updated. Analysts use established analytical processes to gauge likelihood as new information about the target of study becomes available. Nonetheless, models of the flow of unlawful migrants and goods across borders are also characterized by uncertainty, meaning that analysts never know precisely what data to look for. To be useful as a threat indicator, information must be valid relative to the threat being analyzed. In other words, the information must relate to the actual evolution of the threat. Indicators also should be reliably and consistently observable, and the earlier they are visible in the evolution of a threat, the more valuable they are to decision-makers. Likewise, an indicator's persistence over time allows for its repeated measurement and reevaluation. Finally, the more *visible* and the more *unique* indicators are, the easier it is to use them.[39]

For example, the actual attainment of a particular milestone by a terrorist group, such as the successful recruitment of a document forger, may not be especially *visible* to U.S. intelligence agencies. This makes this data point a poor indicator. In other words, effectively identifying a terrorist group's achievement of an indicator requires the capacity to witness it or obtain evidence of it. The more *unique* an indicator is, the easier it is to identify upon achievement. An indicator may be more consistent with a number of activities, not just the one of interest to intelligence analysts. The recruitment of document forgers may not be a unique indication that a terrorist group will cross the U.S. border, for example. The forger may have been recruited to produce unrelated documents.[40]

### Evaluating Potential Consequences of Border Threats

Any given border threat may result in a range of potential consequences, and policymakers may disagree about how to evaluate them. The process of evaluating consequences includes at least three discrete tasks: Defining the scope of a threat (i.e. the types of consequences), measuring the potential impact, and attaching value to the impact.

### Defining Consequences

DHS defines consequences as "the effect of an incident, event, or occurrence, whether discreet or indirect."[41] The first step in evaluating the potential consequences of a given threat is to define its scope: What type of impact may occur? Many traditional risk assessment methodologies limit their analysis to concrete criteria, including *direct economic costs* and *loss of life*. An advantage to defining consequences narrowly in this way is that both of these criteria are relatively easy to quantify (i.e. in dollars and the absolute number of lives lost), and analysts may make specific predictions about these potential impacts.

An alternative approach considers a wider scope of consequences. In its Strategic National Risk Assessment, for example, DHS identifies six broad categories of potential consequences: *Loss of life, injuries and illness, economic costs, social displacement, psychological distress*, and *environmental impact*.[42] An advantage to adopting this more expansive definition is that, for certain types of threats, these additional consequences may be at least as important as the economic and mortality effects. For instance, terrorist attacks are designed primarily to instill fear, i.e. "terror," in the general populace, and thus considering the psychological aspects of a terrorist attack is certainly an important exercise. On the other hand, psychological and sociological effects such as the impact of unlawful migration on the rule of law, or the ways illegal drugs affect the families and communities of users, also may be far more difficult to define and quantify in a bounded or concrete fashion.

### Measuring Consequences

Once the scope of consequences has been defined, a second challenge is how to measure the potential impact of a given threat. One aspect of the measurement challenge concerns how close in time a given consequence must be to be attributed to a particular security incident. Even when focused on the relatively narrow category of loss of life, for example, consider the following two scenarios:

1. A terrorist is smuggled into the United States and creates and detonates a car bomb; an individual is killed in the blast.

2. A drug trafficker smuggles cocaine into the United States; over several months a client continually uses cocaine supplied by this trafficker and eventually overdoses and dies.

Some may argue that because the ultimate impact of both scenarios is the loss of a single life, they should be deemed to have the same consequence. Others may see that the consequences should be defined differently based on the immediacy of the outcome. Both of these scenarios also may have other types of consequences, including economic impacts, injuries and illnesses, psychological effects etc.

Similar measurement questions exist with respect to geographic boundaries and whether and how to estimate second- and third-degree effects of a given threat versus restricting the analysis to immediate impacts. For example, what are the economic consequences of a transnational retail crime network? Members of this network enter the U.S. and operate in a number of criminal capacities including as boosters and fences (a "booster" is someone who steals merchandise and then sells it to a fence for profit. A "fence" is someone who knowingly buys illegally obtained goods from a booster and then sells the goods for a profit, usually legitimately).[43] Retailers incur direct economic costs from the loss of the pilfered goods, and also may incur second-degree costs from security spending to prevent merchandise loss; and federal and state governments may suffer lost tax revenues. There may be third-degree costs if the criminal network sells the stolen products and uses the proceeds to further additional criminal operations. For instance, federal law enforcement has reputedly traced the illicit proceeds from the theft and resale of infant formula to terrorist organizations and insurgent groups, including Hamas and Hezbollah.[44] Are economic costs limited to the duped retailer, or do they also include the associated costs to public and private security agencies charged with investigating the crimes and related criminal activities?

Analysts disagree about the potential consequences of different types of threats. In the case of unlawful migration, even when the analysis is limited to the narrowest economic question of fiscal impact, estimates of net effects vary by wide margins. The measurement challenge may be substantially greater when it comes to the potential consequences of unknown future threats, which may affect a range of different categories, and for which some of the effects are far more difficult to quantify. Indeed, for certain issues, reasonable people may disagree about the very nature of the consequences: Should the growing prominence of Spanish and other languages in American schools be celebrated as a sign of increasing diversity or feared as a threat to the primacy of English as a national language? The latter often see strategy, threats, and security as a zero-sum, binary proposition whereas the former see a more holistic and shared approach to security, where a "pie" or resources can be indefinitely divided and shared.

## Valuing Consequences

How one evaluates potential consequences also depends on who is making the judgment. For example, a smuggler bringing counterfeit medication into the United States impacts a range of individuals from law enforcement officers charged with detecting and preventing the entry of illegal goods, to individuals consuming the counterfeit drugs, to the legitimate manufacturer. Consumers may place the greatest value on the potential health consequences of consuming the counterfeit product. Legitimate manufacturers may perceive the issue primarily in terms of the economic consequences of their lost sales revenues and repetitional costs.

When considering valuing consequences, the border security challenges in the U.S. can be framed in terms of motive: Some threats arise directly from individuals who wish the U.S. ill, others do not. Terrorists targeting the U.S. seek to cause the country and its inhabitants harm, while drug traffickers exist primarily to derive profit. What is more "threatening"? . . . terrorists who intend to harm U.S. interests, or drug traffickers who intend to earn illicit profits but cause mayhem in the process?[45] In the end, should motive enter into any calculation of consequence among border threats? Are the consequences of an incident greater when they represent the culmination of a concerted effort to attack the U.S.?

Ultimately, how one defines the scope of a given threat and how one weighs the various categories of a threat under consideration are subjective considerations (i.e. human opinion enters into the consideration). There is no "correct" way to value the loss of human life, for example, or the destruction of a particular ecological habitat, or disregard for the rule of law.

## CRITICISM OF BORDER PATROL MILITARIZATION

The change in the Border Patrol's mission and increasing use of military and equipment and military tactics has led many advocates and scholars to criticize the agency for an increasing culture of militarization at the southern border. Critics note that border militarization includes not just the use of tactics, technology, and strategy, but the attendant shift in rhetoric and ideology as well. For instance, the first sentence of the Border Patrol mission statement reads,

> The priority mission of the Border Patrol is preventing terrorists and terrorist weapons, including weapons of mass destruction, from entering the United States.

Critics point out that this contradicts the reality of human rights needs at the border, because under this mission statement Border Patrol agents are trained to treat individuals as military combatants rather than as non-combatant human beings. This militarized nature of border enforcement agencies they note is evident in the profile of many Border Patrol agents as well. For instance, CBP and Border Patrol hiring practices favor veterans, and accordingly over a third of CBP officers have previously served in the military. Critics point out that military culture and strategy, along with sophisticated equipment such as drones, sensors, satellite telemetry, and reconnaissance as well as ever-increasing physical fences and walls creates a permanent, low-intensity war zone similar to the Berlin Wall in Germany during the Cold War.[46]

Criticisms of border control and security are legion and serve as the subject of several textbooks. Lawmakers and advocates on both sides of America's political divide point to border enforcement as a symptom of America's ineffective immigration laws because these laws discourage lawful, temporary immigration while criminalizing need-based unlawful migration. Summary findings from a recent study on border apprehensions and incarcerations presented a reasonably comprehensive list of grievances:

• Since 2005, nearly three quarters of a million people have been prosecuted in federal courts for the crime of unlawful migration: 412,240 for improper entry and 317,916 for unlawful re-entry. This escalating system of migrant

**FIG. 4.19** A pre-existing border wall spans the international boundary between Arizona and Mexico. Expansions of this wall in recent years has concerned non-governmental advocacy organizations.

*Source*: Donna Burton, U.S. Customs and Border Protection, CBP Southwest Border Wall, https://farm9.staticflickr.com/8387/8510182328_53b08a32bf_o_d.jpg.

prosecutions is making a significant and growing contribution to mass incarcerations and to overcrowding in the federal prison system;

- Conservative estimates show that costs entailed by the jail and prison terms that result from criminal prosecutions for unlawful entry and re-entry total at least $7 billion since 2005. A large share of this tax burden produces increased profits for the country's leading private prison corporations;

- Economic circumstances and family responsibilities overwhelmingly drive improper migration, and there is no convincing evidence that apprehension, incarceration, or deportation is a deterrent for people facing these pressures. The resulting human costs to those prosecuted, their families and communities are incalculable; and

- The border control, interdiction, apprehension, and deportation system is not seen as effective by most of the judges and lawyers that participate in the process day in and day out. They say that several Border Patrol operations and the related felony prosecutions are driven by politics, not by good policy.[47]

## Unaccompanied Minor Crisis and Deaths

Lending fire to some of the claims and criticisms above was a surge in unaccompanied minors that occurred in 2014. Between October 2013 and September 2014 the Border Patrol apprehended a staggering 68,541 children (all minors) who arrived in the United States *without a parent*. This was a 77% increased from a year earlier and 330% more than during the same period from 2010–11 (Figure 4.20). The vast majority of the minors came from conflict-ridden Central American countries, notably El Salvador, Guatemala, and Honduras. The Rio Grande Valley portion of the border was the area where most of these minors chose to cross. There was a similar surge of individuals who came with other family members, sometimes complete families and other times with only a few members surviving. In most cases apprehending these children didn't require any pursuit on behalf of the Border Patrol. Many willingly turned themselves into U.S. authorities, in some cases affirmatively seeking them out.[48]

**FIG. 4.20** Data from a Government Accountability Office Report that shows the sharp rise in the number of unaccompanied minors showing up the southern U.S. land border in recent times.

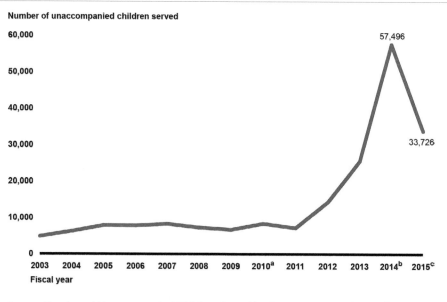

*Source*: Number of Unaccompanied Children Served by ORR 2003–2015, https://farm2.staticflickr.com/1571/25763208021_406839f761_o_d.jpg.

A number of these unaccompanied minors, and other unlawful crossers who aren't minors, often face death as they seek to avoid capture while crossing. The land of the southern border is a harsh, dry, and mostly unpopulated desert and dehydration is the by far the largest killer of unlawful migrants. The Border Patrol reported finding 115 remains of migrants in the Rio Grande Valley in 2014 alone. Generally, the contemporary ratio is one death for approximately every 2,000 crossers who are apprehended. Beyond safety issues for the undocumented who are crossing, recovering and processing migrant remains also increases law enforcement costs for the small local towns that sit at the border.

Several studies confirm that those who choose to illegally cross the southern border do so because they either have no option to legally cross or because their options entail waiting several years for paperwork to process for legal entry into the United States. Thus, unlawful crossers make the decision to cross illegally with the belief that the danger that lies ahead of them (i.e. crossing the border, risking possible death, and possible apprehension) is less than the danger that lies behind, where they live.[49] Unlawful border crossers are also often the poor from various nations, but especially the poor from the poorest nations.

## SIDEBAR 4.4 State and Local Roles in Border Security

Several dozen U.S. states share a land border with either Canada or Mexico. Though border security and immigration enforcement are federal responsibilities, states and local municipalities are nonetheless affected by changing border security policy as well as the lawful and unlawful flow of people and goods across the U.S. land borders. In some cases, when states have found federal immigration enforcement efforts lacking, they have taken it upon themselves to enforce or mediate federal immigration law.

For instance, in 2010, Arizona passed Arizona SB 1070 (the Support Our Law Enforcement and Safe Neighborhoods Act). SB 1070, which is still on the books today, made it a misdemeanor crime for any unlawful, undocumented immigration to be in Arizona while not carrying registration documents (as required by federal law). SB 1070 also authorized state and local law enforcement in Arizona, such as local sheriffs' departments, to carry out federal immigration laws and set forth state penalties for those found to be harboring undocumented immigrants in violation of federal law. In effect, the law proposed its own set of state penalties for the violation of pre-existing federal immigration law.

The law drew significant protest, and eventually a challenge from the federal government that made its way to the Supreme Court. In 2011, the Supreme Court struck down three out of the law's four main provisions. The three provisions struck down: Required legal immigrants to carry registration documents at all times, allowed state police to arrest any individual for suspicion of being an undocumented immigrant, and made it a crime for an undocumented immigrant to search for a job (or to hold one) in the state. All Supreme Court justices agreed to uphold the provision of the law allowing Arizona state police to investigate the immigration status of an individual stopped, detained, or arrested if there is reasonable suspicion that individual is in the country illegally.

## CONCLUSION

Understanding the nuanced security issues posed by the flow of people and goods across U.S. borders is fundamental to shaping effective policy. If this chapter (and the text as a whole) indicates anything it is that there is no objectively correct way to evaluate the relative importance of threats at U.S. borders. Nonetheless, the complexity and subjectivity of border threats and their assessment does not diminish the importance of *some form* of threat assessment by state, local, and federal governments. While the border is a critical nexus for the flow of people and goods, as the Sidebar on the "100 Mile Border" indicates, the strategic breadth of border threats and policy responses extends well beyond the border region.

## HOMELAND SECURITY VOICES: Janet Napolitano

*Janet Napolitano currently serves as the President of the University of California System. Prior to her current post, she was the third Secretary of Homeland Security from 2009 until 2013 under President Barack Obama. She came to DHS after serving as the 21st Governor of Arizona and prior to that the Attorney General of Arizona, the first woman to hold all four positions mentioned here.*

**A perennial issue that arises concerns the way DHS deals with Congress. Particularly, with congressional oversight and how fragmented it is. Why do you think that is the case? What can be done to ease the burden on the Executive Branch and departmental leadership?**

JN: There is a role for Congressional oversight for any executive agency. The problem with DHS is that there is both too much and too little. Too many committees and subcommittees exercise jurisdiction over the department. The members of those subcommittees, and in particular their staff, do not really have a good strategic overview of the department and all of its myriad activities. The problem is that these staffers think their issue is the top, and only issue, for the department. However, DHS has many missions, all of which require multi-tasking at any particular moment in time.

**FIG. 4.21**

Janet Napolitano served as the third Secretary of the Department of Homeland Security and is currently the President of the University of California system.

*Source*: Dep't of Homeland Security, Janet Napolitano, Former Secretary of Homeland Security, https://upload.wikimedia.org/wikipedia/commons/f/f1/Janet_Napolitano_official_portrait.jpg.

During my time as DHS Secretary, I testified more than 55 times before Congress. Preparation for testimony alone takes a great deal of time. It requires preparation of a written statement, which requires staff time, the Secretary has to approve it, and the OMB (Office of Management and Budget) has final approval. Sometimes the deadlines were very unrealistic, reflecting the viewpoint that subcommittees should get priority over everything else.

Now the exceptions are the two authorizing committees in the House and Senate, as well as the appropriations subcommittees see the whole department. Those hearings were very wide ranging and could cover any topic and they provided useful oversight for the Congress and the public. Everything else was surplus. They took more resources than was beneficial.

Oversight is set up the way it is partially because it goes to issues of "turf" in the Congress that is zealously protected by the committees and subcommittees. Those battles were not solved in the haste to build DHS. Congress, particularly the House, has not had the leadership or will to address this issue even though every Secretary (of DHS) and others who know about the department have all said that the oversight is too much and needs to be reformed.

*The silo problem, especially pre-9/11, is partially the reason why DHS was formed. There were information sharing problems within the intelligence and national security community. Do you think DHS has alleviated some of those concerns? If so, what else can DHS do to diminish this problem?*

JN: In terms of DHS' creation, information sharing, particularly with respect to terrorism and counterterrorism, has improved. Mainly due to the National Counterterrorism Center (NCTC) and to some degree with the CIA. We have made some great strides in information sharing, although somewhat less so with the FBI. Part of that is because the country and the Executive Branch is working out who has primary jurisdiction over what, and the need to establish common depositories for information.

*What do you see as DHS' role in the larger Executive Branch and the government overall? The department has had a bit of a tortured path, and sometimes DHS is not seen by other agencies as an important or relevant agency. Do you think that is changing? What do you see the role of DHS going forward?*

JN: DHS plays a critical role in very different areas. Obviously, it dominates the immigration and border security portfolios. The DOJ (Department of Justice) has some role, but immigration has never been a prioritized interest. Disaster management and response has also been handed to DHS. Having both FEMA and the Coast Guard under one roof helps in that regard, although Congress may not have done that intentionally. Cybersecurity is a growing problem and the department needs to develop its capacity. Cybersecurity is too fragmented in the Executive Branch. The NSA, FBI, and DHS all have large roles in cybersecurity, but exactly who has the lead and how information is shared is still an evolving topic. On the counterterrorism side, there exist a myriad of different players, so Congress was not able to locate all of that in one place.

*Do you think it makes DHS' work more challenging, particularly for counterterrorism, to intercept and investigate lone wolf actors and terrorists, such as the Boston Marathon bombers?*

JN: In hindsight, I do not think the Boston Marathon bombing could have been prevented under any reasonable law enforcement or intelligence sharing protocol absent Russia giving us more information about the brothers, particularly them traveling in Russia. Lone wolves, by their very nature, are almost impossible to detect and prevent. The challenge is the ability for immediate response and communities to be resilient in the face of a lone wolf episode. For example, the University of California, Santa Barbara had a lone wolf type incident with a mentally ill individual going on a shooting rampage. Could that have been prevented? Possibly if he was institutionalized, but absent that, you do not have law enforcement resources to watch everyone who may be capable of a lone wolf attack even if you know someone who might fit the personality to do such a thing.

*You brought up the concept of resiliency. Resiliency is often a hard concept to explain. How would you explain it to someone not familiar with it?*

JN: Basically, it is the ability to take a punch and get right back up again.

*What does that look like in terms of DHS' work?*

JN: It depends. It is seen more frequently in the disaster response area. It is the ability to restore infrastructure and get people basic necessities first (power, food, water, healthcare), and then get the community operating again as quickly as possible. The most difficult type of situation is when you have a huge event like Hurricane Sandy where multiple communities are affected and thousands of people needing help simultaneously.

*Turning to a more controversial topic—immigration. The United States has been dealing with the issue of unaccompanied minors for the last several months. In a recent interview you mentioned that DHS was criticized quite a bit about the number of deportations and removals over the past several years, but you stated that those criticizing DHS did not look at the whole picture under the Obama Administration. What would you want them to consider? What is the whole picture?*

JN: The average annual deportation number is 400,000. This number needs to be broken down into who is in that number. One of the changes under the Obama Administration was to move more ICE agents to border communities, and to initiate a process where Border Patrol would pick up border crossers and hand them to ICE for placement into removal proceedings. Therefore, the 400,000 includes those apprehended at the border and put into proceedings. That was not happening before my tenure as DHS Secretary. I believe people criticizing that number have a paradigm in mind that those people being deported have been here for decades with established families and jobs.

Long-term undocumented people are an infinitesimal part of those who are deported. The deportees include those apprehended at the border, those with criminal records, or those who are apprehended in the context of committing another crime and law enforcement then turns them over to be removed from the country. You do not hear arguments concerning those categories. The next largest category are repeat immigration violators. Under the Obama Administration we stopped business raids and made more concerted efforts to sanction employers who continually hired a lot of undocumented. We really tried to shift the administration more toward border violators, criminal offenders, and repeat offenders.

*It's almost like you shouldn't have to do all that work. A lot of this is being done because Congress isn't doing the work they need to.*

JN: That is correct. It is very difficult to tell an ICE agent whose job it is to enforce the immigration law to turn their back on people they come across in the country illegally. But, that is what needs to happen when you set priorities. It is not dissimilar to the DOJ setting prosecution priorities, and the Attorney General stating they will not prosecute low-level drug offenders anymore. That happens because no law enforcement agency has infinite resources. You have to have priorities, so for the first time we instituted new priorities into the immigration enforcement mechanism.

Additionally, another thing people overlook is that under the previous administration Congress had greatly increased the number of ICE and Border Patrol agents. So frankly you have more officers in the field than you did in the past. Under Obama for the first time we had priorities and for the first time we included and had a process for border crossers who were turned over to ICE and put into removal proceedings.

We were criticized by immigration advocates for the number of deportees, although in Washington, D.C., a number of those advocate leaders know what is behind the number. However, that is not helpful to these advocates in terms of mobilizing their base. At the same time, we got criticized by members of Congress as well, particularly by Republican members, that we were not enforcing the law. But that is immigration. That happens when you have a system that no longer matches reality, our economic needs, nor our moral values.

## KEYWORDS

- **territorial integrity**: Is a principle of international law that allows for nations to secure their borders against unwanted excursion and also prohibits other nations from using force to diminish the territory or political independence or another nation.

- **customs**: Usually refers to the inherent authority of a nation to control the flow of goods and people across its borders, including but not limited to the ability to monitor and tax this flow (tariffs); often also used to refer to the name of the government agency that exercises this authority.

- **goods**: Goods are non-person things, or materials that satisfy human wants and needs and provide some utility. When entering the U.S. individuals and companies must "declare" goods being brought into the country to CBP.

- **operational control**: Defined by the Border Patrol as the ability to detect, respond to, and interdict border intrusions in areas deemed as high priority for threat potential or other national security objectives, through varied deployment combinations of personnel, technology, and infrastructure.

- **likelihood**: The chance of something happening, whether defined, measured, or estimated objectively or subjectively, or in terms of general descriptors (such as rare, unlikely, likely, almost certain), frequencies, or probabilities.

- **Sanctuary Cities**: Cities and counties in the U.S. that limit their cooperation with federal immigration enforcement agencies such as CBP and ICE.

---

**KNOWLEDGE CHECK**

1. How have U.S. border security policies changed since the founding of the nation? Over the last 100 years?
2. What are the differences between transnational criminals and terrorists?
3. What government agency is responsible for securing the U.S. land, air, and sea border? What are its component parts?

---

## NOTES

1. Patrick Ettinger, Imaginary Lines: Border Enforcement and the Origins of Undocumented Immigration, 1882–1930 99–100 (2009).
2. Kelly Lytle Hernández, Migra! A History of the U.S. Border Patrol (2010).
3. Robert D. Schroeder, Holding the Line in the 21st Century, U.S. Customs and Border Protection, at 3 www.cbp.gov/sites/default/files/documents/Holding%20the%20Line_TRILOGY.pdf.
4. *Playbook Breakfast: 10th anniversary of DHS*, POLITICO (accessed Aug. 7, 2013) www.politico.com/gallery/playbook-breakfast-10th-anniversary-of-dhs?slide=0.
5. Judith A. Greene, Bethany Carson, & Andrea Black, *Indefensible: A decade of mass incarceration of migrants prosecuted for crossing the border* (2016) http://grassrootsleadership.org/sites/default/files/reports/indefensible_book_web.pdf.
6. David W. Garland, The Culture of Control: Crime and Social Order in Contemporary Society (2001).
7. *The Constitution in the 100-Mile Border Zone*, ACLU (last visited Dec. 27, 2018) www.aclu.org/other/constitution-100-mile-border-zone?redirect=immigrants-rights/constitution-100-mile-border-zone.
8. *Id.*
9. *Detroit Sector Michigan*, U.S. CUSTOMS AND BORDER PROTECTION (Nov. 28, 2016) www.cbp.gov/border-security/along-us-borders/border-patrol-sectors/detroit-sector-selfridge-angb-michigan.
10. Adapted from *Detroit Sector Michigan*, U.S. CUSTOMS AND BORDER PROTECTION (Nov. 28, 2016) www.cbp.gov/border-security/along-us-borders/border-patrol-sectors/detroit-sector-selfridge-angb-michigan.

11. Vox, *How sanctuary cities actually work*, Youtube (Apr. 25, 2017) www.youtube.com/watch?v =XaR5kR8h4es&feature=youtu.be.

12. Adapted from *Canine Program*, U.S. Customs and Border Patrol (June 3, 2014) www.cbp.gov/ border-security/along-us-borders/canine-program.

13 *Domestic General Aviation Law Enforcement Operations*, U.S. Customs and Border Protection, at 6 (Oct. 1, 2014) www.cbp.gov/sites/default/files/documents/Top%20Down%20Review%20 GA_09302014a.pdf.

14. Portions of this and following sections are adapted with permission from the Congressional Research Service's report entitled *Border Security: Understanding Threats at U.S. Borders* by Marc R. Rosenblum, Jerome P. Bjelopera, and Kristin M. Finklea, No. 7–5700, R42969, released February 2013.

15. *CBPs 2011 Fiscal Year in Review*, U.S. Customs and Border Protection (CBP) (Dec. 12, 2011). Cargo flows through U.S. ports (imports plus exports) was valued at $3.7 trillion in 2011, about 25% of U.S. gross domestic product (GDP); and international tourism to the United States (exports) was valued at $134 billion in 2010, about 1% of GDP. *See* Brock R. Williams and J. Michael Donnelly, Cong. Research Serv., RL33577, U.S. International Trade: Trends and Forecasts (2012); *see also* Suzanne M. Kirchhoff, Cong. Research Serv., R41409, U.S. Travel and Tourism Industry.

16. *Quadrennial Homeland Security Review Report: A Strategic Framework for a Secure Homeland*, U.S. Dep't of Homeland Security, at 26 (2010).

17. *Risk Management Fundamentals: Homeland Security Risk Management Doctrine*, Dep't of Homeland Security, at 7 (2011).

18. Marc R. Rosenblum, Jerome P. Bjelopera, and Kristin M. Finklea, Cong. Research Serv., R42969, Border Security: Understanding Threats at U.S. Borders, at 4 (Feb. 21, 2013) available at www.hsdl.org/?view&did=731927.

19. See U.S. Department of Justice, National Drug Intelligence Center, National Drug Threat Assessment 2011, pp. 13–16, www.justice.gov/ndic/pubs44/44849/44849p.pdf.

20. U.S.C.A. § 1182(a)(3)(B)(i) (2018).

21. Louise Richardson, What Terrorists Want: Understanding the Enemy, Containing the Threat 16 (2007).

22. U.S.C.A. § 1182(a)(3)(B)(iii).

23. *Id.*

24. Klaus von Lampe, *Reconceptualizing Transnational Organized Crime: Offenders as Problem Solvers*, 2 Int'l J. of Security and Terrorism 11 (2011).

25. *See* Moises Naim, *Mafia States: Organized Crime Takes Office*, 91 Foreign Affairs 100–111 (May/ June 2012).

26. U.S.C.A. § 1182(a)(1)-(7).

27. Research by the Congressional Research Service, from which this section adapts much of its content, suggests that criminality rates among the foreign-born U.S. population likely is no more than, and perhaps even lower than, rates among the native-born U.S. population. *See*

Marc R. Rosenblum and William A. Kandel, Cong. Research. Serv., R42057, Interior Immigration Enforcement: Programs Targeting Criminal Aliens.

28. Phil Williams, Terrorism, *Organized Crime and WMD Smuggling: Challenge and Response,* 6 Strategic Insights (Aug. 2007).

29. *On a Typical Day in Fiscal Year 2011,* U.S. Customs and Border Protection (Mar. 7, 2012).

30. *Intellectual Property Rights Fact Sheet,* U.S. Customs and Border Protection.

31. Legislative Committee Report, Michigan Liquor Control Commission, Illegal Importation of Alcohol Into Michigan: An Assessment of the Issue and Recommendations (Jan. 15, 2008).

32. William Booth and Nick Miroff, *Stepped-up efforts by U.S., Mexico Fail to Stem Flow of Drug Money South,* Washington Post (Aug. 25, 2010).

33. David E Longnecker & Ricardo A. Molins. A Risk Reduction Strategy for Human Exploration of Space A Review of NASA's Bioastronautics Roadmap (2006).

34. Jennifer E. Lake, Cong. Research Serv., R41189, Homeland Security Dep't: FY2011 Appropriations (Dec. 23, 2010) available at https://fas.org/sgp/crs/homesec/R41189.pdf.

35. Robert D. Schroeder, Holding the Line in the 21st Century, U.S. Customs and Border Protection, at 12, available at www.cbp.gov/sites/default/files/documents/Holding%20the%20Line_TRILOGY.pdf.

36. Risk Lexicon, U.S. Dep't of Homeland Security 20 (2010) available at www.dhs.gov/sites/default/files/publications/dhs-risk-lexicon-2010_0.pdf.

37. *See e.g.,* Options for Estimating Illegal Entries at the U.S.-Mexico Border, National Research Council (Alicia Carriquiry & Malay Majmundar, eds., 2013) www.nap.edu/initiative/panel-on-survey-options-for-estimating-the-flow-of-unauthorized-crossings-at-the-us-mexico-border.

38. Risk Lexicon, U.S. Dep't of Homeland Security 20 (2010) available at www.dhs.gov/sites/default/files/publications/dhs-risk-lexicon-2010_0.pdf.

39. Richards J. Heuer, Jr. & Randolph H. Pherson, Structured Analytic Techniques for Intelligence Analysis 136 (2011).

40. Gregory Treverton, Intelligence for an Age of Terror 42–45 (2011). Indicators described above are predictive and are typically used in intelligence analysis. Law enforcement often also uses backward-looking descriptive indicators "to assess whether a target's . . . behavior is consistent with an established pattern." *See* Richards J. Heuer Jr. & Randolph H. Pherson, Structured Analytic Techniques for Intelligence Analysis 132 (2011).

41. Risk Lexicon, U.S. Dep't of Homeland Security 10 (2010) available at www.dhs.gov/sites/default/files/publications/dhs-risk-lexicon-2010_0.pdf.

42. The Strategic National Risk Assessment in Support of PPD 8: A Comprehensive Risk-Based Approach Toward a Secure and Resilient Nation, U.S. Dep't of Homeland Security, at 5 (2011) www.dhs.gov/xlibrary/assets/rma-strategic-national-risk-assessment-ppd8.pdf.

43. *See* Kristin M. Finklea, Cong. Research Serv., R41118, Organized Retail Crime (Jun. 16, 2010) www.hsdl.org/?view&did=22210.

44. *See* Charles I. Miller, Organized Retail Theft: Raising Awareness, Offering Solutions, National Retail Federation Foundation 4 (2005). *See also Media Reports—Middle East Connection: Organized Retail Crime*, Food Marketing Institute, www.fmi.org/docs/loss/ORCMiddleEast.pdf; Combating Organized Retail Crime: The Role of Federal Law Enforcement, H. Comm. on the Judiciary, Subcommittee on Crime, Terrorism, and Homeland Security, 111th Cong., 1, (Nov. 5, 2009) (testimony by David Johnson, Section Chief, Criminal Investigative Division Federal Bureau of Investigation).

45. The argument can be made that intent is irrelevant; both terrorists and drug traffickers harm U.S. interests and public safety, and drug traffickers perhaps even more given their longer term and more widespread impact on health, psychological well-being, and the economy.

46. Todd Miller, *The US-Mexico Border: Where the Constitution goes to Die*, MOTHER JONES (July 15, 2014) www.motherjones.com/politics/2014/07/shena-gutierrez-us-mexico-border-constitution-die/.

47. Judith A. Greene, Bethany Carson, & Andrea Black, *Indefensible: A decade of mass incarceration of migrants prosecuted for crossing the border* (2016) http://grassrootsleadership.org/sites/default/files/reports/indefensible_book_web.pdf.

48. Adam Isacson & Maureen Meyer, ON THE FRONT LINES: BORDER SECURITY, MIGRATION AND HUMANITARIAN CONCERNS IN SOUTH TEXAS, at 6 (Feb. 2015) www.nnirr.org/drupal/sites/default/files/onthefrontlines.pdf.

49. Tanya Maria Golash-Boza, Deported: Policing Immigrants, Disposable Labor and Global Capitalism 61–62 (2015).

# CHAPTER 5

# *Intelligence*

---

**IN THIS CHAPTER YOU WILL LEARN ABOUT**

How intelligence information is gathered, analyzed, and transformed into intelligence products.

The "Intelligence Community," its constituent members, and how they work together.

The role of Congress, advocacy groups, and others in providing intelligence gathering oversight.

---

## INTRODUCTION

Government agencies rely on intelligence to identify emerging threats, prioritize security, and defense efforts, and inform their operations. Intelligence gathering, analysis, and dissemination is done by a number of government organizations, collectively known as the Intelligence Community (IC). The IC is an essential element in the homeland and national security mission. With a collection of 17 member agencies from throughout the U.S. federal government, the IC gathers a range of information to develop intelligence products that inform the decisions of policymakers, legislators, agency leaders, and partners at all levels of government. This chapter reviews how actionable intelligence is produced, which government bodies produce it, and the various legislative elements that authorize and provide oversight to IC activities.

Since the September 11 attacks, intelligence gathering has played an important role in transforming the national security state. As the need for information about terrorists and criminals has risen, so too has the technology to track, detect, and deter bad actors. Ever-increasing Internet use, as well as the rise of robust social media platforms, has transformed how people around the world share information. Intelligence agencies increasingly rely on the information generated on these platforms to inform senior elected leaders about emerging threats to the homeland.

The government's growing information gathering capability has alarmed civil liberties advocates in the United States. Whistleblowers, such as Edward Snowden, have leaked classified information as part of a desire to inform the American public about intelligence gathering and analysis operations that target the American people, in addition to foreign powers. As the threats from transnational and domestic terrorism increase and evolve, considerations for how best to gather intelligence, while at the same preserving Americans' civil rights and civil liberties, will be an increasingly important and increasingly debated element of the homeland security enterprise.

*Relationship & balance between intel & civil liberties*

## THE INTELLIGENCE CYCLE

Working in concert under the applicable laws and with oversight from two branches of government, the IC collects and collates intelligence, creates intelligence products, and disseminates this information to a range of individuals and organizations. This process of collection, creation, and dissemination is broadly referred to as the intelligence cycle or **intelligence process**. The process converts acquired information into clear, comprehensible intelligence and delivers it to the President, policymakers, and military commanders in a form they can use to make educated decisions.

The process begins by identifying issues in which policymakers are interested and defining the information required to make decisions on those issues. The relevant members of the IC then create a plan for acquiring the intelligence information and proceed to collect it. From the raw intelligence, agencies conduct analyze the information, weigh its relevance to the questions at hand, and prepare summary reports and recommendations (often called "intelligence products") to be delivered to national security policymakers. The answers that intelligence products supply can reveal other areas of

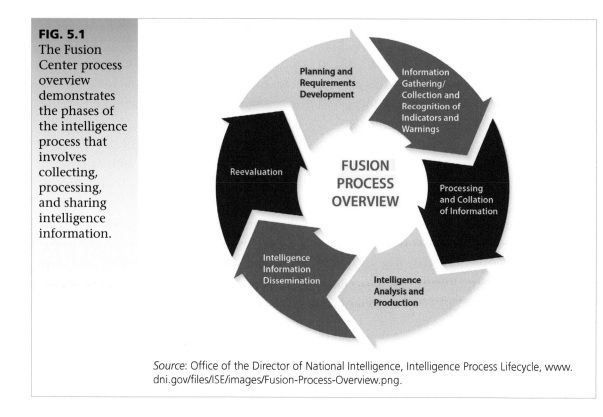

**FIG. 5.1**
The Fusion Center process overview demonstrates the phases of the intelligence process that involves collecting, processing, and sharing intelligence information.

*Source*: Office of the Director of National Intelligence, Intelligence Process Lifecycle, www.dni.gov/files/ISE/images/Fusion-Process-Overview.png.

concern or interest, leading to more questions and intelligence demands. In this way, the end of one cycle often leads to the beginning of another.[1]

Each stage of the intelligence cycle moves towards delivering answers to targeted questions and requires the participation of multiple government authorities.

### Stage 1: Planning and Direction/Management

During this management phase, the IC determines which issues need to be addressed and what information must be gathered to provide the proper answers. Policymakers, including the President, his or her aides, the National Security Council, and other government departments and agencies initiate requests for intelligence based on their areas of concern. Issue coordinators from the IC interact with these public officials to clarify their core concerns and related information requirements. These needs guide collection strategies and allow the IC to produce the appropriate intelligence products.[2]

## Stage 2: Collection

The intelligence gathering strategy is executed, and the IC acquires raw information through activities such as interviews, technical and physical surveillance, human source operation, searches, and liaison relationships. Information can be gathered from open, covert, electronic, and satellite sources.[3] There are several methods of intelligence collection, including:

- *Signals Intelligence (SIGINT)* the interception of signals, whether between people, machines, or a combination of both.
- *Imagery Intelligence (IMINT)* refers to the representations of objects reproduced electronically or by optical means on film, electronic display devices, or other media. It can be derived from visual photography, radar sensors, infrared sensors, lasers, and electro-optics.
- *Measurement and Signature Intelligence (MASINT)* refers to the scientific and technical intelligence information used to locate, identify, or describe distinctive characteristics of specific targets. MASINT employs a broad group of disciplines, including nuclear, optical, radio frequency, acoustics, seismic, and materials sciences. For example, MASINT can identify distinctive radar signatures created by specific aircraft systems or the chemical composition of air and water samples.
- *Human-Source Intelligence (HUMINT)* refers to intelligence derived from people. Collection includes clandestine acquisition of photography, documents, and other material; overt collection by personnel in diplomatic and consular posts; debriefing of foreign nationals and U.S. citizens who travel abroad; and official contacts with foreign governments. To the public, HUMINT is synonymous with espionage and clandestine activities. However, most of HUMINT is accumulated by overt collectors, such as diplomats and military attaches.
- *Open-Source Intelligence (OSINT)* is publicly available information appearing in print or electronic form, including radio, television, newspapers, journals, the Internet, commercial databases, videos, graphics, and drawings.

- *Geospatial Intelligence (GEOINT)* is the collection and creation of imagery and mapping data produced through an integration of imagery, imagery intelligence, and geospatial information. GEOINT is typically gathered from commercial satellites, government satellites, reconnaissance aircraft, or by other means, such as maps, commercial databases, census information, GPS waypoints, utility schematics, or any discrete data that have locations on earth.

## Stage 3: Processing

The collection stage of the intelligence process typically yields large amounts of unfiltered data that requires organization. Substantial U.S. intelligence resources are devoted to the synthesis of this data into a form intelligence analysts can use. Information filtering techniques include exploiting imagery; decoding messages and translating broadcasts; preparing information for

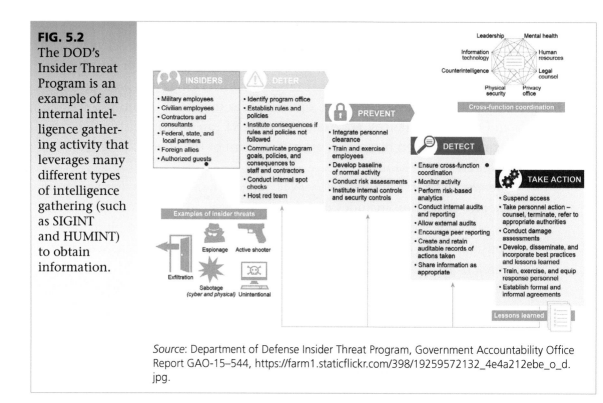

**FIG. 5.2** The DOD's Insider Threat Program is an example of an internal intelligence gathering activity that leverages many different types of intelligence gathering (such as SIGINT and HUMINT) to obtain information.

*Source*: Department of Defense Insider Threat Program, Government Accountability Office Report GAO-15–544, https://farm1.staticflickr.com/398/19259572132_4e4a212ebe_o_d.jpg.

computer processing; storage and retrieval; and placing human-source reports into a form and context to make them more comprehensible.[4]

### Stage 4: Analysis and Production

Once the raw intelligence is converted into basic information, it can be analyzed and turned into documentation that is meaningful and helpful to the requesting government bodies. This includes integrating, evaluating, and analyzing all available data, which is often fragmented and sometimes contradictory. The results of the analysis are then distilled into final intelligence products, which can highlight information on topics of immediate importance or make long-range assessments.

Analysis is conducted by subject-matter specialists in areas like a given culture, region, or technical specialty. These analysts absorb the information, evaluate it, and produce a written assessment of the current state of affairs in a specific area, putting the evaluated information in context. They may also forecast future trends or outcomes. Indeed, analysts are encouraged to include alternative futures in their assessments and look for opportunities to warn about possible developments abroad that could either create threats to or opportunities for U.S. security and policy interests. Analysts also develop requirements for collection of new information.[5]

### Stage 5: Dissemination

When information has been reviewed and correlated with data from other available sources, it is called **finished intelligence**. This is disseminated directly to the policymakers whose needs generated the intelligence requirement. Finished intelligence is hand-carried to the President and key national security advisers on a daily basis.[6]

### SIDEBAR 5.1 Classifying Intelligence

The current system of classifying information was created by the Obama Administration's 2009 Executive Order 13526, which augmented previous

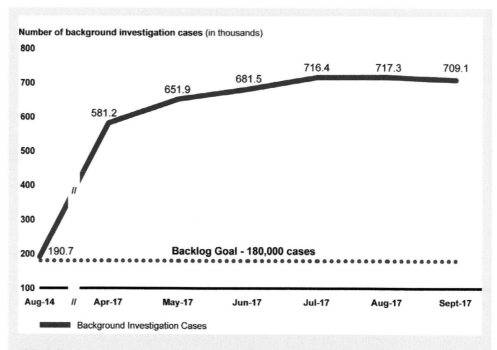

**Number of background investigation cases** (in thousands)

**FIG. 5.3**

The government's security clearance process for employees is meant to identify individuals with criminal histories or other questionable behavior before they receive access to classified information. However, government agencies aren't able to investigate and process these security clearances in a timely manner—and, consequently, have fallen way behind. As of September 2017, there were more than 709,000 incomplete background investigations for federal employees and contractors.

*Source*: Government Security Clearance Backlog, U.S. Government Accountability Office Report GAO 18–29, https://blog.gao.gov/2018/01/25/governments-security-clearance-process-is-high-risk/.

orders.[7] There are three levels of information sensitivity, determined based on the degree of harm that would be caused to U.S. national security if the information were disclosed:

- Top Secret—The highest level of classification. This is information that if disclosed could "cause exceptionally grave damage to national security that the original classification authority is able to identify or describe."
- Secret—Information that if disclosed could cause "serious damage."
- Confidential—Information that could cause "damage."

Some documents, while unclassified, may still require limited dissemination for security reasons and can be marked Sensitive but Unclassified (SBU), with additional designations denoting the limited group for which the information is intended. Common examples include: "Unclassified-For Official Use Only" (U//FOUO), often exempting a document from Freedom of Information Act (FOIA) requests; "Sensitive Security Information" (SSI), which refers to information obtained through security activities, such as airport screening; and Law Enforcement Sensitive (LES), intended for the law enforcement community.

Increasing levels of sensitivity require increasing levels of authority to make the classification. Only the President, the Vice President, or an agency head can designate a document "Top Secret." By Executive Order, information cannot be classified so as to conceal illegality, inefficiency, or administrative error; prevent embarrassment; restrain competition; or "prevent or delay the release of information that does not require protection in the interest of the national security."[8]

There are several kinds of finished intelligence products.

- *Current intelligence products* address day-to-day events, detailing new developments and providing related background to assess the significance of current events, warn of their near-term consequences, and signal potentially dangerous situations in the near future.
- *Estimative intelligence products* look ahead to assess potential developments that could affect U.S. national security in the future. By discussing the implications of a range of possible outcomes and alternative scenarios, estimative intelligence helps policymakers think strategically about long-term threats.
- *Warning intelligence products* serve as an alarm or give notice to policymakers about impending threats that may require policy action. Warning intelligence includes identifying or forecasting events that could cause the engagement of U.S. military forces or highlighting those events that would have a sudden and detrimental effect on U.S. foreign policy concerns (e.g. political coups, third-party wars, refugee situations). This kind of product often involves exploring alternative futures and low probability/high impact scenarios.

- *Scientific and Technical (S&T) intelligence products* examine the technical development, characteristics, performance, and capabilities of foreign technologies, including weapon systems or subsystems. S&T intelligence covers a complete spectrum of sciences, technologies, weapon systems, and integrated operations.
- *Supporting current and estimative intelligence products* are research intelligence products, which can be divided into two specialized subcategories: Basic intelligence and intelligence for operational support. Basic intelligence primarily consists of the structured collection of geographic, demographic, social, military, and political data on foreign countries. The publicly available CIA World Factbook is a well-known declassified example of this kind of finished intelligence product (Figure 5.4).[9] Intelligence for operational support is tailored, focused, and rapidly produced intelligence for planners and operators that incorporates all types of intelligence production (i.e. current, estimative, warning, research, and S&T).

**FIG. 5.4**
The CIA World Factbook is an example of a declassified finished intelligence product available for free use online and in print.

*Source:* Ehsan Zaffar, CIA World Factbook.

## INTELLIGENCE COMMUNITY MEMBERSHIP

Intelligence is produced by the IC, a coalition of 17 agencies and organizations within the Executive Branch that hold intelligence gathering and analysis responsibilities (Figure 5.5). The IC's primary mission is to collect and convey the information the President and members of the policymaking, law enforcement, and military communities require to execute their appointed duties. All IC members share this mission but operate under their own specific and distinct directives.

IC member agencies collect and assess information regarding international terrorist and narcotic activities; hostile activities by foreign powers, organizations, people, and their agents; and foreign intelligence activities directed

**FIG. 5.5**
The Intelligence Community is made up of several dozen intelligence agencies that all report to the Office of the Director of National Intelligence.

*Source*: Members of the U.S. Intelligence Community, Office of the Director of National Intelligence, www.dni.gov/files/documents/USNI%202013%20Overview_web.pdf.

against the United States. As needed, the President may also direct the IC to carry out special activities to protect U.S. security interests against foreign threats.

While all IC member agencies participate in intelligence gathering activities, some play a more regular, prominent role in supporting homeland security.

## Office of the Director of National Intelligence

The Office of the Director of National Intelligence (ODNI) is a federal office tasked with coordinating, parsing, and integrating the IC's intelligence gathering and analysis activities. ODNI directs and manages the actions of the IC and its constituent agencies to ensure the rapid dissemination of intelligence, as appropriate, to the entire community. As such, ODNI primarily employs subject matter experts in the areas of collection, analysis, acquisition, policy, human resources, and management.[10]

The Director of National Intelligence (DNI) is the head of the IC, overseeing and directing the implementation of the National Intelligence Program and acting as the principal advisor to the President, the National Security Council, and the Homeland Security Council for intelligence matters related to national security. Working together with the Principal Deputy DNI, and with the assistance of Mission Managers and Deputy Directors, the ODNI's goal is to integrate foreign, military, and domestic intelligence in defense of the homeland and of U.S. interests abroad.[11] Many IC organization department heads report in some way to the DNI, who in turn reports directly to the President.

The ODNI is a more recent addition to the IC. Before 9/11, the Director of the Central Intelligence Agency (CIA) served as the director of the IC. As discussed in Chapter 2, the National Commission on Terrorist Attacks Upon the United States (the "9/11 Commission") found that major adjustments were needed to coordinate and optimize the U.S. intelligence apparatus. Notably, the 9/11 Commission found that the CIA Director was so burdened with the task of running the agency that he had insufficient time to coordinate the actions of the other intelligence agencies. Furthermore, the 9/11 Commission uncovered that before 9/11, members of the IC routinely refused to share

FIG. 5.6
ODNI interns created this poster, playing on myths that the IC is secretly holding aliens, to promote ODNI's new transparency efforts.

*Source*: Aliens Aren't Being Held Hostage by the Intelligence Community, Office of the Director of National Intelligence, www.intelligence.gov/images/careers/intern-poster.jpg.

information between agencies, even though the information in their possession, if shared, may have helped prevent future terrorist attacks.[12] This resistance to interagency collaboration is often called the "silo effect," with agencies operating independently of one another in unconnected "silos." This mentality can frustrate information sharing with colleagues from other intelligence agencies and law enforcement organizations.

Based on the recommendations in the 9/11 Commission Report, the House and Senate passed bills with major amendments to the National Security Act of 1947. Intense negotiations to reconcile the two bills ultimately led to the Intelligence Reform and Terrorism Prevention Act of 2004 (IRTPA), which established the ODNI.[13] To carry out its duties, the ODNI has been given significant statutory powers. For instance, the ODNI develops and executes the annual IC budget and transfers staff and other resources among the IC as it sees fit.[14]

ODNI is divided into four primary directorates:

- *Enterprise Capacity (EC)*: This directorate focuses the IC's resources, workforce, systems, technology, and infrastructure to obtain results as needed by senior policymakers. It is the logistical programming office of the IC.
- *Mission Integration (MI)*: This directorate delivers strategic intelligence and distinctive insights and helps to allocate various categories of intelligence (HUMINT, SIGINT, etc.).
- *National Security Partnerships (NSP)*: This directorate optimizes ODNI's extensive partnerships to "synchronize activities and engagements on whole-of-nation challenges, leveraging the capabilities, information, and expertise from ODNI partners within the agency and beyond."[15]
- *Strategy & Engagement (S&E)*: This directorate sets the strategy and policy framework enabling the IC's ability to "deliver timely, accurate, relevant intelligence, support, and capabilities and stay ahead of opportunities and risks in the IC's complex, challenging, global and technological environment."[16]

## National Security Agency

The National Security Agency/Central Security Services (NSA/CSS, commonly called NSA) is the government agency responsible for collecting and analyzing SIGINT. NSA's mission to gather and analyze SIGINT includes eavesdropping on radio broadcasting and monitoring the Internet, telephone calls, and other forms of communication that can be intercepted. The NSA is also authorized to intercept and monitor sensitive information from foreign government sources.

Executive Order 12333 delineates NSA's roles and responsibilities, which include:[17]

- Through open source and covert methods, collecting, processing, producing, analyzing, and disseminating SIGINT for foreign intelligence and counterintelligence purposes to support national and departmental missions.
- Acting as the National Manager for National Security Systems as established in law and policy, reporting to the Secretary of Defense and to the ODNI.
- Handling and distribution of SIGINT and communications security material within and among the elements under control of the NSA Director, and exercising the necessary supervisory control to ensure compliance with the regulations.

In addition to its intelligence collection and analysis responsibilities, the NSA is also responsible for securing government communication networks, often through the design of specialized hardware and software.[18] Like the CIA, the NSA is legally limited to gathering information from and about foreign sources and is not permitted to conduct domestic intelligence gathering.

In 2013, however, Edward Snowden, a Booz Allen Hamilton contractor working at the NSA's operation center in Hawaii, copied a large amount of classified U.S. and foreign government files and fled to Hong Kong. While there, Snowden began disclosing the classified documents to journalists.

## SIDEBAR 5.2: Edward Snowden and Metadata

Documents leaked by Snowden revealed the existence of the NSA's bulk metadata gathering programs. Put simply, **metadata** is "data about data," or a set of data that describes other data. For instance, metadata can include the time, date, and information about the sender or recipient of a communication. However, metadata does not include the substance of a communication itself, e.g. the content of an email. Snowden's leaks discussed NSA programs with telecommunications companies that collected metadata on every phone call in the United States, including those of American citizens. Another NSA program discussed in the documents leaked by Snowden, called PRISM, purported to collect enormous amounts of metadata from large Internet companies, like Yahoo!, Google, and Microsoft,[19] with some NSA sites allegedly collecting 20 terabytes of data per day.[20]

The NSA Signals Intelligence Directorate uses a variety of computer programs and algorithms to sort through vast amounts of data and identify connections that might reveal terrorist affiliates or activities. For metadata collection on the Internet, however, the NSA has in the past been found by the Foreign Intelligence Surveillance Court (FISC) to have unlawfully collected and analyzed communications between Americans, which is a breach of the Fourth Amendment (i.e. protection against unreasonable searches and seizures). A declassified FISA court ruling revealed that over a three-year period, the NSA unlawfully collected some 56,000 emails.[21]

**FIG. 5.7**
After Edward Snowden leaked classified information regarding the National Security Agency to the press, several entrepreneurs began capitalizing on the controversy. This is an example of a T-shirt owned by one of the author's students that mocks the NSA.

**The NSA**
*The only part of government that actually listens.*

*Source:* Ehsan Zaffar, National Security Agency Parody T-Shirt.

The Snowden documents drove public interest and debate regarding the NSA's data collection activities, ultimately resulting in the passage of the 2015 USA Freedom Act, which, among other things, imposed some limits on the bulk collection of metadata from phone calls made by Americans. For instance, the Freedom Act now bars the NSA from storing the metadata of Americans on its own servers, but it does allow phone and Internet companies to collect and store this bulk metadata themselves. The NSA can then request the data from the telecommunications providers on an as-needed basis using legal means. Critics argue that because the NSA can always obtain this information from phone companies, the Freedom Act does not represent a meaningful check on the NSA's ability to conduct suspicion-less searches. The Freedom Act also does not limit the bulk collection of metadata from the Internet as a general proposition.

## Central Intelligence Agency

The Central Intelligence Agency (CIA) is responsible for the collection and analysis of HUMINT. Created by the National Security Act of 1947, the CIA was successor to, and inspired by, the Office of Strategic Services (OSS), an intelligence agency that operated during World War II (Figure 5.8). William J.

**FIG. 5.8**

Like all government agencies, the CIA was not created overnight and functioning at full capacity the following morning. In fact, there were various renditions of an intelligence agency for six years prior to the formal establishment of the Central Intelligence Agency. At the beginning of World War II America's first peacetime, non-departmental intelligence organization was created. That organization moved and morphed and changed names and ownership, was dissected and dismantled before President Truman signed the National Security Act of 1947 creating a permanent Central Intelligence Agency.

*Source*: CIA's Family Tree, Central Intelligence Agency, www.cia.gov/about-cia/history-of-the-cia/CIA_Family_Tree.png/image.png.

Donovan, the last serving director of the OSS, proposed that President Franklin D. Roosevelt create a new organization directly supervised by the President to:

> procure intelligence both by overt and covert methods and that will at the same time provide intelligence guidance, determine national intelligence objectives, and correlate the intelligence material collected by government agencies, during peace time and times of war.[22]

From his famous recommendation arose the philosophical underpinnings of what the CIA was to become: A central, civilian intelligence agency to operate abroad in secret and sometimes openly, potentially subversively, but never to operate in a law enforcement capacity within the United States.[23] The CIA does not collect intelligence on the activities of U.S. citizens within the country, but its intelligence gathering activities are not geographically constrained and can take place anywhere.

Today, the CIA has three primary responsibilities. First, the agency is responsible for gathering information about foreign governments, individuals, and public and private organizations. Second, the CIA is responsible for analyzing this information and preparing it for dissemination to other government bodies and leaders, including the President. Third, the CIA is responsible for carrying out covert, tactical operations overseas (at the request of the President) or overseeing other government agencies or the military as they carry out these operations.

The CIA is divided into four directorates:

*The Directorate of Intelligence*—Produces all-source (not just HUMINT) intelligence on foreign and intercontinental issues, often manipulating raw intelligence data from CIA covert operatives to create intelligence products for elected officials, the President, and other Executive Branch officials.

*The National Clandestine Service (NCS)*—Responsible for collecting foreign intelligence, primarily from HUMINT, in a clandestine manner, often undercover and through the use of covert operations. The NCS also coordinates HUMINT collection across the IC. The specific organization and extent of the NCS is classified.[24]

*The Directorate of Support*—Provides support functions such as administrative, technical, and organizational support to the CIA.

*The Directorate of Science and Technology*—Researches technical disciplines related to intelligence gathering and analysis and also creates technical equipment. Many of this Directorate's innovations, once declassified, are used by other parts of the U.S. government or the private sector. For instance, the U-2 high altitude reconnaissance aircraft was researched and manufactured by the U.S. Air Force in cooperation with the CIA. The U-2 was then put into service to conduct reconnaissance and collect imagery intelligence throughout the Cold War.[25]

The 1947 law that established the CIA also vested the Legislative Branch with the responsibility to oversee the agency's covert intelligence activities. Congress assigns oversight responsibility to relevant committees, such as the Intelligence or Armed Services committees. In practice, awareness of CIA's intelligence operations is limited to a handful of high-ranking members of Congress, and the legislative body as a whole has historically had poor visibility into the agency's daily operations and intelligence priorities.[26]

Due to the secrecy and sensitivity surrounding intelligence findings, conclusions, dissemination, and sources and methods, as well as competition between the legislature and executive for influence over and access to them, there have long been concerns about whether intelligence agencies receive appropriate oversight by independent, trusted actors.[27] Concerns regarding effective oversight have been underscored by a number or controversies and matters related to civil rights and civil liberties issues that have arisen over actions the CIA has taken domestically and abroad. For example, in the 1960s and 1970s, the CIA conducted Operation CHAOS, which gathered intelligence on the constitutionally protected activities of anti-Vietnam War protestors in the United States at the time.[28] The CIA's activities abroad have also led to numerous criticisms, especially by human rights organizations. A contemporary example is the CIA's "enhanced interrogation" and rendition program, which relied on a network of clandestine "black sites" around the globe to hold and forcibly question detainees.

## Defense Intelligence Agency

The Defense Intelligence Agency (DIA) is a Department of Defense combat support agency. It is the central manager of all foreign intelligence gathering and analysis operations for the armed forces. DIA provides military intelligence to warfighters, defense policymakers, and force planners, both in the Department of Defense and the IC, in support of U.S. military planning and operations and weapon systems acquisition. With more than 16,500 military and civilian employees worldwide, DIA is a major producer and manager of foreign military intelligence (during times of both war and peace).

**DEFINITION BOX: Military Intelligence**

**Military intelligence** is the discipline of collecting and analyzing information to support commander decision-making. Common military intelligence sources include interaction with the local population, radio broadcasts, captured government documents, telephone traffic, and open-source media.

Prior to the existence of the DIA, each branch of the armed forces maintained its own intelligence organization, individually gathering and analyzing intelligence and issuing separate intelligence products. This resulted in considerable duplication of resources and assets. The DIA was thus designed to combine all these efforts under one agency for the entirety of the armed forces, and it was former Defense Secretary Robert S. McNamara who encouraged the Joint Chiefs of Staff to create the DIA with Directive 5105.21 in August 1961.

The current DIA Director is a three-star military officer who serves as principal adviser to the Secretary of Defense and to the Chairman of the Joint Chiefs of Staff on matters of military intelligence. The Director also chairs the Military Intelligence Board, which coordinates activities of the defense intelligence community.[29] Similar to the CIA, the DIA has its own Clandestine Service, which conducts covert operations abroad, often with a focus on gathering HUMINT.

The DIA is divided into four directorates:[30]

*Directorate of Operations*—Comprised of the Defense Clandestine Service (DCS), Defense Attaché System (DAS), and the Defense Cover Office (DCO). Working closely with the CIA, the DCS deploys teams of linguists, field analysts, case officers, interrogation experts, technical specialists, and U.S. Special Forces to collect and analyze intelligence. The DAS represents the United States in defense and military-diplomatic relations with foreign governments and manages overt HUMINT collection. The DCO works for the agency's intelligence operatives.

*Directorate for Analysis (DI)*—Analyzes and disseminates DIA intelligence products from DIA sources and from partners in the IC. DIA analysts focus on political or economic events in foreign countries and also analyze the capabilities of foreign armed forces, weapons, and emerging foreign terrorist threats. Products from this directorate routinely find their way into the President's Daily Brief on intelligence matters.

*Directorate for Science and Technology (DS&T)*—The IC's primary MASINT collection agency. Sources include radar intelligence, acoustic intelligence, nuclear intelligence, and chemical and biological intelligence.

*Directorate for Mission Services*—Provides administrative, technical, and programmatic support to the agency's operations and analytic efforts. This includes counterintelligence operations.

Although not recognized as one of its main four directorates, the DIA also manages the Directorate for Intelligence, Joint Staff (J2). This directorate advises the Joint Chiefs of Staff on foreign military intelligence matters, including defense policy and war planning.

## National Geospatial Intelligence Agency

The National Geospatial Intelligence Agency (NGA) is the lead federal agency for GEOINT collection and manages a global consortium of more than 400 commercial and government relationships. Aerial photography was first used as an intelligence gathering tool during World War I. Following the development of advanced imagery and satellite technologies, Congress established

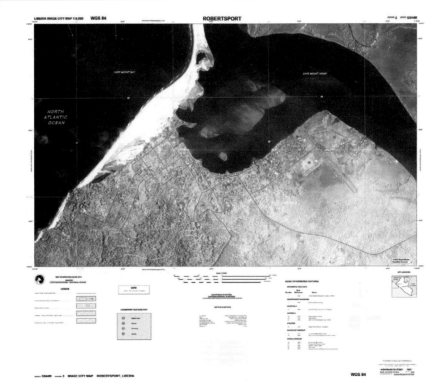

**FIG. 5.9** The National Geospatial-Intelligence Agency released a series of Image City Maps derived from satellite imagery and human geography data sets, which played a key role in the international effort to combat the Ebola crisis in western Africa.

*Source*: Robertsport, Liberia, National Geospatial-Intelligence Agency, www.flickr.com/photos/nga_geoint/16206142426/in/album-72157650126207756/.

the precursor to the NGA in 1997, the National Imagery and Mapping Agency (NIMA).[31] To better reflect its primary role as the GEOINT collector and analysis center for the U.S. government, NIMA was renamed the National Geospatial Agency in 2004.

The NGA delivers strategic intelligence information that informs the decision-making of the President and that of other policymakers on matters related to counterterrorism threats, weapons of mass destruction, and global political crises. The NGA provides timely warnings to military and national decision-makers by monitoring, analyzing, and reporting on imminent threats. The NGA is often the only U.S. agency with the capacity to watch, in real time or near-real time, developments occurring in conflict zones around the world. As well as foreign intelligence production, the NGA also supports homeland security efforts in counterterrorism, counter-narcotics, and border and transportation security.[32]

In addition, the NGA supports security planning for special events, such as presidential inaugurations, state visits by foreign leaders, international conferences, and major public events (e.g. Olympics, Super Bowls). The NGA also assists humanitarian and disaster relief efforts by working directly with the lead federal agencies responding to fires, floods, earthquakes, landslides, hurricanes, or other natural or human-caused disasters.[33]

One of the most significant uses of GEOINT was the deployment of unmanned aerial vehicles (UAVs) in support of the operation to find Osama bin Laden.[34] The NGA's "RQ-170" UAVs provided policymakers and CIA officials with critical data that allowed them to assess the number of individuals living in what was later confirmed to be bin Laden's compound in Abbottabad, Pakistan; create three-dimensional renderings based on imagery and laser radar; and assist the Joint Special Operations Command by creating simulators for the helicopter pilots who flew the mission.[35]

After the September 11, 2001 attacks, the NGA (then NIMA) partnered with the U.S. Geological Survey to inspect the World Trade Center site and determine the extent of the destruction.

- In 2002, the NGA (then NIMA) partnered with other federal agencies to provide geospatial assistance to the 2002 Winter Olympics in Utah. The NGA also helped support the 2004 Summer Olympics in Athens, Greece, and the 2006 Winter Olympics in Turin, Italy.

- The NGA supported Hurricane Katrina relief efforts by providing geospatial information about the affected areas based on imagery from commercial and U.S. government satellites, and from airborne platforms, to the Federal Emergency Management Agency (FEMA) and other government agencies. NGA's Earth website is a central source of these efforts.

NGA employs approximately 14,500 government civilians, military members, and contractors, with approximately two-thirds of the workforce located at the NGA Headquarters at NGA Campus East, on Fort Belvoir North Area in Springfield, Va., and approximately one-third of the workforce located at NGA's two St. Louis facilities. Like the CIA and NSA, by statutory and presidential direction, NGA is limited in the collection of foreign intelligence concerning the domestic activities of US citizens. Collection of information regarding U.S. persons is allowed only for an authorized intelligence purpose; for example, if there is a reason to believe that an individual is involved in international terrorist or international narcotics activities.[36]

NGA's budget is classified.

## National Counterterrorism Center

The National Counterterrorism Center (NCTC) serves as the lead organization in the U.S. government for integrating and analyzing all intelligence pertaining to counterterrorism (except for information relating exclusively to domestic terrorism, which is the sole province of federal law enforcement agencies such as the Federal Bureau of Investigation (FBI)). The NCTC Director reports to the President regarding Executive Branch-wide counterterrorism planning and to the DNI regarding intelligence matters. The Center's mission statement summarizes its key responsibilities:

> Lead our nation's effort to combat terrorism at home and abroad by analyzing the threat, sharing that information with our partners, and integrating all instruments of national power to ensure unity of effort.[37]

The NCTC was established by Presidential Executive Order 13354 in August 2004 and codified by the Intelligence Reform and Terrorism Prevention Act of 2004 (IRTPA). NCTC implements a key recommendation of the 9/11 Commission:

> Breaking the older mold of national government organizations, this NCTC should be a center for joint operational planning and joint intelligence, staffed by personnel from the various agencies.[38]

To this end, NCTC is given access to various classified and unclassified databases to fulfill its mission obligations, including the Terrorist Identities Datamart Environment (TIDE), which it manages directly.[39]

## SIDEBAR 5.3 Centralized Terrorism Databases

The Terrorist Identities Datamart Environment (TIDE) is a centralized, classified database compiled and managed by the National Counterterrorism Center (NCTC).[40] It contains the identities and personal information of individuals with suspected links to terrorist activities, including the names of known or suspected terrorists, as well as those affiliated with known terrorists. The list surpassed one million individuals in 2013, and according to the most recently publicly available information, there are 25,000 U.S. citizens or permanent residents included in TIDE.

Departments across the federal government nominate individuals for inclusion in TIDE, recommending an individual based on the department's intelligence and counterterrorism analysis and investigations. Activities that can merit a nomination to TIDE include committing an act of terrorism or being a member of an international terrorist group; preparing or planning for international terrorism; soliciting funding or recruits for terrorist activity; gathering information on potential targets for terrorism; or providing material support (e.g. funds, weapons) to terrorist activities.

Once included in TIDE, the individual's name, as well as their biographic and biometric information, is available and disseminated to all members of the IC. This reflects the revelation after 9/11 that segregating federal agencies creates national security vulnerabilities. TIDE centralizes the threat information for better distribution across the IC. An unclassified but sensitive list is extracted from TIDE and informs the FBI's Terrorist Screening Database (TSDB),[41] which in turn informs agency-specific watchlists, such as the Transportation Security Administration's (TSA) "No Fly" list and the Department of State's visa database.

NCTC follows the policy direction of the President and National and Home-land Security Councils.[42] It integrates foreign and domestic analysis from across the IC and produces a range of detailed assessments designed to support senior policymakers and other members of the policy, intelligence, law enforcement, defense, homeland security, and foreign affairs communities. Prime examples of NCTC analysis products include items for the President's Daily Brief and the daily National Terrorism Bulletin. NCTC is also the central player in the ODNI's Homeland Threat Task Force, which orchestrates inter-agency collaboration and keeps senior policymakers informed about threats to the homeland via a weekly update.[43]

In addition to these duties, NCTC also conducts strategic operational planning for counterterrorism activities across the U.S. government, integrating all instruments of national power, including diplomatic, financial, military,

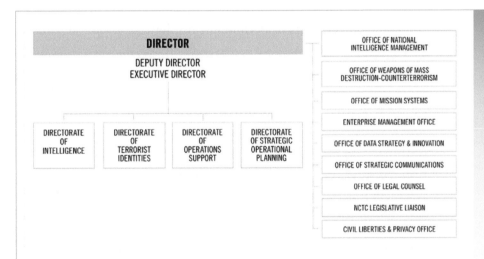

**FIG. 5.10**
NCTC has four primary directorates—Directorate of Intelligence, Director-ate of Terrorist Identities, Directorate of Operations Support, and Director-ate of Strategic Operational Planning—and nine offices that provide critical functions that include intelligence management and acquisition of data to which NCTC has unique access.

*Source*: NCTC Organizational Structure, National Counterterrorism Center, at 7, www.dni.gov/files/NCTC/documents/features_documents/NCTC-Primer_FINAL.pdf.

intelligence, homeland security, and law enforcement. NCTC ensures effective integration of counterterrorism plans and synchronization of operations across more than 20 government departments and agencies engaged in countering and combating terrorism through a single, joint planning process.[44]

## Department of Homeland Security Office of Intelligence and Analysis

The Office of Intelligence and Analysis (I&A) at the Department of Homeland Security (DHS) is the federal government's lead for sharing information and intelligence with state, local, tribal, and territorial (SLTT) governments, as well as the private sector—non-federal partners that increasingly work with the federal government in preventing and responding to evolving threats to the homeland.

As discussed in Chapter 2, one of DHS' fundamental responsibilities is facilitating intelligence flows between all levels of government. As DHS' intelligence arm, I&A was tasked with the specific responsibility to serve as a conduit for information sharing, delivering intelligence gathered by federal agencies to state and local partners while also collecting and disseminating intelligence gathered by state and local law enforcement with the rest of the IC. I&A facilitates this intelligence sharing through state and major urban area Fusion Centers with deployed personnel and systems, training, and collaboration. The National Network of Fusion Centers is the hub for much of the two-way intelligence and information flow between the federal government and its SLTT partners.[45] Fusion Centers are scattered throughout much of the United States and are physical locations where law enforcement and intelligence personnel from every level of government can work together.

Additionally, I&A is responsible for managing the Nationwide Suspicious Activity Reporting (SAR) Initiative (NSI). The NSI developed after 9/11 as a joint collaboration between DHS, the FBI, and SLTT governments. First pioneered by the New York Police Department in the immediate aftermath of the 9/11 attacks, NSI was designed to recruit citizens to spot suspicious activity in public places, such as an unattended package being left at a train station. The now-famous slogan, "See Something, Say Something," soon became a part of

**FIG. 5.11**
DHS' Suspicious Activity Reporting program is prominently used at large events such as the Super Bowl, to encourage reporting of suspicious packages and backpacks.

*Source*: Barry Bahler, DHS Security Efforts at Super Bowl XLIX, U.S. Dep't of Homeland Security, www.flickr.com/photos/dhsgov/16451820805/in/photolist-r4MT9R-r4CTJH-r4H1iY-p37zbq-p3arbR-p37zqJ-pGyJL3-p37yWN-CCEbiZ-DrMnmc-DrMnmH-DxJoHL-DA3QVr-MuGEXS-MuGAVd-MPk1ir-MPjZsZ-MPjXEF-MWNQpp-MWNLrV-MLHiks-MLHhVQ-MuGknu-LZeXLH-MTH2GL.

the lexicon of millions of Americans and was adopted by DHS I&A as part of their nationwide SAR efforts (Figure 5.11).

## SIDEBAR 5.4 Fusion Centers

Fusion centers are *physical* focal points within the state and local environment for the receipt, analysis, gathering, and sharing of threat-related information between the federal government and state, local, tribal, territorial (SLTT), and private sector partners (Figure 5.12).[46] At these centers, personnel from various agencies assist law enforcement and homeland security partners in preventing, protecting against, and responding to crime and terrorism.

Fusion Centers are designed to overcome some of the failures in intelligence, namely, the lack of information-sharing that led to the U.S. government's inability to apprehend the 9/11 hijackers prior to their attack. By physically collocating local intelligence and law enforcement

**FIG. 5.12**
A Fusion Center is a collaborative effort of two or more agencies that provide resources, expertise, and information to the center with the goal of maximizing their ability to detect, prevent, investigate, and respond to criminal and terrorist activity.

*Source*: DHS I&A Managed Fusion Centers, U.S. Dep't of Homeland Security, www.archives.gov/files/isoo/oversight-groups/sltps-pac/SLTPS%20Certified%20Minutes,%2020170726.pdf.

personnel with national-level counterparts, intelligence from around the country can be shared and analyzed at all levels. In addition to being staffed by state and local law enforcement, a Fusion Center may also be staffed by representatives from the FBI, U.S. military, the Bureau of Alcohol, Tobacco, and Firearms (ATF), and DHS.

One of the primary functions of a Fusion Center is to support the National Suspicious Activity Reporting (SAR) Initiative (NSI), which is an attempt by the federal government to standardize suspicious activity identification and reporting.[47] It was developed following the release of the 9/11 Commission Report, the Intelligence Reform and Terrorism Prevention Act (IRTPA) of 2004, and the 2007 *National Strategy for*

*Information Sharing*, which established legislative and executive intent to create locally controlled distributed information systems for analysis to uncover emerging patterns or trends in terrorism and terrorism-related activities.[48]

Fusion centers are located in states and major urban areas throughout the country, and they physically and logistically bring together all government agencies and organizations working on gathering and analyzing intelligence or threat-related information. They are owned and operated by state and local entities, with support from federal partners, such as with deployed personnel. DHS, for example, deploys Intelligence Officers (IOs) and Protective Security Advisors (PSAs).

Fusion Center Guidelines were created to help ensure the effective and efficient operation of all Fusion Centers in a way that protects an individual's privacy and civil liberties. These Guidelines[49] adopt 28 C.F.R. Part 23 as the minimum governing principles for criminal intelligence systems. In part, the federal regulations require reasonable suspicion to collect and maintain criminal intelligence and prohibit the collection and maintenance of information in relation to First Amendment protected activity, unless the information or the individual involved "directly relates to criminal conduct or activity."[50] Many civil liberties and civil rights organizations question the collection standards used by Fusion Centers. In particular, privacy concerns are raised in relation to Fourth Amendment search and seizure protections.[51]

Furthermore, while Fusion Centers serve an important function, a 2012 Senate investigation report revealed that they may be falling short in some ways.[52] Specifically, the report highlights:

- Reporting from Fusion Centers was often flawed and unrelated to terrorism;
- Some Fusion Center reports had "nothing of value," meaning terrorism-related reporting was often outdated, duplicative, and uninformative;
- Many Fusion Centers did not prioritize counterterrorism efforts; and
- Fusion centers may have hindered, not aided, some federal counterterrorism efforts.

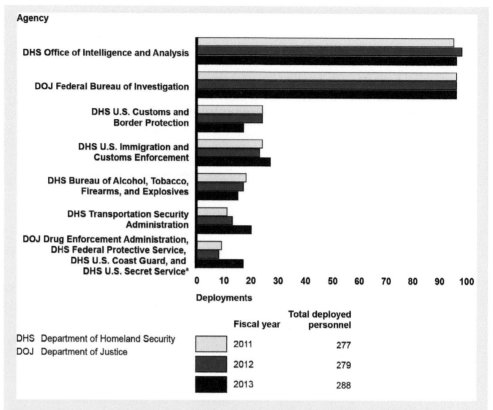

**FIG. 5.13**
A graph detailing the number of federal personnel agencies that reported deploying to Fusion Centers 2011–2012.

*Source*: Fusion Center Deployments, U.S. Government Accountability Office Report GAO-15–155, www.flickr.com/photos/usgao/15159869764/in/photolist-o86ezd-vkUkNu-nL7gSQ-nTktVg-nTktVM-oZE86r-DEhFRD-v4Rpdq-PLwfaF-LBF3YU-UaSKXW-TDvU6A-TZysPE-TDvTXu-nVZr9Z-pQYkUF-nDNjeU-pzFubG-p6Ci7U-CJUqVB-CRa3xt-v94DwR-24uNa2U-QnsugT-MMN6t5-MXTTjB-MUQJiq-M1kS1C-MQrhwa-M1k7cV.

I&A is staffed primarily by Intelligence Officers (IOs) who serve two primary functions: 1) they partner with Fusion Centers to facilitate achievement of the baseline capabilities for State and Major Urban Area Fusion Centers; and 2) they manage the intelligence cycle in their area of responsibility, including threat-related information sharing between state and local partners and the federal government. In addition, IOs provide state and local law enforcement and homeland security leadership access to best practices, lessons learned, and other resources from the federal government and across the National Network of Fusion Centers.[53]

Closely aligned with IOs are DHS Protective Security Advisors (PSAs). PSAs are part of NPPD (another directorate at DHS; see Chapter 2) and not I&A, but they are nonetheless often the first DHS personnel to respond to incidents that may require federal intervention, especially those involving critical infrastructure. During an incident, PSAs work with state and local Emergency Operations Centers and the Federal Emergency Management Agency (FEMA) Regional Offices to advise federal and state and local partners on issues impacting critical infrastructure and help prioritize and coordinate critical infrastructure-related response and recovery activities. As violence and threats of violence to schools, public facilities, and houses of worship have increased in recent years, PSAs now also help public facilities secure themselves against active shooters and other threats of domestic violent extremism (Figure 5.14).

IOs and PSAs have distinct but complementary roles that inform one another's efforts. Combining vulnerability and security information with

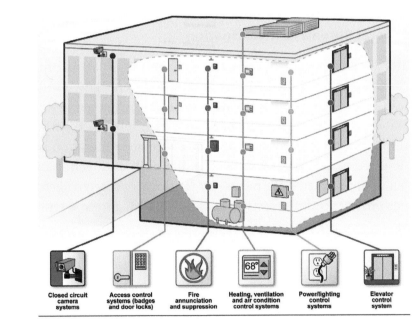

**FIG. 5.14**
DHS Protective Security Advisors often look for vulnerabilities in critical infrastructure, such as federal facilities, and then attempt to address these vulnerabilities proactively.

*Source*: PSA Reviews of Building and Access Control Systems in a Federal Facility, General Accountability Office, Report GAO-15–6, www.flickr.com/photos/usgao/16146831299/in/photolist-2ca5bfv-qAQJp6-pWvLwc-rfPJry-qqz9Us-xAriaE-xTGLJr-xAxLh2.

threat-related information offers a more comprehensive and accurate risk profile for all law enforcement personnel who sit at a Fusion Center. These complimentary roles also align with state, local, and federal law enforcement officers and intelligence analysts who work at Fusion Centers.

In addition to its unique information-sharing responsibilities, I&A also collects a substantial amount of intelligence information, mostly from open sources and publicly available material. From this, I&A creates a variety of intelligence products and employs hundreds of intelligence analysts who continually focus on short-term or operational issues, such as imminent terrorist threats to the homeland. As a part of the DHS Office of the Secretary, I&A is DHS' lead intelligence component. In addition to I&A, several DHS component agencies and offices also play an intelligence gathering and analysis role. This wider "DHS Intelligence Enterprise" consists of components with distinct mission sets, including: Customs and Border Protection (CBP); Immigration and Customs Enforcement (ICE); U.S. Citizenship and Immigration Services (USCIS); the U.S. Coast Guard (USCG); the Transportation Security Administration (TSA); the U.S. Secret Service; and the Federal Emergency Management Administration (FEMA).

**Federal Bureau of Investigation**

The Federal Bureau of Investigation (FBI) is a part of the U.S. Department of Justice and is the nation's foremost federal law enforcement body and lead federal agency investigating counterintelligence activities in the United States. The FBI also undertakes various intelligence gathering and analysis responsibilities, as well as works to counter proliferation of weapons of mass destruction and protect critical information and technology from being stolen or appropriated for misuse by terrorists or foreign agents. In total, the FBI has jurisdiction to investigate nearly 200 categories of federal crime.[54]

**DEFINITION BOX: Counterintelligence**

**Counterintelligence** refers to information gathering and activities conducted to protect against espionage, other intelligence activities, sabotage, or assassinations conducted for or on behalf of foreign powers, organizations or people, or international terrorist activities.

Established in 1908 as the Bureau of Investigation, the FBI now has more than 50 field offices throughout the country and also operates internationally with officers stationed in U.S. embassies and consulates worldwide. The FBI investigated the 9/11 attacks, and the ensuing investigation was one of the most comprehensive in the Bureau's history. At its peak, the investigation involved more than half of the FBI's agents.[55] The attacks led to far-reaching changes at the FBI, transforming it from a law enforcement-focused organization to one that now prioritizes the prevention of terrorist attacks through intelligence-driven procedures and personnel training.[56]

The FBI's National Security Branch (NSB) was created on September 12, 2005, in the wake of recommendations from the Commission on the Intelligence Capabilities of the United States Regarding Weapons of Mass Destruction ("WMD Commission"). The WMD Commission called for a "national security service" to bring the FBI's counterterrorism, counterintelligence, and

**FIG. 5.15**
Future Law Enforcement Youth Academy (FLEYA) students present suggestions for a transgender detention policy for Connecticut law enforcement as part of their group assignment.

*Source*: Future Law Enforcement Youth Academy, FBI, www.flickr.com/photos/fbi/29520187055/.

intelligence assets into a coordinated branch reporting to the Executive Assistant Director (EAD).

The NSB is made up of five divisions:[57]

- *The Counterterrorism Division (CTD)* leads law enforcement and domestic intelligence work. The CTD oversees the Joint Terrorism Task Forces (JTTFs) in 104 cities across the country. As discussed elsewhere in the text, JTTFs are multi-jurisdictional partnerships of federal and SLTT law enforcement, managed by the FBI, whose mission is to develop and share intelligence throughout the FBI and IC and engage in counterterrorism investigations.
- *The Weapons of Mass Destruction Directorate (WMDD)* provides U.S. law enforcement and intelligence with scientific expertise to combat WMD threats to U.S. interests. WMDD is focused on denying WMD materials and technologies to both state- and non-state-sponsored actors.
- *The Counterintelligence Division (CD)* investigates and works to prevent foreign intelligence activity in the United States. In 2011, the FBI joined its counterproliferation components and created the Counterproliferation Center (CPC). The jointly managed CPC includes the WMD Directorate, providing scientific support; the Counterintelligence Division, providing operational support; and the Directorate of Intelligence, providing analytical support.
- *The High-Value Detainee Interrogation Group (HIG)* is made up of members from throughout the IC. HIG uses interrogation resources to collect intelligence from captured terrorism suspects, and it also leads scientific research into interrogation techniques.
- *The Terrorist Screening Center (TSC)* was created to consolidate U.S. terrorism screening efforts into a single multi-agency organization. TSC operates the Terrorist Screening Database (TSDB) and processes the nomination of known or suspected terrorists for inclusion in the TSDB. TSDB is a sensitive but unclassified system, allowing the information it contains to be shared throughout the screening and law enforcement community, most of which does not have the necessary clearance to view classified information. TSC also serves as a liaison between law enforcement, the IC, the homeland security community, and international partners.

In 2014, (now former) FBI Director James Comey established the Intelligence Branch (IB) as a distinct organization within the FBI; the IB previously operated as part of the NSB.[58] Today, the IB is the strategic leader for the FBI's intelligence efforts, focused on cultivating collaboration throughout the FBI and IC with intelligence policy and guidance that balances strategic and tactical initiatives.

## SIDEBAR 5.5 Joint Terrorism Task Force

A Joint Terrorism Task Force (JTTF) is a small cell of highly trained, locally based investigators, analysts, linguists, police, and other specialists from dozens of U.S. law enforcement and intelligence agencies. JTTFs are coordinated by the FBI's National Joint Terrorism Task Force in Washington, D.C., and are the nation's primary terrorism investigation arm. JTTF personnel chase down leads, gather evidence, make arrests, provide security for special events, conduct training, collect and share intelligence, and respond to threats and incidents as needed. As of this writing JTTFs are based in 104 U.S. cities, including in each of the FBI's 56 field offices. Seventy-one of these JTTFs have been created since 9/11, the first being established in 1980 in New York City.[59]

The number of JTTF personnel has grown four-fold since 9/11 to approximately 4,000 individuals. JTTF personnel come from over 500 state and local agencies, and 55 federal agencies (such as DHS, the U.S. Armed Forces, ICE, and TSA). Though JTTFs predated 9/11, the 9/11 Commission recommended an expansion of the program after 9/11 because JTTFs already embodied the intelligence-sharing ethos sought by the Commission in the aftermath of the attacks. Beyond just creating a shared base of intelligence, JTTFs:

> Create a familiarity among investigators and managers before a crisis. And perhaps most importantly, they pool talents, skills, and knowledge from across the law enforcement and intelligence communities into a single team that responds together.[60]

Though much of their work is classified, the FBI has publicly acknowledged that JTTFs have been instrumental in breaking up cells of terrorists such as the "Portland Seven" and the "Lackawanna Six," and have foiled terrorist plots on the Fort Dix Army base New Jersey.[61]

## Department of State Bureau of Intelligence and Research

The State Department acts as the representative of the American government overseas and gathers information through publicly available sources via U.S. embassies and consulates. Specific and actionable intelligence activities are conducted by the State Department's Bureau of Intelligence and Research (INR).

INR's primary mission is to harness intelligence to serve U.S. diplomacy. Using all sources of intelligence (e.g. SIGINT, HUMINT), INR provides independent analysis of international events to U.S. State Department policymakers. INR also works to ensure that all intelligence activities support foreign policy and national security purposes. Finally, INR serves as the focal point at the State Department for ensuring policy review of sensitive counterintelligence and law enforcement activities across the world.[62]

## Department of Justice National Security Division

The Department of Justice's National Security Division (NSD) was created in March 2006 by the Uniting and Strengthening America by Providing Appropriate Tools Required to Intercept and Obstruct Terrorism Act of 2001 ("USA PATRIOT ACT"). The creation of the NSD consolidated the Justice Department's primary national security operations, combining the former Office of Intelligence Policy and Review and the Counterterrorism and Counterespionage Sections of the Criminal Division.[63]

Today, NSD's mission is to combat terrorism and other threats to national security within the means and purview of the Justice Department. The NSD's organizational structure is designed to ensure greater coordination and unity of purpose between prosecutors and law enforcement agencies on the one hand, and intelligence attorneys and the IC on the other, thus strengthening the effectiveness of the federal government's national security efforts.[64]

Of particular note is the NSD's Office of Intelligence, which has grown dramatically in an effort to ensure that IC agencies have the legal authority necessary to conduct intelligence operations, particularly operations involving the Foreign Intelligence Surveillance Act (FISA). The Office of Intelligence also exercises meaningful legal oversight over the IC's various national security activities and plays an active role in FISA-related litigation.[65]

**CRITICAL THINKING QUESTION**

Should the CIA, NSA, and other intelligence agencies be limited from collecting information regarding U.S. persons on U.S. soil? Why or why not?

## Department of Treasury Office of Terrorism and Financial Intelligence

The Treasury Department is the executive agency responsible for promoting economic prosperity and ensuring the financial security of the United States. The Office of Terrorism and Financial Intelligence (TFI) at the Treasury Department is charged with safeguarding the financial system against criminal exploitation that seeks to support terrorist organizations or activities. With its intelligence and enforcement capacity, TFI is also engaged in combating rogue nations, terrorist facilitators, weapons of mass destruction proliferators, money launderers, narcotics traffickers, and other threats to national security.[66]

As part of its work, the TFI works to verify the authenticity of charitable organizations to ensure their work is not a front for terrorist activity. Under Executive Order 13224, TFI works to designate charities as fronts for terrorist financing. This work is part of the Department of Treasury's broader effort to regulate and protect charitable organizations from terrorist abuse.[67] Charities provide essential services, comfort, and hope to those in need around the world, but terrorists (including the 9/11 hijackers) have often exploited the charitable sector to raise and move funds, provide logistical support, encourage terrorist recruitment, or otherwise support their organizations and operations. This abuse threatens to undermine donor confidence and jeopardizes the integrity of the charitable sector.[68]

As such, designations are an important resource in TFI's prosecution of terror financing. With them, TFI is able to freeze the assets of individuals and groups who seek to commit terrorist acts, as well as those entities who attempt to support them. When examining individuals or organizations for potential designation, TFI works in conjunction with authorities from several other nations, and with international organizations, such as the European Union and the United Nations.

---

**CALL-OUT BOX**
**Ten "Fun Facts" About TFI**

1.  Lots of acronyms: Office of Foreign Assets Control (OFAC), the Office of Terrorist Financing and Financial Crimes (TFFC), the Financial Crimes Enforcement Network (FinCEN), and the Treasury Executive Office of Asset Forfeiture (TEO-AF) make up the TFI.
2.  OFAC enforces financial and economic sanctions programs against countries of concern and groups of individuals involved in illicit activity, such as terrorists and narcotics traffickers.
3.  There are currently 5,298 names on OFAC's Specially Designated Nationals List. In 2001, the list was around 2,000 names.
4.  TFFC develops policies and implements strategies to strengthen the integrity of the financial system and safeguard it from terrorist financing, money laundering, drug trafficking, organized crime, and proliferation finance.
5.  Since 2004, there have been over 160 mutual evaluations conducted by the FATF global network. As part of this assessment process, virtually all of these countries have enacted legislation to strengthen their financial crimes laws.
6.  OIA is the only intelligence office in the world based in a finance ministry.
7.  Since the Foreign Narcotics Kingpin Designation Act was passed, more than 1,500 drug traffickers and money launderers have had their access to the U.S. financial system cut off.
8.  FinCEN is the Financial Intelligence Unit of the U.S. and engages with law enforcement on investigative efforts while fostering interagency and global cooperation against domestic and international financial crimes.
9.  TEOAF uses assets forfeited by ringleaders of financial fraud, such as Ponzi schemes or credit card hackers, to pay back financial victims. In 2013, TEOAF remitted (returned) over $76 million of forfeited funds to financial victims. TEOAF uses its funding to help law enforcement stay on the cutting edge of financial investigations.
10. TFI's unprecedented sanctions on Iran have led the way in demonstrating the power and efficacy of TFI's financial measures.[69]

---

### Department of Energy Office of Intelligence

The Department of Energy (DOE) Office of Intelligence (IN) is the IC's technical intelligence resource in four core areas: Nuclear weapons and nonproliferation; energy security; science and technology; and nuclear energy, safety, and waste. Tapping the broad technology base of DOE's national laboratories and the international reach of the DOE complex as a whole, IN accomplishes a three-part mission:[70]

- To provide DOE, other U.S. government policymakers, and the IC with timely, accurate, high-impact foreign intelligence analyses;
- To ensure that DOE's technical, analytical, and research expertise is made available to the intelligence, law enforcement, and special operations communities; and
- To provide quick-turnaround, specialized technology applications and operational support based on DOE technological expertise to the intelligence, law enforcement, and special operations communities.

The DOE intelligence program traces its origins to the days of the Manhattan Project, when the former Atomic Energy Commission was tasked with providing specialized analysis of the Soviet Union's nascent atomic weapons program. Since then, the program has come to reside within DOE. The IN continues to evolve in close concert with changing policy needs and the strengths of DOE's unique scientific and technological base, from the world energy crisis of the 1970s—and consequent demand for intelligence expertise in international energy supply and demand issues—to growing concerns over nuclear proliferation.

## INTELLIGENCE COMMUNITY OVERSIGHT

Broad discretion and powers are granted to those who gather, analyze, and disseminate intelligence. But just like Spiderman, with great power comes great responsibility. A great number of government bodies, both inside and outside the Executive Branch, ensure that IC member agencies are carrying out their work in a responsible manner. In the Executive Branch, the President's Intelligence Advisory Board (PIAB) provides advice to the President on the quality and adequacy of intelligence collection; analysis and estimates; counterintelligence; and other intelligence activities. Unique within the government, the PIAB has traditionally been tasked with providing the President with an independent source of advice on the effectiveness with which the IC is meeting the nation's intelligence needs and the vigor and insight with which the community plans for the future. The PIAB consists of not more than 16 members selected from distinguished citizens outside the government who are qualified on the basis of achievement, experience, independence, and integrity.

## SIDEBAR 5.6 State Secrets Privilege

How does the federal government manage state secrets (gathered by the IC) and ensure they do not become public through courtroom trials and judicial subpoenas? Often, government officials and law enforcement agents rely on the **state secrets privilege**. This is a rule of evidence and legal doctrine that results in the exclusion of evidence from a court case based on sworn statements from government officers.[71] The state secrets privilege seeks to prevent the disclosure of sensitive information that might endanger national security.[72] Only the federal government has the power to intervene in civil and criminal cases to assert the privilege and ask courts not to reveal secrets during the course of a lawsuit.

The state secrets doctrine derives from a 1953 Supreme Court case *United States v. Reynolds*.[73] In *Reynolds*, the widows of three civilians killed in a military plane crash filed a wrongful death lawsuit against the government. To establish their case, the widows sought to obtain the report with details about the accident. The government, however, claimed the report could not be disclosed because it also contained information about secret military equipment aboard the downed flight.

The Supreme Court recognized the government's need to protect this secret information because they reasoned disclosure could harm national security or foreign relation interests if disclosed. Even though the Supreme Court ruled in favor of the government's ability to keep certain secrets in a court of law, they nonetheless placed a restriction on the government, stating that the privilege could only be invoked when there was a "reasonable danger" that disclosure would expose military matters threatening national security interests. The Supreme Court also mandated that the assertion of the privilege had to come from the head of the government department involved in the issue.[74]

In the wake of the 9/11 attacks, individuals and advocacy groups, such as the American Civil Liberties Union, have argued that the state secrets privilege is too broad and is thus used by the Executive Branch to conceal misconduct at trial. In 2009, the Obama Administration released a memorandum addressing those concerns. The memo asserted that the privilege would only be invoked during the occurrence of a genuine and significant harm to national security and to the extent necessary to protect those interests.[75] Further limitations were implemented requiring all invocations of the privilege to first be reviewed by a State Secrets Review Committee.[76] Today, review by this committee requires a final, personal approval by the Attorney General before the privilege is invoked.[77]

As a part of the PIAB, the President's Intelligence Oversight Board (IOB) consists of not more than four PIAB members appointed by the PIAB chairperson. The mission of the IOB is to oversee the IC's compliance with the U.S. Constitution and all applicable laws, Executive Orders, and Presidential Directives. In reviewing the legality and propriety of intelligence activities, the IOB advises the President on intelligence activities that the board believes may be unlawful or contrary to an Executive Order or Presidential Directive; inadequately addressed by the Attorney General, the DNI, or the head of a department or agency; or should be brought immediately to the President's attention.

The Department of Justice's aforementioned NSD Office of Intelligence also oversees IC activities through its Oversight Section, which monitors the activities of IC member agencies and identifies individual and systemic incidents of non-compliance with the U.S. Constitution and applicable U.S. laws. The Oversight Section also fulfills important Department of Justice reporting obligations, such as ensuring that instances of non-compliance with FISC orders are tracked, reported, and resolved.[78]

Also providing IC oversight within the Executive Branch is the Office of Management and Budget (OMB). It reviews intelligence budgets in light of presidential policies and priorities, clears proposed testimony, and approves draft intelligence legislation for submission to Congress. In the Legislative Branch, principal oversight responsibility rests with two intelligence committees: The Senate Select Committee on Intelligence (SSCI) and the House Permanent Select Committee on Intelligence (HPSCI). By law, the President must ensure that these two committees are kept "fully and currently" informed of the activities of the IC, including any "significant anticipated intelligence activities." Both committees must also receive notice of all covert action programs approved by the President, as well as all "significant intelligence failures."[79]

In the Senate, SSCI membership has ranged from 13 to 17 legislators, with the majority party in Congress having one more member than the minority. SSCI members serve eight-year terms. In addition to its role in annually authorizing appropriations for intelligence activities, the SSCI carries out oversight investigations and inquiries, as required. It also handles presidential nominations referred to the Senate for the positions of DNI, Principle Deputy DNI, CIA Director, and CIA Inspector General, as well as reviews treaties referred to the Senate for ratification to determine the IC's ability to verify the provisions of the treaty under consideration.

In the House, HPSCI membership is currently set at 19 members and is proportional to the House's partisan makeup. Members may be appointed for terms up to eight years. Like its Senate counterpart, the HPSCI conducts oversight investigations and inquiries, in addition to processing the annual authorization of appropriations for intelligence. In addition to the intelligence committees, other congressional committees occasionally become involved in oversight matters by virtue of overlapping jurisdictions and responsibilities. The armed services, homeland security, and judiciary committees of each chamber, for example, exercise concurrent jurisdiction over the intelligence activities of the Departments of Defense and Homeland Security, and the Federal Bureau of Investigation, respectively.

## LEGAL UNDERPINNINGS OF SURVEILLANCE

All of the activities of the IC's 17 agencies and organizations are rooted in law, and the relevant legislation spans decades and myriad volumes. Of particular importance, however, is the Foreign Intelligence Surveillance Act (FISA). Enacted in 1978, FISA outlines procedures for the electronic and physical surveillance and collection of foreign intelligence information between foreign powers and/or agents of a foreign power.[80] FISA established a detailed process for the Executive Branch to obtain orders allowing for the collection of foreign intelligence information without violating the Constitutional rights of U.S. citizens, lawful permanent residents, corporations, or foreign corporations employing U.S. citizens and residents.[81] This includes obtaining information related to foreign business records.[82]

FISA permits surveillance if there is sufficient evidence (i.e. "probable cause") to believe the target is a foreign power or an agent of a foreign power, regardless of whether there is a suspicion of criminal activity.[83] If the surveillance target is a U.S. citizen, permanent resident, corporation, or unincorporated association, there must be probable cause to believe the target is engaged in espionage or related activities. Importantly, activities by U.S. targets that are protected by the First Amendment cannot be the sole basis for probable cause.

After 9/11, FISA was amended by the USA PATRIOT ACT to cover activities by rogue terrorists or nations. This amendment expanded the authority of law enforcement to conduct surveillance on terrorism suspects, even if these individuals did not specifically represent a foreign government. In 2004, a further amendment known as the "lone wolf" provision was added to FISA, which changes the definition of "foreign power" to permit FISA courts to issue surveillance and physical search orders on individuals irrespective of their ties to a foreign government or foreign terrorist group. This change has made it easier for government law enforcement agencies, such as the FBI, to gather evidence and intelligence on terrorist organizations, even if they operate within the United States.[84]

Under FISA, Congress authorized the Foreign Intelligence Surveillance Court (FISC), a U.S. federal court overseeing requests for approval of electronic surveillance, physical search and certain other forms of investigative actions for foreign intelligence purposes.[85] Requests for approval, or surveillance warrants, are made by federal law enforcement agencies against suspected foreign intelligence agents inside the United States.[86] As required by statute, most of the FISC's work is conducted in secret.[87] This means FISC hearings and records of the proceedings are closed to the public. Due to the need to protect classified national security information, usually only government attorneys appear before the FISC.[88]

Unlike normal courts, proceedings before the FISC are not adversarial. While the government presents its arguments for why an electronic surveillance order should be granted, there is no opposing party presenting arguments against granting such an order. The FISC issued a letter explaining its review process to Congress, stating that generally, "FISA does not provide a mechanism for the FISC to invite the views of nongovernmental parties."[89]

To obtain electronic and physical surveillance and collection of foreign intelligence information, the government must request a surveillance warrant (commonly called a FISA warrant).[90] The Attorney General must approve the request, and the federal government must then file an *ex parte* order with the FISC.[91] The FISC judge determines if there is probable cause to show that:

1. The target of the electronic surveillance or physical search is a foreign power and/or agent of a foreign power, provided that no U.S. person may be considered an agent of a foreign power solely upon the basis of activities protected by the First Amendment; and
2. For electronic surveillance, each of the facilities or places at which the electronic surveillance is directed is being used, or is about to be used, by a foreign power and/or an agent of a foreign power.[92]

If a FISC judge finds that there is cause, the *ex parte* order is approved, allowing the government to conduct the requested surveillance described in the warrant. Historically, almost all requests for surveillance have been approved. Between 1979 and 2006, only five requests for surveillance out of a total of 22,990 were denied.[93]

## SIDEBAR 5.7 Criticisms of the Foreign Intelligence Surveillance Act

Because of the secret nature of FISC proceedings and because congressional oversight of FISA is closed to public view, it is often difficult to determine whether those carrying out the FISA mandate have broken the law. Nonetheless, FISA itself provides for criminal and civil liability for violations in its statutory language. If the government intentionally engages in electronic surveillance without FISC authorization, the government can be fined $10,000 or the offending personnel may face up to five years in prison. Those who are the subject of unauthorized surveillance can also sue under the act for civil damages.[94]

Given the FISC's closed and secretive nature, various advocacy organizations have raised concerns regarding FISA's constitutionality. Numerous lower courts, however, have found FISA constitutional. In *United States v. Duggan*, the defendants were members of the Irish Republican Army (IRA) and were convicted of various crimes concerning the shipment of explosives and firearms.[95] They attempted to suppress evidence the government had collected pursuant to FISA-approved surveillance showing the defendant's attempts to send weapons to Northern Ireland. In *Duggan*, the court held that FISA wasn't overbroad, didn't violate the Fourth Amendment's warrant requirement, and didn't deprive nonresident aliens of equal protection under the law. Specifically, the Supreme Court found that it made sense to treat foreign individuals differently from American citizens when seeking to protect the United States from foreign threats to its national security.[96]

*United States v. Nicholson* dealt with whether "secret" evidence gathered under a FISA warrant could be admitted into court. The court in *Nicholson* ultimately allowed the use of evidence collected as a result of the defendant's arrest and indictment on espionage charges.[97] More importantly, the court rejected claims that FISA violated several provisions and rights found in the U.S. Constitution, including due process, equal protection, separation of powers, and the right to counsel.[98]

Criticisms of FISA have accelerated in the wake of former NSA contractor Edward Snowden's decision to leak information detailing NSA and IC-run programs that capture the information of U.S. persons, in addition to that of foreign agents and foreign powers. Experts have noted that this "dragnet" surveillance by the NSA may be in violation of the Fourth Amendment. Critics have also argued that FISA should be amended to take newer surveillance technologies and procedures (such as data mining and Internet traffic analysis) into account.[99]

In relation to these emerging issues, the celebrated jurist Judge Richard Posner has criticized FISA for being antiquated and inflexible, noting that:

FISA retains value as a framework for monitoring the communications of known terrorists, but it is hopeless as a framework for detecting new terrorists. FISA requires that surveillance be conducted pursuant to warrants based on probable cause to believe that the target of surveillance is a terrorist, when the desperate need is to find out who is a terrorist. (emphasis added)[100]

Legal experts and civil rights advocates are divided on how to view FISA, particularly in light of the amendments to FISA after 9/11. Considerable evidence in the press obtained through Snowden has lent credence to "nightmare" scenarios predicted by civil liberties advocates, including a government empowered by FISA to conduct warrantless physical searches of personal electronic devices and data belonging to U.S. citizens and residents.[101]

### Telephonic Surveillance

Prior to the advent of ubiquitous Internet and mobile devices, FISA warrants generally sought surveillance by way of physical searches, foreign business records, and phone records. One such target of surveillance was "pen registers." A **pen register** (Figure 5.16) is an electronic device that records or

**FIG. 5.16**
An example of an old pen register manufactured in the mid-20th century.

*Source*: John Nagle, Old Pen Register, https://upload.wikimedia.org/wikipedia/commons/e/e3/Pen_Register.jpg.

decodes dialing, routing, addressing, or signaling information transmitted by an instrument or facility from which a wire or electronic communication (such as a phone call) is transmitted.[102] While a pen register captures outgoing transmissions, a pen-trap is a device that captures the incoming electronic or other impulses.[103]

The FISC may mandate a secret order authorizing the installation and use of a pen register or trap if it finds that the information is likely to be obtained by their installation and use and the information obtained is relevant to an ongoing criminal investigation.[104] Generally, the Fourth Amendment protects the privacy, possessory, and liberty interests of individuals. This means that in most cases searches conducted by the government against individuals within the United States are protected under the Fourth Amendment. However, pen registers do not constitute a "search" as defined by the Fourth Amendment because they collect information already available and recorded by a third party.[105] This is broadly known as the "third party doctrine" and discussed elsewhere in this text. Therefore, the burden of proof for the use of pen registers is much lower than with other surveillance methods. When seeking a FISA warrant for the installation of a pen register, the government must merely show that a pen register would "likely" help in an "ongoing" investigation.[106]

### Expansion to Internet Surveillance

As the Internet became a primary mode of 21st-century communication, the surveillance tools used to record phone call data began to be used to capture Internet data. The passage of the USA PATRIOT ACT expanded the use of pen registers to the Internet,[107] allowing the interception of address information from emails and via user-specific Internet traffic.[108] Just as pen registers allow the government to obtain phone numbers, the same Fourth Amendment analysis (i.e. that the information sought is already in the hands of parties other than the target of surveillance) allows the government to obtain email addresses, IP addresses, and URLs.[109]

The PATRIOT ACT also allows collection of "envelope data" from emails.[110] A variety of state and federal laws already allow the federal government to legally obtain information from the back of physical envelopes. Courts have ruled that the sender of physical mail correspondence has no reasonable expectation of privacy concerning the information on the outside of an envelope because envelopes are used in the open. After 9/11, this standard of privacy was also applied to emails under the PATRIOT ACT.

Thus, under the PATRIOT ACT and regulations stemming from it, an email's metadata (i.e. data about data) can be searched without a FISA warrant. Courts across the United States have held that the metadata information contained in an email header is subject to the same diminished privacy rights as the information contained on the back of an envelope. Thus, information about the sender of an email, the time the email was sent etc. does not have the same legal protections as the content of the email message itself. More importantly, once the metadata information is in the possession of federal law enforcement, they can rely on that information to procure a warrant for the contents of the email itself—as long as the information contained in the metadata satisfies the threshold of probable cause.[111]

## CONCLUSION

As with all other aspects of U.S. homeland and national security, the 9/11 attacks led to a dramatic shift in how the IC coordinated its efforts. With information sharing now a fulcrum of IC organization and operation, the United States is better positioned to deliver timely, actionable intelligence to policymakers, agency leaders, and public servants on the frontlines of the homeland security mission. This is perhaps nowhere more apparent than in the massive expansion of the U.S. transportation security apparatus after September 11, 2001, which we discuss in the next chapter.

## HOMELAND SECURITY VOICES: Bruce Hoffman, Ph.D.

*Professor Bruce Hoffman is currently the Director of the Center for Security Studies, Director of the Security Studies Program, and a tenured professor at Georgetown University's Edmund A. Walsh School of Foreign Service, Washington, D.C. He previously held the Corporate Chair in Counterterrorism and Counterinsurgency at the RAND Corporation and was the Director of RAND's Washington, D.C., office. Professor Hoffman also served as RAND's Vice President for External Affairs and was Acting Director for RAND's Center for Middle East Public Policy. Professor Hoffman was Scholar-in-Residence for Counterterrorism at the Central Intelligence Agency between 2004 and 2006. He was also adviser on counterterrorism to the*

Source: Professor Bruce Hoffman

*Office of National Security Affairs, Coalition Provisional Authority, Baghdad, Iraq during the spring of 2004 and from 2004 to 2005 was an adviser on counterinsurgency to the Strategy, Plans, and Analysis Office at Multi-National Forces-Iraq Headquarters, Baghdad. Professor Hoffman was also an adviser to the Iraq Study Group.*

*He remains a member of several groups and organizations, including the National Security Preparedness Group, the successor to the 9/11 Commission, and a member of the Advisory Committee of the Terrorism and Counterterrorism Program at the Human Rights Watch. Professor Hoffman is a scholar and visiting professor at numerous institutions, including the Woodrow Wilson International Center for Scholars; the U.S. Military Academy at West Point; the Institute for Counter-Terrorism, Interdisciplinary Center, Herzliya, Israel; and the S. Rajaratnam School of International Studies, Nanyang Technological University, Singapore. Professor Hoffman was the founding Director of the Centre for the Study of Terrorism and Political Violence at the University of St Andrews in Scotland, where he was also Reader in International Relations and Chairman of the Department of International Relations. He is Editor-in-Chief of Studies in Conflict and Terrorism, the leading scholarly journal in the field, and editor of the new Columbia University Press Series on Terrorism and Irregular Warfare. A revised and updated edition of his acclaimed 1998 book, Inside Terrorism, was published in May 2006 by Columbia University Press in the U.S. and S. Fischer Verlag in Germany.*

***What did you study in school, and how did you get started in your field?***

BH: Early on in my education, the Munich Massacre made a great impression on me. The Munich Massacre was an incident where 11 members of the 1972 Israeli Olympic team and others were taken hostage and murdered by terrorists. The incident made me start thinking about terrorism as more than just a localized problem, but rather a contemporary and increasingly global phenomenon.

I focused on ballistic missile issues and the NATO-Warsaw Pact. When I entered graduate school four years later, my peers were primarily interested in strategic issues such as intercontinental ballistic missiles and the confrontation between NATO and the Warsaw Pact. There was an East-West standoff and a cold war but terrorists were also just then becoming a big part of the picture. It was around this time that terrorists began coercing governments to behave in ways that caused these governments to modify their own policies and treaty agreements. The ability of a small group of people (terrorists) to have such a disproportionate impact on nations was a phenomenon I found fascinating. It made me think of international relations differently and I began focusing on the impact that terrorism was having on international relations.

While in graduate school I began to realize that non-state actors, such as terrorists, have much greater impact on states than people realized. How was this possible? I also became curious about the terrorists themselves. Many of them were in their 20s, around the same age as myself. Sometimes, highly educated and on the same path I was on as a student, but then they somehow headed off in a completely different direction. I began to ask questions that I have attempted to answer since then: Why do persons become terrorists? Why do they commit the acts they do? What is it that compels persons to embrace violence as a means to achieving fundamental political change?

I went to graduate school in 1976 when nobody was studying terrorism, which is also what made it appealing. My graduate degree was in international relations, but I focused on military and diplomatic history and security studies within that degree.

***If the behavior and motives of terrorists interested you, then why not pursue a field like psychology or cognitive science?***

BH: Though psychology may shed light on why terrorists behave the way they do, it seemed to me even back then, that the impetus to becoming a terrorist was an established narrative—the desire to achieve some fundamental change in a political system that these individuals thought was hostile to them, and the belief that joining a certain group of like-minded believers gave collective meaning to their own anger, feelings, or political leanings. For me, understanding terrorism meant trying to understand the political forces and social movements and the historical reasons that animated war and conflict and impelled individuals to becoming terrorists.

***As someone who has seen the field mature, what kind of changes have you seen in the way individuals and scholars approach this field?***

BH: Because of 9/11 there is greater knowledge about terrorism and the various dimensions of it, than ever before. Today, people instantaneously comprehend the concept of the "terrorist narrative." The differences in comprehension are fairy profound. When I was studying terrorism in graduate school, most of the time there were no one else doing so, and certainly very few established academics at the time interested in it. None of the larger related majors, such as political science or international relations, had courses focused on terrorism.

Practically speaking, it was also rare for people to have witnessed a terrorist attack, or even know someone who had been affected directly by a terrorist attack. This changed after the 9/11 attack. Today, it is not very difficult to meet individuals who have been directly impacted by terrorism. Moreover, people today are also increasingly affected by a terrorist attack even though they did not experience the attack themselves. Policies throughout the country change, laws are passed, and economies shift due to attacks which may take place hundreds of miles away. As tragic as the 1998 U.S. Embassy bombings in Africa were, they did not elicit the same visceral reaction as the 9/11 attacks—such as compelling people to join the armed forces or start studying terrorism. Compared to the 1990s many of my students today have had direct experience with terrorism, in one sense or another, often by serving in the U.S. military or in government. The state of knowledge among my students today about terrorism is completely different, and often informed by some kind of direct or personal experience.

***Would you say that violence is a productive or successful way of expressing grievances and influencing change? Why does terrorism continue to be so pervasive?***

BH: Successful, yes. Productive, I'm not sure. The answer depends on how you define success. If success is achieving long-term goals, then terrorism really isn't a successful way of influencing change. But if success means the ability to attract attention to a cause or belief, then absolutely—terrorism succeeds at this. For terrorists, the first stepping stone is attracting sufficient attention to their cause so as to force it to be thrust upon someone else's agenda. If their issue becomes something others have to deal with, then by that definition the use of violence is successful, because in many cases if terrorists had not resorted to violence, their issues would often be ignored.

### But doesn't the use of violence create barriers to achieving political or social change?

BH: Not as long as terrorists attempt to calibrate their violence. As long as terrorists don't go too far, as they did with the 9/11 attacks, then violence doesn't serve as too insurmountable of a barrier. The modern use of violence is a big difference in terrorism from the late 20th century. During the 20th century, violence almost always seemed calibrated for a specific outcome. The inclusion of a theological imperative, so common and pervasive in the 21st century among terrorists, means that terrorism today has become something of a divine decree, and the sense of restraint or calibration of violence is abandoned. Thus, when the use of violence to achieve political or social change is ad-hoc and uncalibrated, it becomes much less successful. Modern-day terrorist organizations, like al-Qa'ida or ISIS, may get attention or publicity, but no one is going to negotiate with them.

### How would you define terrorism?

BH: Terrorism is use of violence or the threat of violence in the pursuit of political change. It is generally acts of violence designed to have far-reaching psychological repercussions committed by non-state actors that often, but not exclusively, target civilians. States of course use terror and other forms of violence against their own citizens and others—and have done so throughout history. And this is as abhorrent and tragic as terrorism is. But one needs to distinguish between "terrorism"—which traditionally is associated with non-state actors and state "terror," which is what the violence perpetrated by governments against civilians is termed.

### Why the dichotomy between "terrorism" and "hate crimes"—why do you think that the federal government and even academia view certain violent actions as terrorism and others as crime? Should there be a difference?

BH: Hate crimes are terrorism. For instance, the FBI's definition of terrorism includes actions that have a political, social, economic, or religious motive. How the media or politicians define terrorism is a different story altogether.

### Critics, including Congress, have called the Department of Homeland Security out for focusing too broadly on al-Qa'ida inspired terrorism instead

*of combating terrorism from other sources such as white supremacists and anti-government groups. In the context of your definition of terrorism and hate crimes, what are your thoughts on their criticism?*

BH: I disagree with those who say that law enforcement agencies do not regard threats other than those posed by al-Qa'ida as legitimate. For instance, in 2002/2003, just after the 9/11 attacks, the FBI said that the most dangerous terrorist threat to the U.S. came from radical environmentalists or animal rights activists. Acts of terrorism and hate crimes are not necessarily mutually exclusive. Nonetheless, inevitably, law enforcement agencies and others will prioritize certain crimes over others.

Moreover, al-Qa'ida presents a very different, sustained threat which straddles something between a strategic and tactical challenge. Since the government and law enforcement lack endless resources, they have to develop a means to prioritize which crimes and which criminal organizations they will address. Thus, it is important to note that law enforcement isn't ignoring the threat of terrorism or crime unrelated to al-Qa'ida, but rather understand that law enforcement pays attention to all threats, but prioritizes and emphasizes addressing the al-Qa'ida threat.

*Let's take a look at foreign policy. There are allegations by many experts that the collateral damage from U.S. drone strikes abroad creates a lot resentment among citizens of countries like Pakistan and Yemen and this resentment is then used by al-Qa'ida, ISIS, and other terrorist organizations to fuel a narrative of terrorism recruitment and retention. What are your thoughts on that?*

BH: An innocent civilian is an innocent civilian. Innocent civilians should not be killed—and the fact that they are is a problematic aspect of drone strikes. Moreover, drones should be used judiciously. However, it is important to remember that drones are not the source of all animus directed towards the U.S. The animus towards the U.S. already exists; drones are often used by terrorist groups as yet another justification to launch attacks on American targets.

In many instances, too, the tallies of civilian casualties are imprecisely known. Governments tend to downplay civilian casualties and terrorist groups or others with an interest against the government tend to exaggerate the same casualties. Discerning the accurate number is part of the problem. The bottom line is, it is wrong to kill innocent civilians. They should never be killed. We (the United States) need to exercise greater restraint, but at the same time that does not mean drones have not proven to be an enormously effective weapon.

### *Why have drones proven to be enormously effective?*

BH: Though drones will not single-handedly win the war on terrorism, they have nonetheless proven to be enormously effective in targeting terrorist leaders. People often confuse tactics with strategy. Drones are a good tactic, but not a viable long-term strategy. Use of drones alone will not end the al-Qa'ida threat. Nonetheless, drone attacks have eliminated many seasoned, experienced, and highly trusted al-Qa'ida operatives. They have compelled members of al-Qa'ida, especially the senior leadership, to spend as much time worrying about their own security as planning the next terrorist attack. These are all positive developments.

### *You've referred to the "war" several times. Many people contend that the "War on Terror" as both a description and an actual conflict is vague and ambiguous. Moreover, critics contend that a war such as this is one without an end. What are your thoughts on these contentions?*

BH: It was a mistake to call this war a "War on Terror" because terror is an emotion. We should have gotten it right and called it a "war on terrorism." This difference is critical because unlike "terror," *terrorism* is recognizable as a political phenomenon. Whether you can declare war on a political phenomenon is a whole other problem, but it is at least slightly less problematical.

Broadly speaking, there never was a "war on terror" because we were never going to war with terrorists everywhere. At the same time, calling the struggle a "war" may not have been a mistake because labeling it so recognized that the struggle against al-Qa'ida and associated forces had gone beyond the ability of law enforcement to counter. In fact, up until 9/11 the U.S. viewed terrorism as a law enforcement problem. The U.S. would approach terrorists as criminals and throw the perpetrators in jail, while failing to unravel the terrorists' chain of command and thus potentially intercepting other terrorist plots. It was only after 9/11 that the law enforcement and national security community recognized that terrorism had crossed a threshold and become a much more strategic threat that could not be dealt with on a local level.

Secondly, it is important to note that we have wars against a lot of things—drugs, cancer, poverty. None of them have been very successful because they are big, amorphous issues like terrorism. However, you do need some all-embracing, galvanizing word to pull together the disparate strands of governmental effort, though I am still not necessarily sure "war" is appropriate, even while I understand why it was chosen.

*What advice would you give someone in graduate school interested in the work that you do?*

BH: Terrorism is a problem that is not going away. It is a problem that still requires smart minds. Even if opportunities in this field may be shrinking at one point in time, at another point they are just as likely to change. Building knowledge on terrorism is essential to understanding it—and government and industry will always need smart people with critical analytical abilities and a solid foundation of learning and understanding of this phenomenon.

## KEYWORDS

- **intelligence process**: The process of the collection of sensitive information by covert or overt means, its creation into intelligence products, and the dissemination of these products to senior policymakers and elected leaders.

- **finished intelligence**: Finalized intelligence products, such as reports, that have been reviewed and correlated with data from other available sources.

- **metadata**: Is "data about data," or a set of data that describes other data.

- **state secrets privilege**: A rule of evidence and legal doctrine that results in the exclusion of evidence from a court case for reasons of national security and based upon sworn statements from government officers.

- **pen register**: An electronic device that records or decodes dialing, routing, addressing, or signaling information transmitted by an instrument or facility from which a wire or electronic communication (such as a phone call) is transmitted.

### KNOWLEDGE CHECK

1. What steps comprise the intelligence process cycle?
2. What are some member agencies of the Intelligence Community? What kinds of intelligence do each of these agencies collect?
3. How does Congress provide oversight on the Intelligence Community? Why is this important?

# NOTES

1. *How Intelligence Works*, The United States Intelligence Community (last visited July 8, 2016) www.intelligencecareers.gov/icintelligence.html.
2. *Id.*
3. *Intelligence Collection Disciplines (INTs)*, Federal Bureau of Investigation (last visited July 8, 2016) www.fbi.gov/about-us/intelligence/disciplines.
4. *How Intelligence Works: Processing*, The United States Intelligence Community (last visited July 8, 2016) www.intelligencecareers.gov/icintelligence.html.
5. *How Intelligence Works: Analysis*, The United States Intelligence Community (last visited July 8, 2016) www.intelligencecareers.gov/icintelligence.html.
6. *How Intelligence Works: Dissemination*, The United States Intelligence Community (last visited July 8, 2016) www.intelligencecareers.gov/icintelligence.html.
7. Exec. Order No. 13,526, 3 C.F.R. § 183 (2009).
8. *Id.*
9. *The World Factbook*, U.S. Central Intelligence Agency (last visited July 8, 2016) *available at* www.cia.gov/library/publications/the-world-factbook/.
10. *ODNI FAQ*, Office of the Director of National Intelligence (last visited June 17, 2016) www.dni.gov/index.php/about/faq?start=5.
11. *Organization*, Office of the Director of National Intelligence (last visited July 8, 2016) www.dni.gov/index.php/about/organization.
12. *Id.*
13. *History*, Office of the Director of National Intelligence (last visited July 8, 2016) www.dni.gov/index.php/about/history; *see also* Intelligence Reform and Terrorism Prevention Act, Pub. L. No. 108–458, 118 Stat. 3638 (2004), *available at* www.gpo.gov/fdsys/pkg/PLAW-108publ458/pdf/PLAW-108publ458.pdf.
14. *Organization*, Office of the Director of National Intelligence (last visited Jan. 2, 2019) www.odni.gov/index.php/who-we-are/organizations; *see also Organization*, Office of the Director of National Intelligence (last visited June 17, 2016) www.dni.gov/index.php/about/organization.
15. *Organization*, Office of the Director of National Intelligence (last visited Jan. 2, 2019) www.odni.gov/index.php/who-we-are/organizations.
16. *Id.*
17. Exec. Order No. 12,333, 3 C.F.R. § 200 (1981).
18. Ellen Nakashima, *Bush Order Expands Network Monitoring*, Washington Post (Jan. 26, 2008) *available at* www.washingtonpost.com/wp-dyn/content/article/2008/01/25/AR2008012503261_pf.html.
19. Barton Gellman & Laura Poitras, *US Intelligence Mines Data From Internet Firms in Secret Program*, Boston Globe (June 7, 2013) *available at* www.bostonglobe.com/news/nation/2013/06/07/mines-internet-firms-data-documents-show/kWTtVohYV6UvqULjJXeGoO/story.html.

20. Ryan Gallagher, *NSA Targets Internet Users Who Search for "Suspicious Stuff,"* *Newly Revealed Documents Show*, Slate (July 31, 2013) *available at* www.slate.com/blogs/future_tense/2013/07/31/xkeyscore_nsa_targets_internet_users_who_search_for_suspicious_stuff.html (last visited July 8, 2016).

21. *FISA Court Ruling on Illegal NSA E-Mail Collection Program*, Washington Post (Aug. 21, 2013) *available at* http://apps.washingtonpost.com/g/page/national/fisa-court-documents-on-illegal-nsa-e-mail-collection-program/409/.

22. *Factbook on Intelligence*, U.S. Central Intelligence Agency, 4–5 (Dec. 1992).

23. Thomas F. Troy, *Truman on CIA*, U.S. Central Intelligence Agency (Sept. 22, 1993) *available at* www.cia.gov/library/center-for-the-study-of-intelligence/kent-csi/vol20no1/html/v20i1a02p_0001.htm.

24. *Clandestine Service: Who We Are*, U.S. Central Intelligence Agency (last updated Aug. 3, 2016) www.cia.gov/offices-of-cia/clandestine-service/who-we-are.html.

25. Chris Pocock, 50 Years of the U-2: The Complete Illustrated History of The 'Dragon Lady', 404 (2004).

26. James S. Van Wagenen, *A Review of Congressional Oversight*, U.S. Central Intelligence Agency (last updated June 27, 2008) www.cia.gov/library/center-for-the-study-of-intelligence/csi-publications/csi-studies/studies/97unclass/wagenen.html.

27. Loch K. Johnson, Strategic Intelligence: Windows into a Secret World (2004).

28. Timothy S. Hardy, *Intelligence Reform in the Mid-1970s*, U.S. Central Intelligence Agency, (last updated Aug. 4, 2011) www.cia.gov/library/center-for-the-study-of-intelligence/kent-csi/vol20no2/html/v20i2a01p_0001.htm.

29. *About DIA*, Defense Intelligence Agency (last visited Jan. 2, 2019) www.dia.mil/About.aspx.

30. *Organization*, Defense Intelligence Agency (last visited Jan 2, 2019) www.dia.mil/About/Organization.aspx.

31. National Defense Authorization Act for Fiscal Year 1997, Pub. L. No. 104–201, 110 Stat. 2422 (1996), *available at* www.gpo.gov/fdsys/pkg/PLAW-104publ201/pdf/PLAW-104publ201.pdf.

32. *Id.*

33. *Id.*

34. Alexandra Viers, *The Future of Geospatial Intelligence*, The Cipher Brief (Oct 4, 2015) www.thecipherbrief.com/article/future-geospatial-intelligence.

35. Marc Ambinder, *The Little-Known Agency That Helped Kill Bin Laden,* The Atlantic (May 5, 2011) www.theatlantic.com/politics/archive/2011/05/the-little-know.

36. *About NGA*, National Geospatial-Intelligence Agency (last visited Jan. 2, 2019) www.nga.mil/About/Pages/Default.aspx.

37. *Today's NCTC*, National Counterterrorism Center, at 5–8 (2017) www.dni.gov/files/NCTC/documents/features_documents/NCTC-Primer_FINAL.pdf.

38. National Commission on Terrorist Attacks Upon the United States, The 9/11 Commission Report, at 403 (2004) www.9-11commission.gov/report/911Report.pdf.

39. Karen DeYoung, *After Attempted Airline Bombing, Effectiveness of Intelligence Reforms Questioned*, Washington Post (Jan. 7, 2010) *available at* www.washingtonpost.com/wp-dyn/content/article/2010/01/06/AR2010010605158.html.

40. *Terrorist Identities Datamart Environment (TIDE)*, National Counterterrorism Center, (last visited Jan. 6, 2019) www.dni.gov/files/NCTC/documents/features_documents/TIDEfactsheet-10FEB2017.pdf.

41. *Hearing Before the House of Representatives Committee on Homeland Security, Subcommittee on Transportation Security and Infrastructure Protection* (Sept. 9, 2008) (statement of Rick Kopel, Principal Deputy Director, Terrorist Screening Center, FBI) *available at* www.fbi.gov/news/testimony/the-terrorist-screening-database-and-watchlisting-process.

42. *How We Work*, National Counterterrorism Center (last visited Jan. 2, 2019) www.nctc.gov/overview.html.

43. *Id.*

44. *Strategic Intent*, National Counterterrorism Center (last visited July 8, 2016). www.dni.gov/index.php/features/125-about/organization/national-counterterrorism-center/1458-strategic-intent.

45. *Office of Intelligence and Analysis Mission*, U.S. Dep't of Homeland Security (Dec. 7, 2018) www.dhs.gov/more-about-office-intelligence-and-analysis-mission.

46. *State and Major Urban Area Fusion Centers*, U.S. Dep't of Homeland Security (Dec. 17, 2018) www.dhs.gov/state-and-major-urban-area-fusion-centers.

47. *The Nationwide SAR Initiative*, Nationwide SAR Initiative (last visited Jan. 2, 2019) http://nsi.ncirc.gov/?AspxAutoDetectCookieSupport=1.

48. *About the NSI*, Nationwide SAR Initiative, (last visited Jan. 2, 2019) http://nsi.ncirc.gov/about_nsi.aspx.

49. *Fusion Center Guidelines: Developing and Sharing Information and Intelligence in a New Era: Guidelines for Establishing and Operating Fusion Centers at the Local, State, and Federal Levels*, U.S. Dep't of Justice, Global Justice Information Sharing Initiative, (Aug. 2006), *available at* http://it.ojp.gov/documents/fusion_center_guidelines_law_enforcement.pdf.

50. 28 C.F.R. § 23.20.

51. *See e.g.*, Michael German & Jay Stanley, *What's Wrong with Fusion Centers?*, ACLU (Dec. 2007) www.aclu.org/files/pdfs/privacy/fusioncenter_20071212.pdf.

52. Carl Levin and Tom Coburn, Senate Permanent Subcommittee on Investigations, Federal Support For and Involvement in State and Local Fusion Centers Majority and Minority Staff Report, U.S. Senate (Oct. 3, 2012) *available at* www.hsgac.senate.gov/imo/media/doc/10-3-2012%20PSI%20STAFF%20REPORT%20re%20FUSION%20CENTERS.2.pdf.

53. *Deployed Intelligence Officers and Protective Security Advisors*, U.S. Dep't of Homeland Security (May 31, 2017) www.dhs.gov/publication/deployed-intelligence-officers-and-protective-security-advisors.

54. *Quick Facts*, FBI (last visited July 8, 2016) www.fbi.gov/about-us/quick-facts/quickfacts.

55. *Famous Cases & Criminals: 9/11 Investigation (PENTTBOM)*, FBI (last visited July 8, 2016) www.fbi.gov/about-us/history/famous-cases/9-11-investigation.

56. *Ten Years After: The FBI Since 9/11*, FBI (last visited July 8, 2016) www.fbi.gov/about-us/ten-years-after-the-fbi-since-9-11.

57. *Federal Bureau of Investigation: National Security Branch*, U.S. Dept. of Justice (last visited July 8, 2016) www.fbi.gov/about-us/nsb/national-security-branch-brochure.

58. *Intelligence Branch Overview*, FBI (last visited July 8, 2016) www.fbi.gov/about/leadership-and-structure/intelligence-branch.

59. *Joint Terrorism Task Forces*, FBI (last visited Jan. 2, 2019) www.fbi.gov/investigate/terrorism/joint-terrorism-task-forces.

60. *Id.*

61. *Id.*

62. *Bureau of Intelligence and Research*, U.S. Dep't of State (last visited Jan. 2, 2019). www.state.gov/s/inr/.

63. USA PATRIOT Improvement and Reauthorization Act of 2005, Pub. L. No. 109–177 (2006).

64. *About the Division*, U.S. Dep't of Justice (last visited Jan. 2, 2019) www.justice.gov/nsd/about-nsd.html.

65. *Office of Intelligence*, U.S. Dep't of Justice (last visited Jan. 2, 2019) www.justice.gov/nsd/intelligence.htm.

66. *About: Duties and Functions of the U.S. Department of the Treasury*, U.S. Dep't of Treasury (last visited July 8, 2016) www.treasury.gov/about/role-of-treasury/Pages/default.aspx; *see also* Terrorism and Financial Intelligence, U.S. Dep't of Treasury (last visited Jan. 6, 2019) *available at* www.treasury.gov/about/budget-performance/budget-in-brief/BIB19/08.%20TFI%20BIB.pdf.

67. Multiple agencies within the federal government play a role in investigating threats or cases of terrorist financing in the charitable sector. Treasury's Office of Intelligence and Analysis regularly reviews intelligence pertaining to terrorist financing abuse of charitable organizations. The Internal Revenue Service Criminal Investigation Division examines important tax-based information relating to terrorist abuse of charities. Finally, Treasury's Office of Foreign Assets Control plays an invaluable role by implementing and administering terrorist-financing related designations, including those against charities, pursuant to Executive Order 13224.

68. *About: Terrorism and Financial Intelligence*, U.S. Dep't of Treasury (last visited July 8, 2016) www.treasury.gov/about/organizational-structure/offices/Pages/Office-of-Terrorism-and-Financial-Intelligence.aspx.

69. Treasury Department (@USTreasury), Twitter (Jun. 2, 2019, 8:02 AM) https://twitter.com/ustreasury/status/473479796518060033.

70. Steven Aftergood, *Department of Energy: Office of Intelligence*, Federation of American Scientists, (May 12, 2009) *available at* www.fas.org/irp/agency/doe/.

71. Todd Garvey and Edward C. Liu, Cong. Research Serv., R41741, The State Secrets Privilege: Preventing the Disclosure of Sensitive National Security Information During Civil Litigation, at 1 (2011).

72. Carrie Newton Lyons, *The State Secrets Privilege: Expanding Its Scope Through Government Misuse*, 11 Lewis & Clark L. Rev. 99 (2007).

73. *U.S. v. Reynolds*, 345 U.S. 1 (1953).

74. *Id.* at 8.

75. Memorandum from Eric Holder, Attorney General, to Heads of Executive Departments and Agencies (Sept. 23, 2009) *available* at www.justice.gov/sites/default/files/opa/legacy/2009/09/23/state-secret-privileges.pdf (Policies and Procedures Governing Invocation of the State Secrets Privilege).

76. *Id.*

77. *Id.*

78. *Id.*

79. *Id.*; *see also* Memorandum from Alfred Cumming, Specialist in Intelligence and National Security (Jan 18, 2006) *(Statutory Procedures Under Which Congress is to be Informed of U.S. Intelligence Activities, Including Covert Actions) available at* www.fas.org/sgp/crs/intel/m011806.pdf ("In a change enacted as part of the fiscal year (FY) 1991 Intelligence Authorization Act (P.L. 102–88), Congress, for the first time, placed a statutory obligation upon the President to ensure that the congressional intelligence committees are kept fully and currently informed of United states intelligence activities, including any significant anticipated intelligence activity").

80. Foreign Intelligence Surveillance Act, Pub. L. No. 95–511, 92 Stat. 1783 (1978); *see also* 50 U.S.C. ch. 36 (2018).

81. *Id.*

82. 50 U.S.C. §1861 (2018).

83. 50 U.S.C. §1801(b) (2018).

84. 50 U.S.C. § 1801.

85. Foreign Intelligence Surveillance Act, Pub. L. No. 95–511, 92 Stat. 1783 (1978); *see also About the Foreign Intelligence Surveillance Court*, U.S. Foreign Intelligence Surveillance Court (last visited Jan. 3, 2019) www.fisc.uscourts.gov/about-foreign-intelligence-surveillance-court.

86. *Id.*

87. 50 U.S.C. §1805(a) (2018).

88. 50 U.S.C. §1802(a)(3) (2018).

89. Letter from J. Reggie B. Walton to Chairman Leahy, Committee on the Judiciary, U.S. Senate (July 23, 2013) *available at* www.fisc.uscourts.gov/sites/default/files/Leahy.pdf.

90. 50 U.S.C. §1802(a)(3).

91. *Id.*

92. *See* 50 U.S.C. §§1801(h), 1805(a).

93. *Foreign Intelligence Surveillance Act Court Orders 1979–2012*, Electronic Privacy Information Center, (last visited Jan. 3, 2019) *available at* www.epic.org/privacy/wiretap/stats/fisa_stats.html.

94. 50 U.S.C. § 1810 (2018).

95. *U.S. v. Duggan*, 743 F.2d 59 (2d Cir. 1984).

96. *Id.*

97. *U.S. v. Nicholson*, 955 F.Supp. 588 (E.D. Va. 1997).

98. *Id., see also USA v. Abu-Jihaad*, 630 F.3d 102 (2d Cir. 2010) (finding FISA is constitutional on its face and does not violate the Fourth Amendment).

99. K. A. Taipale, *Whispering Wires and Warrantless Wiretaps: Data Mining and Foreign Intelligence Surveillance*, 7 N.Y.U. Rev. L. & Sec. (2006).

100. Richard A. Posner, *A New Surveillance Act*, The Wall Street Journal (Feb. 15, 2006) *available at* www.wsj.com/articles/SB113996743590074183.

101. Barton Gellman, Aaron Blake & Greg Miller, *Edward Snowden Comes Forward as Source of NSA Leaks*, The Washington Post (Jun. 9, 2013) *available at* www.washingtonpost.com/politics/intelligence-leaders-push-back-on-leakers-media/2013/06/09/fff80160-d122-11e2-a73e-826d299ff459_story.html.

102. 18 U.S.C. § 3127(3) (2018).

103. *Id.*

104. 50 U.S.C. § 1842 (2018).

105. *Smith v. Maryland*, 442 U.S. 735 (1979).

106. 18 U.S.C. § 3123(a)(1).

107. USA PATRIOT ACT of 2001, Pub. L. No. 107–56 (2001) § 216 ("modification of authorities relating to use of pen registers and trap and trace devices").

108. *Id.*

109. *Id.*

110. *Id.*

111. *Id.*

# *Transportation*

---

**IN THIS CHAPTER YOU WILL LEARN ABOUT**

The components of the U.S. transportation system.

The role of the Transportation Security Administration and other agencies in securing the transportation system.

## INTRODUCTION

The nation's air, land, and marine transportation systems are designed for accessibility and efficiency. These two characteristics make the U.S. transportation system vulnerable to attack and an attractive target for terrorists.[1] Securing the transportation system is a monumental undertaking. Airlines, trains, waterways, roadways, and other transportation modes carry millions of people and pieces of cargo every day. Thus, the security challenge is to identify the small number of bad actors within the millions of ordinary travelers and carriers—and stop them before they cause harm.

Securing transportation systems is not just about protecting lives. Different modes of transportation (e.g. air, highway) operate as networks, and a disruption in one area impacts the entire transportation network. For instance, the consequences of 9/11 included not just the massive loss of life but also the ensuing shutdown of the entire aviation system. The 9/11 attacks grounded all air traffic (except for military, police, and medical) in the United States and Canada for two days and put a great strain on other means of transport. The grounding of air traffic also affected travelers, cargo, and commerce on an international scale. Thus, taking the disruption of the transportation network into account, the economic consequences of 9/11 were measured in the hundreds of billions of dollars.

Given the enormous impact that can stem from disruptions to transportation networks, there are several federal agencies involved in protecting U.S. transportation systems. While September 11 was the catalyst for the creation of the Department of Homeland Security (DHS), it was the creation of the Transportation Security Administration (TSA) subcomponent within DHS that was the most direct result of the attacks. Even though we call it the "Transportation" Security Administration, today the public sees TSA primarily as an *aviation security* agency. This perception isn't unfounded. Even though TSA's mission requires it to protect all parts of the transportation system, because of 9/11 the TSA has most visibly focused on securing the civil aviation system over other forms of transportation.

Though the TSA emphasizes civil aviation protection, the agency is also responsible for implementing and overseeing the security of all of the nation's passenger and freight transportation systems, including securing rail, surface, and pipeline systems. TSA works closely with other federal agencies, such as Customs and Border Protection, the U.S. Coast Guard, the Federal Aviation Administration, and a host of domestic and international public and private partners. This chapter explores the role of the TSA and other similar organizations as well as the vast challenge of securing U.S. transportation systems.

## THE TRANSPORTATION NETWORK

The United States has a robust transportation network consisting of seven key modes:

*Aviation*: Included are all aircraft, air traffic control systems, and about 19,700 airports, heliports, and landing strips. Approximately 500 of these ports provide commercial aviation services at civil and joint-use military airports, heliports, and sea-plane bases. The aviation transportation network also includes commercial and recreational aircraft (manned and unmanned) and a variety of support services, such as aircraft repair stations, fueling facilities, navigation aids, and flight schools.[2]

*Highway and Motor Carrier*: Encompasses more than 4 million miles of road-way, 600,000 bridges, and 350 tunnels. Traffic transiting this infrastructure includes commercial vehicles like trucks (some carrying hazardous materials), motor coaches, and school buses. This transportation mode also includes vehicle and driver licensing systems, traffic management systems, and cyber systems for operational management.[3]

*Maritime Transportation System*: Consists of about 95,000 miles of coastline, 361 ports, more than 25,000 miles of waterways, and intermodal land-side connections that allow the various modes of transportation to move people and goods to, from, and on the water.[4]

*Mass Transit and Passenger Rail*: Includes terminals, operational systems, and supporting infrastructure for passenger services by transit buses, trolley-buses, monorail, heavy rail (such as subways and metros), light rail, and vanpool/rideshare networks. Public transportation and passenger rail operations provided an estimated 10.8 million passenger trips in 2014.[5]

*Freight Rail*: Consists of seven major carriers, hundreds of small railroads, more than 138,000 miles of active railroads, more than 1.33 million freight cars, and approximately 20,000 locomotives. An estimated 12,000 trains operate daily. The Department of Defense has designated 30,000 miles of track and structure as critical to the mobilization and resupply of U.S. forces.[6]

*Pipeline Systems*: Consists of more than 2.5 million miles of pipelines spanning the country carrying nearly all of the nation's natural gas and about 65% of hazardous liquids, as well as various chemicals. Above-ground assets, such as compressor stations and pumping stations, are also included.[7]

*Postal and Shipping*: Moves about 720 million letters and packages each day and includes large integrated carriers, regional and local courier services, mail services, mail management firms, and chartered and delivery services.

For all transportation modes, there are four principal policy objectives supporting a system of deterrence and protection:

1. Ensuring the trustworthiness of the passengers and the cargo flowing through the system;
2. Ensuring the trustworthiness of the transportation workers who operate and service the vehicles, assist passengers, or handle the cargo;

3. Ensuring the trustworthiness of the private companies operating within the system, such as the carriers, shippers, agents, and brokers; and

4. Establishing a perimeter of security around transportation facilities and vehicles in operation.

The first three policy objectives are concerned with preventing an attack from within a transportation system, such as the one that occurred on 9/11. Security strategies and policies designed around these three objectives ensure attackers do not masquerade as passengers or workers to launch an attack.[8] The fourth policy objective is concerned with preventing an attack from outside a transportation system. For example, terrorists could ram a bomb-laden speedboat into an oil tanker, as was done in October 2002 to the French oil tanker *Limberg*, or they could launch a shoulder-fired missile at an airplane during take-off or landing, as was attempted in November 2002 against an Israeli charter jet in Mombasa, Kenya.[9]

While many potential attack paths can be blocked, it is not possible to achieve absolute transportation security and prevent every attack. Often, system vulnerabilities are revealed only when adversaries apply a novel approach, targeting an aspect of a transportation network with an innovative tactic. As such, policymakers strive to manage risk by balancing security priorities with the fast and efficient transport of people and cargo.

## SECURITY AGENCIES AND METHODOLOGIES

The federal agency most directly engaged in implementing solutions to achieve transportation security policy objectives is the Transportation Security Administration (TSA). A component of the Department of Homeland Security (DHS), TSA employed some 55,600 people in 2016, constituting nearly a third of the entire DHS workforce.[10] Its $7.6 billion budget funds 17 offices addressing all aspects of transportation security, some of which include legislative affairs, intelligence and analysis, the Federal Air Marshal Service, training and development, and public affairs.[11]

TSA works across all transportation modes to identify and address emerging security threats, screen for threatening goods and people moving within

**FIG. 6.1**
A GAO Report
diagram that
explains TSA's
passenger
screening
program.

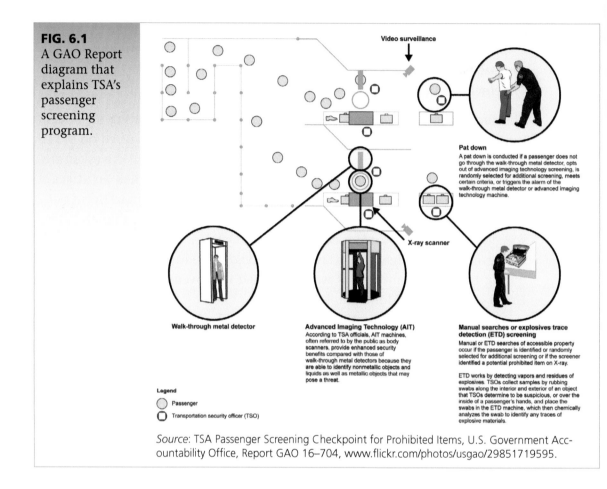

Video surveillance

**Pat down**
A pat down is conducted if a passenger does not go through the walk-through metal detector, opts out of advanced imaging technology screening, is randomly selected for additional screening, meets certain criteria, or triggers the alarm of the walk-through metal detector or advanced imaging technology machine.

X-ray scanner

**Walk-through metal detector**

**Advanced Imaging Technology (AIT)**
According to TSA officials, AIT machines, often referred to by the public as body scanners, provide enhanced security benefits compared with those of walk-through metal detectors because they are able to identify nonmetallic objects and liquids as well as metallic objects that may pose a threat.

**Manual searches or explosives trace detection (ETD) screening**
Manual or ETD searches of accessible property occur if the passenger is identified or randomly selected for additional screening or if the screener identified a potential prohibited item on X-ray.

ETD works by detecting vapors and residues of explosives. TSOs collect samples by rubbing swabs along the interior and exterior of an object that TSOs determine to be suspicious, or over the inside of a passenger's hands, and place the swabs in the ETD machine, which then chemically analyzes the swab to identify any traces of explosive materials.

**Legend**
○ Passenger
▢ Transportation security officer (TSO)

*Source*: TSA Passenger Screening Checkpoint for Prohibited Items, U.S. Government Accountability Office, Report GAO 16–704, www.flickr.com/photos/usgao/29851719595.

the transportation system, set security standards, and work with private sector organizations operating in each transportation mode to develop security plans and encourage best practices. TSA works with other federal, state, and local government agencies. Its partners include many DHS Components, most notably Customs and Border Protection (CBP), and agencies outside of DHS, such as the Federal Aviation Administration (FAA), the U.S. Intelligence Community, and federal, state, and local law enforcement.

For years, TSA focused primarily on advances in scanning technology to improve security and efficiency. The advanced imaging technology (AIT) machines (more commonly called "full-body scanners") throughout U.S. airports are an example of technological advances designed to rigorously scan air passengers. At airports, TSA also scans every piece of checked baggage before it is loaded onto a passenger aircraft. Individually scanning every person and bag at the same level of scrutiny is often called a "**100% screening methodology**." It presumes that all people and baggage present an equally devastating potential threat.

The 100% methodology is especially palatable to the traveling public (and the lawmakers who represent the public). Scanning every person and bag in full provides a valuable sense of security, yielding the perception that if all people and things are subjected to inspection, the terrorist threat is eliminated. This, however, belies the enormous challenge of the transportation security mission. The terrorist threat is constantly evolving, and agencies involved with transportation security must not only address current threats but also imagine and address future exploits. Terrorists look for unaddressed vulnerabilities, not those that already receive heavy scrutiny.

What is more, the 100% methodology demands vast resources and can cause significant delays in the transport of people and cargo. TSA must ensure transportation security without dampening the productivity of a fast and efficient transportation system. While the consequences of a terrorist attack take priority, the economy also suffers from the application of a 100% screening methodology. For example, there are some 87,000 flights every day in the United States, each of which move millions of people and millions of tons of cargo. Scanning all of these people and cargo presents a complex logistical challenge. Disruption or delay in one part of the aviation system has cascading implications at cities hundreds of miles away. Thus, TSA's mission is to simultaneously address current threats and interdict innovative plots to attack the transportation system, all while preserving the supply chain and movement of people that facilitate a productive U.S. economy.

Considering the hundreds of millions of dollars required for scanning technologies, the economic implications of efficient transportation systems, and the constantly evolving threat environment, TSA and its partners have increasingly moved away from a 100% screening methodology and towards a **risk-based screening methodology**.[12] A risk-based methodology acknowledges that not all people and goods present an equal potential threat and focuses limited resources on identifying and disrupting the most likely threats. Using intelligence and a layered approach to security, TSA and its partners implement tools and programs to mitigate the risk of attack. As discussed throughout this chapter, TSA and CBP have initiated a number of risk-based screening initiatives to focus resources and apply directed measures based on intelligence-driven assessments of security risk.

## SIDEBAR 6.1 Trusted Traveler Programs

The risk-based methodology underpins the TSA and CBP trusted traveler programs. TSA's PreCheck is a prescreening program that vets airline passengers prior to their arrival at the airport (Figure 6.2). Passengers submit biometrics (like fingerprints) and receive a background check. If approved, PreCheck participants and their carry-on luggage receive an abbreviated scanning process at the airport. They do not need to remove their shoes or take liquids or laptops out of carryon bags. (Importantly, PreCheck participants can be randomly selected to go through a full scanning process, preserving the unpredictability of airport security meant to

**FIG. 6.2**
TSA's PreCheck program is an example of risk-based screening at work.

*Source*: TSA PreCheck Enrollment Center, U.S. Transportation Security Administration, www.tsa.gov/sites/default/files/pre.jpg.

keep terrorists on their toes.) As of this writing, TSA is on track to process 50% of the entire traveling public through the PreCheck program.

Similarly, Customs and Border Protection (CBP) administers the Global Entry program. Travelers who apply for Global Entry receive a background check and an in-person interview and submit biometrics. Once admitted to the program, travelers receive expedited clearance at U.S. ports of entry. When entering the United States using Global Entry, the traveler has their fingerprints read by a scanner, which are checked against their submitted biometrics, and complete a customs declaration, and they then are moved swiftly towards the exit.[13] CBP also administers the NEXUS and SENTRI programs.[14] NEXUS uses pre-screening to expedite the processing of travelers moving between Canada and the United States at land ports of entry, and SENTRI expedites processing for prescreened travelers at southern land ports of entry.

These programs allow TSA and CBP to distinguish between low-risk and higher-risk travelers and, in so doing, focus limited resources on unknown or elevated-risk passengers. Trusted traveler programs reduce the volume of people that must pass a more elaborate screening process at points of entry and departure. By relying on these programs, TSA and CBP can ensure security of the transportation network while minimizing disruption to the efficient flow of passengers.

## AVIATION SECURITY

While TSA's mandate is to secure all forms of mass transit in the United States, its mission has been dominated by securing the aviation system. This is due in large part to how terrorists attacked the United States on September 11, as well as the persistent terrorist threat targeting the domestic and international aviation system. Aviation security legislation in the aftermath of 9/11 has largely focused on specific mandates to comprehensively screen for explosives and carry out background checks and threat assessments. A Congressional Research Service report on transportation security for the 114th Congress outlined six challenges facing TSA as it seeks to achieve its aviation security mission:[15]

1. Effectively screening passengers, baggage, and cargo for explosive threats;
2. Developing effective risk-based methods for screening passengers and others with access to aircraft and sensitive areas;
3. Exploiting available intelligence information and watchlists to identify individuals who pose potential threats to civil aviation;
4. Effectively responding to security threats at airports and screening checkpoints;
5. Developing effective strategies for addressing aircraft vulnerabilities to shoulder-fired missiles and other standoff weapons; and
6. Addressing the potential security implications of unmanned aircraft operations in domestic airspace.

Before 9/11, the federal government was not in the passenger screening business. Instead, airlines paid for and conducted passenger and baggage security screening themselves. Every airport had slightly different screening policies though the overall policies were regulated by the Federal Aviation Administration (FAA). In 1998, the FAA delivered a report to Congress titled "Civil Aviation Security Responsibilities and Funding." This report detailed two existing aspects of the aviation security system at the time: Air carriers bore the primary responsibility for securing passengers, crews, baggage, and cargo; and the FAA required carriers and airport operators to maintain the minimum security necessary to meet the threat level.

In the aftermath of the 2001 attacks, Congress quickly passed the Aviation and Transportation Security Act, which created the TSA. The Transportation Security Act shifted aviation security responsibilities from private contractors to the federal government, placing TSA in charge of setting aviation security standards and policies and enforcing those standards with a federal workforce of security screeners inspecting airline passengers, baggage, and cargo. Today the TSA vets, either directly or through indirect means, all air passengers moving into, out of, and within the United States through TSA's Secure Flight program.

The transformation of aviation screening from a private to federal security regime introduced advantages and challenges. One advantage was uniformity of system security. Prior to 9/11, the screening approaches applied by the numerous and disparate private security firms were inconsistent. This meant aviation security depended on the capacity and processes of each private company, and it also meant that air passengers had to contend with varying approaches to airport screening depending on the company that was conducting the screening. The creation of TSA ensured a single standard for screening policies, rules, and tactics at every airport.

For instance, today Transportation Security Officers (TSOs) wear standard uniforms, implement generally the same procedures, use the same equipment, and are trained to treat passengers in the same manner. As a result, air passengers encounter a relatively homogenous and predictable screening experience throughout U.S. airports. A standard screening experience, however, also presents a security disadvantage. Predictability can make it easier for terrorists and criminals to identify and exploit screening vulnerabilities at any TSA checkpoint. The challenge for TSA has been to balance a common set of screening protocols while also introducing the randomness that can frustrate terrorist or criminal planning.

One solution has been TSA's Playbook program. Under TSA's "Operation Playbook," TSA uses roving TSO teams, Behavior Detection Officers (BDOs), and Transportation Security Inspectors to conduct random and unpredictable screening and inspection of passengers and employees at secure areas.[16] According to TSA guidelines, the purpose of the Playbook is to "create a transportation security system that increases unpredictability, thereby frustrating terrorist plans and potentially deterring terrorist attacks."[17]

## A Layered Approach to Aviation Security

In securing the aviation system, TSA relies on a layered security approach. Like a combination lock requiring several numbers in the correct sequence to open, passengers and cargo must successfully pass multiple security layers before they gain access to an airport's sterile area; that is, the area immediately after the security checkpoint at an airport, where one boards the airplane. A layered security approach ensures that even if a bad actor manages to circumvent one security layer, they will encounter several more before reaching the sterile area.

By the time a passenger boards a flight, they have been subject to at least 20 security layers.[18] Before a passenger ever arrives at the airport, there are a number of less visible layers at work. TSA intelligence analysts work with

**FIG. 6.3**
Multiple inter-
diction points
for bad actors
make air travel
safer, but also
make TSA's job
harder.

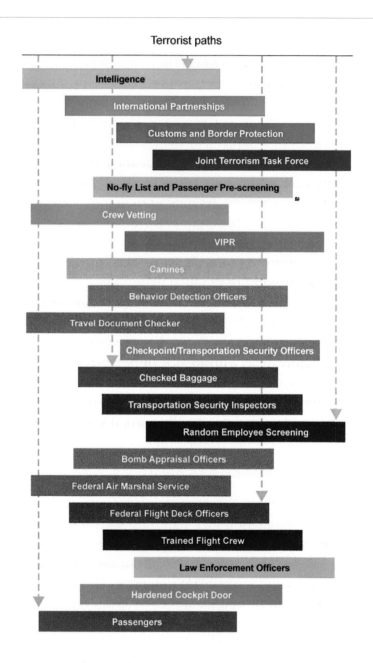

Terrorist paths

Intelligence

International Partnerships

Customs and Border Protection

Joint Terrorism Task Force

No-fly List and Passenger Pre-screening [a]

Crew Vetting

VIPR

Canines

Behavior Detection Officers

Travel Document Checker

Checkpoint/Transportation Security Officers

Checked Baggage

Transportation Security Inspectors

Random Employee Screening

Bomb Appraisal Officers

Federal Air Marshal Service

Federal Flight Deck Officers

Trained Flight Crew

Law Enforcement Officers

Hardened Cockpit Door

Passengers

*Source*: TSA's "Layered Approach" to Security Screening, U.S. Transportation Security Administration.

counterparts in the Intelligence Community, including DHS Intelligence and Analysis and international agencies, to determine imminent threats to aviation security. TSA collaborates with other DHS Components and intergovernmental task forces, such as the Joint Terrorism Task Force (JTTF), on threats and security issues. Passengers are checked against TSA's "No Fly" list, and airplane crews are vetted with similar intelligence tools.

More layers are present throughout the airport. Airports with commercial flights are required to have a TSA-approved security program, covering everything from the type of fencing around the perimeter of the airport to how many police officers are needed to prevent vehicles from being parked or left unattended in loading zones. Airport perimeter security is accomplished by a badging and credentialing system at each airport. This system, including access controls and credentialing of airport workers, is generally the responsibility of airport operators.

TSA requires that access control points into and out of the airport and sterile gate area be secured by security personnel or electronic locks. Airports must provide training for airport personnel to ensure they can identify and challenge individuals who are not authorized to access secure areas. Occasionally, airports may also deploy surveillance technologies and security patrols to protect property from intrusion. These measures are paid for by the airport but approved by TSA as part of the airport's overall security program.[19]

The best security is based on characteristics focused on behavior and intelligence-driven data. Screening based on intelligence and behavior also avoids numerous concerns regarding profiling passengers on the basis of race, religion, or another protected class and encourages screening agencies, such as TSA, to concentrate resources on those passengers whose behavior poses the most risk. To that end, TSA has developed several screening programs driven by behavioral characteristics, such as the early Screening Passengers by Observational Techniques (SPOT) program. Under the SPOT program, Behavioral Detection Officers (BDOs) seek to identify travelers whose behaviors reveal stress or deceptiveness, which could indicate malicious intent. By 2012, the SPOT program had deployed approximately 3,000 BDOs at an annual cost of $200 million.[20]

BDOs participate in Visible Intermodal Prevention and Response (VIPR) teams, which also consist of Federal Air Marshals, local law enforcement, and canine teams that may patrol anywhere at the airport, both before and beyond the checkpoint.[21] Canines are often considered the quickest, most efficient means of detecting explosive substances. The TSA National Explosives Detection Canine Team trains and deploys canines and handlers at transportation facilities to detect explosives. More than 180 of the TSA teams are dedicated to passenger screening at about 40 airports. In addition, canine teams composed of local law enforcement officers and TSA-provided canines may be present. TSA has trained more than 500 teams in partnership with local law enforcement agencies.[22]

## SIDEBAR 6.2 VIPR Teams

Visible Intermodal Prevention and Response (VIPR) teams were implemented to augment the security of U.S. transportation networks. Formed in the aftermath of the 2004 Madrid train bombings, VIPR teams were authorized by 6 U.S.C. Section 112, initially to serve as a force multiplier and visual deterrent for rail, bus, and other non-aviation transportation modes. In time, however, the teams have been deployed to all mass transit hubs, including airports.

VIPR teams are managed through the TSA Federal Air Marshal Service (FAMS) and the Office of Security Operations and Transportation Sector Network Management. These teams supplement and enhance the visible presence of law enforcement at high-profile events involving venues relying on mass transit such as trains, particularly during periods of heightened threat.

VIPR teams are composed of Federal Air Marshals, Transportation Security Officers, Surface Transportation Security Inspectors, canine detection teams, explosives detection specialists, Behavior Detection Officers, and federal, state, and local law enforcement officers.[23] They work to deter terrorism through their *visible* presence. Unlike FAMS, who strive to be inconspicuous on important flights, VIPR teams overtly patrol sensitive transportation hubs and actively search for criminal and terrorist activity. A visible law enforcement presence deters bad actors who may otherwise commit a terrorist attack if they think no one is looking.

In addition to airports and mass transit hubs, VIPR teams detain and search travelers at railroad stations, bus stations, ferries, car tunnels, seaports, subways, truck weigh stations, rest areas, and special events (such

**FIG. 6.4**
Members from Amtrak police, Transportation Security Administration, and local law enforcement agencies participate in Operation RAILSAFE at Washington, D.C.'s Union Station, September 3, 2015. During Operation RAILSAFE counterterrorism assets conducted explosive detection sweeps, random bag inspections, and patrols by TSA's Visible Intermodal Protection and Response teams during high volume travel days to highlight passenger rail systems security.

*Source*: Barry Bahler, Operation RAILSAFE, U.S. Dep't of Homeland Security, www.flickr.com/ photos/dhsgov/21130074012/in/photolist-ycc9QU-yaLVBY-yaAsko-xVuj8u-ycUNJk-xVpAAF- xVzYmK-yd69Br-xVA1Ae-yaAmCw-xgcK6c-xgcMNr-yaLQMh-ydAW2H.

as presidential inaugurations). They are used to guard critical transportation infrastructure, such as the 2.6 million miles of oil and natural gas pipelines throughout the United States,[24] and they are trained to deal with chemical, biological, radiological, and nuclear weapons of mass destruction.

VIPR teams conducted approximately 14,000 operations in 2014.[25] These included National Security Special Events and Special Event Assessment Rating activities, such as the Super Bowl, NCAA Final Four, and the Presidential State of the Union.

Aircraft are screened on a random basis by VIPR teams, as are airport and airline employees. Those with access to the airport's secure and sterile areas, such as food service workers and gate attendants, are subject to random screening in addition to undergoing background checks on a recurring basis. Once at the screening checkpoint, passengers show their boarding pass and ID to a Transportation Security Officer (TSO), who checks the validity of documents, verifying that the person on the ID is indeed the one flying on the plane. Individuals with faulty or duplicitous documents are referred to local law enforcement for additional inspection.

Passengers then must pass through the screening area at the TSA checkpoint. In addition to passengers on commercial airlines, TSA spends considerable time and resources screening cargo and facility personnel for explosives and other harmful agents. Screening passengers for explosives is primarily accomplished with AIT machines and other technologies. Passengers are also occasionally and randomly subjected to an explosives trace detection swab, which searches for samples of explosive residue from passenger carry-on items. Meanwhile, as required by law, TSA scans every checked bag before flight. Scanning machines can check up to 900 bags per hour for explosives.[26]

Federal Air Marshals are TSA law enforcement officers who are trained to operate within the aircraft, providing security to passengers while in flight. TSA also trains private individuals to be aware of their surroundings and respond to threats. For example, through the Federal Flight Deck Officer Program, TSA trains and authorizes pilots and some crew members to carry a firearm aboard the plane. Through the Crew Member Self Defense program, TSA also trains other members of the flight crew to defend themselves inside an aircraft in the event of a hijacking or similar attack. And National Suspicious Activity Reporting (SARS) programs like "See Something, Say Something" provide yet another layer of security, empowering the general public to identify potentially threatening items or people that TSA and other airport security personnel may miss.

The last layer of security is the fortified, locked cockpit door of the aircraft. After the 9/11 attacks, the FAA mandated certain requirements for how cockpit doors are constructed and operated during flight. Cockpit doors must be locked before takeoff and throughout the flight, and in most cases, the doors must be able to withstand a grenade blast.[27]

Collectively, these layers of security ensure no single failure in a screening process can result in a compromise of passenger and flight safety. Coupled with randomized searches and risk-based, intelligence-driven screening, an attack of the kind seen on 9/11 is almost impossible today.

## SIDEBAR 6.3 November 2013 LAX Attack

On November 1, 2013, a gunman targeting TSA employees fired several shots at a screening checkpoint at Los Angeles International Airport (LAX). Transportation Security Officer (TSO) Gerardo Hernandez was killed (the first TSA employee to die in the line of duty) and two others were injured. After the incident, TSA identified several proposed actions to improve checkpoint security: Enhanced active shooter training for screeners; better coordination and dissemination of information regarding incidents; routine testing of alert notification capabilities; and expanded law enforcement presence at checkpoints during peak travel times.

After the attack, Congress passed the Gerardo Hernandez Airport Security Act of 2015. The Act addresses security incident response at airports. It requires airports to put in place working plans for responding to security incidents, such as active shooters, terrorist attacks, and incidents targeting passenger checkpoints.[28] The Act also requires TSA to create a mechanism to share best practices among airports and requires TSA to identify ways to expand the availability of funding for checkpoint screening law enforcement support through cost savings from improved processes. Since TSOs are relatively immobile, unarmed, and not protected by bulletproof vests, having law enforcement respond to incidents is critical to securing an airport screening checkpoint. While some airports place law enforcement officers at dedicated posts, others allow officers (especially those airports with their own airport police) to patrol areas of the airport as necessary.

## Foreign Airport Security

What about the screening practices of foreign air carriers and airports that send passengers to the United States? TSA ensures that foreign carriers sending passengers from abroad to the United States meet standardized requirements regarding passenger and cargo screening. As part of these responsibilities, TSA inspects foreign airports from which commercial flights depart to the United States. TSA representatives assess country compliance against international norms for aviation security. They also work closely with international partners to plan and coordinate U.S. airport risk analyses and assessments of foreign airports. These TSA officials also coordinate the response to terrorist incidents and threats to U.S. citizens and transportation assets and interests overseas.

As of this writing, at least 15 foreign last point of departure airports (eight in Canada, two in the Bahamas, one in Bermuda, one in Aruba, two in Ireland, and one in the United Arab Emirates) have Customs and Border Protection (CBP) "preclearance" facilities where passengers are admitted to the United States prior to departure.[29] Passengers arriving on international flights from these preclearance airports deplane directly into the U.S. airport's sterile area where they can then board connecting flights or leave the airport directly, rather than being routed to CBP screening facilities at those airports. Several international airports have also received preclearance status for checked baggage.

## Air Cargo Security

Air cargo is transported on most commercial passenger flights. In the aftermath of 9/11, the Implementing Recommendations of the 9/11 Commission Act of 2007 ("9/11 Act") included a mandate to screen all air cargo (foreign and domestic) on passenger planes for explosives and threatening items piece by piece. When cargo arrives at the airport, it is often stacked on pallets and wrapped in plastic. To adhere to the 9/11 Act, TSA or the airlines were required to unwrap and individually screen every piece on every pallet. This threatened to dramatically slow the international supply chain, causing massive economic repercussions for businesses, air forwarders (such as UPS and FedEx), and airlines. TSA and the air transportation industry were given three years to comply with the 9/11 Act.

**DEFINITION BOX: Scanning and Screening**

**Scanning** is the physical inspection of people and cargo, including by hand, with trained animals (like dogs), and with technology. **Screening** is the overall process of reviewing risk and ensuring people and cargo do not present a threat. This can be achieved through scanning techniques, but also by using intelligence, passenger data, and other means. Scanning is screening, but screening is not necessarily scanning.

To screen cargo efficiently, TSA recognized that complying with the 9/11 Act would require a different approach. In response, it developed the Certified Cargo Screening Partnership (CCSP) program. CCSP participants, such as airlines, airports, air forwarders, distributors, and manufacturers, receive certification from TSA allowing them to screen cargo at the point of origin, for example, at a manufacturing plant where products are packaged for shipment. Once screened, cargo could arrive at the airport via vendors and carriers who were also vetted CSSP participants, thus ensuring that the cargo did not have to be screened again at the airport.

Though CSSP was effectively implemented domestically, since TSA has no authority to enforce security certification overseas, TSA was unable to implement the law internationally. When the deadline arrived, international cargo began arriving in the United States daily in violation of federal law. TSA exercised its right to extend the deadline and began forming international partnerships with countries from which air cargo departs. In February 2011, President Obama and Prime Minister Harper of Canada released the joint declaration, "Beyond the Border: Shared Vision for Perimeter Security and Economic Competitiveness." Through the implementation of this document, the United States and Canada achieved mutuality in air cargo security programs. Since then, the United States has also reached agreements with Switzerland and the European Commission, which state that their air cargo screening policies and practices are commensurate with the United States. Due to these agreements, cargo originating in or transiting through partner countries in Europe meets the screening requirements set forth in the 9/11 Act.

Air cargo transported on all-cargo planes is continually vulnerable to attack or tampering. In 2010, al-Qa'ida operatives in Yemen created two bombs disguised as printer cartridges.[30] They hid the bombs in two separate packages and sent them by air cargo to the United States, both timed to detonate in mid-air over Chicago. The packages were first separately flown on passenger planes to the United Arab Emirates. One was transferred onto a UPS all-cargo plane destined for a transfer point at the East Midlands Airport in the United Kingdom; the other was loaded onto a FedEx plane in Dubai. Due to intelligence work, both bombs were discovered and defused before they reached the United States.

The plot revealed that terrorists were adapting their plans to exploit relaxed screening for cargo moved on all-cargo planes. For TSA and CBP, this greatly expanded the volume of air cargo requiring screening before it reached the United States. In response, TSA and CBP jointly launched the Air Cargo Advance Screening (ACAS) pilot project.[31] The voluntary project was designed to test the feasibility of receiving "cargo data security files" for all air cargo destined for the United States. Under the program, express, passenger, and all-cargo air carriers, as well as freight forwarders, submitted filing data to CBP's Automated Targeting System to identify high-risk shipments that required closer inspection. ACAS has been extended each year since its inception, and while it remains a pilot program, it is an important part of the United States' overall air cargo security apparatus.[32]

## SIDEBAR 6.4 Unmanned Aerial Vehicles (UAVs)

The advent of affordable and increasingly sophisticated unmanned aerial vehicles (UAVs, or more commonly, "drones") raises a number of potential security risks (Figure 6.5). For example, UAVs could be used to deliver an explosive payload to a public area or building. UAVs operated by law enforcement and government agencies could also be targeted by hackers as part of a broader cyberattack on U.S. infrastructure and as a way to obtain sensor and map data. Numerous examples reveal that security concerns regarding UAVs are real and growing.

For instance, in September 2011, the FBI disrupted a homegrown terrorist plot to attack the Pentagon and the Capitol Building with large model aircraft packed with explosives. The incident heightened the

**FIG. 6.5**

This drone is an advanced prototype model of a UAV. Technology from this drone eventually filters down for use by domestic law enforcement, such as CBP and the FBI. Thereafter, these technologies become available to consumers.

*Source*: Advanced Unmanned Aerial Vehicle, NASA.

concern about potential terrorist attacks using unmanned aircraft. In September 2013, an unauthorized flight at a political rally in Dresden, Germany, came into close proximity with Chancellor Angela Merkel. In January 2015, the crash of a small hobby drone on the White House lawn in Washington, D.C., drew concerns about White House safety and security. A number of drone flights throughout 2015 in Paris raised concerns about security threats, and there are increasing reports of UAVs flying over or in close proximity to airports, restricted airspace, and manned aircraft throughout the United States.

While the payload capacity of drones inherently limits how much damage can be done with a conventional weapon (such as explosives), drones could be used to deploy chemical, radiological, biological, or nuclear weapons, and the resulting damage would be catastrophic. Recognizing the rising security concerns, the FAA has issued guidance to law enforcement regarding unlawful drone operations. It remains unclear how law enforcement agencies can implement such guidance given limited training and technical capacity to respond to this emerging potential threat.[33] Though TSA has broad statutory authority over aviation security issues, as of this writing it has not formally addressed the potential security concerns arising from UAV operations in domestic airspace.

It is important to remember that while drones may pose a risk to aviation security, they are also a valuable homeland security asset. CBP currently employs a small fleet of modified Predator drones and has plans to acquire additional drones to augment its border patrol capabilities. These unarmed drones patrol the northern and southern land borders and the Gulf of Mexico to detect potential border violations and monitor suspected drug traffic. State and local governments have also expressed interest in acquiring and operating drones for diverse missions, such as traffic patrol, surveillance, and security for large-scale events, such as the Olympics. Several federal grant programs have allotted a small number of drones to a few states with specific FAA-limited flight operation instructions. These numbers are likely to grow as the FAA and TSA promulgate more specific rules about localized drone operation.

### Aviation Cybersecurity

As air travel has increasingly come to rely on complex technology, there has been concern over cybersecurity threats to aircraft, air traffic control systems, and airports. Executive Order 13636 provides broad guidance to DHS regarding how it can work with the FAA to identify cybersecurity risks, establish voluntary cybersecurity measures, and share information on cybersecurity threats within the broader cybersecurity framework.[34] Additionally, 49 U.S.C. Section 44912 directs TSA to periodically review threats to civil aviation with a particular focus on specified threats, including the potential disruption of civil aviation service resulting from a cyberattack.[35]

Despite these specific laws and regulations, TSA mostly works on cybersecurity issues through voluntary collaboration with airports, aviation software and hardware manufacturers, and other companies. Under this informal framework, TSA has formed the Transportation Systems Sector Cybersecurity Working Group, which created a cybersecurity strategy for the transportation

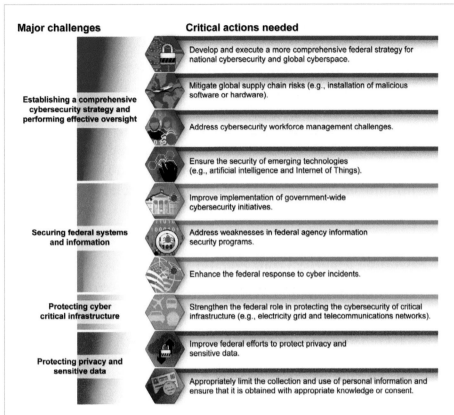

**Major challenges**    **Critical actions needed**

Establishing a comprehensive cybersecurity strategy and performing effective oversight

Develop and execute a more comprehensive federal strategy for national cybersecurity and global cyberspace.

Mitigate global supply chain risks (e.g., installation of malicious software or hardware).

Address cybersecurity workforce management challenges.

Ensure the security of emerging technologies (e.g., artificial intelligence and Internet of Things).

Securing federal systems and information

Improve implementation of government-wide cybersecurity initiatives.

Address weaknesses in federal agency information security programs.

Enhance the federal response to cyber incidents.

Protecting cyber critical infrastructure

Strengthen the federal role in protecting the cybersecurity of critical infrastructure (e.g., electricity grid and telecommunications networks).

Protecting privacy and sensitive data

Improve federal efforts to protect privacy and sensitive data.

Appropriately limit the collection and use of personal information and ensure that it is obtained with appropriate knowledge or consent.

**FIG. 6.6**
A broad infographic, which though not directly relevant to aviation cybersecurity, nonetheless highlights the numerous challenges government agencies like the TSA must face when addressing cyberattacks.

*Source*: Ten Critical Actions Needed to Address Four Major Cybersecurity Challenges, U.S. Government Accountability Office, Report GAO-18–645T, www.gao.gov/assets/700/693405. pdf.

sector in 2012.[36] In coordination with the FBI and industry partners, TSA also launched the Air Domain Intelligence Integration Center and an accompanying analysis center in 2014 to share information and conduct analysis of cyber threats to civil aviation.[37] The program includes analysts from the Office of the Director of National Intelligence (ODNI), the FBI, the FAA, TSA, and DHS Components that work together to share information with the private sector.

For onboard aircraft systems, the FAA requires security and integrity checks as part of a certification and airworthiness process. Large commercial aircraft manufacturers and aviation systems manufacturers now collaborate with software security companies to ensure their software passes the FAA's software security requirements in avionics equipment. The government and the private sector recognize that additional work needs to be done to ensure the safety of aviation software systems, especially in an era of growing foreign cyberespionage. The Government Accountability Office (GAO) has recommended that the FAA develop a comprehensive and coordinated cybersecurity strategy for aviation systems, rather than its current patchwork approach. The GAO also recommended that the FAA better clarify cybersecurity roles and responsibilities, improve management security controls and contractor oversight, and fully incorporate National Institute of Standards and Technology information security guidance into its policies.[38]

### Aviation Security Controversies

TSA's airport operations have been the subject of significant ire from the traveling public, as well as lawmakers, academics, and security experts. Since 2004, the DHS Inspector General's Office issued 115 audit and inspection reports about TSA operations, along with hundreds of recommendations for improving efficiency and effectiveness. As DHS IG John Roth told the House Committee on Oversight and Government Reform in 2015, "we remain deeply concerned about TSA's ability to execute its important mission."[39]

TSOs have been implicated in a range of highly public controversies. Officers have been fired for theft of passenger belongings,[40] and allegations of racial and ethnic profiling against travelers are commonplace. There have also been ongoing issues in the maintenance of AIT machines and training for TSOs who use them.[41] From the public's perspective, the machines have always been controversial.

The first versions of the AIT machines used backscatter X-rays to produce images that showed significant details of the human body beneath clothing (Figure 6.7). They also subjected the individual being scanned to ionizing radiation, albeit in small amounts. This led to broad public backlash, and the FAA Modernization and Reform Act of 2012 mandated that the machines be removed and replaced with a system that secured the traveling public without the negative privacy implications of backscatter technology. These new replacement AIT machines scan passengers using millimeter waves (the same

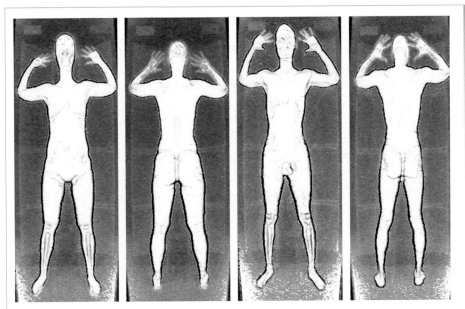

**FIG. 6.7**
An example of a backscatter image produced by some older TSA airport screening machines.

*Source*: Backscatter Image, U.S. Transportation Security Administration.

kind of radio waves emitted by cell phones) that display the items beneath a traveler's clothing on a generic outline of a person (rather a realistic x-ray image).

Meanwhile, the Electronic Privacy Invasion Center (EPIC) sued DHS in 2012 claiming that use of any AIT machine (backscatter or millimeter-wave) constituted a violation of numerous laws and rights, including those granted by the Fourth Amendment.[42] As a result, courts permitted the use of the AIT machines so long as travelers were provided with an alternative screening option, such as a full-body pat-down. The implementation of full-body pat-downs has also drawn significant criticism and resulted in numerous instances of public complaints.

The way TSA uses trusted traveler screening at checkpoints has also drawn criticism. The DHS Inspector General informed Congress in 2015 that as a way to increase checkpoint throughput, TSA used a practice of "managed inclusion," where members of the general public were at times randomly selected to use PreCheck lanes even though they were not program participants and had not been vetted.[43]

*[handwritten margin note: 4th Amendment: search & seizure]*

**CALL-OUT BOX**
**Body Scanner Resolution Rooms Conduct and Privacy**

*Happy new year! Over the holidays, I read an article titled "The TSA Is Laughing at You" talking about what happens in the resolution rooms where body scanner images are viewed. We've talked about this many times in the past, but information is often spread through uninformed sketchy third-hand sources. So, I just wanted to post on privacy issues again.*

*First off, I want to make it clear that since the implementation of new software on our body scanners, many of the rooms are no longer in use. Instead, a generic image is used for millimeter wave scanners. You can read more about the software here.*

*These resolution rooms are still used in locations where backscatter machines are in place. For units that do not yet have the new software, TSA has taken all efforts to ensure passenger privacy. The officer who assists the passenger never sees the image the technology produces and the officer who views the image is remotely located in a secure resolution room and never sees the passenger. The two officers communicate via wireless headset. The resolution room is used only for the viewing of the images and is not a gathering place or break room for other officers as the officer viewing the images has to be focused in order to prevent any dangerous items from entering the airport.*

*Advanced imaging technology cannot store, print, transmit or save the image, and the image is automatically deleted from the system after it is cleared by the remotely located security officer. Officers evaluating images are not permitted to take cameras, cell phones or photo-enabled devices into the resolution room. Initially, it was feared by the traveling public that these images would be leaked and posted online. This has not happened. To further protect passenger privacy, backscatter technology has a privacy filters that blur images.*

*This is the image our officers see from the viewing room.*

*Bob Burns*
*TSA Blog Team*
*January 2, 2013*[44]

Given these types of operational issues, there have been calls to expand the Screening Partnership Program (SPP), which provides for privatized passenger screening similar to the way screening was conducted prior to 9/11. Under this program, private contractors replace the federal workforce at airports and operate under TSA oversight. TSA has resisted SPP, and only a few airports have been allowed to implement the program. There is ongoing conflict between Congress, TSA, and airport owners and operators about if and how this program can be expanded. A 2015 GAO Report indicated that TSA's method for calculating the cost effectiveness of SPP required improvement and that TSA's estimated costs should be provided to Congress.[45]

Given these and other issues, to this day, federalization of airport screening remains controversial. Representative Bill Shuster, Chairman of the House Transportation and Infrastructure Committee, contended that, in hindsight, the decision to create TSA as a federal agency functionally responsible for passenger and baggage screening was a "big mistake" and that frontline screening responsibilities should have been left in the hands of private security companies.[46]

At the same time, TSA has been challenged by Congress in its pursuit of a risk-based methodology. For example, in 2013, TSA announced it would remove penknives 2.36 inches or smaller, as well as golf clubs and novelty baseball bats, from the banned carry-on item list. Then-TSA Administrator John Pistole testified before Congress that intelligence indicated emerging terrorist threats involved explosives, not small knives.[47] Thus, he said that TSOs needed to prioritize their checkpoint screening to focus on the greatest threat (cleverly concealed bombs) rather than negligible threats (small knives or bats). Pistole's proposed strategy was a good example of a risk-based security methodology in practice.

Congress resisted Pistole's decision, even though the International Civil Aviation Organization (ICAO) had already amended restrictions on penknives years earlier, effectively allowing those knives to be carried on flights bound for the United States. Some congressional representatives threatened to write legislation prohibiting TSA from removing penknives from the banned item list, citing passenger safety. In response, TSA was forced to back down, and penknives remain on the banned item list today.

Use of terrorist watchlists has also presented challenges for TSA. The failed al-Qa'ida bombing attempt of Northwest Airlines flight 253 on December 25, 2009, by Umar Farouk Abdulmutallab (the so-called Underwear Bomber) raised policy questions regarding the effective use of terrorist watchlists and intelligence information to identify individuals who may pose a threat to aviation. As noted in earlier in the text, in the immediate aftermath of 9/11, Homeland Security Presidential Directive 6 directed the Attorney General to establish the Terrorism Screening Center (TSC) to monitor and maintain the

U.S. government's consolidated Terrorist Screening Database (TSDB).[48] The TSDB informs TSA's "No-Fly" list, which contains the names of known or suspected terrorists or criminals who are not allowed to board flights into or within the United States. Though the TSDB is an important tool in safeguarding the nation, Abdulmutallab was not included on it, despite intelligence information that indicated he should have been. This incident prompted reviews of intelligence analysis and terrorist watchlisting processes and ultimately led to changes to the criteria for adding individuals to the classified Terrorist Identities Datamart Environment (TIDE), which is used to populate the TSDB, and by extension, TSA's "No Fly" list.[49]

## MASS TRANSIT AND RAIL SECURITY

Bombings and shootings on passenger trains in Europe and Asia have illustrated passenger rail system vulnerability to terrorist attacks. Passenger rail systems, such as Amtrak in the United States, as well as mass transit systems, such as subways in many metropolitan U.S. cities, carry about five times as many passengers each day as airlines. Mass transit and rail systems cover hundreds of thousands of miles of track and include multiple stations designed for easy access, often located in city centers.

The increased focus on securing air travel after 9/11 has led to concerns that terrorists may turn their attention to these "soft" targets. Policymakers are confronted with the timeless challenge of balancing the desire for increased rail passenger security with the efficient functioning of transit systems. They must also consider the potential economic and psychological costs of an attack along with other federal priorities.[50] The volume of ridership and number of access points in the mass transit system make it impractical to subject all rail passengers to the type of screening airline passengers undergo. Consequently, transit security measures tend to emphasize managing the consequences of an attack, even as steps have been taken to reduce the risk of a terrorist attack on mass transit systems.

For example, rail operators, supported by government assistance, routinely conduct vulnerability assessments, plan for emergencies, time emergency response, and measure the performance of emergency personnel through

**FIG. 6.8**
This poster is one of a series created for Amtrak by the Michael Schwab Studio to advertise cross-country routes. The Crescent follows a 1,377-mile route that takes it through 12 states and the District of Columbia.

*Source*: Michael Schwab, Amtrak, https://history.amtrak.com/archives/i-crescent-i-poster-2008.

regular drills. These are usually coordinated with local law enforcement, fire safety, and medical response personnel. Rail operators also train local security personnel for responses to possible threats and install equipment, such as video cameras, to track suspicious packages and passengers.

Unlike the aviation sector, where TSA provides security directly to the airports and airlines by running checkpoints, security at most rail and subway terminals and stations is provided though the rail lines or station owners. Amtrak provides its own security forces at New York Penn Station and Washington, D.C.'s Union Station, and metropolitan police patrol subway systems nationwide. TSA still plays a consistent and increasingly important role in securing U.S. rail systems, but TSA is far less physically present at rail and mass transit hubs than at airports. For the most part, for mass transit and rail systems, TSA's role is one of oversight, coordination, intelligence sharing, training, and assistance to local security forces, rather than actual security screening.

The 9/11 Act included provisions on passenger rail and transit security and authorized $3.5 billion in grants through fiscal years 2008–2011 for public transportation security. The 9/11 Act reclassified public transportation agencies and railroads as high-risk targets and required that owners and operators draft DHS-approved security plans.[51] Other provisions of the 9/11 Act required DHS to conduct a name-based security background check and immigration status check on all public transportation and railroad frontline employees and gave DHS the authority to regulate rail and transit employee security training standards. The aforementioned VIPR teams are most present at rail and mass transit hubs. They occasionally conduct operations with local law enforcement, creating unpredictable visual deterrents with periodic patrols of transit and passenger rail systems.

In 2010, TSA completed a national threat assessment for transit and passenger rail, and in 2011, TSA completed an updated transportation systems sector-specific plan, which established goals and objectives for a secure rail transportation system. According to the plan, there are three primary objectives for reducing risk in rail and mass transit systems:

1. Increase system resilience by protecting high-risk/high-consequence assets (such as critical tunnels, stations, and bridges);
2. Expand visible deterrence activities through the use of canine (VIPR) teams, passenger screening, and anti-terrorism teams; and
3. Engage the public and transit operators in the counterterrorism mission.[52]

TSA transportation security inspectors conduct assessments of transit systems (and other surface modes) through the agency's Baseline Assessment for Security Enhancement (BASE) program. The BASE program sets a security standard for individual system security programs and also provides for a voluntary assessment focusing on categories such as security plans, security training, drills and exercise programs, public outreach efforts, and background check programs. Based upon review, the BASE program helps transit agencies identify ways to further enhance security.[53] This review also gives TSA a broad picture of mass transit readiness, which helps identify system-wide vulnerabilities that can then be addressed.[54]

TSA has also developed the Intermodal Security Training and Exercise Program (I-STEP), a security training and security exercise program for surface transportation modes. I-STEP arose from the recommendations made in the 9/11 Commission report, which called for an exercise and training program for mass transit, freight rail, and over-the-road bus transportation system providers. I-STEP exercises help test and evaluate security plans, including prevention, preparedness, response, and cooperation with first responders. By revealing individual system vulnerabilities and plans, I-STEP supports more effective training and readiness while also advancing partnerships and information-sharing between government and the private sector.[55]

In 2010, TSA launched Operation RAILSAFE, which provides an enhanced visible law enforcement and security presence at certain stations and on certain trains on high-volume travel days. This risk-based program is infrequently implemented, with only 50 RAILSAFE events in 42 states as of 2015.[56] DHS also provides grants for security improvements for public transit, passenger rail, and other surface transportation modes under the Transit Security Grant Program. The vast majority of the funding goes to public transit providers. As well as offering funding for projects that improve security, the grant program gives TSA a mechanism for helping industry prioritize vulnerabilities or aspects of system security plans and readiness.

### Freight Rail Security

Unlike the mass transit and passenger rail system, the U.S. freight rail system is predominantly used to transport cargo (freight) within the country and into Canada and Mexico. Freight rail transport is particularly attractive for its high efficiency over long distances, carrying raw materials and manufactured products across the country and the continent. TSA and the Department of Transportation (DOT) share responsibility for securing the U.S. freight rail system, and their work in this area has primarily focused on securing trains carrying hazardous materials.

Most hazardous materials transported in the United States travel by rail, with DOT estimating upwards of 1.7 million carloads of hazardous materials moved annually.[57] A **hazardous material** is a substance that poses an unreasonable risk to health, safety, and property, including things like petroleum products, toxic chemicals, waste and pollutants, and toxic inhalation hazards (TIH), such as chlorine gas and ammonia.[58] While there have been

**FIG. 6.9**
Railcars such as this one are also regulated by the Federal Rail Administration (FRA).

*Source*: Freight Car, U.S. Federal Rail Administration, https://railroads.dot.gov/sites/fra.dot.gov/files/FRA_locomotive.png.

few terrorist threats to U.S. rail freight, the impact from an attack on the freight system could have enormous consequences. Rail freight is often transported through urban areas, where an attack could spread hazardous materials among a dense population. Additionally, because manufacturing and commerce depends heavily on rail freight, an attack could have an outsized, cascading impact on the U.S. economy.

Because the freight rail system is privately owned, operated, and maintained, securing the system requires close collaboration between TSA, other federal departments, such as the Federal Railroad Administration, and the private sector. TSA's Transportation Sector Network Management office manages all surface transportation security, with one division, the Freight Rail Program office, focusing on freight rail. This division, and TSA and DHS more broadly, are charged with issuing regulations for rail carriers to conduct vulnerability assessments, create security plans, and participate in TSA-led security exercises and training programs. DOT also serves a regulatory function, responsible for ensuring the safety and security of transporting hazardous materials.

To date, TSA has focused almost exclusively on securing freight carrying toxic inhalation hazard (TIH) materials, given their potential impact on public health.[59] A 2004 Homeland Security Council report found that the destruction of a single chlorine gas tank in an urban area would release a gas cloud that could kill 17,500 people, injuring 10,000 more and sowing mass panic.[60] In 2007, there were 105,000 carloads of TIH materials moved in the United States, evidencing the volume of shipments posing a potential threat if attacked or otherwise destroyed.[61]

## HIGHWAY AND MOTOR CARRIER SECURITY

The challenge of securing rail passengers is dwarfed by the challenge of securing passenger cars and buses. In the United States, approximately 76,000 buses carry 19 million passengers on weekdays to hundreds of thousands of destinations throughout the country. Buses are extremely difficult to secure due to their large number and mobility. While TSA provides some information to private companies and public sector organizations (such as schools with bus fleets) on how to secure buses and bus routes, passenger bus security is not part of a comprehensive TSA strategy.

FEMA also plays a role in bus security in their capacity as DHS' grant administration authority. For example, the FEMA Intercity Bus Security Grant Program plays an important role in implementing FEMA's National Preparedness System.[62] The $3 million grant provides funding for protecting intercity bus systems (traveling between cities) from terrorism. The program seeks to assist operators of fixed-route intercity and charter bus services in obtaining the resources required to support security measures, such as enhanced planning, facility security upgrades, and vehicle driver protection.[63]

## MARITIME SECURITY

Maritime security focuses on securing seafaring vessels, the cargo they carry, and the transportation hubs serving these vessels, such as seaports and regional transportation hubs. A key challenge for U.S. policymakers is prioritizing maritime security activities among a nearly unlimited number of potential attack scenarios. A weapon of mass destruction could be smuggled amid the millions of shipping containers that arrive at U.S. ports every year. A bomb-laden speedboat could be rammed into a passenger or military vessel, which is how al-Qa'ida attacked the U.S.S. *Cole* in Yemen in 2000.[64] These are not the only scenarios, but as with all terrorist attacks, there are more potential scenarios than ones that are likely to occur.

Maritime security is one of the basic responsibilities of the U.S. Coast Guard (USCG), a semi-autonomous branch of the armed forces housed within DHS. Several domestic and international laws grant the USCG authority to monitor and secure U.S. territorial waters. The Espionage Act of 1917 mandated that the USCG create and carry out regulations to prevent damage to harbors and vessels during national security emergencies. The Port and Waterways Act of 1972, which was a reaction to several major oil spills and other natural and manmade disasters during the early 1970s, provided port safety authority to the USCG to protect the use of port transportation facilities and to enhance efforts against the degradation of the marine environment.

**FIG. 6.10**
Crew members from Coast Guard Station Curtis Bay provide security during Baltimore's Star-Spangled Spectacular fireworks show.

*Source*: Matthew S. Masaschi, Coast Guard Security Operation, U.S Coast Guard, www.flickr.com/photos/coast_guard/16243259903/in/photolist-qKmXge-rn69rF-rFpWF8-5pdUGY-bAcGmy-q3C2MM-nbxPGS-rFjzvZ-nujhP6-roRdLb-9syGei-bpCvyo-9bCETA-bpyGkm-ro5Hhg-5pdVi1-qKpDYo-5qaTRg-9rzdo4-bCxFKF-qKmXsX-7zMU6L-7zMUbS-5p9Dwx-5qaVFg-5qaWsr-nsKHPT-5qb7rg-rFpWU4–5qff9Q-roRx1C-9sd9oP-dCT9iF-dWG9UV-rn69hT-9spVQn-5qfdYN-5pdUhY-bpCuAG-5p9DJZ-5p9ApP-5qfeAU-bCxxgr-5qff7o-w1bBZu-5p9CqR-5pdTxh-bpCfdW-5qfeSG-pKzc2F.

After 9/11, the Maritime Transportation Security Act (MTSA) of 2002 provided extensive new authorities to the USCG for preventing acts of terrorism on the high seas. MTSA regulates the security of maritime vessels. The MTSA requires owners and operators of seaborne vessels to designate security officers, develop security plans based on security assessments, implement security measures specific to the vessel's operation, such as passenger and baggage screening, security patrols, access control, and surveillance equipment. The MTSA also requires vessels to comply with current maritime security levels set by the USCG.[65] Similar to TSA's risk-based screening, not all maritime vessels are screened or subject to the same level of scrutiny. Rather, screening and security efforts are adjusted and modulated for the amount of risk a particular vessel poses. This requires coordination between the maritime community, port operators, and state, local, and federal governments and agencies, such as the USCG.

While the USCG is the lead federal agency in securing maritime transportation and seaports, TSA provides additional support in passenger screening and port security. Through the aforementioned I-STEP program, TSA provides security training materials for crews of passenger vessels and port terminal employees.[66] TSA also provides maritime-related passenger vessel security training courses covering security awareness, improvised explosive device (IED) recognition and response, crowd control, terrorism and hijacking scenarios, screening procedures, and evacuation procedures.[67]

TSA also administers the Transportation Worker Identification Credential (TWIC), required by the MTSA.[68] It provides credentials for employees who access secure areas of ports and vessels. As with other TSA screening programs, employees receive a threat assessment and are given a TWIC biometric ID card indicating they are cleared to access secure areas. TSA has issued 3.5 million such cards to port employees, truckers, and merchant mariners. In 2016, the DHS Inspector General's Office found that the TWIC program's background check process is in some cases unreliable, owing to ineffective fraud detection, quality controls, and program visibility.[69]

## Maritime Container Security

The bulk of U.S. overseas trade is carried by cargo ships on open water. The consequences of an attack on these ships or the ports where they dock could

**FIG. 6.11**
DHS and the Coast Guard routinely collaborate on research and design projects that further security on the high seas.

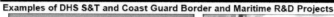

Examples of DHS S&T and Coast Guard Border and Maritime R&D Projects

Source: GAO

Mobile Surveillance System Imager/Radar Upgrade, a retrofit kit developed by S&T BMD for CBP tested at the Arizona-Mexico border.

Source: USCG

Shipboard Vessel Entanglement System developed by the Coast Guard and others for use on Coast Guard vessels.

*Source*: DHS and Coast Guard Collaboration on R&D, U.S. Government Accountability Office Report GAO-13-372, www.flickr.com/photos/usgao/9956867093/in/photolist-gaRxGi-o3aXBQ-9eAkNZ-o5dAeS-hJfmS8-o77civ-o52LS4-o3aLfS-nMQtc1-o52TdF-oZE86r-nMQEaH-rsvrb1-jDPBko-pETyzD-qBA4cy-bv2BZp-nAqgzC-nJ4LaF-aB-4Hbh-jDPBkd-jDPBhN-oZDn7Y-qK49nU-nJ4L8g-paMZnm-pQdtkn-DEhFRD-CRa3xt-211bc9R-V6gprk-TL5Ty7-TCgTQF-pgZnQR-bvSPxC-oZDmNG-C2EPvb-Sw75NB-RvRK9m.

be catastrophic. Just as 9/11 caused massive disruption to the international aviation system, a large attack on a seaport or vessel could disrupt the international supply chain, causing cascading negative implications for commerce and trade around the world.

CBP is primarily responsible for securing goods arriving by sea from abroad. The challenge of screening containers moved over water is enormous. Each year, some 12 million shipping containers arrive at U.S. ports. Currently, all containers arriving at U.S. ports are scanned to detect radiation, and some high-risk cargo receives imaging inspection. However, Section 1701 of the 9/11 Act requires all imported marine containers to be scanned by nonintrusive imaging equipment and radiation detection equipment *at a foreign loading port*. The law set a 2012 deadline for DHS to meet this standard. The deadline, however, was extended three times and as of this writing, the new deadline is 2018.

Like the air cargo screening mandate, the maritime container mandate is rooted in a 100% methodology, and there are two primary challenges in meeting it. First, compliance requires the purchase and implementation of scanning and imaging equipment at foreign ports, which is a logistical challenge. Secondly, obtaining this equipment and implementing scanning overseas is very costly. The Congressional Budget Office estimates that meeting the letter of the law would cost $22 to $32 billion over ten years.[70] The costs would either need to be funded directly by the U.S. government or recouped through shipper fees, which would have a significant economic impact on businesses. An alternative proposal would be to scan only at the 121 foreign ports loading 97% of U.S.-bound containers and re-routing the remaining 3% of containers through those 121 ports. This would still cost between $12 billion and $22 billion over ten years.[71]

While CBP continues to pursue a workable method to achieve 100% screening at foreign ports, it is running innovative and effective risk-based programs designed to identify and inspect U.S.-bound high-risk cargo. For example, the Container Security Initiative (CSI) is a comprehensive security regime to identify and inspect high-risk containers at foreign ports. CBP has stationed teams of CBP officers in foreign locations to work with foreign government counterparts. These CBP officers target and prescreen containers and develop additional investigative leads related to the terrorist threat to U.S.-bound cargo.[72] As of this writing, CSI was operational at ports in North America, Europe, Asia, Africa, the Middle East, and Latin and Central America. Currently, CSI ports prescreen more than 80% of all maritime container cargo imported into the United States.

CBP has identified three core elements of CSI:

1. Identify high-risk containers. CBP uses automated targeting tools to identify containers that pose a potential risk for terrorism, based on advance information and strategic intelligence;
2. Prescreen and evaluate containers before they are shipped. Containers are screened as early in the supply chain as possible, generally at the port of departure; and
3. Use technology to scan high-risk containers. The challenge is to conduct scans without slowing and disrupting trade. The technology used to scan containers includes large-scale X-ray and gamma ray machines and radiation detection devices.

International partnerships are a critical part of ensuring the security of containers that traverse the globe. CBP's international partners share intelligence that CBP uses to identify high-risk containers for closer inspection. One example of international cooperation is DHS' Program Global Shield, which includes 90 participating nations and international organizations. Global Shield allows for the sharing of information by each of these nations' law enforcement entities to combat theft or illegal diversion of chemicals that can be used to make IEDs. As of July 2012, Program Global Shield accounted for 41 seizures of chemical precursors totaling more than 126 metric tons related to illicit diversion of these chemicals.[73]

## SUPPLY CHAIN SECURITY

International trade has been and continues to be a powerful engine of U.S. and global economic growth. In recent years, communications technology advances and trade barrier and production cost reductions have contributed to the expansion of the global trade market, as well as the growth of new economic opportunities. The global system of goods transportation (referred to as the supply chain) is essential to the United States' economy and a critical global asset.

Many entities are responsible for or reliant upon the functioning of the global supply chain, including regulators, law enforcement, public-sector buyers, private businesses, and other foreign and domestic partners. The global supply chain system relies on an interconnected web of transportation infrastructure and pathways, information technology, and cyber and energy networks. While these interdependencies promote economic activity, they also serve to propagate risk across a wide geographic area or industry arising from a local or regional disruption, such as a terrorist attack.[74]

The federal government's plan for securing the supply chain is articulated in the National Strategy for Global Supply Chain Security. The strategy has two goals:

1. Promote the secure and efficient movement of goods; and
2. Foster a resilient supply chain.

By undertaking the first goal, DHS seeks to resolve threats early, improve the verification and detection capabilities to identify goods that may be suspicious

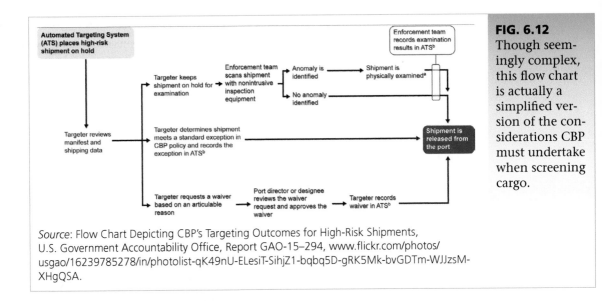

**FIG. 6.12** Though seemingly complex, this flow chart is actually a simplified version of the considerations CBP must undertake when screening cargo.

Source: Flow Chart Depicting CBP's Targeting Outcomes for High-Risk Shipments, U.S. Government Accountability Office, Report GAO-15–294, www.flickr.com/photos/usgao/16239785278/in/photolist-qK49nU-ELesiT-SihjZ1-bqbq5D-gRK5Mk-bvGDTm-WJJzsM-XHgQSA.

or contaminated, enhance security of infrastructure and conveyances, and maximize the flow of legitimate trade.[75] Likewise, by undertaking the second goal, DHS seeks to mitigate systemic vulnerabilities in the supply chain while also promoting trade policies and practices in the wake of a disruption.

In addition to screening maritime cargo, CBP also administers known shipper programs, designed to segregate low-risk cargo from higher-risk, unscreened shipments. Two such programs are the Customs-Trade Partnership Against Terrorism (C-TPAT) program and the Free and Secure Trade (FAST) program. C-TPAT is a voluntary public-private partnership program through which businesses work with CBP to protect the supply chain, identify security gaps, and implement security measures and best practices.[76] The security benefit is two-fold: Businesses working in the supply chain improve and enhance their security practices, yielding a more secure supply chain; and known-shippers are pre-cleared and considered lower risk, allowing CBP to focus attention on the unknown and higher risk businesses and cargo.

Applicants to the program must take several steps to address security issues in their business practices. The benefit for the participating organizations is that the companies and the goods they transport spend less time in customs and are delivered to customers faster. There are more than 10,000 C-TPAT member companies around the world.

CBP also administers the FAST program, a commercial clearance program for low-risk shipments crossing the northern or southern U.S. border. The FAST program is available to truck drivers from the United States, Canada, and Mexico; however, participation in the program requires that all links in the supply chain (manufacturer, carrier, driver, and importer) be C-TPAT certified.[77]

Supply chain companies and organizations also move packages and mail by air and over land. Private companies collaborate with TSA and CBP to move packages and mail in line with the programs and partnerships mentioned in this chapter. Another supply chain stakeholder is the U.S. Postal System (USPS). In the past, the USPS has been exploited to conduct terrorist attacks. Most notable of these were the 2001 anthrax attacks.[78] These attacks took place one week after 9/11 and involved letters containing anthrax spores that were mailed to news organizations and the offices of two U.S. Senators. Five people were killed and 17 were infected. In addition to the cost to life and health, millions of dollars were spent to clean and decontaminate postal facilities, news offices and government buildings.

Today, the USPS uses a mix of human oversight, machine screening, and information-gathering to track suspicious mail and prepare for potential attacks. Every piece of first class mail is scanned for harmful agents by a machine that takes air samples to detect dangerous biological materials. Mail sent to federal agencies and Congress is screened at an irradiation facility where it receives radiation strong enough to destroy bacteria and viruses.[79] Magazines and solicitations are not scanned, as the senders are considered low-risk, nor are Priority Mail and Express mail packages.

## PIPELINE SECURITY

More than 2.5 million miles of pipeline transport natural gas, refined petroleum products, and other commercial products throughout the country (Figure 6.13).[80] The pipeline system includes critical facilities, such as compressor and pumping stations, metering and regulator stations, breakout tanks, and the automated systems used to monitor and control them. Raw materials are critical to the U.S. economy and national security, and an attack on the pipe-

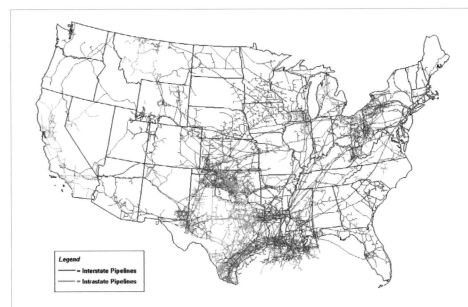

**FIG. 6.13**
The U.S. natural gas pipeline network is a highly integrated transmission and distribution grid that can transport natural gas to and from nearly any location in the lower 48 states. Its breadth and depth present innumerable security challenges.

*Source*: U.S. Natural Gas Pipeline Network (2009), U.S. Energy Information Administration, www.eia.gov/naturalgas/archive/analysis_publications/ngpipeline/ngpipelines_map.html.

line system could result in massive loss of life and have significant economic impact. Disruption of pipelines can impact access to energy, hurt businesses, increase energy costs, and damage the natural environment through spillage.

TSA is responsible for securing the nation's pipelines, using a network of partnerships with pipeline operators to share information and intelligence, training resources, best practices, and security guidelines. TSA's role in these partnerships is to support the owners and operators of the pipeline network by identifying threats, developing security programs to address those threats, and encouraging and assisting the implementation of security programs. TSA serves as a Co-Sector-Specific Agency alongside DOT and USCG for the transportation sector. TSA and DOT co-chair the Pipeline Government Coordinating Council to facilitate information sharing and coordination on activities such as security assessments, training, and exercises. TSA and DOT also work together to integrate pipeline and safety security priorities.

Since the United States imports more petroleum through pipelines from Canada than any other nation, TSA works closely with Canadian security counterparts to secure the U.S.-Canada cross-border pipeline network. TSA and the Canadian National Energy Board coordinate on pipeline security matters, including exchanging information on assessment procedures, exercises, and security incidents. Since 2005, TSA and Natural Resources Canada have cosponsored the International Pipeline Security Forum, an annual two-day conference that enhances the security domain awareness of hazardous liquid and natural gas pipeline operators and provides opportunities for discussion of major domestic and international pipeline security issues.

Physical reviews of pipelines and spot inspections are also an important part of securing the vast transportation network, much of it in rural America. TSA's I-STEP program facilitates exercises to help pipeline operators test security plans, prevention and preparedness capabilities, and cooperation with first responders. TSA also conducts corporate and physical security reviews with pipeline operators, which it has done more than 140 times since its inception.[81]

In addition to conducting actual inspections, TSA provides considerable logistical support and training materials to pipeline infrastructure owners and operators. TSA's Pipeline Security Guidelines provide a security structure for pipeline owners and operators to voluntarily use in developing their security plans and programs, and these guidelines have been broadly adopted. According to TSA, since their publication, there has been an increase in the number of pipeline operators conducting security drills and exercises and increasing coordination with local law enforcement agencies.[82]

Pipelines often employ sophisticated technology that is at risk of cyberattack. TSA supports DHS cybersecurity efforts in support of the National Institute of Standards and Technology Cybersecurity Framework. The cybersecurity framework is designed to provide a foundation for the pipeline industry to better manage and reduce their cyber risk. TSA shares information and resources with its industry stakeholders to support their adoption of the framework. It also distributes a cybersecurity toolkit developed from DHS Critical Infrastructure Cyber Community C3 Voluntary Program materials designed to offer the pipeline industry an array of free resources, recommendations, and security practices.

Additionally, within the pipeline industry, TSA coordinates a voluntary cyber-assessment program with the Federal Energy Regulatory Commission to examine pipeline operators' cybersecurity programs. TSA works closely with the pipeline industry to identify and reduce cybersecurity vulnerabilities, including facilitating classified briefings to increase industry's awareness of cyber threats.[83]

## CONCLUSION

The challenge of securing all of America's transportation modes is vast. As the array of security programs implemented after 9/11 have matured, policymakers have realized that the 100% security screening methodology is impractical. Instead, in many cases CBP and TSA have moved towards a risk-based approach to security that prioritizes screening on targets that pose the greatest danger. This transition continues to encounter political challenges and lukewarm public reception.

Ultimately, threats to the U.S. transportation network cannot be eliminated, though they can be effectively mitigated. The efforts described in this chapter have yielded a safer nation that has not seen an attack on the scale of 9/11 since the creation of DHS. This has meant that DHS' efforts to secure the transportation network yields positive results for every citizen and industry. Indeed, transportation security continues to be the department's most expansive function, rivaled only by its work in border security and immigration.

## KEYWORDS

- **100% screening methodology**: A screening methodology in aviation security that presumes all people and baggage present an equally devastating potential threat.

- **risk-based screening methodology**: An aviation security screening methodology that acknowledges that not all people and goods present an equal potential threat and focuses limited resources on identifying and disrupting the most likely threats.

- **hazardous material**: A substance that poses an unreasonable risk to health, safety, and property, including things like petroleum products, toxic chemicals, waste and pollutants, and toxic inhalation hazards (TIH), such as chlorine gas and ammonia.

---

### KNOWLEDGE CHECK

1. What components comprise the transportation system in the United States?
2. Name three ways in which aviation security has changed after 9/11.
3. What government body is primarily responsible for securing maritime waters?

## NOTES

1. Bart Elias, David Randall Peterman & John Frittelli, Cong. Research Serv., RL 33512, Transportation Security: Issues for the 114th Congress, at 1 (2016) www.fas.org/sgp/crs/homesec/RL33512.pdf.
2. *Transportation Systems Sector*, U.S. Dep't of Homeland Security (last visited Jan. 3, 2019) www.dhs.gov/transportation-systems-sector.
3. *Id.*
4. *Id.*
5. *Id.*
6. *Id.*
7. *Id.*
8. Bart Elias, David Randall Peterman & John Frittelli, Cong. Research Serv., RL 33512, Transportation Security: Issues for the 114th Congress, at 1 (2016) www.fas.org/sgp/crs/homesec/RL33512.pdf.
9. *Id.*
10. *Hearing before the United States Senate Committee on Appropriations, Subcommittee on Homeland Security* (Mar. 1, 2016) (statement of Peter Neffenger, Administrator, Transportation Administration, U.S. Dep't of Homeland Security) *available at* www.tsa.gov/news/testimony/2016/03/01/hearing-fy17-budget-request-transportation-security-administration.
11. *Leadership and Organization*, Transportation Security Administration (last visited Jan. 3, 2019) www.tsa.gov/about/tsa-leadership.
12. Bart Elias, David Randall Peterman & John Frittelli, Cong. Research Serv., RL 33512, Transportation Security: Issues for the 114th Congress, at 1 (2016) www.fas.org/sgp/crs/homesec/RL33512.pdf.

13. *Global Entry*, U.S. Customs and Border Protection (last updated Oct. 2, 2017) www.cbp.gov/travel/trusted-traveler-programs/global-entry.

14. *Trusted Traveler Programs*, U.S. Customs and Border Protection (last updated Aug. 22, 2018) www.cbp.gov/travel/trusted-traveler-programs.

15. Bart Elias, David Randall Peterman & John Frittelli, Cong. Research Serv., RL 33512, Transportation Security: Issues for the 114th Congress, at 2 (2016) www.fas.org/sgp/crs/homesec/RL33512.pdf.

16. Letter from Stephen A. Alterman, Chairman of the Aviation Security Advisory Committee to Melvin Carraway, Acting Administrator, Transportation Security Administration, at 10 (Apr. 8, 2011) *available at* www.tsa.gov/sites/default/files/asac-employee-screening-working-group-04-15.pdf.

17. TSA's Security Playbook, Center for Evidence-Based Crime Policy, George Mason University, at 1 (Jan. 2012) http://cebcp.org/wp-content/publications/PhaseII-Final-Report-Redacted.

18. *Layers of Security*, U.S. Transportation Security Administration (Mar. 24, 2008) www.tsa.gov/blog/2008/03/24/layers-security.

19. Bart Elias, David Randall Peterman & John Frittelli, Cong. Research Serv., RL 33512, Transportation Security: Issues for the 114th Congress, at 8 (2016) www.fas.org/sgp/crs/homesec/RL33512.pdf.

20. Irrespective of its stated aim to *not* violate the civil liberties of Americans, several advocacy groups and members of Congress have argued that BDOs end up engaging in racial and religious profiling. In 2013, the Government Accountability Office (GAO) released a report critical of the SPOT program, noting that it lacked a scientific basis proving whether the program was effective. *See, e.g.,* H.R. 1229, 115th Cong. (2017); H.R. 1385, 115th Cong. (2017); S. 635, 115th Cong. (2017); U.S. Gov't Accountability Off., GAO-14–159, Aviation Security: TSA Should Limit Future Funding for Behavior Detection Activities (2013) *available at* www.gao.gov/products/GAO-14-159.

21. *Layers of Security*, U.S. Transportation Security Administration (Mar. 24, 2008) www.tsa.gov/blog/2008/03/24/layers-security.

22. *Layers of Security*, U.S. Transportation Security Administration (Mar. 24, 2008) www.tsa.gov/blog/2008/03/24/layers-security.

23. Dep't of Homeland Security Office of Inspector General, Efficiency and Effectiveness of TSA's Viable Intermodel Prevention and Response Program Within Rail and Mass Transit Systems (2012) www.oig.dhs.gov/assets/Mgmt/2012/OIGr_12-103_Aug12.pdf.

24. *Securing and protecting our nation's pipelines*, U.S. Transportation Security Administration (July 11, 2016) www.tsa.gov/news/releases/2016/07/11/securing-and-protecting-our-nations-pipelines.

25. *Hearing before the House Committee on Homeland Security, Transportation Security Subcommittee* (July 16, 2015) (statement by Roderick Allison, Director of the Transportation Security Administration) *available at* www.tsa.gov/news/testimony/2015/07/16/testimony-federal-air-marshal-service-and-its-readiness-meet-evolving.

26. Bart Elias, David Randall Peterman & John Frittelli, Cong. Research Serv., RL 33512, Transportation Security: Issues for the 114th Congress, at 8 (2016) www.fas.org/sgp/crs/homesec/RL33512.pdf.

27. FAA Federal Aviation Regulations, 14 C.F.R. Pt. 129, § 28.

28. Gerardo Hernandez Airport Security Act of 2015, Pub. L. No. 114–50 (2015).

29. Transportation Security Administration, U.S. Coast Guard, Congressional Budget Justification FY2017- Volume II, U.S. Immigration and Customs Enforcement (2017) https://www.dhs.gov/sites/default/files/publications/FY%202017%20Congressional%20Budget%20Justification%20-%20Volume%202_1.pdf.

30. *Hearing before the United States Senate Committee on Homeland Security, Subcommittee on Transportation Security* (Apr. 18, 2012) (testimony of Michael C. Mullen, Executive Director, Express Association of America) *available at* https://homeland.house.gov/files/Testimony-Mullen.pdf.

31. Air Cargo Advance Screening Pilot Strategic Plan, U.S. Dep't of Homeland Security (2012) *available at* http://securepackages.org/wp-content/uploads/2016/08/acas_psplan_3.pdf.

32. U.S. Customs and Border Protection, Extension of the Air Cargo Advance Screening Program (July 22, 2016) www.federalregister.gov/documents/2016/07/22/2016-17366/extension-of-the-air-cargo-advance-screening-acas-pilot-program.

33. *Subcommittee on Oversight and Management Efficiency, Committee on Homeland Security, U.S. House of Representatives* (March 18, 2015) (Statement of Chief Richard Beary, President of the International Association of Chiefs of Police).

34. *Fact Sheet: Executive Order 13636 Improving Critical Infrastructure Cybersecurity and Presidential Policy Directive (PPD) 21 Critical Infrastructure Security and Resilience*, U.S. Dep't of Homeland Security (last updated Aug. 22, 2018) www.dhs.gov/publication/eo-13636-ppd-21-fact-sheet.

35. www.gpo.gov/fdsys/pkg/USCODE-2011-title49/html/USCODE-2011-title49-subtitleVII-partA-subpartiii-chap449-subchapI-sec44912.htm

36. Executive Order 13636—Improving Critical Infrastructure Cybersecurity, Section 10(b) Report: TSA's Approach to Voluntary Industry Adoption of the NIST Cybersecurity Framework, U.S. Dep't of Homeland Security (last visited Jan. 3, 2019) https://www.dhs.gov/sites/default/files/publications/ExecutiveOrder_13636Sec10%28b%29Reportv5.pdf.

37. Rachael King, *Aviation Industry and Government to Share Cyber Threats in New Intelligence Center*, Wall Street Journal (Apr. 15, 2014) http://blogs.wsj.com/cio/2014/04/15/aviation-industry-and-government-to-share-cyberthreats-in-new-intelligence-center/.

38. Bart Elias, David Randall Peterman & John Frittelli, Cong. Research Serv., RL 33512, Transportation Security: Issues for the 114th Congress, at 18 (2016) www.fas.org/sgp/crs/homesec/RL33512.pdf.

39. *Committee on Oversight and Government Reform, U.S. House of Representatives* (May 13, 2015) (Statement of John Roth, Inspector General, U.S. Department of Homeland Security) www.oig.dhs.gov/assets/TM/2015/OIGtm_JR_051315.pdf.

40. *The Top 20 Airports for TSA Theft*, ABC News (Oct. 23, 2012) http://abcnews.go.com/Blotter/top-20-airports-tsa-theft/story?id=17537887.

41. *The Transportation Security Administration Does Not Properly Manage Its Airport Screening Equipment Maintenance Program*, Dep't of Homeland Security Office of the Inspector General (May 6, 2015) www.oig.dhs.gov/assets/Mgmt/2015/OIG_15-86_May15.pdf.

42. *Whole Body Imaging Technology and Body Scanners ("Backscatter" X-Ray and Millimeter Wave Screening)*, Electronic Privacy Information Center (last visited Jan. 3, 2019) https://epic.org/privacy/airtravel/backscatter/.

43. *Committee on Oversight and Government Reform, U.S. House of Representatives* (May 13, 2015) (Statement of John Roth, Inspector General, U.S. Department of Homeland Security) www.oig.dhs.gov/assets/TM/2015/OIGtm_JR_051315.pdf.

44. *Body Scanner Resolution Rooms Conduct & Privacy*, U.S. Transportation Security Administration (Jan. 2, 2013) www.tsa.gov/blog/2013/01/02/body-scanner-resolution-rooms-conduct-privacy.

45. U.S. Gov't Accountability Off., GAO-14–19, Screening Partnership Program: TSA Can Benefit from Improved Cost Estimates (2015) www.gao.gov/assets/680/673659.pdf.

46. Keith Laing, *GOP Chairman: TSA was a 'big mistake,'* The Hill, (Mar. 18, 2015) http://thehill.com/policy/transportation/236130-gop-rep-creating-tsa-was-a-mistake.

47. *Committee on Homeland Security, Subcommittee on Transportation Security, U.S. House of Representatives* (Mar. 14 and Apr. 11, 2013) www.gpo.gov/fdsys/pkg/CHRG-113hhrg82579/html/CHRG-113hhrg82579.htm.

48. *Terrorist Screening Center*, Federal Bureau of Investigation (last visited Jan. 3, 2019) www.fbi.gov/about/leadership-and-structure/national-security-branch/tsc.

49. S. Rep. No. 111–199 (2010) *available at* www.intelligence.senate.gov/sites/default/files/publications/CRPT-111srpt199.pdf

50. Bart Elias, David Randall Peterman & John Frittelli, Cong. Research Serv., RL 33512, Transportation Security: Issues for the 114th Congress, at 18 (2016) www.fas.org/sgp/crs/homesec/RL33512.pdf.

51. Implementing Recommendations of the 9/11 Commission Act of 2007, Pub. L. No. 110–53 §§ 1405, 1512 (2007).

52. Department of Homeland Security, Transportation Security Administration, Surface Transportation Security FY2016 Congressional [Budget] Justification, p. 11.

53. *TSA commends 13 mass transit and rail agencies for highest security levels*, U.S. Transportation Security Administration (Apr. 6, 2016). www.tsa.gov/news/releases/2016/04/06/tsa-commends-13-mass-transit-and-rail-agencies-highest-security-levels.

54. *Committee on Homeland Security, Subcommittee on Transportation Security, and Subcommittee on Counterterrorism and Intelligence, U.S. House of Representatives* (Sep. 17 2015) www.dhs.gov/news/2015/09/17/written-testimony-tsa-house-homeland-security-subcommittees-transportation-security (Testimony of Eddie Mayenschein assistant administrator of the TSA Office of Security Policy and Industry Engagement).

55. *Intermodal Security Training and Exercise Program*, American Association of State Highway and Transportation Officials (Aug. 22, 2012) http://onlinepubs.trb.org/onlinepubs/conferences/2012/securitysummit/presentations/Lee_I-STEP.pdf.

56. *TSA supports passenger rail systems security*, U.S. TRANSPORTATION SECURITY ADMINISTRATION (Sep. 3, 2015) www.tsa.gov/news/top-stories/2015/09/03/tsa-supports-passenger-rail-systems-security.

57. U.S. Gov't Accountability Off., GAO-09–243, Freight Rail Security: Actions Have Been Taken to Enhance Security, but the Federal Strategy Can Be Strengthened and Security Efforts Better Monitored (2009) www.gao.gov/new.items/d09243.pdf.

58. *Hazardous Materials*, FEDERAL RAILROAD ADMINISTRATION (last visited Jan. 3, 2019) www.fra.dot.gov/Page/P0444.

59. U.S. Gov't Accountability Off., GAO-09–243, Freight Rail Security: Actions Have Been Taken to Enhance Security, but the Federal Strategy Can Be Strengthened and Security Efforts Better Monitored (2009) www.gao.gov/new.items/d09243.pdf.

60. David Howe, *Planning Scenarios: Executive Summaries*, THE HOMELAND SECURITY COUNCIL (2004) www.globalsecurity.org/security/library/report/2004/hsc-planning-scenarios-jul04_exec-sum.pdf.

61. Lewis M. Branscomb, Mark Fagan, Philip Auerswald, Ryan N. Ellis, & Raphael Barcham, RAIL TRANSPORTATION OF TOXIC INHALATION HAZARDS: POLICY RESPONSES TO THE SAFETY AND SECURITY EXTERNALITY, Harvard Kennedy School (2010) www.hks.harvard.edu/m-rcbg/rpp/Working%20papers/Rail%20Transportation%20of%20TIH.pdf.

62. *National Preparedness System*, FEDERAL EMERGENCY MANAGEMENT AGENCY (last updated Nov. 19, 2018) www.fema.gov/national-preparedness-system

63. *Fiscal Year 2016 Intercity Bus Security Grant Program*, FEDERAL EMERGENCY MANAGEMENT AGENCY, www.fema.gov/media-library-data/1467228711739-80849d36933278d1d70d0ae017d-abe66/FY_2016_IBSGP_Fact_Sheet.pdf.

64. Bart Elias, David Randall Peterman & John Frittelli, CONG. RESEARCH SERV., RL 33512, TRANSPORTATION SECURITY: ISSUES FOR THE 114TH CONGRESS, at 19 (2016) www.fas.org/sgp/crs/homesec/RL33512.pdf.

65. Sarah Janaro, *New Policy Letter—Facility Security Plan, Alternative Security Program, Vessel Security Plan*, COAST GUARD MARITIME COMMONS (Apr. 20, 2016) http://mariners.coastguard.dodlive.mil/2016/04/20/4202016-new-policy-letter-facility-security-plan-alternative-security-program-vessel-security-plan/.

66. *TSA provides support to Coast Guard to secure U.S. ports*, U.S. TRANSPORTATION SECURITY ADMINISTRATION (Aug. 22, 2016) www.tsa.gov/news/top-stories/2016/08/22/tsa-provides-support-coast-guard-secure-us-ports.

67. *Surface Transportation,* U.S. TRANSPORTATION SECURITY ADMINISTRATION (last visited Jan. 3, 2019) www.tsa.gov/for-industry/surface-transportation.

68. *TWIC*, U.S. TRANSPORTATION SECURITY ADMINISTRATION (last visited Jan. 3, 2019) www.tsa.gov/for-industry/twic.

69. Dep't of Homeland Security Office of Inspector General, TWIC Background Checks are Not as Reliable as They Could Be (2016) www.oig.dhs.gov/assets/Mgmt/2016/OIG-16-128-Sep16.pdf.

70. *Scanning and Imaging More Shipping Containers Bound for or Arriving at U.S. Ports*, Congressional Budget Office (last visited Jan. 3, 2019) www.cbo.gov/budget-options/other/51662.

71. *Id.*

72. *CSI: Container Security Initiative*, U.S. Customs and Border Protection (last visited Jan. 3, 2019) www.cbp.gov/border-security/ports-entry/cargo-security/csi/csi-brief.

73 *Cargo Screening*, U.S. Dep't of Homeland Security (last visited Jan. 3, 2019) www.dhs.gov/cargo-screening.

74 *National Strategy for Global Supply Chain Security*, The White House, at 1 (2012) https://obamawhitehouse.archives.gov/sites/default/files/national_strategy_for_global_supply_chain_security.pdf.

75. *Id.* at 3.

76. *CTPAT: Customs Trade Partnership Against Terrorism*, U.S. Customs and Border Protection (last visited Jan. 3, 2019) www.cbp.gov/border-security/ports-entry/cargo-security/c-tpat-customs-trade-partnership-against-terrorism.

77. *FAST: Free and Secure Trade for Commercial Vehicles*, U.S. Customs and Border Protection (last visited Jan. 3, 2019) www.cbp.gov/travel/trusted-traveler-programs/fast#.

78. *Amerithrax or Anthrax Investigation*, Federal Bureau of Investigation (last visited Jan. 3, 2019) www.fbi.gov/history/famous-cases/amerithrax-or-anthrax-investigation.

79. *Mail Irradiation*, U.S. Environmental Protection Agency (last visited Jan. 3, 2019) https://www3.epa.gov/radtown/mail-irradiation.html.

80. U.S. Transportation Security Administration, Pipeline Security Guidelines (2018) www.tsa.gov/sites/default/files/tsapipelinesecurityguidelines-2011.pdf.

81. *Hearing before the United States House of Representatives Committee on Homeland Security, subcommittee on Transportation Security* (Apr. 19, 2016) (Written testimony of Sonya Proctor, Director of the TSA Office of Security Policy and Industry Engagement Surface Division) *available at* www.dhs.gov/news/2016/04/19/written-testimony-tsa-house-homeland-security-subcommittee-transportation-security.

82. *Id.*

83. *Id.*

# CHAPTER 7

# Emergency Management and Hazards

---

**IN THIS CHAPTER YOU WILL LEARN ABOUT**

The various ways emergency management is defined and articulated as a profession, particularly after 9/11.

The organizational principles, strategies, and policies that facilitate the delivery of disaster assistance.

The role of state and local governments in responding to and mitigating the effects of hazards.

---

## INTRODUCTION

Emergency management is a discipline and area of government responsibility that requires a "whole of government" approach, involving the efforts of state, local, tribal, and federal government bodies. When a disaster occurs, the federal government acts primarily as a coordinator and funder of local emergency response efforts. It does so by following the National Response Framework (NRF), a comprehensive set of rules and best practices that govern roles and responsibilities at various levels of government, and outline how non-government actors such as community organizations and private sector partners can support disaster response.

In this chapter we discuss emergency management in terms of an "**all-hazards**" approach. Though still poorly defined, an "all-hazards" approach to emergency management implies that the government should both prepare for specific hazards (such as hurricanes) and also for hazards generally, especially those that may be unpredictable (such as terrorist attacks). In doing so, the government is obliged to develop tools, policies, and practices that can flexibly respond to an emergency situation irrespective of the specific nature of that emergency. This approach became a hallmark of emergency management after the 9/11 attacks. The government adopted the all-hazards approach primarily to fit terrorist attacks within the broader emergency management framework. Note that though these terms are not synonymous, for ease of use, we will use the words "disaster," "emergency," and "hazard" interchangeably in this chapter.

The history of the U.S. disaster response framework is the history of the formation of DHS and the creation of the nation's homeland security infrastructure. This history is detailed in Chapter 1. This chapter discusses contemporary government disaster mitigation, preparedness, response, and recovery policies as well as the government actors tasked with carrying out these policies.

## MANAGING EMERGENCIES FROM THE BOTTOM UP

The U.S. takes a "bottom-up" approach to emergency management. The responsibility for responding to disasters begins locally, with local law enforcement, fire services, and hospitals administering immediate aid to those affected by a disaster. Depending on the size and sophistication of the local municipality, local emergency management professionals, trained specifically to respond to disasters, may also be deployed. If local government resources become overwhelmed, non-governmental voluntary organizations in the community and governments in neighboring jurisdictions may be called upon to provide assistance. For instance, a fire department from a neighboring town may send firefighters to help stamp out a wildfire in the affected nearby region.[1]

If those sources of assistance also become exhausted, state and tribal governments may supplement a local government's resources, which may be coupled with a state governor declaring a state disaster or emergency declaration. The federal government only steps in after even the state's resources have

**FIG. 7.1**
Secretary of
Homeland Secu-
rity Jeh Johnson
comforts a disas-
ter survivor in
the residential
neighborhood
of Plantation
Drive in May-
flower after it
was hit by an
EF-4 tornado on
April 27, 2014.
The Federal
Emergency
Management
Agency supports
local, state, and
tribal govern-
ments and
assists indi-
vidual survivors
in their efforts
to recover from
natural disasters

*Source*: Christopher Mardorf, Tornado Damage In Mayflower, Arkansas, U.S. Dep't
of Homeland Security (2014) www.flickr.com/photos/dhsgov/14793959190/in/
photolist-oxhUDU-oPvK52-puqRLm-pvNxYY-pJMjuW-pvRhMm-pdXBRF-rQjfcQ-
GRTEDd-rSwBVD-rSuwGh-GRTE2w-rA3GPC-qVPeR6-qVBFyy-rSuv1S-rAa99c-rA2p3L-
rQjhPJ-rAahJ8-rSBiRr-rSuA6S-rAacsr-qVPi5F-rA3Fms-GLAntw-qVBvKL-FZoDpf-FkTutD-FkTt4p-
GaiKuZ-FkGYR3-FkHLbw-GdS6Sf-Ggapxi-G7ZY8o-GgaoiK-FR41RY-GdSv33-GdSpPY-us3ZK-
C-FkUnEr-G81sN9-FR4mQL-FR4iVs-FkUbek-G81iBy-GajiN6-GgaER4-GajhvM.

either been exhausted or found to be insufficient to respond to the disaster.
This "last to assist" role of the federal government is outlined in the Stafford Disaster Relief and Emergency Assistance Act and is to "supplement the
efforts and available resources of states, local governments, and disaster relief
organizations in alleviating the damage, loss, hardship, or suffering . . ."[2]

Given the number of disasters occurring in a country the size of the United
States, the relatively small scope of most disasters and the comprehensive
coverage provided by state, local, and tribal resources, most disasters never

reach the federal level and are managed by state and local governments. The Federal Emergency Management Agency (FEMA) and other federal government bodies play a role in only the most extraordinary circumstances.

## WHO IS IN CHARGE?

In most cases, the locally elected chief executive, such as the mayor, leads disaster response for most local communities. When it comes to state responses, the governor is the lead official. Similarly, the chief of a tribe is likely to be the individual responsible for disaster response coordination for a Native American tribe. If state resources are being used to supplement the local response, they are coordinated through a State Coordinating Officer (SCO) as well as the state's emergency management or homeland security agency, though only larger and more populous states tend to have such agencies. If an incident has been declared by the President as an emergency or Major Disaster under the Stanford Act, the President will request that each governor appoint an SCO if they have not done so already.[3] A similar structure is in place at the federal level where the President or FEMA Administrator usually appoints a Federal Coordinating Officer (FCO) to coordinate all federal resources by state. The FCO may operate out of a Joint Field Office (JFO—often structurally similar to the JFOs operated by federal law enforcement agencies such as the FBI) where federal agencies and departments coordinate their activities.

### Disaster Declaration

If the capacities of state, local, and tribal governments are overwhelmed by an incident, they can request assistance from the federal government. In most cases, the first step is to request a declaration of a federal disaster by the President under the requirements set forth in the Stafford Act. The governor or other senior executive must decide whether the incident is severe enough to warrant a declaration. Often, this means assessing the preliminary damage in the immediate aftermath of a disaster by deploying a Preliminary Damage Assessment team. In some cases, if there is a certainty that damage will occur

**FIG. 7.2**
State of Oklahoma and FEMA officials verify that a damage inspection just completed is agreed upon.

*Source*: Win Henderson, Members of a FEMA Preliminary Damage Assessment Team, Federal Emergency Management Administration, www.fema.gov/media-library/assets/images/57316.

even prior to the occurrence of the disaster, the governor may request federal assistance even before the disaster occurs.[4]

A Preliminary Damage Assessment team includes individuals from various state and local agencies, as well as the federal government (typically an official from FEMA's local office). FEMA officials usually brief the PDA team on the factors the federal government considers before classifying a disaster as a federal emergency. The team's findings are presented to FEMA leadership and the President, who can then declare either 1) an emergency or 2) a "Major Disaster" under the Stafford Act. Under both scenarios, once declared, the Stafford Act then allows the federal government to assist the state or other local municipalities with supplemental federal assistance.[5]

### Emergency Declarations

Emergency declarations authorize activities that can help states and communities carry out essential services and activities that might reduce the threat of future damage. Emergency declarations may be declared before an incident occurs to save lives and prevent loss. Thus, the President can declare an emergency for any occasion or instance when the President determines federal assistance is needed. Emergency declarations supplement state and local efforts in providing emergency services, such as protection of lives, property, and public health and safety. The total amount of assistance provided for in a single emergency cannot exceed $5 million (though if the amount is exceeded in any case, the President must submit a report to Congress detailing the reasons why).[6]

In order to receive emergency disaster funds, the governor of an affected state (or the tribal equivalent) must submit a request to the President, usually through FEMA, within 30 days of the occurrence of the incident.[7] The request must be based on a finding that the disaster situation is beyond the capability of the state or regional government to handle and that supplemental federal emergency assistance is necessary to save lives and protect property and public health. The request must also include:

- Confirmation that the governor has taken appropriate action under the relevant state laws to curb the impact of the disaster and has also effectuated the existing state emergency response plan;
- A description of the state or local/tribal government efforts and resources already utilized to alleviate the emergency;
- A description of other federal agency efforts and resources utilized in response to the emergency; and
- A description of the type and extent of additional federal assistance required.

These requirements are extensive and stringent, and perhaps difficult to fulfill especially during and in the immediate aftermath of a disaster. Nonetheless, these requirements exist to guard against the potential for fraud, waste, and abuse because the funds awarded to the states are both extensive and require no repayment.

As noted above, a governor may request an Emergency Declaration in advance of or in anticipation of the imminent impact of an incident that threatens significant destruction likely to result in a Major Disaster. Such requests must meet all of the statutory and regulatory requirements for an Emergency Declaration request (normally made in the aftermath of a disaster).

**FIG. 7.3**
This timeline illustrates key federal actions and events in response to hurricanes Irma and Maria in the U.S. Virgin Islands between August 31 and September 16, 2018.

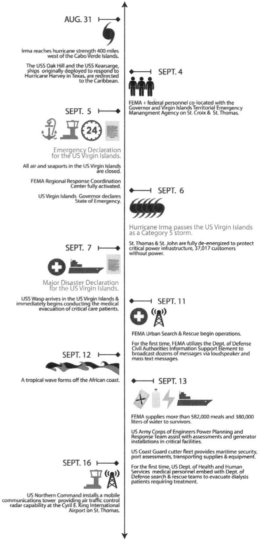

# Hurricanes Irma and Maria
 FEMA
# USVI RESPONSE TIMELINE

AUG. 31 through SEPT. 16

**AUG. 31**

Irma reaches hurricane strength 400 miles west of the Cabo Verde Islands.

The USS Oak Hill and the USS Kearsarge, ships originally deployed to respond to Hurricane Harvey in Texas, are redirected to the Caribbean.

**SEPT. 4**

FEMA + federal personnel co-located with the Governor and Virgin Islands Territorial Emergency Manangment Agency on St. Croix & St. Thomas.

**SEPT. 5**

Emergency Declaration for the US Virgin Islands.

All air and seaports in the US Virgin Islands are closed.

FEMA Regional Response Coordination Center fully activated.

US Virgin Islands Governor declares State of Emergency.

**SEPT. 6**

Hurricane Irma passes the US Virgin Islands as a Category 5 storm.

St. Thomas & St. John are fully de-energized to protect critical power infrastructure, 37,017 customers without power.

**SEPT. 7**

Major Disaster Declaration for the US Virgin Islands.

USS Wasp arrives in the US Virgin Islands & immediately begins conducting the medical evacuation of critical care patients.

**SEPT. 11**

FEMA Urban Search & Rescue begin operations.

For the first time, FEMA utilizes the Dept. of Defense Civil Authorities Information Support Element to broadcast dozens of messages via loudspeaker and mass text messages.

**SEPT. 12**

A tropical wave forms off the African coast.

**SEPT. 13**

FEMA supplies more than 582,000 meals and 380,000 liters of water to survivors.

US Army Corps of Engineers Power Planning and Response Team assist with assessments and generator installations in critical facilities.

US Coast Guard cutter fleet provides maritime security, port assessments, transporting supplies & equipment.

**SEPT. 16**

For the first time, US Dept. of Health and Human Services medical personnel embed with Dept. of Defense search & rescue teams to evacuate dialysis patients requiring treatment.

US Northern Command installs a mobile communications tower providing air traffic control radar capability at the Cyril E. King International Airport on St. Thomas.

*Source*: Hurricanes Irma and Maria USVI Federal Response Timeline, Federal Emergency Management Agency, www.fema.gov/media-library-data/1536074861527-eb50e1b2f4dceabef-485b9ea80590588/USVI_Irma_Maria_One-Year-Timeline_One_of_Two1-01.png.

These pre-disaster requests must demonstrate that the existence of critical emergency protective measure needs prior to impact are beyond the capability of the state and affected local governments and identify specific unmet emergency needs that can be met through the Emergency Declaration.[8] The pre-disaster request may include, but is not limited to personnel, equipment, supplies, and evacuation assistance. Pre-positioning of assets generally does not require a declaration.

When an emergency exists for which the primary responsibility rests with the federal government, the President may declare an emergency without a request from a governor or tribal official. This may be the case when an emergency affects the entire nation, several states, or involves the national defense of the nation. These kinds of pre-emptive federal emergency declarations don't prevent the governor from subsequently requesting a Major Disaster Declaration for other unmet needs caused by the event.

## Major Disaster Declarations

Unlike emergency declarations, major disaster declarations involve more specific situations and the range of assistance available to state and local governments and non-state organizations is broader (Figure 7.4). Under a Major Disaster Declaration, state and local governments and NGOs are eligible for assistance for the repair or restoration of public infrastructure, such as roads and buildings. A Major Disaster Declaration may also include additional programs beyond temporary housing, such as disaster unemployment assistance and crisis counseling, and other recovery programs, such as community disaster loans. The President can declare a Major Disaster for any natural event such as a hurricane, storm, earthquake, drought, or fire, as well as technical and manmade hazards. In order to declare a Major Disaster the President must determine that the disaster or hazard has caused damage of such severity that it is beyond the combined capabilities of state and local governments to respond. A Major Disaster Declaration provides a wide range of federal assistance programs for individuals and public infrastructure, including funds for both emergency and permanent work.[9]

The governor or tribal official must submit a request to the President regarding the declaration of a Major Disaster through FEMA within 30 days of the

**FIG. 7.4**
This GAO chart outlines the complicated, but rigorous process for declaring a Major Disaster. FEMA received 294 declaration requests for Individual Assistance during 2008–2016. Of these requests, the President declared 168 disasters, and FEMA obligated about $8.6 billion in Individual Assistance to 46 states and territories.

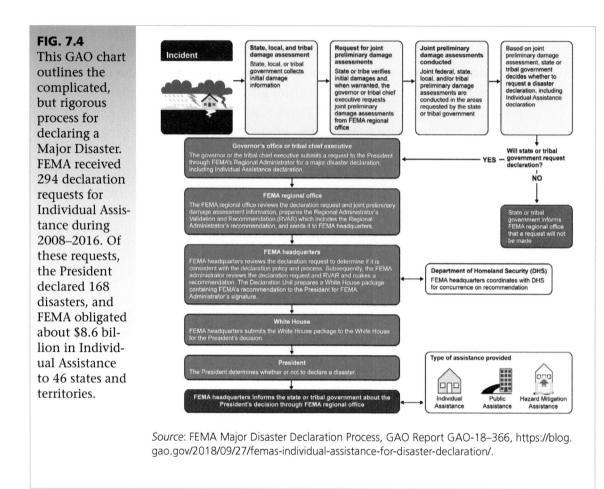

*Source*: FEMA Major Disaster Declaration Process, GAO Report GAO-18–366, https://blog.gao.gov/2018/09/27/femas-individual-assistance-for-disaster-declaration/.

occurrence of the incident. Similar to the request for an Emergency Declaration, the governor has to certify that his or her state is incapable of dealing with the disaster and that supplemental federal assistance is necessary, and similar to the request for an Emergency Declaration, the request must also include:

• Confirmation that the governor has taken appropriate action under state emergency management plans;
• An estimate of the amount and severity of damage to the public and private sector;

- A description of state and/or local government efforts and resources utilized to alleviate the disaster;
- Preliminary estimates of the type and amount of Stafford Act assistance required; and
- Certification by the governor that state and local governments will comply with all applicable cost sharing requirements.

Notice that the reporting requirements for Major Disasters are even more stringent than for emergency declarations. This is because the amount of funds and other federal assistance awarded here is even greater than what is available under an Emergency Declaration.

If a Major Disaster is declared under the Stafford Act, three forms of federal financial assistance are available:

- Public Assistance (PA): Provides grants to tribal, state, and local governments and certain private non-profit organizations so that they can provide emergency protective services, conduct debris removal operations, and repair or replace damaged public infrastructure. For-profit businesses that engage in disaster relief operations are not eligible for these grants.[10]
- Individual Assistance (IA): Provides direct aid to affected households, and can take the form of housing assistance, other needs assistance such as crisis counseling, and legal and disaster unemployment assistance. There are annual limits to these assistance programs set by Congress.
- Hazard Mitigation Assistance (HMA): Funds mitigation and resiliency projects (i.e. steps that can be taken *before* a disaster or hazard occurs to lessen its impact). States often share the cost of these assistance programs. Mitigation projects can include the construction of safe rooms, buyouts of frequently flooded properties, and retrofitting of older facilities to withstand disasters such as earthquakes.

In addition to financial assistance that is available under the Stafford Act, a number of other programs that are not administered by FEMA also provide assistance:

- The Small Business Administration (SBA) provides federally subsidized loans to repair or replace homes, personal property, or businesses that sustained damage not covered by insurance following a disaster. SBA loans are a key source of assistance for the private sector and individual homeowners, but are often passed over by businesses due to onerous reporting and compliance requirements.

- The Department of Housing and Urban Development (HUD) offers Community Development Block Grant program funds that can be used to meet a wide range of disaster needs, but the program typically requires a supplemental Congressional appropriation to meet the high cost of disaster relief.
- The U.S. Department of Transportation's Federal-Aid Highway Emergency Relief Program is a major source of grant funds for the repair and reconstruction of roads on the federal highway system that have suffered serious damage as a result of either a natural disaster over a wide area (such as a hurricane) or a catastrophic failure from an external cause.[11]
- The U.S. Department of Agriculture runs an Agriculture and Rural Assistance programs that provides food, housing, and financial assistance, primarily to agricultural and rural communities affected by hazards. The USDA's Food and Nutrition Service (FNS) also coordinates with state, local, and voluntary organizations to provide food for shelters and other mass feeding sites, distribute food packages directly to households in need in limited situations, and issue Disaster Supplemental Nutrition Assistance Program (D-SNAP) benefits. As part of the National Response Framework, FNS provides nutrition assistance to those most affected by a disaster or emergency. When state agencies notify the USDA of the types and quantities of food that relief organizations need for emergency feeding operations, FNS supplies food to disaster relief organization such as the Red Cross and the Salvation Army for mass feeding or household distribution.
- The U.S. Army Corps of Engineers provides substantial emergency assistance to cities and states by offering to repair damaged infrastructure such as flood control works, dams, and other waterways. The Corps has an emergency response authority under which it performs flood-fighting and other emergency response work.[12]

When evaluating requests for Major Disasters and making recommendations to the President, FEMA considers the following factors:
For the Public Assistance Program, FEMA:

- Evaluates the estimated cost of federal and non-federal public assistance against the population to give some measure of the per capita impact of the disaster. FEMA uses a per capita amount as an indicator that the disaster is of such severity and magnitude that it might warrant federal assistance, and it then adjusts this figure annually, based on the Consumer Price Index.

- Evaluates the impact of the disaster at the county and local government levels, as well as at the American Indian and other tribal government levels, because, at times, there are extraordinary concentrations of damages that might warrant federal assistance even if the statewide per capita is not met. This may be true where critical failures (such as roadway or public building collapse or destruction) are affected or where localized per capita impacts are extremely high. For example, localized damages may be in the tens or even hundreds of dollars per capita, even though the overall per capita impact is low.

- Considers the amount of insurance coverage that is in force in the state (per capita and per organization) or should have been in force as required by law and regulation at the time of the disaster, and reduces the amount of anticipated assistance by that amount.

- Considers the extent to which mitigation measures contributed to the reduction of disaster damage. This is especially significant in those disasters where, because of mitigation, the estimated assistance damages fall below the per capita indicator.

- Considers the disaster history of the state or locality within a 12-month period to better evaluate the overall impact of the recent disaster. A state still recovering from a previous disaster may need more funds than if the most recent disaster had occurred after many disaster-free years. FEMA also looks at how much money, both by the state and by the federal government, has already been spent on previous disasters from which the state may still be recovering.

- Considers programs of other federal agencies, because oftentimes their assistance programs more appropriately meet the needs of the disaster.[13]

For Individual Assistance Programs, FEMA:

- Considers the concentration of damage. High concentrations of damage to individuals, such as destroyed or damaged housing, may indicate a greater need for federal assistance than widespread and scattered damage.

- Considers the degree of trauma to the community, with special attention to large numbers of injuries and deaths, large-scale disruptions to normal community functions and services, and emergency needs, such as extended or widespread loss of power or water.

- Considers the impact of the disaster on special or vulnerable populations such as the low-income, elderly, disabled, unemployed, or other racial or religious minority communities.
- Assesses the capabilities of voluntary, faith, and community-based organizations (such as the members of NVOAD, discussed elsewhere in this chapter), as these entities play an important role in meeting both the emergency and recovery needs of individuals impacted by disasters.
- Considers the level of insurance coverage held by individuals. This is because assistance under the Stafford Act is meant to be supplemental to pre-existing funds individuals may have to cover losses, including insurance payouts.
- Assesses the number and severity of damaged residences. When conducting joint Preliminary Damage Assessments, FEMA evaluates the total number of homes destroyed and damaged, as well as the accessibility and habitability of the dwellings and the communities affected.

The declaration process contains many factors for consideration, and for all but the most catastrophic events, the process moves at a relatively slow speed as information is accumulated from local sources and sent to the federal government for assessment. While this process is informed by that information and its relationship to potential assistance programs, the information that is gathered at the state and local level does not preclude the exercise of judgment by the governor or the President.

## FEDERAL RESPONSE

Though state and local governments and non-governmental organizations are often the first responders to minor and major disasters, it is often the federal government that steps in to provide significant financial and logistical experience in the wake of a disaster or terrorist attack. Types of aid can include, but are not limited to operational, logistical, and technical support; financial assistance through grants, loans, and loan guarantees; and the

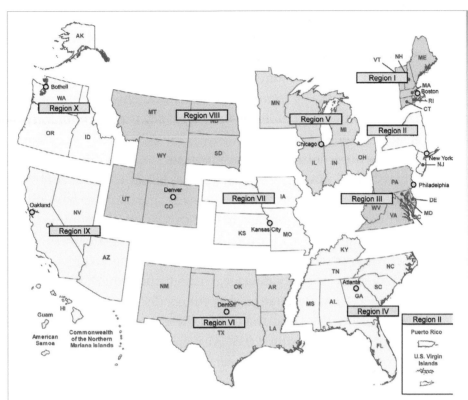

**FIG. 7.5**
FEMA Regional Offices serve as the primary organizational unit for liaison to states and local governments within each region, and non-governmental and private sector entities within each Regional Office's geographical area.

*Source*: FEMA's 10 Regions and Their Member States and Territories, Federal Emergency Management Agency, www.flickr.com/photos/usgao/25323750652/in/photolist-EzLQNy-EzLHS9-EXib3a-pR3yQE-B8ogi8-BFUgYR-Hp9Ykp-BeLmJ9-GDo2vK-DNRpKP-FNJtF5–29scxuP-TDvU6A-TZysPE-TDvTXu-RKpYgb-NoMvpb-NHydh8-N9r7y7-N-jJGNP-Mryhew-HvjS3G-GecS7o-GecQWN-wDAXfp-GzCzp9-GDo76X-rQ7QL3-wKj1W3-wKi-JZd-x2arw1-w5Ucwd-x2Vbap-rSi2LU-rzXzye-rUD9ra-sdPFrU-rXpeC5-uZx6vY-rXwbtK-rR3PkV-LBF3YU-23kDPyS-TCFzwk-UaSKXW-TCgTQF-TL5Ty7-SkaVX2-R3tLtf-MQrhwa.

provision of federally owned equipment and facilities.[14] A number of these aid programs are available after a Major Disaster Declaration has been issued by the President, but some can be had by local municipalities even in the absence of such a declaration.

Beyond the federal assistance programs that are deployed as part of an emergency or Major Disaster Declaration, several other federal departments and agencies have additional programs to assist both individuals and organizations and local governments obtain disaster relief. For example, the Centers for Disease Control and Prevention (CDC) may provide a range of technical assistance on issues relating to public health concerns in the immediate aftermath of a disaster. Some federal agencies are authorized to waive restrictions or reporting requirements in times of disaster to assist in recovery and response efforts. For example, the Environmental Protection Agency and the Department of Energy can issue emergency waivers of certain fuel standards in affected areas.[15]

If another federal agency is called upon to assist during a disaster, they usually receive a mission assignment from FEMA and are reimbursed through a disaster relief fund. Federal government agencies also have numerous authorized deployable federal assets that can support the immediate response to disaster. There are also situations when the federal government or a federal asset will provide immediate assistance, primarily to prevent direct loss of life or significant property damage, without the request rising through the normal Emergency Declaration procedures discussed elsewhere in this chapter. For instance, the Department of Defense (DOD), through its Defense Support of Civil Authorities (DSCA) regulations and policies, authorizes local DOD officials to provide immediate assistance without a formal request rising through the state and lead federal officials.[16]

## Disaster Recovery Programs

The breadth and depth of federal disaster relief programs are enormous. Most individuals seeking federal disaster assistance consult the Catalog of Federal Domestic Assistance (CDFA). The CDFA is a compendium of financial and non-financial programs from across the federal government that provide assistance or benefits—though many programs are not limited to disaster relief. Assistance to individuals may:

> Include funds for temporary housing for victims, individual and family grants to meet disaster-related expenses, and loans to individuals for repair or replacement of real and personal property. Funds may flow directly from the federal government to the individual, or from the federal government to the individual through a state or a subdivision of a state, or from a nonprofit organization to the individual.[17]

Some examples of these programs include block grants from the Department of Housing and Urban Development to Department of Defense labor assistance on breach control and erosion of public land.

### Assistance for Business and Non-Governmental Organizations

Federal government assistance to businesses (such as farms or even single-person operations) is made available when the ability to continue operations is terminated or impaired by a disaster. Such assistance may include loans to help repair a rental property, grants to replace livestock herds, restore damaged commercial structures, or infrastructure, and replace inventories of products.[18]

The Small Business Administration's (SBA) Office of Disaster Assistance is the primary federal body responsible for providing financial assistance to businesses of all sizes (though focused on small businesses such as small landlord operations) and private non-profit organizations, such as colleges and universities and community service organizations. Financial assistance is usually available in the form of low-interest, long-term loans. The SBA also provides "economic injury" assistance to cover small business operating expenses after a declared disaster.

### SIDEBAR 7.1 National Flood Insurance Program

In 1968 Congress created the National Flood Insurance Program (NFIP) to encourage property owners to purchase insurance protection against losses from flooding. The program was necessary because the catastrophic damage caused by flooding made flood insurance policies prohibitively expensive for most individuals and businesses. Instead, the NFIP today effectively allows the federal government to subsidize or pay part of the cost of these insurance policies, thus encouraging individuals and businesses to purchase flood insurance. When homes are thus insured, the burden on FEMA as well as state and local emergency management agencies is lessened because insurance policies cover much of the damage caused by flooding.

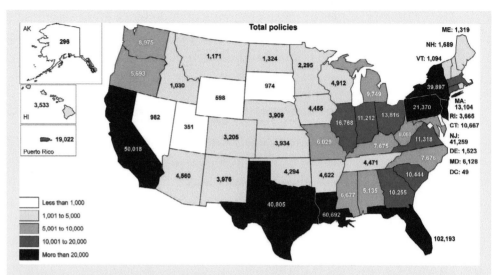

**FIG. 7.6**

Notice the disproportionate number of such policies in states with relatively small populations, such as Louisiana and Georgia, but nonetheless a higher potential for flood damage.

*Source*: Number of Estimated Subsidized Flood Insurance Policies by State, 2013, GAO Report GAO-16–190, www.flickr.com/photos/usgao/25567315133/in/photolist-EzLQNy-EzLHS9-EXib3a-pR3yQE-B8ogi8-BFUgYR-Hp9Ykp-BeLmJ9-GDo2vK-DNRpKP-FNJtF5–29scxuP-TDvU6A-TZysPE-TDvTXu-RKpYgb-NoMvpb-NHydh8-N9r7y7-NjJGNP-Mryhew-HvjS3G-GecS7o-GecQWN-wDAXfp-GzCzp9-GDo76X-rQ7QL3-wKj1W3-wKiJZd-x2arw1-w5Ucwd-x2Vbap-rSi2LU-rzXzye-rUD9ra-sdPFrU-rXpeC5-uZx6vY-rXwbtK-rR3PkV-LBF3YU-23kDPyS-TCFzwk-UaSKXW-TCgTQF-TL5Ty7-SkaVX2-R3tLtf-MQrhwa.

The federal government also encourages adoption of flood insurance policies by requiring flood insurance for all federal loans or lines of credit that are secured by existing buildings. Thus, if your home is damaged by a flood and you seek disaster assistance from FEMA, a prerequisite for receiving this assistance is enrollment in the NFIP. As of August 2017, the program insured about 5 million homes throughout the U.S., mostly in Texas and Florida.[19]

Though well-intentioned, many experts have come to criticize the program as unhelpful, expensive, and inconsequential in terms of increased safety and security. For instance, critics point out that participation in the NFIP doesn't prevent a homeowner from also qualifying for federal or state-based disaster assistance, thus negating the original intent of the NFIP to diminish reliance on federal disaster aid.[20] Because the NFIP provides a measure of safety and security it also encourages construction in flood-prone areas that are often damaged in the wake of a hurricane or storm. As evidence, critics point to the fact that properties covered by the NFIP tend to flood far more frequently than those in similar flood-prone areas that have no flood insurance.[21]

# STATE AND LOCAL GOVERNMENT DISASTER RESPONSE AND ASSISTANCE

## Local Government Response and Recovery

Local governments are primarily responsible for managing the response to and recovery from hazards. At the local government level, the responsibility for protecting citizens belongs to local elected officials such as mayors, city councils, and boards of commissioners. When a local government receives warning that an emergency could be imminent, its first priority is to alert and warn citizens and take whatever actions are needed to minimize damage and protect life and property. If necessary, local governments may order an evacuation. When an emergency or disaster does occur, fire and police units, emergency medical personnel, and rescue workers rush to damaged areas to provide aid.

After this initial response, local governments must work to ensure public order and security. Vital services such as water, power, communications, transportation, shelter, and medical care must be provided. Debris removal must begin, either through government resources or by private contractors. Public and private utility company crews, along with other emergency teams, must be on the job to restore essential services. Local government coordinates its efforts with voluntary agencies who assist individuals and families in need.[22]

When a local government responds to a disaster, the levels of activities and the type of resources required are determined by several factors, including:

- The speed of onset of the emergency;
- The potential need for evacuation;

- The magnitude of the situation;
- The projected duration of the situation;
- The projected duration of the event; and
- The extent of the threat to citizens.

In the aftermath of an emergency or disaster, many citizens will have specific needs that must be met before they can return to their pre-disaster lives. Typically, there will be a need for several different kinds of services, such as:

- An assessment of the extent and severity of damage to homes and other property;
- Restoration of services generally available in communities, such as water, food, and medical assistance;
- Repair of damaged homes and property; and
- Professional counseling when sudden hazards and emergencies result in mental anguish and inability to deal with difficult situations.

Local governments help individuals and families recover by ensuring that these services are available and by seeking additional resources if the community needs them. When an emergency occurs, the local government is often able to use local media to publicize the types of assistance available and how to access this assistance.

Recovery as a part of the Emergency Management Lifecycle is discussed elsewhere in this chapter. Here we focus on local government and community efforts to recover from a disaster. Local recovery from a disaster occurs generally in the short term and in the long term. **Short-term recovery** measures are those intended to return the community to minimum operating standards. **Long-term recovery** includes those steps that return the community to its previous condition, to the extent that is realistically possible.

Short-term recovery could include making houses habitable so that families can move out of temporary shelters and return to their own homes. Short-term recovery also can involve restoring essential services so that people can return to work. At the community level, short-term recovery may require completing repairs to roads and bridges so traffic can start moving again, or restoring power to areas in need. On the other hand, long-term recovery can occur over a period of several months or even years, depending on how severe the disaster was. Long-term recovery often involves significant rebuilding of local infrastructure, both public and private. The disruption and destruction to the community can be so intense that some businesses may never reopen and have to go out of business or relocate. Although a community may appear to be "open for business" a few weeks after an emergency or disaster, it may be years after a severe disaster before the community returns to pre-disaster conditions.[23]

As part of the recovery, communities often consider strategies that lessen the effects of a similar event in the future. We call these "mitigation" strategies and they are discussed elsewhere in the chapter. Undertaken comprehensively, mitigation and preparedness strategies increase a community's *resilience* to disaster. The concept of resilience in the emergency management concept is similar to its application to the broader homeland security context (and defined in Chapter 1), i.e. a community that is resilient increases its ability to recover from or adjust easily to misfortune and change caused by a hazard. For instance, if a community were to undertake measures to mitigate harm caused by a future flood it could help residents raise furnaces to higher floors, encourage business owners to store inventory above traditional flood levels, and help hospitals elevate and move generators and other critical facilities to protected buildings. The local government could also revise ordinances and other local laws to account for the effects of predicted climate change, such as by mandating additional areas as flood plain.[24]

## State Government Response and Recovery

If the emergency situation is such that the local community feels it cannot recover on its own, it may reach out to the state government for additional resources (Figure 7.7). Mutual aid agreements between local municipalities such as cities and counties often already exist to facilitate the provision of assistance by neighboring jurisdictions. This is most commonly witnessed on the news in the form of firefighters called in from nearby cities and states to assist in putting out a large wildfire. However, in a number of cases, these resources from other local communities may be insufficient, particularly if the neighboring communities are also dealing with the same disaster or are affected by their own type of hazard.

**FIG. 7.7**
Texas Governor
Gregg Abbott
holds a news
conference to
update Hur-
ricane Harvey
response and
recovery at the
Texas Division
of Emergency
Management
offices.

*Source*: Steve Zumwalt, Texas Governor News Conference, September 2017, Federal Emergency Management Agency, www.fema.gov/media-library/assets/images/135863.

In these cases, the local government may appeal to the state for assistance. This usually takes the form of local officials submitting a request to the state governor providing specific information about the emergency situation and its effects as well as outlining the type of assistance required. Emergency management offices in each state, or their equivalent, assess such requests on a routine basis and then advise the governor on appropriate actions. Generally, state emergency officials work quite closely with local officials (especially local officials of larger cities or those cities that are frequently impacted by emergency hazards) to ensure that the required documentation for assistance is properly formatted and complete. Close cooperation is also important because if the state government then turns to the federal government for further assistance, it relies on the completeness and validity of local disaster reporting for speedy access to federal funds.

All states have laws that describe the responsibilities of state governments during emergencies. These laws provide governors and state agencies with the authority to plan for and carry out the necessary actions to respond to emergencies and recover from their effects. Typically, the state emergency management legislation describes the duties and powers of the governor, whose authority typically includes the power to declare a state-wide emergency and to decide when to end this declaration.

Many specific responsibilities to carry out the provisions of any state emergency management laws are generally delegated to the state emergency management government agency. Especially after 9/11, almost all states have emergency management government agencies, though their names vary. Some are small, and some rival FEMA in size and scope (though not budget). Some handle multiple responsibilities and others are dedicated solely to emergency management work. Regardless of the title or structure of the emergency management government agency at the state level, its responsibilities are usually the same: To prepare for emergencies and to coordinate the activation and use of the resources controlled by the State government when they are needed to help local governments respond to, and recovery from, emergencies and other hazards.

The state emergency management organization, in its coordinating role, is involved in virtually all serious emergencies and hazards. Typically, this organization is responsible for receiving reports from the local area. Based on these and other data, emergency management officials work in consultation with other agency representatives and members of the governor's staff to determine what types of resources and personnel should be deployed to the impacted area. Using procedures specified in the state emergency management plan, the state emergency management government agency (such as the California Office of Emergency Services) will coordinate deployment of state personnel and resources to the impacted areas.[25]

However, it is not necessary for a governor to declare an emergency or disaster before agency personnel and resources are deployed to monitor situations and provide information. For instance, personnel and equipment are typically used to monitor situations where an area's water supply may become contaminated or when large-scale chemical leakage is possible. State agency personnel would generally be involved in early inspection activities and in making reports back to the state emergency management office and their own agencies for the purpose of determining additional assistance that may be needed.

When a state emergency is declared, the governor (or the director of the emergency management government agency at the state level) can mobilize resources to supplement those of the local government. For instance, the state government could deploy the state national guard to assist in evacuation of an affected area by prescribing evacuation routes and helping to control entries and departures from the disaster area. State and local government can also regulate the movement of persons inside the affected area. For instance, individuals could be prevented from returning to buildings rendered uninhabitable or unsafe by the disaster itself (this kind of state action also intersects with the idea of "quarantines"—see the Sidebar on quarantines elsewhere in this chapter). The exercise of these powers is necessary not only to protect residents of the affected community, but also to make the work of emergency response personnel safer and more efficient.

If the disaster is significant enough, a governor may even suspend local ordinances or state laws if doing so would ease human suffering or speed up emergency response efforts. In some states, after an Emergency Declaration, the governor may establish economic control over resources in the affected area, such as food and wages and over some services, such as the provision of shelter and clothing. Frequently, most governors choose to mobilize the state National Guard when a state-level state of emergency is declared. The National Guard are often granted the power to use all available state resources to respond effectively and efficiently to the emergency. The governor may also draw upon the resources, expertise, and knowledge of other state agencies who do not have a direct emergency management role, in order to assist response and recovery efforts.

## SIDEBAR 7.2 Georgia Emergency Management Agency

Like many states, the State of Georgia has a state-wide emergency management agency known as the Georgia Emergency Management and Homeland Security Agency (GEMHSA). Unlike many similar agencies that were established after 9/11, GEMHSA has been operating since 1981. Nonetheless, GEMHSA changed significantly after 9/11, in particular adding the "HS" component to its name and emphasizing the homeland security policy areas in its mission. This has increasingly meant tackling untraditional emergency management issues such as violent extremism, lone wolf terror attacks, and ensuring the safety and security of regional transportation networks.

Today, GEMHSA works with "local, state and federal governments, in partnership with the private sector and the faith-based community to prevent and respond to natural and man-made emergencies."[26] Like other similar state agencies, GEMHSA sits at the Office of the Governor and operates under statutory authority, in this case the Georgia Emergency Management Act of 1981. Also similar to other state agencies is GEMHSA's mission set, which focuses on the Emergency Management Lifecycle components of mitigation, preparedness, response, and recovery.

Just as some local communities may seek aid from nearby cities and towns, states are also able to request mutual aid from other states. If they have pre-existing agreements in place (such as Emergency Management Assistance Compacts), the provision of this aid becomes easier and faster. States that come to the aid of their neighbors often provide assistance in the form of personnel, equipment, and emergency relief supplies. These kinds of state-to-state mutual aid agreements are a way for states to circumvent or avoid the provision of federal disaster assistance. Notably, and similar to his or her powers to quarantine, under most state declarations of emergency, a governor may also have the power to use or commandeer private property for the purpose of responding to the disaster. Emergency management acts generally grant the governor the power to use, or authorize the use of, contingency and emergency funds in the event of an emergency. In some states, the governor may also reallocate funds when designated funds are exhausted.[27]

**Types of State Assistance**

Typically, States provide respond and provide recovery assistance in two ways:

1. State personnel and resources can be activated and deployed to assist in the response and recovery effort directly (or to manage, similar to what FEMA may do). Search and rescue of individuals trapped in their homes in the wake of severe flooding is an example of this kind of recovery response; and

2. State emergency personnel and equipment can be deployed to perform a variety of monitoring and inspection activities that can ensure the safety of community members and response personnel in the area. Monitoring of the emergency situation or additional follow-ups to the emergency (i.e. the threat of a tsunami in the wake of an earthquake) is an example of this kind of recovery response.

**CRITICAL THINKING QUESTION**

Read the section on state government response and recovery. Notice that states that often assist each other in the aftermath of an emergency might do so to avoid federal government involvement. Why would state governments want to avoid receiving federal aid or assistance for their citizens, especially when the federal government has far more resources at its disposal?

**State Agencies Involved in Emergency Management**

A number of state agencies and organizations are involved in providing assistance in the wake of an emergency situation. Some of these include:

• *Public safety departments*: These state-level agencies may undertake the repair of infrastructures such as bridges and roads damaged by floods or earthquakes. Heavy cranes and other specialized equipment, along with the expertise and skill needed to use this equipment, can often be provided by state transportation or highway agencies. Engineers employed by transportation departments also have the knowledge and skills to conduct accurate damage assessments of bridges and other structures. In addition, they can suggest mitigation methods so that reconstruction includes added protection for future disasters.[28] Public safety experts and personnel can also assist law enforcement in disaster zones with traffic control, security, and search and rescue. The fire marshal's office can deploy personnel to investigate structural fires and to assist in assessing the safety of structures that may be at risk from fires. Some larger departments may be involved in preventing food and water contamination after a disaster, or documenting a disaster for insurance claims or further federal disaster aid purposes.

- *Social service agencies*: Social service agencies at the state level can provide personnel and resources to help in setting up and running shelters for those who are left homeless in the wake of emergencies. They can provide counseling services to alleviate stress (a practice that has significant positive impact early in the disaster management cycle, if handled appropriately). If a federal emergency has been declared, social services agencies usually provide the administrative services to manage several federal programs. Social service agencies also assist voluntary agencies such as the American Red Cross in their efforts to provide relief to disaster victims.
- *The National Guard*: In more serious state-level disasters the governor can deploy the state National Guard to perform a wider array of duties, often those requiring a substantial amount of manpower. The National Guard can assist in flood-fighting activities such as sandbagging, evacuation, and search and rescue or provide civil order to prevent looting and crimes of opportunity in the wake of a natural disaster.
- *Public health agencies*: State public health agencies often deploy medical personnel such as physicians, nurses, and medical technicians, as well as hospital beds and other medication and supplies needed to restore health and safety. State public health agencies also play a critical role in monitoring water supplies since public utility infrastructure may become compromised after a disaster and contaminate the water supply. As was the case in Haiti in the aftermath of the 2010 earthquake, communicable diseases such as cholera may spread quickly where they otherwise would easily have been contained. State public health agencies serve a critical function in allocating medication and controlling these communicable diseases, as well as identifying and quarantining victims.[29]
- *Departments of agriculture*: A state department of agriculture will generally assist when damage to farms and ranches is involved. It may carry out measures to protect the long-term food supply of the affected area. State agriculture departments also inventory food resources and may help procure food for disaster victims. Longer-term assistance provided by agriculture departments includes advising farmers and agribusinesses in mitigation planning and recovering from damages to facilities, crops, and livestock.

- *Natural resource agencies*: State natural resource agencies usually ensure the protection of non-human resources such as livestock, fish, and game resources. They may also deploy personnel to help conduct damage assessments. Occasionally, these agencies help advise local officials and assist them in monitoring and protecting natural resources in the state. For instance, natural resource agencies may be called upon in the wake of a brushfire or a wildfire to assist in the evacuation of wildlife in the path of the fire. Environmental protection agencies may assist in similar ways to help local officials preserve and protect various environmentally sensitive areas and to plan mitigation measures for further disasters. They can also provide technical expertise to help agencies respond to hazardous materials spills that could result from primary emergencies such as floods.[30]

Various other state agencies and organizations have resources and expertise that is often helpful to local communities responding to emergencies. State departments of labor can assist with safety inspections. Education departments can help to run schools and other educational services for children. State management and budget agencies can assist in locating and establishing recovery centers and field operations offices.

**FIG. 7.8**
These kinds of temporary health clinics are often provided by state social service agencies and public health agencies to provide onsite healthcare assistance to remote populations in the aftermath of a disaster.

*Source*: Jack Heesch, Temporary Health Clinic in Eagle, Alaska, Federal Emergency Management Agency, www.fema.gov/media-library/assets/images/56029.

Depending on the severity of the emergency, some agencies become more substantially involved in providing assistance for the community's recovery. For example, treasury departments can conduct post-emergency audits to document expenditures by local governments. In some states, they also provide tax advice for disaster victims. Some state general services agencies can help identify and make state facilities available for use as shelter, as well as to warehouse food supplies. In some states, commerce departments assist in licensing vehicles needed to transport emergency supplies. They may also expedite the recovery of public utilities to affected areas. Personnel from these agencies may also be involved in damage assessment work.[31]

### SIDEBAR 7.3 Quarantines

In December of 2013, 1-year-old Emile Ouamouno died in his small village in Guinea, West Africa. The boy's home was in the vicinity of a bat colony and he had apparently been bitten, though no one had noticed. What his community also hadn't known at the time was that the bat carried a virulent strain of the Ebola Virus—a highly contagious virus that causes fever, muscular pain, rash, and the eventual failure of the body organs of many primates who contract the virus.

Soon after Emile's death, his mother, sister, and grandmother also became ill and died. People infected in Emile's village spread the disease to other nearby villages in Guinea. Because individuals did not perceive Ebola to be local to West Africa, the disease continued to be mis-categorized for several days.[32] By March, over 100 cases had been reported and the disease soon spread to Guinea's capital, killing over 200 by May.

As concern regarding the disease's spread increased, several international organizations, such as the World Health Organization, worked with local governments to set up massive, nation-wide quarantines around several West African nations. A **quarantine** is a limitation on physical movement of individuals in order to prevent the spread of disease. Quarantines often last for a limited period of time, usually until the threat of infection subsides. Though often applied to humans, as was the case with Ebola outbreak described here, quarantines are most often used to isolate animals that may be carrying diseases.[33]

As Ebola spread past the borders of Guinea, many countries considered imposing travel restrictions to or from the region, further quarantining West Africa. Though a full quarantine and travel shut down was never imposed, several health restrictions were set up before travelers were allowed to leave or enter West African nations affected by the Ebola Virus. Among these were mandatory tests for the virus, hand-washing requirements, measuring of body temperature, and military escorts.[34]

If Ebola or another highly contagious disease had broken out of West Africa and into the United States, several U.S. laws would have allowed the President (through the Centers for Disease Control) to impose a quarantine or health cordon. Executive Order 13295 (Revised List of Quarantinable Communicable Diseases, issued April 4, 2003) and its amendments specify that a quarantine may be quickly imposed on populations with symptoms of cholera, diphtheria, infectious tuberculosis, plague, smallpox, yellow fever, viral hemorrhagic fevers (such as Ebola), and influenza among other diseases. In the event of conflict of laws between federal, state, local, or tribal authorities, federal law regarding quarantines is supreme.[35]

The Division of Global Migration and Quarantine (DGMQ) of the U.S. Centers for Disease Control (CDC) operates small quarantine facilities at a number of U.S. ports of entry, of which 19 are airports. Working closely with CBP, the CDC can activate these facilities as needed. Each facility is responsible for quarantining potentially infected travelers entering through nearby ports of entry as well. These facilities are small, capable of accommodating only 1–2 infected individuals, and each one is operated by a few CDC or CBP staff members.[36]

## NON-GOVERNMENTAL DISASTER RESPONSE AND ASSISTANCE

It is often the case that the capacity of local, state, and even the federal government is overwhelmed in the face of significant disasters. This was the case in the aftermath of Hurricane Katrina, Hurricane Sandy, and most recently Hurricanes Harvey and Maria as well as the wildfires in Northern California. Often without being asked, several large voluntary organizations step in to support local and regional communities in the aftermath of major disasters. In some cases, state, local, and the federal government have pre-existing agreements that oblige NGOs to step in to assist in the wake of a disaster (for instance, the American Red Cross is an organization obliged to assist in the wake of a major hazard, and funded partially by Congress as a result of these obligations).

Voluntary organizations are encouraged by the federal government to coordinate their disaster response work under the National Response Framework (NRF, discussed later in this chapter). In some cases, NGOs may actually have specific statutory responsibilities. For instance, the American Red Cross and the National Voluntary Organizations Active in Disasters (NVOAD) have specific responsibilities under the NRF. A large number of American faith-based organizations, both local and national in scope, are also deeply involved in disaster response and recovery. For instance, Catholic Charities, a large NGO organized around many national dioceses, has personnel dedicated to providing disaster relief. One example is the Catholic Charities' Safe Harbor program, which:

> Provides individuals and families impacted by disaster with rent-free, furnished housing and case management services for 90 days . . . as well as temporary housing while clients resolve issues involving home repair and disruption of income so they may return to their pre-disaster living situations.[37]

Since every disaster elicits involvement from a large number of unique and specialized NGO and volunteer-run response organizations . . . state, tribal, or local government officials may generally be the best source of initial information on NGO activities during the disaster. If the incident has been declared an emergency or Major Disaster through the Stafford Act, FEMA's Voluntary Agency Liaisons (VALs) may provide additional support to coordinate the efforts of voluntary organizations bringing relief to afflicted communities.[38]

## NVOAD

National Voluntary Organizations Active in Disaster (NVOAD) is the forum where organizations share knowledge and resources throughout the emergency management lifecycle (e.g. mitigation, preparedness, response, and recovery . . . discussed elsewhere in this chapter) to assist disaster survivors and their communities.[39] Members of NVOAD form a coalition of non-profit organizations that respond to disasters as part of their overall mission. NVOAD was founded in 1970 in response to the challenges many disaster organizations experienced following Hurricane Camille, which hit the Gulf Coast in August 1969.

Prior to the founding of NVOAD, numerous organizations served disaster victims independently of one another. These included government, faith-

**FIG. 7.9**
Cathy McCann (right), Vice-President of Operations at the Community Food Bank of New Jersey, and Ernest Vaughan (left), warehouse manager, smile for the camera during their work with volunteers who sort and pack donated food at the Food Bank. During times of disaster, the Food Bank of New Jersey coordinates its activities through FEMA's Voluntary Agency Liaison (VAL) to provide assistance to disaster survivors.

*Source*: Christopher Mardorf, Community Food Bank of New Jersey assists disaster survivors, Federal Emergency Management Agency, www.fema.gov/media-library-data/ e2c669be-7a39-4e5c-ac3f-1008b5e9d7d6/54106.jpg.

based organizations, and the private, non-profit sector. As a result, help came to the disaster victim haphazardly as various organizations assisted in specific ways. Unnecessary duplication of effort often occurred, while at the same time, other needs were left unmet. There was only limited availability of training for potential volunteers. Information for victims on services during disasters was inadequate and communication among voluntary disaster agencies was very limited while coordination of services to disaster victims remained negligible.[40]

Seeing all of these problems, seven founding organizations came together and committed to a "four C's" program: Communication, coordination, collaboration, and cooperation . . . in order to better serve people impacted by all hazards. Today, NVOAD is the preeminent umbrella organization of NGOs involved in emergency management and serves as the primary NGO point of contact for the federal government in the wake of a national emergency or disaster.

## American Red Cross

For more than 122 years, the mission of the American Red Cross (ARC) has been to help people prevent, prepare for, and respond to emergencies. It is the nation's preeminent non-governmental disaster response organization. The ARCs size, scope, and capacity in some cases dwarfs even that of government efforts and it is often relied upon by Americans for critical disaster recovery services. A humanitarian organization led by volunteers, guided by its Congressional charter and the fundamental principles of the International Red Cross Movement, the ARC is woven into the fabric of American communities with 940 chapters nationwide.[41]

The ARC responds to over 70,000 disasters per year, including house and apartment fires, hurricanes, floods, earthquakes, tornadoes, hazardous materials spills, transportation accidents, explosions, and other natural and man-made hazards. Although not a government agency, the ARC was granted a Congressional Charter to:

> Carry on a system of national and international relief in time of peace and apply the same in mitigating the sufferings caused by pestilence, fam-

ine, fire, floods and other great national calamities, and to devise and carry on measures for preventing the same.[42]

The charter is a grant of power, but also a set of obligations placed on the ARC that make it unique among other volunteer disaster response organizations (such as those that are part of NVOAD). The ARC provides food aid, shelter, health and mental services, and other services to address basic human needs. At the local level, ARC chapters operate using volunteer-staffed Disaster Action Teams. In some cases, ARC even supports the emergency workers of other organizations and state, local, and even federal emergency management organizations. A major misconception among the general public is that ARC provides medical facilities, engages in search and rescue operations, or deploys ambulances. Instead, first responder roles are left to government agencies as dictated by the National Response Framework.[43]

### SIDEBAR 7.4 Volunteer Disaster Response Organizations, Team Rubicon

A number of unique organizations take up the mantle of disaster relief in the United States. One of the newest and most successful is Team Rubicon. Team Rubicon was founded by U.S. Marines William McNulty and Jake Wood in the aftermath of the Haiti earthquake in 2010. Today the organization, which is made up mostly of U.S. military veteran volunteers, is a disaster service organization that helps to re-integrate veterans back into civilian life by involving them in disaster response in the United States and abroad. The name "Rubicon" comes from the phrase "crossing the Rubicon," which refers to Roman Emperor Julius Caesar's crossing of the Rubicon River in order to invade Rome. Once the Rubicon was crossed, Caesar had crossed the point of no return and would be unable to return backwards without incurring the wrath of Rome. Today the phrase has come to refer to any individual or group committing itself irrevocably to a risky or revolutionary course of action.

Since the Haiti earthquake, Team Rubicon has deployed to over 175 operations, including international operations in Pakistan, Chile, and Burma. In the United States Team Rubicon has responded to disasters such as Hurricanes Matthew, Irene, Sandy, and most recently Harvey and Maria. Unique to Team Rubicon's disaster response philosophy is the integration of military principles such as discipline, camaraderie, efficiency, and mental and physical toughness. Team Rubicon is organized in a manner similar to that of the armed forces, with volunteers deployed in squads and battalion-like units over a compressed timeframe.

In particular, Team Rubicon focuses on vulnerable and at-risk populations affected by a disaster. This is because while the initial damage and trauma of natural disasters will impact any population regardless of socio-economic factors, the financial burden of recovery and rebuilding has dramatic and long-lasting repercussions on many rural and urban populations lacking proper insurance and public/private resources. This includes populations without the wherewithal, time, or sophistication to apply for FEMA or state-based disaster assistance. In doing this kind of work, Team Rubicon and other similar non-profit organizations thus fill a policy gap in emergency response and recovery.[44]

## THE NATIONAL PREPAREDNESS SYSTEM

Emergency response and recovery is often carried out in accordance with the National Preparedness System, which despite its name, covers aspects of preparedness, response, and recovery to all hazards. The National Preparedness System (NPS) was established under former President Barack Obama in March 2011. The NPS is designed to help "ensure the Nation's ability to prevent, respond to, recover from, and mitigate natural disasters, acts of terrorism and other man-made disasters."[45] The NPS and its sub-policies set forth the vision of the federal government, one that is informed by various non-profit disaster response organizations, academics, community groups, and other local organizations and governments.[46] The NPS is designed to meet what FEMA calls the National Preparedness Goal. The National Preparedness Goal defines what it means for the emergency preparedness community to be prepared for all types of disasters and emergencies. The goal itself is summarized by FEMA as:

> *A secure and resilient nation with the capabilities required across the whole community to prevent, protect against, mitigate, respond to, and recover from the threats and hazards that pose the greatest risk.* (emphasis added)[47]

These risks may include events such as natural disasters, disease pandemics, chemical spills, and other manmade hazards such as terrorist attacks and cyberattacks. In addition to stating the goal, the National Preparedness Goal describes 32 activities, called core capabilities, that address the greatest risks to the nation. Each of these core capabilities is tied to a capability target. These targets recognize that everyone needs the flexibility to determine how they apply their resources, based on the threats that are most relevant to them and their communities. A Midwestern city, for example, may determine it is at high risk for a catastrophic tornado. As a result, the city could set a target to have a certain number of shelters and medical facilities in place. This also applies across all potential risks, knowing that each risk is different, and that therefore each target is different.[48]

The NPS also establishes methods for achieving the nation's desired level of preparedness for both federal and non-federal partners by identifying **core capabilities**. Congress defines "capability" as:

> The ability to provide the means to accomplish one or more tasks under specific conditions and to specific performance standards. A capability may be achieved with any combination of properly planned, organized, equipped, trained, and exercised personnel that achieves the intended outcome.[49]

A *core* capability is one that is "necessary to prepare for the specific types of incidents that pose the greatest risk to the security of the Nation."[50]

The NPS is managed using a complicated system of tasks, routines, and areas of responsibilities, collectively known as the National Incident Management System (NIMS). NIMS provides a consistent approach for the entire hazard management community to work "together seamlessly and manage incidents involving all threats and hazards, regardless of cause, size, location or complexity—in order to reduce loss of life, property and harm to the environment."[51] The NPS is also subdivided into five mission areas: Prevention, Protection, Mitigation, Response, and Recovery. Collectively these five areas are known as National Planning Frameworks (NPF). Each NPF is supported by a federal interagency operational plan that describes how the federal government aligns its supporting resources and delivers core capabilities. The National Response Framework and the National Recovery Framework are two of the most important of these frameworks and we discuss them below.[52]

## National Response Framework

The National Response Framework (NRF) guides the nation's response to a major hazard, irrespective of how small or large the hazard is or what the cause of the hazard is (i.e. manmade, natural, terrorist, etc.). Any disaster that may require coordination with or by the federal government, including financial assistance from the federal government, is managed under the NRF. Because the NRF is a consistent operational guide, this means that federal, state, and local governments operate similarly during a response to an emergency hazard. Consistent response ensures that each level of government can predict what the other may do, and anticipate the needs and workflow of other large government and non-governmental organizations involved in emergency hazard response operations.[53]

The NRF is further divided into 14 Emergency Support Functions (ESFs) that organize the response capabilities of the federal government (see list of ESFs elsewhere in this chapter). ESFs are grouping categories and place certain federal agencies in "buckets" with other state, local, or federal government authorities as well as other resources and expertise in the same ESF area.[54] For instance, ESF #9 is titled "Search and Rescue," which unifies federal agencies with the appropriate resources and authorities to conduct search and rescue operations in the aftermath of a major hazard such as an earthquake or tornado. One federal agency or a part of a federal agency may be placed in a coordination or leadership role for each ESF. For instance, the Department of Health and Human Services (HHS) is the coordinator for ESF #8, which deals with Public Health and Medical Services responsibilities.

Beyond tasking responsibilities to various federal agencies, the ESF also contains additional guidance describing how the NRF must be used to respond to common hazards. For example, the Volunteer and Donations Management Support Annex outlines how the federal government is obligated to assist and coordinate the use of unaffiliated volunteers, organizations, and donated goods in the aftermath of a major hazard.[55]

**CALL-OUT BOX**
**Emergency Support Functions**[56]

Emergency Support Functions provide the structure for coordinating federal interagency support for a federal response to an incident. They are mechanisms for grouping functions most frequently used to provide federal support to states and federal-to-federal support, both for declared disasters and emergencies under the Stafford Act and for non-Stafford Act incidents.

- *ESF #1* Transportation:

- Aviation/airspace management and control
- Transportation safety
- Restoration/recovery of transportation infrastructure
- Movement restrictions
- Damage and impact assessment

- *ESF #2* Communications:

- Coordination with telecommunications and information technology industries
- Restoration and repair of telecommunications infrastructure
- Protection, restoration, and sustainment of national cyber and information technology resources
- Oversight of communications within the Federal incident management and response structures

- *ESF #3* Public Works

-  Engineering:
- Infrastructure protection and emergency repair
- Infrastructure restoration
- Engineering services and construction management
- Emergency contracting support for life-saving and life-sustaining services

- *ESF #4* Firefighting:

- Coordination of Federal firefighting activities
- Support to wildland, rural, and urban firefighting operations

- *ESF #5* Emergency Management:

- Coordination of incident management and response efforts
- Issuance of mission assignments
- Resource and human capital
- Incident action planning

- Financial management

- *ESF #6* Mass Care, Emergency Assistance, Housing and Human Services:

- Mass care

- Emergency assistance

- Disaster housing

- Human services

- *ESF #7* Logistics, Management, and Resource Support:

- Comprehensive, national incident logistics planning, management, and sustainment capability

- Resource support (facility space, office equipment and supplies, contracting services, etc.)

- *ESF #8* Public Health and Medical Services:

- Public health

- Medical

- Mental health services

- Mass fatality management

- *ESF #9* Search and Rescue:

- Life-saving assistance

- Search and rescue operations

- *ESF #10* Oil and Hazardous Materials Response:

- Oil and hazardous materials (chemical, biological, radiological, etc.) response

- Environmental short- and long-term cleanup

- *ESF #11* Agriculture and Natural Resources:

- Nutrition assistance

- Animal and plant disease and pest response

- Food safety and security

- Natural and cultural resources and historic properties protection and restoration

- Safety and well-being of household pets

- *ESF #12* Energy:

- Energy infrastructure assessment, repair, and restoration

- Energy industry utilities coordination

- Energy forecast

- *ESF #13* Public Safety and Security:

- Facility and resource security

- Security planning and technical resource assistance

- Public safety and security support
- Support to access, traffic, and crowd control
- *ESF #14* Long-Term Community Recovery:
- Social and economic community impact assessment
- Long-term community recovery assistance to States, local governments, and the private sector
- Analysis and review of mitigation program implementation
- *ESF #15* External Affairs:
- Emergency public information and protective action guidance
- Media and community relations
- Congressional and international affairs
- Tribal and insular affairs

## National Disaster Recovery Framework

The National Disaster Recovery Framework (NDRF) is a companion document to the NRF and guides the nation's long-term recovery from disasters.[57] The NDRF provides basic recovery principles, an explanation of roles and responsibilities at various levels of government, and a structure and process to assist short and long-term recovery following a disaster event. Similar to the NRF, the NDRF uses a support-function model to organize federal capabilities called Recovery Support Functions. The six Recovery Support Functions and their respective coordinating agencies are:

1. Community Planning and Capacity Building (FEMA)
2. Economic Recovery Support (Department of Commerce)
3. Health and Social Services Recovery Support (Department of Health and Human Services)
4. Housing Recovery Support (Department of Housing and Urban Development)
5. Infrastructure Systems Recovery Support (Army Corps of Engineers)
6. Natural and Cultural Resources Support (Department of Interior)[58]

The NDRF also establishes three positions that provide focal points for incorporating recovery considerations into the decision-making process following a disaster. Those positions are the Federal Disaster Recovery Coordinator (FDRC), State or Tribal Disaster Recovery Coordinators, and Local Disaster Recovery Managers.[59]

# HAZARDS

### Defining Hazards

Emergency managers at all levels of government have various definitions of what a "hazard" is, irrespective of the type of hazard they may be talking about. Most definitions of "hazard" view it as an event, and most attach the idea of potentiality to that term. For instance, examine this definition:

> **Hazard:** "A condition or event with the potential for harm to the community or environment."[60]

Note that in this definition the author includes threats to the environment, not just human beings.[61] Here is another definition that introduces the concept of *risk* into the definition of hazard:

> **Hazard:** "Hazard is best viewed as a naturally occurring or human-induced process or event with the potential to create loss, i.e. a general source of danger. Risk is the actual exposure of something of human value to a hazard and is often regarded as the combination of probability and loss. Thus, we may define hazard (or cause) as a 'potential threat to humans and their welfare' and risk (or consequence) as 'the probability of a specific hazard occurrence'."[62]

The distinction between hazard and risk from the definition above can be illustrated by this scenario: Two people cross an ocean, one in an ocean liner and the other in a rowing boat. The main hazard (deep water and large waves) is the same in both cases, but the risk (probability of drowning) is much greater for the person rowing the boat. Thus,

> while an earthquake hazard can exist in an uninhabited region, an earthquake risk can occur only in an area where people and their possessions exist. People and what they value are the essential point of reference for all risk assessment and for all disasters.[63]

A commonly accepted definition by FEMA breaks hazards down into three distinct categories:

- **Hazard**: A potentiality or threat of harm to humans, and/or the things they value;

- **Disaster**: The combination of a hazard actuality and the intersection of this occurrence with human values; and
- **Risk**: A measure of the hazard's occurrence or measure of the damage potentiality of the hazard occurrence.[64]

What significance do these multitude of definitions have on the emergency management enterprise within homeland security? For emergency managers and homeland security policymakers, the way we define hazards determines and frames the activities government agencies engage in. For instance, if drought is not a hazard, then a government organization, leader, or employee spends no time, attention, or resources on it. Resources devoted to fighting and mitigating hazards depend on whether policymakers consider them a hazard or not. Moreover, current political considerations may also determine whether an event is considered a hazard. For instance, prior to 9/11 few emergency managers considered a terrorist attack to be a hazard (rather, such an attack was classified as a matter of national security). Likewise, in the early 1990s few emergency managers thought of the West Nile Virus as a hazard to contend with—many do today.[65]

Put another way,

> Which definitions and concepts will be used depend less on their inherent or scientific merits, but more on political considerations—the political arena is the place where in almost all societies differences of opinions and values are fought over and usually 'resolved' in one direction or another. Students who will be emergency managers . . . need to take into account the political contexts in which they will be operating. Scientific evidence or the views of scientists will be only one factor that will feed into that context.[66]

## CLASSIFYING HAZARDS

For the purposes of this text, hazards usually fall into three broad categories: Natural, technological, and manmade. *Natural hazards* are generally weather related, such as earthquakes, flood, hurricanes, or tornados. *Technological hazards* refer to human-caused disasters such as a dam or bridge collapse or the exposure of hazardous waste to humans and the environment. *Manmade hazards* are typically those associated with an intentional human action, such as criminal or terrorist act.[67] There are additional categories of hazards that sometimes get combined with the three categories discussed above, or listed as subcategories. These are:

- *Environmental disasters*: Oil spills, nuclear reactor meltdown etc.;
- *Biological hazards*: Examples include the outbreak of disease such as Ebola, or infestations by living in organisms such as mold or fungi; and
- *Chemical/Radiological hazards or events*: A "dirty" nuclear device, chemicals intentionally leaked into a water system that may be harmful to a person's health.

The U.S. military uses the acronym **CBRNe** as a standard for classifying these hazards. CBRNe stands for chemical, biological, radiological, nuclear, or explosive (which covers terrorism). The lines between these hazards are not always clear-cut. For instance, natural hazards can be compounded by man-made or technological hazards such as when the levees in Louisiana broke (technological hazard) due to the immense water levels caused by Hurricane Katrina (natural hazard). These co-dependent or combination of hazards are often referred to as "hybrid" or "combination" hazards.

## THE EMERGENCY MANAGEMENT LIFECYCLE

Defining hazards in terms of risks and probabilities as well as events points to how governments at all levels respond to hazards. State, local, and federal governments discharge their emergency management responsibilities by taking four interrelated actions: 1) mitigation, 2) preparedness, 3) response, and 4) recovery. We refer to this as the **Emergency Management Lifecycle** (Figure 7.10). The overall goal of the emergency management lifecycle, and emergency management in general, is to minimize the impact caused by an emergency in a jurisdiction.

### Mitigation

Mitigation actions involve lasting reduction of exposure to, probability of, or potential loss from hazard events.[68] Mitigation actions are forward-look-

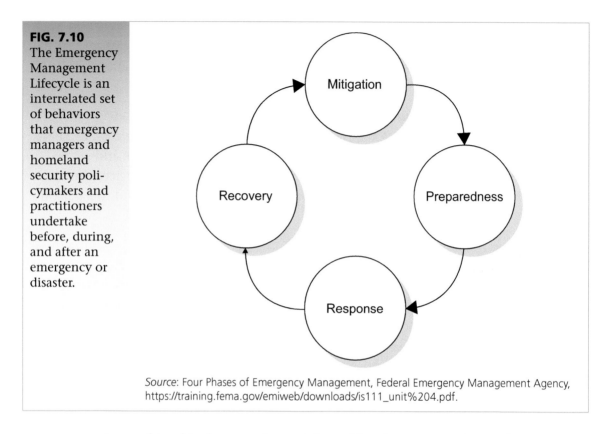

**FIG. 7.10**
The Emergency Management Lifecycle is an interrelated set of behaviors that emergency managers and homeland security policymakers and practitioners undertake before, during, and after an emergency or disaster.

*Source*: Four Phases of Emergency Management, Federal Emergency Management Agency, https://training.fema.gov/emiweb/downloads/is111_unit%204.pdf.

ing and tend to focus on how state and local governments can improve preexisting situations to minimize the impact of future hazards. For instance, a city may mandate that structures in a floodplain be built at a certain height or with a specific kind of foundation to minimize the loss of structures from catastrophic flooding. Mitigation can also involve educating businesses and the public on simple measures they can take to reduce loss and injury, such as fastening bookshelves, water heaters, and file cabinets to walls to keep them from falling during earthquakes.[69]

Cost-effective mitigation measures are the key to reducing disaster losses in the long term. In hazard-prone areas, mitigation can break the cycle of having to rebuild repeatedly with every occurrence of floods, hurricanes, or earthquakes. Ongoing mitigation efforts may include:

• Educating the private sector about what it can do to mitigate the impact of hazards at home and at work;

Since 1989, there have been

**1,485** Major Disaster Declarations

resulting in the availability of

**$13.8** billion

Hazard Mitigation Grant Program funds

Data current as of Feb. 2017

**FIG. 7.11**
A graphic with stats on Hazard Mitigation Program funds that FEMA provides to local and state governments and other bodies to assist with mitigating the effects of a future disaster.

*Source*: Roosevelt Grant for FEMA, 13.8 Billion Hazard Mitigation Grant Program Funds, www.fema.gov/media-library/assets/images/130702.

- Reaching out to local planning, zoning, and development agencies to ensure that hazard conditions are considered in comprehensive plans, construction permits, building codes, design approvals; and
- Creating inventories of existing structures and their vulnerabilities.

Often disaster management organizations and NGOs conduct mitigation efforts in the recent aftermath of a hazard such as a natural disaster because at that time public and private awareness of disasters is high, funds are perhaps more readily obtained, and the disruption in status quo makes it possible to rethink design and location of facilities and infrastructure to make them more resilient to natural and other hazards.[70]

## Preparedness

While mitigation can make communities safer, it does not eliminate risk and vulnerability for all hazards. Therefore, jurisdictions must be ready to face emergency threats and hazards that have not been mitigated sufficiently. Since hazards evolve rapidly and become too complex for effective improvisation, the government can sufficiently discharge its emergency management responsibilities only by taking certain actions beforehand. We call this "preparedness."

Preparedness involves establishing authorities and responsibilities for emergency actions and garnering the resources to support them: A jurisdiction must assign or recruit staff for emergency management duties and designate or procure facilities, equipment, and other resources for carrying out assigned duties. This investment in emergency management requires upkeep: The staff must receive training and the facilities and equipment must be maintained in working order. To ensure that a local government's investment in emergency management personnel and resources can be relied upon when needed, there is often a need for recurring tests, drills, and exercises. Consideration is also given to reducing or eliminating the vulnerability of the jurisdiction's emergency response organizations and resources to hazards that threaten the jurisdiction (for instance, does the emergency management HQ in a city have a backup power supply? Are they able to directly reach law enforcement if their phone lines are sabotaged by terrorists?). Preparedness is thus about planning and a key element of preparedness is the development of plans that link the many aspects of a jurisdiction's commitment to emergency management.[71]

### Response

The onset of an emergency creates the need for time-sensitive actions to save lives and property *while the hazard is occurring or in its immediate aftermath*. This includes actions to stabilize the hazard situation so that the locality can regroup. Such response actions many include notifying emergency management personnel of the crisis, warning and evacuating or sheltering the population if possible, keeping the population informed, rescuing individuals and providing medical treatment, maintaining the rule of law, assessing damage, addressing mitigation issues that arise from response activities, and even requesting help from outside the jurisdiction.[72]

### Recovery

Recovery refers to the steps taken in the immediate aftermath of a disaster to place a community back to where it was before the hazard or disaster occurred. Put another way: "recovery is the effort to restore infrastructure and the social and economic life of a community to normal."[73] For the short term, recovery may mean bringing necessary lifeline systems such as power, communication, water and sewage, Internet services, and transportation . . . up to an acceptable standard that provides for basic human needs. Recovery may also mean providing for the societal needs of individuals and the communities affected by the disaster. These needs may include maintaining the rule of law, providing psychological counseling etc. For instance, the author of this textbook set up a legal clinic in the aftermath of Hurricane Katrina to provide legal care to those affected by natural hazards who were beset by a host of legal and fiscal problems due to the hurricane.

Recovery efforts begin immediately after, or often in conjunction with, response efforts. Usually, once some semblance of stability is achieved, the local community can begin these recovery efforts for the long-term. These long-term efforts may include restoring economic activity and rebuilding community facilities and family housing with attention to long-term mitigation needs.[74]

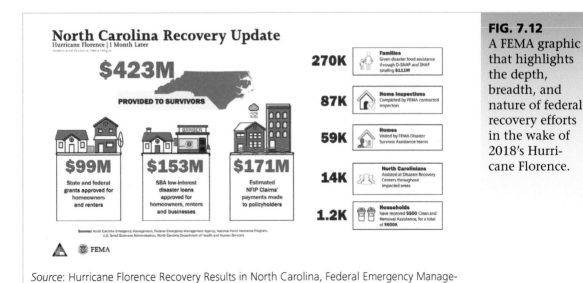

**FIG. 7.12**
A FEMA graphic that highlights the depth, breadth, and nature of federal recovery efforts in the wake of 2018's Hurricane Florence.

*Source*: Hurricane Florence Recovery Results in North Carolina, Federal Emergency Management Agency, www.fema.gov/media-library/assets/images/172641.

### SIDEBAR 7.5 Should Emergency Management Be Part of Homeland Security?

After 9/11 FEMA, the primary disaster response agency in the U.S. government, was made part of the new Department of Homeland Security. In merging FEMA into a security-oriented organization, Congress signaled its intent to treat disaster response as a homeland security rather than emergency management issue. This created confusion and consternation in both fields that has continued to this day.

The differences between DHS and FEMA have become starker as time has passed. Despite its change in mission to focus on "all-hazards," FEMA continues to mostly focus on assistance related to natural hazards. When a terrorist attack occurs, the FBI or another similar federal law enforcement agency is first on the scene, not FEMA. This is because unlike DHS, or the FBI, FEMA is primarily a coordinator of federal support to state and local governments and NGOs. FEMA has few internal assets or investigative personnel and relies on assistance from other federal agencies to coordinate disaster response. For instance, FEMA relies on the Small Business Association (SBA) to deliver disaster relief loans to small businesses.

Nonetheless, FEMA is often called on the handle duties outside its (actual, not technical) mission of providing assistance and coordination for natural hazards. For instance, as the assigned primary grant-vetting organization at DHS, FEMA is responsible for creating, vetting, and delivering grants on issues as diverse as the prevention of online violent extremism to training local law enforcement to interdict active shooter threats. Lacking the expertise on these issues, FEMA personnel often rely on other parts of DHS and the federal government to fulfill this grant-making mission. This often delays and frustrates FEMA's ability to effectively carry out its grant-making goals.

Many have also argued that a FEMA separate from DHS would allow its leadership to more readily focus on providing disaster relief more effectively.[75] Prior to 9/11 the FEMA Administrator would directly speak with the President. Today, he or she vies for the attention of the Secretary of Homeland Security amongst several other DHS Components and departments. Though calls for separating FEMA from DHS are legion, it is highly unlikely this will occur unless another disaster or major event forces Congress and other government leaders to seriously reconsider FEMA's role in homeland security.

## COMMUNITY PLANNING FOR DISASTERS

The abilities of local communities and cities as well as states to respond to and recover from disasters depends on the mitigation measures undertaken before an emergency occurs. This is largely the "mitigation" portion of the disaster response lifecycle discussed above. Prepared localities develop response, recovery, and hazard mitigation plans and routinely revise them. State, tribal, and local officials plan what roles different organizations under their jurisdiction have in the event of an emergency and consider and prepare (through drills etc.) an effective potential response to an emergency in order to avoid duplication of benefits and confusion when an emergency actually occurs.

### Local Response Planning

A community's ability to respond to an emergency begins with the development of a local emergency operations plan. These plans can be flexibly drafted, but FEMA and the federal government often provide assistance to local municipalities so that the plan can fit a standard format. Each local community (such as a city, town, or municipality) plan may include a list of resources that could be deployed in the event of an emergency. Good plans are flexible and often keep in mind the "all-hazards" approach adopted by FEMA and DHS. Thus, in this case, the resources listed would be helpful in the event of a natural hazard, such as a hurricane, or a terrorist hazard, such as a mass shooting. A plan may also include a set of best practices or actions, such as safe and common evacuation routes or the identification of shelters.

An emergency plan would also establish ways to notify community members in the event of an emergency. These plans should and usually do take into account the emergency situation itself. For instance, how should the public be notified of a hazard if the hazard itself has knocked out the electrical power grid? These plans also include mutual aid agreements, discussed else-where in this chapter, that allow for the immediate provision of resources such as rescue boats from neighboring cities and municipalities.

In addition to providing policies, procedures, and an emergency organiza-tion structure, local emergency plans often contain information about the specific emergency conditions under which the plan will be activated. If the conditions warrant, local authorities may declare an emergency. The legal basis for a local state-of-emergency declaration typically is a local ordinance that stipulates who has the authority to declare a state of emergency and under what conditions this can be done. Documentation provided in the plan gives local governments a solid legal foundation for any subsequent request for state or federal emergency assistance and eliminates any confusion about the degree of impact the event has had on the community. Communities that formulate sound plans, establish appropriate emergency-related policies, and test their plans through regularly scheduled exercises will be prepared to assist citizens if an emergency occurs. State governments have similar and analogous emergency response plans. The typical state plan is similar in struc-ture and organization to most emergency operations plans developed by local governments. Sophisticated emergency management professionals endeavor to ensure that the state and local plans are coordinated and that procedures for providing assistance result in an effective combined effort (Figure 7.13).[76]

### Local Recovery Planning

Similar to response planning, state and local governments often develop plans that detail how they will *recover* from emergencies. These plans tend to be less sophisticated than response plans as every disaster often calls for unique and novel means of post-disaster recovery.

A disaster recovery plan establishes the roles, responsibilities, policies, and procedures to be used by state and local governments during the short- and long-term phases of a disaster. The disaster recovery plan may be separate from the emergency operations plan or it may be a smaller subcomponent of it. Some states require their local communities to develop disaster recovery plans as a mandatory measure in order to receive state disaster aid. A good recov-ery plan should identify the roles and responsibilities of local government

**FIG. 7.13**

State, local, and federal governments often assist local communities in planning for future disasters. Here, FEMA representatives and local government personnel are using CommunityViz, a tool for evaluating the cumulative effects of community development decisions using a geographically based analytic platform. The program can help governments or organizations conduct a comprehensive recovery planning process that engages local stakeholders in disaster response and recovery.

*Source*: Kenneth Wilsey, Training Session To Improve Community Planning, www.fema.gov/media-library/assets/images/161015.

staff involved in disaster recovery operations, the organizational structure for the local disaster recovery staff, and policies and procedures that will be used during disaster recovery operations.[77]

Examples of activities covered in disaster recovery plans are debris removal, inspection of damaged structures, assessment of public health and safety infrastructure, establishment of temporary housing for disaster victims, the restoration of community services, and documentation of expenditures for recovery operations.[78]

### State and Local Hazard Mitigation Planning

The Stafford Act requires that the recipients of disaster assistance make every effort to mitigate hazards in the area. In order to comply with this provision (and thus qualify for federal disaster assistance) state and local governments must prepare and implement a hazard mitigation plan outlining cost-effective strategies to reduce vulnerability to specific hazards. Through the plan, state and local governments evaluate the hazards in a disaster area and identify the appropriate actions to mitigate the vulnerability to these hazards.

The Stafford Act specifically encourages the regulation of land use and protective construction standards as part of a long-term and comprehensive approach to mitigation of hazards.[79] The President is also authorized to prescribe hazard mitigation standards and approve such standards proposed by state and local governments. Disaster assistance is often made conditional upon a state or local government's agreement to develop a long-term strategy and mitigation program that will reduce or eliminate the need for future federal disaster assistance should a similar emergency occur. After a Presidential Disaster Declaration, FEMA works with state authorities to develop an Early Implementation Strategy.[80] The strategy outlines activities to help reduce future damages based on damages assessed in the current disaster. This ensures that communities, states, and individuals consider ways to reduce potential damage from the next disaster as they make repairs immediately after a disaster.

## NATIVE AMERICAN TRIBES AND EMERGENCY MANAGEMENT

Because of their unique status in the United States and because they now enjoy many of the rights and benefits of sovereign nations, American Indian and Alaska Native tribal governments have been assigned a separate disaster policy by FEMA that differs from that of state governments. Once the President approves the state governor's request for a disaster declaration, tribal governments that represent areas experiencing a disaster can apply for disaster aid.

Disaster assistance to tribal governments is authorized under the Stafford Act. The Stafford Act authorizes FEMA to provide grants to individuals who do not qualify for other assistance for their unmet necessary expenses and serious needs. Additionally, FEMA has a Public Assistance program that provides supplemental grant assistance to help tribal governments rebuild after the disaster. Finally, the Stafford Act also created the Hazard Mitigation Grant Program that provides grants to implement long-term hazard mitigation measures after a disaster declaration. These grants are provided on a cost-shared basis and normally the recipient (in this case, the tribe) provides 25% of the cost of the repair project.

Based on internal advocacy from FEMA and a number of Native American tribes, President Obama signed the Sandy Recovery Improvement Act of 2013 (SRIA), which amended the Stafford Act to provide federally recognized tribal governments the option to request an emergency or Major Disaster declaration independently of the state in which they are located. Tribes still retain the choice to be considered part of a state's declaration request if they wish.[81]

## SIDEBAR 7.6 Emergency Management in a Changing Climate

The challenges posed by climate change, such as more intense storms, frequent heavy precipitation, heat waves, drought, extreme flooding, and higher sea levels will significantly alter the types and magnitudes of hazards faced by communities and the emergency management professionals serving them. A 2016 White House Presidential Memorandum on climate change and national security sheds considerable light on how a changing climate poses both an emergency management challenge and a broader risk to homeland security:

*Climate change poses a significant and growing threat to national security, both at home and abroad. Climate change and its associated impacts affect economic prosperity, public health and safety, and international stability. Extended drought, more frequent and severe weather events, heat waves, warming and acidifying ocean waters, catastrophic wildfires, and rising sea levels all have compounding effects on people's health and well-being. Flooding and water scarcity can negatively affect food and energy production. Energy infrastructure, essential for supporting other key sectors, is already vulnerable to extreme weather and may be further compromised. Impacts of a changing climate can create conditions that promote pest outbreaks and the spread of invasive species as well as plant, animal, and human disease, including emerging infectious disease, and these can further undermine economic growth and livelihoods. Impacts can also disrupt transportation service, cutting off vulnerable communities from relief immediately after events and reducing economic output. These conditions, in turn, can stress some countries' ability to provide the conditions necessary for human security. All of these effects can lead to population migration within and across international borders, spur crises, and amplify or accelerate conflict in countries or regions already facing instability and fragility.*

*Climate change and associated impacts on U.S. military and other national security-related missions and operations could adversely affect readiness, negatively affect military facilities and training, increase demands for Federal support to non-federal civil authorities, and increase response requirements to support international stability and humanitarian assistance needs.*

*The costs of preparing for, responding to, and recovering from the impacts of climate change are expected to increase in the coming decades. Some meteorological events (i.e. heat waves and intense precipitation) are projected to become more frequent and more severe, occur in geographic areas not previously exposed to such events, inflict more damage, heighten humanitarian needs, undermine development investments, adversely impact public health, contribute to ecological, social, and political instability, compromise diplomatic goals, and undermine national security interests. There is evidence that the rate of climate change and the resulting impacts are accelerating, even as global efforts to curb greenhouse gas pollution are increasing. The United States must take a comprehensive approach to identifying and acting on climate change-related impacts on national security interests, including by maintaining its international leadership on climate issues.*[82]

## CONCLUSION

Local governments are often the first line of defense against emergencies. When needed, they can serve as the link between individuals and the emergency response efforts carried out by the state and federal government. The federal government, meanwhile, serves as the funder of not only local and state response, but also the important work done by non-governmental response organizations such as the American Red Cross and Team Rubicon.

Emergency management is a cyclical discipline, involving work in preparedness, mitigation, response, and recovery from hazards. And hazards, especially after 9/11, continue to be defined in increasingly broad terms. Questions remain over whether emergency management, particularly the response and recovery from natural hazards, should remain in the ambit of governmental homeland security responsibilities, or whether emergency management should remain a separate discipline as it was prior to 9/11.

Nonetheless, despite these structural issues, it is clear that the role of emergency management professionals will only continue to grow, especially as climate change threatens established response mechanisms and new emergencies such as election fraud and cyberattacks continue to threaten the homeland security of the United States. We discuss these threats in the next chapter.

**HOMELAND SECURITY VOICES: Rebecca Katz, Ph.D.**

*Dr. Rebecca Katz is an Associate Professor at the George Washington University School of Public Health and Health Services in the Department of Health Policy. Currently her primary research focuses on the domestic and global implementation of the International Health Regulations. Generally, Dr. Katz's research focuses on public health preparedness, the intersection of infectious diseases and national security, and health diplomacy. Dr. Katz continues to be a consultant to the State Department on issues related to the Biological Weapons Convention, Avian and Pandemic Influenza, and disease surveillance. Previously, she worked on Biological Warfare counterproliferation at the Defense Intelligence Agency, was an Intelligence Research Fellow at the Center for Strategic Intelligence Research in the Joint Military Intelligence College, and spent several years as a public health consultant for The Lewin Group. She also authored a textbook on Public Health Preparedness. Dr. Katz obtained her undergraduate degree in*

*Political Science and Economics, an MPH in International Health, and a Ph.D. in Public Affairs.*

**Tell us a little about yourself and how you came to your current position.**

RK: I'm an Associate Professor of Health Policy and Emergency Medicine. My background is in social science—demography, public policy, and epidemiology, all focused on public health pol-icy. I think, there are many

*Source*: Rebecca Katz, Ph.D.

different avenues for working in the public health preparedness field. Some of my colleagues have hard science backgrounds, but it is not a requirement.

**Is a background in national security law or policy helpful for the work you do?**

RK: Absolutely, some background in these subjects helps.

**What would you advise a student, in terms of their academic career, if they choose to do the work you do on a regular basis?**

RK: One thing that is consistent amongst all of us on our team, even those not formally trained in public health, is that we all take a public health perspective.

**Is it a detriment to your success in the field if you don't have that perspective?**

RK: No. But then you won't be the public health person in the room.

**What do you believe is the most valuable experience you've had in shaping your career?**

RK: My answer for when I was in my twenties is different for my answer for in my thirties, which will be different for my answer for when I'm in my forties. I come from a public health background; many members of my family are public health professionals. I always knew I'd end up in that field. After I graduated from college I was volunteering in maternal and child health clinics in southern India and got very sick. The bug that I was sick with, *Brucella melitensis*, turned out to be a Class B biological weapons agent. It's the first agent the United States ever weaponized, as part of the US offensive biological weapons program in the early 1950s.

***So, I'm assuming you got better once they figured out what you had?***

RK: It took four years. And I still have it. It's endemic in some parts of the world. If you get it through lab exposure you know right away. Otherwise it becomes intracellular and really hard to treat. I spent much of my master's programs hooked up to I.V. medication. I would go in the morning to the medical center to get my I.V. drip then go to class. What was really interesting was, you come back to the U.S. and you have this disease nobody knows about and you have to become, as any patient does, your own expert in your disease. And the best literature on my disease in the U.S. was related to bioweapons. So the interest in my own condition helped me to develop an interest in public health and bioterrorism issues. I thought, "hey I have this social science, political science, international relations, and economics background, and I'm studying epidemiology in international health—and here is this thing, bioterrorism, that brings all of these interests together." So I became really interested in bioterrorism issues and biodefense, and I started going to meetings on these issues after graduate work.

***Talk a little bit more about the gender disparity in your profession.***

RK: Since I've been interested in these issues, the world has changed a lot. Up until 9/11 the people who looked at biological weapons were part of a very small community. Mostly, they were members of the military or intelligence communities. It wasn't a question about gender disparity—there just weren't many people interested in the profession—male or female. I had completed my master's degree and I was working in the public health field and I decided I really wanted to become an expert in this area of disease and security, so I applied for my doctoral degree in 1999. I wanted to do my Ph.D. in epidemiology and the schools of public health almost uniformly told me that they liked me as a candidate but "we're not sure about this 'thing' (biological weapons, bioterrorism) you're interested in." I had a hard time finding faculty who were willing to work with me. I ended up in a policy school for my doctoral work, which was more amenable to multidisciplinary approaches, and I found a mentor who was willing to take me on.

### Still the case?

RK: I wrote a paper on biological weapons as a public health problem and handed it in on Sept. 10, 2001 to my faculty advisor. One day later, 9/11 happened, and there was suddenly a lot of interest in the things I had been studying. The '90s were a time that people were admitting emerging infectious diseases were a problem again. In the 1970s there had been a shift of focus from infectious diseases and onto non-communicable diseases. Cancer was the new thing in public health in the 1970s, and it wasn't until the emergence of HIV, Ebola, and other emerging infectious diseases in the late '80s and early '90s that people in the public health community started talking about infectious diseases again as a problem and starting to focus on the connection between disease and security. For instance, the term "emerging infectious diseases" wasn't even coined until the early 1990s. Really the shift in thinking to infectious diseases as weapons or weaponized agents—didn't start until late in the Clinton Administration.

### Where do you see the field headed?

RK: The Global Health Security Agenda was launched in February 2013. So hopefully that is the future: What actions the global community should take to protect community health and make populations more secure against bio-threats. So the 2000s was about making the intellectual jump that public health and security are connected and now we are looking at what the public health community is going to do about it.

### What challenges do you see coming up in the next 5–10 years in the field?

RK: One of the things that we are thinking about a lot is metrics: Asking how do you measure success? Is your population safe? Yes or no? Do you have disease surveillance? Yes or no? Have you been able to detect outbreaks? It's not as easy as some of the other questions in terrorism-related disciplines. To me, metrics is the next major intellectual challenge. Measuring success is what holds people accountable.

### If you could ask Congress for one thing what would it be?

RK: Money spent wisely. I think investing in building good disease surveillance systems, which means systems and policies which can help detect outbreaks of infectious diseases quickly, is a valuable use of resources. Good disease surveillance means you can also respond quickly to disease outbreaks and save more lives. We don't have these kinds of detection systems in many parts of the world. You can't separate the domestic from the global, so spending the money across the world is in many ways just as useful as spending it at home.

*Let's say somebody graduates from college and is about to embark on a career like yours. They don't really know what you do day to day, but they are passionate about the subject. So what career advice, in terms of courses that are important, internships to take etc., would you give to such a student?*

RK: First, if you want to work overseas, you actually have to get some global experience. The easiest time to do that is right after you graduate college. Life gets much more complicated as you get older. If you have even some idea that you want to do global work, you should try to go abroad. If you want to work in emergency preparedness go spend some time in a local health department. All public health is local, so figure out what that "local" is, whether that is here or abroad, and then go work there.

*So practical, on the ground experience is important?*

RK: If you have practical experience it makes you somebody worth listening to. It's important to have policy skills. Some of these skills can be taught. Some can't be taught and they have to be learned from experience.

## KEYWORDS

- **all-hazards approach**: An approach to emergency management where the government prepares for specific hazards (such as hurricanes) and also for hazards generally, especially those that may be unpredictable (such as terrorist attacks).

- **short-term recovery**: Local disaster recovery measures intended to return the community to minimum operating standards.

- **long-term recovery**: Local disaster recovery measures that return the community to its previous condition, to the extent that is realistically possible.

- **quarantine**: A limitation on the physical movement of individuals in order to prevent the spread of disease.

- **core capabilities**: The institutional capabilities necessary to prepare for the specific types of incidents that pose the greatest risk to the security of the United States.

- **hazard**: A potentiality or threat of harm to humans, and/or the things they value.

- **disaster**: The combination of a hazard actuality and its intersection with human values.

- **risk**: A measure of a hazard's occurrence and/or a measure of the damage potentiality of the hazard occurrence.

- **CBRNe**: A Department of Defense standard for classifying emergency hazards. CBRNe stands for chemical, biological, radiological, nuclear, or explosive (which covers terrorism).

- **Emergency Management Lifecycle**: The process by which emergency management professionals and organizations mitigate, prepare for, respond to, and help communities recover from hazards.

---

**KNOWLEDGE CHECK**

1. What are the various ways to define a "hazard" in the emergency management context? Why is having an accurate definition of "hazard" important?
2. What are the various arguments on both sides regarding whether emergency management should be part of the broader homeland security enterprise?
3. Name and define the four components of the Emergency Management Lifecycle.

---

## NOTES

1. Jared T. Brown, Bruce R. Lindsay, and Jaclyn Petruzzelli, Cong. Research Serv., RL 41981, Congressional Primer on Responding to Major Disasters and Emergencies, at 1–3, (2017) *available at* www.hsdl.org/?abstract&did=804217.
2. 42 U.S.C. § 5122 (2018).
3. *See* 42 U.S.C. § 5143(c).

4. Jared T. Brown, Bruce R. Lindsay, and Jaclyn Petruzzelli, Cong. Research Serv., RL 41981, Congressional Primer on Responding to Major Disasters and Emergencies, at 1–3, (2017) *available at* www.hsdl.org/?abstract&did=804217.

5. *Id.*

6. *The Disaster Declaration Process*, Federal Emergency Management Agency (last updated Jan. 8, 2018) www.fema.gov/disaster-declaration-process.

7. *See* 44 C.F.R. § 206.35 (2018).

8. *Id.*

9. *The Disaster Declaration Process*, Federal Emergency Management Agency (last updated Jan. 8, 2018) www.fema.gov/disaster-declaration-process.

10. *See* 42 U.S.C. §§ 5170b(a)(3)(A), 5172, 5189f, 5192(a)(5) (2018).

11. Robert S. Kirk, Cong. Research Serv., R43384, Emergency Relief for Disaster-Damaged Roads and Transit Systems: In Brief (2017).

12. 33 U.S.C.S. §701n (2018).

13. *The Disaster Declaration Process*, Federal Emergency Management Agency (last updated Jan. 8, 2018) www.fema.gov/disaster-declaration-process.

14. Maria Kreiser, Maura Mullins, and Jared C. Nagel., Cong. Research Serv., RL 31734, Federal Disaster Assistance and Response and Recovery Programs: Brief Summaries (2018) *available at* https://fas.org/sgp/crs/homesec/RL31734.pdf.

15. *See Fuel Waivers*, U.S. Environmental Protection Agency (last visited Jan. 11, 2019) www.epa.gov/enforcement/fuel-waivers.

16. *See* 32 C.F.R. §185.4(g) (2018); *but see* 83 FR 14589 (2018) ("This final rule removes the Department of Defense (DoD) regulation concerning defense support of civil authorities. This part contains DoD policy and assigns responsibilities for Defense Support of Civil Authorities (DSCA). This part also authorizes immediate response authority for providing DSCA, when requested, and authorizes emergency authority for the use of military force, under dire situations. The content of the rule is internal to DoD and does not require codification.").

17. Disaster Assistance: A Guide to Recovery Programs, Federal Emergency Management Agency, at xv (2005) www.fema.gov/media-library-data/20130726-1538-20490-9100/recoveryprograms229.pdf.

18. *Id.*

19. Rachel Witkowski & Leslie Scism, *Hurricane Harvey Threatens Largest Flood Insurer: The Government*, Wall Street Journal (Aug. 26, 2017) www.wsj.com/articles/hurricane-harvey-threatens-largest-flood-insurer-1503771686.

20. Overwhelming risk: Rethinking flood insurance in a world of rising seas, Union of Concerned Scientists (2014) www.ucsusa.org/sites/default/files/legacy/assets/documents/global_warming/Overwhelming-Risk-Full-Report.pdf

21. Greg Hanscom, *Flood pressure: Climate disasters drown FEMA's insurance plans*, Grist (Jan. 13, 2014) https://grist.org/cities/flood-pressure-how-climate-disasters-put-femas-flood-insurance-program-underwater/.

22. How Communities and States Deal with Emergencies and Disasters, A Citizen's Guide to Disaster Assistance, Federal Emergency Management Agency (last visited Jan. 11, 2019) https://training.fema.gov/emiweb/downloads/is7unit_2.pdf.

23. *See* How Communities and States Deal with Emergencies and Disasters, A Citizen's Guide to Disaster Assistance, Federal Emergency Management Agency, at 2–4 (last visited Jan. 11, 2019) https://training.fema.gov/emiweb/downloads/is7unit_2.pdf.

24. *Id.*

25. See generally id. at 2–8.

26. *About*, Georgie Emergency Management & Homeland Security Agency (last visited Jan. 11, 2019) https://gema.georgia.gov/about.

27. How Communities and States Deal with Emergencies and Disasters, A Citizen's Guide to Disaster Assistance, Federal Emergency Management Agency, at 2–8 (last visited Jan. 11, 2019) https://training.fema.gov/emiweb/downloads/is7unit_2.pdf.

28. *See id.* at 2–11.

29. *Id.*

30. *See id.* at 2–14.

31. See id.

32. *Hollow tree in Guinea was Ebola's Ground Zero, scientists say*, Mail & Guardian Africa (last visited Jan. 1, 2016); *see also* Richard Ingham, *Hollow tree was Ebola's Ground Zero, scientists say*, Medical press (Dec. 30, 2014) https://medicalxpress.com/news/2014-12-source-ebola-epidemic-west-africa.html.

33. *About Quarantine and Isolation*, Centers for Disease Control and Prevention (last updated Aug. 28, 2014) www.cdc.gov/quarantine/quarantineisolation.html.

34. *In Sierra Leone's Ebola hot zone: A series of reports*, UN Office for the Coordination of Humanitarian Affairs (retrieved Nov. 2, 2014).

35. Koenig and Schultz's disaster medicine: comprehensive principles and practices 205 (Carl Schultz & Kristi Koenig, eds., 2009).

36. Hollis Stambaugh, Daryl Hensenig, Rocco Casagrande, Shania Flagg, and Bruce Gerrity, Quarantine Facilities for Arriving Air Travelers: Identification of Planning Needs and Costs, TRB's Airport Cooperative Research Program (ACRP) Report 5 (2008).

37. *Disaster Recovery—Restoring Hope and Rebuilding Lives*, Catholic Charities (last visited Jan. 11, 2019) https://catholiccharities.org/our-services/strengthening-families/disaster-relief/.

38. *Voluntary Faith Based Community Based Organizations,* Federal Emergency Management Agency (last visited Sep. 2016) www.fema.gov/voluntary-faith-based- community-based-organizations.

39. *Voluntary Organizations Active in Disaster*, Ready.gov (last visited Jan. 11, 2019) www.ready.gov/voluntary-organizations-active-disaster.

40. *Id.*

41. *Community Preparedness Webinar Series: Red Cross*, Ready.gov (last visited Jan. 13, 2019) www.ready.gov/community-preparedness-webinar-series-red-cross.

42. *Our Federal Charter*, American Red Cross (last visited Jan. 11, 2019) www.redcross.org/about-us/who-we-are/history/federal-charter.

43. *FEMA And American Red Cross Partnership Will Strengthen Mass Care During A Disaster*, Federal Emergency Management Agency (October 22, 2010) www.fema.gov/news-release/2010/10/22/fema-and-american-red-cross-partnership-will-strengthen-mass-care-during.

44. *Who We Serve*, Team Rubicon Disaster Response (last visited Jan. 11, 2019) https://teamrubiconusa.org/who-we-serve/.

45. 6 U.S.C. §§ 743–744 (2018).

46. Jared T. Brown, Bruce R. Lindsay, and Jaclyn Petruzzelli, Cong. Research Serv., RL 41981, Congressional Primer on Responding to Major Disasters and Emergencies, at 2–4, (2017) *available at* www.hsdl.org/?abstract&did=804217.

47. *National Preparedness Goal*, Federal Emergency Management Agency (last updated May 2, 2018) www.fema.gov/national-preparedness-goal.

48. *Id.*

49. 6 U.S.C. § 741(1) (2018).

50. *See Presidential Policy Directive 8: National Preparedness*, The White House, at 2 (Mar. 30, 2011) www.dhs.gov/presidential-policy-directive-8-national-preparedness.

51. *National Incident Management System*, Federal Emergency Management Agency (last updated Nov. 19, 2018) www.fema.gov/national-incident-management-system.

52. Jared T. Brown, Bruce R. Lindsay, and Jaclyn Petruzzelli, Cong. Research Serv., RL 41981, Congressional Primer on Responding to Major Disasters and Emergencies, at 2–4, (2017) *available at* www.hsdl.org/?abstract&did=804217.

53. National Response Framework, Second Edition, U.S. Dep't of Homeland Security, at 17 (May 2013) www.fema.gov/library/viewRecord.do?id=7371. Examples include public health emergencies declared under Section 319 of the Public Health Services Act, *see, e.g.*, 42 U.S.C.S. § 201 (2018), or spills of national significance under the Oil Pollution Act, Pub. L. No. 101–380 (1990).

54. Jared T. Brown, Bruce R. Lindsay, and Jaclyn Petruzzelli, Cong. Research Serv., RL 41981, Congressional Primer on Responding to Major Disasters and Emergencies, at 3, (2017) *available at* www.hsdl.org/?abstract&did=804217.

55. *See Volunteer and Donations Management Support Annex*, Federal Emergency Management Agency (last updated May 6, 2013) www.fema.gov/media-library/assets/documents/3228.

56. Emergency Support Function Annexes: Introduction, Federal Emergency Management Agency (Jan. 2008) www.fema.gov/media-library-data/20130726-1825-25045-0604/emergency_support_function_annexes_introduction_2008_.pdf.

57. *National Disaster Recovery Framework*, Federal Emergency Management Agency (last updated Oct. 22, 2018) www.fema.gov/national-disaster-recovery-framework.

58. *Recovery Support Functions,* Federal Emergency Management Agency (last updated June 1, 2018) www.fema.gov/recovery-support-functions.

59. U.S. Department of Homeland Security, Federal Emergency Management Agency, National Disaster Recovery Framework, at 25 (Sep. 2011) www.fema.gov/pdf/recoveryframework/ndrf.pdf

60. Thomas Drake, Course at the FEMA Higher Education Project: The Social Dimensions of Disaster (1997).

61. Federal Emergency Management Agency, Theory, Principles and Fundamentals of Hazards, Disasters, and U.S. Emergency Management (1996) (Session Title: What are Hazards?).

62. Keith Smith, Environmental Hazards: Assessing Risk and Reducing Disaster (1996).

63. *Id.*

64. Federal Emergency Management Agency, Theory, Principles and Fundamentals of Hazards, Disasters, and U.S. Emergency Management (1996) (Session Title: What are Hazards?).

65. *Id.*

66. E. L. Quarantelli, *Organizational Behavior in Disasters and Implications for Disaster Planning*, Federal Emergency Management Agency Training Center, at 1–3 (1984).

67. Dep't of Homeland Security Office of Inspector General, OIG-10–03, FEMA's Progress in All-Hazards Mitigation, at 2–10 (2009).

68. Federal Emergency Management Agency, Guide for All Hazard Emergency Operations Planning, at 8 (1996) www.fema.gov/pdf/plan/slg101.pdf.

69. *Id.*

70. *Id.*

71. *Id.*

72. *Id.* at 9

73. Federal Emergency Management Agency, Guide for All Hazard Emergency Operations Planning, at 9 (1996) www.fema.gov/pdf/plan/slg101.pdf.

74. *Id.*

75. Frank Cilluffo, Daniel Kaniewski, Jan Lane, Gregg Lord, & Laura Keith, The George Washington University Homeland Security Policy Institute, Serving America's Disaster Victims: FEMA, Where Does it Fit?, (Jan. 13, 2009) https://cchs.gwu.edu/sites/g/files/zaxdzs2371/f/downloads/IssueBrief_3_HSPI.pdf.

76. How Communities and States Deal with Emergencies and Disasters, A Citizen's Guide to Disaster Assistance, Federal Emergency Management Agency, at 2–16 (last visited Jan. 11, 2019) https://training.fema.gov/emiweb/downloads/is7unit_2.pdf.

77. *Id.* at 2–17.

78. *Id.* at 2–19.

79. Robert T. Stafford Disaster Relief and Emergency Act, Pub. L. No. 93–288, 88 Stat. 143 (codified as amended in 42 U.S.C. 5121 et seq.).

80. *Standard Operating Procedures*, Federal Emergency Management Agency (last visited Jan. 12, 2019) www.fema.gov/media-library-data/20130726-1444-20490-6594/365sec2_1_.txt.

81. Federal Emergency Management Agency, FEMA and Tribal Nations: A Pocket Guide (Sep. 2014) www.fema.gov/media-library-data/1414163004909-18662df46f3a3c28f51c1c5b7a209358/FEMA_Pocket_Guide_508_Compliant.pdf.

82. Memorandum from the White House Office of the Press Secretary to the Heads of Executive Departments and Agencies (Sep. 21, 2016) ("Presidential Memorandum—Climate Change and National Security") *available at* https://obamawhitehouse.archives.gov/the-press-office/2016/09/21/presidential-memorandum-climate-change-and-national-security.

# CHAPTER 8

# *Cybersecurity*

## IN THIS CHAPTER YOU WILL LEARN ABOUT

The range of illicit activities that comprise the cybersecurity space.

Governmental efforts and organizational frameworks designed to combat and defend against cyberattacks.

Private sector efforts to tackle cybersecurity threats.

## INTRODUCTION

As the Internet has grown over the past three decades, "cyberattacks" have become more common. Cyberattacks can refer to a range of activities conducted through the use of information and communications technology, including but not limited to the Internet. For instance, distributed denial of service attacks (DDoS) have become a common method of achieving political goals through the disruption of online services or companies. In these types of attacks, a server is overwhelmed with Internet traffic so access to a particular website is degraded or denied. The Stuxnet worm, which was a complex computer virus and considered by some to be the first cyber weapon, targeted Iran's computerized industrial control system on which nuclear centrifuges operate, causing them to self-destruct.

In this chapter we discuss several categories of cyberattacks: Cybercrime, cyberwarfare, and cyberterrorism. These are not the only categories, but are the ones most common in homeland security legal and policy areas.

Policymakers, lawyers, and law enforcement make use of these categories to determine the type and extent of a cyberattack, how best to investigate it and then prosecute the attack if possible. Due to the wide-ranging and nebulous nature of digital networks, actions within these categories may overlap or not fit neatly into the proscribed categories. With the globalized nature of the Internet, perpetrators can launch cyberattacks from anywhere in the world and route attacks through servers of third-party countries. From a homeland security perspective, this makes attacks difficult to counteract, and if no one "pushes back," research indicates that cyberattacks will continue.

It is also important to note that currently there is no clear criteria to determine whether cyberattacks are a form of crime, activism, terrorism, or the use of force by a nation-state. Likewise, no international legally binding instruments have yet been drafted to regulate interstate relations in cyberspace. This becomes especially problematic as cyberattacks are carried out on the Internet, which has no physical boundaries. Thus, in this chapter we discuss a number of "cyber" terms that overlap definitionally with each other: "*cyberattacks,*" which threaten "*cybersecurity*" and come in the form of "*cybercrime,*" "*cyberwarfare,*" and "*cyberterrorism.*" The reader may find it helpful to eliminate the word "cyber" from words like "cybercrime" in this chapter to better understand how a cyber concept is situated definitionally in the "offline" world.

## CYBERCRIME

**Cybercrimes** are crimes that are directed at computers or other digital devices and where these digital devices are integral or central to the offense. Financial gain is often a motivation for committing cybercrime. Examples include identify theft, online fraud, cyberbullying, and distribution of child exploitation material. For the purposes of this text we distinguish cybercrime from cyberterrorism and cyberwarfare, which tend to target nations rather than solely individuals and institutions. By several estimates, cybercrime is the fastest growing category of criminal activity in the United States. The FBI, DHS, and the Department of Justice have overlapping responsibilities in combating various types of cybercrime outlined below.

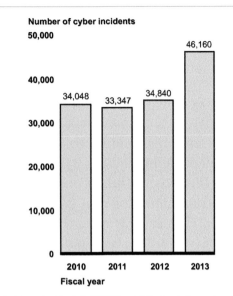

**Number of cyber incidents**

**FIG. 8.1**
The federal government keeps track of the number of cyber incidents, such as cybercrime, reported to the U.S. Computer Emergency Readiness Team (US-CERT) on a yearly basis.

*Source*: Cyber Incidents Reported to US-CERT by All Federal Agencies, GAO Report GAO-14–354, www.flickr.com/photos/usgao/14144289737/in/photolist-wFDUBk-nxTbyr-nQdi8E-nv9rhn-nAqgzC-299trdA-h9ks9K-qAQJp6-dV4nqN-pWvLwc-jzEgvA-qRKwtT-o9NmB8-psTFbv-tntJDH-h9iyg8-r2z6u2-rkTwWZ-qp87ct-JTFYGH-uDPdT1-t5QFe5-tntJRX-S69tcf-RWK2k4-N5qpch-L9PEQU.

## Attacks on Computer Systems

Sophisticated criminals are able to exploit vulnerabilities on computers and other devices. They may hack a computer without permission, implant malicious software such as a virus or Trojan Horse program (collectively known as malware) to monitor a computer's activity, or flood a computer with so much data that it overloads (referred to as a "denial of service" attack). Attacks on computer systems can result in the hacker accessing personal or financial details of the owner of the computer.

## Cyberbullying

Cyberbullying or online stalking is when someone engages in offensive, menacing, or harassing behavior through the use of technology. This behavior can be, and often is, paired with bullying behavior that occurs in person. Cyberbullying isn't limited to young adults and children; individuals at every age are targets and the bullies are often anonymous. Examples of cyberbullying may include:

- Sharing the personal information of an individual online without their permission (usually paired with a hostile or threatening message);
- Sending abusive texts or emails to a target;
- Creating fake social networking profiles or websites that are hurtful or harm the reputation of an individual;
- Excluding or intimidating others online; and
- Any form of communication that is discriminatory (especially on the basis of a protected class such as race, religion, gender etc.), intimidating and intended to cause hurt or make someone fear for their safety.[1]

It is important to note that just like bullying in the offline world, not all cyberbullying is criminal. Nonetheless, certain kinds of behavior can rise to the level of a crime. As Americans have increasingly used online tools, cases of cyberbullying have grown and become more extreme. State and local lawmakers have taken action to prevent this kind of behavior through laws (in state education codes and elsewhere) as well as model policies (that provide guidance to districts and schools). Each state addresses cyberbullying differently. In some cases offline bullying and cyberbullying may be addressed in a single law or addressed separately in multiple laws. In other cases, cyberbullying appears in the criminal code of a state that may apply to juveniles only.

Though there is no federal law that criminalizes cyberbullying, the Department of Education has taken several steps to advise states on the creation of cyberbullying laws and policies, including providing best practices and examples of procedures to allow victims of cyberbullying to report misconduct safely and effectively.[2]

### Email Spam and Phishing

Spam is electronic junk mail (unsolicited messages without the recipient's consent). Spam messages often contain offers of free goods, promises of wealth (often from a former "Nigerian Prince"), cheap products, or other sim-

**FIG. 8.2**
Department of Defense officials work with children like Liam Konczak (2) and his parents so that they understand the impact of cyberbullying from an early age and learn to counteract its affects.

*Source*: Erica Crossen, Officials try to get in front of cyberbullying, U.S. Air Force, www.scott.af.mil/News/Article-Display/Article/766740/officials-try-to-get-in-front-of-cyberbullying/.

ilar offers. In the United States, spam is only illegal if it falls outside of the criteria laid out by the "CAN-SPAM" Act of 2003.[3] Under CAN-SPAM, spam is legal if it:

- Includes a "truthful" subject line;
- Contains no forged information in the technical headers or the sender's address; and
- Abides by other minor requirements.

Notice that the truthfulness of the content of the spam message is not a factor under CAN-SPAM.

**Phishing** is a way criminals trick people into giving out their personal or financial details. Phishing messages often pretend to come from legitimate businesses such as banks or telecommunications providers.[4] Phished messages often look like legitimate requests for information and then direct recipients to enter personally identifiable information, including bank account numbers, into the fake website or email form.

Though phishing often meets the criteria for a number of federal criminal fraud statutes, to date there is no specific crime that targets phishing as a cybercriminal activity at the federal level. Nonetheless, 23 states and Guam have laws that specifically target phishing schemes. The remaining other states have laws that address computer crime, fraudulent or deceptive practices, or identity theft. These laws end up encompassing activities like phishing.[5]

### Identity Theft

Identity theft is a type of cybercrime that occurs when a criminal gains access to an individual's personal information (such as name, birthdate, address, or bank account information) in order to steal funds or gain other benefits. Identity thieves often start with a small amount of information and use it to gain additional information about a victim, pretend to be that individual on an online site, and make transactions under their name for a short period of time before the affected individual or comprised bank or other institution finds out.

In the United States identity theft is considered a cybercrime under the Identity Theft and Assumption Deterrence Act, which amended U.S. Code Title 18, Section 1028's definition of fraud as "related to activity in connection with identification documents, authentication features, and information."[6] The statute makes the possession of any "means of identification" to "knowingly transfer, possess, or use without lawful authority," a federal crime, alongside unlawful possession of identification documents.

### SIDEBAR 8.1 United States Computer Emergency Readiness Team (US-CERT)

US-CERT is a team of computer and security professionals at the Department of Homeland Security. Created in 2003 to protect U.S. Internet infrastructure, US-CERT works to accomplish this mission by coordinating defense against cyberattacks and coordinating with other organizations to respond to cyberattacks on an ongoing basis. US-CERT is also responsible for analyzing and reducing cyber threats and vulnerabilities and disseminating cyber threat warning information to public and private partners, as well as the aforementioned coordination response activities.

This coordination usually takes place between other federal agencies, the private sector, the academic research community, state and local governments, and international entities. By analyzing incidents reported by these entities and coordinating with national security incident response centers responding to incidents on both classified and unclassified systems, US-CERT disseminated actionable cybersecurity information to the public.[7] Some particular collaboration activities of note include:

- The US-CERT website (www.us-cert.gov)—provides government, private sector, and the public with information needed to improve its ability to protect information systems and infrastructure.
- The US-CERT Einstein Program—an automated process for collecting, correlating, analyzing, and then sharing computer security information across the federal government to improve federal cyber-situational awareness.
- The National Cyber Response Coordination Group (NCRCG)—a program established in partnership with the Department of Defense and Department of Justice, serves as the federal government's principal interagency mechanism to facilitate coordination of efforts to respond to and recover from cyber incidents of national significance.
- Government Forum of Incident Response Security (GFIRST)—is a community of more than 50 incident response teams from various federal agencies working together to secure the federal government.
- Internet Health Service—provides information about Internet activity to federal government agencies through the GFIRST community.[8]

## Prohibited Online Content

With a few exceptions, the First Amendment of the U.S. Constitution, as well as analog provisions of state constitutions, prohibit the government from directly censoring the content on the Internet in the United States. Nonetheless, several exceptions exist that have been codified into federal law. Most of these exceptions deal with obscene material or child pornography. Possession or dissemination of these materials online is a cyber crime. Below are a few statutes that criminalize the possession, duplication, and sharing of certain content online in the U.S.:

- *Computer Fraud and Abuse Act* (CFAA): Criminalizes accessing a computer without authorization. Often criticized for its broad scope and difficult application to real world scenarios.
- *Communications Decency Act* (CDA): Only Section 230 of this law remains in effect, the other portions having been found to be unconstitutional. Section 230 frees operators of Internet services from legal liability for the words of third parties (such as their customers) who use their services and also protects ISPs from liability for good faith voluntary actions taken to restrict access to certain offensive materials or giving others the technical means to restrict access to that material.[9]
- *Digital Millennium Copyright Act* (DCMA): Criminalizes the production and sharing of technology that could be used to circumvent copyright protection mechanisms and makes it easier to act against alleged copyright infringement on the Internet.[10]
- *Children's Online Privacy Protection Act* (COPPA): Applies to the online collection of personal information by persons or entities under U.S jurisdiction from children under 13 years of age and details what a website operator must include in a privacy policy, when and how to see verifiable consent from a parent or guardian, and what responsibilities an operator has to protect children's privacy and safety online, including restrictions on the marketing of those under 13 years of age.[11]
- *Stop Advertising Victims of Exploitation Act of 2015* (SAVE): Makes it illegal to *knowingly* advertise content related to sex trafficking, including online advertising.[12]

Beyond these existing laws, a number of proposed bills are currently being considered by Congress. There are also policy-based censorship rules. For instance, the Department of Defense prohibits personnel from accessing certain IP addresses on DoD computers. The sharing of classified information by government employees with a security clearance is also prosecutable (see Sidebar on Edward Snowden in Chapter 5). In the consumer space, sharing trade secrets or the intellectual property of another company online is also a crime.

The National Conference of State Legislatures has also tabulated many state laws that criminalize the sharing or publishing of online content in certain states. For instance, a number of states curb Internet use in public schools, libraries, or other publicly funded institutions:

> The majority of these states simply require school boards/districts or public libraries to adopt Internet use policies to prevent minors from gaining access to sexually explicit, obscene or harmful materials. However, some states also require publicly funded institutions to install filtering software on library terminals or school computers.[13]

### CRITICAL THINKING QUESTION

By criminalizing the sharing of classified information by government employees, doesn't the government assert a right to privacy? How is that possible? The reader may wish to refer to Chapter 9, which notes that the government has no rights, only obligations. How can institution (not a person) have a right to privacy? How do these rules conflict with the Freedom of Information Act (FOIA) discussed elsewhere in this text?

## Online Child Pornography

Child pornography is a form of sexual exploitation of minors (those under the age of 18 in the United States). Federal law defines child pornography as any visual depiction of sexually explicit conduct involving a minor. Images of child pornography may also be referred to as child sexual abuse images.[14] Under federal law, the production, distribution, importation, reception, or possession of any image of child pornography is a federal (cyber)crime.

Because the term "child pornography" is used in federal statutes, it is also commonly used by lawmakers, prosecutors, investigators, and the public to describe this form of sexual exploitation of children.[15] However, the term fails to describe the true horror that is faced by countless children every year.

The production of child pornography creates a permanent record of a child's sexual abuse (which is criminalized under additional state and federal laws). When these images or videos are placed online and shared, the victimization of the child continues. The Department of Justice and its experts agree that victims depicted in child pornography often suffer a lifetime of re-victimization by knowing that the images of their sexual abuse are on the Internet.

The expansion and use of the Internet and other advanced digital technologies has encouraged the growth of the child pornography market. Child pornography images are often disseminated through online forums, social media sites, and file- and photo-sharing sites. According to the Department of Justice, child pornography offenders also connect on Internet forums and networks to share their interests, desires, and experiences abusing children, in addition to selling, sharing, and trading images.[16] These online communities have promoted communication and collaboration between child pornography offenders, thereby fostering a larger relationship premised on a shared sexual interest in children. This has the effect of eroding the shame that typically would accompany this criminal behavior, as well as desensitizing those involved to the physical and psychological damage caused to the child victims.

Those trafficking in child pornography are increasingly being targeted by the Department of Justice, the FBI, and ICE Homeland Security Investigations' respective cybercrime units, but these offenders often use various sophisticated encryption techniques and anonymous networks to avoid detection on the "**Dark Web**." The Dark Web refers to websites that exist on secure, encrypted networks and cannot be found using traditional search methods, such as Google search. According to the Department of Justice:

> several sophisticated online criminal organizations have even written security manuals to ensure that their members follow preferred security protocols and encryption techniques in an attempt to evade law enforcement and facilitate the sexual abuse of children.[17]

Both the FBI and ICE HSI have statutory authorization to combat the rise of child pornography. As part of ICE's Cyber Crimes Center (C3) Homeland Security Investigations uses sophisticated online criminal fighting programs to tackle the ongoing problem of child pornography. One such program is Operation Predator, an international initiative to identify, investigate, and arrest child predators who:

- Possess, trade, and produce child pornography;
- Travel overseas for sex with minors; and
- Engage in the sex trafficking of children.

Collaborating with law enforcement partners from around the world, Operation Predator brings together a number of resources to target child predators. As part of the effort:

- HSI participates on all 61 Internet Crimes Against Children (ICAC) Task Forces across the U.S. These task forces are led by state and local law enforcement agencies.
- HSI runs a National Victim Identification Program at C3, combining the latest technology with traditional investigative techniques to rescue child victims of sexual exploitation.
- HSI is the U.S. representative to the Interpol working group that locates new child sexual abuse material on the Internet and refers cases to the country that the abuse is believed to be occurring in for further investigation. Also, HSI special agents stationed internationally work with foreign governments, Interpol, and others to enhance coordination and cooperation on crimes that cross borders.
- HSI works in partnership with the National Center for Missing and Exploited Children and other federal agencies to help solve cases and rescue sexually exploited children.
- HSI is a founding member and current chair of the Virtual Global Taskforce, joining law enforcement agencies, non-governmental organizations, and private sector partners around the world to fight child exploitation information and images that travel over the Internet.[18]

At the Department of Justice, Child Exploitation and Obscenity Section (CEOS) attorneys work with the High Technology Investigative Unit (HTIU), the FBI, U.S. Attorneys' Offices, and the National Center for Missing and Exploited Children to combat the growing problem of child pornography by investigating and prosecuting violators of federal child pornography laws. This process also involves CEOS attorneys often working with local law enforcement to identify and rescue victims of child pornography from continued abuse. The Internet is global and using it to commit cybercrime like child pornography has blurred traditional notions of a criminal jurisdiction. CEOS thus maintains a coordinated, national-level law enforcement focus to help coordinate nationwide and international investigations and initiatives.[19] CEOS attorneys and HTIU computer forensics specialists travel worldwide and conduct trainings for other international counterparts while also helping design law enforcement strategies, legislative proposals, and policy initiatives related to child pornography laws.

### Online Financial Fraud

Generally referred to as "computer fraud" or "hacking," this catchall category of cybercrime is still an evolving space. Some experts classify the aforementioned email spam and phishing as well as identity theft as forms of online fraud. Usually, however, online financial fraud refers to attempts to defraud larger financial institutions or steal their intellectual property. Most often this presents itself in the form of a data breach. A data breach is a leak or spill of data that is released from a secure location to an untrusted environment. Data breaches usually occur at larger corporations but may also affect smaller companies and involve sensitive, protected, or confidential information that is copied, transmitted, viewed, stolen, or used by an individual or group that is unauthorized to do so.[20]

The U.S. Secret Service maintains several workforces on electronic crimes, which focus on identifying and locating international cyber criminals connected to cyber intrusions, bank fraud, data breaches, and other computer-related crimes. The Secret Service's Cyber Intelligence Section has directly contributed to the arrest of transnational cyber criminals responsible for the theft of hundreds of millions of credit card numbers and the loss of approximately $600 million to financial and retail institutions. The Secret Service also runs the National Computer Forensic Institute, which provides law enforcement officers, prosecutors, and judges with cyber training and information to combat cybercrime.[21]

## CYBERWARFARE

**Cyberwarfare** is usually defined as state vs. state action that would be the equivalent of a physical use of force that would likely trigger an equivalent military response. Those carrying out these attacks can often be classified as "cyber spies." They often steal classified or proprietary information used by other governments or private entities to gain a competitive strategic, security, financial, or political advantage. They may also be called "cyberwarriors," and can be considered direct or quasi-agents of nations who develop capabilities and undertake cyberattacks in support of a country's strategic objectives.

Cyberwarriors may or may not be acting on behalf of the government with respect to target selection, timing of the attack, and type(s) of cyberattack and are often blamed by the host country when accusations are levied by the nation that has been attacked.[22] Frequently, when a foreign nation is shown evidence that a cyberattack is emanating from its country, the victim nation is informed that the perpetrators acted of their own volition and not at the direction of the government being accused. Thus, the structural basis of cyberwarfare, its lack of an easy evidentiary trail, allows perpetrators to claim plausible deniability on a frequent basis.

Additionally, determining who committed cyberwarfare (or any other kind of cyberattack for that matter) becomes difficult due to the "bandwagon effect," when numerous groups claim credit for a successful attack in order to gain notoriety without any effort. For instance, in August 2012 a series of cyberattacks were directed against Saudi Arabia's AramCo, the world's largest oil and gas producer. The attacks compromised 30,000 computers and the computer code was apparently designed to halt and disrupt oil production. Numerous security officials and cyberwarfare experts suggested that Iran may have supported this attack. However, numerous groups, some with links to nations with objectives counter to Saudi Arabia, claimed credit for this incident.

In September 2012, the United States Department of Homeland Security took a public position on whether cyberattacks could constitute a use of force under Article 2(4) of the United Nations charter and international law. According to the legal advisor at the State Department at the time, Harold Koh, "Cyber activities that proximately result in death, injury or significant

**FIG. 8.3**
The U.S. Navy promotes messaging that educates sailors and others about the ongoing threat of cyberwarfare.

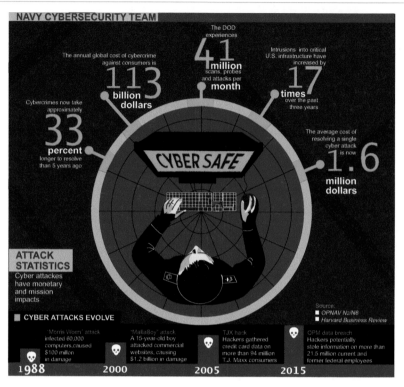

*Source*: U.S. Navy Cyber Safe Campaign, www.doncio.navy.mil/CHIPS/ArticleDetails. aspx?ID=9537.

destruction would likely be viewed as a use of force."[23] "Proximate" causation refers to the event before the final bad act. In other words, a negligent driver may proximately cause harm if she fails to help alert a stranded driver to an oncoming truck that ends up hurting the stranded driver. The negligent driver did not directly harm the stranded driver; the truck driver did. Nonetheless, her absence of action contributed, albeit indirectly, to the stranded driver's injuries.

The same rationale applies to cyberwarfare in Koh's thinking. For instance, Koh offered the following examples of cyberattacks that could be considered a use of force: A meltdown at a nuclear power plant, opening a dam that ends up causing significant flood damage, and causing airplanes to crash by interfering with air traffic control. By focusing on the ends achieved (final causation) rather than the means with which they are carried out (proximate causation), this definition of cyberwar fits within existing international legal frameworks of how crimes in the offline world are defined. Thus, if a cyberterrorist employs a cyberattack to produce effects that warrant an equivalent use of force in the offline force (i.e. if he blows up a dam using physical means) then the use of that cyberattack rises to the level of the use of real-world force.[24]

## CYBERTERRORISM

As with cyberwarfare, there is no consensus definition of what constitutes **cyberterrorism**. One such definition can be found in the USA PATRIOT ACT: "(Cyberterrorism is) acts of terrorism transcending national boundaries."[25]

For purposes of this text a more comprehensive definition is:

> the premeditated use of disruptive activities, or the threat thereof, against computers and/or networks, with the intention to cause harm or further social, ideological, religious, political or similar objectives, or to intimidate any person in furtherance of such objectives.[26]

Attacks of these kind are carried out by "cyberterrorists" who can be defined as "state-sponsored and non-state actors who engage in cyberattacks to pursue their objectives."[27]

Some of the confusion regarding how to define cyberterrorism stems from confusion of the underlying crime of terrorism, which still remains vaguely defined in state, federal, and international law. For instance, some legal scholars define cyberterrorism as the "federal crime of terrorism," which might place cyberterrorism solely in the cybercrime space. Other experts such as Dorothy Denning from the Naval Post Graduate School argue that a definition of cyberterrorism should focus on the distinction between destructive and disruptive action. She argues that cyberterrorism, like offline terrorism, generates fear comparable to that of a physical attack, and is not just a "costly nuisance."[28] In her thinking, though a DDoS attack may not itself yield the kind of fear or destruction of a "real-world" hazard such as a hurricane, the secondary events caused by the attack (such as a flood caused by a malfunctioning dam computer) may do so.[29]

Despite the confusion surrounding how to define cyberterrorism, several government agencies and NGOs have attempted to categorize cyberterrorist attacks. For instance, the Monterey Group organizes cyberterrorism into three distinct levels of capability that can be used by law enforcement as a framework to interdict attacks:

1. *Simple-unstructured*: When a cyberterrorist or group has the capability to conduct basic hacks against individual systems using tools created by someone else. The individual or organization possesses little target analysis, command and control, or learning capability.

2. *Advanced-Structured*: When a cyberterrorist or group has the capability to conduct more sophisticated attacks against multiple systems or networks and, possibly, to modify or create basic hacking tools. The organization possesses an elementary target analysis, command and control, and some learning capability.

3. *Complex-Coordinated*: When a cyberterrorist or group has the capability for coordinated attacks capable of causing mass disruption against integrated, heterogeneous defenses (including cryptography) and the ability to create their own sophisticated hacking tools. The individual or organization is highly capable in target analysis, command and control, and organizational learning capability. The hacking group *Anonymous* would be an example of this level of sophistication.[30]

In some cases it may be more appropriate to call a cyberterrorist a "**cyberactivist**" instead. Cyberactivists are individuals who perform cyberattacks for pleasure, philosophical, political, or other non-monetary reasons. Experts distinguish cyberactivists from cyberterrorists in that their actions are not meant to terrorize a population or use terror as a pressure tactic to achieve a political end. Nonetheless, the actives of cyberactivists can be disruptive or even harmful enough to rise to the level of a crime or national security threat. The group *Anonymous*, which has hacked both corporations and foreign states, is classified by some nations and organizations as a cyberterrorist group and by others as a cyberactivist group (Figure 8.4). The activities of these groups can range from nuisance DDoS attacks and website defacement to the disruption

**FIG. 8.4**
The emblem of Anonymous, an international cyberactivist (or "hacktivist") group known for its cyberattacks on government and private party infrastructure as a way of advancing its beliefs.

*Source*: Anonymous Emblem, https://upload.wikimedia.org/wikipedia/commons/thumb/a/a6/ Anonymous_emblem.svg/2000px-Anonymous_emblem.svg.png.

of state, federal, or international government networks and the disruption of global corporate computer systems.

## SIDEBAR 8.2 "The Cyber Terror Bogeyman"

In his article titled, "The Cyber Terror Bogeyman," Peter W. Singer of the Brookings Institution, a Washington, D.C., think tank, argues that cyberterrorism is not a true threat to the safety of the United States. Or at least not a threat as serious as what has been portrayed by the government and in the media:

*About 31,300. That is roughly the number of magazine and journal articles written so far that discuss the phenomenon of cyber terrorism. Zero. That is the number of people who have been hurt or killed by cyberterrorism at the time this went to press (November, 2012).*[31]

Singer argues that cyberterrorism is the equivalent of the Discovery Channel's "Shark Week," where Americans collectively are entertained by the fear of a shark attack when the chances of being hurt or killed in an accident involving a toilet are 15,000 times higher than those of being attacked by a shark. He argues that part of the problem lies in how the government defines cyberterrorism:

> The FBI defines cyberterrorism as a "premeditated, politically motivated attack against information, computer systems, computer programs, and data which results in violence against non-combatant targets by subnational groups or clandestine agents." A key word there is "violence," yet many discussions sweep all sorts of nonviolent online mischief into the "terror" bin. Various reports lump together everything from Defense Secretary Leon Panetta's recent statements that a terror group might launch a "digital Pearl Harbor" to Stuxnet-like sabotage (ahem, committed by state forces) to hacktivism, WikiLeaks and credit card fraud. As one congressional staffer put it, the way we use a term like cyber terrorism "has as much clarity as cybersecurity—that is, none at all."[32]

He also notes that government bureaucrats and media professionals who do not know much about cyberterrorism often conflate fears of a cyberterrorist attack with reality. It takes a lot to actually pull of a successful cyberterrorism attack that can actually harm or hurt someone: "to cause true damage requires an understanding of the devices themselves and how they run, the engineering and physics behind the target," and this knowledge is hard to acquire and even harder to execute.[33] As George R. Lucas Jr., a professor at the U.S. Naval Academy, put it, conducting a truly mass-scale cyberattack "simply outstrips the intellectual, organizational and personnel capacities of even the most well-funded and well-organized terrorist organization, as well as those of even the most sophisticated international criminal enterprises."

Moreover, Singer argues that the scale of work required in cyberterrorism results in low damage output, whereas low effort in the offline world results in high damage output. For instance, a cyberterrorist could disrupt the power grid in Washington, D.C., and this would cause some inconvenience for a day or two, some financial loss, and perhaps even loss of life for those who require electricity in their homes or a hospital, in order to survive. However, the loss would be minimal, and power would be restored in short order. Moreover, generators at critical infrastructure sites would be able to provide electricity.[34]

On the other hand, a "dirty nuclear bomb could irradiate an American city for centuries," and would be a relatively easy attack to carry out. Though by asking the reader to worry more about a dirty bomb compared to a cyberterrorist attack, Singer may be asking the reader to play into the same fallacy he warns about: The chances of a dirty nuclear bomb exploding in a U.S. city are even less likely than a cyberterrorist attack that ends up taking lives.

**CRITICAL THINKING QUESTION**

Read the Sidebar on the "Cyber Terror Bogeyman" in this chapter. Do you agree with the author's views that the threat of cyberterrorism is overblown? The article discussed in the Sidebar was written in 2012 and cyberterrorism has only grown since then, both in scope and sophistication. Given the alleged hacking of the 2016 American presidential election by Russian agents, do you think the author would revise his views?

## PLANNING FOR CYBERSECURITY

### The Cybersecurity Framework

The United States depends on the reliable functioning of critical infrastructure. Cyberattacks exploit the increased complexity and connectivity of critical infrastructure systems, placing the United States' security, economy, and public safety at risk. Similar to financial and repetitional risks, cybersecurity risk affects a company's bottom line. Cyberattacks can drive up costs and affect revenue and harm an organization's ability to innovate and to gain and maintain customers.[35]

To better address these risks, the Cybersecurity Enhancement Act of 2014 (CEA) updated the role of the National Institute of Standards and Technology

(NIST) to include identifying and developing cybersecurity risk frameworks for voluntary use by critical infrastructure owners and operators. Through, CEA, NIST now creates a Cybersecurity Framework (Framework), which is "a prioritized, flexible, repeatable, performance-based, and cost-effective (document), including information security measures and controls that may be voluntarily adopted by owners and operators of critical infrastructure to help them identify, assess and manage cyber risks" (Figure 8.5).[36]

The USA PATRIOT ACT of 2001 defines critical infrastructure as

> systems and assets, whether physical or virtual, so vital to the United States that the incapacity or destruction of such systems and assets would have a debilitating impact on security, national economic security, national public health or safety, or any combination of those matters.[37]

Due to the increasing external and internal threats to infrastructure (outlined in Chapter 9), organizations that are responsible for critical infrastructure must have a consistent, flexible, and dependable approach to assessing and managing cybersecurity risk. This approach is necessary regardless of an organization's size, threat exposure, or cybersecurity sophistication—especially since cybersecurity threats discriminate less based on size and notoriety. To manage cybersecurity risks, a clear understanding of an organization or business' motives and security considerations specific to its use of technology is required. Because each organization's risk, priorities, and systems are unique, the tools and methods used to achieve these outcomes are described in a variety of ways in the Framework.

The Framework also accounts for the protection of privacy and civil liberties and includes a methodology to protect individual privacy and civil liberties when critical infrastructure organizations conduct cybersecurity activities. Many organizations already have processes for addressing privacy and civil liberties. The methodology in Framework is designed to complement such processes and provide guidance to facilitate privacy risk management consistent with an organization's approach to cybersecurity risk management.

The Framework has also been designed to be technology neutral, especially given the fast pace of technological change and the variety of ways in which various organizations and businesses in the U.S. use technology. The Framework relies on a set of global standards, guidelines, and practices that have

**FIG. 8.5**
Graphic display-
ing the major
components of
Version 1.1 of
the Cybersecu-
rity Framework,
a voluntary
effort to orga-
nize cyberse-
curity efforts
across govern-
ment and the
private sector.

*Source*: N. Hanacek, National Institute of Standards and Technology, "NIST Cybersecurity Framework V. 1.1," www.nist.gov/sites/default/files/images/2018/04/16/framework-01.png.

been developed by the tech industry as well as industry partners that use the technology being protected. Building from these standards, guidelines, and practices, the Framework provides a common language and mechanism for organizations to:

1. Describe their current cybersecurity posture;
2. Describe their target state for cybersecurity;
3. Identify and prioritize opportunities for improvement within the context of a continuous and repeatable process;
4. Assess progress toward a target state; and
5. Communicate among internal and external stakeholders about cybersecurity risk.[38]

The Framework consists of three parts: The Framework Core, the Implementation Tiers, and the Framework Profiles. The Framework Core is a set of cybersecurity activities, outcomes, and informative references that are common across sectors and critical infrastructure. Elements of the Core provide detailed guidance for developing organizational Profiles. Through the use of

Profiles, the Framework helps organizations to align and prioritize their cyber-security activities within business and mission requirements, risk tolerance, and resources. The Tiers provide a mechanism for organizations to view and understand the characteristics of their approach to managing cybersecurity risk, which helps them to prioritize and achieve cybersecurity objectives.[39]

The government leaves the decision of *how* an organization uses the Frame-work up to the organization itself. For example, a social media company like Facebook may choose to use the Framework Implementation Tiers to articu-late envisioned risk management practices. On the other hand, a car manu-facturer like Toyota may use the Framework's five Functions to analyze its entire risk management portfolio. Thus, the Framework complements, and does not replace, an organization's pre-existing cybersecurity program.[40]

## National Cyber Incident Response Plan

Several years of debate about cybersecurity by experts in the national and homeland security field have resulted in a set of shared conclusions about what it takes to respond to a cyberattack. The first of these conclusions was the acknowledgment of the growth of networked technologies and their spread across the globe and in every facet of human life. Networked tech-nologies have driven innovation, nurtured freedoms, and spurred economic prosperity. Even so, the very technologies that enable these benefits offer new opportunities for malicious and unwanted cyber activities. Acknowledg-ment of these risks led to the development of Presidential Policy Directive 41, known broadly as "United States Cyber Incident Coordination," which sets forth principles governing the federal government's response to any cyber incident, whether involving government or private sector entities.[41]

The National Cyber Incident Response Plan (Plan) was developed under the direction provided by Directive 41 and leverages doctrine from the emergency-response oriented National Preparedness System (discussed in Chapter 7) to articulate the roles and responsibilities, capabilities, and coordinating struc-tures that support how the U.S. responds to and recovers from significant cyberattacks posing risks to critical infrastructure. The Plan is not a tactical or operational plan, but instead serves as the primary strategic framework for stakeholders to understand how federal departments and agencies and other national-level partners provide resources to support response operations.[42] The intended audience for the Plan is U.S. organizations. However, it can also enhance international partners' understanding of U.S. responses to cyberattacks.

The Plan is based on several guiding principles that determine the response to any cyberattack.[43] These principles apply to government or private sector entities. They include:

- *Shared responsibility*: Individuals, the private sector, and government agencies have a shared, vital interest and complementary roles and responsibilities in protecting the U.S. from malicious cyber activity and managing cyber incidents and their consequences.
- *Risk-based response*: The federal government will determine its response actions and the resources it brings to bear based on an assessment of the risks posed to an entity, national security, foreign relations, the broader economy, public confidence, privacy and civil liberties, or public health and safety. Critical infrastructure entities should also conduct risk-based response calculations during cyber incidents to ensure the most effective and efficient utilization of resources and capabilities.
- *Respect for affected entities*: To the extent permitted by law, federal staff who respond to a cyberattack should safeguard details of the incident, as well as privacy, civil liberties, and sensitive private sector information, and generally should defer to affected entities in notifying other affected private sector entities and the public. In the event of a significant cyberattack where the federal government interest is served by issuing a public statement concerning an incident, federal responders should coordinate their approach with the affected entities to the extent possible.
- *Unity of governmental effort*: Various government entities possess different roles, responsibilities, authorities, and capabilities that can all be brought to bear on cyber incidents. These entities must coordinate efforts to achieve optimal results. The first federal agency to become aware of a cyber incident should rapidly notify other relevant federal agencies in order to facilitate a unified federal response and ensure that the right combination of agencies responds to a particular incident. When responding to a cyberattack that occurs in the private sector, unity of effort synchronizes the overall

federal response, which prevents gaps in service and duplicative efforts. State, local, and tribal governments also have responsibilities, authorities, and capacities that can be used to respond to a cyberattack and the federal government should coordinate often with these other government actors in the wake of a cyberattack. The transnational nature of the Internet and communications infrastructure requires the U.S. to coordinate with international partners in cyber incidents.

- *Enabling restoration and recovery*: Federal response activities should facilitate restoration and recovery of an entity that has experienced a cyberattack, balancing investigative and national security requirements, public health and safety, and the need to return to normal operations as quickly as possible.[44]

The Plan was authored in close coordination with government and private sector partners with a stake in cybersecurity issues and outlines "lines of effort" for how the federal government will organize its activities to manage the effects of significant cyberattacks when they occur. The lines of effort are: Threat response, asset response, intelligence support, and the affected entity, which undertakes efforts to manage the effects of the cyberattack on its operations, customers, and workforce. A number of government departments and agencies come together to share responsibility for responding to a cyberattack under the Plan; they include:

- *Department of Justice*: Is the lead agency for threat response during a significant cyber incident, acting through the FBI and National Cyber Investigative Joint Task Force. Threat response activities include conducting appropriate law enforcement and national security investigative activity at the affected entity's site; collecting evidence and gathering intelligence; providing attribution; linking related cyberattacks; identifying additional affected entities, exploiting disruption opportunities; developing and executing courses of action to mitigate the immediate threat; and facilitating information sharing and operational coordination with asset response.[45]
- *Department of Homeland Security*: The Department of Homeland Security is the lead agency for asset response during a significant cyber incident, acting through the National Cybersecurity and Communications Integration Center (NCCIC). Asset response activities include furnishing technical

assistance to affected entities to protect their assets, mitigating vulnerabilities, and reducing impacts of cyber indents; identifying other entities that may be at risk and assessing their risk to the same or similar vulnerabilities; assessing potential risks to the sector or region, including potential cascading effects, developing courses of action to mitigate these risks; facilitating information sharing and operational coordination with threat response; and providing guidance on how best to utilize federal resources and capabilities in a timely, effective manner to speed recovery.[46]

- *Office of the Director of National Intelligence*: ODNI is the lead coordinator for intelligence support during a significant cyber incident, acting through the Cyber Threat Intelligence Integration Center. ODNI's responsibilities in the wake of a cyberattack include intelligence support and related activities, including providing support to federal asset and threat agencies and facilitating the building of situational threat awareness and sharing of related intelligence; integrated analysis of threat trends and events; identification of knowledge gaps; and degrading or mitigating adversary threat capabilities.[47]

A federal agency affected by a cyberattack usually engages in a variety of efforts to manage the impact of the incident, which may include maintaining business or operational continuity; addressing adverse financial impacts; protecting privacy; managing liability risks; complying with legal and regulatory requirements (including disclosure and notification); engaging in communications with employees or other affected individuals; and dealing with external affairs (i.e. media and congressional inquiries). Whichever federal agency is affected usually has primary responsibility for this line of effort.

When a private entity is targeted by a cyberattack, the federal government typically will not play a role in its efforts to mitigate the attack, but will remain cognizant of the affected entity's response activities consistent with the principles stated in the Plan and in coordination with the affected private sector entity. The relevant sector-specific agency will generally coordinate the federal government's efforts to understand the potential business or operational impact of a cyberattack on private sector critical infrastructure.[48]

## CALL-OUT BOX
## 2018 National Cybersecurity Strategy

In 2018, the White House issued the nation's first, comprehensive national cyber security strategy. After reading the excerpt below, ponder the release timeline of the Strategy in light of the numerous cybersecurity incidents discussed in this chapter:

### How Did We Get Here?

*The rise of the Internet and the growing centrality of cyberspace to all facets of the modern world corresponded with the rise of the United States as the world's lone superpower. For the past quarter century, the ingenuity of the American people drove the evolution of cyberspace, and in turn, cyberspace has become fundamental to American wealth creation and innovation. Cyberspace is an inseparable component of America's financial, social, government, and political life. Meanwhile, Americans sometimes took for granted that the supremacy of the United States in the cyber domain would remain unchallenged, and that America's vision for an open, interoperable, reliable, and secure Internet would inevitably become a reality. Americans believed the growth of the Internet would carry the universal aspirations for free expression and individual liberty around the world. Americans assumed the opportunities to expand communication, commerce, and free exchange of ideas would be self-evident. Large parts of the world have embraced America's vision of a shared and open cyberspace for the mutual benefit of all.*

*Our competitors and adversaries, however, have taken an opposite approach. They benefit from the open Internet, while constricting and controlling their own people's access to it, and actively undermine the principles of an open Internet in international forums. They hide behind notions of sovereignty while recklessly violating the laws of other states by engaging in pernicious economic espionage and malicious cyber activities, causing significant economic disruption and harm to individuals, commercial and non-commercial interests, and governments across the world. They view cyberspace as an arena where the United States' overwhelming military, economic, and political power could be neutralized and where the United States and its allies and partners are vulnerable.*

*Russia, Iran, and North Korea conducted reckless cyber attacks that harmed American and international businesses and our allies and partners without paying costs likely to deter future cyber aggression. China engaged in cyber-enabled economic espionage and trillions of dollars of intellectual property theft. Non-state actors including terrorists and criminals—exploited cyber-space to profit, recruit, propagandize, and attack the United States and its allies and partners, with their actions often shielded by hostile states. Public and private entities have struggled to secure their systems as adversaries increase the frequency and sophistication of their malicious cyber activities. Entities across the United States have faced cybersecurity challenges in effectively identifying, protecting, and ensuring resilience of their networks, systems, functions, and data as well as detecting, responding to, and recovering from incidents.*

## The Way Forward

*New threats and a new era of strategic competition demand a new cyber strategy that responds to new realities, reduces vulnerabilities, deters adversaries, and safeguards opportunities for the American people to thrive. Securing cyber-space is fundamental to our strategy and requires technical advancements and administrative efficiency across the Federal Government and the private sector. The Administration also recognizes that a purely technocratic approach to cyberspace is insufficient to address the nature of the new problems we confront. The United States must also have policy choices to impose costs if it hopes to deter malicious cyber actors and prevent further escalation.*

*The Administration is already taking action to aggressively address these threats and adjust to new realities. The United States has sanctioned malign cyber actors and indicted those that have committed cybercrimes. We have publicly attributed malicious activity to the responsible adversaries and released details of the tools and infrastructure they employed. We have required departments and agencies to remove software vulnerable to various security risks. We have taken action to hold department and agency heads accountable for managing the cybersecurity risks to systems they control, while empowering them to provide adequate security.*

*The Administration's approach to cyberspace is anchored by enduring American values, such as the belief in the power of individual liberty, free expression, free markets, and privacy. We retain our commitment to the promise of an open, interoperable, reliable, and secure Internet to strengthen and extend our values and protect and ensure economic security for American workers and companies. The future we desire will not come without a renewed American commitment to advance our interests across cyberspace.*

*The Administration recognizes that the United States is engaged in a continuous competition against strategic adversaries, rogue states, and terrorist and criminal networks. Russia, China, Iran, and North Korea all use cyberspace as a means to challenge the United States, its allies, and partners, often with a recklessness they would never consider in other domains. These adversaries use cyber tools to undermine our economy and democracy, steal our intellectual property, and sow discord in our democratic processes. We are vulnerable to peacetime cyber attacks against critical infrastructure, and the risk is growing that these countries will conduct cyber attacks against the United States during a crisis short of war. These adversaries are continually developing new and more effective cyber weapons.*

*This National Cyber Strategy outlines how we will (1) defend the homeland by protecting networks, systems, functions, and data; (2) promote American prosperity by nurturing a secure, thriving digital economy and fostering strong domestic innovation; (3) preserve peace and security by strengthening the United States' ability—in concert with allies and partners—to deter and if necessary punish those who use cyber tools for malicious purposes; and (4) expand American influence abroad to extend the key tenets of an open, interoperable, reliable, and secure Internet.*

*The Strategy's success will be realized when cybersecurity vulnerabilities are effectively managed through identification and protection of networks, systems, functions, and data as well as detection of, resilience against, response to, and recovery from incidents; destructive, disruptive, or otherwise destabilizing malicious cyber activities directed against United States interests are reduced or prevented; activity that is contrary to responsible behavior in cyber- space is deterred through the imposition of costs through cyber and non-cyber means; and the United States is positioned to use cyber capabilities to achieve national security objectives.*

*The articulation of the National Cyber Strategy is organized according to the pillars of the National Security Strategy. The National Security Council staff will coordinate with departments, agencies, and the Office of Management and Budget (OMB) on an appropriate resource plan to implement this Strategy. Departments and agencies will execute their missions informed by the following strategic guidance.*[49]

## CYBERSECURITY AND STATE, LOCAL, AND TRIBAL GOVERNMENTS

Many states and local governments have criminal statutes regarding unauthorized access or damage to computer systems, which could be implicated in a cyberattack. State Fusion Centers (discussed in Chapter 5) are situated

National Cyber Security Awareness Month

# CyberAware

SECURING THE INTERNET IS OUR SHARED RESPONSIBILITY

STOP | THINK | CONNECT

*Source*: FBI National Cybersecurity Awareness Month Campaign Flyer, www.fbi.gov/news/stories/national-cyber-security-awareness-month-2017.

**FIG. 8.6**
The FBI's #CyberAware flyer is an attempt by the federal government to share cybersecurity best practices with individuals and local businesses and organizations.

at the theoretical and physical intersection between federal and local law enforcement. They play a role in sharing threat-related information between federal, state, and local governments and private sector partners.[50] Even so, Fusion Centers vary greatly in their cyber capacity and sophistication. Local governments, especially large cities, play an important role in local response activities. Often times, private citizens and small businesses do not have relationships with, or access to, federal law enforcement involved in incident response activities. Thus, local and state governments usually play a critical role in providing a communication bridge for individuals and local businesses to federal cybersecurity professionals (Figure 8.6). The Cybersecurity Information Sharing Act of 2015 establishes legal protections and important conditions for sharing information with and between the federal government, state, and local government organizations and the private sector.[51]

Ensuring the safety and welfare of citizens is a fundamental responsibility of government at every level. Toward these objectives, key executives, executive leadership, elected officials, and executive staff of each state, local, and tribal government are responsible for ensuring preparedness, response, and recovery activities within their jurisdiction. In cases of cyberattacks, the standard emergency response roles and responsibilities may not be sufficient to address the technical challenges posed by an attack. Each state can choose to develop a plan that describes their role in asset response for entities within their state. The state plans usually reside with the National Response Framework (discussed in Chapter 7) and serve as a cyber annex to their respective state emergency management plan.

The federal government provides a number of resources to state, local, and tribal governments to handle the non-physical-border oriented nature of cyberattacks, including but not limited to:

- Participation in regional homeland security offices and Fusion Centers;
- Multi-state ISACs funded through grants from DHS to support the security of state and local government digital networks; ISACs act as a focal point for critical information exchange and coordination between the state and local community and the federal government; every state has an MS-ISAC primary member, usually the state chief information security officer;
- Local governments may also apply for and receive Urban Area Security Initiative grant funds from DHS; and
- DHS NPPD field personnel can provide information and expertise on cybersecurity issues and work closely with state and local information security officers.

State, local, and tribal governments have a variety of coordination structures available to them for cyberattack response. These structures support information sharing, incident response, operational coordination, and collaboration on policy initiatives among other non-federal governments. As mentioned above, state and local governments can be members of ISACs, ISAOs, or other information-sharing organizations. For incidents on state and local government networks, MS-ISACs provide information sharing and technical assistance to its members and has established relationships with the federal government. As owners and operators of critical cyber infrastructure (such as computer networks and data centers), state and local government agencies are also often members of sector-specific ISACs and may also develop unique structures, tailored to their jurisdiction's needs, to provide coordination and direction to response officials during a cyber incident. Many also collaborate with one another through selected cyber information sharing groups or organizations such as the National Association of State Chief Information Officers or the National Governor's Association (discussed further below).

Though many state and local governments are developing operational coordination structures for cyber incident response, they have not all adopted a standard approach. Some may designate their state or major urban area Fusion Center as the primary contact and information-sharing hub for cyber incident coordination while others choose to leverage their respective emergency or security operations center. For cyber incidents with physical effects, or that have consequences that must managed in collaboration with other emergency management agencies such as fire departments and public health organizations, emergency operations centers provide important information sharing and incident management functions.[52] Emergency operations centers often coordinate resource requirements with federal agencies, including FEMA and the Department of Defense, and provide operational coordination with the National Guard. The federal government encourages state and local governments to provide cross-functional training in cybersecurity for the employees of their emergency operations center.

The Governors Homeland Security Advisory Council also provides a structure through which homeland security advisors from each state, territory, and the District of Columbia discuss cybersecurity issues, share information and expertise, and keep governors informed of the issues affecting homeland security policies in the states. State, local, and tribal Government Coordinating Councils also exist and bring together geographically diverse experts from a wide range of cybersecurity disciplines to ensure state and local government officials play an integral role in national critical infrastructure and resilience efforts.

As a dual force with state and federal roles, the National Guard also plays a critical cybersecurity response function. National Guard forces have expertise in critical response functions and many also have expertise and capabilities in cyber activities. At the direction of a state governor and adjutant general, the National Guard may perform state missions, including supporting civil authorities in response to a cyber incident. In certain circumstances, the National Guard may be requested to perform federal service or be ordered to active duty to perform Department of Defense missions, which could include supporting a federal agency in response to a cyber incident.[53]

Frequently, following a cyber incident, state and local community leaders and stakeholders may be asked to provide advice, support, and assistance to federal departments and agencies on preparedness and response activities related to state and local priorities. Cyber incidents can cause cascading and/or physical impacts that implicate non-cyber incident response activities by state and local governments. Key executives and points of contact have a need for situational awareness of the federal government's asset response activities even when a cyber incident does not affect the state and local government system. This includes being prepared to request additional resources from the federal government, including federal disaster aid assistance under the Stafford Act, especially in the event of a cyberattack that exceeds the local government's capabilities to respond.[54]

State Fusion Centers involve various levels of state government, private sector entities, and the public—though the level of involvement of some of these participants will vary based on specific circumstances. Nonetheless, the Fusion Center process is organized and coordinated, at a minimum on a statewide level, and each state establishes and maintains a Fusion Center to facilitate the fusion process. Though the primary function of Fusion Centers is to provide law enforcement intelligence information to local partners, Fusion Center leadership evaluates their respective jurisdictions to determine what public safety and private sector entities should participate in the Fusion Center. Sometimes, these entities include those with a focus on cybersecurity issues.[55]

## CYBERSECURITY AND ROLE OF THE PRIVATE SECTOR

Private sector entities perform critical roles in supporting threat response activities by reporting and sharing information regarding cyber incidents and malicious cyber activity in a timely manner to appropriate law enforcement agencies or government entities. Private entities bear a significant burden as owners and operators of the vast majority of cyber infrastructure. They are the primary targets for cyberattacks and also have the most to lose from a successful cyberattack. Information, communications, and technology providers and manufacturers, such as Internet service providers (ISPs), common carriers, manufacturers of key networking hardware, and major software companies also play an important role in the threat response to malicious cyber activity, due to the potential exploitation or use of their systems by cyber threat actors.[56]

At the same time, private companies and organizations are responsible for the security of their own systems. They are normally the first to identify a cyberattack and are also often in the best place to respond to it. In some cases, especially if they are receiving federal aid, private entities may have reporting or disclosure requirements related to cyber incidents, which they have to comply with as they respond to the incident. In most cases, these incidents are considered routine and are mitigated by the company using internal resources or with the assistance of contracted services providers. Routine, steady-state information sharing related to cyberattacks, even when mandatory reporting isn't required by federal or state/local governments, alerts other at-risk entities and allows them to mitigate vulnerabilities that may have cascading impacts on their systems.[57]

Private sector providers and cybersecurity practitioners offer critical services, such as managed security services, indications and warnings, cybersecurity assessment, and incident response, which system owners and other asset responders might need when managing an incident. These private sector resources can serve as surge and specialty support to augment an in-house cybersecurity team at an affected entity. Effective coordination between these private sector entities and other response organizations is often essential in a response to a cyberattack.

Critical infrastructure owners and operators work with DHS and relevant sector-specific agencies to implement the National Infrastructure Protection Plan (NIPP) tenets of public-private partnership to improve preparedness and manage risk. Due to the tightly interconnected and interdependent nature of some sectors, companies may also provide information to other entities in the sector or in other sectors, to facilitate shared situational awareness, contain the cyberattack, or mitigate damage. Thus, private companies often look to share and receive information from a variety of sources, including DHS and other federal, state, and local law enforcement organizations and counter-intelligence officials, including the respective Information Sharing Analysis Centers (ISACs) discussed earlier in this chapter.

Most private sector operational information sharing is conducted through ISACs. ISACs are typically a sector-based type of **Information Sharing and Analysis Organization** (ISAO) and operate through a defined-sector based model, which means that organizations within a certain sector (such as the financial sector, energy sector, or aviation services) join together to share information about cyber threats. Although a number of these groups are already essential drivers of effective cybersecurity collaboration, some organizations do not fit neatly into one established sector and have multiple responsibilities or unique cybersecurity needs. Unlike ISACs, ISAOs are a broader category and can also be formed based on geography, the aforementioned substantive sector, or any other grouping in which companies are interested and grouped to analyze and disseminate cyber threat information. Those organizations that cannot join a sector-specific ISAC but have a need for cyber threat information can benefit from membership in an ISAO. Unlike ISACs, ISAOs are not necessarily tied to a specific substantive critical infrastructure sector.[58]

In the case of cyber incidents, especially significant cyber incidents, greater coordination may be needed with the federal government, state and local communities, regulators within the sector, and among multiple sectors. In addition to responding to situations in which private companies are themselves the victims of cyber incidents, private entities also respond to situations in which private sector providers (especially ISPs, managed security service providers, and other technology vendors) provide support for national-level incident response efforts. During such an incident, the private sector often provides support or assistance to federal and state and local departments and agencies on preparedness and response activities. Federal and state/local regulators also have mandatory reporting requirements for certain types of cyberattacks in certain sectors. Depending on the sector and type of incident, some response actions may require regulator coordination, approval, and or regulatory relief.[59]

Private sector entities provide for the security of their networks and security processing of breaches or other incidents through standing in-house or contracted services or the use of external cybersecurity experts. Standing services are a part of (usually larger) private entity network structures and the private sector entity is often encouraged by the federal government to share information with government cyber incident personnel that the standing services develop or pursue concerning a cyberattack. The Cybersecurity Information Sharing Act of 2015 provides liability and other legal protections to private sector and state and local organizations and governments and establishes important conditions regarding sharing information with the federal government, state and local government organizations, and the private sector.[60]

## SIDEBAR 8.3 Russian Interference in the 2016 United States Election

In January 2017, the United States Intelligence Community (IC), specifically the Office of the Director of National Intelligence (ODNI), released a declassified version of a highly classified report entitled, "Assessing Russian Activities and Intentions in Recent U.S. Elections." The report discusses the significant Russian efforts to influence the 2016 U.S. presidential election and

> the most recent expression of Moscow's longstanding desire to undermine the U.S.-led liberal democratic order . . . and demonstrate a significant escalation in directness, level of activity, and scope of effort compared to previous operations.[61]

In the report, the IC concludes that Russian President Vladimir Putin ordered an influence campaign in 2016 aimed at the U.S. presidential election and that Russia's goals were to undermine public faith in the U.S. democratic process, denigrate candidate Hillary Clinton, and harm her electability and potential presidency, while also expressing a clear preference for the electability of Donald Trump. Moscow's influence campaign followed a Russian messaging strategy that blended covert intelligence operations, such as cyberthreats and cybermessaging, with overt offline efforts by Russian government agencies, state-funded media, third-party intermediaries, and paid social media users or "trolls" as well as fake "robot" social media accounts.[62]

The IC noted that Russia's intelligence services conducted cyber operations against targets associated with the 2016 U.S. presidential election, including targets associated with both major U.S. political parties: The Democrats and the Republicans:

> We assess Russian intelligence services collected against the U.S. primary campaigns, think tanks, and lobbying groups they viewed as likely to shape future U.S. policies. In July 2015, Russian intelligence gained access to Democratic National Committee (DNC) networks and maintained that access until at least June 2016. The General Staff Main Intelligence Directorate (GRU) probably began cyber operations aimed at the U.S. election by March 2016. We assess that the GRU operations resulted in the compromise of the personal email accounts of Democratic Party officials and political figures. By May (of 2016) the GRU had exfiltrated large volumes of data from the DNC.[63]

The ODNI and other intelligence agencies found that Russian operatives and their agents released the data collected on U.S. political parties via U.S. websites such as Wikileaks and DCLeaks.com because of these websites' reputation for authenticity. More troubling was the finding that Russian operatives and agents also accessed multiple state and local election boards and had been successful at doing so since 2014.[64] Both the IC and policy analysts in cybersecurity are confident that Russia will continue to interfere in future elections unless stopped by U.S. cybersecurity forces.

## CRITICAL THINKING QUESTION

Many Americans are unconvinced that Russian interference in the U.S. elections was a big deal. Do you think it is important as an American citizen to care about Russian hacking of the American political system? Or is this just a narrow policy issue for Washington, D.C., policy experts to consider? Why do you think it important to consider?

Here is what John Brennan, former Director of the CIA, said in response to a similar question to Congress in 2017:

*Well, for the last 241 years, the nation and the citizens have cherished the freedom and liberty upon which this country was founded upon. Many brave Americans have lost their lives to protect that freedom and liberty and lost their lives to protect the freedom and liberties of other peoples around the world. Our ability to choose our elected leaders, as we see fit, is, I believe, an inalienable right that we must protect with all of the resources and authority and power.*

*And the fact that the Russians tried to influence resources and authority and power, and the fact that the Russians tried to influence that election so that the will of the American people was not going to be realized by that election, I find outrageous and something that we need to, with every last ounce of devotion to this country, resist and try to act to prevent further instances of that. And so, therefore, I believe, this is something that's critically important to every American. Certainly, it's very important for me, for my children and grandchildren to make sure that never again will a foreign country try to influence and interfere in the foundation stone of this country, which is electing our democratic leaders.[65]*

## CONCLUSION

Cybersecurity is increasingly becoming an ever-important part of the broader homeland security mission to secure the nation. Nonetheless, despite the growing threat of both foreign and domestic cyberattacks and interference, U.S. policymakers continue to struggle to understand the cybersecurity landscape. Unlike the legal and policy-oriented fields of immigration security and intelligence gathering, an understanding of cybersecurity threats requires expertise in fast-moving fields like computer science and data engineering. Since most politicians, lawyers, criminologists, and other homeland security professionals have little familiarity with the technical underpinnings of cybersecurity issues, they are often forced to make significant policy decisions on the basis of an incomplete understanding of the cybersecurity landscape.

Uninformed decision-making has serious consequences for homeland security and may lead to significant security gaps that bad actors can exploit. These issues become even more serious when one considers how software and hardware are increasingly becoming intertwined. Today a software exploit, such as a computer virus, can cause major "real world" damage if used to disrupt a physical asset, such as train track signal or a dam. In the next chapter we explore the threats posed to these "hardware" assets as well as how securing the cyber landscape can also help secure national critical infrastructure.

## KEYWORDS

- **cybercrime**: Crime that is directed at computers or other digital devices and where these digital devices are integral or central to the offense.

- **phishing**: Fraudulent attempt to obtain user information via the Internet (e.g. credit card numbers, usernames, and passwords) by disguising as a trustworthy entity.

- **Dark Web**: Websites that exist on secure, encrypted networks and cannot be found using traditional search methods, such as Google search.

- **cyberwar(fare)**: The use of computers, particularly related to the Internet and online networks, for sabotage, espionage, or other offensive action against the cyber-infrastructure of a nation.

- **cyberterrorism**: The premeditated use of disruptive activities, or the threat thereof, against computers and/or networks, with the intention to cause harm or further social, ideological, religious, political, or similar objectives, or to intimidate any person in furtherance of such objectives.

- **cyberactivist**: Individuals who perform cyberattacks for pleasure, philosophical, political, or other non-monetary reasons.

- **Information Sharing Analysis Organization**: A grouping of organizations from the government and the private sector that are defined by certain subject areas (e.g. transportation) and that join together to share information about cyber threats.

## KNOWLEDGE CHECK

1. How are concepts of *cybercrime*, *cyberterrorism*, and *cyberwarfare* different? How are they the same?
2. Name and explain three forms of cybercrime.
3. What role does the private sector play in national cybersecurity efforts?

# NOTES

1. *Cyber-bullying*, AUSTRALIAN CYBERCRIME ONLINE REPORTING NETWORK (last visited Jan. 15, 2019) www.acorn.gov.au/learn-about-cybercrime/cyber-bullying.
2. *Key Components in State Anti-Bullying Laws, Policies and Regulations*, STOPBULLYING.GOV (last updated Jan. 7, 2019) www.stopbullying.gov/laws/key-components/index.html.
3. Hypertouch v. ValueClick, Inc., 192 Cal. App. 4th 805 (Cal. Ct. App. 2011).
4. *Email spam and phishing*, AUSTRALIAN CYBERCRIME ONLINE REPORTING NETWORK (last visited Jan. 15, 2019) www.acorn.gov.au/learn-about-cybercrime/email-spam-and-phishing.
5. *State laws addressing "phishing,"* NATIONAL CONFERENCE OF STATE LEGISLATURES (Jan. 29, 2018) www.ncsl.org/research/telecommunications-and-information-technology/state-phishing-laws.aspx.
6. Charles Doyle, Cong. Research Serv. R42100, Mandatory Minimum Sentencing: Federal Aggravated Identity Theft (Aug. 20, 2015) *available at* https://fas.org/sgp/crs/misc/R42100.pdf.
7. U.S. DEP'T OF HOMELAND SECURITY, UNITED STATES COMPUTER EMERGENCY READINESS TEAM (last visited Jan. 15, 2019) www.us-cert.gov/sites/default/files/publications/infosheet_US-CERT_v2.pdf.
8. *Id.*
9. The law considers this material "to be obscene, lewd, lascivious, filthy, excessively violent, harassing, or otherwise objectionable, whether or not such material is constitutionally protected." See 47 U.S.C.S. § 230(c)(2)(A) (2018).
10. *The Digital Millennium Copyright Act of 1998, U.S. Copyright Office Summary* (Dec. 1998) *available at* www.copyright.gov/legislation/dmca.pdf.
11. *Complying with COPPA: Frequently Asked Questions*, U.S. FEDERAL TRADE COMMISSION (last visited Jan. 15, 2019) www.ftc.gov/tips-advice/business-center/guidance/complying-coppa-frequently-asked-questions.
12. The Justice for Victims of Trafficking Act of 2015, Pub. L. No. 144–22, 122 Stat. 227 (2015).
13. *Children and the Internet: Laws Relating to Filtering, Blocking and Usage Policies in Schools and Libraries*, NATIONAL CONFERENCE OF STATE LEGISLATURES (last updated Oct. 30, 2018) www.ncsl.org/research/telecommunications-and-information-technology/state-internet-filtering-laws.aspx.

14. *Child Pornography*, U.S. Dep't of Justice (last visited Jan. 15, 2019) www.justice.gov/criminal-ceos/child-pornography.

15. *See generally, id.*

16. *Id.*

17. *Id.*

18. *See Child Exploitation Investigations Unit*, U.S. Immigration and Customs Enforcement (last updated Apr. 3, 2017) www.ice.gov/predator.

19. *Child Pornography*, U.S. Dep't of Justice (last visited Jan. 15, 2019) www.justice.gov/criminal-ceos/child-pornography.

20. *Scams and Safety: Internet Fraud*, Federal Bureau of Investigation (last visited Jan. 15, 2019) www.fbi.gov/scams-and-safety/common-fraud-schemes/internet-fraud.

21. *See Combatting Cyber Crime*, U.S. Dep't of Homeland Security (last visited Jan. 15, 2019) www.dhs.gov/topic/combating-cyber-crime.

22. Catherine A. Theohary & John W. Rollins, Cong. Research Serv. R43955, Cyberwarfare and Cyberterrorism, at 3 (Mar. 27, 2015) https://fas.org/sgp/crs/natsec/R43955.pdf.

23. Harold Hongju Koh, Legal Advisor for U.S. Dep't of State, remarks at the USCYBERCOM Inter-Agency Legal Conference, Ft. Meade, MD (Sep. 18, 2012).

24. Catherine A. Theohary & John W. Rollins, Cong. Research Serv. R43955, Cyberwarfare and Cyberterrorism, at 4 (Mar. 27, 2015) https://fas.org/sgp/crs/natsec/R43955.pdf.

25. *Id.* at 9.

26. *Id.*

27. *Id.*

28. Serge Krasavin, *What is Cyber-terrorism?*, Computer Crime Research Center (last visited Jan. 15, 2019) www.crime-research.org/library/Cyber-terrorism.htm

29. Catherine A. Theohary & John W. Rollins, Cong. Research Serv. R43955, Cyberwarfare and Cyberterrorism, at 9 (Mar. 27, 2015) https://fas.org/sgp/crs/natsec/R43955.pdf.

30. Dorothy E. Denning, *Cyberterrorism* (May 23, 2000) *available at* http://palmer.wellesley.edu/~ivolic/pdf/Classes/Handouts/NumberTheoryHandouts/Cyberterror-Denning.pdf.

31. Peter W. Singer, *The Cyber Terror Bogeyman*, Brookings (Nov. 1, 2012) www.brookings.edu/articles/the-cyber-terror-bogeyman/.

32. *See id.*

33. *Id.*

34. *Id.*

35. National Institute of Standards and Technology, Cybersecurity Framework 1.1, at V, https://nvlpubs.nist.gov/nistpubs/CSWP/NIST.CSWP.04162018.pdf.

36. *Id.*

37. 42 U.S.C. § 5195c(e) (2018).

38. National Institute of Standards and Technology, Cybersecurity Framework 1.1, at V, https://nvlpubs.nist.gov/nistpubs/CSWP/NIST.CSWP.04162018.pdf.

39. *Id.*

40. *Id.* at 2.
41. U.S. Dep't of Homeland Security, National Cyber Incident Response Plan, at 4 (Dec. 2016) www.hsdl.org/?view&did=798128.
42. *Id.*
43. *Id.* at 7.
44. *Id.* at 8.
45. *Id.* at 4.
46. U.S. Dep't of Homeland Security, National Cyber Incident Response Plan, at 5 (Dec. 2016) www.hsdl.org/?view&did=798128.
47. *Id.*
48. *Id.*
49. The White House, National Cyber Strategy of the United States of America, at 1–3 (Sep. 2018) *available at* www.whitehouse.gov/wp-content/uploads/2018/09/National-Cyber-Strategy.pdf.
50. U.S. Dep't of Homeland Security, National Cyber Incident Response Plan, at 8 (Dec. 2016) www.hsdl.org/?view&did=798128.
51. U.S. Dep't of Homeland Security, National Cyber Incident Response Plan, at 8 (Dec. 2016) www.hsdl.org/?view&did=798128.
52. *Id.* at 27.
53. *Id.* at 17.
54. *Id.*
55. *Id.* at 20.
56. U.S. Dep't of Homeland Security, National Cyber Incident Response Plan, at 8 (Dec. 2016) www.hsdl.org/?view&did=798128.
57. *Id.* at 13.
58. *Id.* at 15; *Frequently Asked Questions About Information Sharing and Analysis Organizations*, U.S. Dep't of Homeland Security (Oct. 6, 2016) www.dhs.gov/isao-faq.
59. From U.S. Dep't of Homeland Security, National Cyber Incident Response Plan, at 15 (Dec. 2016) www.hsdl.org/?view&did=798128.
60. *Id.*
61. Intelligence Community Assessment, Assessing Russian Activities in Recent US Elections, at ii (Jan. 6, 2017) *available at* www.dni.gov/files/documents/ICA_2017_01.pdf.
62. *Id.*
63. *Id.* at 2.
64. *Id.* at 3.
65. Domenico Montanaro, *Why the Russia Investigation Matters and Why You Should Care*, NPR (May 24, 2017) www.npr.org/2017/05/24/529781094/why-the-russia-investigation-matters-and-why-you-should-care.

# CHAPTER 9

# Infrastructure Protection and Technology

> **IN THIS CHAPTER YOU WILL LEARN ABOUT**
>
> The changing nature of critical infrastructure protection before and after 9/11.
>
> Sixteen critical infrastructure protection sectors used as a framework to protect national critical infrastructure.
>
> The role of various federal, state, and local agencies as well as the private sector in protecting critical infrastructure.

## INTRODUCTION

The wealth, health, and security of the U.S. is reliant on the consistent production and distribution of goods and services. The physical assets, functions, and systems that produce these goods and services are often referred to as **critical infrastructure**. Critical infrastructure is the "body of systems, networks and assets that are so essential that their continued operation is required to ensure the security of a nation, its economy and the health and well-being of its populace."[1] An example would be the infrastructure that ensures the nation's continued supply of electricity, the power plants that generate it, and the electric grid upon which the electricity is distributed and shared.

A disruption of critical infrastructure can be devastating for a nation. For instance, in May 1998 the PanAmSat Galaxy IV satellite's onboard controller malfunctioned, disrupting service to an estimated 90% of the nation's pagers (fewer people used cellular phones at that time), causing problems for hospitals trying to reach doctors on call, emergency workers, and people trying to use their credit cards at gas pumps, among other serious problems.[2] A number of factors can cause these disruptions, including poor design of the critical infrastructure, destruction due to natural hazards (such as an earthquake or hurricane), or damage due to intentional human actions (i.e. a criminal act or act of terrorism). As discussed in Chapter 8 on cybersecurity, the majority of critical infrastructure in the U.S. is owned and operated by private actors, many of whom have taken measures to guard against and quickly respond to the threats to their property. Nonetheless, 9/11 and subsequent attacks and threats to infrastructure have demonstrated the need to reexamine how critical infrastructure is protected in light of the terrorist threat.

## CRITICAL INFRASTRUCTURE BEFORE 9/11

A number of laws, including those passed by Congress and those passed as Executive Orders by the President, set forth a basic policy and strategy for protecting U.S. critical infrastructure. The federal government works with states, localities, and the owners and operators of private and publicly owned critical infrastructure to identify those specific assets and systems that constitute U.S. critical infrastructure. Together, these entities assess critical infrastructure vulnerability to manmade or natural threats, determine the level of risk associated with possible terrorist attacks, and identify policies that can be implemented to reduce those risks.[3]

Though the primary responsibility for critical infrastructure protection lies with owners and operators of the infrastructure, the federal government can and does intervene in those areas where owners and operators are unable or unwilling to provide what the federal government may assess to be adequate protection or response.[4] Modern-day thinking about the government's critical infrastructure responsibilities began prior to 9/11, but the role of the federal government in critical infrastructure protection expanded dramatically in the aftermath of 9/11. In 1996, the President's Commission on Critical Infrastructure Protection (Commission) met to share the following with the President:

- The scope and nature of vulnerabilities and threats to nation's critical infrastructure (including cyberthreats);
- Recommend a comprehensive national policy and implementation plan for protecting critical infrastructure; and
- Determine the legal and policy issues raised by proposals to increase protections and propose statutory and regulatory changes necessary to effect recommendations.

The Commission's final report to the President found no immediate crisis to the nation's infrastructure (though it did recommend strong action be taken to protect computer networks, which were new and growing at that time).[5] The report included a strategy of action that recommended that the government:

- Facilitate greater cooperation and communication between the private sector and appropriate government agencies by setting up a top-level policy-making office in the White House;
- Establish a council that includes corporate executives, state and local government officials, and cabinet secretaries and also set up an information clearing house with best practices about critical infrastructure protection that could be accessed by owners and operators;
- Develop a real-time capability of attack warning;
- Establish and promote a comprehensive awareness and education program;
- Streamline and clarify elements of the legal structure to support assurance measures (including learning jurisdictional barriers to pursuing hackers electronically); and
- Expand research and development in technologies and techniques, especially technologies that allow for greater detection of intrusions.

## CRITICAL INFRASTRUCTURE POST-9/11

The Commission's report resulted in Presidential Decision Directive (PPD) No. 63, which set as a national goal the ability to protect the nation's critical infrastructure from intentional attacks (cyber and physical) by 2003.[6] Many of the PPD recommendations were subsumed into Executive Orders that were passed in the immediate aftermath of 9/11 when President Bush signed two Executive Orders relevant to critical infrastructure protection. One of these was the Executive Order that established the original Office of Homeland Security (which soon thereafter became DHS itself) including among its comprehensive national strategy:

> strengthening measures for protecting energy production, transmission, and distribution; telecommunications; public and privately owned information systems; transportation systems; and the provision of food and water for human use. (And) . . . to coordinate efforts to ensure rapid restoration of these critical infrastructures after a disruption by a terrorist threat or attack.[7]

Another was Executive Order (E.O. 13231) signed on October 16, 2001, which stated that it would be U.S. policy

> to protect against the disruption of the operation of information systems for critical infrastructure . . . and to ensure that any disruptions that occur are infrequent, of minimal duration, and manageable, and cause the least damage possible.[8]

E.O. 13231 also established the President's Critical Infrastructure Protection Board, a National Plan on Critical Infrastructure, created a Special Advisor to the President for Cyberspace Security position, and established the National Infrastructure Advisory Council, which provides advice to the President on the security of information systems for critical infrastructure. Many of the reforms and strategies of the Bush Administration related to critical infrastructure continued under the newly formed Department of Homeland Security and expanded further during the Obama Administration's eight-year tenure.

## CRITICAL INFRASTRUCTURE SECTORS

The critical infrastructure discipline within homeland security relies on a framework of 16 critical infrastructure sectors as a way to organize critical infrastructure policy nationwide. These 16 critical infrastructure sectors and the related assets, systems, and networks, whether physical or virtual, are considered so vital to the U.S. that their incapacitation or destruction would have a serious, debilitating effect on security, national economic security, national public health or safety, or any combination of these areas. Several policy documents, laws, and Executive Orders (discussed in later sections of this chapter) mandate national policies to strengthen and maintain infrastructure in these sectors against threats.

### Chemical Sector

The Chemical Sector is an important part of the U.S. economy. Businesses and other organizations that make up the Chemical Sector manufacture, store, use, and transport potentially dangerous chemicals upon which a wide range of other critical infrastructure sectors rely. Securing these chemicals against growing and evolving threats requires extreme vigilance from both the private sector owner and operators, and the public sector. Presidential Policy Directive 21 (PPD 21) identifies DHS as the Chemical Sector-Specific Agency to lead the Chemical Sector's public-private partnership and work with companies to develop tools and resources to enhance the sector's security and resilience.[9]

The Chemical Sector is composed of several hundred thousand U.S. chemical facilities in a complex global supply chain that converts various raw materials into more than 70,000 diverse products that are essential to modern life. Based on the end product produced, the sector can be divided into five main segments, each of which has distinct characteristics, growth dynamics, markets, new developments, and security issues. These are:

- Basic chemicals
- Specialty chemicals
- Agricultural chemicals
- Pharmaceuticals
- Consumer products

### Commercial Facilities Sector

The Commercial Facilities Sector includes a diverse range of sites that draw large crowds of people for shopping, business, entertainment, or lodging.

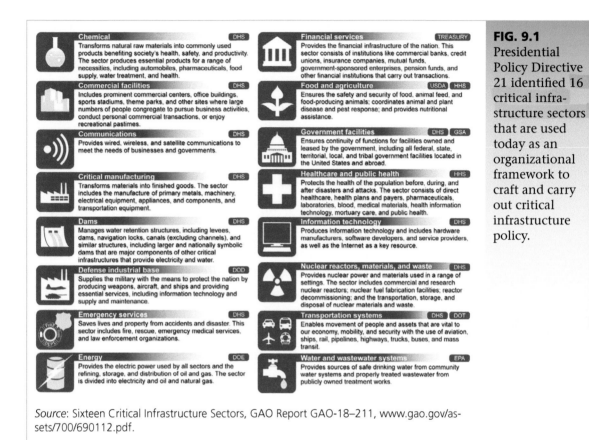

**Chemical** [DHS]
Transforms natural raw materials into commonly used products benefiting society's health, safety, and productivity. The sector produces essential products for a range of necessities, including automobiles, pharmaceuticals, food supply, water treatment, and health.

**Commercial facilities** [DHS]
Includes prominent commercial centers, office buildings, sports stadiums, theme parks, and other sites where large numbers of people congregate to pursue business activities, conduct personal commercial transactions, or enjoy recreational pastimes.

**Communications** [DHS]
Provides wired, wireless, and satellite communications to meet the needs of businesses and governments.

**Critical manufacturing** [DHS]
Transforms materials into finished goods. The sector includes the manufacture of primary metals, machinery, electrical equipment, appliances, and components, and transportation equipment.

**Dams** [DHS]
Manages water retention structures, including levees, dams, navigation locks, canals (excluding channels), and similar structures, including larger and nationally symbolic dams that are major components of other critical infrastructures that provide electricity and water.

**Defense industrial base** [DOD]
Supplies the military with the means to protect the nation by producing weapons, aircraft, and ships and providing essential services, including information technology and supply and maintenance.

**Emergency services** [DHS]
Saves lives and property from accidents and disaster. This sector includes fire, rescue, emergency medical services, and law enforcement organizations.

**Energy** [DOE]
Provides the electric power used by all sectors and the refining, storage, and distribution of oil and gas. The sector is divided into electricity and oil and natural gas.

**Financial services** [TREASURY]
Provides the financial infrastructure of the nation. This sector consists of institutions like commercial banks, credit unions, insurance companies, mutual funds, government-sponsored enterprises, pension funds, and other financial institutions that carry out transactions.

**Food and agriculture** [USDA] [HHS]
Ensures the safety and security of food, animal feed, and food-producing animals; coordinates animal and plant disease and pest response; and provides nutritional assistance.

**Government facilities** [DHS] [GSA]
Ensures continuity of functions for facilities owned and leased by the government, including all federal, state, territorial, local, and tribal government facilities located in the United States and abroad.

**Healthcare and public health** [HHS]
Protects the health of the population before, during, and after disasters and attacks. The sector consists of direct healthcare, health plans and payers, pharmaceuticals, laboratories, blood, medical materials, health information technology, mortuary care, and public health.

**Information technology** [DHS]
Produces information technology and includes hardware manufacturers, software developers, and service providers, as well as the Internet as a key resource.

**Nuclear reactors, materials, and waste** [DHS]
Provides nuclear power and materials used in a range of settings. The sector includes commercial and research nuclear reactors; nuclear fuel fabrication facilities; reactor decommissioning; and the transportation, storage, and disposal of nuclear materials and waste.

**Transportation systems** [DHS] [DOT]
Enables movement of people and assets that are vital to our economy, mobility, and security with the use of aviation, ships, rail, pipelines, highways, trucks, buses, and mass transit.

**Water and wastewater systems** [EPA]
Provides sources of safe drinking water from community water systems and properly treated wastewater from publicly owned treatment works.

**FIG. 9.1**
Presidential Policy Directive 21 identified 16 critical infrastructure sectors that are used today as an organizational framework to craft and carry out critical infrastructure policy.

*Source*: Sixteen Critical Infrastructure Sectors, GAO Report GAO-18–211, www.gao.gov/assets/700/690112.pdf.

Facilities within the sector operate on the principle of open public access, meaning that the general public can move freely without the deterrent of highly visible security barriers. The majority of these facilities are privately owned and operated, with minimal interaction with the federal government and regulatory entities.

The Commercial Facilities Sector consists of eight subsectors:

• Entertainment and media (such as motion picture studios, broadcast media);
• Gaming (such as casinos);
• Lodging (such as hotels, motels, and conference centers);
• Outdoor event venues (such as theme parks, fairs, and campgrounds);

- Public assembly venues (such as arenas, stadiums, aquariums, zoos, and convention centers);
- Real estate (such as large office and apartment buildings, condominiums, and storage facilities);
- Retail (such as large shopping malls and retail centers); and
- Sports (such as large sporting events and sports league gatherings).

## Communications Sector

The Communications Sector is an important part of the U.S. economy and is the framework for the operations of all businesses, public safety organizations, and the government at all levels. PPD 21 identifies the Communications Sector as critical because it "provides an enabling function" across all other critical infrastructure sectors. Over the last three decades, the Communications Sector has changed dramatically from being predominantly a provider of voice services into a diverse, competitive, and interconnected industry that now provides terrestrial, satellite, and wireless transmissions systems that carry interminable amounts of data around the world. The transmission of these services has become interconnected as well. Satellite, wireless, and wireline providers depend on each other to carry and terminate their traffic and companies routinely share facilities and technology to ensure interoperability.[10]

The private sector, as owners and operators of the majority of communications infrastructure, are primarily responsible for protecting Communications Sector infrastructure and assets. Working with the federal government, the private sector is able to predict, anticipate, and respond to sector outages and understand how they might affect the ability of the national leadership to communicate during times of crisis, impact the operations of other sectors, and affect response and recovery efforts.

The Communications Sector is closely linked to other sectors, including:

- The Energy Sector, which provides power to run cellular towers, central offices, and other critical communications facilities and also relies on communications to aid in monitoring and controlling the delivery of electricity.

- The Information Technology Sector, which provides critical control systems and services, physical architecture, and Internet infrastructure, and also relies on communications to deliver and distribute applications and services.
- The Financial Services Sector, which relies on communications for the transmission of transactions and operations of financial markets.
- The Emergency Services Sector, which depends on communications for directing resources, coordinating response, operating public alert and warning systems and receiving emergency 911 calls.
- The Transportation Systems Sector, which provides the diesel fuel needed to power backup generators and relies on communications to monitor and control the flow of ground, sea, and air traffic.

## Critical Manufacturing Sector

The Critical Manufacturing Sector is crucial to the economic prosperity and continuity of the United States. A direct attack on or disruption of certain elements of the manufacturing industry could disrupt essential functions at the national level and across multiple critical infrastructure sectors.[11] The Critical Manufacturing Sector includes several industries:

- *Primary metals manufacturing*: Including iron and steel mills, aluminum production and processing, and nonferrous metal production and processing;
- *Machinery manufacturing*: Including engine and turbine manufacturing, power transmission equipment manufacturing, and earth moving and mining equipment;
- *Electrical equipment, appliance, and component manufacturing*: Including electric motor manufacturing; and
- *Transportation equipment manufacturing*: Including vehicle and commercial ships manufacturing, aerospace products and parts, and transit/rail car manufacturing.

Products made by these manufacturing industries are essential to many other critical infrastructure sectors. The Critical Manufacturing Sector focuses on the identification, assessment, prioritization, and protection of nationally significant manufacturing industries within the sector that may be susceptible to manmade and natural disasters.[12]

## Dams Sector

The Dams Sector delivers critical water retention and control services in the United States, including hydroelectric power generation, municipal and industrial water supplies, agricultural irrigation, sediment and flood control, river navigation for inland bulk shipping, industrial waste management, and recreation (Figure 9.2). Its key services support multiple critical infrastructure sectors and industries. Dams Sector assets irrigate at least 10% of U.S. cropland, help protect more than 43% of the U.S. population from flooding, and generate about 60% of the electricity in the Pacific Northwest of the United States.[13]

**FIG. 9.2**
Dams are an important critical infrastructure asset. Here, the Big Tujunga Dam is under construction to reinforce the walls due to an increased debris flow from recent severe winter storms.

*Source*: Adam DuBrowa, The Big Tujunga Dam in California, www.fema.gov/media-library/assets/images/57775.

There are more than 90,000 dams in the U.S. and more than 65% are privately owned. Approximately 80% are regulated by state dams safety offices. The Dams Sector has interdependencies with a wide range of other sectors, including:

- *Communications*: Communications networks enable remote Dams Sector operations and control;
- *Energy*: Hydropower dams provide critical electricity resources and black-start capabilities;
- *Food and Agriculture*: Dams Sector assets provide water for irrigation and protect farmland from flooding;
- *Transportation Systems*: Navigation lock systems in the Dams Sector enable all inland and intracoastal waterway freight movements. Major roads may traverse dams; and
- *Water*: Dams Sector assets provide drinking water supplies and pumping capabilities.

## Defense Industrial Base Sector

The Defense Industrial Base Sector is the worldwide industrial complex that enables research and development, as well as design, production, delivery, and maintenance of military weapons systems, subsystems, and components or parts, to meet U.S. military requirements. The Defense Industrial Base partnership consists of Department of Defense Components, more than 100,000 Defense Industrial Base companies and their subcontractors who perform under contract to the Department of Defense, companies providing incidental materials and services to the Department of Defense, and government-owned/contractor-operated and government-owned/government-operated facilities.[14]

Defense Industrial Base companies include domestic and foreign entities, with production assets located in many countries outside the U.S. This sector provides products and services that are essential to mobilize, deploy and sustain military operations. The Defense Industrial Base Sector does not include the commercial infrastructure of providers of services such as power, communications, transportation, or utilities that the Department of Defense uses to meet military operational requirements.[15]

### Emergency Services Sector

The Emergency Services Sector (ESS) is a community of millions of highly skilled, trained personnel, along with the physical and cyber resources that provide a wide range of prevention, preparedness, response, and recovery services during both day-to-day operations and incident response (Figure 9.3). The ESS includes geographically distributed facilities and equipment in both paid and volunteer capacities organized primarily at the federal, state, local, tribal, and territorial levels of government, such as city police departments and fire stations, county sheriff's offices, Department of Defense police and fire departments, and town public works departments. The ESS also includes

**FIG. 9.3** The mission of the ESS is to save lives, protect property and the environment, assist communities impacted by disasters, and aid recovery during emergencies. Five distinct disciplines compose the ESS, encompassing a wide range of emergency response functions and roles.

*Source*: The Emergency Services Critical Infrastructure Sector, www.dhs.gov/sites/default/files/images/ip/ESSDisciplines.JPG.

private sector resources, such as industrial fire departments, private security organizations, and private emergency medical services providers.[16]

## Energy Sector

The U.S. energy infrastructure fuels the modern-day national and global economy. Without a stable energy supply, health and welfare are threatened and the U.S. economy cannot function. Presidential Policy Directive 21 identifies the Energy Sector as uniquely critical because it provides an "enabling function" across all critical infrastructure sectors—allowing all other sectors to function. More than 80% of U.S. energy infrastructure is owned by the private sector. This sector supplies fuels to the transportation industry, electricity to households and businesses, and other sources of energy that are important to growth and production across the U.S.[17]

Energy infrastructure is divided into three interrelated segments: Electricity, oil, and natural gas. The U.S. electricity segment contains more than 6,413 power plants with approximately 1,075 gigawatts of installed generation. Approximately 48% of electricity is produced by combusting coal (which is transported by rail), 20% in nuclear power plants, and 22% by combusting natural gas. The remaining generation is provided by hydroelectric plants (6%), oil (1%), and renewable resources such as solar, wind, and geothermal (3%). The heavy reliance on pipelines to distribute products across the nation highlights the interdependencies between the Energy and Transportation Systems Sector.[18]

The reliance of virtually all industries on electric power and fuels means that all sectors have some dependence on the Energy Sector. The Energy Sector is thus the most sophisticated actor in the critical infrastructure space, well aware of its vulnerabilities, and is leading a significant voluntary effort to increase planning and preparedness for a hazard or attack. Cooperation through industry groups has resulted in substantial information-sharing of best practices across the sector. Many Energy Sector owners and operators have extensive experience abroad with infrastructure protection and have more recently focused their attention on cybersecurity.[19]

**CALL-OUT BOX**
**Energy Subsector Risks**

Considerable media attention has been devoted to the threats to energy infrastructure, including cyber threats and possible terrorist attacks. Despite the generalized concern about threats to the Energy Sector, the types of threats faced by the diverse subsectors such as the electricity, oil, and natural gas industries, vary widely. Below is an excerpt from DHS' 2015 Energy Sector-Specific Plan that highlights the diversity of risk (and thus the difficulty in ameliorating these risks) faced by some specific subsectors:

### 2.1.1 Electricity Subsector Risks and Threats

*Many organizations conduct a wide variety of risk assessments of the Electricity Subsector. For example, the North American Electric Reliability Corporation (NERC) assesses risks in terms of the potential impact to the reliability of the bulk power system (i.e., did an event result in the loss or interruption of service to customers?), while private companies and utilities examine risks and threats as they relate to the operational and financial security of each company (i.e., could a threat negatively impact the company's financial health?). Based on a review by some of the largest U.S. electric utilities (in terms of revenue) as well as the analysis by NERC, a wide variety of issues were considered threats in the Electricity Subsector. Despite the differences in what constitutes risk, the Electricity Subsector identified several issues as the key risks and threats to its infrastructure and/or continuity of business in 2012 and 2013:*

- *Cyber and physical security threats;*
- *Natural disasters and extreme weather conditions;*
- *Workforce capability ("aging workforce") and human errors;*
- *Equipment failure and aging infrastructure;*
- *Evolving environmental, economic, and reliability regulatory requirements; and*
- *Changes in the technical and operational environment, including changes in fuel supply.*

### 2.1.2 Oil and Natural Gas Subsector Risks and Threats

*The Oil and Natural Gas Subsector, particularly the oil industry, faces a diverse risk landscape due to its worldwide geographic presence, the hazardous and evolving exploration, production, and operating conditions, as well as the various domestic and in some cases foreign regulatory jurisdictions under which it operates. Based on a survey of the 100 largest U.S. exploration and production companies, the following were identified as key risks the oil and natural gas industry faced during 2012:*

- *Natural disasters and extreme weather conditions;*
- *Regulatory and legislative changes—including environmental and health—as well as increased cost of compliance;*
- *Volatile oil and gas prices and demands;*
- *Operational hazards including blowouts, spills, and personal injury;*
- *Disruption due to political instability, civil unrest, or terrorist activities;*
- *Transportation infrastructure constraints impacting the movement of energy resources;*
- *Inadequate or unavailable insurance coverage;*
- *Aging infrastructure and workforce; and*
- *Cybersecurity risks, including insider threats.*[20]

## Financial Services Sector

The Financial Services Sector represents a vital component of U.S. critical infrastructure. Large-scale power outages, recent natural disasters, and an increase in the number and sophistication of cyberattacks demonstrate the wide range of potential risks facing the sector.

The Financial Services Sector includes thousands of depository institutions, providers of investment products, insurance companies, other credit and financing organizations, and the providers of critical financial utilities and services that support these functions. Financial institutions vary widely in size and presence, ranging from some of the world's largest global companies with thousands of employees and many billions of dollars in assets, to community banks and credit unions with a small number of employees serving individual communities.[21]

## Food and Agriculture Sector

The Food and Agriculture Sector is almost entirely under private ownership and is composed of an estimated 2.1 million farms, 935,000 restaurants, and more than 200,000 registered food manufacturing, processing, and storage facilities. This sector accounts for a staggering one-fifth of the United States' economic activity. The Food and Agriculture Sector has critical dependencies with many sectors, but particularly the following:

- *Water and Wastewater Systems*: For clean irrigation and processed water;
- *Transportation Systems*: For movement of products and livestock;
- *Energy*: To power the equipment needed for agriculture production and food processing; and
- *Chemical*: For fertilizers and pesticides used in the production of crops.[22]

The Food and Agriculture Sector is particularly vulnerable to attack and disruption as corrupting one element of the sector, for instance cattle feed, can have downstream impacts on the rest of the sector and the nation, for instance in the form of poisoned beef (Figure 9.4).

**FIG. 9.4**
The Food and Agriculture Critical Infrastructure Sector is mostly privately owned, yet critical to the health and well-being of all Americans. Damage recovery efforts to this sector are often prioritized by state, local, and federal government agencies.

*Source*: Andrea Booher, Damage to Barns and Farm Infrastructure in Puerto Rico, FEMA, www.fema.gov/media-library/assets/images/148275.

## Government Facilities Sector

The Government Facilities Sector includes a wide variety of buildings, located in the U.S. and overseas, that are owned or leased by federal, state, local, and tribal governments. Many government facilities are open to the public for business activities, commercial transactions, or recreational activities while others that are not open to the public contain highly sensitive information, materials, processes, and equipment. These facilities include general-use office buildings and special-use military installations, embassies, courthouses, national laboratories, and structures that may house critical equipment, systems, networks, and functions. In addition to physical structures, the sector includes cyber elements that contribute to the protection of sector assets (e.g. access control systems and closed-circuit television systems) as well as individuals who perform essential functions or possess tactical, operational, or strategic knowledge.[23] Additional subsectors include:

- *Education Facilities Subsection*: Covers pre-kindergarten through 12th grade schools, institutions of higher education, and business and trade schools. Notably, this subsector includes facilities that are owned by both government and private sector entities.
- *National Monuments and Icons Subsector*: Encompasses a diverse array of assets, networks, systems, and functions located throughout the U.S. Many national monuments and icons are listed in the National Register of Historic Places. These can often be targets for terrorists or other bad actors because of their cultural significance and the psychological impact their destruction would have on the American psyche.
- *Election Infrastructure Subsector*: Covers a wide range of physical and electronic assets such as storage facilities, polling places, and centralized vote tabulation locations used to support the election process. These assets and other facilities may also be used to gather information and communications technology such as voter registration databases, voting machines, and other systems to manage the election process and report and display results on behalf of state and local governments.

## Healthcare and Public Health Sector

The Healthcare and Public Health Sector is an important sector because its protection secures the U.S. from terrorist attack, infectious disease outbreaks, and natural disasters. Like other sectors, the vast majority of this sector is owned by private actors and thus collaboration and information sharing between the public and private portions of this sector is essential to increasing the resilience of the overall sector.

Operating in all U.S. states, territories, and tribal areas, the Healthcare and Public Health Sector plays a significant role in response and recovery across all other sectors in the event of a natural or manmade disaster. While healthcare tends to be delivered and managed locally, the public health component of the sector, which is focused primarily on population health, is managed across all levels of government: National, state, regional, local, tribal, and territorial. The Healthcare and Public Health Sector is highly dependent on fellow sectors for continuity of operations and service delivery, including but not limited to the Communications, Emergency Services, Energy, Transportation Systems, and Information Technology sectors.[24]

## Information Technology Sector

The Information Technology (IT) Sector is central to the nation's security, economy, and public health and safety as businesses, governments, academia, and private citizens are increasingly dependent on Information Technology Sector functions. These virtual and distributed functions produce and provide hardware, software, and information technology systems and services and—in collaboration with the Communications Sector—the Internet. The sector's complex and dynamic environment makes identifying threats and assessing vulnerabilities difficult and requires that these tasks be addressed in a collaborative and creative fashion.[25] Often protecting the IT Sector becomes the responsibility of government agencies with a cybersecurity mandate, such as NPPD at DHS (see Chapter 8 for more information on cybersecurity and securing IT Sector assets).

IT Sector functions are operated by a combination of entities, often owners and operators and their respective associations, that maintain and reconstitute the network, including the Internet. Although information technology infrastructure has a certain level of inherent resilience, its interdependent and interconnected structure presents challenges as well as opportunities for coordinating public and private sector preparedness and protection activities.

## SIDEBAR 9.1 Security Tenets for the Internet of Things

Critical embedded systems, whether medical devices, cars that connect to the Internet, Supervisory and Data Acquisition (SCADA) tools, industrial control systems (ICS), or other systems . . . play a crucial role in today's increasingly tech-focused world. As more and more of these systems become interconnected to the "Internet of Things" the need to properly secure these systems from hackers and cyberattacks is becoming increasingly important.[26]

The **Internet of Things (IoT)** refers to the network of physical devices, vehicles, home appliances, and other items embedded with electronics, software and sensors that allows them to connect to the Internet and exchange data. This creates opportunities for more direct integration of the physical world into computer-based systems, resulting in efficiency improvements and economic benefits, but also the potential for malfeasance.[27] Examples of these systems in the consumer world are the now-common "smart speakers" such as Amazon's Echo and television devices like Apple TV. Researchers have been able to remotely take control over these devices as well as medical technology embedded in the human body such as pacemakers and insulin pumps.

DHS' critical infrastructure organizations meet the need for securing the IoT by providing basic security guidelines meant to ensure that embedded systems across all industries that are critical to health and safety (often referred to as "life critical embedded systems") have a common understanding of what is needed to protect human life, prevent loss or severe damage to equipment, and prevent environmental harm. The intent of DHS' work is not to create a mandate or set of regulations, but rather to specify a set of prioritized, core technical principles that can be applied across any industry or organization with life critical embedded systems.[28] Attacks using or against the IoT have increased by as much as 280% over the last several years and this increase has prompted other federal agencies, such as the Department of Commerce, to create security standards for industry groups.

A declassified U.S. National Intelligence Council report summarizes both the advantages and challenges the IoT poses to the future of the United States:

> If the United States executes wisely, the IoT could work to the long-term advantage of the domestic economy and to the US military. Streamlining—or revolutionizing—supply chains and logistics could slash costs, increase efficiencies, and reduce dependence on human labor. Ability to fuse sensor data from many distributed objects could deter crime and asymmetric warfare. Ubiquitous positioning technology could locate missing and stolen goods. On the other hand, we may be unable to deny access to networks of sensors and remotely controlled objects by enemies of the United States, criminals, and mischief makers. Foreign manufacturers could become both the single-source and single-point-of-failure for mission-critical Internet-enabled things. Manufacturers could also become vectors for delivering everyday objects containing malicious software that causes havoc in everyday life. An open market for aggregated sensor data could serve the interests of commerce and security no less than it helps criminals and spies identify vulnerable targets.
>
> Thus, massively parallel sensor fusion may undermine social cohesion if it proves to be fundamentally incompatible with Fourth-Amendment guarantees against unreasonable search. By 2025, social critics may even charge that Asia's dominance of the manufacturing of things—and the objects that make up the Internet of Things—has funded the remilitarization of Asia, fueled simmering intra-Asian rivalries, and reduced US influence over the course of geopolitical events.[29]

This same report lays out signposts for policymakers that indicate the direction and pace with which any field of uncertainty in IoT is advancing:

- The size and nature of demand for expedited logistics in commerce and military organizations;
- The effectiveness of initial waves of IoT technology in reducing costs, thereby creating conditions for diffusion into vertical application

areas including civilian government operations, law enforcement, healthcare, and document management;

- The ability of devices located indoors to receive geolocation signals, possibly distributing such signals by leveraging available infrastructures (cell towers, broadcasters, and other means);
- Closely related technological advances in miniaturization and energy-efficient electronics, including reduced-power microcomputers and communications methods, energy harvesting transducers, and improved microbatteries;
- Efficient use of radio-wave spectrum, including cost-effective solutions for wide-area communications at duty cycles that are much smaller (e.g. the equivalent of a few minutes per month) than those of cell phones (averaging many minutes per day); and
- Advances in software that act on behalf of people, and software that effectively fuses ("makes sense of") sensor information from disparate sources.[30]

## Nuclear Reactors, Materials, and Waste Sector

From the power reactors that provide electricity to millions of Americans, to the medical isotopes used to treat cancer patients, the Nuclear Reactors, Materials, and Waste Sector covers most aspects of America's civilian nuclear infrastructure. The Nuclear Reactors, Materials, and Waste Sector includes:

- Ninety-nine active and 18 decommissioning power reactors in 30 states that generate nearly 20% of the United States' electricity. In the U.S. there have been no civilian deaths associated with the operation of a nuclear power plant since the technology's introduction over 60 years ago, making nuclear power one of the safest forms of energy in the U.S. However, the potential catastrophic damage to the homeland should a disaster occur can be great;
- Thirty-one research and test reactors located at universities and national labs. These reactors produce medical and industrial isotopes used to treat cancer and perform radiographic services, as well as to conduct academic research across multiple fields, including chemistry, physics, and material science;

- Eight active nuclear fuel cycle facilities that are responsible for the production and reprocessing of nuclear reactor fuel. These facilities take natural uranium from the ground and enrich it to approximately 5% Uranium-235. This enriched uranium is turned into solid Uranium Dioxide fuel pellets for use in nuclear reactors;
- More than 20,000 licensed users of radioactive sources. These radioactive sources are used for medical diagnostics and treatment in hospitals, depth measurements at oil and gas drilling sites, sterilization at food production facilities, research in academic institutions, and examining packages and cargo at security checkpoints; and
- Over three million yearly shipments of radioactive materials. Special security measures are taken when radioactive materials are shipped to ensure the safety of the transportation workers and to prevent theft or sabotage of the radioactive material itself.[31]

The Nuclear Reactors, Materials, and Waste Sector depends on other critical infrastructure sectors and they depend on it, including the:

- *Chemical Sector*: Chemicals are used daily in the production of electricity and other power sources, including nuclear power plants.
- *Emergency Services Sector*: The Nuclear Sector's uniquely hazardous characteristics require trained emergency responders during any hazard occurrence.
- *Energy Sector*: Nuclear facilities both supplying electricity and also depending on large amounts of uninterrupted power for continuous safe operation.
- *Healthcare and Public Health Sector*: North America performs about 20 million medical procedures per year using radioactive materials.
- *Transportation Systems Sector*: Nuclear and radioactive materials are shipped worldwide via air, rail, highway, and water.
- *Water and Wastewater Systems Sector*: Nuclear power plants use large quantitates of water for cooling. Interrupted water supply may require shut down.

### Transportation Systems Sector

The U.S. transportation system quickly, safely, and securely moves people and goods through the country and overseas. DHS and the Department

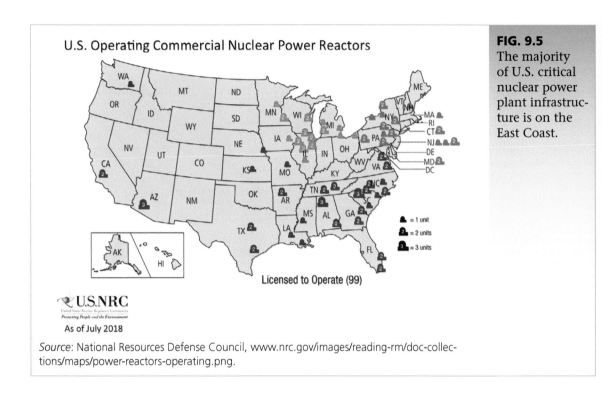

**FIG. 9.5**
The majority of U.S. critical nuclear power plant infrastructure is on the East Coast.

U.S. Operating Commercial Nuclear Power Reactors

▲ = 1 unit
▲ = 2 units
▲ = 3 units

Licensed to Operate (99)

U.S.NRC
United States Nuclear Regulatory Commission
*Protecting People and the Environment*
As of July 2018

*Source*: National Resources Defense Council, www.nrc.gov/images/reading-rm/doc-collections/maps/power-reactors-operating.png.

of Transportation are designated as the Co-Sector-Specific Agencies for the Transportation Systems Sector. The Transportation Systems Sector consists of seven key subsections (or modes): Aviation, highway and motor carrier, maritime transportation systems, mass transit and passenger rail, pipeline systems, freight rail, and postal and shipping. These modes are discussed in detail in Chapter 6.[32]

## Water and Wastewater Systems Sector

Safe drinking water is a prerequisite for protecting public health and all human activity. Properly treated wastewater is vital for preventing disease and protecting the environment. Thus, ensuring the supply of drinking water and wastewater treatment and service is essential to modern life and the U.S. economy. There are approximately 153,000 public drinking water systems and more than 16,000 publicly owned wastewater treatment systems in the

**FIG. 9.6**
A graphic that highlights the numerous federal agencies, personnel and non-government partners that work together to secure critical port infrastructure in the Transportation System Critical Infrastructure Sector.

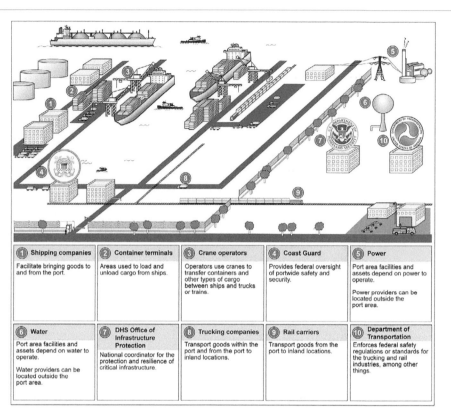

| ① Shipping companies | ② Container terminals | ③ Crane operators | ④ Coast Guard | ⑤ Power |
|---|---|---|---|---|
| Facilitate bringing goods to and from the port. | Areas used to load and unload cargo from ships. | Operators use cranes to transfer containers and other types of cargo between ships and trucks or trains. | Provides federal oversight of portwide safety and security. | Port area facilities and assets depend on power to operate.<br><br>Power providers can be located outside the port area. |
| ⑥ Water | ⑦ DHS Office of Infrastructure Protection | ⑧ Trucking companies | ⑨ Rail carriers | ⑩ Department of Transportation |
| Port area facilities and assets depend on water to operate.<br><br>Water providers can be located outside the port area. | National coordinator for the protection and resilience of critical infrastructure. | Transport goods within the port and from the port to inland locations. | Transport goods from the port to inland locations. | Enforces federal safety regulations or standards for the trucking and rail industries, among other things. |

*Source*: Key Partners Involved in Port Critical Infrastructure Operations and Oversight, GAO Report GAO-13–11, www.flickr.com/photos/usgao/8148001081/in/photolist-wFDUBk-qRKwtT-nAqgzC-G1TiWY-S69tcf-N5qpch-dq1CRg-pgZnQR-dV4nqN-jzEgvA-xAriaE-xTGLJr-xAxLh2.

U.S. More than 80% of the U.S. population receives their potable (i.e. drinkable) water from these systems and about 75% of the U.S. population has its sanitary sewage treated by these wastewater systems.

Because of its depth and breadth and the necessity of water consumption to life, the Water and Wastewater Systems Sector is vulnerable to a variety of terrorist attacks, including contamination of the water supply with deadly agents; physical attacks, such as the release of toxic gaseous chemicals; and cyberattacks on water and wastewater systems. The result of any attack could be large numbers of illnesses or casualties or a denial of a water delivery service that could impact public health and national economic vitality.[33]

This sector is also vulnerable to natural disasters. Earthquakes can cause pipes to burst and contaminate drinking water. They are difficult and time consuming to repair. Critical services, such as firefighting and healthcare (hospitals) and other dependent and interdependent sectors such as the Energy, Food and Agriculture, and Transportation Systems sectors would suffer negative impacts from a disruption in the Water and Wastewater Systems Sector.[34]

# DHS AND CRITICAL INFRASTRUCTURE PROTECTION

As mentioned in previous chapters, the Homeland Security Act established the Department of Homeland Security and assigned DHS the mission of preventing terrorist attacks, reducing the vulnerability of the nation to such attacks, and tasking it with responding rapidly should such an attack occur.

The Homeland Security Act also transferred a number of agencies and offices with critical infrastructure protection responsibilities to DHS. These various offices were integrated into the National Protection and Programs Directorate (NPPD). Today, NPPD's Office of Infrastructure Protection leads and coordinates national programs and policies on critical infrastructure security and resilience and is responsible for establishing partnerships across all government and private sectors. The office conducts and facilitates vulnerability and consequences assessments to help critical infrastructure owners and operators and state, local, and tribal and territorial partners understand and assess risks to critical infrastructure. The Infrastructure Protection Office provides information on emerging threats and hazards so that appropriate actions can be taken. The office also offers tools and training to partners to help them manage the risks to their assets, systems, and networks.[35]

The Office of Infrastructure Protection has several subdivisions that conduct important critical infrastructure protection work; they include the following offices

## Infrastructure Information Collection Division

The Infrastructure Information Collection Division (IICD) leads DHS' efforts to gather and manage vital information regarding the nation's critical infrastructure. Protecting U.S. critical infrastructure requires detailed, accurate, and consistent data to better prepare for, respond to, and recover from natural or manmade disasters. IICD helps to ensure that the necessary infrastructure data is available to homeland security partners by identifying information sources and developing applications and tools to support data collection, management, and visualization.

One such tool is the Infrastructure Protection Gateway (IP Gateway) tool, which serves as a single interface through which DHS mission partners can access a range of integrated tools and data to conduct comprehensive vulnerability assessments and risk analysis.[36] Web-based infrastructure surveys and assessments available through IP Gateway allow users to capture valuable data on a facility's physical and operational security and its resilience to attacks and natural hazards. The collected data is analyzed to determine the facility's relative security and resilience in comparison to the national average for similar facilities. This information is used to develop dashboards that equip the facility's owners and operators with the knowledge to detect and prevent physical, cyber, and natural threats, and better respond to, recover from, and remain resilient against "all hazards."[37]

The IICD also establishes standards, requirements, and procedures to help ensure the consistency and relevance of data collected through NPPD's information systems. As part of this effort, IICD develops and maintains the DHS Infrastructure Data Taxonomy program, which provides a common terminology for communication about critical infrastructure. The success of DHS' critical infrastructure and resilience program relies on participation from critical infrastructure owners and operators. To protect critical infrastructure information voluntarily shared with the government from disclosure and to enhance information-sharing efforts among the public and private sectors, IICD runs the Protected Critical Infrastructure Information program (PCII), which provides congressionally mandated protections from public disclosure to qualifying critical infrastructure information. Thus, the PCII encourages private sector owners of critical infrastructure to participate in programs with the federal government because they are assured that their sensitive information will be protected.[38]

Lastly, IICD also manages infrastructure information partnerships with homeland security geospatial stakeholders in state and local governments, as well as the private sector. These partnerships include working to define better geospatial information requirements, improving data sharing, creating geospatial data sets for use by partners, serving as focal points for state and local data needs, and managing workshops to address future geospatial information issues in homeland security and emergency response.[39]

### Infrastructure Security Compliance Division

The Infrastructure Compliance Division (ISCD) is an IP division that is responsible for implementing the Chemical Facility Anti-Terrorism Standards (CFATS)—the United States' program to regulate security at high-risk chemical facilities. ISCD also leads the DHS effort to secure other high-risk chemical facilities in the U.S. and works to prevent the use of certain chemicals in a terrorist act on the homeland through systematic regulation, inspection, and enforcement of chemical infrastructure security requirements.

The CFATS program, which ISCD enforces, was passed by Congress in 2007 (and reauthorized in 2014). The program uses a risk assessment process to identify high-risk chemical facilities. Facilities identified as high-risk must meet and maintain performance-based security standards appropriate to facilities and the risks they pose. ISCD chemical security inspectors work nationwide to help ensure facilities have security measures in place to meet CFATS requirements.[40]

### SIDEBAR 9.2 Chemical Facility Anti-Terrorism Standards (CFATS)

DHS' Chemical Facility Anti-Terrorism Standards (CFATS) is the United States' first regulatory program focused specifically on security at high-risk chemical facilities. DHS administers CFATS though its Infrastructure Security Compliance Division (ICSD). The program involves DHS working closely with chemical facilities to ensure they have security measures in place to reduce the risks associated with certain hazardous chemicals and also prevent these facilities from being exploited in a terrorist attack.[41] Under CFATS a chemical facility is defined as any establishment (or individual) that possesses or plans to possess any of the 300 chemicals of interest (COI) listed in Appendix A of DHS' Screening Threshold Quantity Standards documentation. A number of facilities, not just those traditionally considered to be chemical facilities, fall under CFATS regulation, including chemical manufacturing, chemical storage and distribution facilities, energy companies and utilities (for instance, nuclear power plants), agriculture and food industries (for instance, those that store fertilizers that can be highly combustible), explosives and weapon manufacturers, mining, electronics, plastics, universities and laboratories, and healthcare and pharmaceutical companies. Chemical facilities must report their chemical holdings to DHS via an online survey known as "Top Screen." DHS uses the Top Screen information a chemical facility submits to determine if the facility is considered high risk and whether it must develop a security plan.

Once a facility submits their chemical holding information to DHS, they either receive an Authorization Inspection (which validates the information submitted) or an ongoing Compliance Inspection (which ensures that the chemical facility is implementing existing and planned security measures).[42]

## National Infrastructure Coordinating Center

The National Infrastructure Coordinating Center (NICC) is a dedicated 24/7 coordination and information sharing operations center that maintains situational awareness of the nation's critical infrastructure for the federal government (and is part of the Infrastructure Protection Office) (Figure 9.7). When an incident or event affecting critical infrastructure occurs and requires coordination between DHS and the owners and operators of U.S. infrastructure, the NICC serves as the information-sharing hub to support the security and resilience of vital assets.

Due to President Obama's 1) Executive Order on Improving Critical Infrastructure Cybersecurity and 2) Presidential Policy Directive on Critical Infrastructure Security and Resilience, cybersecurity and physical security information sharing now occurs regularly between the NICC and the National Cybersecurity and Communications Integrations Center (NCCIC)

**FIG. 9.7**
Former DHS Secretary Jeh Johnson spends a day at the National Infrastructure Coordinating Center (NICC) in Arlington, VA, in 2017.

*Source*: Jetta Disco, DHS Leadership at the National Infrastructure Coordinating Center, Dep't of Homeland Security.

to enhance the efficiency and effectiveness of the U.S. government's work to secure critical infrastructure and make it more resilient.[43]

Among other roles, the NICC is responsible for:

- *Situational Awareness*: Collecting, maintaining, and sharing information about threats to infrastructure;
- *Information Sharing and Collaboration*: Integrating and disseminating information throughout the critical infrastructure partnership network;
- *Critical Infrastructure Assessment*: Coordinating and evaluating infrastructure information for accuracy, importance, and implications;
- *Decision Support*: Providing recommendations to critical infrastructure partners and DHS leadership; and
- *Future Operations*: Supporting decision-makers and providing actionable information 24–72 hours before and after a critical infrastructure-related event.

### Protective Security Coordination Division

The Protective Security Coordination Division (PSCD) is one of the most important IP Office divisions because it often works directly with owners and operators of critical infrastructure and provides programs and initiatives to help develop resilience against a future threat. PSCD helps critical infrastructure owners and operators and state and local responders:

- Assess vulnerabilities, interdependencies, capabilities, and incident consequences;
- Develop, implement, and provide national coordination for protective programs; and
- Facilitate critical infrastructure response to and recovery from all hazards

This is accomplished through a combination of data collection, assessment, and analysis to give government officials and private sector owners and operators enhancement options to mitigate risk and build resilience. The PSCD's activities also inform DHS initiatives, such as infrastructure protection grant programs and research and development requirements. Notably, the PSCD has a field office program staffed by Protective Security Advisors. PSAs are professionals who work locally throughout the U.S. and help owners and operators of critical infrastructure conduct vulnerability assessments and training, support incident management, and provide a vital communication channel between state and local officials, private sector owners and operators, and DHS (see the Sidebar on PSAs in this chapter).[44]

### SIDEBAR 9.3 Protective Security Advisors

PSAs serve as critical infrastructure protection and security experts to federal, state, and local government, and private sector partners. Though IOs and PSAs serve in different capacities, they complement each other and work together to support homeland security partners and ensure the safety and security of the nation.

PSAs are deployed by the DHS Office of Infrastructure Protection and are trained critical infrastructure protection and vulnerability mitigation subject matter experts. They conduct specialized site visits to gather critical infrastructure security information, which informs the national risk profile, and they provide information and guidance to state and local government and private sector partners on critical infrastructure protection issues. The PSA program focuses on three core areas: 1) infrastructure protection, 2) critical infrastructure-related incident management, and 3) information sharing with critical infrastructure owners and operators and the private sector.

PSAs enhance infrastructure protection by coordinating critical infrastructure-related training and vulnerability assessments for state and local partners and owners and operators of critical infrastructure. PSAs also advise law enforcement and homeland security leaders about ongoing state and local critical infrastructure security efforts and assist them in maturing their infrastructure protection capabilities, including working with Fusion Center analysts. Like IOs, PSAs facilitate information sharing across all levels of government and the private sector with specific emphasis on infrastructure-related vulnerability and physical security information. PSAs provide an invaluable on-the-ground perspective to DHS' national risk profile by identifying, assessing, monitoring, and minimizing risk to infrastructure at the regional and local levels.

Because PSAs are deployed strategically across the United States, they are often the first DHS personnel to respond to incidents that may require federal intervention, especially those involving critical infrastructure. During an incident, PSAs work with state and local Emergency Operations Centers and the Federal Emergency Management Agency (FEMA) Regional Offices to advise federal and state and local partners on issues impacting critical infrastructure and help them prioritize and coordinate critical infrastructure-related response and recovery activities. For instance, a PSA may be called upon to provide training and expertise to a local power plant or house of worship to ensure that these facilities are equipped to handle an active shooter incident.

## Sector Outreach and Programs Division

The Sector Outreach and Programs Division (SOPD) builds stakeholder capacity and enhances critical infrastructure security and resilience through voluntary partnerships and provides key tools, resources, and partnerships. The division operates the council and stakeholder engagement mechanisms for the critical infrastructure security and resilience community. SOPD also serves as the sector-specific agency for six of the 16 critical infrastructure sectors and collaborates with the other ten. The SOPD's services for enhancing critical infrastructure security and resilience across the sectors include:

- Serving as the sector-specific agency for six of the critical infrastructure sectors.
- Coordinating critical infrastructure protection responsibilities across all 16 critical infrastructure sectors.
- Providing expertise in critical infrastructure security and resilience.
- Enabling critical infrastructure security partnerships and managing the Critical Infrastructure Partnership Advisory Council.
- Developing and delivering stakeholder education, training, and exercises.
- Facilitating information-sharing and managing the critical infrastructure information sharing environment.[45]

## ROLE OF STATE, LOCAL, AND TRIBAL GOVERNMENT IN INFRASTRUCTURE PROTECTION

Ownership of most critical infrastructure in the United States sits in the hands of the private sector, and the federal government is the primary security coordinating and funding body for critical infrastructure protection. Nonetheless, state, local, and tribal governments play an important role in protecting critical infrastructure in their territories.

State, local, tribal, and territorial governments execute the critical infrastructure mission as entities responsible for ensuring the security and resilience of their jurisdiction and/or as owners and operators of assets, systems, and networks. State and local government critical infrastructure programs actively implement a partnership approach to security and resilience; prioritize sharing information across the critical infrastructure community; and ensure coordinated, comprehensive risk management. State and local government owners and operators of critical infrastructure provide for a wide range of services necessary for a safe and functioning society. A failure or

**FIG. 9.8**
Liane Richardson, a County Administrator in Alabama, participates in a nuclear disaster mock training exercise. Whenever critical infrastructure is under threat, local government is first on the scene.

*Source*: Shannon Arledge, Local County Administrator Participates in Critical Infrastructure Protection Training, FEMA, www.fema.gov/media-library/assets/images/68048.

disruption to state and local government-owned critical infrastructure could result in significant harm or loss of life, major public health issues, long term economic loss, and/or cascading disruptions and escalating impacts to other critical infrastructure.

## Structure

Due to their diversity and number, state and local governments tend to establish critical infrastructure programs to formalize their approach to achieving the security and resilience of infrastructure critical to their communities' sustainability. In addition, state and local agencies own and/or operate assets in several critical infrastructure sectors: Communications, Dams, Emergency Services, Energy, Government Facilities, Healthcare and Public Health, Transportation Systems, and Water and Wastewater Systems. The human, physical, and cyber assets in these sectors provide for many essential services necessary for a secure society, including government operations, energy and water utilities, education systems, public health, and emergency response. Risks to the ability for state and local government operators to provide these essential services include managing an all-hazards portfolio, operating in a resource-constrained environment, and needing to increase knowledge and awareness of critical infrastructure issues, tools, programs, and policies.[46] Despite their diversity, some common characteristics can generally describe state and local government critical infrastructure programs in terms of their location, staffing, priorities, and primary focus areas.[47]

State and local critical infrastructure programs continually struggle with issues that usually do not concern their federal and private sector counterparts. For instance, concerns about sustaining program operations contribute to decisions about program management, staffing, and priorities, particularly in light of reduced Homeland Security Grant Program funding nationwide, loss of Urban Area Security Initiative status for many jurisdictions, and constraints on state and local government budgets for competing priorities (many state and local government critical infrastructure program staff are located in Fusion Centers or maintain significant relationships with DHS Fusion Centers).[48]

Over time, state and local programs have shifted from single mission support (e.g. exclusively supported by emergency management) to joint mission support (e.g. supported by both emergency management and homeland security agencies) or to Fusion Centers and homeland security agencies, where programs are guided by the nature of the all-hazard mission of their home organization. In addition, many state and local programs are becoming more formalized and are located at the department level. For instance, California's critical infrastructure program now sits at the California Department of Homeland Security and Emergency Management.

## Staff

State and local critical infrastructure programs are staffed by government personnel rather than private contractors; however, the number of staff and their specific activities varies widely between jurisdictions. Many programs employ critical infrastructure directors or coordinators, who often maintain additional responsibilities, depending on their organizational location (e.g. managing broader homeland security, emergency management, and/or Fusion Center activities or agencies). More advanced and long-standing programs (typically for state and local regions with multiple major metropolitan areas, such as Texas) generally employ several dedicated personnel, including experienced critical infrastructure directors.

Minimally staffed programs (typically for fledging programs or jurisdictions with lower population density) have comparatively few, part-time personnel. Often, these programs manage additional priorities that compete for already scarce local resources. In addition to directors and coordinators, common state and local program personnel include planners who focus on developing and implementing strategic documents, and analysts that identify critical infrastructure, conduct risk and threat assessments, and analyze risk information.[49]

## Priorities

State and local critical infrastructure programs are driven primarily by lifeline sectors, economic drivers critical to their jurisdictions, threat information, mass gathering and special events, and dependencies and cascading effects among sectors. Currently, common constraints that affect these priorities include cybersecurity risks, increased frequency of extreme weather events, prevalence of mass gathering events, evolution of threats to soft targets, aging infrastructure, local and private sector risk management needs, and requirements from federal and other state and local agencies.

Critical elements of state and local critical infrastructure programs usually include implementing a partnership approach to security and resilience, sharing information with partners, and ensuring coordinated comprehensive risk identification and management. Primary activities of state and local critical infrastructure programs include:

- *Identifying Infrastructure*: Though some programs at the local level have a relatively long history of identifying and assessing critical infrastructure, near-term priorities change with the risk environment in which new, emerging threats influence the focus on types of infrastructure to identify and assess.

- *Assessing and Analyzing Risk*: State and local critical infrastructure assessment is a collaborative effort among state and local government, Fusion Center, and DHS IP personnel, with DHS Protective Security Advisors serving as highly valued and relied-upon sources of support.
- *Setting Goals and Objectives*: The majority of state and local programs have formalized program strategies by either developing stand-alone critical infrastructure strategic plans (often modeled on national programs) or incorporating critical infrastructure elements into an overarching homeland security strategy. Either approach requires periodic updating.[50]

### Assets

State and local government critical infrastructure consists of assets, systems, and networks composed of human, physical, and cyber components. The security and resilience of these components are addressed by the specific risk management methodologies implemented by the state and local government owners and operators of critical infrastructure. The human assets of critical infrastructure at the state and local level are also very important components. Millions of career and volunteer critical infrastructure practitioners actively serve every community in the United States. Considerable federal and private critical infrastructure often has state and local employees working to secure these assets.

Below is a summary from the State and Local SSP Annex to the NIPP of eight local critical infrastructure sectors and the role state and local governments play in securing them.[51] These sectors attempt to align themselves with the federal sectors discussed earlier in this chapter.

- *Communications*: State and local governments own, operate, and rely on a wide array of communications systems and equipment, especially for emergency response and recovery efforts (remember that state and local governments are almost always the first responders to natural disasters). Key examples include public alert systems, 911 centers, emergency operations centers, and associated equipment. Specific radio frequency spectrum bands (e.g. 400 and 800 megahertz), upon which Emergency Services Sector communications operations rely, are often only available to state and local governments. In addition, public and private sector communications assets are frequently co-located (e.g. privately owned communication towers may grant space to state and local-owned equipment). The coordination of such critical communication systems and equipment requires significant coordination among public and private sector stakeholders.[52]

- *Dams*: Approximately 25% of this sector's infrastructure is owned and operated by state and local governments, including thousands of small and medium-sized dams dispersed throughout the United States. Select regions and critical industries depend heavily on these assets for hydroelectric power, nuclear plant cooling water, water storage, and protection from catastrophic flooding.[53]

- *Emergency Services*: A majority of Emergency Services Sector personnel are state and local personnel and volunteers. State and local Emergency Services Sector operations provide the first line of defense for nearly all critical infrastructure sectors and the American public during natural disasters and other physical emergencies.[54]

- *Energy*: State and local government personnel operate public utilities for electricity and natural gas. State public utility commissions regulate utilities at the state level and are engaged in a variety of critical infrastructure activities (such as cost-recovery, energy supply curtailment plans, emergency response, and cybersecurity). Local governments comprise a large set of Energy Sector stakeholders, representing the interests of cities, towns and municipalities in sector security, protection, and emergency preparedness. Tribal agencies play significant roles in electricity transmission corridors, especially in the southwestern part of the United States, and in various energy supply resources, including coal and potentially the growth of wind and other renewable energy sources.[55]

- *Government Facilities*: State and local government facilities (e.g. city hall), including educational facilities, are a major component of this sector. Office buildings and government support facilities used for the storage and maintenance of physical or cyber assets are naturally critical to the secure operation of state and local governments. Public education facilities (e.g. public K-12 schools and public universities) are a very important part of American society overall.

- *Healthcare and Public Health*: Public health departments and agencies are critical portion of this Sector, including the purely state and local components that comprise millions of healthcare personnel, more than a thousand hospitals, hundreds of thousands of ambulatory services, thousands of nursing and residential care facilities, and state health insurers. Public health personnel and agencies are often the first responders to health emergencies (such as pandemics and infectious disease outbreaks) and are therefore actively engaged in health preparedness and response for the American public.

- *Transportation Systems*: A considerable portion of the U.S. transportation infrastructure is owned and operated by state and local governments, including large portions of highways, roads, bridges, railways, airports, and inland navigable waterways. Local jurisdictions are well-positioned to address specific transportation security needs and preparedness and response capabilities. In addition to providing safe transport of people and commerce, state and local departments of transportation are intricately involved in disaster preparedness, response, recovery, and mitigation with other critical infrastructure sectors (e.g. coordinating response fleet movements across jurisdictions and providing situational awareness of transportation capabilities) and in adaptation planning (e.g. conducting vulnerability assessments on climate impacts and adopting adaptation strategies).

- *Water and Wastewater Systems*: Public water utilities are operated by state and local government personnel, supporting and managing more than 150,000 public water systems (for drinking water) and more than 16,000 local government-owned treatment works (for wastewater) in the United States. These critical state and local professionals are deeply integrated into the security and resilience of this lifeline sector and are therefore very important contributors to the security and resilience other interconnected, independent sectors.

### Risks

Critical infrastructure owned and operated by state and local governments face risks from innumerable sources. "Risk" (as defined in Chapter 7) is the measure of a hazard's occurrence and/or a measure of the damage potentiality of a hazard occurrence. Below are several significant risk areas as outlined by the State and Local SSP Annex to the NIPP.[56] These risk areas encompass vulnerabilities to critical infrastructure and their associated risks, including the ability of state and local governments to ensure security and resilience in their jurisdiction. These risks develop from the complexity of managing all hazards, resource limitations, and the lack of knowledge or awareness of critical infrastructure issues, tools, and programs.

- *Physical Threats*: State and local governments are constantly threatened by physical attacks on their critical infrastructure. High profile state and local government facilities such as a city hall or government sports venues, as well as government-run services and systems, are frequent targets of those who wish to harm, impede, or sabotage local government or steal government property. Public utilities, which often are at least partially owned or controlled by local government, are targeted for extensive detrimental effect. The increasing use of unmanned drones presents a new risk, as these aircraft may be able to surpass common, established security systems. Emergency operations centers (often setup in the aftermath of a natural disaster) are physically connected to state and local government resources, and may be targeted to hinder emergency response and recovery efforts. Similar dependencies between state and local infrastructure and infrastructure owned by private actors as well as the federal government may be exploited.
- *Cyberthreats*: Examples discussed in Chapter 8 include phishing attempts, hacking, and use of outdated software to manipulate a system. These attempts are a rising and continually changing threat to cyber systems owned by state and local governments. Moreover, personnel throughout the cyber sector have varying degrees of cybersecurity knowledge and understanding of attacks. This is an area of growing concern for state and local governments because of the pervasive dependence on cyber infrastructure within state and local governments, as well as throughout the sectors. It is further complicated by the necessity of cybersecurity to go beyond securing stationary assets to securing mobile information systems needed during emergency response.
- *Natural Hazards*: As discussed elsewhere in this chapter, preparedness, response, and recovery to natural disasters is a primary state and local government responsibility. As natural disasters and weather hazards become

more frequent and intense due to climate change, a timely response and recovery by government entities will become more challenging, taxing already limited government resources.

- *Mass Gathering Events*: State and local venues host the majority of mass gatherings in cities, such as sporting events and concerts. As has been seen on numerous occasions (the 2017 Las Vegas shooting being a recent and notable example of this), mass gatherings also provide an ideal opportunity for those with harmful intent to potentially cause a great deal of damage to people and infrastructure. Active shooter events and violent extremism are a growing concern to state and local governments responsible for the safety and security of their citizens and first responders.

State and local governments also have to manage a number of risks in various broader subject areas. For instance, to manage the risk of cyberattack, state and local agencies consider a multitude of issues, many of which are classified as "unknowns" or are subject to knowledge deficiencies (i.e. staff does not understand technology). Although the cyber risk environment is individualized—based on each entity's security capabilities and infrastructure vulnerabilities—common cybersecurity issues are repeated across jurisdictions. These include cyber-physical system dependencies, increasing dependence on technology, potential cyber-vulnerability exploitation by nefarious actors, access control, information security deficiencies, and personnel and knowledge gaps. Two of the major cyber risk areas that state and local agencies focus on are information security and infrastructure system access control. Managing and securing the complex collection of personal, consumer, and financial information and controlling the access to that information and infrastructure are seen as priorities for governments and businesses alike.[57]

Soft targets are another risk area for state and local critical infrastructure personnel to pay attention to. **Soft targets** (unlike hardened facilities) are more vulnerable to attack because they allow for open access and have limited security barriers. Examples include banks, shopping malls, apartment buildings, houses of worship, and places of recreation and entertainment. The vulnerability of soft targets is a growing concern due to the comparative ease with which bad actors can compromise or execute these structures and evade pre-operational detection, efforts that may be more difficult to execute on hardened facilities. The increasing number of special events and mass gatherings around the U.S. (e.g. open access sporting events and parades) are of particular concern to state and local agencies that must prevent or mitigate risks in densely populated and accessible areas. Violent extremist threats from a range of violent extremist groups and individuals, including the domestic terrorist and homegrown violent extremist, further complicate the issue of soft-target security. Increasingly sophisticated use of the Internet, social media, and information technology by actors with nefarious intent adds an additional layer of complexity.[58]

Lastly, natural disasters, the most common incidents that state and local agencies manage, pose a unique risk for state and local agencies when the disaster threatens critical infrastructure. Frequent and extreme weather events can increase response demands, which may drain sector personnel, assets, and capabilities and may also threaten key services that enable a state and local response. In many cases natural disasters (such as a major hurricane) are not localized and may impact an entire region's infrastructure.

Whether resulting from natural hazards, technological hazards, or intentional acts such as terrorism—incidents like these can quickly expand beyond the local level and affect the entire United States. For example, biological agents or infectious disease can quickly spread through numerous jurisdictions and greatly strain state and local resources (such as local public health facilities, personnel, and supplies), impacting the health and safety of large numbers of public and first responders. The risk from such incidents is compounded by the challenge of containing incidents at the local level. The medical community, of which state and local public health departments and agencies are critical components, and state and local personnel must receive appropriate instruction and messaging on quarantine and isolation measures.

## Risk Management

We discuss risk management in the context of state and local government critical infrastructure responsibilities, but the content herein also applies to the work of the federal government and even the private sector. **Risk management** is an approach to making and implementing informed security and resilience decisions for physical, cyber, and human elements of critical infrastructure and is the cornerstone of the national effort to strengthen critical infrastructure security and resilience and is relevant at all levels of government. Risk management is the strategy employed to manage and ameliorate the risks discussed earlier. Vital to this effort are state and local government agencies that manage a wide range of risks through their critical infrastructure programs and activities. Their ability to make risk-informed decisions on the most effective solutions during crisis operations is important in ensuring security and resilience and reinforces the United States' economic, public health, and national security.

To manage the risks from significant threats and hazards to physical and cyber critical infrastructure, state and local government agencies embrace an integrated approach encompassing diverse public and private sector partners and conduct a variety of risk management activities. Across the United States, state and local critical infrastructure programs construct different priorities depending on the risk environment, underlying constraints, and risk tolerance. Risk tolerances can vary greatly, depending on the jurisdiction, organizational structure, resources, regulatory environments, and infrastructure criticality and dependencies.[59]

State and local emergency management agencies often establish formal programs with a critical infrastructure coordinator and develop strategic plans that are structured as a standalone plan or built into a homeland security or emergency management strategy. Common plan elements include topical

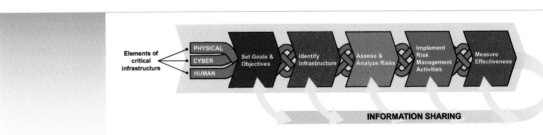

**FIG. 9.9**
Collaborating to manage risk includes five primary functions, each supported by a feedback loop facilitated by information-sharing.

*Source*: NIPP Risk Management Framework, www.dhs.gov/sites/default/files/publications/nipp-ssp-sltt-gcc-2015-508.pdf.

focus areas, asset identification and management, information sharing, building partnerships, and risk management program activities (e.g. training, exercises, and infrastructure assessments). States may formalize plans to provide a standard for local plans, provide templates and program technical assistance, or incorporate plan and program areas from other states. Some programs/plans decentralize critical infrastructure program implementation, shifting responsibility from the state to the local or regional level.[60]

Some states incorporate various localities and disciplines (such as homeland security, emergency management, emergency services, or intelligence analysis) into their planning efforts. This reflects the "all-hazards" approach discussed in Chapter 7 and includes building cross-agency relationships, establishing diverse working groups, building multidisciplinary strategy and assessment teams, or co-locating with or detailing personnel to another agency. Part of risk management also includes identifying critical assets, systems, and networks and then understanding their dependencies and interdependencies. Based on their unique risk environment, state and local agencies may view critical infrastructure differently than their federal and private sector counterparts. However, all agencies recognize the importance of a modern system or program to collect data to achieve risk-informed decision-making. State and local agencies use asset identification, collection tools, and leverage partnerships to contribute to the management of physical, cyber, and human assets.

Additionally, state and local agencies seek to identify dependencies, interdependencies, and cascading effects in order to comprehend the consequences of a disruption or attack on an asset, system, or network. To accomplish the identification of dependencies, state and local agencies significantly engage in information sharing with stakeholders across the critical infrastructure community, in addition to building relationships and partnerships across disciplines and jurisdictions. Agencies may also use exercises and trainings to identify key lifelines sector dependencies.[61]

## SIDEBAR 9.4 Assessing and Analyzing Risks to Critical Infrastructure

Critical infrastructure is often assessed in terms of threat, vulnerability, and consequence. State and local agencies perform critical infrastructure risk assessments to inform their risk management program decision-making using a broad range of methodologies. To fully understand the risk environment, state and local agencies utilize comprehensive risk assessment methodologies. State and local agencies also perform specific-purpose risk assessments, such as threat, vulnerability, and consequence assessments to better understand specific components of risk. To effectively assess risk, state and local agencies rely on timely, reliable, and actionable information regarding threats, vulnerability, and consequences.[62]

We define a **threat** in this context as the natural or manmade occurrence, individual, entity, or action that has harmed or indicates the potential to harm life, information, operations, the environment, and or/property. When assessing risk, the threat of an intentional hazard is estimated as the likelihood of an attack that accounts for both the intent and capability of the adversary. Threat assessments are the most frequent type of specific-purpose assessment utilized by state and local agencies. In assessing threats, agencies consider the full spectrum of intentional and unintentional threat sources, including natural hazards (e.g. hurricanes, fire, pandemics), technological hazards (e.g. power failure, train derailment, radiological release), and human-caused incidents (e.g. biological attack, cyber incident sabotage). State and local agencies recognize that threat assessments are most effective when applied to a specific geographic region, state, or locality, and threat source.[63]

Relatedly, a **vulnerability** is defined as the physical feature or operational attribute that renders an entity open to exploitation or susceptible to a given hazard, while a **consequence** is defined as the effect of an event, incident, or occurrence that reflects the level, duration, and nature of the loss resulting from the incident. Common consequences state and local agencies seek to understand include public health and safety, economic, psychological, and governance or mission impact.

## Implementing Risk Management Activities

Risk management activities are central to state and local critical infrastructure programs. By systematically conducting risk assessments to assess state and local assets, systems, and networks, state and local agencies are able to make informed decisions and increase the defensibility of resource allocation decisions. Agencies may prioritize risk management activities based on various elements, such as activity costs, potential for risk reduction, and varying levels of infrastructure criticality. All elements are shaped by the different views across jurisdictions and the unique risk environment. The following are various risk management activities state and local agencies conduct:

- *Assessments*: State and local agencies conduct a variety of assessments depending on the threat environment and are increasingly asked to conduct soft target security surveys and provide options for consideration to increase critical infrastructure security posture. Assessments can range from comprehensive (e.g. inclusive of threat, vulnerability, consequence, and dependencies) to specific purpose (e.g. threat only).
- *Training and Exercises*: State and local agencies not only undergo regular training to improve security capabilities (e.g. active shooter incident response), but they also sponsor robust training programs designed to improve the capabilities of public and private sector stakeholders. Trainings and exercises are typically conducted onsite; however, FEMA's Emergency Management Institute and public-private partnerships offer online critical infrastructure training. The most commonly deployed topical trainings and exercises include those related to cybersecurity, active shooter attacks, and natural hazard incidents.
- *Partnerships*: Ensuring security and resilience requires an engaged "whole of community" approach. This means that federal, state, and local governments, owners and operators of infrastructure, regional entities, non-profit organizations, and academia must all be involved together in protecting infrastructure. State and local agencies recognize the criticality of partnerships and continually make them a cornerstone of their programs. Partnerships provide subject matter experts, training programs, educational opportunities, information-sharing mechanisms, and a connection to the private sector.
- *Information-Sharing*: Information-sharing underlies all components of the risk management framework, facilitates collaborative problem-solving, and is critical to a common operating picture, particularly during expanding incidents or incidents that affect multiple jurisdictions simultaneously. State and local governments use several mechanisms to share information

with other critical infrastructure stakeholders. For instance, they may use secure online portals like the Homeland Security Information Network (HSIN). Fusion centers also work closely with state and local critical infrastructure personnel. Lastly, public-private partnership organizations like InfraGrad, government and private sector councils, working groups, ISACs, academic institutions, and interagency relationships also provide unique opportunities for two-way information sharing on hazards, threats, sector interdependencies, and best practices.

### SIDEBAR 9.5 Homeland Security Information Network (HSIN)

The Department of Homeland Security's standard mandate is to share critical law enforcement and national security-related information received by the federal government with state and local governments, law enforcement, and first responders so that they may be prepared to respond appropriately to a homeland security incident. To advance this mission, DHS runs the Homeland Security Information Network, which is an online information-sharing network that shares sensitive (but unclassified) information with local governments and the private sector (particularly those private sector partners that own or operate critical infrastructure) (Figure 9.10).[64]

An example of how HSIN can support critical infrastructure protection comes from the 2017 HSIN Annual Report:

#### HSIN Supports Fifth Consecutive Super Bowl

*Super Bowl LI marked the fifth consecutive year HSIN has provided real-time information sharing support for the NFL's championship game. The Houston Police Department used HSIN to collaborate and share information with partners from DHS, the FBI and other agencies during the event. Since 2013, HSIN has played a major role in the Super Bowl's planning stages and operational support by successfully providing real-time information sharing solutions. This ongoing work enables first responders to protect thousands of spectators and participants while they enjoy the largest and most watched public event in the world. Having demonstrated best practices, strategy and mature approaches for planning and support, HSIN's continued involvement with the Super Bowl has allowed host cities to see, first-hand, the enhanced and seamless collaboration HSIN can provide homeland security partners.*[65]

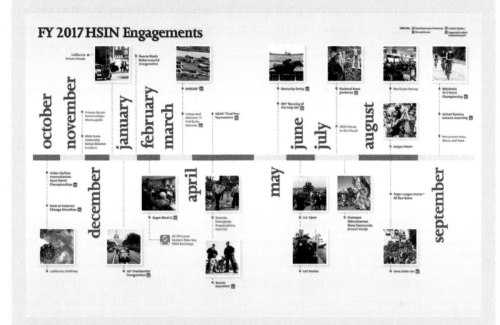

**FIG. 9.10**
Timeline of how HSIN has been used throughout 2017 by various government and private sector partners.

*Source*: HSIN Engagements, www.dhs.gov/xlibrary/hsin-annual-report-2017/hsin-at-a-glance/hsin-engagements.html.

## Measuring Effectiveness

Measurement efforts are an important step in the risk management process and facilitate the determination of effective investments, programs, and activities. Although not yet widely integrated throughout all the state and local critical infrastructure programs, some state and local agencies use a variety of indicators to measure the efficacy and continuous improvement of their security and resilience risk management activities. Performance measurement effort activities include reviewing program goals and tracking implementation, developing metrics for conducting assessments and follow-up visits, measuring outcomes related to capability targets identified through the jurisdiction's THIRA and State Preparedness Report, disseminating information products complete with a feedback form, hosting formal and informal discussions with sector partners on activity effectiveness, and conducting exercise after-action activities to share strengths and areas for improvement.[66]

### Resource Constraints

Unlike their federal government and private sector counterparts, state and local governments also operate under a significant number of constraints when seeking to secure their critical infrastructure. For instance, the continuity of state and local infrastructure programs and activities is constantly hindered by limited and diminishing resources (especially to maintain dedicated program personnel), predominantly as a result of inconsistent funding or loss of funding from federal critical infrastructure grants. This forces state and local governments to focus on highest-priority activities and restricts governments to being reactive rather than proactive. Program continuity is also threatened by the loss of knowledge due to the turnover of personnel (from changing local government administrations), including those at the federal level. Additionally, resource constraints limit the capacity for state and local programs to address the expansive portfolio of assets within a jurisdiction.[67]

There are also a number of constraints when state and local governments endeavor to build partnerships. Major challenges to sustaining public-private partnerships include time, resources, and personnel constraints limiting partnership outreach; the need to consistently deliver products and events that are highly valued by partners to secure consistent participation; and time between disasters leading to diminished participation (due to a sense of complacency). In addition, information security concerns and bidirectional information-sharing prohibitions may impact the flow of critical information to ensure full public and private sector knowledge of risks, capabilities, and mitigation efforts.[68]

**State and Local Government Coordination With Federal Partners**

The State, Local, Tribal and Territorial Government Coordinating Council (SLTTGCC) is run by DHS and serves as a forum to ensure that state and local homeland security partners are fully integrated as active participants in national critical infrastructure security and resilience efforts and to provide an organizational structure to coordinate across jurisdictions on state and local government-level guidance, strategies, and programs. The SLTTGCC also provides information on state and local government-level security and resilience initiatives, activities, and best practices.[69]

The primary functions of the SLTTGCC include:

- Providing senior-level, cross-jurisdictional strategic communications and coordination through partnership with DHS, the sector-specific agencies, and critical infrastructure owners and operators;
- Participating in planning efforts related to the development, implementation, update, and revision of the National Infrastructure Protection Plan (NIPP), Sector-Specific Plans (SSP), or aspects thereof;
- Coordinating strategic issues and issue management resolution among state, local, tribal, and territorial partners and federal departments and agencies;
- Coordinating with DHS to support efforts to plan, implement, and execute the nation's critical infrastructure protection mission; and
- Providing DHS with information on state, local, tribal, and territorial-level critical infrastructure protection initiatives, activities, and best practices.[70]

The SLTTGCC maintains a minimum of 25 representatives of state, local, tribal, and territorial governments who have critical infrastructure expertise and experience. Additional members may be nominated for inclusion on the SLTTGCC.

# ROLE OF PRIVATE SECTOR IN INFRASTRUCTURE PROTECTION

As discussed previously, over 80% of the critical infrastructure in the United States is owned by private owners and operators. Power grid operators, chemical plant workers, and IT service personnel are often the first to identify and respond to any threat to critical infrastructure. Thus, the first line of defense to critical infrastructure attack lies outside federal and state government control. DHS is responsible for coordinating a national protection strategy, including formation of government and private sector councils and working groups as a way to allow the private sector to collaborate with the federal government on critical infrastructure. These councils, among other things, identify the most critical private sector assets, assess the risks they face, and identify protective measures using sector-specific plans that comply with DHS' National Infrastructure Protection Plan (NIPP).

DHS' responsibilities in this area arise from Homeland Security Presidential Directive 7 (HSPD-7). This directive instructs sector-specific agencies to identify, prioritize, and coordinate the protection of critical infrastructure to prevent, deter, and mitigate the effects of attacks. HSPD-7 makes DHS responsible for, among other things, coordinating national critical infrastructure protection efforts and establishing uniform policies, approaches, guidelines, and methodologies for integrating federal infrastructure protection and risk management activities within and across sectors. HSPD-7 requires DHS to produce a national plan summarizing initiatives for sharing information, including providing threat warning data to state and local governments and the private sector. HSPD-7 also requires DHS to establish the appropriate systems, mechanisms, and procedures to share homeland security information (including information on critical infrastructure protection such as threat-warning data) with other federal departments and local governments and the private sector in a timely manner.[71]

According to the NIPP, additional DHS responsibilities regarding critical infrastructure protection include developing and implementing comprehensive risk-management programs and methodologies with private sector partners; developing cross-sector and cross-jurisdictional protection guidance; recommending risk management and performance criteria and metrics within and across sectors; and establishing structures to enhance the close cooperation between the private sector and government at all levels. As discussed earlier, the NIPP relies on a sector partnership model as the primary means of coordinating government and private sector critical infrastructure protection efforts. Under this model, each sector has both a government council and a private sector council to address sector-specific planning and coordination. Each council is to work in tandem to create the context, framework, and support for coordination and information-sharing activities required to implement and sustain that sector's critical infrastructure protection efforts. The council framework allows for the involvement of representatives from all levels of government and the private sector, so that collaboration and information sharing can occur to assess events accurately, formulate risk assessments, and determine appropriate protective measures.[72]

Under the model, critical asset owners and operators are encouraged to be involved in the creation of sector councils that are self-organized, self-run, and self-governed, with a spokesperson designated by the sector membership. Members of the sector councils are generally representative of the asset owners and operators within the sectors. Because some of the councils are newer than others, council activities vary based on the council's maturity and other characteristics, with some younger councils focusing on establishing council charters while more mature councils focus on developing protection strategies.[73]

Sector council membership varies, reflecting the unique composition of entities within each, but is generally representative of a broad base of owners, operators, and associations—both large and small—within a sector. For example, members of the drinking water and water treatment systems sector council include national organizations such as the American Water Works Association and the Association of Metropolitan Water Agencies and also members of these associations that are representatives of local entities, including Breezy Hill Water and Sewer Company and the City of Portland Bureau of Environmental Services. In addition, the commercial facilities sector council includes more than 200 representatives of individual companies spanning eight different subsectors, including public assembly facilities; sports leagues; resorts; lodging; outdoor events facilities; entertainment and media; real estate; and retail. According to sector council representatives, memberships generally represent the majority of private industries within each sector. This provides the councils opportunities to build the relationships needed to help ensure critical infrastructure protection efforts are comprehensive.[74]

Many sectors are exploring a relatively new DHS information sharing mechanism, the Homeland Security Information Network (HSIN). This network, in particular the portal for critical infrastructure protection called Critical Sectors (HSIN-CS), is a suite of tools that sector councils can use for information sharing, coordination, and communication about alerts, incidents, and planning efforts within the sector.

## CONCLUSION

Critical infrastructure protection is vital to our national security, economic vitality, and public health. Significant damage to critical infrastructure and key resources could disrupt the functioning of business and government alike, underscoring the need for the private and public sectors to take a coordinated approach to critical infrastructure protection. Yet the task of securing the dams, bridges, power plants, schools etc. that make up the nation's vast and growing infrastructure is difficult and complicated.

Though the government can offer membership in the coordinating councils, frameworks, and plans discussed in this chapter, these policies are useless if private sector owners and operators of critical infrastructure choose not to be involved in protecting their assets. One reason private sector cooperation with critical infrastructure becomes a challenging endeavor is due to the great cost that private owners and operators must incur in order to harden and protect soft targets and other critical infrastructure. These and other challenges remain on the horizon for homeland security experts in the growing subfield of critical infrastructure protection.

## HOMELAND SECURITY VOICES: Mark Camillo

*Mark Camillo is internationally recognized as a law enforcement and security professional, with exceptional expertise in the area of emergency preparedness operations. He currently serves as the Senior Vice President for Strategic Planning at Contemporary Services Corporation, and was recently named chair of the Public Assembly Facility Subsector Council. Camillo began his career as a Special Agent in the U.S. Secret Service, completing a distinguished 21-year career that included assignments at the White House, and advancing to the position of Deputy Assistant Director. Most notably he was appointed the Olympic Coordinator for the 2002 Salt Lake*

*Winter Olympics, directing the Secret Service to plan and implement the Federal operational security plan for the Games. Currently, Camillo is a member of several organizations, including the American Society of Industrial Security's Global Terrorism/International Crime Council, the International Association of Chiefs of Police, and Chair of the Board of Trustees for the Academy for Venue Safety and Security. He also serves as a senior fellow at George Mason University's Center for Infrastructure Protection.*

**FIG. 9.11**
Mark Camillo.
*Source*: Photograph provided by Mark Camillo

### What advice would you give students who would like to work in the homeland security field, particularly those who would like to work for the Secret Service?

MC: I would advise students to pay attention to their behavior before they even apply for any position. Prudent lifestyle choices are important when working in this field. If your lifestyle includes run-ins with law enforcement, drug abuse, or other outrageous behavior, then it will be difficult for you to obtain and maintain employment in homeland security-related positions. These kinds of behavior can make you vulnerable to blackmail and extortion or jeopardize an important case in the future. Identify role models who hold jobs you would one day like, watch how they behave, and try to emulate their good habits. Both before and after your employment in the homeland security field—when in doubt about whether you should engage in a certain kind of behavior, err on the side of caution. In today's social-media driven world, your actions can easily be taken out of context.

### Speaking of social media, what effect has the rise of social media had in the homeland security field?

MC: As Internet usage has continued to grow, discretion in communication has declined. People don't realize that emails, often written in haste and thought of as impermanent, can backfire—especially for defendants in criminal cases where email correspondence is increasingly used as evidence. Likewise, the instantaneous availability of information has led to an explosion of information, but you have to be careful that the information out there is accurate.

***Is the rise of the information economy and the Internet helpful or a hindrance to someone in your position?***

MC: It is tremendously helpful as long as you remain vigilant about vetting the information. In the Intelligence Community, you never know if the information you are considering in a case, for instance, has been deliberately released to mislead you. Social media and the Internet provide great tools for law enforcement work, but also considerable risk.

***What led to your career in the Secret Service and beyond?***

MC: Actually, my background is in teaching. I taught school for six years at an institute where I worked with hearing-impaired children. Learning American Sign Language helped me see the importance of breaking down perceived barriers in communication. Law enforcement organizations today cannot do their job effectively without maintaining an internal collaborative environment. There is more cross-communication than ever in law enforcement agencies today due to electronic mail and interdepartmental working groups.

The Secret Service has a statutory responsibility to investigate and suppress US counterfeit currency. My technical background in graphic arts and photography caught the attention of the Secret Service and I began my career working in the Philadelphia Field Office. I started as an entry-level Special Agent advancing to the Senior Executive Service position of Olympic Coordinator, where I was responsible for overseeing the federal security operations at the 2002 Salt Lake City Winter Olympics. Soon after, I was reassigned as the deputy special agent-in-charge of the Presidential Protective Division responsible for security operations at the White House complex where I remained until being reassigned to assist in the development and establishment of DHS. I finished my career as a Deputy Assistant Director, overseeing the Secret Service technology divisions. Though I am not an engineer, I understood the mission well enough to ensure that procuring technologies was done in an efficient and effective manner, and remained mission critical.

***What are the challenges you faced securing different facilities and structures?***

MC: Security and law enforcement are not synonymous. Law enforcement is responsive—when you have an incident or crisis, law enforcement personnel are first responders at the scene. On the other hand, security is mostly preventative. Good security operations are designed to detect, deny, and disrupt threats before they occur. At particularly high-profile events, such as the Olympics or important public buildings, such as the White House, the federal government often serves as the security lead. The Secret Service is responsible for designing, planning, and implementing the security operation in these locations. But they aren't the only agency working on security. Other federal agencies, such as DHS' Federal Protective Service as well as state and local organizations, work in concert to secure these locations and events.

The process is collaborative. We have a name for these kinds of security operations when applied to an event of national significance: In 1998 the federal government began calling them National Special Security Events (NSSE). Usually, the Secretary of Homeland Security in conjunction with the Attorney General designates an event as an NSSE and when they do so, the Secret Service, FBI, and FEMA begin working immediately with the event hosts and local public safety organizations and other stakeholders on a plan to secure the event. There have been over 40 NSSEs since 1998; the largest of these was the Salt Lake City Winter Olympics. Since Salt Lake, all other NSSEs have essentially utilized the same security model.

### *How does DHS determine whether an event will be classified as an NSSE?*

MC: The Department of Justice employs a Special Event Readiness Level (SERL) test when considering how many resources to bring towards securing an event. Historically, the Boston Marathon or the Super Bowl, with the exception of the 2002 game, had not met the criteria to be classified as an NSSE. However, as an event satisfies more of the determining risk factors, it can be elevated all the way up to SERL 1, which is classified as an NSSE. There are multiple elements that are weighed against an event to determine the degree of support it should receive from the federal government. Iconic events with a history of threats coupled with worldwide media attention will always be carefully considered for a NSSE designation. Strong local resources and capabilities may reduce the designation to a lower SERL rating.

SERL classifies all events on a scale from 1 to 4. The classification level determines how many resources are provided by the federal government in order to secure the event and how many federal government entities will be involved. It is important that any security plan emphasize both the prevention and crisis response aspects of security. Of course, the risk level determines the intensity of both the prevention and crisis response plans. And "risk" itself is determined by identifying in advance the vulnerabilities and threats present at each event.

### What organization comes up with best practices for securing an event?

MC: For a sporting event, it is often the sporting league, such as the National Hockey League (NHL) or the National Basketball Association (NBA). In other cases it may be trade groups such as the International Association of Venue Managers and the Stadium Managers Association. DHS' Office of Infrastructure Protection shares best practices on securing critical infrastructure with these groups.

### How does one go about encouraging implementation of best practices?

MC: First, venues should have facility managers that are skilled, open-minded, and willing to implement security practices.

It's also helpful if private venues have facility managers that are skilled, open-minded, and willing to implement security practices. Additionally, security and facility professionals need to constantly look for ways to increase their understanding of current threats. They have to be willing to argue with decision-makers regarding when upgrades and advancements to security procedures should be made. Today's threat is not necessarily tomorrow's threat. It is not a matter of if, but when. An emergency management plan should be part of every facility's toolkit; however, the plan doesn't have much value if it isn't exercised.

### How did you make the transition from the Secret Service to critical infrastructure protection?

MC: I went from the public sector (Secret Service) to the private sector (security industry). There are a lot of similarities and differences between the two and a lot of overlap. Remember that government agencies such as DHS aren't the only ones responsible for securing critical infrastructure. The venue, whether it be a stadium or a convention center, has the authority to decide how they would like threats to their facility to be addressed. Speaking broadly about my work on critical infrastructure: We try to use an all-hazards approach. Since I can't tell my clients when an attack might occur, I have to rely on informing my clients about how they can reduce the risk of an attack occurring. For instance, severe weather events cause a lot more damage to critical infrastructure than any other kind of threat—and prevention practices borne from an all-hazards approach are a lot more useful in preventing damage from severe weather events.

### Can you speak further on weather and its impact on critical infrastructure?

MC: Studies have concluded that most fatalities at sporting events occur as a result of weather-related events or other non-terrorist acts, such as structural collapse or fires. Though we are seeing a recent rise in active shooters and targeted violence in the country, weather-related events still cause by far the most damage. Casualties from single assailants in public places are not new—but as humans we tend to focus on them rather than on natural hazards such as hurricanes.

***Where do you think security is headed in the future? Where do you think it should be headed?***

MC: Security is headed to a kind of convergence—a blend of proven technologies, trained personnel, and proven best practices all coming together to secure a space—including cyberspace. Another upcoming trend is to protect associated venues that provide critical resources. For example, if someone can't enter your venue then maybe they can get to the venue's power source, water source, or transportation infrastructure. With cyber-driven attacks, securing a venue is becoming increasingly complicated and planners have to think outside the box.

## KEYWORDS

- **critical infrastructure**: The body of systems, networks, and assets that are so essential that their continued operation is required to ensure the security of a nation, its economy, and the health and well-being of its populace.

- **Internet of Things (IoT)**: Refers to the network of physical devices, vehicles, home appliances, and other items embedded with electronics, software, and sensors that allows them to connect to the Internet and exchange data.

- **soft targets**: Locations that are easily accessible to large numbers of people and that have limited security or protective measures in place, thus making them vulnerable to attack.

- **risk management**: An approach to making and implementing informed security and resilience decisions for physical, cyber, and human elements of critical infrastructure.

- **threat**: The natural or manmade occurrence, individual, entity, or action that has or indicates the potential to harm life, information, operations, the environment, and or/property.

- **vulnerability**: The physical feature or operational attribute that renders an entity open to exploitation or susceptible to a given hazard.

- **consequence**: The effect of an event, incident, or occurrence that reflects the level, duration, and nature of the loss resulting from an incident.

---

### KNOWLEDGE CHECK

1. How has the field of critical infrastructure protection changed meaningfully after 9/11?
2. Name at least eight critical infrastructure sectors and their importance to homeland security.
3. How are concepts of threat, vulnerability, and consequence different? How are they the same?

---

## NOTES

1. Margaret Rouse, *Critical infrastructure*, WHATIS.COM (last updated Mar. 2016) https://whatis.techtarget.com/definition/critical-infrastructure.
2. John D. Moteff, Cong. Research Serv. RL30153, Critical Infrastructures: Background, Policy and Implementation, at 1 (June 10, 2015) https://fas.org/sgp/crs/homesec/RL30153.pdf.
3. *Id.* at 2.
4. U.S. DEP'T OF HOMELAND SECURITY, NATIONAL STRATEGY FOR HOMELAND SECURITY, at 33 (July 2002) *available at* www.dhs.gov/sites/default/files/publications/nat-strat-hls-2002.pdf ("The plan will describe how to use all available policy instruments to raise the security of America's critical infrastructure and key assets to a prudent level. . . . In some cases the Department may seek legislation to create incentives for the private sector to adopt security measures. . . . In some cases, the federal government will need to rely on regulation.").
5. President's Commission on Critical Infrastructure Protection, Critical Foundations: Protecting America's Infrastructures (Oct. 1997) *available at* https://fas.org/sgp/library/pccip.pdf.
6. *See* The White House, Presidential Decision Directive 63: Critical Infrastructure Protection, (May 22, 1998) *available at* https://fas.org/irp/offdocs/pdd/pdd-63.htm.
7. John D. Moteff, Cong. Research Serv. RL30153, Critical Infrastructures: Background, Policy and Implementation, at 8 (June 10, 2015) https://fas.org/sgp/crs/homesec/RL30153.pdf.

8. Exec. Order No. 13,231, 86 Fed. Reg. 202 (Oct. 18, 2001) ("Critical Infrastructure Protection in the Information Age").

9. *Chemical Sector*, U.S. Dep't of Homeland Security (last visited Jan. 19, 2019) www.dhs.gov/chemical-sector.

10. *Communications Sector*, U.S. Dep't of Homeland Security (last visited Jan. 19, 2019) www.dhs.gov/communications-sector.

11. *Critical Manufacturing Sector*, U.S. Dep't of Homeland Security (last visited Jan. 19, 2019) www.dhs.gov/critical-manufacturing-sector.

12. *Id.*

13. *Dams Sector*, U.S. Dep't of Homeland Security (last visited Jan. 19, 2019) www.dhs.gov/cisa/dams-sector.

14. *Dams Sector*, U.S. Dep't of Homeland Security (last visited Jan. 19, 2019) www.dhs.gov/defense-industrial-base-sector.

15. Id.

16. *Emergency Services Sector*, U.S. Dep't of Homeland Security (last visited Jan. 19, 2019) www.dhs.gov/emergency-services-sector.

17. *Energy Sector*, U.S. Dep't of Homeland Security (last visited Jan. 19, 2019) www.dhs.gov/energy-sector.

18. *Id.*

19. *Id.*

20. U.S. Department of Homeland Security, Energy Sector-Specific Plan, at 5 (2015) www.dhs.gov/sites/default/files/publications/nipp-ssp-energy-2015-508.pdf.

21. *Financial Services Sector*, U.S. Dep't of Homeland Security (last visited Jan. 19, 2019) www.dhs.gov/financial-services-sector.

22. *Food and Agriculture Sector*, U.S. Dep't of Homeland Security (last visited Jan. 19, 2019) www.dhs.gov/food-and-agriculture-sector.

23. *Government Facilities Sector*, U.S. Dep't of Homeland Security (last visited Jan. 19, 2019) www.dhs.gov/government-facilities-sector.

24. *Healthcare and Public Health Sector*, U.S. Dep't of Homeland Security (last visited Jan. 19, 2019) www.dhs.gov/healthcare-public-health-sector.

25. *Information Technology Sector*, U.S. Dep't of Homeland Security (last visited Jan. 19, 2019) www.dhs.gov/information-technology-sector.

26. *Id.*

27. Ovidiu Vermesan & Peter Friess, Internet of Things: Converging Technologies for Smart Environments and Integrated Ecosystems (2013) *available at* www.internet-of-things-research.eu/pdf/Converging_Technologies_for_Smart_Environments_and_Integrated_Ecosystems_IERC_Book_Open_Access_2013.pdf.

28. *Information Technology Sector*, U.S. Dep't of Homeland Security (last visited Jan. 19, 2019) www.dhs.gov/information-technology-sector.

29. National Intelligence Council, Disruptive Civil Technologies: Six Technologies With Potential Impacts on U.S. Interests Out to 2025 (Apr. 2008) *available at* https://fas.org/irp/nic/disruptive.pdf.

30. *Id.* at 31.

31. *Nuclear Reactors, Materials, and Waste Sector*, U.S. Dep't of Homeland Security (last visited Jan. 19, 2019) www.dhs.gov/nuclear-reactors-materials-and-waste-sector.

32. *Transportation Systems Sector*, U.S. Dep't of Homeland Security (last visited Jan. 19, 2019) www.dhs.gov/transportation-systems-sector.

33. *Water and Wastewater Systems Sector*, U.S. Dep't of Homeland Security (last visited Jan. 19, 2019) www.dhs.gov/water-and-wastewater-systems-sector.

34. *Id.*

35. *Infrastructure Security Division*, U.S. Dep't of Homeland Security (last visited Jan. 19, 2019) www.dhs.gov/office-infrastructure-protection.

36. *Infrastructure Information Collection Division*, U.S. Dep't of Homeland Security (last visited Jan. 19, 2019) www.dhs.gov/iicd.

37. *Id.*

38. *Id.*

39. *Id.*

40. *Infrastructure Security Compliance Division*, U.S. Dep't of Homeland Security (last visited Jan. 19, 2019) www.dhs.gov/iscd.

41. *Chemical Facility Anti-Terrorism Standards (CFATS)*, U.S. Dep't of Homeland Security (last visited Jan. 19, 2019) www.dhs.gov/cisa/chemical-facility-anti-terrorism-standards.

42. *CFATS Covered Facilities and Inspections*, U.S. Dep't of Homeland Security (last visited Jan. 19, 2019) www.dhs.gov/cfats-covered-chemical-facilities.

43. *National Infrastructure Coordinating Center*, U.S. Dep't of Homeland Security (last visited Jan. 19, 2019) www.dhs.gov/national-infrastructure-coordinating-center.

44. *Protective Security Coordination Division*, U.S. Dep't of Homeland Security (last visited Jan. 19, 2019) www.dhs.gov/about-protective-security-coordination-division.

45. *Sector Outreach and Programs Division*, U.S. Dep't of Homeland Security (last visited Jan. 19, 2019) www.dhs.gov/sopd.

46. U.S. Dep't of Homeland Security, State, Local, Tribal, and Territorial Government Coordinating Council, at IV (2015) www.dhs.gov/sites/default/files/publications/nipp-ssp-sltt-gcc-2015-508.pdf.

47. *Id.* at 2.

48. *Id.* at 3.

49. *Id.*

50. *Id.*

51. U.S. Dep't of Homeland Security, State, Local, Tribal, and Territorial Government Coordinating Council, at 4–5 (2015) www.dhs.gov/sites/default/files/publications/nipp-ssp-sltt-gcc-2015-508.pdf.

52. *Id.* at 4.

53. *Id.*

54. *Id.*

55. *Id.*

56. *Id.* at 5–6.

57. U.S. Dep't of Homeland Security, State, Local, Tribal, and Territorial Government Coordinating Council, at 5–6 (2015) www.dhs.gov/sites/default/files/publications/nipp-ssp-sltt-gcc-2015-508.pdf.

58. *Id.* at 14.

59. U.S. Dep't of Homeland Security, State, Local, Tribal, and Territorial Government Coordinating Council, at 9 (2015) www.dhs.gov/sites/default/files/publications/nipp-ssp-sltt-gcc-2015-508.pdf.

60. *Id.* at 10.

61. *Id.* at 11.

62. *Id.*

63. *Id.*

64. *Homeland Security Information Network,* U.S. Dep't of Homeland Security (last visited Jan. 19, 2019) www.dhs.gov/what-hsin.

65. Homeland Security Information Network, 2017 Annual Report, at 17 (2017) *available at* www.dhs.gov/sites/default/files/publications/HSIN-2017-Annual-Report.pdf.

66. U.S. Dep't of Homeland Security, State, Local, Tribal, and Territorial Government Coordinating Council, at 13 (2015) www.dhs.gov/sites/default/files/publications/nipp-ssp-sltt-gcc-2015-508.pdf.

67. Id. at 5–6.

68. *Id.* at 6.

69. *Critical Infrastructure Sector Partnerships,* U.S. Dep't of Homeland Security (last visited Jan. 19, 2019) www.dhs.gov/critical-infrastructure-sector-partnerships.

70. *State, Local, Tribal, and Territorial Government Coordinating Council,* U.S. Dep't of Homeland Security (last visited Jan. 19, 2019) www.dhs.gov/sltt-gcc.

71. U.S. Gov't Accountability Office, GAO-07-39, Critical Infrastructure Protection: Progress Coordinating Government and Private Sector Efforts Varies by Sectors' Characteristics, at 11 (Oct. 2001) available at www.gao.gov/assets/260/252603.pdf.

72. *Id.* at 14.

73. *Id.* at 15.

74. *Id.* at 19.

# CHAPTER 10

# *Civil Rights, Civil Liberties, and Privacy*

---

**IN THIS CHAPTER YOU WILL LEARN ABOUT**

Basic civil and human rights protections such as the freedom of speech, freedom of religion, and freedom of the press.

How civil rights are affected by homeland security policy.

Homeland security policy arguments that result in perceived or actual diminishment of civil rights.

---

## INTRODUCTION

**Civil rights** and, more broadly, human rights, are sets of moral principles or norms that describe standards of human behavior. They are often practically expressed as laws and policies both obligatory on and protected by the government. Human rights are more appropriately understood as "inalienable" or fundamental rights that cannot be separated from the person. In other words, a person has the right to life, liberty, or safety merely because they are a human who exists. Thus, human rights apply to all humans irrespective of their nationality, language, religion, or ethnicity. On the other hand, civil rights are a more specific subset of human rights. They must take effect through the rule of law, i.e. in a statute or governing constitution. Thus, because the laws and people of each nation are different, civil rights protect a specific class or classes of people and differ from country to country. For instance, in the United States, the Second Amendment to the United States Constitution guarantees Americans the right to bear arms. This right to bear arms is unique to only a few other countries besides the United States.

Some examples of modern human rights would be the right to life, the right to free movement, the right to safety and security. Examples of civil rights, for instance, those found in the United States, would be the freedom of expression and speech, the right to vote, and the freedom to petition to government for grievances.

In this text we focus mostly on civil rights. Because homeland security is a vast discipline encompassing immigration, border security, natural hazards, transportation safety, and port security, among other issues—and because the field of civil rights law and policy is indeed even more complex, thinking about both areas simultaneously is an extraordinarily complicated enterprise. Issues of rights often "rub up" against issues of security. Some scholars view these two topics as balanced on a scale. This view holds that in order to increase security, a government must diminish the rights of the people it wishes to protect with that increased security. Other scholars see this as a false tradeoff and are of the view that additional security policies need not diminish the rights and privileges enjoyed by the population protected by these policies.

In this chapter, we examine the history of civil rights, and the relationship of civil rights to security and law enforcement in the U.S. The latter half of the chapter discusses several case studies that further explore the relationship between rights and homeland security in modern times. In doing so we attempt to assess both the "balanced scale" and "false tradeoff" frameworks outlined above.

## LIMITATIONS

It is important to note that in almost all cases, rights are not unlimited. Reasonable limitations are applied by law and policy to the expression of all human and civil rights. For instance, though Americans enjoy freedom from government interference in their speech, this right is not unlimited: All U.S.

law students learn that they are not protected from yelling "fire" in a crowded theater lest their exclamation cause a stampede and trample other patrons. In the United States, as in many other countries, speech is not protected if it causes imminent harm to another person, especially if the harm intended by the speech was intentional. Later parts of this chapter will explore some other limitations on speech and protections granted to certain kinds of speech such as political speech.

Human rights as moral principles, and then later as codified rules and laws, have been around since the dawn of civilization. As the idea of nation-states has become refined, so too have the laws that govern them, including human rights laws. The effectiveness of rights is often determined by the consistent application of the rule of law, and by extension the quality and character of the biases of legal and government institutions. Thus, the strength of human and civil rights laws is often mediated by institutional and structural discrimination, and furthered by racial equity and a recognition of identity-based privilege.

## THE DEVELOPMENT OF CIVIL RIGHTS

As originally ratified, the U.S. Constitution primarily addressed the structure of the government and provided for few individual liberties. Instead, these rights were set forth later in the Bill of Rights, comprised of the first ten amendments to the Constitution. A bill of rights was demanded by many states in return for ratification of the Constitution itself. Though the Constitution continues to undergo a process of formal amendment and interpretation by courts, the fundamental principles on which this country was founded remain at the core of this document more than 200 years later.

The Bill of Rights remained little more than an empty promise of individual freedom until 1803, when the U.S. Supreme Court held in *Marbury vs. Madison* that the Supreme Court had the authority to strike down legislation it found unconstitutional (Figure 10.1).[1] Even then, the Bill of Rights applied only to the federal government and failed to bind individual states until the late 1890s, when the Incorporation Doctrine began to take shape. Through a series of decisions beginning in 1897, the Supreme Court held that the

Fourteenth Amendment ensured that portions of the Bill of Rights were enforceable against the states and not just the federal government. Since then, the rights enshrined in the Bill of Rights have been progressively enumerated by the Supreme Court as worthy of constitutional protection irrespective of whether government interference is the result of state or federal action. These rights are said to be "incorporated" against the states through the Fourteenth Amendment.

A prominent and relatively recent example of this incorporation can be found in *Gideon v. Wainwright* where the Supreme Court unanimously held that states were required under the Sixth Amendment to provide counsel in criminal cases to represent defendants unable to afford their own attorneys.[2] The Gideon decision dramatically transformed the rights of indigent, low-income, and unsophisticated litigants throughout the country. The decision effectively created and then expanded the need for public defenders, which

**FIG. 10.1**
A quote from the U.S. Supreme Court case of *Marbury v. Madison* that enshrined the doctrine of judicial review.

*Source*: Swatjester, Quote from Marbury v. Madison at the U.S. Supreme Court Building, Washington, D.C., https://commons.wikimedia.org/wiki/File:Marbury_v_Madison_John_Marshall_by_Swatjester.jpg.

had previously been rare for non-federal cases. For example, immediately following the decision, the state of Florida required public defenders for all parties in each of the state's circuit courts.

Chief among the ten amendments is the first one. The First Amendment is primary for a reason: It bestows among the most comprehensive and expansive of rights upon the American polity. The First Amendment protects the free exercise of religion, the freedom of speech and the press, and the freedom to petition the government and assemble as a group to protest or express grievances. A discussion of the development of a few of the most important of these rights, the freedom of religion and the freedom of speech and the press, is instructive because these rights are foundational to the American ethos, due mostly to the circumstances of religious and state-sponsored persecution that spurred the creation of the United States. Understanding these specific rights is also important because they often end up being the subject of significant homeland security legal and policy disputes.

## Freedom of Religion

The First Amendment protects religious freedom in two ways: It forbids Congress from establishing a national religion (Establishment Clause) and prohibits Congress from passing any law that impedes the freedom of Americans to practice their faith however they wish (Free Exercise Clause). In general, both clauses proscribe governmental involvement with and interference in religious matters.

The freedom to practice a faith, or no faith at all, arose from the historical sense of persecution many American colonists felt under British rule. Up until the late Renaissance, almost every nation in Western Europe had an established and official church. Those Europeans who did not join the church were often denied rights, banished, jailed, tortured, or murdered. Some of these persecuted communities fled England and other nearby nations to become the first American colonists. During this time, wars driven by religious feuds were also common in mainland Europe. The Americas were seen as a refuge from these religious conflicts. It was natural then for many of the framers of the Constitution, such as Thomas Jefferson, to seek to wall off the excesses of a religious state by creating a "wall of separation between church and state."

Despite these noble intentions, in practice, religious freedom has not always been guaranteed in the United States. Throughout the 18th and 19th centuries, non-Protestants were often not seen as trustworthy leaders and "religious tests" were common for those who wanted to hold public office. Though the Constitution banned such tests for federal office, states were slow to implement non-discriminatory provisions and it wasn't until 1961 that the Supreme Court found Maryland's religious test for public office unconstitutional.[3]

Like other civil rights, the Supreme Court has placed freedom of religion on a spectrum of rights, from most protected to least protected. Given the United States' history, the "freedom to believe or not believe" is given the highest judicial deference, meaning that the government cannot interfere with a person's right to practice their faith, except in cases where the government must do so for extenuating circumstances outlined in caselaw. Despite these significant protections, the Supreme Court has drawn a distinction between religious belief and religious conduct. Unlike religious belief, religious conduct must occasionally yield to government interests. The Free Exercise Clause "embraces two concepts—freedom to believe and freedom to act. The first is absolute, but in the nature of things, the second cannot be."[4] In such instances, courts must consider both the government's interest in taking a particular action and the religious rights affected by that action. Only if the governmental interest in limiting conduct is "compelling" and if no alternative forms of regulation would serve that interest, can the individual asserting their rights be forced to yield.

More recently, the Supreme Court has gone so far as to uphold government action that affects religious conduct so long as the resulting restriction is not the purpose of the action but merely incidental to it. For instance, Oregon passed a law prohibiting the possession of *peyote*, a powerful hallucinogenic traditionally used in Native American religious rituals. Although the new law infringed on the religious conduct of Native Americans, the Supreme Court upheld the constitutionality of the law because the primary purpose of the law was to protect people from a harmful drug, not to target Native American religion. A few years later, however, a different decision was reached in a case involving the Santeria religion, which practices animal sacrifice. That case stemmed from a city ordinance passed in Hialeah, Florida, after city leaders learned a Santeria church was about to be established within city limits. The ordinance prohibited the "unnecessary killing of an animal in a public or private ritual ceremony not for the primary purpose of food consumption." The Supreme Court found the ordinance unconstitutional because it targeted the Santeria religion without a compelling reason to do so.[5]

As is often the case, when conflicting court decisions are not resolved by the Supreme Court, Congress can and does step in. In light of these divergent decisions on religious conduct, Congress decided to take action to safeguard long-held religious protections. In 1993, Congress passed the Religious Freedom Restoration Act, which restored the requirement that the federal government have a "compelling interest" before intruding in religious practices. The Supreme Court subsequently held that the law did not apply to states. To overcome this judicial decision, Congress then passed the Religious Land Use and Institutionalized Persons Act of 2000 (RLUIPA), which protects religious institutions from burdensome zoning law restrictions and protects inmates' rights to exercise religious practices. RLUIPA has most frequently been used to prevent local states and municipalities from discriminating against minority religious congregations by using zoning regulations in a discriminatory manner, often without the need for a lawsuit.

For instance, in Berkeley, Illinois a mosque had operated in a former school building on a 4.5-acre parcel for more than 20 years. The mosque sought to build a 13,000 square foot addition to accommodate its congregation (which had grown to the point that worshipers spilled into the hallways during services) and to make exterior changes to give the building a more mosque-like appearance, including adding a minaret. The expansion project faced community opposition and repeated permit denials. The Civil Rights Division of the Department of Justice opened an investigation under RLUIPA in 2007 and in March 2008, the city agreed to allow the mosque project to move forward.[6] Most recently, the First Amendment's religious freedom guarantees have been implicated in the form of a challenge to President Trump's "travel ban," which barred non-citizens from mostly majority Muslim countries entry into the United States. Challengers to the executive order asserted that the order "targeted Muslims for opprobrium, denigration, and discrimination based solely on their faith."

### Freedom of Speech and the Press

The First Amendment protects individual expression by guaranteeing the freedom of speech. The Supreme Court has broadly interpreted "speech" to include Internet communication, art, music, clothing, and even "**symbolic speech**," such as flag burning. Freedom of the press generally allows for newspapers, radio, television, and many online sources to publish articles and express opinions representing the public dialogue without interference or constraint by the government.

At the time it was written, the Constitution's First Amendment established one of the strongest standards for the guarantee of free speech worldwide. Although the First Amendment, as written, is rather absolute in its protection of free speech, those rights protected by the Bill of Rights required the promulgation of revised judicial standards over time (Figure 10.2). In the U.S., these standards evolved through decisions of the Supreme Court to expand freedom and reduce restrictions on the media and other means of expression. For example, slander and national security were traditionally common justifications for restricting speech until recent times.[7] Likewise, the freedom of the press was written into the Constitution primarily to allow an appropriate outlet for free expression. Unlike other nations, the U.S. does not police its press but nonetheless expects them to be responsible and inform the public on current events and important issues so that citizens can make sound decisions, such as which electoral candidates and ballot measures to support. In many ways, the media also provide a check on the government by asking questions of public officials that citizens may not be able to ask.

The First Amendment's free speech and freedom of press guarantees are seen as the cornerstone of the Bill of Rights and are generally premised on three deeply held beliefs by the original drafters of the Constitution. First, the belief that the government of the "people by the people" cannot exist without unfettered debate and disagreement within a free and open space that allows citizens to engage in self-government by using reason and practical judgment. Thus, because people communicate on political matters so that they can intelligently participate in the democratic process, without free speech, self-government becomes impossible.[8]

**FIG. 10.2**
The Bill of Rights protects freedom of speech, press, religion, and assembly, among many other rights. The document on permanent display in the National Archives Rotunda is the enrolled original Joint Resolution passed by Congress in 1789, proposing 12 amendments to the Constitution. The ten that were ratified became known as the Bill of Rights.

*Source*: Photograph, Original Bill of Rights on display at the National Archives.

Second, that the idea first articulated in Western thought by John Stuart Mill, and found later in the court's rationale in *Abrahms v. United States*, is that freedom of speech is important because, in a marketplace of ideas, the better ideas will eventually prevail through competition. Under this framework, one form of speech isn't more valuable than any other form of speech; rather, the value of speech depends on its popularity. This belief has important implications for the persistent homeland security issue of "hate speech." A belief that speech (and thus ideas) should compete in a marketplace of ideas gives rise to the uniquely American belief that even "hate speech" or offensive and abhorrent speech, is as protected as pleasant speech. Thus, in the United States, the best way to combat hate speech isn't for law enforcement to censor it, but instead to encourage the public to respond with "good speech." In a marketplace of ideas, the good speech should "win out" over hate speech.

---

**CRITICAL THINKING QUESTION**

After reading the section on Freedom of Speech and the Press, where would you draw the line on free speech? When does hate speech go from mere words to violent action? Would curbing hate speech, whether it's espousing violent overthrow of a nation, or violence against a religious minority, prevent the violent actions from that speech from coming to pass? How does today's national political climate affect your answer?

---

Lastly, the idea that free speech promotes every individual's self-fulfillment and autonomy was an important belief valued by the Founding Fathers. Under this rationale, non-political speech such as artistic expression is fully covered; as with the marketplace of ideas rationale, there is no hierarchy of speech. On the other hand, under this approach one wonders what is so special about freedom of speech inasmuch as other provisions of the Constitution (like substantive due process) similarly promote self-fulfillment and autonomy. None of these rationales capture the complexity of free speech issues or the actual free speech jurisprudence of the Supreme Court and the policies and regulations that are informed by that set of laws. [For example, the self-government rationale does not explain why artistic expression and scientific speech *Very complex* should be protected by the First Amendment. Similarly, the marketplace of ideas and self-fulfillment/individual autonomy rationales do not satisfactorily explain why obscene speech or child pornography are not protected by the First Amendment.] The inadequacy of these models highlights the fact that like other rights guaranteed in the Constitution, freedom of speech has its limits. For now, the Supreme Court has found that the First Amendment prohibits the state and federal government from restricting speech based on content or by imposing prior restraints on speech.

## SIDEBAR 10.1 Social Media and Hate Speech

**Hate speech** is speech that is meant to attack an individual, or a group on the basis of gender, race, ethnic origin, sexual orientation, disability, or other legally protected category. In some countries, hate speech is illegal, especially if it encourages the listener to take violent action against the subject of the speech. The U.S. does not have hate speech laws. The Supreme Court has repeatedly ruled that laws criminalizing hate speech, no matter how abhorrent this speech may be, violate the constitutional guarantee to freedom of speech (there are some categories that are not protected and they are discussed in elsewhere in this chapter).

The unregulated nature of hate speech has increasingly become a problem due to the proliferation of social media platforms such as Facebook, YouTube, and Twitter—all of which rely on free expression and user-created content to remain in business. Many terrorist organizations, such as ISIS, disseminate hate speech by publishing incendiary posts that act as subtle calls to action. Recently, these tactics have also been adopted by far-right and white supremacist organizations online. Though content analysis algorithms used by many social media companies attempt to capture and delete instances of hate speech, they are only intermittently successful.

Unregulated and intermittently policed hate speech is fast becoming a homeland security and law enforcement concern. Recent studies have found that individuals who frequently visit Facebook pages that include hate speech are much more likely to engage in unprovoked violent attacks against refugees and other foreigners.[9] The study notes that "wherever per-person Facebook use rose to one standard deviation above the national average, attacks on refugees increased by about 50 percent." The correlation between hate speech and violent acts holds true globally. For instance, in Myanmar, Facebook has been used for years to foment hatred against the Rohingya ethnic minority, contributing to their ongoing genocide.

Despite these rising homeland security concerns, hate speech remains difficult to police both technically and legally. For instance, in many cases the law itself protects social media and other communication companies, above and beyond the First Amendment's guarantee of free speech. One notable example is the Communications Decency Act, passed in 1996, which offers social-media platforms significant protections. The law states that:

> *No provider or user of an interactive computer service shall be treated as the publisher or speaker of any information provided by another information content provider.*

It also states that intermediaries don't lose their protection even if they moderate content. This means that platforms such as Facebook, Twitter, and YouTube are not liable for most of their user-generated content.

## Safety-Based Limitations on Speech

Broadly speaking, then, most forms of speech are protected by the First Amendment, but exceptions are made for speech that does not add to public debate or may cause harm. These exceptions include:

- *Obscenity* (though the laws in the United States regarding what is obscene are relatively progressive)
- *Defamation*
- *Incitement to violence*
- *"Fighting words"*
- *Harassment*
- *Privileged communications* such as those between an attorney and her client
- *Classified material* or other material critical for the national security of the nation
- *Copyright, patents, and trade secrets*
- *Military conduct*
- *Political speech*
- Some *commercial speech* such as advertising

*[handwritten margin note: Impedes on other rights? right to life & safety]*

Moreover, speech that is part of an act the law traditionally considers criminal is not protected by the First Amendment. For example, publishers cannot distribute magazines containing child pornography since the manufacturing, distribution, and possession of child pornography is illegal. In instances like this, protecting children from exploitation is deemed to be more important than any message provided in the magazine. Additional nuances exist that effectively act as limitations on speech. For instance, the First Amendment by its terms applies only to laws enacted by Congress and not to the actions of private persons (through interpretation of the Fourteenth Amendment, the prohibition extends to the states as well).[10] Therefore, social media companies such as Facebook or Twitter may freely limit the speech of their customers without legal consequence.

Another important limitation on speech is defamation, or speech that contains false or derogatory statements that injure a person's reputation. Defamation can occur though the spoken word (slander) or written communication (libel). Issues of defamation arise most frequently when public figures are involved.

The Supreme Court established the legal standard for libel, and by doing so, the limits of written speech, in the landmark case *New York Times Co. v.*

**FIG. 10.3**
Protestor in Washington, D.C., exercising her right to free speech and assembly in the wake of the 2016 U.S. presidential election.

*Source*: Rosemary Ketchum Under Pexels License, Protestor in Washington, D.C., www. pexels.com/photo/woman-holding-protest-sign-1464205/.

*Sullivan. New York Times* was not only a landmark freedom of speech case, but a case that further strengthened the freedom of the press in the United States.

## Other Important Constitutional Amendments

Other important amendments include: The Third Amendment, which stems from the anger the colonists felt when the King of England forced them to house military troops, even in times of peace. Although not a problem in recent times, the Supreme Court has held that the Third Amendment's prohibition against the quartering of soldiers, "in any house in time of peace without the consent of the owner," is the foundation of the right to privacy. Thus, while the Constitution does not specifically provide for a right to privacy, the First, Third, Fourth, and Fifth Amendments create "zones of privacy" around a citizen's property and person.

The Seventh Amendment protects the right to a jury trial in most federal civil lawsuits. The right to a jury trial was especially important to the framers of the Constitution, who felt unfairly treated by the British government, which often forced colonists to be tried by a single military judge. Both the Ninth and Tenth Amendment explain that if certain rights are not explicitly set forth in the Bill of Rights, they are retained by the people. Finally, the Fifth Amendment also protects the property rights of citizens by limiting the government's power of eminent domain, which is the government's right to take property (usually land) for public use. For example, if the government proposes to build a new highway where a house now stands, the government may legally take the land, but it must pay the homeowner the fair market value for the property.[11]

Despite these aforementioned rights, their application prior to modern times was laughably discriminatory. When the Declaration of Independence was signed in 1776, discriminatory treatment was rampant among different races, social classes, and genders. Since the founding of the United States, virtually every race and nationality has fallen victim to discriminatory treatment at one time or another. From the founding of the United States, reality did not reflect the rights guaranteed under the law. Despite "all men being equal," slavery was permissible in large parts of the United States. Moreover, the Constitution counted slaves as just three-fifths of a person. Slavery went on to plague political debate for decades and by the 1850s slavery had been eradicated in the northern states and the Northwest Territory but still thrived in the South. In 1857 the *Dred Scott* decision intensified the division between the states and contributed to the start of the Civil War.

The government's victory in the U.S. Civil War ensured the passage of the Thirteenth Amendment. Far more than ensuring an end to slavery, it ensured that no people, regardless of race or other characteristic, may be forced into labor against their will. Because of the Thirteenth Amendment's guarantee against forced labor, courts today generally refuse to require specific performance as a remedy for breach of a service contract. For example, if someone enters into a house-cleaning contract at a hotel but fails to follow through, the hotel may sue for breach of contract, but the court most likely will impose financial damages rather than order the individual to complete the house-cleaning tasks.

Following the civil rights movement of the 1950s and 1960s, the Supreme Court validated Congress' power under the Thirteenth Amendment to enact civil rights legislation that prohibited private racial discrimination. In *Jones v. Alfred H. Mayer Company* (1968), a real estate developer refused to sell housing or property to African Americans. An African-American couple sued the developer under a federal law mandating all U.S. citizens the same property rights as white citizens. The Supreme Court upheld the law, ruling that Congress has the power to enact laws that directly affect the acts of individuals, thereby making the Thirteenth Amendment the first and only constitutional provision applicable to private citizens as well as to the state and federal government.

## CIVIL RIGHTS IN THE MODERN ERA

Although the Thirteenth Amendment to the Constitution and other laws passed after the Civil War guaranteed equal rights to all Americans, many U.S. citizens—especially African Americans—still experienced discrimination and segregation on a wide scale. Southern states passed "**Jim Crow**" laws, which required African Americans and white people to be separated in most public places, such as schools or restaurants. African Americans had to ride in the back of buses and use separate public restrooms.

In the North, African Americans could vote, and segregation was less notice-able, but prejudice still restricted opportunities for them. From an early time, many Americans objected to the unfair treatment of African Americans, and in 1909, a group of mostly African-Americans founded the National Associa-tion for the Advancement of Colored People (NAACP). The NAACP worked through the courts to challenge laws and customs that denied African Ameri-cans their constitutional rights. In 1910, other concerned citizens formed the National Urban League to help African Americans find jobs and reach eco-nomic parity with other Americans. These and other groups built a civil rights movement supported by millions of people across the United States.

In 1948, President Harry Truman ordered an end to segregation in the nation's armed forces; and in 1954, the Supreme Court ruled in favor of NAACP lawyers in *Brown v. Board of Education*, deeming racial segregation in public schools unconstitutional under the Fourteenth Amendment's equal protection principle. In the 1950s, Dr. Martin Luther King, Jr., a Baptist min-ister and a central leader in the civil rights movement, inspired others to join the movement through marches, boycotts, and demonstrations that expressed non-violent resistance to and peaceful protest of discriminatory laws and practices. Some African-American students participated in "sit-ins" at lunch counters reserved for white people, while other African Americans, along with many white citizens, teamed up as "Freedom Riders" to ride buses together throughout the South to protest segregation. On August 23, 1963, more than 200,000 people marched in Washington, D.C., to demand equal rights regardless of skin color. Finally, in 1964, Congress listened to the demands of the people and passed the Civil Rights Act, which prohibited dis-crimination in public facilities, employment, education, and voter registra-tion based on race, color, gender, religion, and national origin. Then in 1965, the Voting Rights Act was enacted, further ensuring that minorities gained equal access to the polls.[12]

This broad period from the end of World War II until the late 1960s is often referred to as the "Second Reconstruction," a time when grassroots move-ments, coupled with gradual but progressive actions by elected leaders and the judiciary, granted all Americans full political rights (at least in name).

This "Second Reconstruction" and the civil rights movement that arose before, during, and after Dr. King's passing encouraged the passage of statutes expanding the application of constitutional amendments in other, more modern, areas of public life. State and federal statutes passed throughout the 1950s and 1960s addressed civil rights in the context of education, employment, housing, and most importantly for our purpose, law enforcement.

These statutes typically outline the scope of the penalties and remedies against interference with the right, and often create a government agency or office (such as the Equal Employment Opportunity Commission or EEOC) to enforce the right through investigation, penalties, and prosecution.

## RIGHTS VS. SECURITY

The remainder of this chapter discusses several case studies that compare how civil rights are or may be affected by homeland security law and policy.

As is evident from the earlier portions of this chapter, the concerns regarding threats to civil rights often arise during, in the immediate aftermath of, and for some time after a conflict or imminent threat to the territorial integrity of the United States. When the U.S. finds itself threatened, lay leaders often seek to curb liberties in order to make the work of managing a crisis easier. U.S. history is replete with instances where elected representatives have found the diminishment of rights and liberties to be an effective way of securing the nation. Arguably, in some cases, these efforts have resulted in dissatisfaction, litigation, rebellion, and even violent conflict.

These periods of history, of which the 9/11 attack and its aftermath is one, follow a familiar 10-step pattern:

1. An unprecedented and sudden attack occurs on U.S. soil or against U.S. persons or assets;
2. The population becomes fearful of another similar attack;
3. Precipitated by the desire to diminish fear and prevent another domestic attack, political leaders such as the President and Congress pass laws to secure the nation;
4. These laws often seek to make it easier for law enforcement, the armed forces, and national and homeland security agencies to do their job. They also seek to make it difficult for the enemies of the U.S. to determine the methods and sources of U.S. efforts to counter them;

5. Because fear and uncertainty, as well as feelings of camaraderie and patriotism, are much higher in the immediate aftermath of the crisis, these measures are embraced by the public and indeed are often quite popular. For instance, less than two weeks after the attacks on 9/11, the PATRIOT ACT passed the Senate by a vote of 98 to 1;

6. As time passes, the public may begin to chafe at some of the limitations these laws present, usually because these laws also curtail civil rights and civil liberties as a way to achieve homeland security objectives. As time passes, civil society actors who were once sympathetic to security measures in the immediate aftermath of a crisis begin calling for these security measures to end and for the restoration of civil rights and liberties as they existed prior to the crisis;

7. Nonetheless, "rolling" back new laws and security measures remains a long, slow, and sometimes impossible process because those calling for roll-back may be seen as "traitors" to the country or as those who would sell the safety of the nation in return for additional, ephemeral freedoms;

8. Likewise, political leaders, often fearful that they may be blamed if another crisis were to occur once these security measures are removed, continue to present these laws and security measures as practical necessities; unflinching support of these security measures comes to be seen as a sacrosanct patriotic duty;

9. Concomitantly, the machinery of the state and judicial system works actively to stifle deliberation of these laws in the name of security. For instance, lawsuits brought to challenge the diminishment of civil rights are often thrown out because the evidence to challenge civil rights violations is often classified and cannot be aired in court. Likewise, Freedom of Information Act (FOIA) requests to obtain such evidence from public government records is often not turned over or when it is, the evidence is often heavily redacted; and

10. Thus, it is often decades, if ever, that the civil rights and civil liberties status quo returns to a pre-crisis era. For civil rights to advance in the name of security imperatives usually requires another crisis or a charismatic figure, such as Dr. Martin Luther King, to rally a dispirited and frustrated populace to call for change.

## FIG. 10.4

Examples of when the 10-step cycle response to conflict has occurred throughout the history of the United States.

| THREAT | RESPONSE | DIMINISHMENT |
|---|---|---|
| **U.S. Civil War** (1861-65) | President Abraham Lincoln suspended the writ of habeas corpus. | Suspending the writ removed a prisoner's ability to contest their detention by the government and effectively allowed for indefinite detention without cause until Lincoln lifted the suspension. |
| **World War I** (1914 -18) | Congress passed a number of laws such as the Espionage Act of 1917 and the Sedition Act of 1918. | These laws served to silence dissent. Newspapers were censored and politicians who criticized the government were jailed. War protestors were arrested by federal officials. |
| **World War II** (1939 – 45) | President Franklin Roosevelt issues Executive Order 9066 | Executive Order 9066 resulted in the forced removal and detention of Japanese - Americans (almost all of them U.S. citizens) solely on the basis of their ethnicity in internment camps across the U.S. for several years. |
| **Cold War** (1948 – 91) | Senator Joseph McCarthy institutes hearings on communists; Congress ramps up the work of the House Un - American Activities Committee and passes related legislation. | McCarthy's efforts and those of others like him in the government led to a series of government -affiliated and sponsored suspicion -less witch hunts against suspected communists, often destroying the personal lives and careers of thousands of innocent Americans. |
| **9/11, War in Afghanistan, Iraq War** (2001 – Present) | Congress passes a series of measures including the Patriot Act. | The Patriot Act and oth er related measures altered freedoms in a number of ways including allowing the government to bypass warrant protections for obtaining personal information; conducting suspicion -less searches and monitoring the personal communications of American citizens without a warrant. |

This pattern of threat, countermeasure, and diminishment of civil rights is a hallmark of U.S. history as well as national and homeland security policy. Balancing the desire for safety and security with the guaranteed rights that comprise a free state can be a complex undertaking (though this chapter presents arguments later that it need not be). Figure 10.4 shows several examples of when the 10-step cycle above has occurred throughout the history of the United States, outlining briefly the threat encountered by the country, the government's response to the threat, and the resulting diminishment in civil rights laws that occurred (only to be withdrawn slower than the initial imposition of the law itself).

Thus, in times of grave threat, the U.S. has not always lived up to its ideals. Scholars argue that the post-9/11 era in which we now live is one of these times.

As earlier chapters in this text show, 9/11 and the legislative, policy, and military actions thereafter radically transformed the country, resulting in the largest reorganization of the federal government since World War II. Moreover, the attacks resulted in the passage of new laws such as the PATRIOT ACT, the Aviation Security Act, and the Homeland Security Act. Many of these laws, especially the PATRIOT ACT, contained several controversial counterterrorism measures, some of which arguably diminished the privacy rights of American citizens. Anticipating advocacy against these measures by civil society, Congress mandated the creation of DHS' Office for Civil Rights and Civil Liberties and the DHS Office of Privacy when DHS was created. Nonetheless, questions continue to surface about the efficacy of congressional measures to protect civil rights in a post-9/11 policy landscape. We examine these questions using several case studies below.

## RIGHTS VS. SECURITY: CASE STUDIES

### Countering Violent Extremism and the Freedom of Religion

Because of its domestic nature, issues surrounding the freedom of religion arise more frequently in homeland security than in national security (which is limited to work done overseas to protect the territorial integrity of the

United States; see Chapter 1 for a discussion on the differences between these two concepts). As the "supreme law of the land," the Constitution usually applies in its entirety to most homeland security policy areas. Thus, though the federal government is not obligated to respect the rights foreign citizens, it is obligated to respect those of U.S. citizens as outlined in the Constitution.

In the aftermath of 9/11, the U.S. government sought several ways to counter the rise of extremism and radicalization. In particular, it sought to interdict those groups like al-Qa'ida and ISIS that began recruiting individuals in the U.S. to commit terrorist attacks on U.S. soil to further these groups' political goals. This recruitment did and continues to take place online through various websites, particularly social media channels such as YouTube and Facebook as well as the Dark Web. The Dark Web is Internet content that exists on websites and services that require special software and authorization to access and is not available through searches on popular search engines (defined further in Chapter 8).

Though the majority of individuals recruited or "radicalized" through these means often did not end up committing any acts of terror, some did. For instance, on May 5, 2010 Faisal Shahzad (the "Times Square Bomber") attempted to detonate an explosive in New York's Times Square. Two American Muslim street vendors alerted NYPD after they spotted smoke coming from Shahzad's vehicle. NYPD discovered that a bomb had been ignited but failed to explode. Incidents like these convinced the U.S. homeland security establishment that 1) terrorist recruitment online was a threat to the U.S. and needed to be countered and 2) aside from "hard" counterterrorism measures such as intelligence gathering and law enforcement investigations, local communities and affinity groups such as the street vendors who spotted Shahzad needed to be recruited to counter online radicalization efforts by terrorist groups.

These insights led to the development of a national strategy and Strategic Implementation Plan (SIP) for countering violent extremism (often referred to as "CVE"—the acronym also refers to the set of programs that arose as a result of the SIP). Though there are a number of definitions, the government broadly defines **violent extremism** as "ideologically, religious, or politically motivated acts of violence" perpetrated inside the United states by white supremacists, anti-government groups, and "radical Islamist entities," such as the Islamic State of Iraq (ISIS)[13] as well as by groups with extreme views on abortion, animal rights, the environment, and federal ownership of public lands.[14]

Primarily led by the Departments of Homeland Security (DHS) and Justice (DOJ) through an interagency task force, the federal government's leadership in CVE efforts is aimed at educating and providing resources to communities

**FIG. 10.5**
Each circle or octagon represents a single attack with the size measuring the number of fatalities. The Extremist Crime Database (ECDB) is a database that includes information on publicly known violent crimes committed in the United States by radical Islamist violent extremists, the violent far right, and far left violent extremists from 1990 through 2015. For 2016, attacks resulting in homicides by ideological violent extremists in the United States were provided to us by email updates from ECDB researchers. The ECDB includes information on the incidents themselves, as well as their perpetrators, related organizations, and victims. There were no attacks since 1990 by persons associated with extreme leftist ideologies that resulted in fatalities to non-perpetrators.

*Source*: Attacks in the United States by Domestic Violent Extremists from September 12, 2001 through December 31, 2016, GAO-17–300, www.gao.gov/assets/690/683984.pdf.

for preventing violent extremist acts. The activities outlined in the SIP are aimed at enhancing the ability of local law enforcement, community organizations (such as religious, educational, and non-profit entities) to provide information and resources to communities targeted by violent extremists for recruitment, as well as for individuals who may have started down a road to violent extremism. These activities generally aim to provide alternative messages and options to terrorists or violent extremist recruitment and radicalization efforts through civic engagement. In this way, these federal efforts mimic local law enforcement community gang intervention efforts.

The SIP defines the federal government approach to CVE as "proactive solutions to counter efforts by extremists to recruit, radicalize, and mobilize followers to violence."[15] The SIP approach is premised on three foundational concepts:

1. Empowering communities and civil society to fight terrorism;
2. Encouraging or directly creating messaging and counter-messaging; and
3. Addressing the causes and drivers that lead someone down the path to violent extremism.

Thus, the federal CVE effort encompasses preventative aspects of counterterrorism as well as interventions to undermine the attraction of violent extremist movements and ideologies that seek to promote violence. For instance, under the SIP the federal government works to support community efforts to disrupt radicalization processes before an individual engages in criminal activity. This may involve meeting with the community's lay or religious leaders or the vulnerable individual's peers or sharing information in outreach activities between law enforcement and community members. For example, the FBI aims to provide tools and resources to communities to help them identify social workers and mental health professionals who can help support at-risk individuals and prevent them from becoming radicalized. Details on what "community" is being engaged on these issues is sparse, but largely these efforts are targeted towards the American Muslim community.[16]

It is these interventions that begin to present thorny issues surrounding the First Amendment's guarantee of the freedom of religion. For instance, civil liberties experts argue that when American government officials intervene in the free exercise of religion, by "telling" communities that the appropriate version of their religion (peace-loving, non-confrontational) is acceptable and that another version (radical, confrontational, polemic) is not acceptable, they create legal and policy problems.[17] In a seminal *New York Times* article and later academic work, Sam Rascoff points to two stories of CVE efforts that highlight this problem. In one, John Brennan, President Obama's top advisor on counterterrorism, speaks to members of an American Muslim law student group and outlines the U.S. government's position on *jihad*, an Islamic religious term that literally means "holy struggle" in Arabic. In another story, Rascoff outlines how someone who has received federal funds to engage in "counter-messaging" only speaks to those American Muslim leaders the federal government finds "acceptable" rather than those it does not, for fear of not receiving of continued federal funds.[18]

Why are these behaviors a potential problem? Remember from earlier in this chapter that the First Amendment prohibits government action, "respecting an establishment of religion." Though challenging violent extremist ideologies and narratives is ostensibly good for homeland security,

> The problem is that when American officials intervene in Islamic teachings— interpreting them to believers in a national-security context and saying which are or are not acceptable—they create tensions, both legal and strategic.[19]

For instance, is the government really the credible authority on the interpretation of Islam? Unlikely. Rascoff argues that interpretations of religious beliefs are ideas best left to religious scholars. When the government seeks to determine what a contested concept (such as *jihad*) within a religion such as Islam means, or which religious leaders have the right to speak for a particular religious community, they violate the Constitution's rule that a secular state shall not become the decider of religious content. As discussed earlier in this chapter, this "separation of church and state" has deep roots in American history. The framers of the First Amendment were wary of the government's ability to control the church or other religious institutions. Many American colonists had left Great Britain and surrounding nations because they saw how the British Monarchy used the Church of England to stifle dissent.

Rascoff, and other scholars like him, argue that the government violates not only the Founding Fathers' belief in the separation of church and state, but also the First Amendment when, beyond playing the role of theologian through official pronouncements on contested concepts like jihad, the government inappropriately serves as missionary when it looks to convert would-be radicals and backs up its efforts with taxpayer-financed outreach.

This is primarily because CVE programs go beyond the government's clear legal authority to address concrete threats to public safety (discussed in the many other chapters in this text) and instead places secular officials in the "dubious enterprise" of sharing the beliefs, however noble, of American Muslims.

Does this imply that the government cannot have conversations with religious communities regarding radicalization? Not really. Similar to the many other case studies that arise when rights contend with security, the answers often require forethought, resources, nuance, and most importantly, trust. One solution Rascoff and others propose is for the federal government to completely extricate itself from discussing the tenets of religion and merely offer funding to reputable religious organizations and let them determine how best to identify and counter-message radical elements in its community.[20] This would mean that sometimes the message may not be what the federal government wants to hear, but as any civil libertarian would say, "disappointment is sometimes the price for freedom."

Another solution, and one that was belatedly implemented by the federal government in recent years, would be to diversify engagement not only with American Muslims, but other violent extremist groups, such as white supremacists and eco-terrorists. The fact that the federal government chooses to engage with American Muslims over and beyond any other group, even when self-professed members of this community only commit 9% of all terrorist attacks in the U.S., highlights another bias of the federal government and another potential freedom of religion issue.

## SIDEBAR 10.2 Violent Extremism

This chapter discusses civil rights issues, particularly those related to the freedom of religion, that arise when the government attempts to counter violent extremism. Here, we discuss how the FBI defines the foundational concept of violent extremism.

The FBI defines violent extremism as "encouraging, condoning, justifying, or supporting the commission of a violent act to achieve political, ideological, religious, social or economic goals."[21] Violent extremists often use propaganda, such as misleading or biased information, that supports a particular point of view, to trick people into believing their ideologies. Propaganda isn't just a tool used by violent extremists; governments employ this tool, often during wartime, to convince populations to support one side or another. The goal of propaganda is to create a compelling narrative that viewers and listeners may buy into.

Violent extremist propaganda can be found anywhere, but violent extremists today often use online tools like email, social media, and webpages on the Dark Web. According to the FBI, extremist groups and individuals often appear in communities struggling with social or political issues. Rather than improving these situations or their own lives through constructive actions, violent extremists often place the blame on another person or group. They argue that the only solution to these problems or injustices is to violently oppose and even destroy those they claim are responsible. The FBI refers to this as the "Blame Game" where placing blame is an effective way to recruit people with feelings of frustration and turn them into a group united by a sense of purpose. It enables violent extremists to invent an "enemy" that must be destroyed. This makes violence seem like the best solution and perhaps even a moral duty.

The FBI notes that violent extremists can be driven by "twisted beliefs and values" tied to political, religious, economic, or social goals. For example:

- Many violent extremist ideologies are based on the hatred of another race, religion, ethnicity, gender, or country.
- Violent extremists often think that their beliefs or way of life is under attack and that extreme violence is the only solution to their frustrations and problems.
- Despite what they sometimes say, violent extremists often do not believe in fundamental American values like democracy, human rights, tolerance, and inclusion.
- Violent extremists twist religious teachings and other beliefs to support their own goals.

The FBI notes that violent extremists leverage the power of groups to achieve their goals. Groups can be a powerful way to bring people together to achieve common goals. "Groupthink" happens, however, when those in the group stop stating their opinions or using critical thinking because they wish to avoid conflict. This can result in poor decision-making. Violent extremist organizations are highly vulnerable to groupthink. They are often led by a strong leader who is rarely challenged. Ideas different from those espoused by this leader are not accepted. Violent extremist groups also often work in secret, not only because their activities and plans are often illegal, but also because they wish to keep contrary opinions from influencing their narrative.

According to the FBI no single reason explains why people become violent extremists, but the transition to violence often happens when someone is trying to fill a deep or personal need. For example, a person may feel alone or lack meaning or purpose in life. Those who are emotionally upset after a stressful event may also be vulnerable to recruitment. Some people also become violent extremists because they disagree with government policy, hate certain types of people, don't feel valued or appreciated by society, or think they have limited chances to succeed.

Violent extremists have joined many popular social networking sites that let a user share pictures and personal information. On these sites, violent extremists create fake profiles and look for people who are vulnerable to recruitment. Violent extremists also spread propaganda on these sites through videos, pictures, and messages that glorify their causes. Violent extremists are also now using popular smartphone applications, or apps, that keep a person's identity and conversations totally private. On these apps, violent extremists may ask for money or share secret information. They may even start fake romances to trick teens into traveling to other countries to join them.

### CRITICAL THINKING QUESTION

Why do you think the security program discussed earlier is called Countering *Violent* Extremism? Why not call the program Countering Extremism instead? Based on what you have read in this chapter, why do you think adding the word "violent" is important or necessary?

### War Reporting and the Freedom of the Press

In the United States, the press and media enjoy near limitless freedom to operate and create content without government regulation. As noted earlier in this chapter, this freedom arises from the U.S. Constitution and the Founding Fathers' desire to create a bulwark to the excesses of the state. When criticized for their zeal in pursuing the truth, journalists often embody this ethos and respond that the "people have a right to know" as a justification for publishing controversial information.

In the days following 9/11, then Attorney General John Ashcroft said that criticism by the media of the Bush administration "only aids terrorists" and "gives ammunition to America's enemies." Then White House Press Secretary Ari Fleischer warned that "all Americans need to watch what they say and what they do." Television executives were often told that the government preferred they not air videos from terrorists like Osama bin Laden (and later ISIS) because these could contain code messages to other terrorists.[22]

Statements like these sparked widespread concern in the U.S. media establishment of increasing indirect restrictions on the freedom of the press. These concerns have only intensified after the ascension of the Trump Administration, which often directly attacks the press and its right to publish material, even material that criticizes government homeland security policy. Moreover, since 9/11 legal efforts to compel journalists to reveal confidential government sources are prevalent, and without a federal law shielding reporters, journalists facing a federal subpoena confront going to jail if they refuse to reveal their confidential sources. On the other side, those national and homeland security employees that leak information to the press, especially classified information, irrespective of whether they believe there is a good reason for doing so, may be imprisoned.[23] In another example of diminishing press freedoms, during its military operations overseas in Iraq and Afghanistan, the U.S. military detained journalists without charge for long periods. Related criticisms of the government's efforts to stamp out press freedom were allegations that the military failed to adequately investigate the documentation of the killings of 16 journalists by U.S. forces "friendly" fire.[24]

The examples above do not show a direct restraint by the government on the freedom of the press. Nonetheless, these indirect pressures often have a cumulative effect of diminishing the ability of the press to do its work. This is often referred to as a "**chilling effect**" on freedoms, such as those of the press and the freedom of speech, among others. For instance, when a reporter fears that the President will criticize her directly on national media for asking a question, or when a network executive fears that sharing vital information may aid those who seek to harm the U.S., however unlikely the chance, both these individuals are "chilled" or discouraged from conducting reporting they otherwise would have. The federal government is the largest organization in the United States, and the homeland security and national security establishment is this government's largest and most well-funded constituent part. Its workings are shrouded in mystery and secrecy. Though secrecy is often necessary in order to conduct the kind of security efforts outlined earlier in this text, oversight of this work is also necessary to prevent abuses of power, which tend to happen more frequently in secret.

## Right to Privacy

On September 18, 2017, the Department of Homeland Security proposed a new policy that would further interpret the Privacy Act of 1974 in an expansive way. Specifically, when asking for data from those seeking immigration benefits (such as a visa, or citizenship status) DHS argued that the Privacy Act allowed for the collection not only of biodata such as the name, age and birthdate of the applicant . . . but also for the collection of social media handles and relevant information from social media accounts.[25]

Specifically, DHS proposed to update the system and method of the collection of this information in the "A-File," which is the official record system of the U.S. government for holding and tracking information related to an individual's application for immigration benefits. The A-File is used in immigration proceedings before Department of Justice (DOJ) immigration judges and the Board of Immigration Appeals (BIA), and is the official record used in Federal court litigation and other official agency business transactions. Though USCIS, ICE, and CBP create and use information that is added to the A-File, USCIS is the official custodian of the A-File and the documents contained within it.

DHS also noted that

> Consistent with DHS' information sharing mission, information stored in the A-File system would be shared with other DHS components that have a need to know the information to carry out their national security, law enforcement, immigration, intelligence or other homeland security functions.[26]

Prior to October 18, 2018, DHS collected identifiable biodata and voluntarily disclosed information that was collected. The new proposed policy would begin collecting information from all publicly available social media accounts, as well as any "associated identifiable information and search results" deemed "relevant" to an individual's application for immigration benefits.[27] The information would come from "publicly available information obtained from the internet, public records, public institutions, interviewees, and commercial data providers." The information wouldn't just be collected on those applying

**FIG. 10.6** User-generated data online via social media apps is increasingly subject to government surveillance.

*Source*: Pexels, Social Media Apps on a Mobile Device, www.pexels.com/photo/apps-blur-button-close-up-267350/.

for immigration benefits, but also those naturalized U.S. citizens who had previously applied for and been granted U.S. citizenship.

These new policy proposals set off alarms among U.S. privacy watchdog groups and lawyers who expressed concerns about how DHS would use the information collected. A summary of the questions raised by privacy experts shows how changing homeland security public policy can have wide-ranging implications for privacy rights:

- *How long would the social media information be stored?* People change and information about individuals used a decade later to reach decisions about immigration status doesn't necessarily reflect the same person currently applying for those benefits.
- *What kinds of information would be collected?* Who defines what social media content is relevant to an immigration application? Social media information often doesn't reflect the life individuals lead, but the lives they want others to think they lead. Would DHS' policies take account of the unreliable and often contradictory nature of social media information? What if someone was denied an immigration benefit on the basis of social media information that was faulty? How would they know they were denied on this basis? Would they be able to appeal the decision and provide accurate information?
- *How would the information collected be secure from hackers and foreign agents?* This is especially a concern given that the U.S. government's information collection system for security clearances was hacked in 2015. Moreover, the FBI and other homeland security-related agencies have found that foreign powers such as Russia and China have often infiltrated U.S. government systems to collect information on individuals and used this information to influence political campaigns (as noted in Chapter 8).
- *What other agencies would have access to the information?* In the field of data privacy this is called the "**secondary use**" problem. Secondary (or third etc.) use of data occurs when data is used for purposes other than those for which it was originally collected. For instance, would the social media data that would be collected by DHS to assess immigration benefits be used later to determine that same person's fitness to obtain a security clearance if they ever applied for a federal job? Or to obtain a gun permit? The secondary

use problem sheds light on a greater issue: The constructive creation of a "**dossier**" or a collection of documents about a particular person that attempts to paint a picture of that individual. Would social media information collected for purpose A and then used to assess that person for purposes B, C, and so on, essentially a create a "file" on that person that the government could use to judge this individual in all their interactions with the government?

- *Would the social media information be used to adjudicate other crimes?* What if social media information in an applicant's profile contains evidence that they engaged in horseplay and arson several years back? Arson is a crime, and the government is obliged to act upon any evidence of a crime it receives. Presumably this evidence would be turned over to local law enforcement to begin an investigation and prosecution for the crime. Privacy advocates fear that social media collection for immigration benefits gives law enforcement a gateway to collect immense amounts of potentially incriminating information without a warrant (and thus avoiding the Fourth Amendment's constitutional protections). These "dragnet" searches are exactly what the Fourth Amendment and other similar laws were drafted to prevent.

- *What if the applicant for immigration benefits (such as a visa) declined to share their social media handles etc., on the application?* Would this limit their ability to obtain the benefit? What if the applicant is older and doesn't remember or understand how to list their social media handles? What if they have an account and forget to list it on the application? Would their application be penalized because of their mistake?

- *Would knowledge that social media data would be collected alter the way applicants express themselves online and thus wouldn't the government be limiting their free speech rights?* This kind of indirect limitation on speech is referred to as a "chilling effect" on free speech discussed earlier.

- *What about the information of non-applicants, such as U.S. citizens, that would undoubtedly be collected due to the "shared" nature of social media?* For instance, what if a U.S. citizen wrote something on an immigrant applicant's Facebook "wall"? Would this information also be collected? U.S. citizens usually enjoy higher privacy protections than those applying for immigration benefits who are not U.S. citizens, and this kind of data collection would certainly violate some of those privacy rights. This is the same issue that occurred when the National Security Agency (NSA) sought to collect telephonic and other data on non-U.S. persons, but in the process also captured a large amount of data on U.S. persons as well.

The list of privacy issues continues and cannot be resolved in this text, but should give the reader an understanding of the significant concerns that arise when the government seeks to collect information and use it to make all kinds of decisions such as whether to adjudicate benefits or make decisions about awarding security clearance, or permits to protest on federal property.

## SIDEBAR 10.3 Third-Parties and Data Collection

Below is a transcript from a video from Google that details how the company handles requests for user data from state, local, and federal law enforcement agencies.[28] Do you find their methods to be effective? Do you feel that your personal information is protected from unnecessary intrusion by state, local, and federal government?

*Transcript*

In the course of a criminal investigation, sometimes the government requests information on Google users. Here's how we protect users' information from excessive requests, while also following the law.

Let's say the federal authorities want information from Google about user "HughDunnit22." Google protects your rights by upholding the Fourth Amendment. The law requires authorities to use a search warrant when seeking private content—like email. If there's enough evidence to support an application for a search warrant, the Investigator heads to court.

The Judge inspects the application, and if satisfied, issues a search warrant.

Then it's served on Google. First stop? The Screener. The Screener sorts and prioritizes search warrants. If it's an urgent matter like child safety, it's given high priority. Next stop—the Producer. The Producer examines warrants and protects users by catching errors and determining what information to provide.

They fix glitches so we don't access someone else's account. Sometimes they're illegible, or the user name is misspelled. Or the request is meant for a different company.

Sometimes, the data request is so vague and broad we have to go back, narrow it down, and play catch up. So, we'll get a hold of investigators to narrow the warrant or go back to court to ask the Judge to amend the warrant.

If legal and appropriate, Google notifies the user that law enforcement made a data request. And looks closely at the warrant, to see exactly what data to produce.

Say the FBI wants all information and content on HughDunnit22's account.

We'll need to clarify.

Below Dialogue's list is not available in APL style, hence we treated as SbarUL list, please check and confirm.

PRODUCER: *Hey it's Google, about that warrant.*

INVESTIGATOR: *Yep.*

PRODUCER: *You need everything for all services?*

INVESTIGATOR: *Yep.*

PRODUCER: *Gmail, YouTube, Photos—*

INVESTIGATOR: *Everything.*

That's a lot of information that may not have anything to do with the case. So, we'll look to narrow the warrant.

PRODUCER: *This sounds like a case where only email from the last month matters. How about we go with that?*

INVESTIGATOR: *Ok. That'll do.*

We can then move forward. We then gather the information, carefully and accurately. Done. Data is then sent to Investigators, along with a Certificate of Authenticity. Matter closed for good? Not yet. We may need to show up in court and present the data. A Producer may serve as Custodian of Records. The Custodian of Records travels and appears in court. They may travel to authenticate the records, verifying that the data is exactly what Google provided.

JUDGE: *The records are hereby admitted into evidence. Have a nice flight back.*

Matter closed.

Let's recap. The Judge signs the warrant. The Screener sorts it. Producer takes over. Oops there's a problem. Wrong company. Wrong user. Vague request? Broad request? Go back and play catch up. Whoa!

> Narrow the scope, okay, time to gather data, gathering, double-checking. . .
> Deliver the data. Now hand it over to the Custodian. He flies to court, authenticates, matter closed. That's how we respond to a US search warrant, while working hard to protect our users' privacy and security.

## RIGHTS VS. SECURITY: ARGUMENTS AND FALLACIES

The case studies as well as the 10-step pattern shown earlier in Figure 10.4 highlights the United States' long and sometimes unfortunate history of reacting to crisis by diminishing civil rights. In each instance, despite ample historical evidence that showed how these policies did not necessarily enhance security, the U.S. nonetheless chose to abridge civil rights in the name of increased security. Often, these rationales are posed as tradeoffs or arguments. We discuss some of them here:

### Small Price to Pay Argument

Beyond some of the rationale discussed in the 10-step process, those Americans who seek to challenge crisis-based security restrictions on constitutional freedoms are often asked to consider the relative weight of the freedom (argued to be small and only valuable for the individual) versus the relative gain in security and safety for society (argued to be large and valuable to all of society or a specific community). The argument goes something like this: "We all have to make sacrifices during a time of war. Some of these sacrifices may include forgoing your right to trial or limiting your speech against the government. These are only temporary restrictions and minor compared to the very real danger of bodily harm or death to oneself, their community, or the entire nation. Thus, an individual diminishment in rights is a small price to pay for a large gain in societal security." A related corollary to this argument is the assurance that once the crisis or wartime effort is over, the government will restore the freedom lost as a result of the threat or crisis.

The U.S. Supreme Court made a similar argument in *Korematsu v. U.S.*, the case that upheld the forcible removal and suspicion-less imprisonment of Japanese-Americans merely because of their ethnicity when the Court noted that "hardships are part of war, and war is an aggregation of hardships."[29] In *Korematsu* the Supreme Court upheld the constitutionality of Executive Order 9066, which ordered that Japanese Americans be forcibly removed from their homes and imprisoned in camps across the U.S. throughout the duration of World War II without cause, and regardless of citizenship.[30] The Court's rationale in ruling against Japanese Americans was that the government's need to protect the nation against espionage outweighed the rights of Japanese Americans. As in similar historical Supreme Court cases that most Americans now find reprehensible (such as the *Dred Scott* decision, which held that African-Americans were three-fifths of a white man), the U.S. government has since conceded the error of its legal defense against this practice. In 2011, the Department of Justice filed an official notice conceding that the Solicitor General's defense of the government's internment policy at the time had been in error.[31]

It is important to note that the "small price to pay" argument is not limited to the United States and arises most often in circumstances surrounding crises that shift national perception of a threat, often with the implicit or explicit support of various governments. These governments often promote a sense of hysteria by exaggeration, manipulation, and distortion of information. The goal of the government in fostering such public anxiety may be either to make it easier for it to gain public acceptance of measures it seeks to impose or to gain partisan political advantage, or both.[32]

---

**CALL-OUT BOX:**
*Korematsu v. U.S.* **Excerpts**

> *Korematsu v. United States* was a landmark Supreme Court case concerning the constitutionality of Executive Order 9066, which ordered the forcible removal and detention of Japanese Americans into internment camps throughout World War II. In *Korematsu*, the court sided with the government's decision to imprison Japanese-Americans on the basis of their ethnicity and without any

specific suspicion. Below are excerpts from the case setting forth the rationale and arguments from both the majority (the law) as well as a concurrence with the majority and then dissenting arguments from the minority.

The legal precedent v established remains highly controversial and has been repeatedly repudiated by legal scholars.

Majority opinion:

> *Korematsu was not excluded from the Military Area because of hostility to him or his race. He was excluded because we are at war with the Japanese Empire, because the properly constituted military authorities feared an invasion of our West Coast and felt constrained to take proper security measures, because they decided that the military urgency of the situation demanded that all citizens of Japanese ancestry be segregated from the West Coast temporarily, and, finally, because Congress, reposing its confidence in this time of war in our military leaders—as inevitably it must—determined that they should have the power to do just this.*[33]

> —Justice Hugo Black

Concurrence (agreement) with majority:

> *According to my reading of Civilian Exclusion Order No. 34, it was an offense for Korematsu to be found in Military Area No. 1, the territory wherein he was previously living, except within the bounds of the established Assembly Center of that area. Even though the various orders issued by General DeWitt be deemed a comprehensive code of instructions, their tenor is clear, and not contradictory. They put upon Korematsu the obligation to leave Military Area No. 1, but only by the method prescribed in the instructions, i.e. by reporting to the Assembly Center. I am unable to see how the legal considerations that led to the decision in Hirabayashi v. United States, fail to sustain the military order which made the conduct now in controversy a crime. And so I join in the opinion of the Court, but should like to add a few words of my own.*

> *The provisions of the Constitution which confer on the Congress and the President powers to enable this country to wage war are as much part of the Constitution as provisions looking to a nation at peace. And we have had recent occasion to quote approvingly the statement of former Chief Justice Hughes that the war power of the Government is "the power to wage war successfully". Therefore, the validity of action under the war power must be judged wholly in the context of war. That*

*action is not to be stigmatized as lawless because like action in times of peace would be lawless. To talk about a military order that expresses an allowable judgment of war needs by those entrusted with the duty of conducting war as "an unconstitutional order" is to suffuse a part of the Constitution with an atmosphere of unconstitutionality. The respective spheres of action of military authorities and of judges are, of course, very different. But, within their sphere, military authorities are no more outside the bounds of obedience to the Constitution than are judges within theirs. "The war power of the United States, like its other powers . . . is subject to applicable constitutional limitations". To recognize that military orders are "reasonably expedient military precautions" in time of war, and yet to deny them constitutional legitimacy, makes of the Constitution an instrument for dialectic subtleties not reasonably to be attributed to the hard-headed Framers, of whom a majority had had actual participation in war.*

*If a military order such as that under review does not transcend the means appropriate for conducting war, such action by the military is as constitutional as would be any authorized action by the Interstate Commerce Commission within the limits of the constitutional power to regulate commerce. And, being an exercise of the war power explicitly granted by the Constitution for safeguarding the national life by prosecuting war effectively, I find nothing in the Constitution which denies to Congress the power to enforce such a valid military order by making its violation an offense triable in the civil courts. To find that the Constitution does not forbid the military measures now complained of does not carry with it approval of that which Congress and the Executive did. That is their business, not ours.*

— Justice Felix Frankfurter

Dissent (disagreement with the majority opinion):

*I dissent, therefore, from this legalization of racism. Racial discrimination in any form and in any degree has no justifiable part whatever in our democratic way of life. It is unattractive in any setting, but it is utterly revolting among a free people who have embraced the principles set forth in the Constitution of the United States. All residents of this nation are kin in some way by blood or culture to a foreign land. Yet they are primarily and necessarily a part of the new and distinct civilization of the United States. They must, accordingly, be treated at all times as the heirs of the American experiment, and as entitled to all the rights and free-doms guaranteed by the Constitution.*

— Justice Frank Murphy

Dissent (disagreement with the majority opinion)

*Korematsu was born on our soil, of parents born in Japan. The Consti-tution makes him a citizen of the United States by nativity and a citizen of California by residence. No claim is made that he is not loyal to this country. There is no suggestion that apart from the matter involved here he is not law abiding and well disposed. Korematsu, however, has been convicted of an act not commonly a crime. It consists merely of being pres-ent in the state whereof he is a citizen, near the place where he was born, and where all his life he has lived. . . . His crime would result, not from anything he did, said, or thought, different than they, but only in that he was born of different racial stock. Now, if any fundamental assumption underlies our system, it is that guilt is personal and not inheritable. Even if all of one's antecedents had been convicted of treason, the Constitution forbids its penalties to be visited upon him. But here is an attempt to make an otherwise innocent act a crime merely because this prisoner is the son of parents as to whom he had no choice, and belongs to a race from which there is no way to resign. If Congress in peace-time legislation should enact such a criminal law, I should suppose this Court would refuse to enforce it.*

— Justice Robert Jackson

## CRITICAL THINKING QUESTION

Read the Call-Out Box on the *Korematsu* case. What do you think of the Supreme Court's argument in *Korematsu*? Do you believe that some crises, such as the attack by Japan on the United States at Pearl Harbor, are so grave that American civil rights and civil liberties should be diminished or eliminated to keep everyone safe? What about the argument that the detention of Japanese-Americans was only temporary and that when they were returned they suffered only a few years of inconvenience? What about the opposite argument that only soldiers sign up for "hardships" and not innocent American citizens? How would your answer change, if at all, when you consider that the laws made at the time of the Japanese-American internment, were made not by minorities, dissidents, or anyone resembling those who were imprisoned?

## The All-or-Nothing Fallacy

Daniel Solove, a privacy expert at George Washington University's School of Law, discusses another fallacy in his work that he terms the "All-or-Nothing Fallacy," and describes as such in the context of the specific right to privacy:

> The All-or-Nothing Fallacy is the view that privacy and security are mutually exclusive—that any increase in privacy is a decrease in security and vice versa. People often ask whether we want a particular security measure or privacy. After the NSA surveillance program was brought to light—a program that involved warrantless wiretapping of phone calls by American citizens in violation of a federal statute—pollsters asked: "Should the NSA engage in surveillance in the war against terrorism?" Most people said yes. But the question was cast incorrectly. The question assumed that security and privacy were all or nothing. We could either have the NSA engaging in surveillance and being protected against terrorism or have privacy and be left exposed and unprotected. Of course most people said yes to the surveillance. But protecting privacy doesn't mean no government surveillance. Protecting privacy doesn't mean that a security measure must be scrapped. Under the Fourth Amendment and various privacy laws, the government can engage in searches and surveillance. Privacy is protected by judicial oversight and by requiring the government to justify its activities. For example, the Fourth Amendment even allows the government to enter and search a person's home with a warrant and probable cause. So we shouldn't ask "Do you want the government searching people's homes?" The question is wrongly put. With regard to the NSA surveillance, the question should have been: "Do you want the NSA to engage in surveillance in the war on terrorism without a warrant, probable cause, or any judicial oversight or do you prefer the NSA to engage in such surveillance with a warrant, probable cause, or some form of judicial oversight?[34]

Thus, this logical fallacy fails to assume other alternative middle grounds between the government's duty and desire to protect the public and the public's right to certain protections from government overreach. Answering this question appropriately often leads to an easy compromise between rights and security, e.g. surveillance, but with the use of appropriate warrants.

### Nothing-to-Hide Argument

Solove also attacks the validity of the Nothing-to-Hide Argument, which posits that an individual need not worry about sharing information with the government if they have "nothing to hide" from the government. In undercutting this argument, Solove notes that privacy, like all other rights, often has value beyond its primarily understood meaning. For instance, privacy isn't just about keeping dirty secrets or hiding bad things from the government. Privacy as a concept may involve many different yet related things such as the right to know about how your data is being used and having the ability to correct errors about that data or keep it secure and prevent fraud and identity theft.

There are good reasons law-abiding citizens want to maintain privacy about certain things even they are not embarrassing or disgraceful. Even having done nothing wrong, individuals may want privacy about certain things because they don't want to have to justify their actions or explain their behavior to government officials. In his 2013 documentary *Terms and Conditions May Apply*, filmmaker Cullen Hoback discusses the case of a screenwriter in Los Angeles who spent considerable time researching how to murder homeland security officials in LA. His search history, viewed without context, presents a specific and dangerous threat to homeland security. The additional context not available is that his Google searches reflect attempts to research scenes for upcoming episodes of his cold-case murder television show. Nonetheless, despite his innocent purpose, he has a desire to keep this search history private, because viewed without context (such as without a warrant and particularized suspicion), this search history portrays the screenwriter as a terrorist rather than as a professional researching a series of episodes.

## CONCLUSION

This chapter introduced some of the many challenges that exist when attempting to balance the government's obligation to ensure civil liberties with its obligation to also secure the nation. There are far too many challenges to discuss in one chapter, but the case studies presented herein should provide the reader with a basic understanding of the depth and scope of the challenges civil rights lawyers, both inside and outside the government, deal with when assessing new security policies.

There has often been a tension between rights and security, though some now argue that this tradeoff is a false one. While the U.S. has often taken politically popular but morally reprehensible actions, such as the internment of Japanese Americans during World War II, it has also learned from its mistakes and the collective security establishment has endeavored to do better. For instance, particular attention was paid after 9/11 to protecting the rights of American Muslims who, it was feared, would be targets of misdirected anger against the 9/11 hijackers. President George Bush continued to clarify that American Muslims "were not the enemy" but that al-Qa'ida was. The few sparse calls for the wholesale internment of American Muslims were shot down immediately and new government departments such as DHS were staffed with robust civil rights and privacy offices.

Nonetheless, the threat to civil rights still remains, and by some estimates the tide is turning. Recently, the federal government has attempted to limit the entry of individuals from several Muslim-majority countries into the United States (often referred to as the "travel ban"). This travel ban is currently being challenged in court by several states and civil rights groups as evidence of the government's desire to profile individuals only the basis of their religion rather than any actual, fact-based threat they present to the United States.

While challenges in balancing civil rights with security will always continue, the best homeland security professionals can do is to protect these rights and ensure security . . . in equal measure.

## HOMELAND SECURITY VOICES: John Esposito, Ph.D.

*Dr. John Esposito is a Professor of Religion and International Affairs at Georgetown University and the founding Director of the Prince Alwaleed Bin-Talal Center for Muslim-Christian Understanding. Dr. Esposito is also the Editor-in-Chief of Oxford Islamic Studies Online and the Oxford Encyclopedia of the Islamic World. He has published more than 45 books, the most recent entitled Islamophobia and the Challenge of Pluralism in the 21st Century. Dr. Esposito obtained a B.A. in Philosophy from St. Antony College and his Ph.D. in Islamic Studies from Temple University.*

Source: John Esposito, Ph.D.

***According to a recent Pew Poll: When asked if "violence is ever justified to espouse religious views," American Muslims, more than any other American religious group, answer in the negative, in other words by saying that violence is never justified to espouse religious views. Given the worldwide rise of Islamist terrorism, do you think their response is a by-product of some post-9/11 pressure on American Muslims to conform?***

JE: No. It's realistic. Empirically and historically, violence is part of the history of all religious traditions. Including the scriptures of religious traditions, even those traditions we usually say are not violent. For example, the tendency in the popular imagination has always been to say that those who practice Hinduism and Buddhism do not use violence under religious pretense. That is just not true, not even today if one looks at Hindu-Muslim and Hindu-Christian conflicts or the persecution of the Rohingya (Muslims) by Buddhists, including monks, in Burma.

Polls such as the one you cite above also depend on the audience polled. If I look at the Palestinian and Israeli situation and the history of American Jews and their attitude towards Israel's use of violence, is there an issue there? What if I look at the use of violence by the United States, which sees itself as a Christian country, and a country where a significant number of the population are conservative Christians. More recently under George W. Bush, Evangelicals and Baptists went against mainstream Christians who all condemned the invasion of Iraq as an unjust war. Where you get the disconnect is that generally all Christians separate the idea that "my religious belief is not a religion that believes in violence," from the reality that America, as a Christian nation, is a nation that often relies on military violence to achieve its goals. The question is whether they believe in the legitimate or illegitimate use of force. In that case, when you jump to the Muslim situation, historically, many Muslims are honest to both the real history of their tradition and the Qur'an, which says legitimate violence is not abhorrent. The Qur'an does not say turn the other cheek. When the Christians answer these poll questions, they generally cite the New Testament and not the entirety of the Bible they embrace (both the Old and New Testament). Therefore, they look to Jesus and not at what many Christians came to believe in committing violence in the name of a just (e.g. legitimate) war. Therefore, the results of the poll also reflect the audience you interview, and how they have been conditioned and raised to think about the issue of religious violence.

I think there is conditioning, especially in American public discourse, that violence and Islam go hand in hand. And this conditioning, again, affects the results of these polls. For instance, when I first came to Washington, D.C., there was an event on Capitol Hill about the Arab World, and one of the speakers stated, "Islamism or Islamist groups are fine as long as they are nonviolent." This, of course, is unfair. Americans of all stripes believe in the legitimate use of violence. After the event, a number of the audience members questioned this statement: Why do only Islamic groups have to be non-violent to be "okay"? Aren't there other religious groups that are equally as violent, yet we don't make these kinds of statements about them.

In summary, I think the Pew data is good, but you really have to say to yourself "who is the audience and how is the audience hearing this question"? Many Muslims only have the sense of the history of Islam, just as Jews and Christians have, for example, the sense of the conquest of Joshua and David. However, for many Muslims their modern experience is one of Muslim-majority countries dealing with invasion and violence. In the American context—these issues are glossed over—but they tend to affect American-Muslims differently, since many are on the receiving end of discrimination, hate speech, and violence (Islamophobia) in the U.S. On the other hand, not many Americans do enormous soul-searching about the nuclear bomb we dropped on Hiroshima near the end of World War II. In most instances, when this is brought up, Americans tend to just say that dropping the bomb ended the war early. In my opinion, not many would think deeply about what the cost of life was in ending the war. The poll is fine on its surface, but dig deeper and I think it is troubling because Pew is just reading the data and not realizing you have to know who your audience is and how they are hearing this question.

***This brings up the larger issue of how Islam is portrayed in the West, and particularly through the lens of popular media. Islam and Muslims are often negatively portrayed by the media or almost exclusively associated with terrorism. How does this affect Americans' perceptions of Muslims and American Muslims' own perceptions of themselves?***

JE: Media Tenor, an organization based in Switzerland, monitors primarily European and American media. In a 2012 study examining 975,000 European and American media pieces that covered Islam and the Muslim world, the study found that in 2001, 2% of the coverage concerned Islamic extremism, and 0.1% provided any wider context about Muslim-majority countries. In 2011 the amount of coverage on Islamic extremism rose to 28% yet stories that shed light on the wider Muslim world and provided additional context remains at 0.1%. In a related study, Media Tenor concluded that for a variety of reasons 8 out of 10 stories about Muslims and Islam tend to include a discussion of extremism or include leads and introductions related to extremism.

The media is conditioned by the realities out there, so a number of stories begin with Islamic extremism as the lead, even though the wider story may be about some other topic related to the Muslim world. Since many folks only read the beginning of these stories, the image that comes across is one of the entire Muslim world as extremist. These stories do not provide the reader with a broader reasonable context within which to frame stories about Islam and the Muslim world. I tried to delve into this issue further, by asking what do the majority of Muslims think about these issues? That is why we did this book with Gallup, to answer the question, "what a billion Muslims really think." In the book (titled the same as the preceding question), we have tried to provide the right context for these kinds of questions—additional information that can help you find meaning in the data.

The research leading up to the book uncovered some interesting information: Amazingly, Muslims are more optimistic than non-Muslims about their future because they are upwardly mobile. At the same time, more than 50% of Muslims polled say that within the last ten years, they or their friends have experienced negativity (on the basis of their religion). Obviously, if you are being discriminated against on the basis of your religion alone, you are unlikely to provide responses which are honest and truthful. Rather, you are more likely to stay quiet (out of fear) or more prone to speak out. This can distort responses to poll questions and these distortions can manifest in public discourse.

For example, let's take the common encounter of an American Muslim returning to the U.S. from abroad. Frequently, Customs and Border Protection (CBP) agents may stop this person at the airport and inappropriately ask this person why they were in a Muslim country, do they have any friends there, do they believe in *jihad*, have they ever handled a Kalashnikov (a gun)? These kinds of questions are often followed by follow-up questions such as "do you believe in violence or religious violence?" Given the context of the first question, the traveler's response to the second question may be very hesitant or defensive. Even assimilated establishment American-Muslims may feel that they are "not American" since they are receiving treatment other Americans would not receive in the same situation. The CBP agent is then likely to interpret this defensive response as a form of deception, a potential threat, and un-American. And all this context lies buried deep; it is unsaid in the interaction between the CBP agent and the American-Muslim traveler.

***A lot of what you are talking about focuses on the importance of language.***
JE: Yes, language and contextualization.

***Can you talk a little bit about that? For instance, one of the initiatives that the Department of Homeland Security works on is scrubbing intelligence products, such as intelligence reports, for inappropriate language. As an example, DHS avoids using the word "jihadist" or "jihadi" to describe violent terrorists who use Islam as an ideology. The rationale behind this is that use of these words legitimizes the terrorist actors who then use these words to recruit others. Another example is not using the word "radical" or "extremist" because it is perfectly acceptable to be a radical or extremist in the United States, but not to be a violent radical or violent extremist. Why do you think this nuanced and perhaps more accurate use of language has not caught on, especially with the general public?***
JE: When popular culture and media accept certain terms, then they become commonly used. For example, let's take the term "fundamentalism." There was a big dispute when the term first came out. I was against using it and I would never use it in my writing. However, I ended up attending a panel entitled "Islamic Fundamentalism." When I was asked why the word "fundamentalism" was part of the title, I was told, it would draw in the audience—increase the number of people attending the

conference. Once popular culture appropriates a term such as "fundamentalism," the term becomes legitimate.

There is a life cycle to this legitimacy as well. We have seen similar terms take on legitimacy through usage in the media, from "fundamentalism" through to the term "political Islam" and then "Islamist." The first person that used the term "Islamist," used it in a book I reviewed. In my review I suggested it not be published if the term "Islamist" was used in the book. They published it nonetheless. Eventually the term "Islamist" got so common it started to be used by the U.S. government.

Language is critical, but society often determines what it means and people change the meaning of words as time passes to suit their motivations. George Bush himself fell into this trap. After 9/11 he was very clear in noting that Muslim extremists and not the religion of Islam was behind 9/11—but then started talking about "Islamo-fascism" when it became part of popular language. This should be corrected, but given the size of the government and political realities in Congress, it will not happen.

Language is modifiable if it is carefully contextualized and defined. You can use an imprecise word, but if you qualify it then it is fine. I used the word "militant" in a way that does not necessarily mean armed, but how most people understand it, so I will use it as a qualifier to indicate it meaning violent. It is critical for DHS and other agencies to use language carefully. *Jihad* in mainstream Islam is a long-established positive term when used in the *Qu'ran* and by Muslims to refer to the obligation of Muslims to strive or exert themselves in following God's will, in leading a good and moral life. Terms like "radical" and *"jihad"* are capable of multiple meanings when they pass from mainstream usage to the language and discourse of militant extremists.

***Let's take this a step further. Why do you think these words, such as "radical" and "militant," are applied overwhelmingly to describe the illicit acts of the American-Muslim minority in America and around the world? Especially when violent radicals and militants are from different backgrounds, etc.***

JE: There are a couple of reasons. You start with the trauma of the Iranian Revolution. For most Americans, the initial discovery of Islam and Muslims looked like angry people protesting, destroying property, this massive outpouring of anger in Iran—people yelling, "Death to America!" For example, if I meet a new ethnic group I do not know, and one or two are heavy drinkers, then I am more likely to conclude that the entire ethnic group do it. Thus, many Americans "met" Muslims for the first time this way, as angry revolutionaries shouting anti-American slogans in Iran—and this helped to form their initial negative opinions of Muslims, or at least make them susceptible to seeing the religion of Islam and most Muslims through the lens of "militant Islam" and thus the negative stereotypes of Muslims. Again, you have to look at the context; there are so many different and diverse Muslim countries and a lot is happening.

To see what I mean about context, let's turn the question on its head: Americans are largely seen throughout the world as the most militant of people, in terms of the number of wars we have started in the past and then also post-9/11, including the invasion and occupation of Iraq and Afghanistan—yet many Americans don't see themselves in this context but rather believe that the U.S. has defended American interests as well as freedom and liberty abroad. When Americans see the "other," whether it be American-Muslims or not, they absorb and are affected by the limited information on Islam and Muslims from the media (which focuses on headline events, on conflict for, as the saying goes, "If it bleeds, it leads") and by social media, which is awash with anti-Muslim (Islamophobic) and anti-immigrant websites and some politicians like Newt Gingrich, Michele Bachmann, Rick Santorum, or media commentators like O'Reilly or Sean Hannity. Consider the issues raised about whether President Obama is a Muslim, the extent to which Republican presidential candidates in 2012 and 2016, and Congressional candidates in 2010, often raised the issue of the religion of Islam or questioned the loyalty of American-Muslims, the 29 states that have attempted to pass anti-Shariah laws and major polls by Gallup and Pew that on the one hand demonstrate the significant negative attitudes of many Americans towards Islam and Muslims (not just militants) and on the other hand the educational, economic, and political mainstreaming of majorities of American-Muslims.

## KEYWORDS

- **civil rights**: Sets of moral principles or norms that describe standards of human behavior; often practically expressed as laws and policies both obligatory on and protected by the government.

- **symbolic speech**: A legal term describing actions that convey a specific message to those viewing it.

- **Jim Crow** (laws): State and local laws in the United States (but mostly in the South) that enforced racial segregation.

- **violent extremism**: Ideological, religious, or politically motivated acts of violence perpetrated inside the United states by white supremacists, anti-government groups, and radical Islamist entities, or groups with extreme views on abortion, animal rights, the environment, and federal ownership of public lands.

- **chilling effect**: The inhibition or discouragement of the legitimate exercise of rights by the threat of legal sanction or the use of force or intimidation.

- **secondary use problem**: Secondary (or third etc.) use of data occurs when data is used for purposes other than those for which it was originally collected.

- **dossier**: A collection of documents about a particular person that attempts to paint a picture of that individual.

---

**KNOWLEDGE CHECK**

1. What is the difference between civil rights and human rights?
2. How does homeland security policy come into conflict with the freedom of the press?
3. Name and explain three arguments/fallacies discussed in this chapter.

## NOTES

1. *See generally*, Marbury v. Madison, 5 U.S. 137 (1803).
2. Humphrey v. Moore, 375 U.S. 335, 372 (1964).
3. Ehsan Zaffar, *Civil Rights Law and Policy*, in Law and Public Policy, at 355–56 (Kevin J. Fandl, ed., 2018) *available at* www.routledge.com/Law-and-Public-Policy-1st-Edition/Fandl/p/book/9780815373919.
4. Cantwell v. Connecticut, 310 U.S. 296, 304 (1940).
5. U.S. Attorney's Office—District of Minnesota, Know Your Rights, A guide to the United States Constitution, at 3 (2011) *available at* www.justice.gov/sites/default/files/usao-mn/legacy/2011/09/16/MN%20Civil%20Rights%20FINAL.pdf.

6. *Combatting Religious Discrimination and Protecting Religious Freedom*, U.S. Dep't of Justice (last updated Aug. 6, 2015) www.justice.gov/crt/combating-religious-discrimination-and-protecting-religious-freedom-21.

7. Ehsan Zaffar, *Civil Rights Law and Policy*, in Law and Public Policy, at 357 (Kevin J. Fandl, ed., 2018) *available at* www.routledge.com/Law-and-Public-Policy-1st-Edition/Fandl/p/book/9780815373919.

8. *Id.*

9. Karsten Müller & Carlo Schwarz, *Fanning the Flames of Hate: Social Media and Hate Crime* (last updated Dec. 6, 2018) https://papers.ssrn.com/sol3/papers.cfm?abstract_id=3082972.

10. *See* U.S. Const. amend. XIV; *See* also Herbert v. Lando, 441 U.S. 153, 168 n.16 (1979).

11. U.S. Attorney's Office—District of Minnesota, Know Your Rights, A guide to the United States Constitution, at 3 (2011) *available at* www.justice.gov/sites/default/files/usao-mn/legacy/2011/09/16/MN%20Civil%20Rights%20FINAL.pdf.

12. Ehsan Zaffar, *Civil Rights Law and Policy*, in Law and Public Policy, at 367 (Kevin J. Fandl, ed., 2018) *available at* www.routledge.com/Law-and-Public-Policy-1st-Edition/Fandl/p/book/9780815373919.

13. The organization referred to as the Islamic State of Iraq and Syria is alternatively known as the Islamic State of Iraq and the Levant, the Islamic State, and occasionally, "Daesh." Radical Islamist entities incorporate a militant ideology aimed at creating a worldwide community, or caliphate, of Muslim believers by any means necessary, including violence. Radical Islamist extremist groups include al-Qa'ida and ISIS, among others.

14. U.S. Gov't Accountability Office, GAO-17–300, Countering Violent Extremism: Actions Needed to Define Strategy and Assess Progress of Federal Efforts (Apr. 2017) *available at* www.gao.gov/assets/690/683984.pdf.

15. *Id.*

16. *Id.*

17. Samuel J. Rascoff, *Uncle Sam is No Imam*, NY Times (Feb. 20, 2012) www.nytimes.com/2012/02/21/opinion/uncle-sam-is-no-imam.html.

18. *Id.* There are numerous examples in Rascoff's article: "There are other examples like these around the country. The Ohio Department of Public Safety has produced and distributed literature that declares, 'When extremists attack and kill in the name of jihad, mainstream Muslims consider such acts as a total deviation from the true religion of Islam.'" Homeland Security officials were signed up for a 2010 conference in which one topic was "Seeking a Counter-Reformation in Islam." In 2004, an inspector general criticized the Bureau of Prisons because it failed to "examine the doctrinal beliefs of applicants for religious service positions to determine whether those beliefs are inconsistent with B.O.P. security policies."

19. *Id.*

20. Samuel J. Rascoff, *Establishing Official Islam? The Law and Strategy of Counter-Radicalization*, 64 Stan. L. Rev. 1, 10 (2012) www.stanfordlawreview.org/print/article/establishing-official-islam/.

21. Material on CVE adapted from the Federal Bureau of Investigation's "Don't be a Puppet" interactive exercises. *See Don't Be a Puppet*, Federal Bureau of Investigation (last visited Jan. 21, 2019) https://cve.fbi.gov/whatis/.

22. Joel Simon, *How 'war on terror' unleashed a war on journalists*, CNN (Sep. 9, 2011) www.cnn.com/2011/OPINION/09/08/simon.press.freedom.911/index.html.

23. Scott Shane, *Complaint Seeks Punishment for Classification of Documents*, NY Times (Aug. 1, 2011) www.nytimes.com/2011/08/02/us/02secret.html.

24. *CPJ seeks Pentagon investigation in Iraq journalist deaths*, Committee to Protect Journalists (Apr. 26, 2010) https://cpj.org/2010/04/cpj-seeks-pentagon-investigations-in-iraq-journali.php.

25. U.S. Dep't of Homeland Security, Notice of Modified Privacy Act System of Records, 82 Fed. Reg. 43,556 (Sep. 18, 2017) *available at* www.federalregister.gov/documents/2017/09/18/2017-19365/privacy-act-of-1974-system-of-records.

26. *Id.*

27. *Id.*

28. Google, *Way of a Warrant*, YouTube (Mar. 27, 2014) www.youtube.com/watch?v=MeKKHxcJfh0.

29. Korematsu v. United States, 323 U.S. 214, 219 (1944).

30. *Id.*

31. *Confession of Error: The Solicitor General's Mistakes During the Japanese-American Internment Cases*, U.S. Dep't of Justice (last updated Apr. 7, 2017) www.justice.gov/archives/opa/blog/confession-error-solicitor-generals-mistakes-during-japanese-american-internment-cases.

32. *Civil liberties in wartime*, ShareAmerica (Apr. 6, 2015) https://share.america.gov/civil-liberties-wartime/.

33. Korematsu v. United States, 323 U.S. 214, 223 (1944).

34. Jay Stanley, *Q&A with Daniel Solove on How Bad Security Arguments Are Undermining Our Privacy Rights*, ACLU (July 14, 2011) www.aclu.org/blog/national-security/qa-daniel-solove-how-bad-security-arguments-are-undermining-our-privacy.

*Index*

Note: Page numbers in italic indicate a figure indicate a table on the corresponding page.